Moffat High Street at the end of the 19th century.

MEMORIES OF MOFFAT

Emilio 'Jack' Dicerbo
6/9/04.

My mother 'Pasquo' and dad 'Tony', mid 1930's.

To Adeline, Fiona and Evelyn

and to the memory of

'Tony' and 'Pasquo' & Philip.

Memories of Moffat
by Emilio Dicerbo

'Memories of Moffat' is really two books in one.

Firstly, it is the autobiography of a young boy during the years of the Second World War, the experiences he encountered at this time in a small border town and some of the events that changed many townspeople's lives.

Secondly, it contains photographs and facts relating to places long-gone. The Hydropathic Hotel, Railway Station and Coxhill Duck Farm to name but a few, and delving further back in time gives the reader an insight into Moffat's earlier history.

Many aspects of the 1950's and 60's are also mentioned adding further interest for today's Moffatonians.

The main storyline and historical parts are intermingled throughout to provide a balance that the reader will soon find easy to follow.

Emilio Dicerbo, September 1999.

An aerial view of the town in the mid-1920's.
Noticeable are the Railway Station, the Gasworks (founded 1837) and Holm Street with houses on both sides. Holm Street was only 4 metres wide at its narrowest point.

MEMORIES OF MOFFAT

BY

EMILIO DICERBO

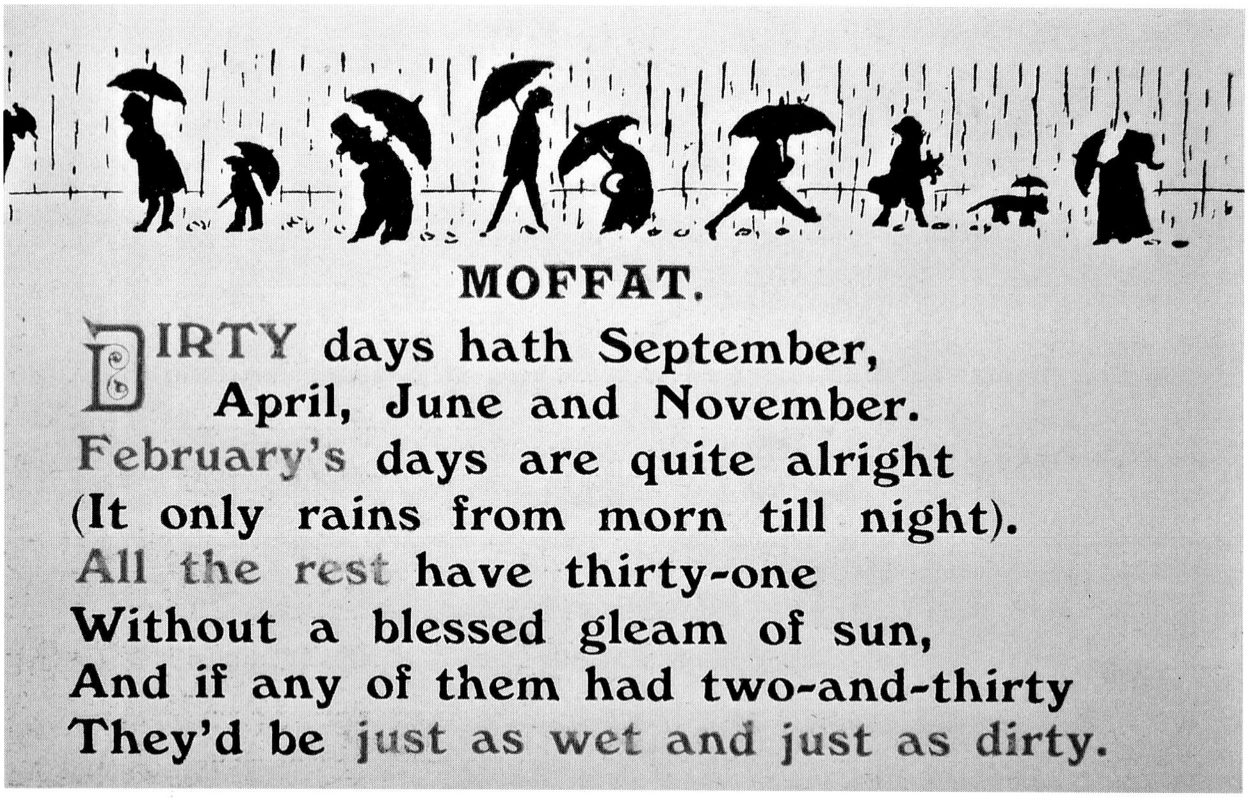
MOFFAT.
DIRTY days hath September,
April, June and November.
February's days are quite alright
(It only rains from morn till night).
All the rest have thirty-one
Without a blessed gleam of sun,
And if any of them had two-and-thirty
They'd be just as wet and just as dirty.

First published in Dumfries, Scotland 1999.
Enlarged and revised edition published in Dumfries, Scotland 2004.

This book has been designed and printed by Solway Offset, *the* Printers. Tel: 01387 262960.

ISBN 1 899316 52 3

Contents

The High Street in holiday mood on the Duke of York's wedding day in 1893; he was crowned King George V in 1910. The second building on the left, now Gemini Jewellers, during the war was owned by Willie K. Mitchell, Electrician and Wireless Engineer, who attended to some of the townspeople's wireless accumulators. Every winter he would carefully strip down his trusty M.G. and rebuild it again in the spring.

Introduction

Moffat lies in a valley, bordered by hills to the north, east and west, some of whose peaks are over 2,000ft. above sea level. The High Street is only 300ft. above sea level, and the southern exit from the town follows the course of the River Annan as it winds it way through a multitude of farms towards the Solway Firth.

Fifty years ago, farming throughout the district was quite different from that of today. Many thousands of sheep grazed the uplands where now there are conifer trees, and the average farm was more diverse in its range of stock.

There were also more smaller farms and smallholdings, where hens roamed freely about the stock yards and hay sheds. Many kept a few pigs, and in those days a visit to practically any farm could introduce children to every type of farm animal.

In the autumn there was always haymaking and potato gathering ('tattie howking'), for some of the older pupils from Moffat Academy. 'Tattie howking' for some of us was a way of having a few days away from class, and though it could be quite a chore, we were paid a shilling an hour, or 5p in today's money, but in those days, a shilling went a long way.

W. K. Mitchell and his M.G.

From near the Grey Mare's Tail, an impressive waterfall situated about 7 miles up the Moffat Water Valley, on the A708 to Selkirk, the Moffat Water follows the valley bottom to the 'Meetings of the Waters', approximately 2 miles to the south-east of the town.

At the 'Meetings', the Moffat Water joins the River Annan which rises near the Devil's Beef Tub, on the A701 to Edinburgh, and borders the west side of the town. A little further west beyond Golf Hill, the River Evan, which runs close to the M74 and main west coast railway line, tumbles through a rocky course before levelling out into the valley bottom near Beattock, where it joins the Moffat Water and the River Annan.

In the early 1950's, shops and businesses in the town differed significantly from those of today.

Moffatonians, fifty years ago, could find all their personal and household needs within the town, as the diversity of shopping and services was adequate, but like many other small towns, the increase in private transport saw one service shop after another having to close its doors, as people travelled farther afield to shop.

Ironically, for those living in Moffat today travel is necessary to purchase men's clothing, footwear, furniture and other items that could, some years ago, be procured simply by walking a few hundred yards.

On the other hand, modern Moffat has much to offer its residents, with attractions for visitors ever on the increase.

The view from St. Andrew's Church Tower in the mid-1930's.
The Well Road Church is prominent in the top right-hand side of the photograph.
It was demolished in the mid 1960's, only 100 years after its construction.

From a similar view point, 50 years later (1985).

Our shop at 8 High Street, before being rebuilt in 1966.

Our Butchers and Bakers are famed far and wide for their products. Lloyd Grossman, convivial host of "Master Chef", said of Little's the Bakers "There is a wonderful bakery in Moffat that makes drop scones you would kill for." Most visitors pay a 'toll', as they suck a Moffat Toffee or lick a freshly made ice cream.

The Delicatessen is exceptional in its range of cheeses and cold meats, the Wine Shop stocks an impressive worldwide range, and the Pet Shop caters for pets of all kinds.

The Wool, Tweed and Gift Shops, of which there are many are second to none in the range and quality of their wares, from trinkets to jewellery, tartan ties to ladies' tweed suits, and a variety of crafts to suit everyone's taste and purse.

Grocers, Newsagents, Jewellers, Chemists, D.I.Y. Ironmongers, and Baby Clothes' shops are all well established, some dating back many years, and all manned by caring and friendly staff. More recently, Sports Goods, Lingerie and Health Care are now on offer.

The Book Shop is well stocked with material and works by many popular and well known authors, covering all manner of subjects, and a search service for difficult to find books is also provided. The Book Exchange, although a more recent venture, has a steady turnover of good quality, second-hand books, and again, the range is extremely varied.

The Arts are also well represented within the town, in the form of an Art Gallery, a well-supported Theatre, and for those interested in 'days gone by', the Museum is a must for a visit.

Ladies' Hairdressers are booked well in advance and the Gents' Barber keeps old and young alike nice and trim for a very reasonable price.

Local Tradesmen ply their individual trades to a very high standard and again most have been established for many years.

It goes without saying that Moffat's Hotels, B&B's, Restaurants and Tea Rooms are of a standard equal to any found throughout Scotland. The number of hotels and eating places points to the fact that Moffat is a very popular place for long- or short-stay visits.

The Caravan Park borders the Moffat Fishery and the Tweedhope Sheepdog Centre. These activities add further attractions to outdoor enthusiasts who enjoy the sporting and leisure pursuits previously available, such as golf, tennis, green bowls and walking.

For ramblers, the Waterside and Station Park suit those who prefer a casual stroll, but for the more rugged scenery, coupled with solitude, there is a wide choice of tracks to follow, through fields, woodlands and our Moffat Hills.

The Station Park, with its boating pond, putting green, children's play area, and floral displays is Moffat's crowning glory, and over the years the many awards achieved in the 'Scotland in Bloom' and 'Britain in Bloom' competitions are a credit to the superb efforts of all concerned in promoting the town – the people of Moffat.

The author in the shop in 1958. Check the ice cream prices:
cones = 3d; 4d; 6d; (approximately = 1½ p to 2½ p).
99's = 9d, less than 5p. Quarter of a pound of large imperials also cost 9d.

The £1 notes of the 1940's and 1950's.
Eight different banks issued £1 notes. The National merged with the Commercial and the North of Scotland merged with the Clydesdale. Both mergers produced further £1 notes, bringing the total of different £1 notes to ten!

Coinage and Banknotes of the Day
(1940's ~ 1950's)

During the 1940's and 50's, Pounds, Shillings and Pence were the monetary units in the country, with 240 pennies to the £1 (pound).

Decimal currency is certainly easier to understand but much less interesting. The farthing, halfpenny and penny are of no value in today's system and the half-crown (two shillings and sixpence) was only equal to 12½p.

Even more interesting were the old Scottish £1 notes, with no fewer than eight different banks issuing them. Two mergers, namely the National and the Commercial, and North of Scotland and the Clydesdale resulted in another two different £1 notes being issued.

Today, three main Scottish banks issue banknotes with only the Royal Bank of Scotland carrying on the tradition of the £1 note.

The photographs' illustrate the 10 x £1 notes that were in circulation during the 1940's and 50's (collectable items today).

At that time Moffat was served by three banking establishments: The Bank of Scotland; The British Linen Bank and the Union Bank of Scotland.

Compare the size of today's £1 note with those of yesteryear.

A Childhood Memory

Emilio Dicerbo 4/12/93

1 Deep in thought one winter's night
While sitting all alone,
Surrounded by material things
That people like to own,
I pondered on the years gone by
When as a little boy
I'd wander through the countryside
My young heart filled with joy...

2 For everywhere I chanced to look
GOD's wonders could be seen.
With woodlands, fields and meadows
Dressed in countless shades of green.
The burns and rivers sparkled
As they flowed down to the sea.
O'er rocks and glides through deep, dark pools
That held such mystery...

3 But those dark pools, they are no more,
The mystery has gone.
For man bulldozed the river beds
To move the water on.
No snags to hide the salmon
On his journey up the river.
No pools to hide the monster trout
For they are gone forever...

4 Through spring and summer every year
The Kerr's wonders were revealed.
But no such moorland is there now
Just one great empty field.
No reeds to shield the curlew
That thrilled me with his call.
Of all the springtime sounds I heard
His was the best of all...

5 The spangled, golden plover
Nests no longer on the knowe.
For once again man intervened
With his gigantic plough.
The cotton grass and heather
Were overturned with ease.
And the scenes I loved to savour
Are now lost among the trees...

6 So many happy hours
I would pass by reedy ponds.
To catch the newts and tadpoles
That hid among watery fronds.
These curious, natural wonders
As a child, I'd often seen.
All I can show the children now
Is where the newts have been.

7 Now fifty years have come to pass
Since I was just a lad.
And though the changes I have seen
Leave me a trifle sad.
A GRANDCHILD's smile lights up my heart
And helps me to carry on...
Towards the future – for it is theirs,
And accept what's gone is gone...

Southern end of High Street in 1946, with the author on a bicycle (borrowed)!

Early Days

I have always regarded myself as being extremely fortunate to have lived in Moffat all my life. From a very early age, all things natural took my interest, and on looking back to when I was very young, I can see Moffat and its surrounding countryside as it was, over sixty years ago.

I remember chasing and trying to catch butterflies as they flitted about on the High Street, on a hot, sunny afternoon. I would pause, as everyone did at that time, to look at a little car being driven past, only resuming my activities as it disappeared out of sight. Cars and other vehicles always attracted my attention, but nothing came close to my favourite, the mighty steam road roller that was garaged down in the council yard.

The sight and sounds of the huge steam roller as it rolled the whinstone chips into the marvellously smelling hot tar fascinated young and old alike while old Watt Bell turned the massive wheel to control the machine as it moved back and forth.

Willie Harkness would control the flow of hot tar from the tar boiler, and the 'chips' would be spread by big Dave Thomson and other council workers with shovels.

Later, after the steam roller had been garaged, if I was lucky, the fire engine's garage door would be open and I'd admire the gleaming red and brass appliance with its leather-covered seats and wooden ladder on top, as I thought to myself, how brave the firemen were.

Businesses of the 1950's

Peter Hepburn's Cycle Depot.
This was the second home of the Moffat Cycling Club.

At that time every home had coal fires, resulting in chimney fires' being commonplace. As soon as the alarm was raised, rattling bicycles, pedalled by puffing firemen, would race down Church Street to the council yard. Soon they returned on the fire engine, with clanging bell and a host of children chasing after it.

Occasionally, Willie Harkness would take one of the big council horses to be shod at the blacksmiths' and he'd take me with him to another of my favourite places. Mr.

J. Barr & Son 'Treasure House of Moffat' is now Moffat Woollens.

Businesses of the 1950's

James Sinclair's, Grocers is now McGarey's, Grocers.

Donaldson, the Smithy, was another man whom I would watch in amazement as he plied his skills. He would fashion and fit the horseshoes in a way that always made me wince, as the nails were hammered home and then nipped off when the points emerged through the hoof. The smell that then arose from the hot iron shoe being fitted, although not bothering the men, always forced me to take a few steps backwards.

Life was leisurely, the surrounding countryside was really wild with all manner of wildlife only a few hundred yards from our house. Not only did the Annandale Field Burn contain sticklebacks, but lovely, brown trout found sanctuary under the low bridge at the council yard, where a stealthy approach would reward one with marvellous sights before the trout darted under the bridge.

The Glebe was marshy, with wee, reedy ponds containing newts as well as frogs, and I remember carrying a beautifully marked red and white toadstool home and placing it in a box – the next time that I looked in the box my find had turned to mush, leaving me quite upset.

Hedges were thick and bushy, and grass grew long until the council men cut it with scythes. They then stacked it into little ricks at the drying green. On escorting my mother, who was hanging out the washing, I'd dive head first into one and emerge covered in hay, which was easier removed than tar. At this time, in hot weather I would be running around with bare feet, and tar bubbles were tempting little eruptions to pop with one's toes.

Some mornings I would help my older brother in the 'chippy', by turning the handle on the potato peeler. To achieve this I had to stand on an upturned lemonade crate, but I never tried my hand at cutting the potatoes into chips. I left that task to my mother, brother and sister, with the chop, chop, chopping of sharp knives on wood resounding until the large white sink and enamelled bath were full of chips, submerged in water.

I much preferred, however, to be taken for a walk up to the second waterside, to Geddes's, where there was a favourite swimming hole.

On one occasion, when the pool and riverbank nearby were really crowded, I wandered deep into the willow- and alder-strewn copse by the riverside. Picking my way carefully through the undergrowth, I came across a most exciting find – a small pool, with water trickling in but without any obvious outflow. The water was gin-clear and the aquatic life abundant – a natural aquarium, with sticklebacks, minnows, young trout and all manner of water insects and caddis swimming around, and crawling about on the stones at the bottom of the pond.

From where I stood, in the shade, I was unnoticed and the light was perfect. I could see every movement. I must have watched for ages and, when someone called my name, I was loath to leave this special place.

Some Saturday mornings would find me rummaging about in the ashes of the joiner's fire, at the waterside. The apprentice from Mr. Henry, the joiners, would push a wheelbarrow load of wood shavings and small pieces of scrap wood to a spot where the contents would be tipped out and set alight.

When the ashes were cool enough, I would collect bent nails, and try to straighten them by tapping the bend with a stone, but this resulted in more bashed fingers than

Spur Tea Room, now Bank of Scotland.

The Old Road Bridge at Station Park which was originally much narrower. When it was widened the added section was at a slightly different level, forming perfect cavities in which dippers nested and roosted for many years. There are no nesting sites in the new bridge.

straightened out nails and a collection of more bent than straight ones – not that it mattered much anyway, as I was too young to do anything with them.

On the other hand, this was the age of the cigarette card, the ultimate items for wee boys to collect and every empty packet found would be eagerly probed, to see if the card had been left inside.

I remember vividly, one evening I was in our shop when a man came in to buy a packet of cigarettes and I enquired if I could have the card. The answer was "yes", but I had to post a letter for him first. I was across the road to the post office and back, as fast as my wee legs would carry me. When I got back, the card was lying on the table – a battleship – one I didn't have. But as I tried to pick it up, much to my dismay, it had been licked on

The new bridge which could barely cope with the flood waters of November 1972.

the gummed back and stuck down. I never did like the man after that.

It was also at this time, that shooters, as well as anglers, would converge on the town in good numbers. The fishing was excellent, and game plentiful, as were gamekeepers who kept 'gibbets', with all manner of vermin nailed to them. I would spend ages looking at any 'gibbet' that I came across on my wanderings. Weasels, stoats, rats, crows, hawks and even the odd heron, could find themselves crucified on a 'gibbet' – and once again, I wanted to take them all home.

The game, in the shape of pheasant, partridge and grouse, attracted many sportsmen to the town and every hotel had a gun room, and a cold room for game. The regular clientele who returned season after season, brought welcome income to many shopkeepers and traders.

Then, not all at once but gradually, a change took place. Fishing rods, shotguns and game bags were exchanged for rifles, tin helmets and gas masks – and I was five years old!

Malcolm McLachlan in Moffat Club jersey.

Moffat Cycling Club

Before the Second World War, Moffat had a well-supported cycling club which was formed in 1935.

Immediately after the war the Moffat club, affiliated to the Scottish Lowlands Cycling Club, re-grouped, with Sunday mornings eagerly looked forward to by members who enjoyed both the company and the open road.

Destinations varied far and wide with St. Mary's Loch and Sandyhills two of the shorter runs.

Harold Rae & Vincent Dicerbo

Friendly races were also organised with Malcolm McLachlan and Hayward Banton almost certainly among the winners.

Some of us younger boys, when bicycles were available, would also go for runs. The 'three fish suppers' – Lockerbie, Lochmaben and Dumfries – it was one of our favourites, though one fish supper was usually enough.

This run could take most of the day and on returning home I for one was more than a wee bit saddle-sore.

Harold Rae, Hayward Banton, Jimmy Hill, Malcolm McLachlan.

Well Street at the turn of the century.

A window display like this would have raised a few eyebrows then!

This series of six local views was compiled in the early 1900's, the subjects and quality earning them a special place in 'Memories'.

The photographs were processed by Solway Offset from glass slides of the type used for projection by the old "magic lanterns".

The photographer is unknown, as are the people who posed in the compositions but the locations are all well known to locals and many regular visitors alike.

A leisurely stroll through the Gallow Hill Woods at the height of their popularity.

Also in the Gallow Hill Woods, the Queens Chair, at the point where well-trodden paths met from four different directions: sadly, long forgotten by most.

Another well-trodden path by the waterside, near the Edinburgh Road (A701) Bridge.

Looking northwards along the Old Edinburgh Road (Beechgrove).

The walker has passed the gateway to Dumcrief on his way to the town.

Elegance personified in both watcher and watched. How many times was this scene depicted in the Station Park over the years?

Old Shops

Looking south towards the Old Meal House c. 1873.

The same view after the Bank of Scotland and the Colvin Fountain has been built c. 1876.

John Young standing in the doorway of his shop previous to it being rebuilt to match Burnie's Drapery.

In the photograph above, Burnie's Drapery is the prominent building while John Young's grocery, to which customers had to climb the stone steps to reach, is quite insignificant.

Provost John Young, while standing in his doorway one morning in the late 1880's, appears to have given this some thought, as he had his premises demolished and rebuilt to match Burnie's.

The result was a fine new attractive building from where he continued his grocery business with the upper storeys suitable for his three sisters to take in paying guests.

George Young (no relation), purveyor of tea, wine and provisions, originally traded from premises purchased from Nettleship in 1901, between Henderson Street and Rae Street. This shop is unoccupied at the moment.

John Young sold the building and business to George Young who then moved his existing grocery store to the new premises in 1917.

David Young, George's brother took over the shop on George's death and together with his son Eric, continued to run the business which remained in the family until Eric's retirement in 1974.

The new building completed in 1880.

The picture above shows the two business premises as they are today. One is the Post Office, the other the "Rumblin' Tum", a popular coffee house.

Previous to the mid 1920's, David Young, like most other wine merchants in the town, blended his own whisky. Four different fine Highland whiskies were carefully mixed together to produce "The Annandale" Blend.

John Young and staff at the new shop front.

George and David Young at the shop George bought from Nettleship in 1901.

Following the move by George Young from the shop between Rae Street and Henderson Street in 1917, it was bought by my great uncle, Joe Coletti, who ran it as a confectioner and tobacconist. Joe was a well known and popular character whose exploits are often referred to with humour by older members of the community.

When Cunningham, Jeweller and Watchmaker, moved to new premises in Well Street in 1911, the business changed to a bakery, Weatherhead's.

When Cunningham, the Jewellers, moved from the west side of the High Street to new premises at 11 Well Street in 1911, the shop changed to James Weatherhead, Baker and Confectioner and has followed along those lines to this day.

James Reive followed Weatherhead and during my boyhood days it was owned and run by John Mitchell and family. John was also the name of Mr. Mitchell's younger son and

In 1930 it was still a bakery but had a change of ownership, James Reive.

My brother Philip (left) with John Mitchell (right) of the High Street Baker's family soon after joining the R.A.F. The chap in the middle is unknown to me.

he and my brother Philip were great friends. They had their own band and at the outbreak of the Second World War, joined the R.A.F. together.

Alec was the older brother and I would visit him in the upper part of the bakery where a hot pancake was usually presented at my appearance.

Alec followed the advance of the Allies on a large map on the wall and would point things out to me that I never really understood but he was a good friend and it was due to his generosity that I eventually owned a bike with drooped handlebars.

In the mid 1950's, Mitchells became Little's, family bakers since 1932. One of the oldest family businesses in the town.

John Mitchell and family continued the trend throughout the war years (1939-45) and in the mid 1950's another family of bakers, Little's developed the business as it is today. The Little family have been established bakers since 1932.

J. Smith, Tea, Wine & Spirit Merchant.

Somerville, Robertson, Smith, Taylor and Stewart, all family grocers who occupied for a time, the shop now known as Fantasia, between Grieve's Newsagents and the Annandale Hotel.

The Robertsons briefly owned the shop in the early 1900's, until a tragedy forced Mrs. Robertson to give it up.

Mr. Robertson sadly came to an untimely end when he was gathering primroses for Primrose Week from the steep, rocky bank of the Hind Gill, near the bridge over the burn at Archbank.

His widow, Agnes, couldn't manage to run the business on her own and eventually sold it.

With two wee boys to raise, Agnes took in washing to earn a living for her family which couldn't have been very lucrative as Reive the Baker's message boy, Ewan Paterson, sensed her plight and decided to help her out. When delivering her order for one roll, he pushed another through the letter box!

Miller's, Draper, Clothier and Silk Mercer.
In the photograph Miller's Drapery is situated on the east side of the High Street.
At the turn of the century Miller's occupied premises which later became the renowned Spur Tearoom on the west side. Today the Bank of Scotland has a branch there.
During the 1950's Thomas Fortune's Drapery, like Miller's before him, was well supported by the townspeople. These premises are now the celebrated Moffat Toffee Shop.

East side of the High Street, mid 1950's.

W. Henderson & Co.,

Fashionable Bootmakers,

Robert Gunn Budge and William Henderson: Boot and Shoemakers.

William Henderson and Co., established in 1863 traded from premises at 3 Well Road, before moving into 1 Well Road when 3 Well Road was bought by Robert Gunn Budge.

William Henderson died in 1906 followed by his wife, Catherine Burnett in 1920.

Robert Gunn Budge married their daughter, also called Catherine Burnett Henderson and in 1932 the entire footwear business moved into 17 Well Street.

The original shops were demolished and a fine sandstone building, Hepburn's Bakery, was built on the spot. Robert Gunn Budge was Provost in Moffat from 1929 to 1938.

J. & W. Locke and Wm. M. Gillespie, Footwear Manufacturers.
Locke and Gillespie were another two bootmaker families who were successful in the town. At the turn of the century, with a population of around 1700, there were many feet to protect and decorate. Rough roads, walking to and from work, as well as the work itself all played their part in wearing out soles. Hence the need for the dozen or so footwear manufacturers in the town at that time.

Smart, Grocer.
In the early 1900's John Smart ran his family grocery business from 7 Well Street then moved across to 8 Well Street. On the opposite side to where Mr. McIlwrick's wine shop is today.
In 1897 this was owned by Mr. Neill, Watchmaker, when its architecture was radically different, pointing to the fact that it must have been altered about this time.
The words Tea and Wines appeared on many of the shop fronts until Grocers became more popular.

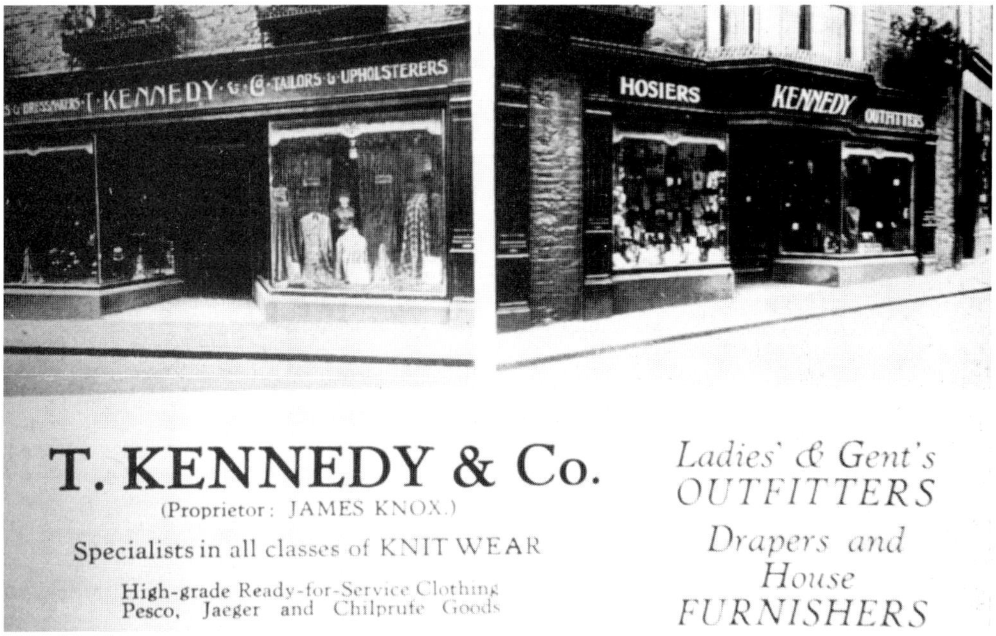
HOSIERS
KENNEDY
T. KENNEDY & Co.
(Proprietor: JAMES KNOX.)
Specialists in all classes of KNIT WEAR
High-grade Ready-for-Service Clothing
Pesco, Jaeger and Chilprufe Goods
Ladies' & Gent's
OUTFITTERS
Drapers and
House
FURNISHERS

T. Kennedy & Co., Ladies and Gent's Outfitters, Drapers and House Furnishers, traded from numbers 22, 24 and 26 Well Street in the early 1900's from premises that today house Lothorien Emporium, Antiques and Collectables and Harvest Time, Delicatessen and Health Foods.
Kennedy also had a Gentlemen's Outfitter and Footwear outlet at 4 Well Street.

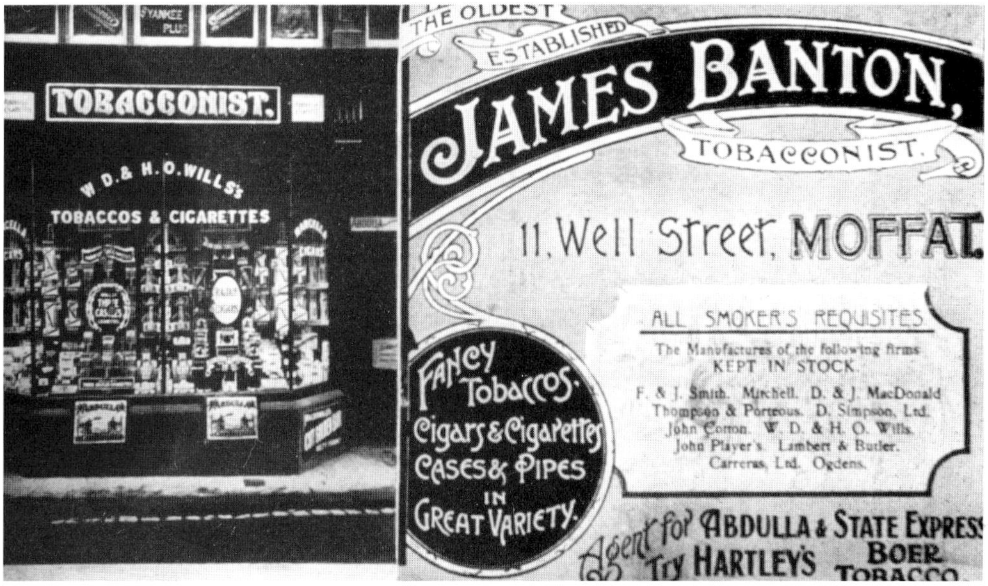

Banton's Tobacconist.

James Banton, Tobacconist traded from 11 Well Street, now House of Beauty, then moved down to 7 Well Street, when John Smart moved across the road to number 8.

Banton's was the specialist tobacconist in the town with a most impressive array of pipes, tobaccos, cigars, cigarettes and cases, in fact every item of smokers needs could be found in the shop.

A selection of cigarettes stocked by tobacconists in the 1950's.

After the Second World War, Mrs. Banton although continuing to trade as a tobacconist was more of a greengrocer and this proved a great advantage for her son Hayward.

One summer evening the usual crowd were 'dooking' at the Caul on the River Evan, when "Banty" appeared and immediately climbed a massive fir tree on the river bank. Minutes later a banana skin landed on the rocky bank where some of us were sitting, then another and another, till no fewer than five littered the area – and there was strict rationing at that time! I think it was one banana per person with deliveries to the shops about once a month!

Hayward was later killed in action during the Korean War while serving with the KOSB.

Boys at the Caul Swimming Pool on the River Evan, c.1946. Top (l to r): Frank Lessels, Jacky Thomson. Bottom (l to r): Terence Eagles, Fred Hyslop, Gordon Hyslop, "Bobo" Kerr and Norman "Peesie" McNeil.

The celebrated Moffat Toffee Shop.

Mrs. Blacklock, Blair Blacklock's grandmother at the celerated toffee shop in Holm Street c.1905. The young lad is 'Mathie', Blair's dad.

At their first shop on the High Street, which was situated at the bottom of the Causeway on the right hand side, at the end of sweetie rationing. I remember as a lad savouring the aroma of freshly made toffee and tablet. No better tablet was made then or since. Vanilla, ginger and walnut, all delicious. Unfortunately, a quarter of a pound of mixed flavours provided just a small portion of each, so it was not for sharing!

Today, Moffat toffee is still one of the most sought after locally made products by visitors to the town.

James Sinclair & Co. Ltd., Grocer and Wine Merchant.

As well as grocers and wine merchants, 'bottom' Sinclair's, under Alex. Cameron ran a successful cattle-feed business, the feed being delivered throughout the district by the company's own lorry. The 'bottom' shop also had two vans on the road delivering groceries etc. to outlying houses and farms.

'Top' Sinclair's, at the top of Well Street, was under the charge of Mr. Duncan Mundell, and as well as the usual groceries and provisions, ironmongery, cutlery, glass and china were all stocked.

The words 'top' and 'bottom' were used by the townspeople to distinguish between the two shops.

James Inglis, Chemist and Druggist, Well Street.

J. Inglis, Chemist and Druggist, occupied premises at 36 Well Street in 1901. When Mitchell bought the business from Inglis it would appear that changing the name boards was top priority as there are no other changes in the two photographs.

Mitchell was the owner in 1915 and 10 years later the premises were those of the first Moffat Co-op Society.

Mr. Samuel Anderson's Fish and Poultry Depot, c.1900 at 17 Well Street.

Johnnie Morgan c1880. Johnnie travelled the south of Scotland, visiting farmhouses and cottages selling the usual packman's wares. His faithful companions were Tommy, his donkey and Quharrie his dog. He died in Thornhill Poorhouse in 1901, aged 85. Although there was a fair number of travelling traders plying their various wares from carts at the turn of the century, Johnnie's must surely have been one of the more basic. Sand for scythe strakes (curved-bladed) and keel for reddening the hearth stane were two of his meagre commodities.

The Treasure House of Moffat was aptly named as there was no better way to describe the business of J. Barr and Son. The exterior of the premises were most attractive, with the original curved windows on either side of the doorway a unique feature. The window displays themselves were always greatly admired, especially from my point of view, the one that contained the boxes of toy soldiers, farm animals and dinky toys. During the war years (1939-45) these toys were non-existent, so they were much sought after as soon as they appeared. Returning home after school, there was always a gathering of lads and lasses at the toy window. Adults were also well catered for as can be seen in the photo of the interior. Selecting a gift in such surroundings must have, on occasion, found the buyer spoilt for choice.

Dickson House.

Dickson House was built in the late 1760's by James Dickson, the town's Stamp Master (Post Master today). His son, Will Dickson, was active with William Wilberforce, the parliamentary leader of the campaign against the slave trade which was eventually abolished in 1807.

The building was altered considerably in 1934 by James Barr & Son to accommodate the Treasure House of Moffat and continued in this vein when it was bought by Donald Lyon in 1956.

A few years later a more modern but less attactive alteration to the shop front was made by Moffat Weavers.

Gemini Jewellers, Campbells.

Syme Street, the narrowest street in Scotland?

In 2003 when Gemini Jewellers received a facelift, it came to light that many years and various owners had come and gone since it too was Tea and Wines, Campbell's.
It's interesting to note that the narrow opening at the right hand side of the photo is actually Syme Street, only 3 feet wide, less than one metre. Moffat has the narrowest hotel in the British Isles, the Star. The shortest street in Scotland, Chapel Street.
Do we have the narrowest street as well?

Jimmy and Ricky are a bit bemused at the 'discovery'.

William Forrest, House Agent, Bookseller, Stationer and Newsagent occupied the site where Grieve's is today.

Armstrong, Gentles, Brown and finally Wallace Brothers, over 100 years of butchers dealing from the same premises at the bottom of Well Street. Similar meats but drastic changes in hygiene and much quieter times since the Tower Clock stopped striking the hour.

The last four owners of the shop occupied by Little's have all been family bakers. The Bank of Scotland's previous owners were flooring furnishers, drapers and restaurateurs.

The Bank of Scotland building at Church Place where, for over 125 years the community were served with efficiency and dignity. Modern banking policy called for a more secure situation, hence the move to new premises on the High Street which proved a bit of a culture shock for many of the populace.

The premises of the previous Co-op store in Holm Street for almost 60 years is now Manse Furnishings.

Today's building, the Moffat Co-op caters for a wider range of shoppers.

Miss Muir's fancy goods and pottery warehouse at 1 Well Road.

J. BARR.
Visitors will find a large variety of well-selected Dainty Souvenirs in Gold and Silver. Scotch Pebble Goods a speciality. We hold a splendid selection of Souvenir and Thistle Spoons.
J. BARR & SON,

J. Barr and Son owned the shop after Miss Muir. According to the advertisement, a wide range of gifts were available, though not quite as extensive as those displayed in their High Street shop.

1 Well Road as it is today, R. Matchett and Son, Electrical Contractors.

ANNANDALE HOTEL
ADVERTISING BROCHURE 1920

D. J. MACDONALD, Annandale Hotel,
MOFFAT.

TARIFF.

Apartments.
For one person, including light and attendance - 3/6
For two persons - - - 6/-
Private Sitting Room - 5/-

Breakfast or Tea.
Cup of Tea or Coffee - 6d.
Plain, with Preserves - 1/6
With Eggs or Cold Meat 2/-
Fish or Meat Breakfast - - 2/6
Afternoon Tea - - - - 1/-

Luncheon or Dinner.
Basin of Soup - - - - 6d.
Cold or Hot Joint, Vegetables and Cheese - - - - - 2/-
Soup, Joints, Sweets and Cheese 2/6
Dinner - - - - - - 3/6

Fires, 1/- and 2/- Baths, Hot 9d., Cold 6d., in Bedroom, 1/-
For Wines, see Hotel List.
SPECIAL BOARDING TERMS.

W. H. PENMAN,
Cycle & Motor Agent.

NEW MOTOR GARAGE OPENED.

CARS FOR HIRE.

Michelin, Dunlop & North British Tyres always in stock.
Petrol. Oils. Accessories. Repairs.

Visitors wishing to purchase a thoroughly reliable Motor Car, or to hire one by the hour, day or week, are recommended to apply to . .

Penman's Garage, Station Road,
MOFFAT.

CHEMIST TO THE HOTEL.

James INGLIS, Established 1863.

Prescriptions accurately dispensed with the Purest Drugs by the Principal only.

Dispensing and Photographic Chemist,

The Spa Pharmacy, Well Street.

Complete Stock of Toilet, Nursery and Sick Room Requisites. - -

Aerated Waters in Syphons & Bottles.

Night Bell—20 Well Road.

Sulphur Bath Powders and Effervescent Aperient Salts, as recommended to be used along with the Moffat Mineral Waters.

Amateur Photographic Materials. Complete Stock of Plates. Films and all Accessories. PLATES & FILMS DEVELOPED AND PRINTED.

DARK ROOM.

SPECIALISTS IN LADIES' AND GENT'S WEAR.

T. Kennedy & Co.,
Milliners, Drapers . and Clothiers, .

22-24 Well Street, MOFFAT.

Highly Recommended for Dresses, Costumes, Hats.

Always the Latest in Ladies' & Gent's Neckwear and Gloves.

HARRIS, SHETLAND & COTTAGE HOMESPUN TWEEDS.

Shetland Shawls and Hosiery.

The Moffat Toffee Shop.

A. H. BLYTHE,
Confectioner,

Station Road,
(Opposite Established Church.)
MOFFAT.

A large assortment of the best makes of Toffee & Confectionery.

Makers of the Celebrated Moffat Toffee.

ANNANDALE HOTEL
ADVERTISING BROCHURE 1920

Mrs. HOOD, Well Road, MOFFAT.

Branch Studio—
Townhead, Lockerbie.
Visits Residences if required.

ENLARGEMENTS.
CHILDREN'S PHOTOS.
AMATEURS' WORK.

These branches are all Specialities, and are superintended by persons of **Long and Practical Experience.**
You are cordially invited to visit Mrs. Hood's Studio and inspect the **Latest Productions in Portraiture.**

The Newest Processes and Styles are represented. All beautifully suited for Enlargements. These can be reproduced from any Old Photo or Negative and are characterised by beautiful workmanship and finish.

DAVID ANDERSON,

Furnishing Ironmonger & Iron Merchant,

MOFFAT.

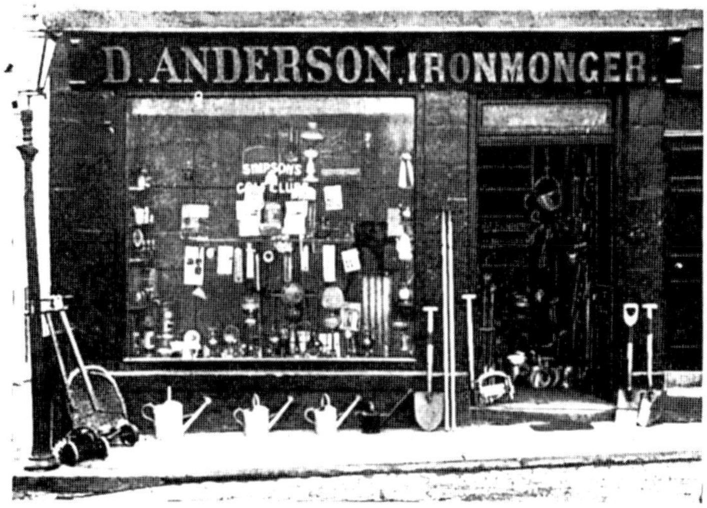

Open and Close FIRE RANGES, STOVES Etc., INTERIOR GRATES and TILES.

Cutlery and Electro-plated Goods of best make and quality.

GUN AMMUNITION.

REPAIRS of all kinds - - promptly executed.

FISHING TACKLE. FLIES, LINES and RODS specially suitable for the District.

MOFFAT'S OFFICIAL GUIDE 1938

A Good Tobacco
DESERVES
A Good Pipe
You can get both from
James Banton
7 WELL STREET
MOFFAT
Phone 201

THE OLDEST ESTABLISHED
: TOBACCONIST IN TOWN :

Fine Selection of
PIPES, POUCHES, Etc.

Ladies' Hairdresser
Telephone 121

Janet L. M. Waugh
2 Queensberry Place
WELL ROAD, MOFFAT

MACDONALD and OLGA
PERMANENT WAVING

A. DICERBO
8 HIGH STREET
6 CHURCH STREET
MOFFAT

Fish Restaurant

DELICIOUS ICES
Made from Purest
Materials

LAUNDRY
AND
Household Service

E. MUIR
"The Corner Shop for Bargains."
1 WELL ROAD
MOFFAT
Tel. No. 8 Tel. No. 8

Agent for 'RICHMOND PARK'
The Complete Laundry Service
HOLIDAY LAUNDRY and Cleaning Service for Visitors

CAMERON'S
BALMORAL HOTEL
THE OLD SPUR INN
WITH ITS BURNS ASSOCIATIONS
MOFFAT
OPPOSITE THE MINERAL BATHS

FULLY LICENSED

LUNCHEONS
DINNERS TEAS
PARTIES CATERED FOR

TERMS MODERATE
SPECIAL WEEK-END
RATES

LOCK-UP GARAGES

FREE TROUT FISHING ARRANGED FOR

PROPRIETOR DONALD ROSS CAMERON TELEPHONE 28

PURVEYORS
OF
HIGH-CLASS
BUTCHER MEAT

Telephone
18

Corned Beef
Salt Rounds
Pickled Tongues
and Sausages
Home-cured Bacon
Town and
Country Orders
Punctually
attended to

W. BROWN & SONS
2 WELL STREET
MOFFAT

T. Hetherington
Dispensing & Photographic Chemist

24 hours'
Developing
and Printing
Service

Photographic
Supplies

Kodak
Cameras and
Films

Established
1844

High Street, Moffat
(1 minute from G.P.O.)

LUNCHEONS, TEAS
REFRESHMENTS

HOME-MADE
CAKES and
SCONES

FLORAL CAFE
HIGH STREET

MORNING
COFFEE, TEA

PARTIES (35-40), TEA
CATERED
NIGHT ACCOMMODATION
W. H. HOY, Proprietor

PRINCELO
CAIRN KENNELS
ANNANLEA, MOFFAT
DUMFRIESSHIRE
Telephone 159 Railway L.M.S.

Champion "PRINCELO JESTER"
Bred and Owned by the proprietor
W. ALLAN GOODWIN
PUPPIES and ADULTS for Sale
Inspection of Kennels invited

THE UNION BANK OF
SCOTLAND, LIMITED
Established over 100 Years
Capital (Paid up) - £1,200,000
Reserve Fund - £1,800,000
NORMAN L. HIRD
General Manager
Head Offices:
GLASGOW - St. Vincent Street
(With Specially Organised
Foreign Exchange Department)
EDINBURGH - George Street
212 Branches throughout
Scotland
Small Savings Accounts
bearing Interest
Sums of 1/- and upwards
received
Passbooks and Home Safes
issued
LOCAL BRANCH—
High St., MOFFAT
AGENT—
NICOL J. McGREGOR

GEORGE YOUNG
GROCERIES - PROVISIONS
WINES AND SPIRITS

Special Value in
Empire Products:—
Teas, Wines, Fresh,
Canned and Dried
Fruits, Canned
Vegetables, Butter,
Cheese, Flour, Hams
Bacon, etc.

HIGH ST. MOFFAT
(Next to Post Office)
Telephone ——— Moffat 26

Careful and prompt attention to all orders

MOFFAT'S OFFICIAL GUIDE 1938

TO MAKE YOUR HOLIDAY MEMORABLE

MOFFAT, with its wealth of natural charms, and many outstanding landmarks—described in detail in other pages—can provide you with a most memorable holiday. You may record these happy memories in tangible and lasting form for yourself and your friends if you

VISIT "THE TREASURE HOUSE OF MOFFAT"

There you will find a wonderful selection of Local and Scotch Souvenirs in Jewellery, Scotch Pebbles and Stones, Crystal, China, Brass, Clan Tartans, Crest Novelties, etc., all at most moderate prices.

ESSENTIAL SERVICES OFFERED BY J. BARR & SON

- Qualified Optical Service—J. GLEN BARR, F.S.M.C., F.B.O.A.
- Repairs of every description to Watches, Clocks, Jewellery, etc.
- Official Shipping and Tourist Agents for all Lines.
- Local View Post Cards, Maps, and Souvenirs.

T. N. HOPKIRK & Co.

GENERAL CARRIERS AND CONTRACTORS

Holm St., MOFFAT

Regular Service between Edinburgh, Glasgow & Moffat

Glasgow Depot
62 Bell Street
Telephone Bell 1403

Edinburgh Depot
22 Grassmarket
Telephone 24891

Careful Reliable Moderate

TELEPHONE EIGHT SEVEN

CROOKS PARK GARAGE

EDINBURGH ROAD
MOFFAT. R.A.C. A.A.

PUBLIC GARAGE AND PRIVATE LOCK-UPS
CENTRAL HEATING

All Classes of Repairs promptly executed by competent mechanics

CARS AND BUSES FOR HIRE

PETROLS AND OILS

TELEPHONE MOFFAT 15

OPEN NIGHT AND DAY

JOHN D. GILMOUR

BUTCHER, POULTERER AND BACON CURER

SPECIALIST IN
COOKED MEATS
AND OWN :: ::
CURED BACON

One Quality Only—THE FINEST

Telephone Moffat 56

TOP OF

Well Street, Moffat

Elmhouse
Boarding
Establishment

NICELY SITUATED IN QUIET SURROUNDINGS

COMFORTABLE
HOMELY
MODERATE

Tariff on application to the Proprietrix, Miss M. Denholm

Phone 165

Moffat House Hotel

MOFFAT

PHONE 39 A.A.

This fine old Manor House, occupying a central position in the town, is beautifully situated in private grounds, finely stocked with ornamental trees, and artistically laid out.

Central Heating has been installed, also hot and cold running water in bedrooms.

Lit throughout with electricity, and each bedroom has a bedside light.

Special attention and care is devoted to cuisine and only the best is served at table. Guests on special diet are carefully catered for on particulars being supplied to proprietrix.

Open to Non-residents. Brochure from Proprietrix

STAR HOTEL
MOFFAT

R.A.C. R.S.A.C. A.A.

THE LOUNGE

Conveniently situated (in High Street) for Tennis Courts, Bowling Green, Golf Course, etc. Recent extensive alterations, redecorations and refurnishings have brought the "Star" up to modern requirements.

Hot and Cold Running Water in Bedrooms

Fully Licensed . .
Electric Light . .
Private Garage . .
Moderate Tariff on application . . . .

Under the constant personal supervision of the Proprietors, Mr and Mrs Oswald W. Butler . . . .

Telephone - - Moffat 34

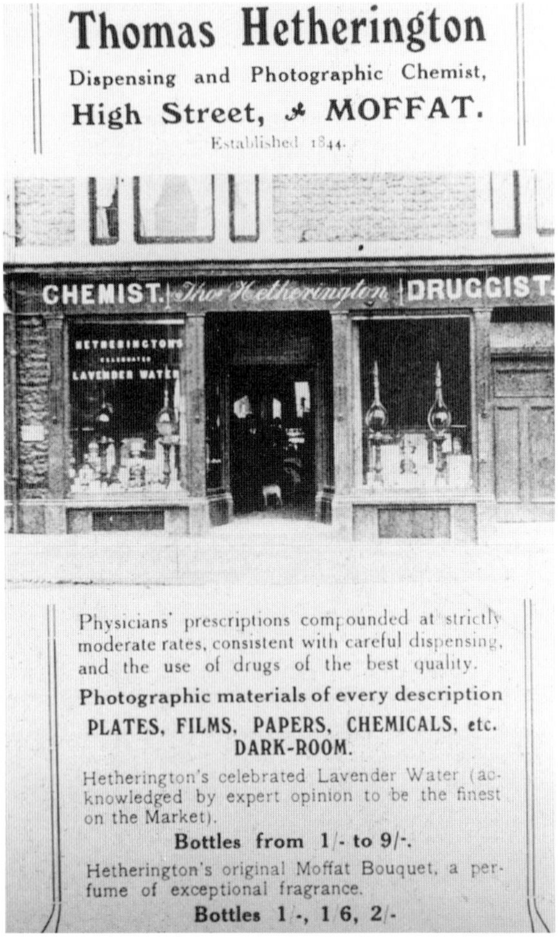

PLATES, FILMS, PAPERS, CHEMICALS, etc.

Hetherington's celebrated Lavender Water (acknowledged by expert opinion to be the finest on the Market).
Bottles from 1/- to 9/-.
Hetherington's original Moffat Bouquet, a perfume of exceptional fragrance.
Bottles 1/-, 1/6, 2/-

Thomas Welsh, M.P.S.,
Dispensing and Family Chemist,
HIGH STREET, MOFFAT.
LAVENDER WATER
Physicians' prescriptions compounded at strictly moderate rates, consistent with careful dispensing, and the use of drugs of the best quality.
CHEMIST · THOMAS WELSH, M.P.S. · PHARMACIST
CHEMIST
DRUGGIST
The Dispensing of Prescriptions is here performed by the Principal only, with the skill and accuracy acquired by many years of the best city experience.
All kinds of Photographic Material kept in stock.
Amateurs' Films and Plates developed.
High-class Ærated Waters, Perfumery, and all Toilet and Sick-room Requisites.
Sole Agent in this community for Rexall Specialities. Rexall Preparations are all sold with the Rexall guarantee — satisfaction or money back.

Thomas Welsh, Chemist and Pharmacist and G. Little, Chemist and Druggist both occupied the premises at 10 High Street during the early 1900's. Today the site houses the very popular Café Ariete.

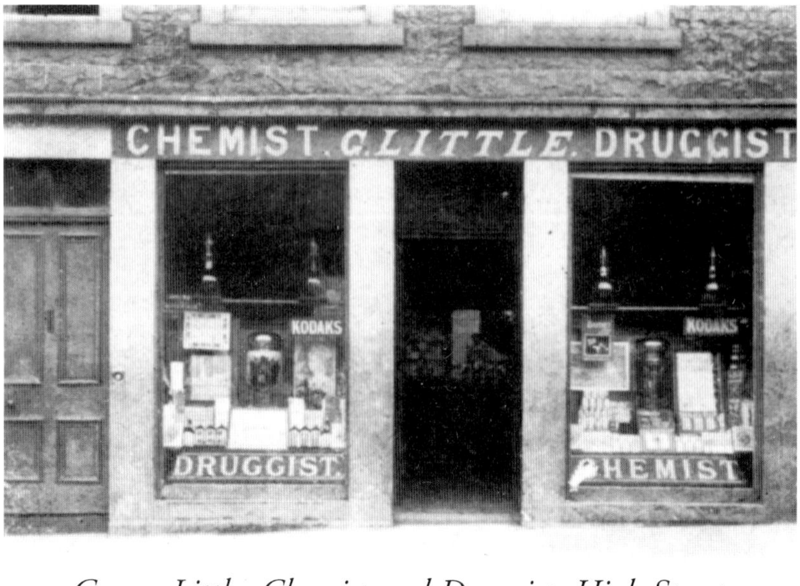

George Little, Chemist and Druggist, High Street.

Tony the Ice Cream Man at his favourite stance, the Station Park Gate, 1930's.

The Second World War: Internment

Over 60 years ago, in September 1939, a great adventure was about to start for a wee 5 year-old boy, an adventure that no other 5 year-old will ever experience in the history of the British Isles ever again. That wee boy was me, Emilio Dicerbo.

At the time, our family consisted of:

Dad, Antonio, 'Tony': 44 years
Mother, Pasqualina, 'Pasquo': 44 years
Oldest Brother, Francis: 18 years
Only Sister, Bettina: 16 years
Philip: 14 years
Vincent: 11 years
and myself, the youngest at 5 years old.

Di Cerbo

Family Name History

The Italian surname Dicerbo has several origins. Firstly, it is of patronymic origin, deriving from the personal name of the father of the original bearer of the name. In this instance, the surname derives from the name Gerbo, a variant of Gerbino, which arose as a hypocoristic or pet name form of Germanic names such as Gerbega and Gerberto. The existence of Italian personal names which are ultimately of Germanic origin may be explained by the fact that during the Middle Ages, Italy was invaded by several Germanic tribes, including the Lombards and Franks. Since the prefix "di" means "of", and most frequently appears in surnames of patronymic origin, we may interpret Dicerbo as meaning "son or descendant of Gerbo". This name was first documented in Florence in the "Libro di Montaperti" ("Book of Montaperti") in 1260 as "Gerbinus".

Alternatively, the surname may be of toponymic origin. In this case, the surname derives from the place name Gerbo. The town of Gerbo is located in the province of Torino, situated in the northwestern Italian region of Piedmont. When viewed in this manner, the surname means "one who hailed from Gerbo". It is important to note that the letters "c" and "g" frequently interchange in Italian surnames, as shown by Cervaso, a variant of Gervaso, and Castaldi, a variant of Gastaldi. Thus, variants of the surname Dicerbo include Gerbi and Gerbino. References to the surname Dicerbo or to its variants include the record of a noble family bearing the surname Gerbi from the Piedmont region. A family bearing the surname Gerbino was founded by one Giovanni, who was a royal soldier in 1542. Although he established his family in Mazzara, members later settled in Palermo.

BLAZON OF ARMS: Or, a fess azure; overall a tree eradicated vert, to the sinister a lion proper, crowned or.
Translation: Or (gold) symbolizes Generosity.
CREST: The lion of the arms.
ORIGIN: ITALY

7458/0

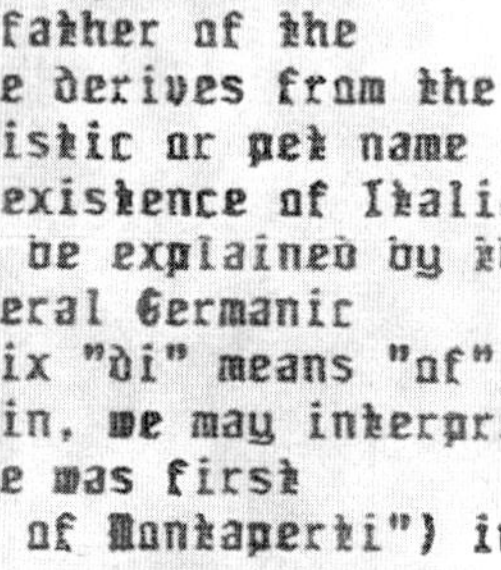

12795

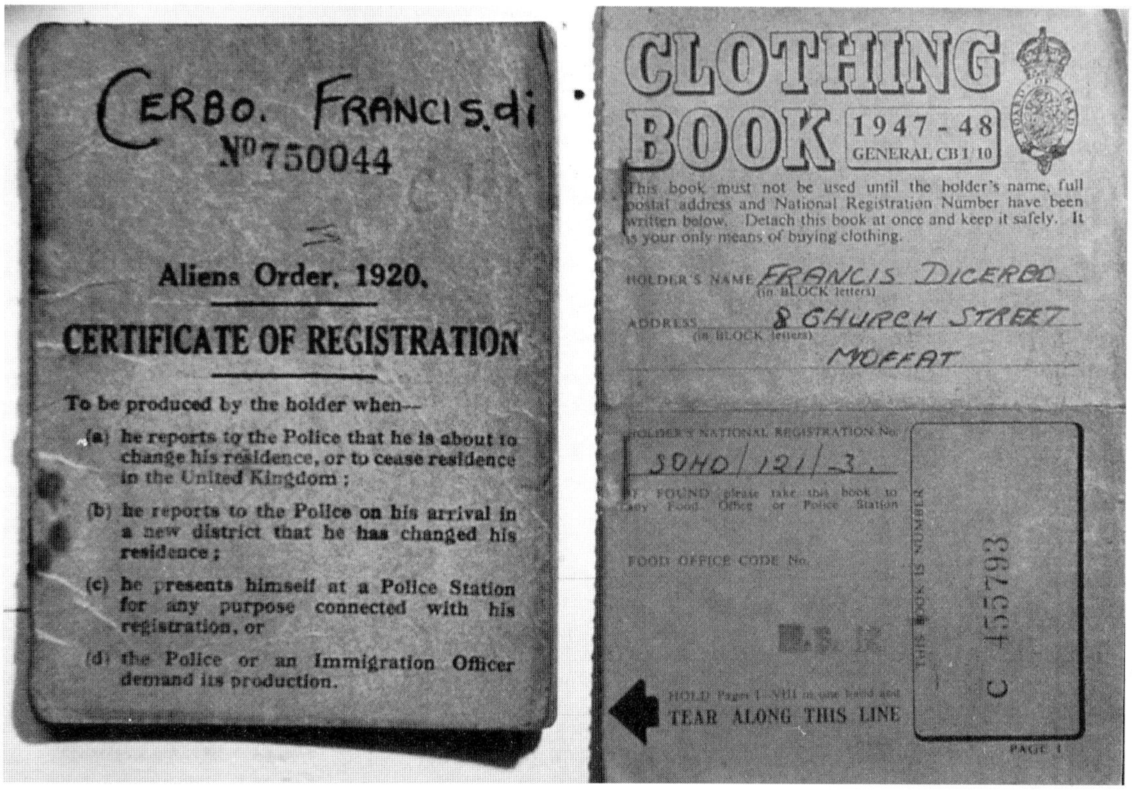

*My brother Francis' Certificate of Registration (1920 Aliens Order)
and book of clothing coupons as issued during and after the war.*

As you can see from our name, our family was Italian, and that meant that at the beginning of the hostilities of the Second World War in 1939 we were aliens, looked upon as potential spies, saboteurs and enemies of the state. So much so that my father Tony, local ice cream merchant who had arrived in Scotland seventeen years before on 20th March 1922, and my oldest brother Francis, who had been only one year old at that time and was now eighteen, received a rude awakening by the authorities in the middle of the night. Bundled into transport and driven to Dumfries Police Station, they were locked in cells together with other poor unfortunates from throughout the county, a dozen or so at a time.

I was very young, and slept soundly, knowing nothing of my dad's and brother's removal until the following day. I cannot remember the sadness that must have engulfed our family at that time. It is a blessing that toddlers don't often remember the darker moments of their early lives.

Every move by the internees, from one place of confinement to another, was conducted through the night. It was when the bus passed through Moffat High Street, en route from Dumfries to the camp at Milton Bridge, that a young passenger heard someone call to the back of the bus, "Hey Francis, there's your place down there." Francis acknowledged, and pointed out that he also worked over at the other side of the High Street, at James Sinclair's, as a storeman.

The young passenger, a seventeen year old, and myself became good friends some years later and I spent many happy hours with him when he was proprietor of the Annandale Hotel. It was Peter Toni.

Peter explained in graphic detail the events that followed from when they arrived at the camp at Milton Bridge, and it is to him that I am most grateful for the account of the rest of this chapter.

At Milton Bridge the internees slept under canvas, and it wasn't long before they found just how meagre their food supply was to be. Breakfast consisted of one slice of bread and marmalade while lunch was a plate of soup. To add insult to injury the kitchens were run by other internees, like themselves, who had arrived at the camp some time previously.

As rationing had not yet come into force, it was still possible to buy biscuits, fruit and chocolate from a little shop outside the camp. One enterprising sergeant would take orders for bits and pieces from some of the men who had not foreseen the dire state they now found themselves in.

Fortunately, most had some cash, not that it would have lasted any length of time, as the sergeant charged 2/6 ($12^1/_2$p), for a chocolate bar costing only 2d (less than 1p). Justice prevailed though, and this particular sergeant got his just desserts from his superiors shortly afterwards.

About a fortnight later, the company was on the move once again. They duly arrived in Bury, billeted in Wharf Mills, a huge empty, cold warehouse-type building with concrete floors and a pile of mattresses stacked against one wall, from which the men were told to take one each and find a place to settle down.

Francis as a teenager late 1930's.

Customers liked to try their hand at making their own 'sliders'. Jim Young is obviously happy with his attempt – too much ice cream on the scoop, Jim!

The stay in Wharf Mills was also quite brief and on orders being given for yet another move, this time the procedure followed a different pattern. The roll was called and the men were ordered to gather at the main gate. As they assembled they realised that some names were being missed out.

The assembled men, including my dad, Francis and Peter, were once more on the move arriving at some unknown port from where they embarked on a boat. Many times they asked various seamen and harbour workers where they were bound, but any replies they received made them none the wiser.

At one time during the crossing, Peter discovered a little kiosk which was boarded-up and as he stood close by, one of the crew approached, asking his name and where he came from. On discovering that Peter had come from Annan, he mentioned that his wife also came from Annan. At this point he disappeared into the kiosk, re-appearing with some fruit and chocolate, which he concealed under Peter's jacket, while whispering to him that their destination was the Isle of Man. Perhaps the sailor knew Peter's family, or just felt sorry for him, but either way he told him not to mention the goodies or the destination to anyone.

On disembarking at Douglas, the men were once again split up, but this time it was the end of their journey. They had at last arrived at the place that would house them for the duration of their internment – an internment which for some would last a few weeks, but for others, several months.

My dad was billeted in the Palace Camp, while Francis and Peter were billeted in the Alexandra Camp, two large hotels, close together and surrounded by a high, wire fence.

As I never at any time discussed their stay on the Isle of Man with my brother, my knowledge of this period is rather vague, except for the fact that parcels of cigarettes and various other items, sent over by my mother, occasionally arrived having been slightly tampered with. On the other hand, there must have been great comradeship among the internees, as all parcels received from loved ones were duly shared among friends.

Both my dad and Francis spent over a year in internment, but Peter, being only seventeen, was more fortunate and was sent home after only a few weeks.

Peter's situation, like our own, was rather bizarre. His brother, a British soldier, visited him at the camp – a seventeen year old interned by the British, while his brother was in the British army – what a farce! There must have been hundreds of families in similar situations. Following his brother's visit, Peter was informed that he had to apply to a tribunal regarding his release. On doing so, after answering all the relevant questions, he was told to leave the office, and that he would find out whether or not he was successfull in the course of a few days.

On leaving the office, one of the staff asked Peter how he'd got on. "I don't know,: answered Peter, at which the member of staff replied "Were the panel smiling?" "They were at the end," said Peter. "Then you're OK," was the reply – and these words proved to be correct a few anxious days later.

Two other internees were waiting for interviews on that particular morning, one of whom introduced himself to Peter, saying he was the Queen's portrait painter, who signed himself 'The Baron'. Were the panel smiling after his interview? I'd say odds-on that they were grinning from ear to ear!

Peter later discovered that his release, apart from the fact that he was only seventeen years old, was mainly due to a reference from Dumfriesshire's Chief Constable Black. On his return home to Annan, a friend asked him why he had left his other half behind, a comment referring to his obvious loss of weight.

Many months were to pass before my dad and Francis were allowed home, and the date on Francis's Certificate of Registration (Aliens Order 1920), shows that he was finally released on 2nd May 1941. Mainly this was thanks to Alex Cameron of Sinclair's, who repeatedly asked for him to be returned to his old job.

My dad was released some time later, and one morning he appeared at my bedside with a little porcelain pig. I don't suppose he could find any toys, but that little pig, and his old fishing rod, I cherish to this day.

Now let us return to Bury, to the time when the internees were first separated, to discover what happened to those who were left behind.

They also boarded a ship, but for a voyage that was meant to be much longer than a trip to the Isle of Man. The destination was Canada, but the ship they sailed on was reputedly carrying gold bullion from the British Mint for safe storage in Canada and it was torpedoed in the North Atlantic.

The ship was the 'Arrandora Star', and many crew members and Italian prisoners were lost at sea. (Did the authorities hope that a shipload of Italian internees would be left alone by German U Boats?)

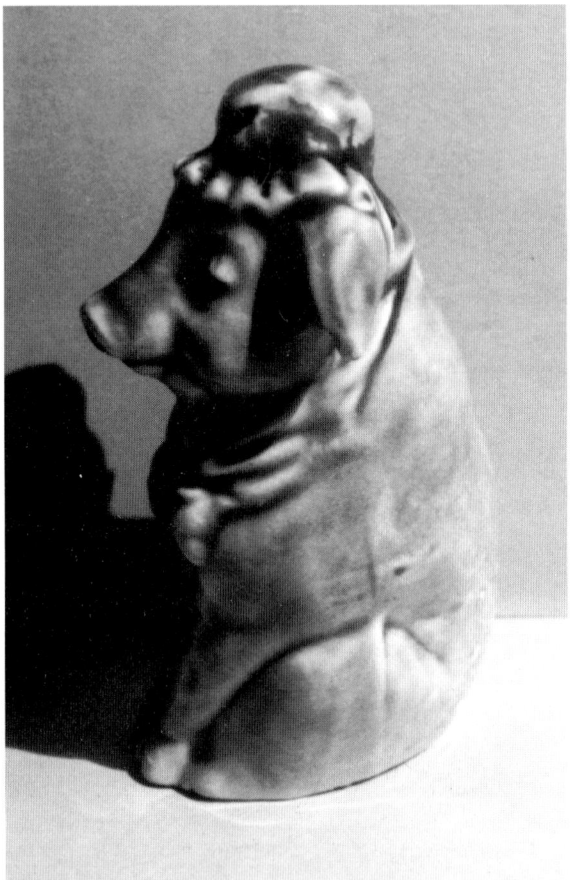

The wee porcelain pig that my dad brought me from the Isle of Man.

One survivor was from a well-known ice cream biscuit manufacturing family. His name was Zaccardelli, and the company of 'Zaccardelli and Cervi' supplied cones and wafers to us for many of my 45 years in the ice-cream trade.

It is rumoured that there are plans afoot to salvage the cargo of the sunken 'Arrandora Star'.

Coaching Days

Travelling in the early coaches was more of an endurance test than a pleasure as the journey along deep-rutted, boulder strewn dirt tracks found the passengers battered, bruised and definitely "under the weather" on arrival at their destination.

Even so, one writer at the time stated that the men who travelled in them were wimps as no true horseman would even consider giving up his mount for such a means of transportation. In truth, coaching journeys were so hazardous that many gentlemen about to embark on even a relatively short journey, made a will. One traveller wrote home: "After heavy rain the roads became covered with water to such an extent that the coach got stuck and the passengers had to swim, and one was drowned, which prevented me from travelling for many hours."

The Annandale Arms Hotel in 1815.

By the mid 1700's the increase in coach travel meant that a much improved road system was required so a toll system was introduced to fund the project.

There were two toll cottages in Moffat. One at the bottom of what is now Golfhill (the Langshaw Toll) and the other at the top of Academy Road on the site where Windygates stands today.

A long distance passenger coach of the early 1800's.

The Annandale Hotel stables were situated at the back of the building where the kitchen is today. There were also stables lining a cobbled driveway that led to a large cow house. There was stabling for 50 horses at the Annandale in 1788, where four fresh horses were hitched in fifty seconds. At that time, the speed increased from 6 to 7 miles per hour. Every coaching inn stabled horses and 620 were required on a journey from London to Edinburgh.

The Toll Cottage at the northern end of the town. In 1795, even though the tolls had been inexistence for some time, the roads were in a dilapidated state, so much so that the Provost of Glasgow was informed that the Glasgow to Carlisle mail might have to be discontinued in favour of the old route by the Crook and Edinburgh, which involved the loss of a whole day.

Moffat circa 1900, from the south. In the foreground is the Toll Cottage where my mother-in-law, Mrs. Robert Adamson was born in 1902. The station park is under construction and the Auld Free Kirk (now the council yard) is on the extreme left (built 1843).

The Toll Cottage at the northern end of the town in the early 1920's.
At this time it was a dairy and confectioner's. The lady in the photograph is Mary Dalling.
'Windygates' stands on the site today.

The Moffat Temperance Hotel.
Advertised as 'a home from home' in the early 1900's it is
better known nowadays as The Balmoral Hotel.

The Old Coach Bridge across the River Evan behind the Old Brig Inn at Beattock. The bridge that replaced it, at the northern approach to the village, was designed by Thomas Telford and built by John Macdonald in 1819.

The commemorative sandstone on the Telford designed bridge.

By the end of the eighteenth century coach travel was slightly more bearable with the introduction of a simple spring like suspension formed by leather straps. Previous to this wagons and coaches ran on solid axles, a fourteen day journey from Edinburgh to London must have been almost unbearable.

In 1799 several mail coaches were snowed in during a severe snow storm on 1st February and weren't able to proceed until 27th April. In 1806 following another freezing journey through a snow storm the driver arriving at his destination, found that his guard had froze to death.

Two well known road engineers were born at this time. John Loudon McAdam was born in Ayr in 1756. He developed tar macadam at Dumcrief and died in Moffat in 1836.

Thomas Telford, who designed the bridge over the River Evan at the Old Brig Inn in 1819 was born in Westerkirk near Langholm in 1757 and died in 1834.

The Edinburgh Road, as it is today, was formed in 1823. In 1818 the Trustees met, agreed the layout with contractors and also decided that the Toll Cottage at the head of the town should be built.

On 1st February 1831, James McGeorge, guard and John Goodfellow, driver perished in a blizzard near Tweedshaws while attempting to reach that place on foot carrying mail bags, weighing almost 100lbs, after their mail coach got stuck in a snow drift.

Two lady passengers who were en-route to Edinburgh were rescued by Mr. Cranstoun of the Spur Inn when he heard of their predicament from Mr. James Marchbank. Mr. Marchbank, a road surveyor of the Burgh who knew the road well, had agreed to escort the coach to Tweedshaws on foot. Only two miles from Moffat the horses could no longer proceed, so McGeorge and Goodfellow decided to carry the mail bags the further five miles to Tweedshaws. It was at this time that Mr. Marchbank returned to Moffat for assistance for the ladies who were in a fearful state of mind.

The following morning Mr. Marchbank set off on foot to see if the two men had reached Tweedshaws, but returned to Moffat exhausted and heavy hearted on learning that neither of the pair had made it to their proposed destination. The following day Mr. Marchbank and Mr. Henderson, the district surveyor and about 150 volunteers from Moffat with shovels and poles renewed the search.

It was eventually discovered that the pair had wandered some way from the main road before perishing in the deep snow, but before succumbing had hung the mail bags on a snow post which bore the marks of frostbitten, bleeding fingers.

The last mail coach from Beattock to Glasgow Post Office arrived at 5.45pm on 14th February 1848, as mail trains had taken over, thus coaches, horses, inns and staff were no longer required in their previous numbers.

The date was the first day of February in the year 1831. On that morning a considerable quantity of snow had fallen, and the wind was rising. The Edinburgh Mail, which left Dumfries at ten o'clock, completed the first part of its journey all but within scheduled time. James MacGeorge was guard.
MAIL COACH HEROES 80 YEARS SINCE.

The Broken Bridge got its name on Tuesday 25th October 1808.

The Broken Bridge

On the night of 25th October 1808 part of a bridge over the River Evan about eight miles from Moffat collapsed into the river.

The bridge spanned the River Evan near the spot where it is joined by the Biddies Burn and during a raging spate which was in progress at the time, one parapet and about half the width of the surface collapsed into the river.

The London mail coach had left Glasgow at 2pm with Alexander Cooper, a Moffat man, coachman and Thomas Kinghorn, guard. There were four inside passengers, one lady and three gentlemen. Two outside passengers were a Mr. Lund of Bond Street, London and Mr. William Brand, an Ecclefechan merchant. These two gentlemen must have been attending to urgent business to be travelling as outside passengers in such inclement weather conditions.

Shortly after 10 o'clock, Cooper, with blinding sleet lashing his face, coaxed his team onwards down the gradient and crashed into the raging torrent which immediately doused the lamps, leaving the panic stricken survivors in total darkness.

Fortunately the lady passenger managed to clamber onto a rock midstream and even though the noise of howling wind and roaring water was horrendous, her screams were heard by the driver of the mail coach approaching from the opposite direction, who stopped just in time to avert a second disaster.

The bridge was midway between Carlisle and Glasgow and the up and down coaches used to pass there each night on their relative journeys.

The lamps of the newcomer illuminated the scene to reveal the wrecked coach, three dead horses and the bodies of Mr. Lund and Mr. Brand, amid the tangle of reins, wood, steel, baggage and mail bags.

The coachman, Mr. Cooper was found following a search, jammed between two rocks. His arm was broken and he also suffered internal injuries from which he died three weeks later in Moffat, where during his confinement the townspeople subscribed a goodly amount for him and his family.

The three gentlemen passengers who were inside the coach all survived, aided by the coachman and guard who in so doing, put their own lives at risk, but the lady who at this time was still crouching on her little island proved to be more of a problem.

It fell upon John Geddes, the down guard to implement her rescue and when he was lowered down the rock face on a rope, he stopped short when modesty held him back. "Whaur?", he asked. "Whaur will I grup her?" "Grip me where you will," cried the lady. "So you grip me tight." Thus reassured, Geddes soon had her safe on the bank, then proceeded to save some of the mail bags from being swept away.

Other mail bags were saved by a number of men who arrived at the scene with Mr. Rae, the Postmaster and Mr. Clapperton, a surgeon who took care of the injured including Kinghorn who had sustained head injuries.

The bridge became known as the "Broken Bridge" and was rebuilt in 1816 when a grant of £50,000 was passed for a new road to be constructed from Carlisle to Glasgow. The new road which followed the Evan Water Valley was opened in 1819.

The Black Bull Inn.

The High Street

The Colvin Fountain or Moffat Ram was funded by William Colvin of Craigielands, Beattock at a cost of £600, and was donated to the town of Moffat in 1875.

Moffat. Colvin Fountain. An ornamental drinking fountain, surmounted by the figure of a Ram in bronze, a gift to the town at a cost of £600, from the late William Colvin, Esq., of Craigielands. William Brodie, R.S.A., Sculptor. *Annandale Series, Weir. Photo., Moffat.*

The sculptor was William Brodie and the subject was selected because of the close association between the town and the sheep industry.

William Colvin, an iron industrialist, took up residence at Craigielands Estate in 1855 together with his sister and ailing mother who died in 1858. At the time of the inauguration ceremony in 1875, William was in ill health, so his brother, Dr. Robert Colvin from Edinburgh, represented him. William died a few years later in 1880 and was buried in Beattock Cemetery.

There is a tale describing the fate of another ram called "Old Charlie". Madge Wildfire or "Feckless Fanny" was a shepherdess who roamed the countryside with a small flock of sheep and a faithful old ram called "Charlie". Madge spent most of her nights outdoors when her flock would close in to keep her warm and safe. In the mornings Charlie would make his way through to her and assist her to rise by allowing her to grasp his horns as she stood up, gently raising his head as Madge found her footing. The story goes that old Charlie led the flock into a vegetable garden where he met his untimely death by being killed by a mastiff. He was buried in the Leddy's Knowe which came to be known as Ladyknowe c.1800.

The High Street c. 1912
The first trees were planted in the 1890's but failed.
In the photograph the subsequent planting is thriving.

The High Street c. 1935
The light-coloured building (our shop) on the left bears a shield-shaped sign 'Tony's Delicious Ice Cream' and the Buccleuch Hotel has its own petrol pumps.

The Ram was removed for restoration work in December 2003 and returned in March 2004.

In March 2002 it was discovered that the Ram was in dire need of repair, a hole had appeared at its backend and cracks were found in the bodywork. It was removed for remedial work in December 2003 and returned in March 2004. Fully restored, it is now floodlit, pumped water keeps the troughs filled, and railings have been erected. The total cost of the restoration project was in the region of £57,000.

Crumb scoop.

Over the years a number of establishments have included the word 'ram' in the name of their business etc. Some of the more recent being Ram Lodge, Ram Antiques and Moffat Rams Rugby Team.

During the early 1900's, one particular business, namely J. Barr and Son, "The Treasure House of Moffat", went one better by adopting the ram as its registered trade mark and included the symbol on some of its merchandise, such as companion sets, door knockers and crumb scoops, like the one illustrated.

The Moffat Ram

from 1875 to 2004

He's stood so proud atop his cairn
Well ower a hundred years
And heard so many people say
"The poor thing's got no ears".
But nobody's sure if thats the truth
Or where his ears might be
As tucked-in tight behind his horns
They're difficult to see.

He's stood so proud there on his own
Through every kind of weather
While hardy members o' his kin
Cavorted through the heather.
To reproduce the bonny lambs
That gambol in the spring
And when he saw them herded by
He felt just like a king.

But herding days are long since gone
Which makes him feel so sorry
The ewes he catches glimpses o'
Now whiz past in a lorry.
No time to notice if they smile
Or gie him the "come-hither"
But what he misses most of a'
Is the sheepish "bah-bah" blether.

He's stood so proud there for so long
From carts to motor cars
He's seen the good times and the bad
And survived the two great wars.
But time waits not for man nor beast
So came that fateful day
When a keen-eyed townie pointed out
That he'd started to decay.

It took three hours to prise him free
From off his lofty cairn
And sent down south to be repaired
All wrapped up like a bairn.
When he returned and was unveiled
His pleasure was immense
For railings, lights and water pump
Were his – at great expense.

Jock Dicerbo
16/4/2004

Shortly before the appearance of the 'Ram', the Bank of Scotland moved from Well Street to its new site at the southern end of the High Street, the site of the old Meal House. Some time later, the lower part of Dickson House became the 'Treasure House of Moffat', which at the moment is owned by Moffat Woollens.

The archway in the building on the south side of the Causeway was enclosed, and became the 'Annandale Estates Office' which is today another shop selling tweeds and woollens.

In the late 1890's, two rows of hybrid lime trees were planted, and in November 1920, the War Memorial was unveiled.

By the end of the 1960's, the two business premises, our ice-cream and confectionery shop and the tea room on the corners of Church Street and High Street, had been altered.

The Garden Centre was built and the remaining open roadway was laid out in a manner more suitable for modern traffic.

Hotels, changing hands from time to time, mostly remained as they were but shops, as well as changing ownership, on occasion changed their business completely.

The High Street c. 1954
The shop on the extreme left was that of J. Barr & Son, the Treasure House of Moffat, Jewellery, Gifts, Toys etc. The original curved windows at the entrance, added to the already most attractive shop front on the High Street.

Moffat Cadet Force, ready for their camp at Sandyhills 1935.
Front Row (L to R): *John Torrance, Andy Little, Peter Richardson, Norman Currie, Bill Wallace, Davy Bullman, John Black, Gillie Turnbull, Mathie Rankine, Peter Richardson, Andrew Richardson, Willie Hunter, Tommy Burns, Geordie Glendinning, Capt. Walter Lockerbie.*
Back Row (L to R): *Rob Little, Jim Halliday, Jim Hogg, Alan Galligan, John Richardson, Sidney Little, Tom Currie, Sandy Turnbull, Willie Moffat, Robert Richardson. 'Lord' John Torrance as he was affectionately called, was a tailor to trade and made all the cadet uniforms - made to measure!*

Miss MacDonald's Girls' Training Corp. (GTC) (1947).
Front Row (L to R): *Margaret Edgar, Margaret Telfer, Miss MacDonald, Mary Black, Agnes Halliday.*
Middle Row (L to R): *Daphne Cowan, Eleanor Moffat, Margaret Moffat, Violet Richardson, Sheila Moffat.*
Back Row (L to R): *Nessie Suttie, Joyce Maxwell, Chrissie Caruthers, Helen Turnbull.*

A friendly Polish soldier with a young Elliot Johnstone "Claudie" on his knee – his big brother Jimmy standing behind and a host of young pals including Jacky Maltman, Billy Duncan and Dick Sneddon.

At the Beginning

Following the internment of my dad and Francis, the earliest memory that I have of the war was the appearance of bell-tents in the Holm Road Playing Fields, and wandering among them in the company of some older boys.

The soldiers were indulging in various activities, washing, polishing, some in small groups sitting talking and smiling as I passed by. Another early memory was the arrival of a number of Polish soldiers.

Some were billeted in sheds at Ladyknowe while the higher ranks were more comfortably off, enjoying the hospitality provided by a number of Moffat families in their homes.

I don't remember how long these soldiers were billeted here, but some of their officers attended classes at Moffat Academy, being taught English, and one of the teachers involved was Miss Rankin, who was my teacher at that time. All this took place in September and October 1940.

Round about this time, preparations were well under way for the defence of the country. There was the Home Guard; Army Cadets; Auxiliary Fire Service; Air Raid

St. Ninian's School was a fee-paying school, founded by Sir Hugh Dowding's father in the latter part of the 19th century. Lord Dowding, who was born in 1882, was educated there. During the late 1940's and early 1950's, St. Ninian's became St. Austin's, when it housed Roman Catholic boys as an approved school. When they left, after lying empty for a while, it was re-opened as Duncan House Boys' School. Following the closure of this establishment, the buildings fell into disrepair, but as fate would have it, the Dowding name has reappeared. The buildings have been completely re-developed into a splendid residential block of flats, providing accommodation for ex-RAF personnel and their dependents – Dowding House.

The Masonic Hall was built in 1886 to accommodate the pupils from Morrison's School (The Seceder Academy) in Well Street. The Seceder Academy was originally built in 1839 with an endowment of £2,000 for the poorer children of the town. William Morrison was born in Moffat in 1796. Following a successful mercantile career in New York and Calcutta, he died on board ship returning home and was buried at sea in 1837.

At the top of Academy Road can be seen Moffat Academy, as it was, a single storey building, after its construction in 1834.

Precautions; Air Training Corps; Women's Rural Institute, and other organisations, as well as the blackout, rationing, gas masks and salvage.

Other forms of precaution were also applied at this time, including protecting the occupants of buildings from flying glass from bomb blasts, by sticking strips of sticky paper diagonally across window panes. Moffat Academy's windows received special attention by having heavy fabric mesh glued to them.

Cars', lorries', vans' and buses' headlamps were blacked out, with only narrow slits, to allow two or three tiny beams to shine through and all vehicles had white paint along the running boards and bumpers. Edges of pavements etc. were also painted white, to make them slightly more visible in the black out. Iron railings were removed from the town hall,

Moffat Academy before the reconstruction in 1933.

The original part of Moffat Academy, as it is today, an attractive sandstone and whinstone building built in 1933. I spent my entire school days there.

St. Andrew's Church, St. Mary's Church, the police station and many other buildings both public and private. Special Saturday matinees at the town hall cinema, were free to all children bringing any old piece of scrap, glass jars or old rubber hot water bottles – anything that could be recycled and used for the war effort.

There were a number of local worthies, both male and female who took active parts in organising functions and "doing their bit", while the young men and women of the town were on active service.

One local character who was deeply involved in protecting the town was Mr. Tom Hopkirk, owner of the haulage firm based on the site of the Ladyknowe garage, by the Mill Burn Bridge.

Tom, or rather Tam as he was known locally, was a Canadian Mountie before he came to Moffat, and he was involved from the very beginning.

His fleet consisted of about nine or ten lorries and he employed half a dozen drivers including Geordie Stewart, Davy Seaton, Wullie Reive, Alan Galligan and at that particular time in late 1939 a young fourteen-year-old apprentice called John 'Jock' Park.

Apparently, Tam had received orders stating that if the church bells chimed, he was to "destroy all the petrol pumps in the town". Needless to say, on one occasion, when Tom returned to Moffat from a meeting in Edinburgh, the bells were chiming away for all they were worth. (It was some practice or other that Tam knew nothing about.)

He stopped at the garage, ran out and grabbed a sledge hammer, jumped into his wee car, and before anyone could stop him, drove off. Pulling up only yards away at Andy

Warriston College, Warriston. Originally housing a girls' college, it then became a boys school before finally ending its days as an educational establishment, a boarding school for girls. By 1990, the Warriston/Holm Park Complex was in a state of dereliction. It will however, be restored to a fine residence and block of six luxury flats.

Fingland's garage, he jumped out, duly landing a couple of hefty blows on one of the pumps, before one of his drivers caught up with him and explained the chiming bells.

Tam took air-raid precautions seriously and would at times, show small groups of people, including his drivers, how to deal with incendiary devices.

His equipment for demonstration purposes consisted of a bucket of sand, a bucket of water, a stirrup pump and a bottle with a piece of cloth pushed into the neck with only the slightest hint of petrol on the cloth.

The cloth was ignited, the bottle pushed over, covered in sand and doused with water. As this took place on a stone floor, there was no fear of any damage – until one particular evening when one of the company decided to liven things up by slightly increasing the volume of petrol, and the demonstration became an incident.

Tam by nature was a jolly soul, but now and again his more serious side would show through. One afternoon, when Tam was working on an engine, he told young Jock Park to go and tidy up the bench at the back of the garage.

Jock proceeded as instructed and as he tidied up the tools he found a wallet lying on the edge of the bench. He opened the wallet and saw a £5.00 note, so he took the wallet to Tam, who also opened it, looked inside, and promptly stuck it in his back pocket, without a word.

Three years later, when Jock was leaving Moffat to join the Fleet Air Arm, Tam called him into his office and said, "You're an honest lad, Jock Park, do you remember when you found yon £5.00 note? Well, I put it there to test your honesty – so here ye are, put it in your pocket – something to go away wi'." Five pounds was a lot of money in 1943.

Moffat Academy Sports Team 1937 with a trophy won at Dumfries.
Standing (L to R): Winnie McDonald; Henry Lockhart; Mabel Chapman ; Johnstone Edgar; Nell Gibson; Eric Young; Aileen Galligan; Donald McLachlan; Margaret Adamson.
Seated (L to R): Mr. Shaw, Rector; Mr. Gordon.
Seated at front row: Ian Harper.
Aileen Galligan was Dux of the Academy the same year.

The open-air swimming pool at Warriston, built by the boys themselves c. 1934.

WARRISTON SCHOOL,
MOFFAT, N.B.

THE DINING HALL.

A 1930's advert for Warriston School.

*A Moffat Academy Primary Class c. 1931.
Back Row: Teacher: Miss Fleming, Willie Richardson, Willie Moffat, Ian Harper, Norman Young, Donald McLachan, Gordon Welsh, Cameron Taylor, ? Stevenson.
2nd Back Row: Margaret Corbett, Jack Raffel, Mathew Rankine, Tommy Burns, Jim Clark, Jim Richardson, Peter Richardson, Sybil Young.
Seated: Marion Murray, Mamie Currie, Janet Denholm, Hannah Boa, Ina Stitt, Olive Wilson, Ella Cuthil, Sheila Hill, Betty Fairbairn.
Front Row: Joe Proudfoot, ?, Margaret Thompson, Elizabeth Black, Bettina Dicerbo, Jim Gentles.*

1937
School Dux Medallists

Jack Raffel, Dux Medallist at Moffat Academy.

Margaret Adamson, High Street, Moffat, and Donald M'Lachlan, Mearsdale Park, Moffat, who won the schools sports championships of Moffat Academy.

Aileen Galligan, Dux Medallist at Moffat Academy.

Rockhill Rest House on Beechgrove in the 1930's.
The iron railings, like those of many other residences were removed for the war effort.

Gas Masks and Salvage

Gas mask drills at the Academy always ended up with the teachers becoming rather irate, the reason being the rude noises that could be produced by placing one's hands over the filter and blowing, forcing the air to escape from between the sides of the gas mask and one's cheeks. It caused great hilarity among us young pupils.

I was now seven years old and could wander around as I pleased. Every Thursday found me down at the council yard, waiting for the council lorry to arrive, with its load of tins and other pieces of light metal scrap for the war effort. The tins and scrap, would be tipped out at the 'tin dump', and as it was emptied, there was always a small group of boys waiting to see what they could find.

Throughout the earlier months of the war, many a fine toy was found among the empty tins and the bigger lads would try all manner of persuasion towards us younger kids to make us part with our treasures, but we were never bullied into parting with anything. In fact I never experienced bullying throughout the entire war years.

Old Willie Harkness, Dave Thomson and Adam Tait were the council workers who looked after the scrap and baled waste paper, which was kept in a locked shed called the 'paper dump' and on any occasion that I chanced to visit them, there were always a few comics. On one very special day even a stamp album had been put aside for me – only a few dozen stamps in it, but it was magic.

Willie Harkness with the Corporation Ash Cart in the early 1940's. 'Old Willie', as I knew him, showed me much kindness when by dad was interned, and I often ponder those days when I pass the 'Auld Kirk' on my way down to the waterside.

Arrival of Evacuees

The earlier part of the war years saw another major change throughout the town, the arrival of evacuee families from Glasgow and Clydebank. The popluation at that time numbered 1970. With the evacuees numbering 948, Moffat's population increased by 42%, whereas in Dumfries the population only increased by 10.8%. Some of them were housed in empty houses and shop properties, while children unaccompanied by adults were found temporary homes in households where they soon became accepted as part of the family.

Three, from the many boys in this situation, were brothers who stayed with Mr. & Mrs. Anderson of Annanside. They were Ian, Billy and Freddy. Billy and I became good friends and were often in each other's company until he eventually left Moffat to return to his home in Glasgow. We soon discovered that we had similar likes and dislikes, with both of us keenly interested in nature study, poking about the burns and ponds and looking for birds nests. In these early years, as a child, one of the poems I liked to read in class contained the lines:

"Down the river and over the lea,
That's the way for Billy and me."

Even today, I can look back and see in my mind's eye two wee boys, chattering excitedly as they hastened along the waterside path, on yet another adventure.

Moffat Fire Brigade 1909
The horse-drawn fire appliance of the early 1900's with the firemen displaying the various pieces of fire-fighting apparatus in use during that period.
In the photograph are: ***Front Row (L to R):*** *Bailie W. Edgar; Lieut. D. Nicholson; Provost Wm. Forrest; Firemaster J. Johnstone; Councillor Tom Welsh.*
Middle Row (L to R): *J. Blythman, Driver; J. McBride; J. Hawthorne; J. Dempster; A. Dunbar; T. G. Tweedie.* ***Back Row (L to R):*** *T. Burgess; A. Moffat.*

Moffat Brigade National Fire Service 1940's.
Front Row (L to R): *Mr. Proudfoot; Mr. Noble; Davy Little; Jim Forrest.*
Middle Row (L to R): *Bob Stewart; Peter Hepburn; Wm. 'Binno' Adamson; Adam Edgar; ? ; Willie Murray.* ***Back Row (L to R):*** *Jim Hendry; ? ; Willie Little; Jack Thomson.*

Moffat Fire Brigade 1920's – 1930's.
Personnel on appliance: ***Top (L to R):*** *Mr. Adamson, Mr. Little, Mr. Murray.*
Middle (L to R): *Mr. D. Thompson, Mr. A. Moffat, Mr. F. Proudfoot, Mr. T. Murray, Mr. B. Maxwell.*
Front Row (L to R): *Mr. Gilmour, Mr. Gunn Budge, Mr. Maxwell, Mr. Fitzsimmons.*

This was the fire engine that raced to the Moffat Hydro in the early hours of the morning on Monday 2nd June 1921. With today's modern fire-fighting appliances there is a good chance that most of the building could have been saved. Unfortunately Moffat Fire Engine didn't carry enough hose to reach a sufficient water supply, the nearest being the River Annan. A further appliance was summoned from Gretna, but sadly by the time it arrived the massive structure was well ablaze. One hundred and forty staff and guests were in residence at the time, incredibly no lives were lost.

The little fire engine was presented to the town by Col. Gardiner. It was garaged in the council building, in the part more recently used as the Burgh Surveyor's office, and latterly where council staff spend their tea breaks. The highly polished helmets lined the walls on pegs that also supported leather belts and axes – an awe inspiring sight for a six-year-old.

Round the corner, old Willie Harkness would stable the two council work horses away for the night, the clatter of the big heavy feet on the cobbles and the rattle of the harness are sounds long since gone. The snow plough always fascinated me, the council workmen built it themselves. It was 'V'-shaped with a huge U-bolt attached at the point of the 'V', which in turn was attached with chains to the horse's harness. The horse would drag the plough through the snow, which at times would swerve from side to side, forming a nice zig-zag pattern as the horse plodded up the road.

The Auld Kirk.
The council yard on one occasion when there was an abundance of water for the appliance. The windows in the building are the only indication that it was once a church. With the building of the church in 1843, the 'Wide Close' as it was known was re-named Church Street.

The Old Churchyard.
In 1747 the headstones in the old graveyard were removed and over a metre of soil was added to accommodate further burials. The disturbance could have been the reason part of the small church collapsed during a service some years later. The minister of the day kept calm and ushered the congregation to safety without anyone sustaining injury.

Buried in the cemetery are John Goodfellow and James McGeorge who perished in the snow above the Beef Tub en route from Dumfries to Edinburgh with the Royal Mail Coach (1st February 1831).
Full report of tragedy in "Coaching Days" on page 70.

John Loudon Macadam of road surfacing (tarmac) fame was buried there in 1836.

The remains of the ancient Chapel of The Knights of St. John, dating from the 12th century. The window arch can be seen at Chapel Farm.

The Grandfather – part of the gable end of the old pre-reformation church as it can be seen in the Old Kirkyard today.

A few metres in to the right-hand side from the gate of the Old Cemetery is a small misshapen piece of sandstone block – "The Kickin' Stane". It was reputed to be the last resting place of an unknown person who burned a bible; apparently residents were told to kick the stone when visiting the cemetery.

The Parish Church 1790 - 1888.
Referred to as 'the Father' and also as 'the Flying Spur'.
Part of 'the Grandfather' can still be seen in the old kirkyard, but as yet I have not heard present-day St. Andrew's referred to as 'the Son'!

Churches

High on a hill, to the west of Moffat stands a monument to the 12th century Knights of St. John (Knights Templar or Red Friars). The monument is an arched window, all that remains of the chapel that in those far-off days welcomed all and sundry to take shelter in their times of need.

St. Andrew's Church as it was shortly after being built, close to the site of 'the Flying Spur'.

St. John's Episcopal Church. Situated on Millburn-side, and erected in 1872 by the late J. T. Lawrence, Esq., a Liverpool merchant, long-resident in Craigieburn House. The church was very comfortable and had a fine organ.

Although the main settlement was at Chapel Farm, much of the land on both sides of the River Annan was farmed by them with much success.

A rich and influential order during crusading times, they professed the defence of the Holy Temple and in so doing evoked the disapproval of the Vatican and were finally suppressed in 1316 by Pope Clement V.

In 1189 the Earl of Huntingdon led 5000 men, 1000 from Annandale and mostly Hallidays, to aid Richard the Lionheart on the third crusade.

Down in the valley, in the old churchyard, stands another monument to the memory of by-gone religion, it is the gable end of the Pre-Reformation Church, in which a

Situated on the south slope of the Gallowhill, with a Western aspect the villas in this part of the town, were much prized by visitors. The Well Road U.F. Church is also seen.

Well Road in 1862 when the foundation stone for the United Presbyterian Church in Old Well Road was laid.

congregation worshipped throughout most of the 18th century until decay forced its closure in 1790.

This church was known as the 'Grandfather'. From the old churchyard, the congregation moved to, and worshipped in, the Parish Church which was built about the same time. This church, as well as being referred to as 'the Father' was also known as 'The Flying Spur'.

The emblematic weather-vane atop the steeple, was incorporated in the crest of the Earl of Hopetoun, who donated the land on which the church was built.

In 1863 the building was complete – a magnificent achievement for the masons and other tradesmen of the period. The church was demolished in the 1960's. The photographer who captured the before and after shots picked his/her spot well.

St. Andrew's today with two major changes – addition of clock faces in 1932 and removal of gas ventilators from roof.

St. Mary's United Free Church in 1892 replaced the 'wee free', presently the council work place.

Mr. Duncan McLachlan and wedding coach. St. Andrew's Church c1919. During the 1914-1918 war, Mr. McLachlan drove the horse-drawn ambulance for the auxiliary hospital.

About a hundred years later, in 1887, St. Andrew's Parish Church was built on a site adjacent to the old church. Apart from one or two obvious alterations and additions, the impressive edifice stands today, as it was constructed, with sandstone blocks cut from Corncockle Quarry near Templand.

In 1843 the Free Church was built at the foot of Annanbrae. This building is now the council work place, and for many years was known as the 'Auld Kirk'. The congregation from this church moved to the towering St. Mary's United Free Church in 1892 and sadly, just over one hundred years on, its future is in doubt.

The cost of upkeep for this type of building is astronomical, so perhaps it will follow in the wake of the United Presbyterian Church in Old Well Road, and eventually be demolished.

The United Presbyterian Church in Old Well Road opened in 1863.

In 1961, the congregation merged with St. Andrews' Parish Church and a few years later the main building was demolished. The Church Hall, however, was left intact and purchased by the Upper Annandale Dramatic Society, who produced performances there for over 25 years before converting it to the 'state of the art' theatre, that it is today.

The Proudfoot Institute. During the Great War, 1914-1918, it was Moffat's Red Cross Auxiliary Hospital for the sick and wounded. During the Second World War, 1939-1945, soldiers were billeted in the building. It later resorted to its previous role, a place of leisure and relaxation for the townspeople.

Carpet bowls was always a favourite with both ladies and gents, here Bob Borthwick and Jock Campbell measure the 'shots' for a ladies tournament.

The winning rink.
Back: Jean McMillan, Isa Traquair.
Front: Sadie McMillan, Betty Smith.

Green Bowling has also been a long-standing favourite game for Moffat ladies.

Looking towards Moffat from the south. As both the 'Flying Spur' Church and St. Andrews can be seen it places the year to be 1887. The 'Flying Spur' also known as 'The Father' was replaced by St. Andrews in 1888.

HOUSE AT MOFFAT, formerly a Tavern,
celebrated in the song "O, Willie
brewed a peck o' maut."

This old house stood at the gateway to the Old Cemetery.

Tennis

JIM TUTON

The South of Scotland Lawn Tennis Championships have been held in Moffat for over 100 years, played on the Beechgrove courts.

Many famous players have graced the tournament. It was therefore quite an occasion when Jim Tuton created a bit of history when he became the first Moffat born player to win the singles trophy for the first time in 1952. He went on to retain the title the following year and was later to be runner-up on three occasions. His record has stood for over 50 years.

South of Scotland Lawn Tennis Championship Tournaments c.1910 at Beechgrove Tennis Courts, Moffat.

South of Scotland Lawn Tennis Championship Tournaments mid 1950's. Both Ladies and Mens Doubles in progress. The same venue but a noticeable change in dress.

Jim Tuton, with his tennis trophies.

Jim won a great number of other tournaments and when his playing days began to wane, he became a qualified coach and Wimbledon Umpire. He was district 'Grass Roots' organiser for 25 years, a National Squad coach and Scottish Team Captain at several competitions. Finally he served on the Scottish Council for ten years.

For his efforts he received awards from the Scottish Sports Council, Scottish Lawn Tennis Association and also one from the Lawn Tennis Association, Great Britain. The latter award being the first one given to a Scotsman.

Although now in his seventies, Jim still manages to coach the local youngsters.

Jim in action.

Moffat Golf Course c. 1910.

In 1904 Ben Sayers of North Berwick was asked to lay out an 18-hole course on Coates Hill, on land where the Laird and his friends previously played on a privately owned 9-hole course.

The present course was inaugurated on 22nd April 1905, the first ball being driven by Lady Younger with a driver presented by Major Mackenzie-Grieve, the captain of the club for that year.

Immediately after this interesting ceremony an exhibition match was played by Sir William Younger and Ben Sayers versus their respective sons.

The Edinburgh Road Bridge as it was during my first introduction to egg collecting, 1942.

Birds Nesting and Egg Collecting

During my early years at the Academy, my favourite times, like those of many other children, were when the stories were read to us by the infant teachers. The simple talks on natural history I found even more enthralling, especially when it involved birds, and I never missed a single word – I was hooked!

It was at this time that I was first introduced to birds' egg collecting and my first experience will stay with me for as long as my memory serves.

I was walking home from school one afternoon when two boys, much senior to myself, approached saying that if I wanted a bird's egg, which was very hard to find, I should go with them and they would show me the nest.

I knew both these boys and had recently seen one of their egg collections. It was in a big wooden box with the eggs laid out in rows, from the largest to the smallest. I was absolutely fascinated.

Off we went along the waterside, to a point where the riverbank had been strengthened by a wall of whinstone blocks.

A tiny crack, just big enough to allow a hand as small as mine, was occupied by a pair of nesting Coal Tits. When one of the boys prodded the entrance with a piece of stick, there was a snakelike hissing sound, which made me somewhat apprehensive. I then gingerly inserted my hand, fingers straight out, with thumb pressed tightly against the palm.

The jagged edges of the whinstone started to bite into the fleshy part of my forearm as it wedged in the hole and just as I was about to withdraw my hand having failed, as I thought, to reach the nest I dropped my fingers slightly and touched a small fluffy object.

It was the parent Coal Tit, sitting tight on her eggs, so I carefully edged her from the nest with my finger tips, and was then instructed to pull the edge of the nest towards the entrance of the hole, and then withdraw my hand. On so doing I saw for the first time in my life, a wild birds' nest full of eggs.

As the boys could now reach the nest for themselves, and my talents as an extractor had been exploited to the full, I was handed a tiny egg and told to go home.

I walked slowly down the river path, pondering the incident which had taken place. No matter how I tried to justify the tiny glistening acquisition in the palm of my hand, the nauseating feeling increased every time I thought about that tiny, fluffy ball that had guarded her eggs so defiantly. Even though I was only seven years old, "one egg would be sufficient to take from any bird's nest," was my first rule for egg collecting.

Since the mid-1950's egg collecting is strictly illegal, and rightly so, but before that date there were even dealers to whom you could write and buy every species of bird's egg available. A few examples at that time were:

Blackbird	1d (old penny)	Golden Eagle	60/- to 100/- (£3 to £5)
Bittern	5/- (25p)	Kingfisher	1/- (5p)
Corncrake	1/- (5p)	Peregrine	10/- (50p)
Dotterel	15/- (75p)		

It makes me cringe when I look at this list, but today on reflection the two most endangered species did not reach this sorry state solely through egg collecting, but by loss of breeding habitat and modern farming methods.

Goldcrests. A prized egg was given to me by my brother Philip, the smallest bird's egg found throughout the country.

The Waterside (Annan Wood) where egg collecting preceded bird study and photography, the subjects of my two previously published books – "Birds of Scotland" and "The Birdwatchers' Almanac".

Soon after this episode, seeing my obvious enthusiasm to collect eggs, my older brother Philip produced an old shoe box from under our bed, and said "Here, you can have these." I opened the lid and inside were about two dozen assorted eggs. Most of them were broken, but among the broken egg shells and cotton wool was a small, round, metal box with a glass top and inside was a tiny egg which I was informed was a 'Basket Hanger', the local name for a Goldcrest. I have both the container and its contents to this day.

Like Philip, most of the schoolboys who collected eggs throughout the spring and early summer months kept them in old shoe boxes and the like. Invariably they were broken before the following spring. Thus their collections never got beyond a few of the more common species, and whatever names were conjured up to identify them. 'Stiggies', were Starlings; 'Stankies' were Moorhens; Hens, the farm variety; Speckled Hens, a rarer species; Wild Ducks; Park Ducks; Farm Ducks; Tree Blackies and Hedge Blackies.

These were all different species, or so I was told during my first year as an egg collector. But on acquiring a few old bird books, and reading them avidly, the following spring I binned the assortment of hens' and ducks' eggs as well as a few Blackbirds'. It was now time to get serious, so the eggs were given their proper names.

Some of the boys who collected eggs hunted in small groups. If a nest was found in a tree, as one of the boys climbed up, the others would yell "Bags I first egg", and so on, which would inevitably result in that particular nest being harried. Needless to say, I shunned these groups and Billy (who never collected eggs) and myself clocked up a good number of species on our own.

It was also at this time that by studying my bird books, I found that some of our birds only spent the summer here. Others came in autumn, leaving the following spring – these were winter visitors. Then our breeding birds were divided into residents and summer residents. I meticulously listed 'our' birds into groups, as there were many species illustrated which came nowhere near Moffat and this saddened me somewhat. Later I was able to add a good number of species to my collection through the dealers mentioned earlier – a disappointing way to obtain an egg, when I'd never even seen the bird. And as I didn't have much money, I could only afford the poorer-marked varieties.

Collecting eggs in the woods around Moffat, in the early years of the war, was also quite hazardous, as there was a rather active old gamekeeper patrolling them – protecting game and persecuting vermin such as crows, stoats and, at that time, sparrow hawks. He didn't take lightly to small boys roaming through 'his' woods, so if perchance he happened to approach us on the far bank of the river, we'd promptly run across in our boots and socks, as he drew nearer, shouting and pointing his shotgun in the air. Old 'Boots', as he was nicknamed by us local boys, was dreaded, and God only knows what would have happened if ever he had caught hold of one of us.

When we'd put enough distance between ourselves and the 'gamie', we'd stop to take off our boots, beat our socks on stones to remove most of the water, then replace them and no one was any the wiser as to where we come from.

Some birds' eggs were obviously good to eat, and Lapwings were the most popular. One evacuee lad who was particularly fond of hunting for Lapwings', or as they were locally known, "Peesies" eggs, was called Norman and as he was often seen in the arable fields at Hammerlands Farm gathering the eggs, he soon earned the nickname which has stuck to him to this day – "Peesie". These eggs though, were not for eating but for an artist who mixed the egg-white with tints for painting.

The word 'gathering' might raise a few eyebrows, especially when the numbers of breeding Lapwings throughout the whole of Annandale, is so low at present, but I can remember, in fact I have it recorded in one of my notebooks, that even in the 1960's I

Mute Swans, the subjects of the dramatic tale of Gordon's egg, lay the largest birds egg found in this country.

Corn stooks in Chapel Farm fields when Corncrakes could be heard in many such fields throughout the district.

located 20+ Lapwing nests containing eggs in one single potato field at Barnhill. Once again I would stress, it was not the collecting of eggs but changes in farming policy, including drainage, that decimated the population of these birds.

The fields at Hammerlands and surrounding moorlands, 'The Kerr' were favourite hunting grounds of mine and occasionally I'd meet up with Jimmy Johnstone who was one of the 'sensible' egg collectors, and who was partial to the odd Curlew's or as he called them, "Whaup's" egg. Like the Lapwings, they too were plentiful, as were Snipe, Redshank, Larks and Pipits, and a myriad of other birds, including the shy Water Rails that nested in the boggiest areas, with the gorse bushes providing a breeding habitat for many pairs of Buntings and Linnets. I think I should mention here that the Corncrake was a common bird, breeding in many hayfields throughout the district but, as with the

An old Massey Ferguson that must have seen many changes in farming policy throughout its active service. The driver, somewhat older, must have seen many more.

poor little Grey Partridge, it has succumbed to modern farming practices.

I would like to close this paragraph on birds nesting with a tale in slightly lighter vein.

Together with another boy Gordon, a year or so older then myself, I visited the park pond where he showed me the huge nest of a pair of Mute Swans, built close to the edge of the 'small' island. We knew that swans were dangerous, having heard tales about limbs being broken by them while defending their nests, but the thought of adding a swan's egg to a collection was overpowering. Both Gordon and I had good collections, but neither of us had a Mute Swan's egg.

The swans were well out of sight behind the big island, so Gordon decided to go for it. Off with shoes and socks and in he went, muddying the water as he waded through and eventually reached his goal.

There were five eggs in the clutch so, grabbing one, Gordon turned to head back to where I was standing, in his hand an egg which, even at that distance, seemed enormous – then it happened.

I don't know from where, but one of the swans was racing towards us with huge flapping wings (that could break my bones), neck stretched straight out in front, taking great strides across the surface of the pond. I was off through the gate and pelting along the waterside path, soon to be joined by a rather pallid Gordon clutching his shoes and socks, but no egg!

"Where's the egg?" I dared ask, "I dropped it," was the reply and we both made our way home for dinner.

Less than an hour later I returned to the scene, not by way of the waterside, but down the High Street.

The pen was sitting on her eggs, the cob was cruising some way off, the water had cleared and the big, beautiful egg was lying in the mud on the bottom of the pond, only an arm's length away from the bank. After over 55 years, I still have "Gordon's Egg".

The combine harvester, together with the silage harvesters ensure that Corncrakes will remain unheard.

The Well Hill and the Well Burn (see on next page).
The area was in constant use as a firing range and for army manoeuvres during World War II, consequently many clean-up operations were carried out in the post war years to rid the area of dangerous material.

The Summer Months

MESSING ABOUT ON THE RIVER AND BREN GUN CARRIERS

I don't know whether it is a true fact or just imagination, but when I look back to the late 1940's and 50's, summers were truly summers with plenty of long, sunny days and winters always provided us with snow and ice.

As the bird-nesting season ended, youthful energies were then applied to other forms of enjoyment, and the best places to play and pass the time were in or near the burns and rivers.

We would paddle, catch tiddlers, build dams, learn to swim, learn how to guddle trout – and later, help the soldiers to clean the Bren Gun Carriers.

Building dams across the river down at the waterside was always a favourite pastime for the boys in summer, big and small, young and old, everyone mucked in to make the swimming hole a success by raising the water level over a metre.

Well Burn.

The Well Burn, or Mill Burn, at Burnside; the Millpond was fed by water from Birnock Burn. It then surged through the Mill Race to drive the Meal Mill, and later the Saw Mill at Taylor and Smith's. Many years ago the burn was diverted and during the high waters, houses with cellars near the river banks today stay dry, whereas houses and shops on the old river course find water seeping into their cellars.

The Old Railway Bridge (now removed), where the Well Burn joins the River Annan.

From the swimming hole there were offshoots to various other activities to keep us out of doors for many hours, building dens and dugouts in the wood bordering the river, building campfires and roasting tatties (for which I had an endless supply) by the riverside. As well as being taught all the dos and don'ts regarding the lighting and control of camp fires, I was taught how to guddle trout, and this became one of my favourite activities, in which I gained expert status in a very short time.

The metal bridge over the River Annan at Barnhill, near the meetings of the waters in October 1974. The bridge collapsed after a 17-ton load 'tested' the stated 5-ton limit. Local anglers Jim Marrs and Archie Wilson view the damage.

From the 'Meetings of the Waters' to Cogries Railway Viaduct, the fishing is controlled by Upper Annandale A.A. Although catches are not as they were 50 years ago, the river is still popular with anglers of all ages. Here the Evan and Moffat waters contribute their floods to the Annan, which they join about two miles below the town. At this point it becomes a stream of considerable volume flowing on to the Solway.

Mill on the Annan, Johnstone Bridge.

The Moffat Mill originally a Meal Mill, but at the end of its days, a Saw Mill – Taylor & Smith's.

The Moffat Mill

The Moffat Mill was originally a three storey building when it was a meal and corn mill owned by Hamilton and Williamson from 1825 to 1856.

Taylor and Smith ran their sawmill and joinery business there from the early 1930's to 1965, during which time Martin Taylor, as an apprentice joiner, made the two long boxes in which the body parts of Dr. Buck Ruxton's victims were placed while the gruesome tasks of their reconstruction was undertaken by the police pathologists at Moffat Cemetery Lodge (see page 235).

The Mill was a very progressive business in its day, being the first place in Moffat to produce and use its own electricity and also the first place where corrugated iron was used on a shed roof.

Myself with a 20½ lb. salmon in November 1959, caught at the 'plum', Woodfoot. Taken on a spinner. In 1997 I passed the 500 mark of Salmon caught in Upper Annandale.

Guddling

All those years ago, the upper reaches of the River Annan were well stocked with good-sized trout, and the river level, dwindling to a mere trickle at times, didn't dry up completely as often as it does today.

There were also many deeper pools, under trees and at bends where previous spates had gouged out sand and gravel, leaving trailing roots and cavities under the overhanging banks. These were the places that yielded the better fish, the occasional fine brown trout over one pound in weight, with half to three quarter pounders commonplace.

Many a summer evening would find two or three guddlers working our way up-river beyond the Edinburgh Road bridge with a couple of bearers carrying most of our clothes and also our 'catch'. To be most successful in some of the deeper pools, it was necessary to wear an old pair of trousers or trunks and something on our feet, old shoes or plimsoles were favoured.

When we thought that we had travelled far enough upstream, we would don dry trousers and shirts, divide our catch, and make our way home to eagerly awaiting elders with frying pans at the ready.

Each of us would have three or four decent-sized trout to take home, and no matter how often we covered the same stretch of the river, stocks never appeared to lessen.

Penman's Garage and Shop (early 1900's).
The garage became the premises of Tait and Anderson's until the 1960's and the Sportsman's Emporium was later a confectioners, Miss Blyth's original Toffee Shop c.1910.

Aggie Blyth moved into Penman's Sportsman's Emporium c.1910. The aroma of boiling Moffat toffee was much more appreciated than the smell of engine oil and old rubber!

The Mercury Hotel at the southern entrance to the High Street, has stood empty since its closure on 31st August 1999.

*The Black Bull, approaching Moffat from the south,
pre - St. Andrew's Church, Penman's Garage and the Railway Station, circa. 1860.*

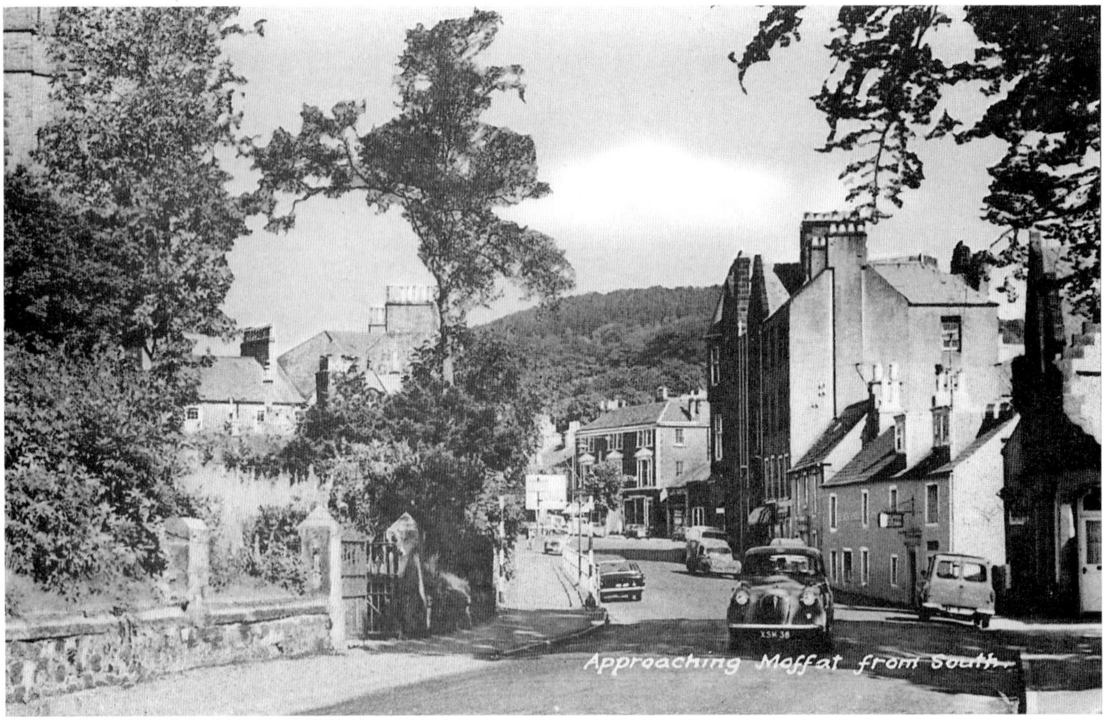

The southern approach to the town, with the Black Bull Hotel on the right, 1950's.

Established as early as 1568, the Black Bull is the oldest hostelry in the town. Over many years it has had a very chequered history. Claverhouse, alias 'Bloody Clavers', alias 'Bonnie Dundee', was billeted there for about 3 years during which time 'The Killing Times' occurred. In 1685 the Moffatonians were ordered to take the 'Test Oath' in the Old Kirkyard.
Robert Burns also fancied the ale and comforts of the establishment on his occasional visits to the district and during one particular sojourn looking through a window, saw two ladies riding by, one a slim, young beauty, the other somewhat larger, giving rise to the verse he scratched on a window pane:

"Ask why God made the gem so small;
And why so huge the granite?
Because God meant mankind should set
The higher value on it."

Osborne Row, off Holm Street and the old Police Station, which is now a popular Italian restaurant. The new Police Station has been sited on the High Street since 1973.

Circa 1930. Holm Street when buildings lined the right-hand side from Osborne Row all the way to the old Kirkyard Gate. The Gasworks were on the left.

Some of the buildings that were demolished to widen the road which at that time was only four metres wide. These were the houses in Holm Street in which the soldiers were trained in locating and de-fusing booby traps during the Second World War (1939-45).

The Annandale Hotel with garage entrance to the left. During the Second World War, Bren Gun carriers clattered through the close, to and from their base. Peter Toni was proprietor from 1968 to 1987.

Bren Gun Carriers

It must have been about the mid-war years when we saw our first bren gun carriers. By this time there were many army personnel stationed in the town, in places like the Masonic Hall and Proudfoot Institute, with Moffat House and Mount Charles housing the higher ranks.

As usual, a few of us youngsters were messing about at the waterside, when two bren gun carriers, or 'brennies' as they came to be known, arrived having been out on manoeuvres.

Their caterpillar tracks, springs and rollers, were covered in mud, so the drivers would drive up the river for a short distance, swivel round and return to the place of entry. But this was when stones would wedge in the mechanism and we were employed as 'stone removers', being paid by a run in the 'brennie' up Church Street and then down behind the Annandale Hotel to the large garage which was their base.

The Masons were tempted to leave working on the Annandale Hotel for an extra penny a day (from 8d to 9d), to work on Moffat House in 1762.

Bullets and Bangs

Some days later, after having attended to a solitary 'brennie', an older lad and myself were making our way back down to the waterside when he strolled into the council yard and stopped beside the remains of an ancient piece of machinery, originally used for grading gravel, a huge iron drum with various sizes of holes in it.

He put his hand into his pocket and brought out what he informed me was a ·303 rifle bullet. He then inserted the point of the bullet into one of the smaller holes, and with the palm of his hand, pushed the casing until it broke in two. He snapped the two pieces apart and then proceeded to give another two bullets the same treatment.

On reaching the waterside, one or two older lads had the usual campfire going, and when I enquired what he was going to do with the bullets, he answered, have you never seen cordite? "No," I replied. "It's great," he said, "watch this." He inserted a pin into the bullet case and worked out some spaghetti-like strands, about 4cm long, placed a few end to end and lit one end with a match. The small flame shot along the line, leaving a mark on the stones. Soon I was emulating him and smiled as I watched the little flame dance along a trail that I had laid out on a flat stone.

"Right men," shouted my big pal, "take cover," and we all dived over a banking as he dropped the three empty bullet cases onto the fire. "Keep your head down," yelled someone as I poked my head up to see what was happening. There was a sharp 'peow', then another two in quick succession. "All clear lads," a voice said, then we walked over to the fire where I remarked, "it nearly blew the fire out." "That's nothing, just watch this," said another of our company. "What's that you've got?" I asked, "Och, it's a dummy bullet, they make a bigger bang." And he showed me the ·303 blank. It was a similar casing, but instead of having a point, it was crimped in at the top. Once again, "take cover," was the order, as the blank was thrown on to the well-restored fire. A short pause, then "Bang!" Bits of burning faggots were strewn about and there was very little fire left burning. "These are great, where do you get them?" I asked, wide-eyed. "Under the brennie seats, didn't you know that?" I knew now.

During the course of the next few weeks, I learned all about 'tracers', 'stens' and 'tommies' as well as 'thunderflashes', but the latter was a mere toy compared to some of the ammunition, mortars, flares, grenades, electric detonators and such like, that I was fortunate to have experiences with before I was ten years old.

Ex-Service Men's Club Trustees, 1919.
Front Row (L to R): *Mr. Carmichael; ? ; ? ; ? ; W. J. Little; Mr. Dixon (Banker); Jimmy Dixon.* ***Back Row (L to R):*** *Andrew Lockhart; Nat. Wallace; C. C. Turnbull; ? ; Dod Irvine; ? ; Mr. Stewart.*

Moffat Cadet Force 1937
Band members (L to R): *Pipe Major W. Proudfoot, Archie Porteous, Bert Richardson, Davy Little, Tucker Porteous, Tom Porteous.*
Cadet Force (L to R) Front Row: *Jackie Bullman, Tommy Douglas, Tom Telfer, Capt. W. Lockerbie, Maj. Gen. Sir Eric Girdwood, Sonny Armstrong, Andy Little, John Park, Bunny Noble.* ***Middle Row:*** *Peter Murray, ? Fraser, ? Beattock lad, Jimmy Bryden, ? Beattock lad, John Sutherland.* ***Back Row:*** *Tommy Rankine, ? Beattock lad, ? Beattock lad, ?Beattock lad, Robin Watson.*

Moffat Academy Cadet Camp 1937.
Colonel Dubs of Craigdarroch inspecting.
Captain J. J. Kydd, Lieutenant J. Torrance.

Hairless

However, life is not always a bowl of cherries. There's always a down side. I recall my very first 'downer', which happened some months earlier behind the cadet hut.

A small Nissen hut, surrounded by barbed wire, attracted our attention one evening and my older companion found the barbed wire no obstacle as he wriggled through, entered the hut and re-appeared with what I thought was a bottle of milk.

I don't remember much of what happened next, but the bottle was smashed and I lost some hair, most of it actually.

I suppose that first narrow escape would have been enough for any normal child, but no, there were many more to follow before the victory bells eventually sounded throughout the country.

My mother 'Pasquo' indulging her favourite pastime, tending her garden.

Indoor Fireworks

Another 'downer' that I remember very well, was one that taught me not to leave bits and pieces lying around, to be picked up by people who were not familiar with them.

I had left a 'dummy' lying somewhere in the house, and obviously my poor mum had no idea as to what it was.

In our living room we had a coal fire, and the living room doubled as a bedroom for my sister Bettina. Under the fire, the can to catch the ashes was a half-sized biscuit tin, and as you can imagine, it got extremely hot.

My mother, in tidying up, had found my ·303 blank, and thinking it to be harmless, threw it into the ash can. Fortunately, in more ways than one, I was out at the time and missed the drama. The blank exploded. The detonator blew a hole through the ash can and landed on my sister's bed cover – burning a hole in it, and the living room was covered in ash.

I was glad that it wasn't a 'pineapple' that I'd so carelessly left.

I think my poor mum got too much of a fright to wallop me on that occasion, but that was soon to follow.

The Station Park soon after its formation in the 1890's.

The Station Park

In the mid 1700's, the River Annan meandered on a winding course down the Annan Water Valley, from its source near the Devil's Beef Tub. It bordered the west side of the town, winding its way towards the 'Kerr', through the Annandale field, the 'Glebe' and grazing land.

Over a hundred years later, from a point near the new cemetery, the river course was diverted to the much straighter route that it follows today, with evidence of bank

An early 1900's study at the entrance to the park, with the 'wee' pond in the foreground.

A 1920's view of the 'big' pond with the swans an obvious attraction.

construction noticeable at various places along the waterside, especially following a spate, when long fir trunks and posts that have been covered for many years become exposed.

This is the reason that the area floods from time to time, as the river, in raging spate, seeks out its old course.

Over fifty years ago, the 'wee' pond was lined with concrete to form the paddling pond, the work mainly carried out by Italian war prisoners. Throughout the years, thousands of children have frolicked about in the water without any obvious harm: today paddling is banned!

The 'middle' pond, shrubbery and well-kept paths (early 1900's).

When the river was settled in its new course, the 'Glebe' and beyond was still damp, a perfect base on which to create a park with ponds and thus, in the 1890's, the three ponds were formed, the 'wee' pond, the 'middle' pond and the 'big' pond.

Water feeds into the wee pond from a burn which borders the Annandale field from where it originates in spring form somewhere beyond. It then runs into the middle pond, and from there runs into the big pond (Boating Pond).

A more reliable spring-fed burn also runs into the boating pond, near the River Annan. In 1984, when the Annandale field burn dried up completely, water continued to flow in

The small island on the left was later removed for extra boating space.
A lone boatman and a nanny enjoying her walk with her two charges (early 1900's).

Station Park in seasonal mood.

this burn, but unfortunately, not enough to sustain a level suitable for boating, resulting in the only instance during my lifetime when boating couldn't take place.

There were originally three islands in the boating pond, and when a small one was removed from the bottom end, near the sluice, pieces of crockery were found bearing the

The floral arch at the main gate in high summer.
The arch, and flower beds are the subject of many visitors' and locals' cameras.

Moffat Hydro motif, pointing to the fact that in an earlier period the area was waste ground, used as a rubbish tip.

Paths followed the contours of the ponds, flower beds were cultivated, an attractive pavilion built, and a putting green was developed. In the late 1940's the wee pond was made suitable for paddling, but recently this has had to cease, which is unfortunate for the hundreds of children who every summer enjoyed the relative safety of the park, while mums watched from nearby, ready to dispense tattie crisps and soft drinks.

Throughout the years, social functions of all kinds have benefited from this attractive situation, and occasionally the park becomes a sanctuary, providing a temporary habitat for young trout and salmon when the river course dries up during drought conditions.

In 1996, a change in the river course near the park resulted in many young trout and parr becoming trapped. As the water level in the old course dropped, my grandson Richard and myself rescued over four hundred of these little fish and liberated them in the feeder burn which runs parallel to the river. The result was a noticeable rise of feeding trout in the boating pond on summer evenings.

Shortly after its formation in the late 1800's Mr. Ewen Cameron was employed as Park Keeper, Gardener and Boatman in the Station Park.

Mr. Cameron, Martin Taylor's grandfather was previously a gardener by trade and this is reflected in early photographs in some of which the primitive implements can be seen.

Ewen Cameron with Flora and Duncan his daughter and son: taken 1930's at Moffat.

Hand propelled lawn mowers and basic hand tools kept lawns and paths in tiptop condition, and boatmanship was explained to, and appreciated by, many visitors of all ages throughout the summer months.

This poem was penned by one such grateful visitor.

TO EWEN CAMERON'S RETIRAL FROM STATION PARK, MOFFAT.

1. Ah, Ewen! stay and see me through –
'Twas you who taught me to canoe
Out o'er the Station Lake.
My holiday will soon be due –
I wish again to see but you –
Yes! just for old times' sake.

2. 'Twas your advice – example too –
That when a youth made me, then rue
The tricks we on you placed:
How, when we should have been ashore,
Like Oliver, we wished for more,
And round the islets raced.

3. And how you threatened if we splashed
The swans, as o'er the pond we dashed
At Segrave's rate.
Our ignorance you motive gave,
'Twas but twin shadows on the wave
We tried to separate.

4. How long before the last half hour,
Relentingly you gave us power
To spend the time afloat:
And how you watched and lingered by
Keeping a keen and constant eye
On rower and on boat.

5. I hoped my boy would follow, too,
And learn the boatman craft from you,
But you must go, alas!
Another must now fill your place –
But it will be your form and face
I'll see when next I pass.

6. The soft kind eye, the high command,
The light step and the hard brown hand
The gunwale rail to grasp.
All that will now be at an end –
So "Good-bye" Ewen Cameron! – friend
Your honest hand I clasp.

Ewen's Station Park. Note the signal box which was in use in Moffat Station's early day.

Bob Tweedie in his role as Park Keeper in 1974.

A few years later another and perhaps better known Park Keeper to many of us, took on the task of presenting the Moffat Station Park to locals and visitors alike in a manner second to none. The late Mr. Bob Tweedie.

From the age of 15, except for war service with the 8th Army's 'Desert Rats', until the age of 72, Bob Tweedie worked in, or rather dedicated his life to, maintaining Moffat's Station Park.

He was a true Moffat character whose sense of humour endeared him to locals and visitors alike, especially when the latter hired a boat. "Battleship or submarine?" Bob would enquire, and "watch the sharks around the island", was another of his favourites.

Bob grew the flowers and plants for the beds from seed in the little greenhouse near the railway bank and on frosty nights he would be there, stoking the boiler fire. It was this sense of duty and love for his job that played a major part in making the Station Park one of the most attractive in the south of Scotland.

His scotch thistles were famous and probably are still famous today. Councillor John Frood from Crewe was given seeds from which he actually grew a thistle 9 feet tall. His son, a biology teacher from Berkshire, has also grown them to 7 and 8 feet. In both locations they are much admired by locals.

As Bob was the receipient of the Queen's Award for Long Service, surely a commemorative seat would be a fitting tribute from all of us who enjoyed the park for so many years when Bob was the "parky".

Council Staff c. 1973
Back row: L. to R. Jimmy Johnstone, Jimmy Rogerson, Stewart Johnstone, Adam Tait, Fred Hyslop.
Middle Row: Geordie Stewart, John Black, Billy Rogerson.
Front Row: Jock Campbell, Bob Tweedie, Gordon Hyslop, Willie Smith.

Moffat Railway Station. The Moffat to Beattock Passenger Service ran from 1883 to 1954 and for a further ten years carried freight. Photo circa 1912.

The Moffat to Beattock Railway Line

The Moffat to Beattock branch line opened to passenger traffic on 2nd April 1883.

By 1890, because of Moffats' popularity as a 'Spa' Town, no fewer than twelve trains per day were running in both directions, with as many as fifteen in the height of summer.

The first service was 'push-and-pull', so called because the engine always stayed at the same end. The three passenger coaches were attached to a Drummond 0-4-4T., No. CR.194, which was based at Beattock.

During the 1930's and 40's the Moffat Bus, or 'Puffer' as it was more affectionately known, was introduced. The 'Puffer' was a steam railcar which was engine and coach combined with 2d. the price of a one-way ticket and 3d. for a return.

The 2-mile journey took about 5 minutes and for children it was a real treat.

Leaving Moffat platform, the train soon crossed its first bridge, a small one which allowed access from the Station Park to the Ladyknowe, then only a few yards further and it was over the River Annan.

No. 57568 with chain attached to a 60ft. section of lines and sleepers.

Finally, a left-hand curve crossed the River Evan before straightening out for the last quarter mile into the docking platform at Beattock.

The passenger service's life came to an end on 6th December 1954, but the line was kept open for freight until 1964. Shortly afterwards the lines were lifted for scrap.

A few minutes later a steady pull drags the entire section along the line to be dismantled and scrapped. The Beattock to Moffat Branch Line was also dismantled in this fashion. Wattie Robson is one of the three onlookers.

Phil Kerr and Willie Hunter (42192), in the pilot sidings at Beattock.

Bert Saunders, Dod Smith and Willie Kennedy, local railway men who crewed the Class 4's that piloted heavy goods trains up to Beattock Summit in the day of steam engines.

Harthope Viaduct.

The class 4 pilot engines or 'pugs' as they were affectionately called by many connected with the railway were based at Beattock Station where they were also maintained.
Although the mighty steam engines could cope with lengthy goods trains on most lines, the 1 in 75 climb to Beattock Summit necessitated the aid of a pilot.
A pilot assisted northbound train on the Harthope Viaduct, just north of Beattock, near the area of ground consecrated by Michael Russell, Bishop of Glasgow in 1847.
Here 37 of the many thousands of navvies working on this section of the Caledonian Railway were buried. It is said that they died from a plague-like disease.
The completed line to Glasgow opened in 1848.

ERECTED
1916
IN MEMORY OF
THIRTY SEVEN WORKMEN WHO DIED
WHILE ENGAGED IN THE CONSTRUCTION
OF THE CALEDONIAN RAILWAY, AND
WERE BURIED IN THIS GROUND WHICH
WAS CONSECRATED 12TH AUGUST 1847, BY
MICHAEL RUSSELL, BISHOP OF GLASGOW.

The last passenger train in service from Moffat to Beattock.
The 3.05pm on 6th December 1954.

The last train to arrive in Moffat Station was a Railtour. Engine No. 80118, crewed by Phil Kerr and Jock Hunter. The track was lifted soon afterwards.

Mr. Grierson on the station dray at the coal office, before making a delivery in the town.

The same office being demolished in November 1999.

For a number of years after the closure of the Moffat Railway Station in the mid 1960's, an area at the southern end was occupied by Reive's Grain and Animal Feed Warehouse.

A harness embelishment from Burns, Saddlers of Moffat and Lockerbie.

The Moffat to Beattock 'Puffer' in the 1930's - George Gray, Driver and James Orr, Fireman.

Beattock ~ Change for Moffat!

Summers melted into autumns, and back in the school playground, it was conkers and marbles for the boys, while the lasses chanted all manner of

Updated in the 1940's.

As well as Grocers and Wine Merchants, James Sinclair & Co. (Alex Cameron) ran a successful cattle feed business (1948). His Austin delivery lorry travelled many miles a week and on this occasion the driver was George Dawson.
This load was collected from Dalkeith and delivered to Badlieu but unfortunately the hay proved to be of poor quality and was refused by the farmer. Fortunately however, another local farmer accepted it thus dispensing with a long return journey.

daft rhymes when they played at skipping. 'Beds' were also fun at this time, with boys and lasses playing together, 'beds' being the local name for hop-scotch.

Autumn was also the time of year when we would go a wee bit further afield, by way of the wee Moffat to Beattock 'puffer' and for 3d. you could get a return ticket. Sometimes, just to pass the time we'd take the 'puffer' to Beattock and walk back along the road or the railway track.

When we walked along the road we would yell our heads off at Lochhouse Tower, or 'Echo' Tower as it was then, and marvellous echoes it produced. Then a little further up the road, we would run like the clappers past the 'Standin Stanes' because they were haunted, and if you looked at them all manner of evil would befall you.

I often think of one particular Saturday afternoon when I must have inadvertently glanced at the stones on the way down to Beattock in the 'puffer'. They made me suffer!

During 1959/60 the Glasgow to Carlisle Road was upgraded to dual carriageway. King's company quarried sand and gravel from Barnhill and here pausing for a breather are driver Sam Smith and a young employee Shug Thomson.

As the volume of traffic on our roads increased more A.A. Patrols were required to deal with the inevitable breakdowns. There were three Patrols based in Moffat, Jack Lees, Bob McClelland and Bob Adamson who can be seen here on his R.S.O. (Road Service Outfit). Motorcycle combinations, R.S.O.'s, were in use from 1920 to 1968 when they were superseded by Mini vans.

Lochhouse Tower as it stood for many years. The distant echoes and the close proximity of the "Standin' Stanes" were the source of many 'spooky' tales among young and old alike!

Lochhouse Tower – renovated as it stands today.

The Three Standin' Stanes on the right-hand side of the Moffat to Beattock Road, one mile from the town. Originally, the road passed at the other side of the stones, but upgrading the Glasgow – Carlisle road to the A74 resited the road. There is said to be a connection between the three standin' stanes and the defeat of the usurper in a battle on 16th December 1332, but some historians believe that they are druidical in origin. It is amazing that so many local people pass these monuments today without any knowledge of their existence.

The sinister remains of the Frenchland's Tower, near the cottage hospital.

Peel Towers and Ruins

The close proximity of Moffat to the English border necessitated the construction of stone Peel Towers during the 15th and 16th centuries, to protect the inhabitants, their goods and livestock, not only from the English raiders but also from marauding Scottish Clans.

There were at least half a dozen of these Peel Towers within a few miles radius of the town, but the only one which has survived, and is inhabited to day is the Loch House or 'Echo' Tower, on the Moffat to Beattock Road, with fairly recognisable remains of the Frenchlands Tower, a mile or so from the town on the Selkirk Road.

Frenchland's Tower was built in the late 16th century and was added to in 1620. It was then occupied by the French family till 1746. From 1746 until 1790 it was the home of the Veitches of Eliock. It was then sold to the Johnstones of Dumcrieff who eventually allowed it to fall into disrepair.

Others, in the Moffat Water and Evan Water Valleys, have long since deteriorated into various sizes of piles of rubble.

The Lochwood Castle, is a fine example of the fortifications of the period, and although it was destroyed by fire in the late 16th century by the Maxwells, the remains have been partially restored, showing the original layout to perfection.

Also, bordered as it is by the old oak wood, on the Raehills Estate, it is well worth a visit from those interested in our ancient or natural history.

The Black Russians!

Kenny had in his possession a packet of 20 Black Russian cigarettes, he also had about 3/- (15p) in his pocket.

We knew that there was a half-crown (12½p) down one of the gratings on the pavement outside Knight's, so we boldly walked in and asked if someone could go down into the cellar and retrieve it for us, and to add credibility to our request we produced the 3/- and said that it was for a message for some woman or other and that this was the rest of the money.

Once in receipt of the half-crown, it was round to Hetheringtons for a large bottle of Ovaltine tablets, as neither of us had any sweet coupons. Then it was down to the station for our tickets, laughing and joking as we munched away at the Ovaltine tablets and puffed the cigarettes.

Arriving at Beattock, we left the 'puffer' and walked up the Crooked Road to the wee hut at the top – smoking and chewing all the way there and back. By the time we arrived back in Moffat all tablets and cigarettes had gone and, needless to say, I suffered. I was ill, sick as a dog – what an experience, but I never smoked again!

Hetherington's Chemist, dating from 1844 is the oldest established pharmacy in Scotland. This was the shop that Kenny and I made a bee-line for once in possession of our 'sneaky' half crown. Hetherington's was one of the last premises to radically change its interior layout from the fascinating older style of family business to the 'trendy' modern version.

The Waterside in a raging spate, November 1972.

Cauld Winter

Winters were cold – no such things as anoraks in those days. So after skating about on the ice on the park pond (without skates) and clowning about in general, we would make our way down the 'Kerr' to the 'first burst', (the first place that we came to where there was a mass of stones,

The Waterside in a different mood in 1996. The pole in the centre of the picture is similar to the one carrying power cables to Golf Hill at the bottom of the track – the pole that Francis climbed!

Gallowhill, where sledging was popular with many boys when conditions were suitable.

left by a previous spate). There were three such places, the first, second and third burst and at the third burst the river had changed course.

As well as stones, there was also a lot of driftwood so it wasn't long before we had a massive bonfire going. For kids to do the same thing today, it would be "Help, Murder, Polis!" When our heater was reduced to a few dying embers, there was always someone

Craigielands, Beattock as it was after having an extra floor added in the early 20th century. At that time curling was well organised with tournaments commonplace.

Later in the century, if the pond did freeze sufficiently to allow a game, locals enjoyed time on the ice.

with a couple of 'dummies' in his pocket. In they went, and off we went like the clappers, to spend the afternoon sledging at Golf Hill, or Gallow Hill if there was any frozen snow on the ground.

The Baths Hall Cinema was by far the best place to spend a cold winter's night – no matter what was showing. There were two different shows a week, Monday and Tuesday for one and Thursday and Saturday for the other.

Sledging at Gallow Hill was great fun, with some of the sledges themselves being real museum pieces. Mostly they were home-made jobs that only lasted a few runs. Once the snow became hard packed, after one or two frosty nights, the run was really fast. A heavy wooden sledge with polished runners and a body lying full length, would bump and rattle at incredible speed down towards the fence, where one's only hope of stopping was to drag one foot on the snowy ground and will your sledge to stop.

The act of dragging one foot on the ground forced the sledge to broadside, and the sudden, broadside movement, at such speeds invariably caused one of the runners to collapse under the strain. The body would then roll off and if he was too near a fence post, yet another poor soul would hobble down towards the town, with the sledge left lying in pieces, just one more hazard for those coming behind.

For the weak-hearted, there was always Craigielands at Beattock, where they could go to watch the curling.

Looking back to those far-off days, it isn't difficult to convince oneself that winters were WINTERS, and summers were SUMMERS!

Lack of practice allowed the odd wobbly delivery to occur.

50 years earlier, in the early 1900's,
curling on Craigieland's pond was a more organised event.

Craigielands in the 1960's when by kind permission of the owners, Mr. & Mrs. David Henry, we were allowed to wander the grounds and search the outbuildings in pursuit of bird subjects to photograph.

Whither Shall I Wander?

Whither shall I wander? Practically anywhere, was the simple answer, even when the soldiers were training in the Annandale field (school playing fields), down the waterside, in adjacent woods, in the grounds of Moffat House and on the park pond.

Ladyknowe was also a place where I would rummage about in the old sheds, as there were always lots of ammunition boxes containing clips of empty ·303 bullet cases, with many just lying loose. It was among these that the occasional misfire could be found, as well as live ·303's.

If I was very lucky, I would find a 'tracer' with a slightly longer bullet, and red rim round the detonator, and although most of us boys had ·303 bullet heads, tracers were scarce indeed!

One afternoon while heading home from school, the rattle of a sten gun emitting from the grounds of Moffat House Hotel attracted me like a magnet and I casually walked in to find two officers firing stens into a pit in the ground.

The Old Laundry as it stood for many years, at least 30 of which found Barn Owls using the loft as a nest site.

Another characteristic purpose-built building that added interest to our frequent visits.

I stood and watched from a distance of a few metres, and as soon as they'd finished, I walked forward and collected a dozen or so empty cartridges for my souvenir collection, while they were still warm. Delving into the soft soil also produced a fair number of small bullets, most of which were in good condition.

Down the waterside, occasionally a few hand grenades ('pineapples') would be thrown from the other side of the path onto waste ground. But as this mostly took place at night, it wasn't until the following morning that I'd find the craters, and search for pieces of shrapnel.

The large, heavy screws from the bottom of grenades were always the easiest parts to find, and the clips would be lying on the ground at the other side of the path from where the grenades were lobbed, but these were no great prize.

The best mornings were those following a night when a few parachute flares were fired from Moffat House above the field, as the odd one failed to ignite.

These were easily spotted because of the white, silk parachute lying on the ground – a double prize, as the flare could be removed to be ignited later and the parachute fetched at least half a crown from the womenfolk who fashioned them into scarves, head squares or other garments of a more intimate nature.

Leaving the loft.
Barn Owls in the Old Laundry at Craigielands, Beattock 1964.
Sadly the Old Laundry was demolished about 20 years later.

Returning with a vole to feed the young.

The female brooding her young.

The Riverside Path at the Barrels, which has stood the test of time, many high waters (with no doubt more to come) and explosive devices!

Thunderflashes

In the park one morning, there was some sort of exercise taking place.

There were two ropes stretched right across the pond, tied to a tree at either side, and two rubber dinghies were steadily approaching, with about half-a-dozen soldiers crouched in each one, towards the bank from where I was watching.

As they neared the bank, an officer was striking and throwing thunderflashes into the pond around the dinghies, where most of them landed flat with fuses burning before they exploded with a flash and a bang. Some were extinguished by landing in the water fuse-end first, so I gathered a good number and placed them into one of the empty boxes.

I intended to take them up the waterside where I could later cut off a short piece of the fuse to expose the live powder, thus rendering them usable again. But the officer picked up my box and carried it off, I don't know why, as boxes of thunderflashes were easy to obtain!

More often than not, one of the older boys would be given a boxful as we walked past the Moffat House garage, on our way home after school. They were piled high in the garage, which was used as a store.

A Near Miss?

Another morning which I remember well was one when my guardian angel was hovering close by. In fact 'He' or 'She' must have been delegated to watch over me for the entire duration of war – and beyond!

I was playing around in the council yard, when a 'brennie' passed by, en route from being washed, back to the garage behind the Annandale Hotel.

Two of the older boys were enjoying the usual run so I headed for the waterside and on arriving at the place where the 'brennie' had been washed, started poking about in the long grass by the riverbank and found a most peculiar item.

I was familiar with thunderflashes and hand grenades but this thing had a longish handle and a tape attached to it. I deduced that the tape was for pulling and the handle for throwing, so I decided to do just that.

I made my way over stepping stones into the wood, found a suitable old stump where I could crouch, tugged the tape from this 'thing' and lobbed it as far as I could among the trees. I heard it hit the ground but nothing happened, so I crouched for a few minutes before venturing out to see what had gone wrong, and very gingerly picked it up. It wasn't even ticking (I don't known why I thought it should), so I laid it on the ground, dug a hole with a stick and buried it.

Shortly afterwards the same two boys were searching the place where I had found the 'thing', and when they saw me twirling the short, white tape around my fingers they demanded to know where their Mills bomb was.

After the war, bomb disposal was widely carried out in the Moffat and Beattock Hills; even today there is still the odd find that has to be dealt with.

The Cook House or Dining Hall of the early 1940's, or as it is today, Currie and Borthwick's Joinery Business. Previous to the Second World War, the building was the garage for the Buccleuch Hotel.

The Cook House

As the army personnel throughout the district increased in numbers, the Buccleuch Garage was converted into a large dining hall, with kitchens added to the back of the building and sleeping quarters for the chefs and other kitchen staff above the kitchens.

The cook house as it was commonly known, was a magnet for some of us who lived nearby, and one of our favourite playgrounds was up on the corrugated iron roof. How the poor cooks put up with the noise of us clattering about is beyond me, but never once were we told to come down. We would sit in the valley of the adjoining roofs of Sinclair's store and the cook house on a sunny day making plans, away from other boys whom we didn't particularly want to find us.

At night, depending who was on night shift, at times they must have been glad of our company as toast was always on the menu, with margarine and greengage jam and a 'pint-pot', a huge mug of tea, that I could barely hold and never finish.

The cook house was also the venue for the concert parties who travelled around the country entertaining the troops and occasionally a soldier would take you in, but mostly it was our sisters who were invited.

Church Street, Moffat.
My address for my entire 65 years. On the left is the chip shop below No. 8 and on the extreme right is the tattie store, where the potatoes are stored for the chippy. This insignificant looking store holds a well kept secret. Almost 200 years ago it was a bakery (Henry Wilson, proprietor) and in the cellar the ovens are intact. Well out into the street, under the snow is a spacious oven, the door of which can be seen (next page).

The Chip Shop

At tea-time our chip shop was a very popular place with the troops as they would come in through the back door, buy some chips and take them to the cook house to supplement their meal. I often wondered why, when they had a meal waiting for them – perhaps it was boiled potatoes and they preferred chips.

I was very fortunate in having the 'chippy' in our family. It was a meeting place for many in the evenings, and a place of sanctuary for me, on dark winters' nights when I was very young, especially during the period of my dad's and Francis's internment, as we had no electricity in the house, only gas, and I preferred to be in company.

A couple of years later the dark winters' nights were no problem as I roamed the streets with others playing 'chasing', going to the cinema, or staying indoors listening to the radio and reading books and comics. For by this time, my brother Vincent had drilled a hole in the 'chippy' ceiling and fed flex through the hole to the living room above, giving us our first electric light.

Another benefit provided by our family owning the 'chippy', was the 'Tattie House'.

The oven door in the cellar which is almost 200 years old.

Tattie House: Venue of Many Activities

The Tattie House was, and still is today, the potato store for the chip shop, and over the years from when I was very young until I recently retired, it served many purposes for me.

All through the war years, it had "Andrew Reive Fruit Store" in big letters on the outside, so obviously it has been that at one time, but before my day.

It has an even more interesting past history though, inasmuch as it is probably the oldest bakery in town still in existence with the ovens still intact in the cellar (I recently traced the date of the baker to 1806). Every time a vehicle travels down Church Street it passes over the top of the huge cavity of the main oven.

The 'Tattie Store'.

This was the place I was going to make for if we ever got bombed by the Germans.

As well as a proposed air-raid shelter, the Tattie house has served as the first meeting place of the Moffat Masons, bike shed, den, place where I built model landscapes, aquariums, budgie house, chicken coop, workshop, dark room for photography, air-gun shooting range, log store, model railway site, general store, canary house, chemistry lab, pet mouse house, gym and last but not least my pigeon loft.

The Town Clock, The Old Court House and Grammar School
In 1953, dry rot was discovered in the clock tower and it was rebuilt lower than it was originally in the early 1770's. The building (now Wallace Brothers' Butchers) housed the Court House, Town Jail and Grammar School. The latter had moved from the original Grammar School building which was situated where the War Memorial stands today. This original school was built with an endowment of £1,000 from the will of Dr. Robert Johnstone in 1639. The Old Grammar School has a rather gruesome past, as it was in this school that the Rector, a man called Robert Carmichael, flogged one poor pupil to death. Carmichael was arrested and taken to Edinburgh for trial where he was convicted, sentenced, flogged and banished from the country.

Local tradesmen who carried out repairs:
(L to R) Martin Taylor, Tommy Nelson, Willie Smith and Willie Murray.

*The unveiling of the war memorial in November 1920 by Dumfriesshire MP Major Murray. Originally built with six sections in the pillar, following a gale in October 1949, when it was blown over,
it was rebuilt with only four sections in the pillar. The other main change was the addition of the names of those killed in action during the Second World War.*

Clock and memorial as they are today.

The east side of the High Street in the 1930's with both the Clock Tower and the War Memorial at their original heights.

War Memorial Blown Over

On 16th October, 1949 a great gale blew over the tall pillar of the war memorial on the High Street. Previous to being rebuilt the monument was 33ft. high. I was watching and waiting for all my pigeons to get in from the blustery rain and wind, from the bay window in our house opposite the loft. One little brown chequered hen was reluctant to enter, preferring to sit on the roof against the wall of the adjoining building. The skylight, which was the entrance to the loft, was supported on a single metal bar, and as it was wavering in the wind I had visions of it clattering down onto the landing stage with pieces of broken glass falling onto the street below.

I waited for a few minutes more, then decided that it was time to go over and close the skylight. As I was heading from our house door towards the Tattie House, I happened to be looking towards the High Street, just as the War Memorial blew over. It never even wavered, but just tumbled towards the south, as if a giant hand had pushed it over from the top. I walked to the top of Church Street and there wasn't a soul in sight – was I the only person to witness the incident?

My brother Philip just before his first active posting: 1943 Sergeant Flight Engineer.

The War Memorial

The War Memorial was unveiled in November 1920 by Dumfriesshire M.P. Major Murray, in memory of the men who died in the Great War, and when it was built the tall pillar consisted of six sections. When it was rebuilt, the main pillar was reduced to four sections and has remained thus to the present day with the only changes, apart from the removal of the railings, being the addition of the names of those killed in the Second World War, including that of my brother Philip.

Philip was one of the keen young men, I suppose they were only boys really, who as members of the A.T.C. (Air Training Corps) met to be instructed on aspects of the R.A.F. in the premises at present occupied by Jumpers.

An Avro Lancaster.
Lancasters were the mainstay of RAF bomber command. They first flew in January 1941 and over 7,000 were built. Eleven Victoria Crosses were won by Lancaster crews, including the one awarded to Wing Commander Guy Gibson of Dam Busters' fame. The expected life-span of a Lancaster was only three months.

At seventeen years old, he joined up together with other lads from the town, gained his wings as a Sergeant Flight Engineer and was soon in the thick of the action.

A few years ago I was given a copy of the 'Brevet', the official magazine of the Dumfries and Galloway Branch of the Aircrew Association, and in it was a full account of Philip's final flight operation with the 'Pathfinders". It read as follows:

THE FIFTH TRIP WITH PFF

"PHILIP'S LAST OPERATION"

Roy Last of the Taunton Branch ordered a copy of 'Valiant Endeavours' and read of my operation to Stuttgart. Apart from a little flak, which modesty forbade me to mention in the book, I did refer to us almost running out of fuel.

This prompted Roy to give his experience on the same operation which was somewhat different to mine.

The background to this operation, which was on 24/25th July 1944 was that his crew had completed 14 ops. with 101 Sqn. and then joined 582 Sqn. (PFF) and this trip was their fifth with this Sqn.

Philip 'Jock' Dicerbo (F/E) from Moffat was a Scot of Italian extraction (his father and brother were interned in the Isle of Man). His skipper, Paddy Finlay, completed a 100 ops by the end of the war and then flew with Aer Lingus, was from Eire, his Navigator, Bomb Aimer and W/Op. were Aussies and the two gunners were from London.

The raid was recorded the next day in the diary of the W/Op., Tom Thomson.

On this occasion we were detailed to attack the important German target of Stuttgart where Mercedes Benz factories are situated. Such a long trip was not greatly appreciated. We started badly. The H2S did not seem to be working as well as it should and the Nav 11 took bearing on two cities (B and C) when it should have been A and B. This put us south of the track and we passed Stuttgart by ten minutes so had to turn around and rejoin the stream, bombing nearly twenty minutes late but fortunately there were others still bombing and we nearly collided with one.

Over the target I had to stand-by at the flare chute to make sure that the photoflash drops when the bombs are released. If it stuck and ignited in the chute it would destroy the aircraft. It stuck, but dropped when I gave it a furious shove.

It was just after leaving the target that we nearly ran head first into another Lanc. which was on a reciprocal course.

I returned to the radio and was listening to the base broadcast when there were a couple of explosions and the plane went into a dive as if to corkscrew. I jumped up and put one leg over the main spar and wondered what was going

The Spitfire, champion of Lord Dowding's fighter command 1940.

A 'Shackleton', the last in service from RAF Kinloss flew over Dowding House as a mark of respect to the residents (May 1991). Shackletons were based at Kinloss, RAF coastal command over 40 years ago when I served my national service there. Equipped with high tech. radar, together with American Neptunes, they kept a wary eye on submarines around the coasts. Lord Dowding was born and educated at St. Ninian's, which was run by his father, before his service career presented him with the task of master-minding the planning for the defence of the country with his fighter command, during The Battle of Britain 1940.

on, then realised that I was switched out of the full intercom circuit. I switched over in time to hear Paddy Finlay, the Pilot, calling for assistance to pull the plane out of its dive as he could not do so alone. The Navigator, Alan Rogers, went to his assistance and we levelled out.

What had happened was that Fred Jones, our rear gunner saw a burst of tracer fire and did not realise until shells began to hit our aircraft that they were aimed at us. At the same time another aircraft attacked from starboard low down and bursts of fire hit us simultaneously. Fred gave the order to corkscrew and away he went. He also fired a burst which he observed to hit the belly of the attacking JU88 as it broke away port quarter up but dived away from sight when hit.

While all this was going on Roy Last, the mid-upper gunner floated up as we dived and instead of his seat resuming its position locked down by his weight, it missed the hook and was flung heavily out of the bottom of the turret onto the floor in a bundle of intercom leads, suit heating leads and oxygen hose.

The Bomb Aimer, Graham Corran, grabbed his parachute and dived for the escape hatch in the nose. The Navigator, Alan, put on his 'chute and prepared

Dowding Memorial, Station Park.
As Churchill said of the pilots of fighter command in 1940:
"never in the field of human conflict was so much owed by so many to so few".

to follow. I was sitting on the spar fully expecting orders to abandon the aircraft as it seemed to be plunging in a most erratic manner. Whilst preparing to dive out through the escape hatch Graham found the Engineer, Jock Dicerbo lying over the exit and that he had been killed instantly by a cannon shell which entered the bottom of the bomb bay and hit Jock in the left side.

Paddy ordered me to check on Roy, whom I found untangling himself and helped him back into the turret and then gathered all the portable oxygen bottles and moved to the cockpit to help Paddy to control the aircraft.

Fred Jones suggested that it may be a good idea to head for Switzerland and after a pause of what seemed like ten seconds, someone said, "No, let's press on."

Paddy asked for something to help hold the control column back so I gave Alan my sheath knife and he cut the dinghy rope from its position near the rest bed. I tied it to the control column and I pulled it in front of Paddy and started to tie it to his right hand arm rest, but he wasn't happy with that as it would hamper him if he had to get out in a hurry so we changed it to around the back left hand side of his seat and a couple of hitches around his arm rest and for the next $3^1/_2$ hours I hung on to that and we watched the artificial horizon to make sure we were not heading downwards. After about ten minutes of this my oxygen had run out and I was in danger of passing out, so we reorganised the fixed oxygen hoses and I connected to one of those.

Coxhill Duck Farm as it would have appeared on the night of 20th July 1940 when three German bombs exploded near the duck houses.
This photograph was taken in 1965.

Coxhill as it is today, 1999.

Three village lads in October 1936, at the entrance to Coxhill Duck Farm examining their 'finds' where workmen were clearing an area. The cobbled floor was uncovered to reveal what was possibly a smiddy. Some say Robin Tamson's smiddy, frequented by Robert Burns.

Roast Duck? Not Quite

THE BOMBING OF THE DUCK FARM

Previous to the formation of the Duck Farm in 1925, the area was a 9-hole golf course.

At one time eleven men were employed, enough for their own football team and on occasion ducklings were sent by rail to Buckingham Palace.

In 1936 an interesting discovery was made when workmen unearthed the remains of what could have been the site of an early blacksmith's.

Some of the objects found, horseshoe, nails, spoons and coins.

On 20th July 1940, Moffat received its first real baptism of the war, when three bombs fell and exploded at Coxhill Duck Farm.

The bombs were dropped from a German bomber, possibly returning from a raid on Clydebank or other strategic target, and having bombs left in its bomb bay. It is a possibility that in the moonlight, the glinting roofs of the duck houses appeared as an army camp.

Fortunately, the duck houses remained intact, with the only damage being the three large craters, around which some of the townspeople searched for pieces of shrapnel to keep as war souvenirs. I remember finding an assortment of pieces but gave them all away. I wonder if there is any piece lying forgotten in some place or other in the town today.

Even the Home Guard were called out on that memorable night, but as yet they had no proper weapons. Later, the duck houses were covered with branches to camouflage them, but I don't think that the poor ducks were in any further fear of their lives – at least from German bombers.

The duck farm continued to thrive well after the war, in fact it eventually ceased production in 1980.

Staff at the Duck Farm, 1955.
Front Row (L to R): *Jimmy McMillan, Jim Clark, Sandy Clark, Stobbie Adamson (my father-in-law). Standing behind is the owner, David Ralston, who was a Major in the Home Guard. Two prettier staff during the war years were landgirls Elizabeth Black and Jean Nairn.*

The pole carrying power to Golf Hill across the River Annan, which Francis climbed, almost costing his life.

A Near Tragedy

Shortly after his release from the Isle of Man, Francis was back with his cronies and as well as working at Sinclair's, he was also one of the projectionists at the Baths Hall Cinema.

On Sunday afternoons, he and his friends would meet at the top of Church Street before setting off for a daunder, which usually took them round by 'Toot", then via Barnhill and Beattock Road, before turning up the waterside towards home.

On this occasion, Francis was in the company of Tommy Wallace, Archie Porteous and Willie Rankine and as they arrived at the junction of the paths at the bottom of Annanside, Francis decided to climb the high pole which carries the electricity supply up to Golf Hill.

Off he went, hand over hand, up one of the supporting wire stays, but when he reached the top he inadvertently swung over and caught the high tension cable.

Eleven thousand volts shot through his body, as the electricity supply to Golf Hill was shut off, and he fell to the ground, flat on his back. Although no bones were broken, at first they said he was dead. Tommy ran up the road to tell my mum, while meantime Mr. Glen Barr, the owner of the gift and toy shop on the High Street, arrived on the scene walking his dog.

He must have been well instructed on the art of first aid, as he immediately took control and sent some of us young boys to the nearby houses for containers of hot and cold water.

I was in a state of shock myself on seeing my brother lying there and don't remember much, but Francis regained consciousness, was taken to Dumfries and eventually returned home to convalesce.

My only other memory of that time is that when visited by a friend and asked how he was getting on, Francis replied "I'm OK but my **** is burning," as there was a massive burn on his backside at the point where his hip pocket, containing a large bunch of keys, made contact with his flesh. If Francis hadn't had the cinema keys in his hip pocket, and the electricity had not surged towards the metal, the outcome might have been a lot different.

The 'Kerr' was at one time common grazing land for the townspeople's animals. The boggy areas, reed bed, hawthorns and gorse provided a sanctuary for bird life. Sadly, more recently, it has become arable field.

A Slim Benefit

All through the war years, I was never at any time what one would call well built, in fact I was a little on the thin side. But this had its advantages, especially for accessing places where most other boys were restricted and this gave one a position of superiority.

Old Robbie Anderson was the keeper of the hens for the Buccleuch Hotel, in two hen houses in the field bordering Schoolar's builder's yard. I was nosing around in my usual way one morning at the hen houses, when I discovered that although the hen houses were locked I could gain access by squeezing through the wee hole used by the hens. So I soon set this to my advantage – a couple of fresh eggs and back home.

Being rather naive at that time, I let one of the bigger boys into my secret and he soon had me passing him out twelve eggs. "Why twelve?" I wondered. I soon found out, "Come on," he said and off we went to the back door of the Buccleuch, where he brazenly went in, returning some time later with some money – I don't know how much as I wasn't given any. So needless to say I steered well clear of him at any time when I fancied an egg.

Poor old Robbie must have thought that his hens had "gone off the lay" on that fateful morning.

Fireworks

It was shortly after this when Verey cartridges became the vogue, much better than ·303 bullets as they were ready-made fireworks. All that was needed was a knife and a match.

The knife easily cut through the cardboard casing of the Verey light. Placing the small round flare on a surface, all one had to do was touch the top of it with a lighted match and you had a brilliant red or green 'volcano'-type firework.

Verey cartridges were readily available from many sources including the 'brennies' as the drivers would sometimes give them to us as payment for helping to wash their vehicles.

The soldiers knew we could use them as fireworks with relative safety. But relative safety goes hand in hand with downright stupidity when in the hands of a clot.

I was walking home, up Holm Street one night when as I passed the old cemetery gates (which I usually ran past for all I was worth), two teenagers asked me if I had a match. I always had matches somewhere on my person so I said yes, thinking that this would be the end of it if I gave them a few.

"Do you know how to set off these Vereys?" was the curt demand from one of my two big companions. "Yes." "Then come and show us," and off we went – inside the cemetery gates, where the Verey flare was placed on a big flat gravestone.

Hairless II

After a few attempts at trying to ignite the flare, all useless because of the dampness of the evening, I suggested that if the flare's surface was scraped with a knife, the resulting powdery surface would ignite easier. I soon wished that I'd kept silent.

The Moffat Cottage Hospital (above), as it stood at the opening in 1906 and greatly changed (below) as it stands today (1999).

Moffat Cottage Hospital with Doctors and Staff, shortly before alterations in 1969.
Doctors: Hugh Sinclair; Hamish MacLeod; Walter Gillies; Hector MacLean.
Matron: Nancy Bastin. Sisters: Mrs. Shaw; Mrs. Wilkins; Mrs. Watson.
Staff Nurse: Mrs. Robison. Auxiliary Nurses: Mrs. Black; Irene Smith; ?.
Cook: Emma Currie.
Major rebuilding in the early 1980's resulted in the Moffat Hospital as it is today.

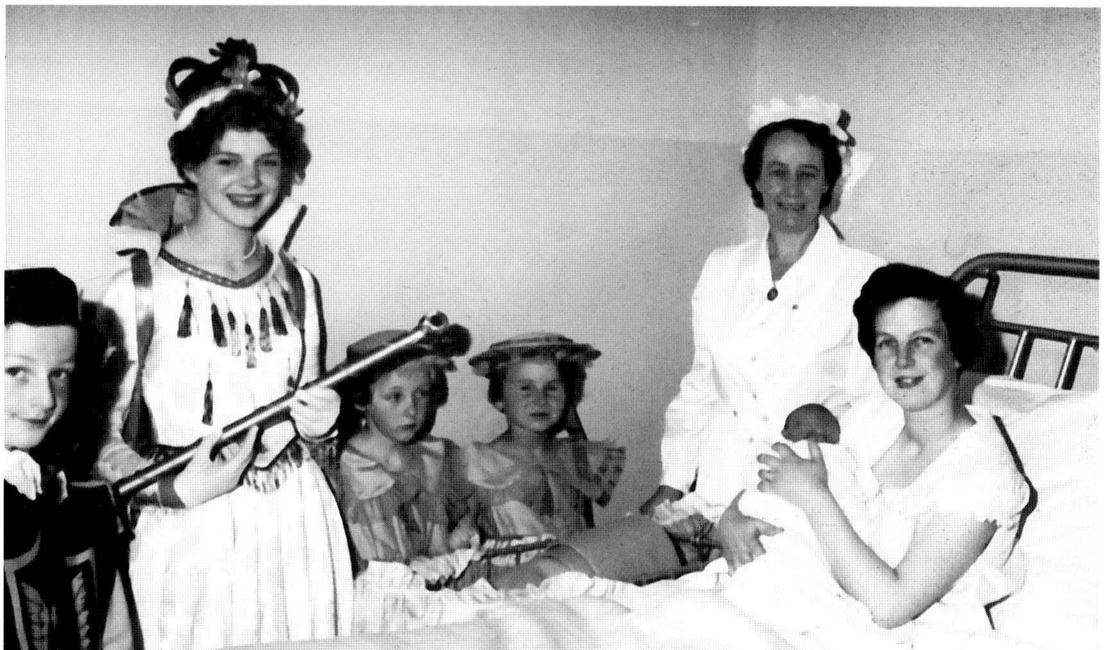

Gala Day 1961. Margaret Gibson, Gala Queen with her page and attendants visiting Mrs. Mary Stirling with one of her twin boys in the Cottage Hospital.
The Matron was Miss Strathern.

"Coorie doon" was the next command, and as I bent over to help keep the drizzle from dampening the powder, the clown touched it with a lighted match. Before I could withdraw – for the second time during the war years – I lost most of my hair. I wasn't burned, only annoyed, so I let them know exactly what I thought of them. This turned out to be another stupid thing to do, as an old piece of rope was found and I spent at least half an hour tied to a headstone in a graveyard, on a dark night, terrified, until they eventually returned to release me. I hated that pair for years!

My ability to squeeze through small apertures came in handy on yet another occasion, but this one was much more daring.

Dr. Pringle, presented with gifts to mark the occasion of his retirement after over thirty years as a medical practitioner in Moffat, December 1959.
Dr. Pringle was Provost from 1951-57, and the presentation is being made by Andy Fingland, Provost of Moffat from 1957-75.
Also in the photograph are Margaret Pringle, Eric Young and seated (l to r) Mrs. Fingland, Mrs. Pringle and Mrs. Young.

Two-inch mortars, mostly harmless parachute flare cases, but there is always an exception to the rule.

3" Mortars

The slaughterhouse at Ladyknowe was always a favourite place to birds-nest. Starlings, House Sparrows, Swallows and Wagtails all found nest sites within its walls, and one morning found me standing outside the big main gate.

Changes had taken place as the gate was securely locked and all around the top of the wall and the gate itself were rolls of barbed wire. It was now being used as an ammunition dump, and had been made secure. No way – the hole at the bottom of the wall, just to the right of the gate, where the slaughterhouse workers would swill out the muck, was open and it was larger than a hole for hens to enter a hen house.

I was on my own – there was no one around – so I got down on my belly and had soon wriggled through the hole. The ammunition boxes were stacked high, so high in fact that I had to climb up to gain access to one and they were big and heavy.

The first box I opened contained 3" mortar bombs, so I lifted one out and unscrewed the cap at the back of the fin and discovered a plastic container with something that I found later burned well. But these things were way out of my league, and they were heavy – so I replaced the mortar, closed the lid and left the same way that I had entered. Then it was up the waterside to find out what this thing was.

EPISODE II
Liza Tuton, M. Fleming, M. McLachlan, N. Sloan, Annie Tuton, Robert Richardshon, W. Harkness, Adam Edgar, Fiddler.

HIGHLANDERS, VILLAGERS and BORDER RAIDERS
R. Cargen, W. Johnstone, D. Cargen, M. Corbett, W. A. Richardson, A. J. Richardson, J. Proudfoot, A. Sharp, J. Corbett, G. Edgar, M. Welsh, J. Hyslop, J. Edgar.

PART III

EPISODE I

1745

THE JACOBITES IN ANNANDALE.

Prince Charlie's men camp on Poldean Meadows.

HIGHLAND DANCING.

EPISODE II

1643

THE "FLYING SPUR."

The Story of the Moffat Coat of Arms.

DANCING.

EPISODE III

1585

THE BURNING OF LOCHWOOD CASTLE.

The ancient stronghold of the Johnstones is burnt by their foes, the Maxwells.

ACADEMY DANCING TROUPE

BROWNIES.

S. Young, M. Thomson, M. Fleming, N. Sloan, B. Edgar, E. Black, B. Dicerbo, M. Cameron, Margaret Fleming, M. Murray, M. Adamson, M. Seaton, M. Gibson, W. Blyth, L. Rankine, J. Kerr.

HIGHLAND DANCERS.

L. Rankine, J. Kerr, H. Gibson, M. Gibson, W. Blyth, N. Roddick, M. Miller, M. Seaton.

LADIES-IN-WAITING.

N. Cranston, O. Wilson, B. Fairbairn, M. Miller, S. McDonald, M. Chapman, E. Cruickshank, H. Gibson, J. Kirkup, W. Blyth, M. Corbett, E. Scott, M. Burgess, A. Galligan, M. Adamson, I. Tuton.

PLAYERS IN THE PAGEANT

EPISODE I

Mary Shankland, May Paterson, Doreen Shaw, John Edgar, T. Fortune, Wallace Park, P. Hepburn, Walter Jackson, Robert Jackson, J. Adamson, G. Turnbull, T. Burgess, J. Corbett, J. Hyslop, A. Edgar, Pipe-major Proudfoot, Piper Richardson.

EPISODE II

Liza Tuton, M. Fleming, M. McLachlan, N. Sloan, Annie Tuton, Robert Richardson, W. Harkness, Adam Edgar, Fiddler.

HIGHLANDERS, VILLAGERS and BORDER RAIDERS

R. Cargen, W. Johnstone, D. Cargen, M. Corbett, W. A. Richardson, A. J. Richardson, J. Proudfoot, A. Sharp, J. Corbett, G. Edgar, M. Welsh, J. Hyslop, J. Edgar.

The two young riders are Robert and Walter Jackson from Woodfoot Farm.

LADIES IN WAITING
N. Cranston, O. Wilson, B. Fairbairn, M. Miller, S. McDonald, M. Chapman, E. Cruickshank, H. Gibson, J. Kirkup, W. Blyth, M. Corbett, E. Scott, M. Burgess, A. Galligan, M. Adamson, I. Tuton.

PAGEANT EXECUTIVE

Convener	Mr J. Glen Barr
Pageant Episodes	Adapted and written by Mrs Park
Dramatic Producers	Messrs J. J. Kydd and W. J. Gordon
Stage Manager	Mr W. A. Armstrong
Dancing Producer	Miss W. Young
Scenic Artist	Mr T. Fairbairn
Costumes	Mrs Hunt, Mrs Bruce Sinclair and Miss R. Gunn Budge
Lighting Effects	Messrs J. J. Beattie and J. Simmons
Broadcasting	"*Scottish Daily Express*" Melody Van
Announcer	Mr J. J. Kydd
Incidental Music	arranged by Mrs Park and Mr Oswald W. Butler
Pipe Band	Moffat Academy Cadet Corps
Procession Marshal	Mr J. Dickson
Fireworks	by "Standard Fireworks"
Firework Operators	Mr W. Penly and Assistant
Hon. Secretary	Mr T. D. Thomson
Hon. Treasurer	Mr R. T. F. Knight

Moffat Town Hall, decked with bunting and thronged with onlookers at the gala celebrations as they were in the 1950's.

Moffat and District Gala Day

THE SHEPHERD AND HIS LASS MEMORIAL SERVICES

The Edinburgh Trades' fortnight ends, the Glasgow Fair begins and Moffat and District Gala Day all fall on the same Saturday in mid-July. Add to this a little sunshine and Moffat is bursting at the seams.

In the late 1940's, the Children's Gala Day was eagerly attended, with the Hope Johnstone Park thronged by both young and old enjoying the event, which was sponsored by the Scottish Co-operative Society. Children's sports, entertainment, highland dancing, competitions and last, but not least, a bag of buns and bottle of lemonade for every child.

In 1950, the Shepherd and his Lass were re-introduced, and the previously named 'Carnival Week' was revived by the Town Council who changed the name to Moffat Gala Week.

The following year, 1951, saw the introduction of the "Queen of Upper Annandale" with other annual events including the children's fancy dress parade, decorated vehicles, election of the Gala Princess, sponsored road races and many more sporting competitions now in place.

Shepherd and Lass, 1958.
Russel W. Young and
Margaret A. Matchett.

Shepherd and Lass, 1965.
Leslie Porteous and Rosemary Linton.

A 1950's Gala Day in Hope-Johnstone Park.

During the mid-1930's the Shepherd and Lass held the grand title of 'Shepherd and Shepherdess of the Hills'. The appointment took place in June in Carnival Week and there was also a children's day when sports and entertainment took place. The photograph depicts a typical group of the period (1935).

On Friday and Saturday, open-air evening entertainment takes place at the Town Hall with a torchlight procession and bonfire later in the evening.

Over the years the 'Baths Hall', now Town Hall, has served many purposes, from cinema to dance hall, and from Council Chambers to childrens' party venue.

Gala Queen 1957, Violet Jackson.

Gala Queen 1958, Vanda Johnstone.

Early 'Old Folks' Treats' and concerts were always well attended, and well-attended-to were the company, by Mrs. Mulvey and her staff from the Balmoral Hotel.

'Old Folks' are now 'Senior Citizens' and previous to their entertainment, groups dine at various hotels in the town. Needless to say, it is an event enjoyed by all.

Gala Queen 1959, Beckwith Mundell.

Functions were splendidly catered for by The Balmoral Hotel, owned and run by Mrs. Mulvey. At that time Balmoral Staff numbered about forty, six of whom pose for a photograph with Hall Keeper, Geordie Stewart.
(L to R): *Bessie Nelson, Gertie Little, Mary Little, Esther Caird, Nellie Coupland, Mrs. Davies.*

In November, the Armistice Day Service is held at the War Memorial on the High Street when townspeople gather to remember those who fell in two World Wars. And in September there is an R.A.F. service held in the Station Park in commemoration of Lord Dowding, mastermind of the Battle of Britain in 1940.

One of the many popular functions of the day, as it was at that time 'the Old Folks' Treat'.

Pipe Major Bert Richardson, with two of the multitude of young dancers who benefitted from his expert tuition, over the many years of his association with the Moffat Pipe Band. On this occasion they are entertaining the elderly. Dancers: left Janet Stitt, right Elizabeth Stitt.

Moffat Pipe Band 1946. Pipe Major W. Proudfoot, Bob McGregor, Davy Little, Tom Porteous, Andy Kerr, Jimmy Beattie, Tucker Porteous, Archie Porteous, Tom Wylie.

Moffat Pipe Band 1956. Pipe Major Bert Richardson, Helen Nelson, Rob. Chisholm, Jimmy Beattie, Billy Harkness, Denis Salmon, Tom Wylie, are some of the members.

The Battle School 1943
This group photograph taken in 1943, shows the diversity of regiments represented while training at the Battle School based in Moffat. As can be seen by their caps, officers and other ranks from a variety of regiments were based here at that time and although I was only nine years old at that time, I recognised many of the faces. The most obvious being, front rank centre, my brother-in-law, eighteen year old George Dawson. At least 20 local lasses married soldiers stationed in Moffat.

The Battle School

The formation of the battle school, together with the arrival of the S.S. Commandos in the town was better than a fun fair, as the structures that were erected for their training by the Royal Engineers were like a giant adventure playground.

The main structure was built with scaffolding at the top end of the Annandale field – a massive affair, about twelve metres high. It was oblong, and though I cannot remember for certain how long or broad it was, I know that when I was up on top of the big flat deck, it was a fair jaunt to get from one end to the other.

There were access holes in the deck with thick ropes dangling all the way to the bottom. As scaffolding tubes and planks for the cross sections were at four different levels, one could stand on a plank and, by swinging from rope to rope, could traverse from one end to the other, just like 'Tarzan' did in the movies.

There was also a huge net hung over one side, which didn't quite reach the ground, so one had to negotiate the ropes and scaffolding to gain a foothold on the net before being

A good number of these regimental badges were seen in Moffat during the war years (1939-45). (Part of the Billy Duncan collection.)

able to continue to the top. Returning to ground level was easier. We just slid down the ropes, being careful not to burn our hands.

It was an exciting place to play and though it was very popular with us boys, and some girls, I can't remember anyone being hurt or injured in any way.

Provost Duncan welcoming Sir Stafford Cripps, Chancellor of the Exchequer, to the town in 1947. On this occasion Sir Stafford assisted in the distribution of clothing coupons for a brief period.

He Flew through the Air

Over in the Annan Wood, there was a mock landing barge in which the Commandos would crouch, ready for a beach landing. Then suddenly the front would drop flat to the ground, and out they would run, over the rough ground to the burn where the banks had been strengthened by corrugated sheets, leaping the burn, then on up the hill, and always in full battle kit.

In those days, the steep bank at the south end of Moffat House grounds was wooded, with sturdy beeches, limes and fir trees, and this whole area was also developed as an assault course with long fir tree trunks from one tree to another a good height from the ground.

Swinging platforms, and thick ropes from tree to tree angled upwards at different heights – that allowed one to set off at ground level and finish up from five to ten metres above ground – were also a great attraction and challenge for the bolder among us.

I can't say that I was one of the boldest, but I did make a gallant attempt one evening to reach the highest point to where a rope was attached.

I was climbing up steadily, hand over hand, achieving a good height, when I felt the rope sway from side to side. I glanced downwards and saw 'Big Tommy' swinging the rope back and forth with mighty sweeps for all he was worth.

I grasped the rope as tightly as I could, swinging back and forth almost parallel to the ground, then inevitably I let go, and flew through the air like 'that daring young man', but without the trapeze.

I landed at the bottom of the steep bank and smashed my hand against a fence post, breaking my wrist in the process.

Everyone skedaddled, including my brother Vincent (he was supposed to be looking after me). I was left to pick myself up and, holding my broken wrist with my good hand, negotiate three fences and the burn before I could make my way home, sobbing and in pain.

Arriving at the chip shop, I managed to tell my mother between sobs, that I had hurt my hand, so on taking a look at the mucky state I was in she grabbed me by the arm and promptly marched me upstairs to the big, white sink in the back kitchen.

Upsetting Mother – Again!

I was still clutching my wrist, and when my mother pulled my good hand away to wash it, she saw my injured wrist.

Still holding on to my good hand, she walloped me, which at the time I felt wasn't very fair because my broken hand was flapping about like a flag, quite useless in defence.

Thinking back though, I only got what I deserved, as my poor mother must have been utterly frustrated. Only months before, Francis had almost got himself killed while climbing, my dad had recently been confirmed as having contracted T.B., and Philip had recently joined the R.A.F.

My wrist was set in plaster at Dumfries Infirmary, where I spent a couple of days, during which time I received a visit from my poor old dad, who was quite upset.

Down in the Long Grass ~ No Way!

A few days later I was back at school, back to Miss MacDonald's daft dancing games, and I hated them. The one that had got underway while I was absent was "Down in the long grass, one summer's day, Tommy and Betty stepped this way."

My fellow pupils had been paired off to perform this absurdity, holding hands and lifting their feet knee-high while pretending to step over the long grass.

I don't know if poor Sylvia had also been absent or whether she was just short of a partner, but we were paired together and started prancing around the circle chanting the words.

Not for me, not for any self-respecting eight-year-old who threw bombs, stripped bren guns and knew all about mortars and flares. My good old wrist – I complained that it was bothering me and was duly excused dancing or whatever. I'm sure that Sylvia must have been pleased too.

Softly, Softly, Catchee Monkey

I must have been about ten years old when I took up the gauntlet for the ultimate challenge, booby-traps.

The old houses in Holm Street, bordering the old cemetery, which were demolished shortly after 1945, served a useful purpose during the latter part of the war – to instruct Commandos and Officers how to locate and defuse booby-traps.

Access was gained by crawling through a small window facing the cemetery as it was almost level with the ground. As it was the first place that I encountered a booby-trap, one of the older boys gave me step-by-step instructions on how to dismantle and defuse it.

The booby-traps themselves looked like toy cannons with a flat base, into which a small cartridge was loaded, and into the cartridge a length of what we called 'fizz-bang' fuse was inserted, but obviously without an explosive charge!

If the wire attached to the booby-trap was pulled or tripped, the firing-pin would be released causing the cartridge to fire, and the fuse would bang – a small bang for a short fuse and so on.

Obvious places, easy to locate, were across dark landings and stairs, with room- and cupboard-doors next, but they were a bit trickier to defuse; and the nastiest of all were the ones in the loos.

If one managed to get through the door without setting one off, there was always the one ready to give you a nasty fright if you lifted the pan seat, and finally there was always the obvious one when the chain was pulled.

When a booby-trap was located it was a simple enough matter to render it safe and remove the cartridge and 'fizz-bang'; and it was the 'fizz-bang' that was the real prize, with lengths of almost a metre being found on occasion, especially in the pans, but this was a rare occurrence with the usual length being much shorter.

To make a firework similar to today's "Little Demon" banger, all one had to do was cut off a piece of 'fizz-bang' about 5cm in length, insert a single strand of cordite from a •303 bullet, lay it on a surface and light the cordite with a match. Louder bangs could be achieved by using longer pieces of fuse.

Mighty Midgets

Close on the heels of the booby-traps came, in my estimation, the most fearsome little explosive device that I encountered throughout the entire span of the war years – the electronic detonator.

The electronic detonator was a small, silver cylinder, slimmer than a pencil and only about 6cm in length with two thin, white wires protruding from one end.

Varying lengths of flex were required depending on the purpose, the flex being joined to the two existing wires of the detonator and run back to some safe spot where the only other requirement was a cycle-lamp battery.

Although I exploded a fair number of these innocent-looking little items, I never found from where they originated, as any that I did have were given to me by one of the much older lads.

To give some idea of the power in these little tubes, one inserted in a crack in the concrete at the "barrels" down at the waterside, when detonated would blast large pieces of concrete into the river.

The 'barrels' as the name suggests were originally wooden barrels filled with concrete and stacked together in such a way that when the concrete set hard and other concrete ledges were added, the resulting structure was a superb riverbank flood barrier, which is still in place today.

Another use that the detonators were put to was one employed by both soldiers and civvies alike. A detonator dropped into a deep pool containing salmon could be exploded, with the result that a few fish would be stunned and float downstream into shallower water from where they could be retrieved. Today, an act like this would carry a heavy fine, with perhaps even a prison sentence. For as long as fifteen years after the end of the war it was possible to count over fifty spawning salmon between the Beattock Road Bridge at the Station Park and the Edinburgh Road Bridge at the other end of the town, at the 'back-end' of the season.

Nowadays, half a dozen would be nearer the mark, not because of anglers etc. in the upper reaches, but on account of the large numbers netted in the estuaries, in the tidal stretches of the rivers, on the high seas and river pollution since the 1960s.

Queen Victoria's Diamond Jubilee 1897.
No need for bunting or illuminations in those days, local greenery plus Moffatonian labour and ingenuity was all that was required for decoration.

Moffat's Illuminations

Nearing D-Day, on 6th June 1944, with the Allies very much on the offensive, even far-flung places like Moffat were involved in some way or other in the mighty invasion that was about to take place. Most noticeable was the convoy of trucks parked overnight, that stretched all the way from the Wells to Wamphray.

Moffat High Street in 1897 – was this the material used to decorate the bottom of Well Street for Queen Victoria's Diamond Jubilee – or perhaps it being removed?

In the mid 1950's, the spacious High Street was uncluttered. Measuring 300 x 50yds, there was plenty of room for the traffic of the day. Today the layout is more suited to the demands of modern motoring, but double-decker buses have long since disappeared from the scene.

Brand new Dennis light 15cwt. trucks with canvas backs, were parked nose to tail for about seven miles down the back-road, and as unobtrusively as they arrived, they were gone the following day.

I suppose, on reflection, the smaller 15cwt. trucks would be more manoeuvrable in the landings than the more cumbersome, heavier troop carriers.

It was also about this time that a few new gadgets were appearing on the scene in the "flash and bang" department and with boxes containing all sorts being left around willy-nilly, one of my regular visits to Mount Charles produced a trip-flare, the likes of which I'd never come across before.

The Provost and Magistrates of Moffat proclaiming the Accession of King George V, at the Market Cross on 10th May 1910.

The trip flare was hidden near the cook house where it lay concealed until one night the soldiers must have been in the process of being moved out. The cook house was full of kit-bags, masses and masses of them piled high, row upon row.

Who could resist playing among such obstacles? Not us, but as we were running to and fro along the aisles in the dim light, the powerful beam of a flashlight heralded the arrival of the special constable, and as he proceeded up one aisle we crouched low until he was at the far end, then we rushed towards the door.

This particular special constable had been close on our heels for months, determined to catch us at it, but it was a friendly chase and quite often he would get just so close, but not close enough, and I'm sure he knew who we were anyway.

Leaving the cook house behind us we pelted down towards the waterside only pausing for me to pick up my flare which I had hidden near the path. We knew that we would be followed as this was usual procedure when discovered involved in mischief, so we headed up the waterside towards the Edinburgh Road Bridge but en route we decided to test the flare.

The flare itself was a 'bakelite' container about the size of a small syrup tin, with a braided wire attached to a pin at the top. The flare was secured at one side while the wire was stretched across the path and fastened round a post. We didn't have long to wait, as minutes later we were lined along the parapet of the bridge in total darkness. Sooner, rather than later, it happened – the countryside was brilliantly illuminated, with our friendly 'special' dancing around in a frenzy. After watching for a minute or so, we were all agreed that these flares were the 'tops', then we turned on our heels and headed for the sanctuary of our homes to swap comics and listen to the radio.

Armistice Day 1964.
Provost Fingland, Bailie J. Cockayne, Town Clerk H. Simpson and Council Members.
Graham Minto, Shepherd and Alison Stitt, Shepherdess.

Two wee lads, Alan and George (Dodo) Cunningham look on as the coach "Annie Laurie", driven by Duncan McLachlan arrives at the well. Earlier coaches in the mid-1800s were "The Ettrick Shepherd" from the Annandale Arms Hotel driven by George Cavers and "The Tibbie Shiels" from the Buccleuch Hotel driven by John Muir.

Coaches preparing to leave from the Annandale hotel c.1900.

Moffat. The Wells.

Never was a town more sweetly
Spread beneath more kindly skies;

All who sigh for healing waters,
Come to Moffat and be wise.
Professor J. S. Blackie.

Annandale Series. J. Weir, Photo., Moffat.

Today, the small shed-like structure is all that is left – similar in fact to improvements made in 1657, when Oliver Cromwell, the Lord Protector, allowed John, Earl of Hopetoun, £25.00 to upgrade the well.

By 1827 the Baths Hall (now Town Hall) was catering for many visitors who wanted to bathe in the "Healing Waters" which were piped from the well to the hall. Charges for baths varied according to the amount of water and temperature, 2/– for a hot mineral bath

The Well Cottage and the Tea Room which was big enough for dances to be held there in the earlier part of the century.

The Mineral Baths and Town Hall, Moffat in 1909.

and 1/– (5p) for a cold one. (Normal baths were available for many years after which time the mineral water had lost its appeal.)

As more and more people converged on the town, trading improved to such an extent that even with the addition of the Annandale Hotel (King's Arms), and Balmoral Hotel (Old Spur Inn), more accommodation was needed.

A donkey cart outside the Town Hall in the late 1800s. The cart was used to deliver mineral well water to the Annandale Hotel where it was decanted and sold by the glass.

This led to the building of the Moffat Hydropathic – a magnificent structure which sadly had a very short life span of only 43 years. Moffat, I feel, would be a more thriving town today had it been spared.

On only one occasion did I drink "Well Water", when an entry in the visitors' book mirrored my opinion. "I'd heard it tasted awful, but it didn't – it was worse!"

The "Hartfell Spa" discovered by John Williamson in 1748, produced 'chalybeate' water (containing iron) and though not as famous as the mineral water, was sent abroad in large quantities.

The Devil's Beef Tub.
The old road from Moffat to Edinburgh ran along the bottom of the valley and climbed steeply behind Ericstane summit. This route crossed the modern road about three quarters of a mile to the south then crossed the present road again at the rim of the Beef Tub. The road as it is today was surveyed in 1815 and completed in 1823.

The Devil's Beef Tub.
An earlier name for this valley was Corrie of Annan. In the sixteenth century it was used by the Johnstones to hoard cattle stolen in predatory raids and it became known as the Beef Tub or the Marquis of Annandale's Beef Stand.

The Covenanter's Monument on the rim of the Beef Tub was erected to the memory of John Hunter who was fleeing from Douglas's Dragoons in the company of a companion, namely James Welsh. Welsh managed to escape but Hunter, having to pause for lack of breath, was murdered by the Dragoons in 1685.

Roman Roads

55 B.C. TO 407 A.D.

The first Roman Wall built in Scotland was from the Forth to the Clyde (36 miles), the Antonine Wall.

The area from this wall to the English border was difficult to keep under control so Hadrian's Wall was built between the Solway and the Tyne (60 miles).

After subduing the English, the Romans found the residents of Annandale and Evandale a race with a culture of their own who were more organised than those south of the border and prepared to fight in defence of their families and homes.

Roman roads paid no heed to hills or bogs but followed near straight lines from one fortification to another. The style of their fixed axle carts dictated this. The Roman road through Upper Annandale from Hadrian's Wall, crossed the River Annan near Girthhead, continued west of Nether Murthat, where is it marked on the OS map and continued to Tassieholm, near Milton.

After passing between Lochhouse Tower and the Three Standin' Stanes, it proceeded straight over Cotes Hill (the ridge between Annan and Evan Waters), through Chapel Farm then over Ericstane Moor where it crossed the present Edinburgh Road near Auldhousehill Bridge, south of the Devil's Beef Tub. It then veered off in a westerly direction.

After passing between Lochhouse Tower and the Three Standin' Stanes, the Roman Road proceeded through Chapel Farm.

Departure of the Romans

REIVERS AND CRUSADERS

Following the departure of the Romans in 407 A.D. the roads were vandalised in many places by the local inhabitants who used the material for various building projects.

Dirt tracks such as those followed by Border Reivers were then used by the valley and hill dwellers to travel from place to place.

The Devil's Beef Tub, a well-hidden favoured place used by the Reivers, not only held stolen cattle but was also used as a disposal depot for brandy, silks and salt smuggled into Dumfriesshire along the Solway coast. The goods were then moved into Tweedsmuir and beyond.

Southern Scotland, when the Romans left was at the mercy of the Vikings, Danes and Angles – this period kept the country moulded into one kingdom and laid the foundation of a rugged and hardy people and prepared the way for Wallace and Bruce.

Heavy rainfall caused this landslide at Birkhill, Moffat Water in 1931. In the top left hand of the photograph part of the rocky crag of Dob's Linn can be seen, where Hab Dob and Davie Din built their bothy.

A view of the Hartfell area where William Moffat conducted his conventicles.

Moffat's Covenanting Days

There is no doubt that there was much covenanting activity in and around Moffat in the 17th century, especially in the Moffat Water region, or Moffatdale as it was known at that time.

Many accounts have gone to press covering Claverhouse, Douglas, his Dragoons, "The Killing Times" and Covenanters Halbert Dobson (Hab Dob), David Dunwoodie (Davie Din) and John Hunter. The latter remembered by a fine memorial at the Devil's Beef Tub on the A701 Moffat to Edinburgh Road.

The previous pair played a major part in Moffatdale's Covenanting history, or were their exploits a figment of James Hogg's fertile imagination.

Hogg appears to have had a fixation with the 'Evil One', who were he omitted from the tales, would have rendered them more readily acceptable.

Follow the exploits of Dob and Din and we end up with four Covenanters executed by Claverhouse, buried in Ettrick Kirkyard. "Not true," some say, while others such as one historian in particular with whom I discussed the subject, assuring me he had seen the graves.

During the reign of the Stuarts the scottish people struggled for religious freedom. Mr. Whiteford, the father of Rachel who discovered the Moffat Mineral Well in 1633, came to Moffat as minister in 1610. Whiteford, although reluctant to come to Moffat because he found the inhabitants 'wild and woolly', ministered to their needs until 1638 when, by order of the Bishop he had to introduce the new Episcopalian service.

Moffatonians were staunch Presbyterians and Whiteford knew that there would be trouble if he followed the Bishop's instructions so he planned his first sermon in such a way as to offend neither Bishop or congregation.

Very early on the Sabbath morning, Whiteford, his wife and servants entered the Kirk where he promptly locked the doors, read the service, and then hastily left for home, but an angry crowd had gathered outside and the party barely made it back to the house without injury. Whiteford left the town soon afterwards...

Also in 1638, the government produced the National Covenant to renunciate Popery and the General Assembly of the Church in Glasgow were determined to abolish Episcopacy by 'fair means or foul'.

In Westminster in 1643, the Covenant was favourably accepted by the English Parliament and returned to Scotland with orders that it should be 'subscribed throughout the kingdom'.

The Scottish Commissioners signed with much enthusiasm and entreated Charles to do likewise but he signified his willingness to sacrifice his crown and life rather than leave the religion he had so long supported.

Charles defended his faith at the Battle of Naseby in 1645, where he was defeated by Cromwell's Roundheads. He was then imprisoned and eventually executed in 1649.

From 1653, until his death in 1658, Cromwell ruled England, Scotland and Ireland, favouring the Puritans and Covenanters, but when Charles 2nd became King in 1660, the persecution of the Covenanters was increased, so much so, that the field Coventicles which were previously allowed became strictly illegal in 1663.

During these troublesome times the people of Moffat manifested a dislike to the local Curate so they hired the services of one called Harkness to persuade the Curate to leave the district in peaceable manner. The Curate agreed to the 'request'. (Curates entered the pulpit by order of the Bishop and not by the choice of the people.)

Harkness was a Covenanter from Lochmaben. He was later imprisoned in Edinburgh in 1663, but escaped about a year later and lived for another 39 years.

John Grahame of Claverhouse was created Viscount Dundee (Bonnie Dundee), and in 1678 he soon set about adding fuel to the flames of Scottish troubles.

Engagements with Covenanters frequently resulted in many of them being slaughtered, the Battles of Pentland and Rullion Green were two examples, then after the Battle of Drumclog where the Covenanters were victorious, Claverhouse routed them at Bothwell Bridge with a ferocity that he had not displayed before.

In 1682, 'Clavers' wrote to his superiors saying that all was well and at peace around Moffat. Nothing was further from the truth, in fact, one William Moffat who dwelt in the inhospitable region of Hartfell held Conventicles there, which were well supported. During the reign of Charles 2nd many Covenanters sought refuge in this mountainous region as did many of the fugitives from the Battle of Boswell Bridge.

While preaching a sermon to a large gathering at a Conventicle at Hartfell on one occasion William Moffat noticed the sheep and lambs approaching them in an unusual manner. Immediately sensing danger he ordered the gathering to disperse and before the Dragoons could fall upon those present, they had all disappeared into a mist which conveniently rolled down from the mountain top at that particular moment in time. (An Act of God, as it was said later.)

In the afternoon of that same day, William Moffat had another lucky escape while being pursued by Dragoons along the banks of the River Evan. He managed to evade capture by hiding in a small cavern on the river bank before crossing the peat bog to Elvanfoot.

James Douglas, a Colonel in a regiment of Dragoons, while in pursuit of John Hunter and James Welsh at the Straight Steps in the Devil's Beef Tub, caught up with Hunter as he lay exhausted among the heather and shot him like a dog. This murder took place in 1685 and there is now a memorial to John Hunter at the Devil's Beef Tub.

On 12th February 1687, a proclamation was issued to the effect that 'moderate' Presbyterianism would be allowed but that all field meetings (Conventicles) should be prosecuted with the utmost rigour of the law.

Claverhouse was then sent to suppress these field meetings which he did with such brutality that he soon became known as 'Bloody Clavers'. The period became known as the 'Killing Times' and the 'Test Oath' was forced on many Moffatonians.

In Turnbull's "History of Moffat" (1871) it states that the older Moffatonians still spoke of 'Clavers' with hatred, and that he was indeed in league with the 'Evil One', because of the wondrous deeds he performed on his famous, black charger while in pursuit of his prey.

In the late 1680's many Covenanters took refuge in the Moffat Water Hills where the farmers at Chapelhope and Bodesbeck turned a blind eye to the disappearance of the odd lamb or ewe. It is said that many of those who hid and sheltered in caverns during the day ventured out at night to undertake tasks for these sympathetic farmers, giving rise to the tale of the 'Brownie of Bodesbeck' (see page 259).

Halbert Dobson and David Dunwoodie, better known as Hab Dob and Davie Din were two Covenanters who built and lived in a small bothy-like structure on a high ledge in Dob's Linn, Moffat Water.

The pair were plagued by nightly visits from the 'Evil One', who tried to persuade them to jump off the high ridge into the valley bottom. One night Hab and Davie

The Moffat Hydropathic Hotel

The Hydro (above and below).
Moffat Hydropathic Hotel was built in 1878 mainly to cater for the many visitors who came to partake of the benefits of the mineral well. Coaches ran on a regular basis to The Wells and St. Mary's Loch and guests were treated in resplendent fashion, with all facilities of the day readily available.

Beechgrove, the road that must have witnessed many fine coaches and occupants to-ing and fro-ing from the Hydro in the late 19th and early 20th century. Beechgrove is also the gateway to Annan Water.

Costing £87,000 to build, the palatial Moffat Hydropathic Establishment opened its doors to the public in April 1878.

Built with red sandstone, the magnificent edifice was said to have incorporated in its structure, three hundred and sixty-five windows, one for every day of the year.

The Hydro stood 500ft. above sea level and commanded a view of the loveliest portion of Annandale for over forty years before it was eventually destroyed by fire in 1921.

The Hydro Avenue as the Groundsmen pause for the photographer.

The spacious garages, coach houses and stables in the Hydro grounds.

The hotel contained over three hundred rooms, which included a spacious dining hall, capable of seating three hundred diners, an elegantly furnished drawing room and a luxurious lounge.

There was also a spacious billiard room, smoking room, and reading and writing room.

The handsome ballroom doubled as a recreation room and as well as having extensive cycle and motor car accommodation, there were also large stables and coach houses.

The cuisine was said to be unequalled at any similar establishment in the country, and as the Hydro was originally built to cater for the many hundreds of people wishing to take the benefit of the 'waters', it is not surprising that the list of baths available was so extensive including: Turkish, Vapour, Spray, Douche, Sitz, Plunge, Brine and Medicated. There was also a fair-sized indoor swimming pool.

Included in the 25 acres of well-kept grounds, were tennis and croquet lawns and a putting green. Back indoors there was a dark room for amateur photographers.

The hotel was heated throughout, lit by electricity and boasted a passenger elevator.

"Salubrious" was how Moffat's climate was described, being particularly beneficial for those suffering from diseases of the chest, and an experienced physician visited the hotel daily.

Towards the end of its existence, support for the Hydro dropped considerably, as the 'waters' began to lose their appeal to the masses. Finally, after serving as a convalescing hospital for officers during the First World War, it had a very short life indeed. Today, a hotel with as much to offer as the Hydro would be well supported by business conferences and the like and Moffat would surely benefit!

The Hydro at the height of its popularity c. 1900.

20 years later, just before it was destroyed by fire.

The Hydro at the height of its popularity c. 1900.

The Inner Hall as it was at the time the Hydro was destroyed by fire in 1921.

The popular tennis and croquet lawns were kept in immaculate condition as were the lawns and paths by the Groundsmen.

Drawing Room, elegance, luxury and comfort.

Morning preparations, not quite so grand in 1920.

Dining Room, perfectly ventilated, separate tables, various sizes.

The interior was palatial as can be seen in the dining room (above). After being destroyed by fire in 1921, the grounds became a popular walk with the townspeople who could now add the Hydro grounds to a Beechwood or Gallow Hill walk. During the war years, the ruins were frequently used for fire drills and manoeuvres by the Fire Service and Home Guard.

Main entrance.

A four-in-hand about to set off for St. Mary's Loch.

Swimming Bath – beautifully tiled, comfortably heated.

Recreation Hall and Ballroom.

the burning building he inquired if the inmates had been removed, and was assured that they had all made their escape.

On being satisfied that everyone was out of the doomed building, the Provost turned his attention to the work of combatting the flames. By this time the local firemen had placed their engine in position, connected up their hose pipes with the hydrants, and some of the men had taken up positions on the roof. All their effort was of no avail, however, for it was found when everything was in readiness that there was

NO WATER.

The Hydropathic is something of a self-contained institution, providing its own water and lighting supply. Owing to the drought which has been experienced during the last two months the water supply was low, and there was not sufficient pressure to meet this emergency. The only alternative was to connect up with the town supply, but as the nearest fire standard is several hundred yards distant, and as the local brigade is not equipped with such an extensive line of hose, this scheme was found impracticable. There was nothing to be done but to await the arrival of the Gretna brigade, which had been summoned at 2am. The Provost was of the opinion that if water had been available at this juncture it would have been possible to have prevented the outbreak from spreading, and to have saved all but a very small portion of the establishment. At 3.30 the Gretna brigade arrived, and very soon water was being poured into the burning pile, but the fire had obtained too good a hold on the interior woodwork, and despite the best efforts of the skilled fire fighters from Gretna, it spread steadily throughout the whole length of the building.

WANT OF ORGANISATION.

Questioned with regard to the amazing circumstance that so few peple had removed their personal belongings, although the fire originated in a distant part of the building, the Provost expressed the view that much of the loss sustained by the inmates was unnecessary. The cause was entirely due to want of organisation.

Most of the sleepers had ample time to dress and remove their property, and if anybody had taken charge of the situation at the outset almost all the personal effects of the inmates would have been salved. The only person who seemed to have been equal to the occasion was a minister from England, who, after conveying his wife and mother-in-law to positions of security, returned to his rooms, packed all the property of his party in three bags, and removed them beyond danger of destruction.

INTERVIEW WITH
MANAGING DIRECTOR.

HIS STORY OF THE DISASTER.

Bailie Robert Wilson, managing director of the Hydro. Company, in the course of an interview, said:

"I came down from Glasgow on Friday night in order to see that certain financial arrangements, such as the paying of accounts, wages, etc., were carried out. Everything went on in the building in the ordinary way until the fire broke out on Monday morning about one o'clock. Dinner was served on the Sunday night as usual about 7.30. At 9 o'clock a short service was conducted by the Rev. Mr. Somers, of the Parish Church. I sat on in the drawing-room until 10 o'clock. An hour later I went into the board-room with Mr. Norris, of London, and we sat discussing the future of the Hydro. until midnight. Our bedrooms adjoined on the south wing. Mr. Norris went to his room and I went to mine.

"I knew nothing afterwards until about one o'clock in the morning when I heard Miss Gardner, the manageress, shouting out the Hydro. was on fire, and calling on the guests to get up. I immediately got up, and the first thing I observed was the reflection of the fire through the window of my room. On looking out I saw that the upper part of the building, or at least the roof, was already ablaze. The fire had evidently broken out on the northern part of the roof, and as there was a stiff breeze blowing from the north it soon fanned the flames until they were running the whole length of the building.

So quickly indeed did the fire spread that by the time the alarm was raised and the firemen has been summoned to the spot from Moffat, it was apparent that nothing could be done to save the building from destruction. The Moffat firemen did their utmost to cope with the conflagration, but it was soon seen that the outbreak was beyond their resources. A 'phone message was sent to Gretna, and the brigade from that centre was on the spot sometime between three and four o'clock in the morning. By that time, however, the whole centre of the building was enveloped in flames, the great towers had fallen, and it was deemed futile to endeavour to save the building.

ENGINEER'S EXPERIENCE.

Mr. James Inglis, master of works and resident engineer, whose residence is within the grounds of the Hydropathic, also gave some interesting particulars in the course of a brief interview. 'I received word of the outbreak,' he said, 'shortly after one o'clock, and proceeded to the main building where I immediately applied the fire extinguishers, and got all the water valves set agoing, but it was a case of "life first". I saw that from the very beginning, so rapidly were the flames getting a hold upon the roof and the upper stories. Along with the staff, therefore, I did everything possible to get the guests removed to safety. I soon saw that there was very little chance of saving the building, but I directed the water from the cisterns in as great a volume as I could secure, and had the hydrants going at their full pressure. Some idea, however, of the fierceness of the flames may be got when I mention that fanned by the strong northerly wind which was blowing the sparks flew right down to the garage 332 yards along the avenue, and actually set it on fire. I had a couple of fire extinguishers in the house, however, and we soon got that little outbreak in hand. The fire in the main building spread with such rapidity that the whole edifice, with the exception of a portion of the northern wing was practically in ruins within three and a half hours.' After paying tribute to the splendid work done by Dr. Huskie and Dr. Park and Miss Gardner in attending to the alarmed guests, he said it was very difficult to state how the fire originated, but it was possible that as Bailie Wilson had said that it had originated in a vent.

The Buck Ruxton Murders

15th SEPTEMBER 1935

"Ruxton's Dump"

As reported in the local press, 1996.

Remains in the Ravine. The original winding road.

Sixty years ago this week, one of the most notorious murder trials in the history of British crime was heading towards its dramatic conclusion.

As the evidence in the headline-hitting case of Dr. Buck Ruxton unfolded, every nitty-gritty fact was devoured by the newspaper-reading public, not least the people of Dumfriesshire.

They had a special interest in the harrowing tale of jealousy, deceit and brutal killings which first came to light with the discovery of human remains in a boulder-strewn ravine near Moffat.

The grim find sparked off a massive cross-Border police investigation by several forces and New Scotland Yard, culminating in the arrest of Dr. Ruxton and, five months later, his appearance in the dock at Manchester Winter Assizes charged with the murder of his common law wife.

The newspapers called it The Crime of the Century. The investigation broke new

The road (A701) and bridge as they are today.

The Gipsy Bridge about a mile further up at Holehouse Linn is often mistaken for Ruxton's Dump.

ground in forensic science and trial, during the first fortnight of March 1936, featured some of the most eminent men of the day.

In the Crown prosecution team were Maxwell Fyfe and Hartley Shawcross while the defence was led by Sir Norman Birkett, and the list of 106 Crown witnesses included celebrated forensic medicine professors John Glaister and Sydney Smith.

Remains

The remarkable story began to unforld on the bright but chilly afternoon of Sunday, September 29, 1935, when Susan Haines Johnson, a young holiday-maker from Edinburgh, went for a stroll on the Moffat – Edinburgh Road.

As she looked over the parapet of a bridge above Gardenholme Linn, a stream tumbling into the River Annan near the Devil's Beef Tub, she spotted what she thought was an arm protruding from some wrapping in the gully below.

She rushed back to her hotel in Moffat, two miles away, told her brother Alfred what she had seen and had a whisky to steady her nerves. Together, they returned to the bridge where Alfred took a closer look and discovered various body parts wrapped in newspapers and cotton sheets.

He rushed back to Moffat and told the police. Sergeant Robert Sloan, of Dumfriesshire Constabulary, was soon on his way to the scene where he confirmed there were four bundles of human remains including two heads.

Among the wrappings were pages of newspapers including the Sunday Graphic of September 15, 1935, and a pair of children's canary-coloured woollen rompers – which proved to be among the most vital clues in the investigation.

Sergeant Robert Sloan.

Sergeant Sloan sent for Inspector Henry Strath at Lockerbie and together they took the ghastly bundles to the mortuary at Moffat cemetery where they were examined by two local doctors.

Two days later, Professor Glaister, Professor Smith and Dr. W. Gilbert Millar, a pathology lecturer at Edinburgh University, arrived in Moffat and began the task of piecing together the gruesome human jigsaw.

They concluded at first that the pieces were from a man and a woman – wrongly, as it turned out – and had been deliberately mutilated to prevent identification, obviously by someone with medical knowledge. Death was believed to have taken place about 10 days before the bodies were found.

The remains, labelled 'Body No. 1' and 'Body No. 2' were put in two rough coffin-like boxes made by a local joiner.

(Made by Martin Taylor, Apprentice Joiner at Taylor & Smiths Mill.)

Meanwhile intense searches over the next few weeks by the local constabulary, police-firemen from Lanarkshire and bloodhounds revealed further body fragments in the Linn and River Annan and at Johnstonebridge, nine miles away, bringing the total number to about 70.

Task

Police concluded that they had been thrown into the stream when the water was in spate and had been depositied on the banking when the level fell.

They were removed to Edinburgh where a high-powered forensic team undertook the task of meticulously reconstructing the bodies, complete except for one trunk and a few other small parts. The eventual conclusion was that they were two women.

Glaister found the small hyoid bone in the older woman's throat was broken – a sign of strangulation – while the younger woman had a skull injury indicating she had been battered to death with a blunt instrument.

The Moffat Ravine Mystery, as it came to be known, presented an appalling and highly baffling case for Dumfriesshire county police force. A check on missing persons proved unproductive and inquiries about any unusual movements by car owners led nowhere.

Had the murders been committed by some mentally deranged medical man or someone else with anatomical knowledge? Who were the victims, where had they been butchered and how had the remains been trasported to Moffat? Was there a madman on the loose who might strike again?

As the inquiry continued, under the gaze of the nation's press, there were many red herrings and false trails. But a dramatic breakthrough came on October 9. It was discovered that the Sunday Graphic which had been used to wrap parts of the bodies was a 'slip' edition of 3,700 copies with pictures of the Morecambe Carnival and had been sold only in Morecame, Lancaster and the surrounding district.

On the same day, Dumfriesshire Chief Constable William Black was informed of an article in the Daily Record about the disappearance, three weeks earlier, of a young woman, Mary Jane Rogerson, who was nursemaid in the house of a Parsee doctor, Buck Ruxton, in Lancaster. The Chief could have been excused for shouting "Eureka!"

Police showed a blouse found at Gardenholme Linn to Mary's mother Jessie Rogerson and she recognised it from a patch as belonging to her daughter. The woollen rompers, also recovered at the scene, were traced back to a woman in Grange over Sands who had given them to Mary for the Ruxton children. They were positively identified by a knot in the elastic.

Mrs. Holme with the child's rompers that she knitted and in which some of the body parts were wrapped.

● HANDSOME Dr Buck Ruxton: convicted of murder 60 years ago this week.

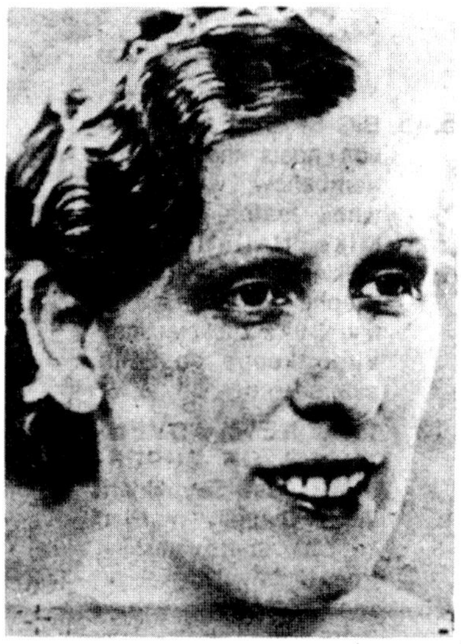

● THIS picture of Isabella Ruxton was matched with a photograph of one of the skulls to help confirm the identification.

The investigation was focused on the 36-year-old handsome Bombay-born doctor whose name was originally Bukhtyar Rustomji Ratanji Hakim before he changed it by deed poll to Buck Ruxton. A graduate of Bombay and London Universities, he had served in the Indian Medical Corps and risen to the rank of captain before buying his Lancaster practice in 1930.

The police there were well aware of the stormy and passionate relationship between the highly emotional GP and his Scottish common law wife Isabella whom he had met in Edinburgh where she was a waitress.

There was a history of bitter quarrels between the couple and allegations that the insanely jealous Ruxton had accused Isabella of being unfaithful, assaulted her and threatened to kill her. But they both enjoyed making up. As Ruxton later said from the witness box during his trial: "We were the kind of people who could neither live with each other nor live without each other."

While the inquiries in Dumfriesshire were in progress, Ruxton had reported Isabella and the maid missing from home. He made a statement to the police saying he was very anxious to find his wife and was annoyed at suggestions in the press that there might be some link between her disappearance and the finds at Moffat.

At the earlier stage in the investigation, when the remains had been described as those of a man and a woman, he had commented confidently: "It's not our two!" Later he told police: "All this damned nonsense is ruining my practice" and asked "Can nothing be done to stop all this talk?"

Evidence

When police began quizzing him closely he became indignant and almost hysterical. But the net was closing. There was damning evidence of unpleasant smells in the house, of attempts to remove bloodstained carpets and a suit, of marks on the bath, and of the doctor's injured hand which he said he had cut while opening a tin of peaches.

It was also emerged that he had been involved in a minor accident with his Hillman Minx car at Kendal on

Family parties would set off on the lengthy walk past Dumcrieff, then climb the hill for a further mile or so, to the Breconside road end, or take the short cut over the hill to join the farm track.

If they went directly to the farmyard, they would probably pause by the 'Covenanters' Pulpit', before traversing the hillside to reach the glen. But mostly it was the walk along the bottom of the glen that was more popular, as the glen was wooded with broadleaves and there were convenient bridges over the burns.

For many years after the Second World War, the Beldcraig remained a popular place – nowadays it is almost inaccessible.

Breconside House as it stood in 1988. Recent renovation has restored it to a desirable residence once again.

The Covenanters' Pulpit, under a large ash tree, which blew down in a storm a few years after I photographed it.

Auchen Castle, Moffat.

Auchen Castle

Auchen Castle was built in 1849 by the Hon. Henry Butler-Johnstone who was influenced by military campaigns when he named the cottages on the estate.

Egypt, Rosetta and Valenciennes must at times have caused townsfolk to ponder as they passed their gates when walking to and from the Garpol Glen.

Twenty years after its completion, the property was enlarged (following a fire), by adding two round turrets to the left of the building, the larger housing a staircase.

At the turn of the century the estate was owned by the Younger family, and when Sir William was in residence, Garpol Glen was Lady Younger's favourite walk.

Stone steps, iron railings, well-defined paths and bridges ensured her safety as she enjoyed the scenic beauty and seclusion of the silvan glen.

Shortly after the Second World War, Auchen Castle was a popular youth hostel, today it is a prestigious hotel.

The two picturesque waterfalls in Garpol Glen, near the Auchen Castle Hotel, Beattock.

Garpol Glen

Although an excursion to the 'Garpol' in the early 1900's cost the same as an excursion to the Beldcraig, namely 1/6d (7½p), the Garpol had much more to offer in the way of scenic beauty and panoramic views. There is also a spa within the glen, two cascading waterfalls and close by are the ruins of the old Auchen Castle.

Residents of both Moffat and Beattock found the walk to and round the glen most agreeable and here too there were many picnic areas. At the top of the glen, the woodland glade was dotted with summer seats and shrubs, the paths were well maintained throughout, and bridges spanned the Garpol Burn at strategic and picturesque points. All in all, a lovely place to spend the better part of a summer's day, as wildlife abounds.

From Moffat, the walk would take us over the golf course to the Auchen Castle Hotel driveway then, by turning left once over the railway bridge, the track allowed access to the glen.

From then on, it was a walk round the glen, then back the way we came, or over the railway lines (which is frowned upon nowadays) and down the Evan side to Beattock from where we had the choice to walking home by either road or railway track, to the Station Park.

From the point where the Garpol Burn flows through the tunnel to join the River Evan, under the railway lines, there was a well-constructed path that led to a small concrete dam, from where water was piped to Beattock railway station for the steam engines but this path, like most of the Garpol Glen, is now in a dire state of repair.

I sincerely hope that within the next few months the generous donation from Barr Construction will be put to good use – the glen will then return to being a very popular place.

The tunnel through solid rock where the Garpol Burn flows into the River Evan. Above the tunnel runs the Glasgow to Carlisle Railway Line. The Garpol was a favourite walking place of Lady William Younger of Auchen Castle in the 1930's. Today, through a generous donation from Barr Construction, it is hoped to re-instate the glen as a walk to be enjoyed by locals and visitors alike. There is also a spa situated within the glen.

Moffat Dale

From only 300 feet above sea level on the High Street, it is only a few miles, as the crow flies, to reach the peaks of the Moffat Water Hills, some over 2000 feet.

Moffat Dale, is the Moffat Water Valley – a valley where scenic beauty excels and where the undulating and winding road is never far from the river.

On rounding each and every bend, the traveller is greeted with dramatic landscapes and every mile travelled is steeped in fascinating, historical facts and legends.

Fifty years ago, the Moffat Water Hills supported thousands of sheep but, acre by acre, the slopes were planted with conifers, until only a fraction of the open hills remains.

I wonder how the writer of the poem on page 255 would describe the same journey today!

The Buccleuch Hotel Coach (c. 1900).
Mr. Fingland and some of his staff pose with the driver, Mr. Muir and his passengers (all well wrapped up), previous to their journey to St. Mary's Loch.

Buccleuch Hotel 1999.

Balmoral Hotel 1999.

Hetherington's Chemist 1999.

In the early 19th century the Beattock Bridge Inn was built. Following many changes of ownership and a variety of uses the classic Georgian building is now the Old Brig Inn incorporating the Telford Restaurant.

Beattock and the River Evan Bridges

During the coaching days of the 1820's the Kings Arms (Annandale Hotel) in Moffat was deprived much of its traffic with the opening of the Beattock to Elvanfoot route and the new Beattock Bridge Inn.

The Telford-designed bridge of 1819 with the older coach bridge a short distance upstream.

Tranquillity now reigns where once 12 to 15 trains crossed daily and re-crossed the bridge over the River Evan on the Beattock to Moffat branch line.

This new route was probably the reason for the construction of a new bridge over the River Evan, designed by Thomas Telford and built by John Macdonald in 1819.

Today, the bridge carries the main road through the village from the north and during the 1950's was a favoured place to watch the competitors in the Monte Carlo Rally as they sped south from Glasgow.

The cold, grey, concrete construction of the bridge carrying the M74(6) service road (A.P.R.).

The third bridge across the River Evan was built c1882 when the Moffat to Beattock railway branch line was laid, previous to the opening of the station in April 1883.

Today from the point where this bridge crosses the river at the Repeating Station, there is a waterside walk along the west bank which ends where the Garpol Burn underpasses the Glasgow/Carlisle railway line.

Almost eighty years after the completion of the railway bridge, the construction of the A74 found the necessity of yet another road bridge being built over the river to carry a dual carriageway and this bridge was of a completely new design.

Gone was the familiar attractive arched construction, and in its place concrete and steel spanned the river straight across from bank to bank, the trend of todays engineers.

Less than forty years on, during the late 1990's, the dual carriageway was reduced to a conventional two-way road, the A.P.R. (all purpose road). The A.P.R. is the service road for the new M74(6) motorway that crosses the river at a new location a few metres downstream. This massive structure of concrete and steel will carry traffic for many years to come.

Certainly needed to cope with the volume of todays traffic, the latest structure to cross the River Evan at Beattock on the M74(6) motorway.

Kirkpatrick-Juxta public school.

Beattock Village

Kirkpatrick-Juxta or as it is more often called Beattock's school in the earlier part of the 20th century was in a similar class to the early bridges in its architecture with both the character and building materials of the period in its construction. The new school which opened in 1968 reflects the character and building materials of today.

The main Glasgow/Carlisle road through the village which saw a vast increase in the volume of traffic after the Second World War quietened considerably with the opening of the A74 by-pass in 1965.

Looking north through Beattock Village in the early 1900's.
On the left is Craigielands Village while the right-hand side is known as Beattock Park.

Porteous's garage, petrol pumps and tea-room in the mid 1920's.
Father and son, both called William, are in the photograph.

Nowadays, the amount of vehicles passing through is a mere fraction of the previous numbers, many of which would pull-in for petrol etc.

In the centre of the village there is the shadow of what was once a thriving garage, filling station and tea-room, which for many years was owned and run by the Porteous family. The tea-room was added to the already well-established business in 1923 and continued catering for patrons until the outbreak of the Second World War.

The garage continued in service for many years later.

Well into the 20th century many households in Beattock were supported by the menfolk's work connected in one way or another with the railway and station. Engine drivers, firemen, cleaners, signalmen, engineers, linesmen, clerical staff and many others were all necessary for the smooth running of the station, with its pilot engines and sidings still in continual use until the early 1970's.

Throughout this period residents could buy provisions and household goods from the village shops and stores. There was even a branch of the S.C.W.S. that traded in a wooden hut which previously held the Railwaymen's Mission. The Post Office was in service for almost 100 years, the premises changing many times. Nowadays, however, Moffat's Post Office supplies resident's needs.

For the past 75 years the familiar red buses of James Gibson & Son have stopped in the village to pick-up or drop-off passengers as they travelled to and from work or from shopping in Moffat or Dumfries. The original service, founded in 1919, only ran between

Beattock Post Office at 10 Craigielands Village in the early 1900's with Mr. Steel (?) at the gate.

St. Anns and Dumfries, but three years later the service extended to Moffat, remaining thus to this day, ably run by Jimmy and Margaret Gibson. The cross-channel tours undertaken by Jimmy today, are a far cry from the late 1940's when no fewer than seven buses were required to carry the many sun-seekers who boarded them early on a summer Sunday morning for a day trip to Sandyhills, organised by Mrs. Adamson and Mrs. Little of Holmend.

Jimmy Gibson, todays joint proprietor of James Gibson and Son with his father (the previous owner) in the mid 1960's.

Part of the Gibson fleet of buses in the late 1960's.
The double deckers have long since disappeared from the service,
trees and bridges proving to be too much of an obstacle.

One of the buses in service during the late 1940's when trips to places like
Sandyhills and Mystery Tours were the vogue.

A Moffat Memory

ANON CIRCA 1910

The following amply covers 'Moffatdale', or Moffat Water, in rhyme, in an anonymous poem, possibly written by one of the cycling party, about to set off from the Hydro to the Rodono Hotel at St. Mary's Loch.

1 A lovely day! The breezy sky,
Dappled with white fantastic forms;
How restful to the weary eye,
These fleecy wrecks of bygone storms!

1

2

CYCLING—"ON SHINING 'WHEELS' AWAY WE SPED."

2 On shining "wheels", away we sped,
Where Moffat's dark-brown
waters wind;
The glorious sunshine overhead,
And cares and worries far behind.

3 The wind blew keenly from the north,
But with it brought no wintry gloom,
For every hedge was bursting forth,
And every whin ablaze with bloom.

3

4 Sweet views, each lovelier than
the last,
Entranced our eyes at every turn,
As through the leafy lanes we passed
That skirt the wood of Craigieburn.

5 The budding larches tender green
Relieve the sombre pine-clad hill,
While here a primrose bright
was seen,
And there a dainty daffodil.

6 The thrush poured forth his
mellow song,
The blackbird whistled loud
and clear,
And robins joined the happy
throng –
All singing gaily, "spring is here!"

7 The mountain tops were white
with snow,
As if for winter's winding sheet,
And from the sheltered field below,
We heard the lambkins
plaintive bleat.

8 By many cheery ups and downs,
We reached the open moorland
road,
Where saddleyolk majestic frowns
O'er Bodesbeck's Brownie's
wild abode.

9 We passed the Grey Mare's
snow-white tail,
Then climbed the hill nor stopped
to rest,
Till looking down on yarrow vale
We paused for breath on Birkhill's
crest.

10 The road now ran by stream
and linn
To where, above the steep
loch-side,
Rodono's hospitable inn
Invited us to break our ride.

11 Good cheer and grateful rest
were ours,
Then back we turned our steeds
of steel,
Just halting by St. Mary's Bowers
To see the home of Tibbie Shiel.

12 Right loth to leave, we
homeward rode,
But many a time we turned to take
A lingering look at hill and wood
And lone St. Mary's lovely lake.

Tibbie Shiel and her son Wullie.

The Brownie of Bodesbeck

In verse eight of the previous poem there is a reference to the 'Brownie of Bodesbeck'. A poor stunted wee soul who shuffled along almost bent double with his hands behind his back.

Whether his deformity was from birth or from wounds received in the struggle against 'Bloody Clavers' during the Killing Times is uncertain but beings of his stature were popular and welcome on the hill farms as they were looked upon as having supernatural powers.

The name 'Brownie' was applied to these wretched little characters who eked out a miserable existence by hiding during the day, usually in a hillside cavern, and venturing out at dusk to do a few chores on the farm.

Payment would be made in the form of food which was left out for them after they had received their orders for the night.

So zealously did the 'Brownie' undertake to pen all the sheep from the hillside one night that he also collected a few hares.

On being congratulated on his prowess the following day, as not a single sheep had been left on the hill, the 'Brownie' replied – "Confound thae wee broon anes, they cost me mair bother than a' the rest o' them pit thegether."

Acknowledgements

With special thanks to:

Alastair Barr; Mary Borthwick; Joyce Byers; David Carroll *(Annandale in Old Photographs)*; Causeway Resources; Jean Cockayne; Bettina Dawson; Dumfries and Galloway Branch of the Aircrew Association; Billy Duncan; Ian Fair; Peter Farrell; Margaret Gibson; Adam Gray; Alistair Hepburn (Moffat Fire Brigade); Sheena Johnstone; Andy Little; Norman 'Peesie' McNeil; Janet McTeir; Davy Moffat; Brian Orr; Harold Rae; T. A. Rankin; Margaret Renvoize; Mr. & Mrs. Bobby Robison; Billy Rogerson; Wendy Simpson; Edith Smith; Martin Taylor; Peter Toni; Jim Tuton; Margaret Walker; Edith Wallace; Tommy Wallace; Tom Wylie; Eric Young; for information, photographs and other material.

And to Vincent, whose photographic expertise prompted this publication.

As much as 90% of the photographic material used comes from the authors own private collection.

GW01164556

SECRETS OF THE LAST NAZI

SECRETS OF THE LAST NAZI

IAIN KING

bookouture

Published by Bookouture

An imprint of StoryFire Ltd.
23 Sussex Road, Ickenham, UB10 8PN
United Kingdom

www.bookouture.com

ISBN: 978-1-910751-10-7
eBook ISBN: 978-1-910751-09-1

To the real Helen Bridle

'No matter how weak an individual may be, the minute that he acts in accordance with the hand of Fate, he becomes more powerful than you could possibly imagine.'

Adolf Hitler,
Nuremberg, 1936

All references in *Secrets of the Last Nazi* to latitude and longitude are matters of fact – you can verify them on the NASA website. Historical events in the book really did occur on the dates mentioned in the book.

The relationship between natural events and human affairs explained in this book is true.

PROLOGUE

9th July, 1945
US Army Garrison Garmisch-Partenkirchen
Near Munich (US Zone of Occupation), Germany

SS Captain Werner Stolz watched as Corporal Bradley brought over the coffee. He eyed his interrogator, then thanked him for the drink and took a large swig.

Bradley sat down opposite, checked his watch, and began a countdown in his head. He waited almost a minute – allowing the Nazi to get comfortable – before he restarted the questioning. 'So, Werner,' he asked gently. 'How does it work?'

Stolz just looked blank. He took more of the coffee, aware of the unusual taste but drinking it nonetheless.

'Please, Werner,' Bradley insisted. 'Just tell me.'

'What else can I say?' shrugged the Nazi. His eyes glowered straight at the American, then glanced towards the young Russian scribbling in the corner, finally turning back to his interrogator. 'I'm very sorry, Corporal,' he offered. 'Really. I can't explain it, either.'

Corporal Bradley took off his glasses to sweep the hair back over his sweaty scalp, then flicked uselessly through the notes once more. He turned to his Soviet Liaison Officer. 'Kirov – any ideas?'

Kirov put down his pencil, twisted around and faced the Nazi. 'The Americans are treating you very well, Stolz,' grinned the Russian. 'They could treat you much less well.'

'I know,' agreed Stolz, trying to remove any trace of arrogance from his Austrian accent. 'I also know neither of you will harm me.'

Bradley put his hand to his face, then glanced at his watch, calculating he had less than three minutes left. He needed a new tack.

'OK then, Stolz,' the American ventured. 'You've got all the answers. What's going to happen next?'

Stolz looked sympathetically at his interrogator, hugging his coffee with both hands as he spoke. 'You'll not get your investigation until we're both dead, which is seventy years from now. It'll be an international …'

'Wait,' interrupted Bradley, 'I'm going to live another seventy years?'

'I said we'd both be dead in seventy years,' clarified Stolz, starting to sway on his chair.

Bradley tried to decode what he'd just heard, wishing he had more time. 'You mean, one of us is going to live another seventy years?'

'Yes,' murmured Stolz, beginning to slump on the table. 'My English is faulty. I mean, one of us dies today ...'

Stolz seemed to switch off. Bradley tried to support him, hoping there was time for just one more question, but the Nazi was starting to collapse. Stolz's chair clattered beneath him, and he spilled his drugged coffee over himself as he fell.

Bradley bent down to check his prisoner's pulse. Stolz had been too sensitive to the scopolamine. Bradley made sure the half-conscious SS man could breathe and checked his watch again: somehow his timings had been wrong.

He was just about to fetch some water for Stolz when the door opened. A single man entered, distinguished-looking and with a silver moustache. Bradley had never seen the officer before, or his regimental crest, but noticed he was wearing an immaculately pressed uniform – a sure sign he'd only just flown in to liberated Europe. Then he saw the single metal star on his shoulders: the insignia of an American Brigadier-General. Bradley jumped to attention.

'At ease, Corporal.'

Corporal Bradley relaxed only enough for his eyes to check on Stolz, who was spluttering under the table.

The Brigadier-General pointedly ignored the Nazi prisoner. 'So you're Bradley; the letter-writer,' sneered the Brigadier, as he walked around the upturned chair. 'You're new to the army, aren't you ...'

'Yes, Sir.'

'Tell me, Bradley ...' the Brigadier glanced down at Stolz, who was writhing on the floor, before he turned back to the Corporal, 'What did you do before the war?'

'Er, High school teacher, Sir,' replied Bradley, frowning to try to look serious. 'Math, Sir.'

The Brigadier paused for several seconds before he answered. 'Good, Bradley.' The Brigadier's voice relaxed, as he finally made eye-contact with Bradley. 'We'll be needing mathematicians now the war's over ... the war against the Nazis ...' Then he lifted Bradley's papers, talking as if his mind was elsewhere, 'And these are the only notes you have on Stolz?'

'There are also two filing cabinets full. Next door, Sir,' replied the Corporal.

'But that's all – all in this building?'

'Yes, Sir.'

The Brigadier accepted Bradley's response and replaced the papers.

Bradley was about to tell the general why the Stolz interrogation was so peculiar when he became distracted by the Brigadier adjusting his uniform – the general seemed to be unbuttoning his jacket. Gently, the Brigadier moved him aside.

The Brigadier raised his eyebrows towards the Russian in the corner. 'And you must be Lieutenant Kirov?'

The Soviet Liaison Officer started to nod. Then, like Bradley, he reacted to a double-clunk noise, and a supressed mechanical cough. For a short moment Kirov's body contorted, then he collapsed to the floor.

Instinct told Bradley to rush towards his friend, but quickly he saw that the Russian was beyond help. Kirov had fallen face-down and was now completely still, except for the blood slowly pooling around his chest. Bradley stared in shock. Then he noticed the Brigadier held a side-arm with a long silencer attachment.

'We don't want to investigate mumbo-jumbo – do we, Bradley?' The Brigadier made eye contact with Bradley as he returned the pistol into his concealed holster, then wafted away the smell of gun oil and cordite.

'No, Sir.'

'And we don't want to burden our Allies with it either. Understood?'

'Yes, Sir,' answered Bradley obediently. He knelt to support Stolz's feverish body as the Nazi prisoner began to recover on the floor.

The Brigadier strutted back towards the door, carefully stepping around Kirov. He took the Russian's pencil-written notes, wiped off splatters of blood, and folded them into his pocket.

'Oh, and Bradley?'

'Sir?'

'A little less scopolamine in the coffee next time,' he cautioned, smoothing down his uniform. 'We want these Nazis to spew up their secrets, not their guts.'

The Brigadier left, closing the door behind him. Bradley never saw him again.

SEVENTY YEARS LATER

DAY ONE

CHAPTER 1

Altersheim Sonnenuntergang (Sunset Nursing Home)
Potsdam, Near Berlin, Germany
2.12 a.m. Central European Time (1.12 a.m. GMT)

Werner Stolz's eye squinted at the lens of the telescope. His failing vision blurred the image into two small crescents. But they were definitely planets, and they were exactly where they were meant to be: together, just above the western horizon.

It was confirmation. His eye retreated, but he knew there was no escaping what he had seen.

Sitting alone in the dark, he removed the bookmark from his ephemeris and let it close.

Slowly, he reached towards the table lamp. As the light came on, Stolz caught himself in the mirror. Shadows made the lines on his face seem even deeper. With only one side of his head illuminated, his image had split in two. One half revealed skin marked by a lifetime of wrinkles. The other half was still hidden.

For a hundred-and-three years he had known that face. He had watched it grow, mature and wither. Now his head had lost its hair and his skin had lost its colour.

Only his eyes remained fully alive. They glowered back at him, one last time. They had kept both his secrets well.

He looked up at the pictures framed on his wall. A photo from when Germany was winning the war: the young Stolz, with his new SS uniform and a cocky grin. Then another, taken several years later, soon after he had been released from the custody of the US army – Stolz looked much thinner.

Then the image of him retiring young, opening champagne in a Sixties shirt. He often wondered whether he should have given up so soon. He could have earned so much more. But every time he wondered, he always concluded the same thing: he had retired at exactly the right time. Retiring was the only way he could keep both his secrets. If he had tried to win too much, he would have lost it all.

Stolz cleared his throat. It became a cough. Gently, he thumped his chest to stop the spasm. Then he waited for his body to settle, and allowed himself several minutes to become calm.

He listened to check No one was outside.

No one – not yet.

Careful to control his breathing, Stolz twisted off the bottom of the table lamp. The pill case was still there. He plucked it out, and wiped the enamel cover with his thumb.

He remembered receiving it – within sight of the Reichstag, just as the centre of the capital had come under artillery fire for the first time. Others shuddered as the shells blasted around them, but he knew he'd be safe.

Now, just holding the small container gave him pleasure. He inspected it. No one would manufacture a lid like that anymore. The design was antique, and the crooked cross on it – a tiny Swastika – had been outlawed in the new Germany. The little tin belonged to an age gone by.

Just like SS Captain Werner Stolz himself.

Then he noticed some rust around the rim. He scratched it in disappointment. Just like the Reich, the tin would not last a thousand years. The war had forced his great nation to make steel which decayed.

Germany will be great again, and the time will come soon.

He knew exactly when it would become great again – the day, month and year – and how it would once again lead all of Europe.

He wished he would be alive to see that day. But he knew he wouldn't.

Stolz gripped as tightly as he could and tried to prise off the lid. Applying all his strength, and his much greater determination, he succeeded.

He peered inside, perturbed to find the liquid in the sealed glass tube was no longer translucent. Now it was dark and opaque, a murky brown colour.

Would it still work?

He picked it up and wondered, rolling it on his palm.

Then he remembered his ephemeris, the computer, the telescope …

Yes, it would work.

Quivering, he lifted the glass vial towards his mouth. Carefully, he placed it between his teeth, and closed his lips around it.

Stolz turned out the light and waited for the footsteps he knew would come.

CHAPTER 2

Imperial War Museum,
London, United Kingdom
7.25a.m. Greenwich Mean Time (GMT)

Myles didn't turn his head to see the mock-up of the trenches - complete with duck-boards, theatrical mud and artificial smells. The vintage machine guns, both German and British, which had caused so much slaughter in the Great War, didn't register with him at all. He even ignored the Spitfire hanging above him, the old German Jagdpanther tank, and the V1 and V2 'Wonderweapons' used by Hitler in his desperate last months.

That was all history. An outdated vision of war. Misleading, even. War wasn't like that, not any more, as he told his students in some of Oxford University's best attended lectures.

Myles knew. He'd been there.

Even the Cold War had been distorted. The superpower confrontation between the United States and the Soviet Union wasn't what most people said it was. Myles walked right past the big photo-posters showing scenes from 1989, when the Berlin Wall disintegrated in the bright glare of TV lights. Frozen in time, some faces were celebrating, while East German police stood around, not believing the impossible had come true.

The only scene he couldn't ignore was the most sinister: a faded photograph, blown-up into a large display, which showed a bureaucrat in front of a queue of Jewish refugees. The man was sitting at a table, registering details from the families as they offloaded from the cattle trucks. The bureaucrat and his paperwork were in control. The refugees clutched their suitcases and precious possessions, leaning forward to speak to the man at the desk, trying to help him with information. The poor men and women were oblivious that they had only minutes left to live.

Myles shook his head in disgust, cursing the bureaucrats ...

He walked on. He had not come here to browse, but to help Frank, his old university friend of almost twenty years.

Myles held the glass door open with his foot as he heaved the last cardboard box inside. 'When do the public arrive?'

'Ten,' replied Frank. 'We've still got time.'

Myles nodded, as he continued through the main entrance area. 'Downstairs with the rest?'

'Yes – thanks. I'll come with you.'

With Frank limping behind him, Myles led the way down the metallic stairs, careful to duck his head under the beam. The museum's walkways had been designed for children, not tall university lecturers. Frank pointed to a pile of other possessions, and Myles placed the box beside them.

'Cheers, Myles,' said Frank, tapping the box with his walking stick. 'That's the last one.'

Together they stared at the cardboard dump. Half a lifetime: just three boxes.

'Really, that's all you've got?'

'It's all I could salvage before it sank - but on the bright side, if I'd been asleep when my houseboat started leaking, I might have drowned!' Frank tried to laugh, but the chuckles came out flat.

'You sure the museum won't mind you using their space, Frank?' Myles asked.

Frank held his stick while he pushed his glasses back into place. 'I hope not – I am the curator. And if they do sack me, I'll have to ask you for advice …' Then the curator's face reacted, as he had another thought. 'In fact, I think …' He started to limp along the underground corridor, looking up at the small cards which explained what each storage unit contained. He stopped opposite a tall cabinet labelled *Terrorism - UK*, then climbed on a small stool to retrieve a box file. He called back to Myles. 'We've still got it somewhere …'

Myles' fingers rubbed his forehead. He didn't want it. 'It's OK, Frank. I've seen it before.'

But Frank had already pulled out the file. He hobbled back down the ladder, and unfolded the tabloid as he returned to Myles.

The headline still screamed at him, all those years later.

Myles Munro: Misfit Oxford Military Lecturer is Runaway Terrorist

Frank was grinning. 'You see – we still have all sorts of war records!' He paused with a half-smile, realising he'd just told an unfunny joke. Then he folded the newspaper back up and patted Myles on the back, realising he needed to change the subject. 'You did well to recover. Very impressive.'

Myles didn't respond. 'Impressive' didn't matter to him.

Frank nudged him. 'Come on – how's it all going?'

Myles tipped his head to one side. 'Predictable, sometimes.'

'Predictable bad or predictable good?

Myles paused to frame his thoughts, tried to explain. 'Most people have very set ideas. Military history just means Hitler to most of them. Even the open-minded ones aren't open to anything too challenging.'

'So you're looking for something else, Myles?'

'Maybe,' accepted Myles. 'Not looking very hard though ...' Myles was distracted by the large vaults looming above them both. 'So what's the Imperial War Museum planning next?' He could see his old friend become enthused.

'My new exhibition: *War and the Natural World.*'

Myles raised his eyebrows. 'Interesting ...'

'It's joint with the Science Museum – you know, for kids,' explained Frank. 'We're trying to show how natural events have a big impact on war.' Frank hobbled around, guiding Myles towards a half-finished display called *World War Two and the Moon.* Then he gave Myles a handout to read.

Myles was impressed. 'Looks like fun.'

'Yes - and the displays go right back to Alexander the Great. The eclipse just before his greatest battle was an omen that the Empire of Persia would be defeated – and it was!'

Myles smiled, only half buying it. He let Frank continue.

'And it wasn't just ancient times,' lectured Frank. 'The Crusades, the Korean War - even World War One began with an eclipse, too. Did you know that?'

'No, I didn't.'

'That's right – in August 1914, on the day that German and British troops first clashed. And the centre of the eclipse was exactly over where the first big battle took place. It was probably the most important battle of the whole war.' Frank lifted his stick towards a map of Europe.

'Battle of Tannenberg?'

'Correct – and World War Three started with an eclipse, as well.'

Now Myles knew he was being ribbed. 'We haven't had World War Three.'

Frank chuckled. 'No – but we almost did. Remember 1999, when the NATO commander ordered his troops to take Kosovo's main airport – the one held by the Russians? The attack was only stopped when a subordinate refused to obey. He "Didn't want to start World War Three", he said. Well, I discovered the centre of the big eclipse in the summer of 1999 was just a few miles from ... wait for it ... Kosovo!'

Myles looked sideways at his friend, wondering whether Frank was taking the eclipses too seriously. Frank hadn't noticed – he was too absorbed.

'... And there was also a very local solar eclipse, exactly over Iceland in October 1986, when Reagan and Gorbachev held their big summit there. Some people say it was the summit which ended the Cold War. Did you know that?'

Myles didn't answer, as he realised his old friend had become even more eccentric with the passing years. Trying to find sense in the movement of planetary bodies was not a good sign.

Ting ...

The faint metallic noise came from far off, further down the corridor. They looked at each other, surprised.

Both men remained silent for a moment.

Frank shrugged, but Myles couldn't dismiss it. He started walking, then jogging towards the noise – along the underground corridor, to where the lighting wasn't so good.

He stopped to listen again.

Nothing.

His instincts were confusing him. He halted, tried to sense what could have caused the sound, then wondered if he had imagined it. He was about to turn back when he noticed an empty box file on the vault floor.

He picked it up and called over to Frank. 'Was this you?'

Frank indicated it wasn't.

Myles looked at the label on the empty file.

De-Nazification interviews, 1945 – box 4

It must have fallen down somehow – although that didn't explain why it was empty.

He peered into the darkness, looking for a shelf with a space on it.

Something didn't seem right. The shelves were messy, as if someone had been rummaging through the archives. But there was something else, too.

Myles froze, and heard movement close by.

Someone was there.

He peered into the gloom, searching for whatever he could find, whatever didn't belong.

Then he saw them: a pair of eyes.

Scared eyes.

They were looking straight back at him.

Suddenly a man rushed out, ramming into Myles who tumbled to the floor, box files raining down on his head.

He could see the intruder running away. The man had something clutched in his hands. He was heading back towards the stairway.

Myles called out, 'Frank – stop him!'

But Frank was too shocked to react. The thief fled past him.

Myles jumped back to his feet and started chasing him down the corridor, pounding up the museum's metallic stairs three steps at a time. His clumsiness made him trip, but he recovered.

Myles raced back past the trench exhibition, ducking under the beam as he ran up the main staircase and towards the ground floor.

He heard Frank's call out behind him. 'I'll get the police ...'

But there was no time to get the police.

Myles stumbled again as he reached the top of the stairs, falling onto the polished surface of the main hallway. Quickly he pushed himself back up.

He scanned the exhibits: rockets, the American army jeep, tanks, information displays, a submarine ... The museum was full of hiding places.

Then he heard a clank: *the outside doors.*

Myles swivelled to see the exit doors were still moving – the thief must have just barged through them and escaped.

Myles dodged a donations bin near the entrance and grappled with the heavy glass door which swung back in his face, slowing him down. Finally he reached the park outside. At last he could see the thief again. The man was racing away from him – past the souvenir section of the Berlin wall, over the well-kept grass, towards the main road...

Myles tried calling. 'Hey you…'

The thief turned around to see Myles' tall frame at the entrance of the museum, and the man's eyes filled with terror.

Quickly he turned and kept running.

Myles sprinted on as fast as he could. Gradually he was catching up. He could see the thief's rucksack. The man's canvas jacket. His trainers…

The thief was approaching the end of the path, forced to slow down as he approached the busy road. The rush-hour traffic was too fast to cross. Myles had him trapped.

Myles saw the man turn and face him again, his eyes flickering around in panic. Myles was getting closer, still running straight at the man. His arms reached out to grab him, but the thief swiftly stepped aside and Myles stumbled, off balance again.

Myles saw the man dash into the traffic. A small car braked as the thief ran in front of it. Back on his feet, Myles manoeuvred around the stopped car. An angry commuter honked at him, but Myles kept on, still chasing the thief.

Their eyes connected again.

That was when Myles felt the huge force of a van smash into his side. He felt his leg bend, and his body twist away. For a moment, he was weightless as he was flung high into the air.

Then agony surged through his leg.

Cars stopped around him, and backed up all along the road. People climbed out and moved towards him.

But Myles soon realised the people were not interested in him. He tried to see through the crowd, through the cars and through the pain and saw people helping the thief, desperately trying emergency medical procedures on his blood-covered face. None of them were any use.

The man Myles had been chasing was dead.

CHAPTER 3

Sonnenuntergang (Sunset Nursing Home), Potsdam, Berlin

8.45 a.m. CET (7.45 a.m. GMT)

The breakfast maid who discovered Werner Stolz's body was not shocked by it. It was the third dead body she had found in three weeks. People came here to die, she'd been told, so dead bodies were only to be expected.

Still, she didn't want to look at the corpse too closely. That was for the nurse. Calmly, she pressed the buzzer and waited.

Stolz hadn't left much, so there wasn't much for her to tidy. There were a few framed pictures on his desk. She made sure they were arranged neatly. She recognised America in one – the middle-aged Stolz seemed to be enjoying a holiday. She tilted her head to see the pictures of Stolz as a young man in military uniform. He had been quite handsome back then, she thought.

Then she saw his computer, and his 'ephemeris' book. She flicked through it: lots of tables and numbers, with dates and funny symbols. Old Werner had been reading some odd things before he died.

Her thoughts were disturbed by footsteps in the corridor. A nurse appeared.

The nurse acknowledged the maid with a nod, then moved straight to the body. She knelt down, ready to place two fingers on his neck and check for a pulse. It was a routine confirmation: the old man was obviously dead, but she had to follow procedure, just to make sure …

Then she noticed his ear. It was bloody. And behind it was a small dark red hole. She turned Stolz's corpse on the floor, to reveal a much greater mass of body fluids on the carpet underneath him.

A gun tumbled from the dead man's hand: an old 7.65 mm Luger pistol with a long silencer.

The breakfast maid felt the need to leave immediately. 'Entschuldigen Sie,' she apologised, hiding her eyes from the sight by staring down at her cleaning trolley.

The nurse held the door open for her, and waited until the maid had gone. Then she began the next test on Werner Stolz's body.

Quietly, she bent down to examine the dead man's mouth. She peered closely and, as she expected, the dead man's lips were blue and covered in a white froth.

She nodded to herself, her diagnosis confirmed. Like so many men of his generation, one-time SS Captain Werner Stolz had chosen to die a short time before death was inevitable. And his preferred method of death, a cyanide pill followed closely by a self-administered bullet through the brain copied the most famous suicide in history: Adolf Hitler's.

It was only as the nurse was leaving that she noticed a scratch on the door frame. The nurse looked closer: the mark looked clean. It must have been made recently. Then she saw the metal doorframe was buckled, as if the door had been barged open.

Someone had broken in.

CHAPTER 4

St Simon's Monastery,
Israel
10.35 a.m. Israel Standard Time (8.35 a.m. GMT)

Father Samuel lowered his knees onto the cold marble, and allowed his ample midriff to flop into his lap. Eyes closed, he bowed his head, and kept the rosary wrapped tightly around his wrists. He was sure he didn't have long to wait.

Faintly, he heard the chapel door open, and listened to the clipped sound of shoes approaching.

'Father Samuel.'

Samuel concluded his prayer, pocketed his rosary, then turned to see the familiar face. He judged the man's expression, and guessed his prayers were being answered even sooner than he had hoped. 'So, how is the Last Nazi?'

'Dead, Father.'

Samuel absorbed the information, celebrating silently to himself. Then he sensed the man had more to tell. 'Anything else?'

'Stolz killed himself.'

Father Samuel stared at the man, trying to understand the news.

The man nodded slowly.

Father Samuel paused and frowned. 'Why would a man who has already lived such a long life choose to cut it short?' He closed his eyes in contemplation, tensing his jaw as he thought. Then he stared directly at the man obediently waiting for his next instructions. 'We're still missing something – you understand?'

The man bowed his head in acknowledgement and walked briskly out of the chapel once again.

Father Samuel returned to prayer, far less happy at the announcement of Stolz's death than he had expected to be.

CHAPTER 5

St Thomas' Hospital,
Central London
10.45 a.m. GMT

The accident had happened not long before the peak of the morning rush hour. The A3202, the main road outside the Imperial War Museum and one of London's main thoroughfares, was blocked.

Within a minute, traffic had backed up half a mile to the river Thames. Several of the drivers stuck in the jam had called for an ambulance, and just four minutes later a team of paramedics was on the scene.

Myles was checked, loaded onto a stretcher and quickly driven to nearby St Thomas' Hospital. Then he was rushed through a series of procedures: X-rays, an MRI scan, blood tests, an injection, a drip … Finally, Myles' trolley was pushed into a private room.

Myles was oblivious to it all – he could only think about the thief. What had the man been trying to steal? What had been worth rushing into the traffic to protect?

The door creaked open. Frank poked his head in. 'Myles, I'm so sorry.' Frank's face was sweaty and apologetic.

Myles waved his hand. 'No need to apologise.'

'What do the doctors reckon?'

'Might just be a ligament thing,' said Myles, looking down at his leg. 'No real damage. But there's also something to do with the brain scan. They won't say what.'

'If that's your only injury, then you'll just be limping around like me.' Frank raised his own polio-ridden leg, trying to make a joke of it.

Myles smiled, then felt a shot of pain from his tibia.

Frank looked apologetic again. 'You better stay still,' he said. 'They'll put something on it soon.' Frank was about to tap Myles' leg in sympathy but, when his hand was mid-air, he decided not to – just as both of them realised it would hurt.

Frank looked embarrassed again, still out of his depth. Same old Frank - he'd always been that way, ever since Myles first met him.

'Frank, can you get Helen for me?'

'Your American woman? Yes, I'll get her,' nodded Frank.

Myles watched as Frank limped off to make the call, then wondered exactly what it was about his brain scan which had interested the doctors so much.

CHAPTER 6

Ministry of Foreign Affairs
Central Moscow, Russia
11.51 a.m., Moscow Standard Time (8.51 a.m. GMT)

Zenyalena Androvsky stopped in the middle of Smolenskaya Square to admire the twenty-seven-storey building in front of her. She felt comforted by the Stalinist architecture: it was a steadfast monument to Soviet glory which had never compromised with capitalism; a single finger poking up into the Moscow skyline, telling the defeatists where to go.

Then she felt her orange trousers swish in the wind, and saw the security men at the entrance to the Ministry react to her femininity. She flirted back. It felt good to be home.

She was soon in her new office, back in the European Affairs Directorate after assignments in Cuba and Venezuela which had seemed more like distractions than proper foreign affairs work. Anonymous staff had already unpacked her effects, right down to the picture taken in 1987 of her father in his full uniform kissing goodbye to Zenyalena, then a gawky teenager. The photograph was the last image of Colonel Androvsky alive. Just ten days later, his helicopter had been eviscerated by a shoulder-launched surface-to-air missile, fired up by a lucky Mujahedeen guerrilla. Zenyalena had never blamed the Afghan who pressed the initiator. Responsibility for her father's death, she was sure, lay with the cowardly organisation which had supplied the hardware: the CIA.

Eager to work and to make her mark as quickly as she could, Zenyalena Androvsky spent just a few moments leafing through the general briefing pack which had been left for her. Then she pressed a buzzer.

An older man entered, grey-suited and pale, refusing to notice Zenyalena's bright clothing. 'Ms Androvsky – welcome to your new post.'

'Don't tell me what I know already.' She tossed the briefing pack to a distant part of her desk. 'What's happening in Europe today?'

Trying not to undermine his new boss's authority, the man reached into the discarded briefing pack to pull out a one-page list of news items. 'Your headlines for today, Madam.'

Zenyalena ignored the slight – her eyes were already devouring the list. Single-sentence headlines outlined events in Ukraine, Spain, Liechtenstein … she stopped when she reached an item two-thirds of the way down the page. 'What's this? And who was 'Werner Stolz'?'

The older man turned the page towards him to check the name, 'Er, I can find out for you, Ms Androvsky.'

'Please do – this morning.'

It took only an hour for the pale man to return clutching a hefty pile of documents. Some looked even older than him, their yellowed edges straying out of the tattered cardboard.

Zenyalena swiftly filleted the files. Within minutes she had spotted yet another opportunity to embarrass the Americans. She called her secretary back in.

'Ludochovic. You read the stuff in these files about Lieutenant Kirov, right?'

Ludochovic indicated that he had.

'Tell me - how do you think he died?'

The grey-suited man looked at Zenyalena's desk as he answered. 'On balance, I think the American report is probably true, Ms Androvsky. Soviet interrogators also experienced SS captives grabbing weapons and going wild.'

Zenyalena's eyes narrowed. 'Yes, but we never let one kill a liaison officer working for a foreign power.' She pulled out another sheet with Soviet-era typewriting on it. 'And look: Kirov died just days after he flagged this Captain Stolz as "special interest". The Nazi even spent time living in the States after the war. I tell you: this one smells.'

Ludochovic accepted her superior logic. 'How do you want to proceed, Madam?'

Zenyalena sank in her chair, fully aware that the best information about Stolz would have been lost in the turmoil of post-war Germany, seventy years ago. But there was still a chance to win one over on the Yanks.

'Ludochovic: I want you to prepare a Demarche. Demand a full investigation of Stolz. If the Americans refuse, we'll know they're hiding something. Send it today.'

The secretary understood. 'To be delivered by our embassy in DC?'

Zenyalena was about to agree, but then stopped herself, her lips pursing into a mischievous grin. 'No – New York. We're going to do this through the United Nations. The *old* United Nations.'

CHAPTER 7

St Thomas' Hospital,
Central London
10.05 a.m. GMT

A serious-looking man in an open shirt and white coat breezed into Myles's room, then paused before he spoke. 'Mr Munro?'

Myles nodded.

The doctor approached Myles' trolley-bed, then exhaled, as if he had some difficult news to tell. Myles remained silent.

'Mr Munro – er, can I call you Myles?' asked the doctor.

'If it makes it easier. Yes. Myles is fine.'

More silence.

'How do you feel, Myles?'

Myles raised his eyebrows – how *did* he feel? 'Er, well, I feel pain. I feel a little thirsty. I feel like I don't like hospitals much …' He mused some more. '… I feel you're about to tell me.'

Myles watched as the doctor tried to explain.

'You see, Mr Munro, we did a scan,' began the doctor, barely managing to speak to Myles' face. 'Two scans, actually – an X-ray of your leg, and an MRI. A brain scan …' The doctor paused again. 'Well, Mr Munro, in a way it's fortunate that you broke your leg, because it allowed us to look inside your head.'

Myles nodded, thoughtfully. 'So what did you find there?'

'Mr Munro – Myles – you see, I've heard of you. You're the military history guy with the unusual theories about war, right?'

Myles didn't respond. He didn't care about his reputation. His silence confirmed the doctor was right.

The doctor checked Myles' bandages as he continued. '... And you see, Mr Munro, every brain is different. They're unique – like fingerprints. And yours is unique too.'

Myles tried to understand the diagnosis. 'So my brain is unique, like everybody else's?'

'Yes. But yours is very unique – different,' said the doctor. 'Let me show you the images, to explain.'

Myles waved his hand, 'Don't bother with that, just tell me what it means.'

'Well, you might think in an unusual way, Mr Munro.' The doctor watched to see Myles' reaction. There was none; Myles just stared back at the doctor.

Myles already knew he was odd. 'Highly gifted but too ready to challenge authority', was one official description. Some had said he was a misfit. Others said he was clumsy, couldn't spell and had a problem reading aloud. His memory was extraordinarily good for abstract facts and dates, but hopeless for normal things, like where he'd left his keys.

'So I'm different. So?' asked Myles.

The doctor nodded, calmly observing Myles' face. Then he tried to cushion his words. 'It means, Mr Munro, that you may experience life a little differently to other people.'

'Everybody experiences life differently – don't they?'

The doctor was stumped, and started picking at his white coat. 'If we may, we'd like to put you on a research programme. We think there might be a link between the shape of people's brains and the lives they lead. We want to study you – to see if there's a match between your brain and your behaviour ...' The doctor could see Myles was unsure about the idea. '...Oh, and we'd pay you.'

The offer of money had no impact on Myles. 'Would I have to come back here?'

'Probably,' confirmed the doctor. 'Yes.'

Myles started shaking his head. 'Then, Doctor, the answer is no.'

The doctor nodded his understanding. 'You're probably still in shock from your accident. Let me know if you change your mind. It's actually quite amazing that you've not had problems before. Anyway, I think you're booked for another examination in about half an hour, in the fracture unit in the east wing, ground floor. I'll check.' The doctor retreated from the room, humbled.

Alone again, Myles thought more about the doctor's offer. Research – Myles did enough of that in his university job. But research for him meant reading – or at least trying to read, since he was not very good at it. Myles would dig up old military facts from obscure sources and try to make sense of them. He'd never been the *subject* of research before. Apart from that one time, when the media had decided to research everything about him.

Although Myles was usually curious, nothing made him curious about himself. There were so many more interesting things to discover.

But deep down, Myles knew the real reason he didn't want to be 'researched'.

He looked up at the hospital ceiling. It was antiseptic white. Dead white.

He remembered coming to a room just like this one when his mother was thin. Deathly thin, like all those concentration camp survivors liberated from the horrors in 1945. His mother had died just a few days later – at the hands of the medical establishment. Cancer. They had said it was treatable. All the statistics, all the odds, all the numbers said she should have survived. It was a minor cancer – treatable, removable. Curable.

Yet they had all failed.

They'd put her on a drug trial. A *double-blind, randomised control* trial – funny pills twice a day, given to her and lots of other desperate people. Only after his mother was dead did Myles learn her pills were only placebos. Fakes. Had her death helped to prove something? Had she helped the numbers? To the teenage Myles, it seemed more like his mother had been sacrificed for the statistics.

No calculus of chance and statistics was going to dictate his life. Not any more – the drug trial had already dictated his mother's death, and that was enough. As the nurses came to collect his trolley, Myles knew he would refuse to take part in the research.

And if the doctors really could use a scan of his brain to predict his behaviour, then they should have predicted his answer already.

CHAPTER 8

Quai D'Orsay,
Paris, France
2.15 p.m. CET (1.15 p.m. GMT)

Flight Lieutenant Jean-Francoise Pigou exhaled in disgust, shaking his head and tutting loudly at the TV. The only customer in the café, he raised his hand at the screen, inviting the café manager to red card the referee with him.

The café owner smiled: Pigou might not be the most gifted military secondee ever to stride through the ornate halls of France's Foreign Ministry, the Quai D'Orsay, but he could be relied upon to keep everyone up-to-date with the progress of the Paris St Germain football team. The flight lieutenant's enthusiasm for the game had filled the whole café more than once. He had charm, even if he was completely undiplomatic. It would be a pity when Pigou's secondment ended, and the officer would return to his normal work, with the French air force.

Jean-Francoise's anger at the referee's decision evaporated when a young, professional-looking woman came towards him, a thin folder of papers in her hand. Jean-Francoise stood up to meet her. 'Carine – you've come to watch with me?'

Carine smiled, but sat down with her back to the TV. 'No, but I knew I could find you here. Is the game over yet?'

'Not yet,' said Jean-Francoise, gesturing, 'but the result is known.'

'Good, then I can give you this.'

The flight lieutenant took the folder with a puzzled expression. 'Thank you. What's inside?'

'A short trip for you – to Berlin.'

Jean-Francoise tipped his head in gratitude. 'Tell me more.'

Carine settled herself in her seat as she explained. 'There's a very old German guy, Werner Stolz, who just died. He used to be SS. The Russians démarched the Americans about him.'

Pigou had just learned enough from his immersion in the Foreign Ministry to understand that a démarche was an official reprimand issued by one country to another, diplomat to diplomat. 'So how did I win a trip to Berlin?'

'The Americans agreed to an investigation, calling the Russian's bluff. I reckon it means there must be nothing to investigate. Your assignment could be short.'

Jean-Francoise chuckled, 'I understand: I am the perfect choice for an unimportant mission.' He made clear he wasn't at all insulted. 'I like Berlin. But why do they want a Frenchman?'

Carine's face reacted to show that even a French career diplomat could be surprised occasionally. 'Well, you see, the Russians have been a bit clever. They did their démarche through a very old protocol – from the Yalta conference, of 1945. It means the United States have to give equal status to Russia, and equal access to all assets of the defeated Germany, including all the Third Reich's information. As a side-effect, it means there's also a role for the other Allied powers, France and Britain.'

'So this treaty means I'm going along as a side-effect?' queried the French airman.

'Yes, Jean-Francoise, but I'm sure you'll put yourself in the centre of things.'

CHAPTER 9

Foreign and Commonwealth Office,
King Charles Street, London
1.35 p.m. GMT

Simon Charfield, assistant deployments manager at the British Foreign Office, arrived back at his computer, still eating his sandwich. He entered his password one-handed, and waited for the new emails to load up. Meanwhile, his eyes drifted out of the window – towards the queue outside Churchill's cabinet war rooms. The bunker from which the British Prime Minister had sheltered from the Blitz always drew tourists. As a human resources specialist in the diplomatic service, Simon often wondered what the holidaymakers did for work, and whether any of the British ones might just be suitable for the 'ad hoc assignments' it was his duty to fill.

The manager turned back to the screen, and immediately discounted the diplomatic telegrams – 'Diptels' – which analysed events around the world. The Middle East peace process, the latest news from Zimbabwe, details about a key election in the Far East – none of it was for him. There was another email chain, all about a British secondee whom he had selected recently for the border monitoring mission in Georgia, which he just ignored. The most important email, he understood quickly, was one from UKMIS – the British diplomatic mission to the United Nations in New York.

IMMEDIATE: UK Secondee required for International Investigation Team (Berlin).

Simon read the email and understood quickly: a UK national was required to join a team also comprising nominees from the US, France and Russia. The Briton on the team, the email reckoned, would add most value if he or she was expert in military history, able to travel swiftly to Germany, and felt comfortable accepting a US lead. Immediately, he knew who he should send.

He double-clicked on his database icon, and a separate window opened on the screen. Simon whizzed through the fields, ticking boxes for 'short-term assignment', 'Europe', and 'previous experience of multi-national work', then, in the box for additional criteria, typed in the words, 'military history expert'. As ever, the computer took less than a second to check through the thousands of pre-cleared deployable civilians on the database. But, because Charfield had added the extra requirement of 'military history expert', it meant far fewer names came up than usual. In fact, just one name:

Myles Munro.

Just as he had expected. And because there was only one candidate and the appointment was urgent, he wouldn't even need to bother with an interview.

Other processes, though, would still have to be followed. Dutifully, he clicked on the name. More information came up, which he scrolled through:

Name:	Myles Munro
Occupation:	Lecturer in military history, Oxford University
Previous work:	Various.
Psychological:	Detached, problem-solver;

Exceptionally intelligent (0.1%);
Not recommended for leadership positions,
or work requiring compliance;
Authority issues *

Charfield had put the asterisk there himself, a reminder that there was a story about the person which was too sensitive for the computerised records. Usually, he scribbled it on a removable yellow post-it note. If ever there was a Freedom of Information request about the individual, he could peel off the note, so it didn't need to be submitted. He kept reading.

Physical description: Height – 6'4' (1.93cm)
Weight - 168lbs / 76 kg
BMI – 20.4 (slim)
Fitness Assessment - very fit*

Previous assignments…

Another asterisk? He'd hadn't noticed the second asterisk on Munro's file before. Succumbing to his curiosity, he moved over to the filing cabinet and fetched out the slim cardboard cover which bound together the sheets of A4 on Myles Munro. The first yellow note fluttered out as he opened the folder. It was the note he had scribbled himself:

Myles Munro may be healthy and physically very fit. But I don't know how the hell he passed his driving text – he can barely tie his shoelaces. He's less coordinated than a kitten on YouTube.

Simon Charfield laughed at his own wit, but quickly sensed others in the office were turning towards him, so he pretended to cough instead, and buried his head in the folder.

He searched for the other note. What was there on file about Myles Munro's 'authority issues'? He looked, but couldn't find it. All he could see was something else handwritten – again, in his own handwriting - slipped into the 'previous assignment' parts of his notes. It bore just one word:

Exonerated.

It was true. Myles Munro had been accused of terrorism, and lambasted by the newspapers for it. There were probably people who still thought he was guilty. But Charfield knew the truth: Myles Munro was the most effective individual on his database. Even if he was sometimes a little bit too individual.

Charfield knew he had to confirm Myles Munro's security clearance for an assignment like this. He checked: Munro had been tested, and passed. The only remark listed under 'noteworthy risks' referred to his long-term partner, who was a journalist and a foreign national. The assistant deployments manager recognised the woman's name – he'd seen her interviewing important people on TV, usually ripping them apart. Then he remembered the words from the Diptel: 'Candidate must … be comfortable accepting a US lead'. Munro was perfect for the job.

He flicked to the contact details. Stuck over the address and telephone number for Munro's college in Oxford was yet another small peel-off square of yellow. He had found the missing note on 'authority issues' – more hand-written words, this time written in a loopy, feminine script, from one of his predecessors:

This candidate asked me if I was a bureaucrat. When I admitted I was, he wasn't interested.

He wondered about the words. What if Myles Munro turned down this assignment?

Simon glanced outside again and, watching the queue of tourists outside Churchill's war-room bunker, an idea came to him – a plan which would make sure Myles Munro said 'yes'.

CHAPTER 10

St Thomas' Hospital,
London
4 p.m. GMT

Helen thanked the nurse for directing her to the room then, when she saw Myles was asleep, crept in as quietly as she could. She stood over him and examined the small cuts on his face, until she was satisfied the damage was only superficial.

She squeezed his hand and held it for a moment. When there was no reaction, she whispered into his ear. 'Myles, it's me, Helen.' Then she kissed him.

Myles rolled his head on the pillow, squinting as he turned towards the lissom silhouette standing next to him. Helen put her hand on his forehead. 'Well, your brain's still together.'

'Thank you.'

'So – you looked left when the traffic came from the right, huh?' She still found it funny that Myles had trouble with his left and right.

Myles smiled. 'I didn't have you looking after me,' he said, touching her forearm. 'No, I was chasing someone.'

Helen nodded. 'And your leg? The doctor told me you'd need a special bandage …'

Myles' expression made clear what he thought of the doctor.

'When you're better … no more thief chasing please.' She moved to sit down beside him.

Myles motioned his eyes towards the medical file on his bedside table. 'What did the doctor say about my scan?'

Helen smiled. 'He asked me about your personality. He said, "We know he's very intelligent, but do you have any evidence of Mr Munro being odd?"' She tried her best to emulate the English doctor's accent. 'I told him it was a silly question. Looks to me like the oddball is the doctor ...'

'They're trying to do research on people,' Myles explained. 'Using brain scans to predict personality.'

Helen screwed up her face in revulsion. 'I hope you said no – I don't want you to be experimented on, Myles.' She paused. 'Although it would be interesting to see what the research said.'

The door opened. Frank's head appeared, flustered, as usual. He was carrying a bag which bulged and made it hard for him to walk with his stick. 'Helen – I'm not interrupting, am I …?'

Helen welcomed him in and gave up her chair.

Frank sat down and placed his walking stick on the floor. 'So they put something on your leg, then, Myles?'

'Yeah – a flexi-thing.' Myles lifted up the grey wrapping around his knee, turning it in curiosity. 'What do you think?'

Frank nodded in appreciation of the medical handiwork. 'You'll only be limping for a few weeks. After that you'll be fine.' Then he delved inside his bag and pulled out some papers. 'Myles – I remembered what you said about your day job. History's all happened, and all that? Well, I got you this.'

He passed a printed-out email to Myles, who held it for Helen to see. 'It's a job,' explained Frank. 'A short-term assignment – in Berlin … I've been asked to see if you might be interested.'

Myles frowned, already looking sceptical. 'Why didn't they ask me directly?'

'Something about last time, I was told,' replied Frank, baffled. 'It's from a friend of mine in Whitehall.'

'Simon Charfield?' suggested Myles.

'Yes – how did you guess? Anyway, they need a military historian – someone British – to join a Frenchman, a Russian and an American.'

'The old Allied war powers?'

Frank nodded.

Helen read through the text with her eyebrows raised. 'So, a Brit, a Frenchman, a Russian and an American go to Berlin …' She smirked at Myles. 'It sounds like the beginning of a joke.'

Frank wanted them to take it seriously. 'Come on, it's easy work. There's some guy who died. An old Nazi. Russia's insisting that an old protocol means the man's papers have to be looked at again, now he's dead.'

Myles and Helen didn't answer immediately. They kept reading the page. Helen finished first. 'It doesn't say what was so special about this guy,' she said, looking up at Frank. 'Er …' She scanned the email for the old man's name. '… Captain Werner Stolz. Why him?'

Frank shrugged his shoulders.

Myles was looking pensive. 'So this means getting inside the head of an old Nazi bureaucrat?'

'Yes, Myles. You'd get an insight into how the Nazi system really worked.' Frank hoped his words might sell the idea to Myles. Instead, they put him off.

It wasn't just that Myles hated bureaucracy – he didn't like studying the Second World War at all. It meant accepting the old-fashioned theory of war: that war was between countries, not people. War as described by most TV documentaries, including their obsession with World War Two, was misleading. Worse than that, it was dangerous. Most modern wars are inside countries, not between them, as Myles lectured his undergraduates. Students loved Myles for his radical views.

Myles put the paper down, next to the image of his brain scan. ‘Thanks Frank. But I’ll pass for now.’

‘Are you sure, Myles?’ Frank was surprised Myles was turning down the offer. ‘It’s work you can still do with a bad leg … It’s just, if you are interested, Whitehall will need to know in a day or two.’

‘Yes, Frank, I’m sure.’

Helen tried to change the subject. ‘Any idea what that guy was trying to take from your museum?’

Frank stretched his face in an expression which said, *I can help with that one*. He dug into his bag again and fished out some papers, which he placed on the table. ‘Here.’

Helen looked at them, not sure how to react. ‘These are what he took?’

‘Yes. The police gave them back to me.’ Frank turned his head to look at the file as he spoke. ‘They’re papers from my new exhibit, mainly. All about how the natural world impacts on war. But one, I know will fascinate both of you …’ Frank opened a cardboard file with some ceremony, and revealed a single sheet of typewriting.

Myles still looked bemused. ‘What is it, Frank?’

‘It’s a real “Hitler letter”,’ Frank answered, proudly. ‘It’s a note which allows the bearer to draw on “All Resources of the Reich” in the performance of their duty. And look: here’s the signature.’ Frank pointed to an illegible squiggle near the bottom of the page. The dictator hadn’t put much effort into writing his name.

Myles sat up in bed. ‘So you think the museum thief was a trophy hunter?’

‘Could have been – working for a private collector, maybe. An Adolf Hitler signature can earn quite a bit at auction,’ explained Frank. ‘Funny to think that Hitler – probably the most evil man in history – is still causing people to die.’

Even Frank was still fascinated by the dead dictator. Like so many of Myles' pupils, Frank was drawn in by the Hitler myth.

Myles refused to look at the signature. Instead, he focussed on the small print at the bottom. He pointed out a name.

'"SS Captain Werner Stolz", it says. Is that who this "Hitler letter" was for, Frank?'

Frank peered closely at the name, then slowly pulled his face back. 'Yes, the same guy who just died in Berlin,' he said, mildly amused. 'Well, isn't that funny?'

Helen and Myles looked at each other. Neither of them believed it was a coincidence.

Myles turned towards the other papers, and thanked Frank with his eyes. 'Reading material for while I get better, huh?' He flicked his thumb up the edge of the pages, glimpsing the material inside. Most of the documents were in German – a language he couldn't read. 'Simon Charfield should get a German speaker for this – not me,' he said.

He waved to Frank, who stood up to leave. Helen showed the museum curator out of the room. By the time she returned, Myles was asleep.

Helen sat back down and started leafing through the papers. A page slipped out and fluttered to the floor. The paper had yellowed and the words on it were from an old-fashioned manual typewriter. As she bent down to collect it, she saw the title was simply 'Communism', and began to read.

The event of 1917, which we associate with the revolution in Russia, is first repeated between November 1952 and July 1953. This major change in communism will soften the ideology; it will become

> defensive and diplomatic. Stalin's style of communism will be no more. The event happens again in March 1989, June 1989 and November 1989. The first of these could end the monopoly of communism in government; the second – in June – will see governments oppose the people; and on the third, in the second week of November 1989, the people will rise up against communism – and win.

This was history she knew well: March 1989 was when non-communists were first allowed to take their place in the Russian parliament. On 3rd and 4th June 1989 the government of communist China cracked down on democracy protestors in Tiananmen Square. And the evening of 9th–10th November was when the Berlin Wall tumbled down, taking with it communism in Eastern Europe.

She turned it over, searching for a date. When she spotted it at the bottom, Helen found herself involuntarily shaking her head at the information in front of her.

She tucked her hair behind her ear, trying to remain calm as she realised she wasn't holding a report about world events. It wasn't a report at all. It was far, far more important than that. The papers she was holding had the potential to shape world events.

CHAPTER 11

5.15 p.m. GMT

On the fourth floor of St Thomas' hospital, while Myles slept, Helen started to rifle through the rest of the file – papers a thief had tried to steal from the Imperial War Museum, at the cost of his life.

The first few pages seemed to be a series of newspaper clippings. All about Rudolf Hess, Hitler's trusted second-in-command, until he mysteriously flew to Scotland in 1941 and tried to cut a peace deal.

Next were documents about how weather forecasts helped Eisenhower plan D-Day, then some typed letters between an American Corporal Bradley and his major from 1945.

She checked the front of the file. A small white sticker had the words 'World War 2 – war/natural world' scribbled on it. The documents were background research papers for Frank's new exhibition.

Then she returned to the page marked, 'Communism' and rubbed the old paper between her fingers. If it was a hoax, it had been done very carefully. She peered closer to notice the paper had been torn. She was holding only part of the page - the bottom half had been ripped away. Someone had taken the prediction seriously enough to tear it in two.

Suddenly she jolted upright.

The movement made Myles stir. 'Helen?' He was still drowsy.

Helen put her hand on his shoulder. 'I've got something for you.'

Myles took a moment to focus, then hauled himself upright, into a sitting position to listen.

'The papers. They're from World War Two, but they seem to predict the fall of the Berlin Wall …' She showed him the document. '… See – November 1989. How did they do that?'

Myles shrugged. 'One of Frank's practical jokes, I guess.'

He glanced at the rest of the papers. Most were in German – he couldn't read them.

Then he was drawn to the correspondence between Corporal Bradley and his superiors, and started to read.

Munich, July 11, 1945

Major Smith, Sir

With greatest respect, Sir, I believe we would be placing the United States at great risk if we halted the investigation into Captain Stolz.

Yours Faithfully,
J Bradley, Cpl.

He turned the page to see a short typewritten reply from the Major.

Corporal Bradley,

Stolz's papers will be filed with the Military Commission for analysis at a future date, as yet undetermined.

Smith

Then another letter from Bradley, this one dated a fortnight later.

Munich, July 27, 1945

Major Smith, Sir

Whilst I have every respect for the wisdom of the military, Sir, to file Stolz's papers with bureaucrats could turn out to be the greatest mistake ever made by Western Civilisation. Bureaucrats will never understand the potential of Stolz's research. His work, Sir, simply <u>must</u> be investigated further by people with more open minds.

Bradley.

The word 'must' had been underlined – probably by Bradley himself. Myles was growing to like Corporal Bradley: the man shared his own disrespect of authority. The letter was followed by a curt military telegram:

Corporal Bradley: reassigned to Alaska, with effect from August 2nd, 1945.

Myles imagined Bradley being taken off his work, and shook his head. Poor Bradley – he had lost his battle, and the bureaucrats had reassigned him to freezing Alaska as a punishment. 'Helen, do you reckon you might be able to track down this guy, Corporal Bradley?'

Helen's face opened up at the possibility. 'I could try, if he's still alive. He'd be very old by now.'

Myles wondered. Whoever Bradley was, he had found some reason to think the German SS Captain Stolz was very important. Myles didn't care for the Second World War, and worried even less about satisfying the governments of Britain, France, the USA and Russia. Helping Bradley beat the bureaucrats, though – that made sense. 'So, what do you reckon about taking up Simon Charfield's assignment, and following up on Bradley's advice – seventy years late?'

Helen nodded. 'Yep, I think you should.' Then she looked again at the 'Communism' page, with its eerie predictions about 1989. 'Be careful, Myles.'

Using Helen's mobile, Myles called Simon Charfield directly to accept. Relieved that he had his man, Charfield printed off a standard Contract of Short Term Assignment, or COSTA, and carried it along Whitehall, across Westminster Bridge, and into the hospital.

He passed the contract to Myles, with a pen, and waited. Only when he had the signed COSTA, and was about to leave to arrange air tickets, did he ask, 'Were you persuaded to come along by the Bradley letters?'

'You put them in the middle deliberately, didn't you,' answered Myles.

'I did, yes,' admitted Charfield. 'To make you feel like you'd found something.'

Myles accepted the answer, then shook his head. 'It wasn't the letters from Bradley which persuaded me,' he said. 'It was the replies.'

DAY TWO

CHAPTER 12

Heathrow Airport
United Kingdom
5.45 a.m. GMT

Gripping his economy flight ticket with his teeth, Myles manoeuvred his injured knee onto the plane. His height and the aluminium crutches made it awkward. Along with his briefing pack, there were too many things to hold. But at least his briefing pack was slim: a few emails printed out, a scanned photo of Stolz, and a last page with just a single sentence on it.

Ref: Doc 1945/730306
– Debrief report (W Stolz, SS Captain)
(Allied War Powers Act)

Myles checked the back of the paper: nothing. That was it.

The emails were correspondence between five people he'd never heard of with others copied in. Then he looked at the email addresses: mostly fco.gov.uk – the British Foreign Office. But there was also an @state.gov – the US State Department, and one from someone using @diplomatie.gouv.fr, which meant the Quai D'Orsay – the French Foreign Ministry. He scanned through the pages. The very first message had come from the Russian Government, but they'd been left off the rest of the email chain.

He read the text. Some mention of Werner Stolz, but he wasn't the main subject of the emails. Most were about whether or not to re-open a joint investigation into Stolz, as the Russians demanded. Much of it was legal jargon, debating how much of the agreements reached in the closing months of World War Two still applied.

Myles put the papers down and looked out of the plane window, wondering what had he stumbled into.

The airline stewardess was leaning towards him. 'Your seatbelt, Sir?'

Still thinking about Stolz, Myles registered the instruction and clumsily tried to fit one part of the mechanism into the other. He watched the runway as the plane accelerated, about to take off, and pondered why were the Russians so interested in such a very old man who had just died. What made this low-level SS officer so special?

The plane shuddered as the nose began to rise. Myles read the emails again. He was missing something. This was a puzzle he couldn't solve – not yet. He didn't have enough pieces. And he knew most of the pieces of the puzzle dated from the end of World War Two. Some would be lost, some buried, and – if they were important enough – some hidden. It meant that to solve it, he'd have to investigate the world as it was at that time. The world when it was at war. The world which still obsessed so many of his students.

He knew he'd get help from Helen. If anybody could track down the former Corporal Bradley, it was her. It would make a great story, potentially for broadcast. But he would have to learn more about Stolz himself. Who was this man, and what sort of life had he lived?

Myles began to imagine Stolz when he was a soldier. A time when people gave hysterical support to Hitler, when Germany seemed able to conquer the world, then – as the war turned against the Nazis – when the Third Reich crumbled and collapsed. How had Stolz reacted to it all?

Myles woke to find the plane landing at Berlin's Tegel airport.

Back on his crutches, handed to him with the stewardess' goodbye, Myles hobbled towards the aircraft steps. Halfway down, he paused to breathe in the surprisingly fresh Berlin city air. Then he was disturbed by a call from below.

'Munro?' It was an American voice.

Myles peered down. The man who had called out had already turned away, scanning around to see who might be watching.

As he reached the bottom of the steps, Myles tucked one of his crutches under his arm and offered a handshake.

The American ignored it. 'You got any baggage?'

His voice was cold and purposeful. Myles noticed his whole head was shaved in an extreme buzzcut: this was a man who coped with baldness by eradicating any trace of hair from his scalp. The American had an ex-military bearing. He obviously kept himself in shape. Probably in his late forties, but it was hard to tell. 'I said, you got any baggage?'

'Yes. One bag. I couldn't really take much carry-on.'

The man kept scanning around, avoiding eye contact with Myles when he spoke. 'So, you're the history professor from Oxford University?'

'Just a lecturer, but yes, at Oxford.'

The American let the words settle before he replied. 'And you do the Nazis?' He said 'Nazis' with his mouth pulled wide, as though saying the words was a painful instruction from a dentist.

'It's hard to be a war historian without covering the World Wars. So, yes, I "do" the Nazis.' Myles wondered whether to explain his unorthodox theory of war. But first he wanted to know more about the frosty American who was guiding him through the arrivals terminal. 'Sorry, your name is?'

The American looked at him sideways, then offered Myles a hand to shake. 'Glenn. You can call me Glenn.'

Myles stopped on his crutches to accept the gesture. 'Hello, Glenn. Just "Glenn"?'

'I said you could call me Glenn. I didn't say it was my name ...'

The American supressed a smirk. Myles had come across people like 'Glenn' before. Probably a spook – they often worked on just a first-name basis. That way, even if they said something notable, nobody could quote it. All that could be reported was that there was someone called 'John' or 'Sarah' working on a particular topic in the national intelligence agency. Myles understood: 'Glenn' could be a firstname, middlename, surname, nickname, code-name or just a random designation given to the well-honed American official standing beside him.

Glenn pointed upwards, directing Myles' eyes towards a sign. Myles duly pulled out his passport, ready to be checked. Glenn waited by Myles while he queued. '... So, you read up much about Werner Stolz?'

Myles shook his head. 'Not sure there's much to read, is there?'

The American didn't reply immediately. Myles sensed the man was measuring his words before he said them. 'That's the thing. There might be more to read than we thought.'

Myles presented his official document to the German border official, who flicked straight to the photo page.

'Welcome to Germany.'

'Thank you.'

Myles was curious about the fact the American didn't show anything to the official – he just made eye-contact and was waved through. Myles kept up with his questions. 'More to read about Stolz, you mean?'

'Sort of,' explained Glenn. 'It looks like there might be a problem with the original file. You see, it looks like something went missing ...'

Neither of them noticed the 'tourist' testing his camera near the passport queue.

CHAPTER 13

Tegel Airport
Berlin, Germany
9.10 a.m. CET (8.10 a.m. GMT)

Glenn took Myles' bag and led him to the airport's parking lot. 'I guess you can't drive – with your leg.' The American nodded towards Myles' knee brace.

'Yeah,' accepted Myles. 'But the doctor reckons I should be out of this in about a fortnight.'

'Good,' said Glenn, as he put Myles' bag in the trunk and opened the passenger door. The American had hired an anonymous mid-range car.

Myles thanked him, threw his crutches in the back, then hauled himself inside.

The radio came on with the ignition, and a German woman's voice started speaking. Probably an advert for something. Although he couldn't understand the language, Myles tried to work out what she was selling.

Glenn switched it off. Silence.

The barrier to the parking lot lifted as they left the airport.

'So, Myles – you've worked with Americans before?'

'Yes.' Myles sense Glenn already knew his answer.

'So, tell me,' Glenn checked the rear-view mirror as he spoke. 'What happened between you and those terrorists?'

Myles sighed. Always the same. The only thing he was known for: false allegations. Glenn had probably googled his name to read all about it.

'I was the patsy.'

'Patsy, huh, Myles? Like Lee Harvey Oswald?' Glenn was teasing Myles for a reaction. 'So who do you blame?'

Myles paused and thought. Glenn's response was odd. Most people, when he explained he had been set up, suspected he was still guilty somehow. But Glenn seemed to take for granted that the authorities were wrong, even though he was employed by them. Glenn *was* the authorities.

Glenn was still concentrating on the road, not really expecting Myles to answer. 'You see, Myles,' he continued. 'I don't care who you blame for your problems, as long as you don't blame the Americans.'

'OK …' Myles puzzled through Glenn's answer. '… So why shouldn't I blame the Americans?'

'Because there are more important things at stake here. Americans and Brits need to stick together.'

'Like during the war, Glenn?'

'Yes, Mr Military Historian,' Glenn relaxed properly for the first time since Myles had met him. 'Like during the war.'

The roads were fast and well-maintained. Glenn drove the car past a few of the city's most famous sites. Myles recognised the Reichstag, Germany's parliament, with its new glass dome. The design had won almost every architectural award there was. It topped a building which rose high above the grassy Platz der Republik, where tourists meandered between flowers and greenery, admiring Berlin's post-war renaissance, while also still fascinated by its horrific past.

Myles spotted the nearby parking lot, and recognised it at once: buried underneath was the infamous Hitler bunker, where the dictator spent much of his last year. The thick concrete walls and its location deep underground had foiled Soviet attempts to destroy it after the war. A memorial to the holocaust had been built nearby, just in case anyone tried to resurrect Hitler's reputation.

Myles saw the main river, the Spree, clean and fresh-looking as it flowed slowly through the city. A small boat carried more tourists, who were being spoken to by a guide. Myles guessed they were learning how the river divided the city between East and West Berlin for more than four decades, looking out for signs of the Cold War on the river banks. He remembered the famous quote from Karl Marx, the prophet of communism:

'He who controls Berlin controls Germany. He who controls Germany controls Europe. He who controls Europe controls the world ...'

Now he had seen Berlin, he understood what Marx had meant a little better.

As they drove into the suburbs, the houses appeared carefully maintained. The lawns were smart and many of the buildings had recently been painted. This was the rich metropolis at the centre of New Europe. No sign of the nation's troubled history at all. But then, that was all a long time ago.

The car slowed and pulled into the forecourt of a hotel. Myles glimpsed the sign.

Schlosshotel Cecilienhof, Potsdam

Myles knew it immediately: this was where the Potsdam conference had taken place in July 1945. It was in this building that the new US President Truman, the Soviet dictator Stalin, and the British Prime Minister had carved up post-war Europe – days before Churchill had been kicked out by the British electorate, and just before the Cold War started in earnest. Now it had been converted into a top-class hotel. Whoever had booked it for them had a wry sense of humour.

The concierge, dressed smartly in a formal uniform, approached the car to open the door. When he saw Myles' scruffy clothes, he supressed a sneer, but upon seeing the artificial support around Myles' knee, he offered an arm to help him climb out and up some steps.

Through a pair of double doors at the top, Myles found himself in the hotel lobby. He was greeted by an attractive brunette. 'Mr Munro. Welcome.' The receptionist beamed, blushing slightly. Myles was about to respond when the woman gestured to the inside of the building. 'Let me guide you to your party, Sir.'

She directed him past the lobby area, along a refurbished corridor, around a couple of corners and up a small flight of stairs. 'These executive rooms have been hired for your group's privacy, Sir.' She pointed towards two heavy but modern-looking doors. They were probably sound-proofed.

Inside, sitting around a table beside Glenn, were two unfamiliar women and a man.

The man, who was wearing a casual jacket, quickly stood up and offered a handshake. 'Mr Munro?' The words came with a heavy French accent. He leaned forward.

'Pigou. Jean-François Pigou, Flight Lieutenant, French air force.' The Frenchman was enthusiastic. Myles sensed he was eager to get going.

'Good to meet you, Flight Lieutenant Pigou. I'm Myles Munro.'

The two women also stood up. The first, slightly older and considerably taller, wore make-up and a beret. 'Zenyalena Androvsky,' she said. Although she was obviously Russian, Zenyalena's dark blonde hair was in a Western style. Her suit was bright orange but stylish. 'You may call me Zenyalena.' She squared up to Myles, looking him in the eye as she shook his hand.

Just from her face Myles could tell she was unorthodox. There was something about her eyes, too, which drew his attention – they seemed to be open too wide, as if she was too alert.

'Glad to meet up, Zenyalena.'

Zenyalena shook his hand with a jolt, hurting Myles' wrist. When he reacted, the Russian woman gave a satisfied grin, then sat down again.

Myles turned to the younger woman. Dressed in practical clothes, she seemed plain, dowdy even. With the manner of a librarian, she was much less showy than the Russian. But something about her face told Myles she was highly intelligent.

'My name is Heike-Ann Hassenbacher. I'm your interpreter, from Germany.' There was only a slight German accent in Heike-Ann's words – she spoke English better than many English people.

'I'm Myles Munro. Good to meet you. I'm guessing you're not just an interpreter.'

'Correct. I'm with the diplomatic police, here in Berlin. My work is looking after foreign diplomats and dignitaries. I'm here to facilitate your investigation.' The woman patted her stomach. 'And before you wonder, yes, I *am* pregnant, although I may be fat, too.'

'Congratulations – when's it due?'

'Thank you. Mid-term at the moment,' said Heike-Ann, peering down at her bulge. 'About four months to go.'

Aware that the introductions were over, Glenn positioned his body in a way which made clear he was in charge. 'Good, we've all met each other, so let's start.'

The group seemed to nod at once. Glenn spread out some papers on the table. Myles, Jean-François and Heike-Ann all leant forward to look.

Only Zenyalena held back. Myles sensed she had an issue with the American assuming command. She was looking round at the team, not following Glenn's lead.

Glenn either didn't notice Zenyalena's reaction or just ignored it. 'So, our mission is to investigate Werner Stolz and his papers …' the American said. He continued with his eyes down at the paper, '… And the mandate for this comes from an edict agreed by our respective governments after the war – before any of us were born.'

'Can you just stop there, please?' It was Zenyalena.

Glenn looked up. 'Yes?'

'Mr Glenn, I think before we start, we need to appoint a chairman.'

Glenn lifted his eyebrows.

Zenyalena turned to the others. 'Jean-François, would the French government object to us appointing a chairman?'

Jean-François was also surprised. He smiled, then shrugged. His expression made clear he didn't care one way or the other.

'Good.' Zenyalena scanned towards Heike-Ann, and seemed to consider asking her, then decided not to. Their interpreter was German: she didn't have a vote. Zenyalena moved on to Myles. 'And the British? Do you mind?' She stared at him for an answer, not blinking.

Myles paused, and caught Glenn's eye as he spoke. 'I suppose there's a good precedent for it: November 1943. When FDR, Churchill and Stalin first met at the Tehran Conference, Stalin said exactly the same thing. He proposed the American President as chair, just to make sure it wasn't the Englishman.'

Glenn lifted his head. 'So Myles, you think it's the turn of the Brits to chair this time?'

Zenyalena spoke before Myles could answer. 'Well, the Russian delegation would like to propose these meetings are chaired by France.'

Jean-François looked surprised again, but took the invitation with a small laugh.

Zenyalena pressed her point home. 'Jean-François, would you mind being chairman?'

'Yes, no problem.'

Glenn caught Myles' eye again. His expression was clear: the American could object, but only if he had British back-up.

Myles wasn't so sure. This wasn't the time to fight. Instead, he proposed a compromise. 'How about this: France to chair for now. We'll pick another chair in a week or so. Yes?'

Zenyalena slowly began to nod, followed by Heike-Ann and Jean-François.

Then Jean-François clapped his hands, and spoke to the team. 'So that's agreed. I'll chair for now. Another chair later. Good.'

The Frenchman leaned over the table, slightly embarrassed. He placed his large hands over the papers which had been in front of Glenn, and slid them towards himself. Then he tried to sort them out. 'So … so …' He picked out a faded yellow page with old typewritten text on it. It was a list. 'So this is the original Allied report. From 1945 …?'

Glenn nodded, still smarting from being evicted from his team leader role. 'Yes. The page you're holding is the inventory on Stolz's papers.'

'And do you know who typed it up?'

Glenn shook his head. 'Some part of the de-Nazification team. Someone in 1945, at an American army base south of Munich. But I don't know who exactly.'

'Can we find out?' asked Jean-François.

'Maybe, but whoever it was, they might be dead by now.'

Jean-François nodded sympathetically, accepting there were limits to what they could learn. He turned back to the papers. From the second pile he drew out a more modern-looking sheet.

This page was white, not faded. The letters on it had come from a computer printer using a contemporary font. He pushed it to the middle of the table. 'And this is the list of papers found in Stolz's apartment?'

Glenn turned to Heike-Ann, encouraging her to speak.

Heike-Ann duly obeyed. 'Yes, that's correct,' she said. 'That is the list made by the Berlin city police team in his apartment yesterday.'

Jean-François continued to interrogate Heike-Ann, ever so politely. 'And all the papers on this new list are from 1945 or earlier?'

'Yes.'

Jean-François considered the two lists. He compared them, putting them next to each other in front of him on the coffee table. Then he spoke softly.

'Now, I don't want to accuse. But does anybody know why the list written in 1945 is incomplete?'

The whole team looked blank.

Jean-François asked again. 'So nobody knows why, in 1945, they didn't list all of the papers?' He looked at all four of the people sitting around him in turn, wondering if any of them might volunteer something. They all remained silent. Jean-François continued, drawing out the final piece of paper. He turned to Zenyalena. 'And does anybody know why the Russian government has decided that Stolz's papers would need to be re-examined after his death?'

The Russian diplomat was about to answer, but Glenn interrupted. He had a sarcastic tone. 'They probably thought it would be amusing.'

Jean-François accepted Glenn's humour. 'OK, so we go through all of Stolz's papers. We read them all, and report on anything which might still be "amusing" seventy years later. Is that agreed?' He looked straight across at Zenyalena. 'Zenyalena – is Russia happy with that?'

'Yes: Russia is content.'

Jean-François turned to Myles. 'Britain?'

'Fine.'

'And finally, the US. Glenn?'

Glenn shrugged his shoulders, much as Jean-François had earlier. The Frenchman took it as consent.

'Good. Then let's start looking through what we've got …'

Myles raised his hand.

Jean-François acknowledged him. 'Yes – Great Britain.'

'Plain "Myles" will do. It's just – I wonder if we'll learn more about this man, Stolz, if we see where he lived. Can we visit his apartment?'

Myles' suggestion was met with accepting faces.

Jean-François nodded in agreement. 'Right – so we look through the papers we have, and we do it in Stolz's old apartment.'

CHAPTER 14

St Hedwig Hospital,
Berlin
10.48 a.m. CET (9.48 a.m. GMT)

Werner Stolz's skin had become grey many years ago – the same colour as his hair, his old photos, and his eyes, which just stared up at the ceiling.

The stiffness which had overtaken his body in the hours after his death had now passed from his limbs. When the autopsy assistant placed his corpse on the inspection slab, Stolz's expression was relaxed – serene, even. The single bullet which had passed through his brain, leaving an entry wound in one temple and a larger exit wound in the other, had done nothing to remove the satisfaction from his face.

'Danke.' The forensic pathologist invited her assistant to stand back from the body. He duly retreated. Then she bent down for a closer look at the head wound. Satisfied that it was just a single bullet, she spoke calmly to her assistant. 'Greifzirkel, bitte.' *Callipers, please.*

She held out her palm to receive the implements. Then she closed the aperture and held them next to Stolz's ear, over the entry wound.

'7.6-7.7 mm.' The pathologist said the numbers as if they were no surprise at all. She had seen other men of Stolz's generation kill themselves this way. They all used 7.65 mm bullets.

It also meant she knew where to look next. Checking her latex gloves were clear of nicks and holes, she probed a short aluminium rod into his mouth, and pushed his tongue to one side. It was there, as expected. 'Pinzette, bitte.'

The assistant duly gave her some tweezers, and for the next three minutes, the pathologist used them to pluck tiny fragments of glass from his gums and cheek. She collected the fragments in a shiny metal bowl, then she took a small ball of cotton wool to soak up the remaining saliva. She placed the swab in the bowl and passed it to her assistant.

The assistant nodded. He didn't need instructions – he already knew he would have to test for cyanide.

It was a common pattern: a man, usually born between 1900 and 1925, who knows he's about to die. He looks for meaning in his life, and decides his most fulfilling moments were in the service of the Führer. De-Nazification is forgotten, and he decides to die as he would have died with the Third Reich: crunching a cyanide capsule just before sending a 7.65 bullet through his head. Exactly the same death as Adolf Hitler himself.

The phenomenon even had a nickname: Führoxia – *death caused by the Führer.*

The pathologist knew how to confirm the diagnosis: blood and saliva tests for cyanide, and a final check that the victim fired the bullet themselves, through tests for traces of gunpowder on their hands.

The pathologist gently lifted Werner Stolz's wrists and wiped another swab of cotton wool along his fingers. She dropped the second swab into a second metal bowl, and passed it over to her assistant, who was already testing the first sample. 'Blut auch, bitte,' she instructed.

The assistant nodded again, confirming that he would also check Stolz's blood.

The pathologist began taking off her gloves, confident of her initial diagnosis: Führoxia, even though it was becoming increasingly rare. But then, Werner Stolz had been one hundred and three years old. There were few of his generation left.

The assistant quietly mixed the chemicals, being as careful with the sodium hydroxide solution he used for the test as he was with Stolz's poisoned blood.

As expected, the cyanide test was positive.

Next, he took a pair of sterile tweezers and lifted the finger swab from the aluminium bowl. The assistant dropped it in a small plastic bag and added a few drops of reagent. Then, while he waited the six minutes for the test to complete, he tidied the old man's body.

Six minutes later, he was perplexed: the gunpowder test was negative.

He stared at the results for a moment, certain there had been a mistake.

He repeated the test, making sure to collect a proper sample of residue from Stolz's fingers this time. More reagent, and another six-minute wait. But it still came back negative.

The assistant re-read the initial report. That made clear that Werner Stolz had been found in the middle of his carpet. There was no sign of anything which could have protected his fingers.

The assistant froze, alarmed by what the science was telling him: that someone else had put the Walter PPK to Stolz's temple and squeezed the trigger – after Stolz himself had bitten the cyanide pill.

That could make it assisted suicide – or even murder.

Finally, the assistant smiled to himself. He had proven the pathologist wrong.

It was not Führoxia at all.

CHAPTER 15

St Simon Monastry,
Israel
1 p.m. IST (10 a.m. GMT)

Father Samuel stared down at his device, and the three words on its small display.

Not suicide. Killed.

He used his thumbs to type back a two-word response.

By whom?

As he pressed 'send', the rotund priest became concerned about the strength of the encryption between the two mobile communication units. Even if the content of his messages were safe, he was sure someone, somewhere would be monitoring the connection between Israel and Germany.

But he became even more concerned, one minute later, when he received the reply.

Guess.

He let out a breath of exasperation, cursing to himself.

Father Samuel rolled his eyes to the Heavens, where he saw his monastery's magnificent ceiling. It was the artwork of religious devotion: years of dedicated craftsmanship, reminding him that his people had endured centuries of suffering.

They had survived before, and it was his duty to ensure they would survive this.

More calmly, he typed back just three words.

No more deaths.

Another minute passed, before he received his answer.

You won't need to pay extra.

Then he sat down to wonder whether he needed to do more to ensure a satisfactory outcome in Berlin. The chance of a *real* problem remained extremely low, but if it did happen, the impact would be unimaginably huge.

CHAPTER 16

Berlin

11.05 a.m. CET (10.05 a.m. GMT)

Within two hours of their first meeting in the exclusive Cecilienhof Hotel in Potsdam, the team of five had driven into the centre of Berlin.

Myles gazed out of the car window, wondering at the sights around him. He saw a woman in a hijab pushing a pram, and two men with tight haircuts holding hands. T-shirts were loud and even the office workers seemed casually dressed. German society had rebelled against everything the Nazis stood for.

Even more dramatic was the evolving cityscape. Cranes and construction equipment seemed to be everywhere: Berlin was being refashioned. Concrete and Prussian brick were being replaced by slick metal trimmed with wood and high-quality plastic. It was a very visual departure from the past.

Meanwhile, scars from the Cold War – including the great wall which had divided the city for more than twenty-eight years – had mostly disappeared, and bomb damage from the end of the Reich was completely gone. Myles noticed not a single street sign bore a bullet hole, which meant those which had been damaged in the intense battle for the city in the spring of 1945 must have been replaced. There were no scorch marks from explosions, or any of the tell-tale chipped concrete he'd seen in other former war zones. The Soviet assault had involved two-and-half million troops, yet all trace of their presence, in this part of Berlin at least, had been erased.

Glenn, in the driving seat, allowed the satellite navigation device to direct him through the traffic.

'Turn left, one hundred yards,' instructed the computerised voice.

Glenn duly obeyed, pulling the hire car quietly into a secluded cul-de-sac.

'Am Krusenick 38. You have arrived at your destination.'

Zenyalena was the first to open a door. She stared up at the building in front of her. 'He hid this away pretty well …'

She was right. Stolz had bought an apartment in former East Berlin. Although the street had been laid down in the 1890s, the whole district had been flattened by bombing raids in the war. Number 38 was a functional and dour five-storey block, built by the Communists over the pre-war foundations. Myles imagined it was probably damp inside, and cold in the winter. There were signs it had been renovated, probably not long after 1989, when the city was reunited. Some of the upper floors had been repainted more recently, but it still looked stark.

Myles sniffed the air: he could smell the city's main river, the Spree, which ran nearby.

Heike-Ann pulled out the police envelope which contained the keys, unsure whether to offer them to Glenn or Jean-François. Glenn deferred to the Frenchman, who took them with a grateful nod. 'Thank you, Heike-Ann,' he said, sizing up the building in front of them all. He began testing the keys in the lock. The first didn't fit, nor the second. But the third one did. He turned his wrist, then gently pushed open the door. 'Let's go in,' he said, as he searched for and quickly found a light switch.

Glenn, Zenyalena, and Heike-Ann followed inside, with Myles hobbling along behind, battling with his crutches.

They were in the shared lobby of the apartment block. The ceiling was high, and the floor carpeted with a plastic mat. A wire-metal door locked off the small space which housed machinery for the lift. It had been swept recently, but not a thorough clean: the dirt had just been brushed under the mat, not taken away.

Heike-Ann pointed them towards the single door on the ground-floor: Stolz's apartment. Myles noticed the paint was worn and neglected. It was a sad place for Stolz to spend his final years.

Jean-François guessed which of his remaining keys fitted this inside door, and got it right first time. He unlocked Stolz's apartment and led them inside.

The interior was much better kept than the outside of the flat would suggest, but certainly nothing special. The walls were painted an old shade of beige, and the furniture seemed like it hadn't been used much. Perhaps Stolz hadn't invited many friends over. Perhaps there had been no friends to invite.

The main living room was dominated by an expensive-looking dining table, with four cardboard boxes on top. Glenn approached them and started opening. Other members of the team watched in silence.

Each box contained the same thing: a set of old files. Glenn pulled one out and peeled open the cardboard. There were several sheets of paper inside.

The American looked up at the others. 'So these are all his papers?'

Heike-Ann nodded. 'Yes. All the papers in the flat – which is all the papers he had relating to the period before May 1945. They're all here.'

Glenn absorbed the information as he leafed through some of the titles. Then, believing he had the rest of the team's permission, he started to read some of them out. 'So we have here a box with a German title: 'Militärische Operation Werwolf – Technologie'. Heike-Ann, what does that mean?'

Heike-Ann tried to take the question seriously, even though it barely needed any translation. 'In English, it means "Military Operation Werewolf – Technology".'

Zenyalena looked puzzled. 'Werewolf?'

Myles recognised the reference. 'Operation Werewolf was Hitler's plan for resistance in Germany once the country was occupied by the Allies. The Führer expected thousands, perhaps millions of his followers to keep fighting after his death.'

Jean-François lifted his head back as if a half-memory about Operation Werewolf had returned to his mind. 'So you think these papers relate to technology for Operation Werewolf?'

'Perhaps,' answered Myles. 'But most resistance to occupation is very low-tech – it uses technology everybody already knows. If this is high-technology and secret, then it might be about the wonder weapons Hitler believed could bring victory when he was losing.'

Zenyalena registered the point. 'Good,' she said, speaking firmly. 'Then we must examine all these papers. There are four boxes and, not counting Heike-Ann, there are four of us.' She had already gone towards the table. 'One each,' she said, picking a box and pulling it to one side.

Jean-François was happy to oblige, and stood next to the box nearest to him.

Myles offered the choice between the remaining two boxes to Glenn, who lifted a file from one of the boxes, then read the title: 'Wirtschaft'. *Economy*. He pushed it across the table to Myles. Myles accepted it, leaving Glenn to take the last one.

Jean-François looked around. The American, Russian and Brit had already started peering into their boxes, lifting out obscure papers to see what they could find.

The Frenchman clapped his hands to gather their attention. 'So: we all take our boxes back to the hotel and read through them tonight. Then we meet again tomorrow at ten in the morning to report back.' Jean-François spoke with a certain charm that made it hard to say no. 'Is that agreed?'

Only Zenyalena managed to quibble. She directed her words to Heike-Ann. 'Half-agreed – Heike-Ann, you said these were only his papers relating to the period before May 1945. Do you know where his other papers are – his papers from after 1945?'

'I understand they are with his lawyers,' replied Heike-Ann.

'Then we must get them,' Zenyalena instructed, matter-of-factly.

Glenn stopped what he was doing, as if the Russian had just said something outrageous. 'No. There's no reason to do that.'

Zenyalena turned her body to the American, facing him squarely. She seemed to have expected objections from Glenn. 'Yes, there is a reason. We want to examine all that Stolz knew at the end of the war. That means reviewing things he wrote afterwards, as well as before.'

Glenn didn't reply immediately. Instead he paused, then pulled from his pocket a folded print-out of an email. He scanned down it, then stopped and picked on a phrase. 'Here, your request: "The team shall re-examine all papers and other materials belonging to SS Captain Werner Stolz." We can't re-examine papers if they weren't examined already. Your words, Zenyalena.' Glenn waved the paper towards the others. 'Our inquiry is limited to papers from 1945 and earlier.'

Zenyalena shook her head. 'You're reading it wrongly,' she said, her tone dismissive. "All papers and other materials". That means all. Recent ones included.'

'But how can we re-examine them, Zenyalena? They were never "examined" in the first place.'

She shrugged, gloating with a satisfied grin. 'Easy,' she said. 'We examine them twice.'

Jean-François seemed insulted that the team were arguing. 'We must all agree,' he suggested. 'If the American delegation doesn't want to re-examine the more recent papers, that is no problem. But the others can.'

Glenn snorted, unimpressed by the Frenchman's weak answer. He turned to Myles, hoping for a better response.

Myles began to speak carefully, thinking as he spoke. 'Glenn certainly has a point. "Re-examine" does suggest only the papers which had been looked at already. But, if there is some mystery to this man, Werner Stolz - an important mystery – then only by looking at his whole life can we find out what it is.' Myles raised his eyebrows, half-apologising to Glenn, who seemed to be losing most of the arguments at the moment.

Glenn returned his glance - the American was accepting Myles' point. But he was also making clear that soon he would need Myles' support. The special relationship – Britain and America – mattered here. Silently, Myles acknowledged it too.

'Good,' said Jean-François, seeming happier. 'Then I will go now to the lawyers who are holding Stolz's other papers. Heike-Ann, I will need you with me because my German is very poor. Does anybody else want to accompany us?'

Zenyalena raised her hand. 'I will come.'

'Excellent. Anyone else?'

Slowly the American raised his hand, copying Zenyalena. 'Well, I don't want this to be a purely Franco-Russian affair,' explained Glenn. He tried to say it as a joke, but the humour was flat. Geo-politics seemed to matter too much to him.

'Welcome along, Glenn. And Myles - you coming, too?'

Myles had already started on the material from his box. Someone had scribbled a translation in English on a large section of the text and he was absorbed by what he was reading.

'Myles?'

Myles looked up to see the four faces inviting him out. 'Oh, no thanks. I'll make a start here. And it's hard for me to travel, with my leg. You'll be back soon, right?'

Jean-François nodded firmly.

Heike-Ann and Zenyalena waved their goodbyes, while they followed the Frenchman out of the room. Glenn patted Myles on the back, and then left with the others. Myles heard the outside door close behind them.

He glanced up from the files and through the window. He could see the four of them standing outside the car, arguing about who should drive. Glenn eventually tossed the car keys over to Zenyalena, who began to adjust the seat.

Myles looked back into the room. Something didn't seem right, but he couldn't work out what it was.

He studied the walls. Stolz had collected a lifetime's worth of books and memorabilia. On a shelf stood a framed photo of the man looking middle-aged next to the Olympic rings. The 1974 Munich Olympics: Stolz must have had VIP tickets to the event.

Stolz had obviously been wealthy. Yet his main apartment, on the ground floor in the centre of Berlin, was dark. It was close to the River Spree, but had no riverside view. It seemed damp - Myles could smell the river inside the building. Surely Stolz could have chosen a better place to live than this?

Myles edged towards the bookcase. The titles were all in German. Even though he couldn't translate the words, he could deduce what they were about. Some science, some history, some travel, and an old Prussian novel. Myles noticed an encyclopaedia of the twentieth century, which had been flicked through many times. The only other book which seemed to have been read so much was titled, 'Ephemeris'. Myles peeked inside: it was a strange timetable, full of symbols and numbers, a different month on every page. Carefully, Myles placed it back, not sure what he had found. He ran a finger along the shelf – some dust, but not much.

Diagonally above the book case was an airvent, which seemed out of place. Stolz had connected a filter to it – a man determined to keep out the carbon from the city traffic?

Myles opened a drawer and found all sorts of small things: train tickets, receipts, a faded set of instructions to some household device. Stolz was a hoarder, but not of large things – the dead German seemed to have collected items which carried information. Myles picked out a photo of the man in his mid-twenties, posing while a jubilant crowd was gathering behind him. Stolz was grinning, as though he had just won tickets to see some big attraction. Myles noticed an out-of-focus swastika in the image. On the back was scribbled simply, 'Vienna, 1938'. He replaced the picture, trying to leave it untouched.

From the lobby of the apartment block, Myles heard the gentle whirring of the lift start up. One of the other residents would be returning to their flat above him.

The distraction made Myles focus. The papers: that was where Stolz's secret lay. That was where Myles had to search.

His thumb moved along the top edges of the papers in his file. Many of the pages were worn: someone had flicked through them before.

Then he noticed more handwritten scribbles under the typewritten text. He gently lifted out the page, careful not to pull too hard in case the paper tore. It was another translation. The words had been done with a fountain pen and the black ink had faded. Myles guessed the scrawls were from the 1940s. It was probably from one of the first people to interrogate Stolz - perhaps from Corporal Bradley himself.

He placed the sheet flat on the table, stretching out the wrinkles with his palms. It was entitled, 'Cross-Border Economic Systems'. Myles began to read.

Our calculations have established the dates on which this happened before, and the historical events associated with those times. These are:

October 1823 to February 1824 –	US President declares his authority over Americas.
December 1852 –	Napoleon III becomes French Emperor and promotes free trade.
1884 –	Berlin Conference sets borders in Africa and international conference agrees on time zones

December 1913 –	US Federal Reserve established
June 1939 –	Pact of Steel unites economies of Germany and Italy.

Myles wondered what the event was: what had happened in June 1939 to coincide with the Pact of Steel? What else had happened when the US Federal Reserve was founded in 1913? For every date, Stolz had told his interviewer about a change in the way money and power operate across borders, but what was he linking to it? Myles noticed the interval between the dates was not even.

He kept reading.

This history and symbolism mean we expect future events to occur on these dates, and have these characteristics:

January 1957 – April 1958 -	Bureaucracy and organisation set up to regulate cross-border trade.
October 1971 –	International economic organisation replaced by negotiation.

August 1984 –	Economic protection is abandoned.
January 1995 –	The way of trade across the world is transformed.
November 2008 –	Lending becomes strict and banking starts to reform.

Myles read it again, amazed.

In 1957 and 1958: the European Economic Community – the future EU – was established, a cross-border bureaucracy to regulate trade in Europe.

October 1971: President Nixon abandoned the rules which fixed the dollar to the price of gold, and brought in a currency based on negotiated power.

August 1984: Economic deregulation dominant in many developed countries.

January 1995: the World Trade Organisation was formed.

November 2008: the credit crunch, causing great problems for banks around the world.

Each one of Stolz's predictions had come true.

He read the rest of the paper.

January 2024 and November 2024:	Technology will replace tradition as the basis for trade; crisis for international organisations.

March 2043 and January 2044:	Technology of world trade abandoned in confusion (efforts to save it in Sept 2043).
May 2066 to January 2068:	War and power settle cross-border economy.

Would these predictions become true, too?

Then Myles looked down at the bottom of the page. There was a simple reference. It had not been translated, because it didn't need to be.

Myles stared at it, stunned.

5. Juli 1940.

It meant the original German words on this page had been typewritten in the summer 1940, many years before the events they predicted.

Myles recoiled from the table.

There were lots of possible explanations. Most likely, the page was written later and the date at the bottom was a lie. How else could the predictions and their precise timings have been made?

But then he began to wonder - why would someone fabricate these predictions? And surely, if it was a hoax, the team from 1945 would have rumbled it?

Behind him, he could still hear the whirr of the lift motor. It had been running for several minutes now. Odd: surely most rides within the five-storey apartment block would take just a few seconds …

Myles slumped down in a seat, taking the weight off his healing knee. He was feeling tired and light-headed. Sick, even.

He looked around the room – his head seemed to be spinning. Perhaps his vision was failing.

He wondered if it was the shock of discovering the old Nazi had been making such accurate predictions. Unlikely – it wasn't enough to explain his intense nausea.

Could the paper have been poisoned somehow? Something chemical or even biological – a clever trap by Stolz to protect his papers? Revenge on anyone who tried to take his secret?

He examined the papers again. The documents were dry, there was no sign of any powder, and Myles had barely touched them. If he was being poisoned, it wasn't by Stolz.

The pages in the box were fluttering slightly, as if there was a gentle breeze within the room. Staggering to his feet, he forced himself back to the boxes. He put his hand on top of them and felt warm air tumbling onto it. Slowly, with his balance failing, he lifted his arm, tracing the source of the draft. His hand reached back to the filter. Warm air was blowing in through it.

He fell backwards, and his head hit the floor. He felt his muscles stiffen, and his stomach convulse, as if it wanted him to vomit. He tried to get back on his feet again, but this time he couldn't.

Suffocating, and with his muscles stiffening by the second, Myles realised he had become completely helpless.

CHAPTER 17

Berlin

11.45 a.m. CET (10.45 a.m. GMT)

Jean-François opened the door to the lawyer's office for Heike-Ann, who accepted the gesture politely, and Zenyalena, who was much less gracious. The three of them had entered a waiting room. Zenyalena was the first to sit down, and choose the largest seat.

Glenn followed on behind, distracted by the English-language version of the Berliner *Morgenpost*, which he accessed on his mobile. He soon found what he was looking for.

> *Werner Stolz made his name in the 1950s and 60s as a financier, and later as a philanthropist. But the man was not always so well-intentioned. Originally from Austria, Stolz began working for the Nazis following the* Anschluss *between his native country and Germany in 1938. He soon found himself working for Hitler's deputy, Rudolf Hess, and, after Hess's bizarre flight out of Germany in 1941, for Heinrich Himmler. It was during this time that he became part of the notorious SS, rising to the rank of captain. But Stolz was never accused of any involvement in war crimes or the wider atrocities associated with the Nazis: he was part of the unit which investigated ancient and pagan wisdoms for the Third*

Reich. His work intrigued the Allies, who interviewed him following Germany's defeat in 1945 …

Glenn could tell most of Stolz's obituary was old. It was common practice for junior reporters to collect material on people like Stolz for use later. Every few years – usually in slack periods, like August and over the Christmas break – the obituaries would be reviewed and occasionally updated by the next generation of trainees.

… Stolz became a successful investment manager, with a reputation for achieving reliable returns and anticipating unexpected events. The great wealth he amassed in the 1950s and 1960s was then spent on a series of good causes. Werner Stolz became a familiar face as a donor to many charities in the mid-sixties. Cynics accused Stolz of trying to buy off his guilty conscience and make up for his time in the SS …

The cynics were probably right. Glenn continued reading.

… Stolz retired at the young age of fifty-five, then became obscure – he is thought to have left Germany for most of the 1970s and 1980s. Soon after the fall of the Berlin Wall in November 1989, Stolz bought a humble apartment in former East Berlin, where he lived for more than two decades, before retreating to a nursing home in Potsdam a few weeks ago …

Finally, Glenn reached the last paragraph. He scanned it, then – suddenly reacting to the words - leaned forward, as he read the text again. Then he exhaled deeply, wondering at the significance of what he had just seen.

He passed his phone to Jean-François, who held it so Heike-Ann could read it at the same time. Zenyalena made a point of using her own phone to find the same website.

Glenn watched Jean-François' face, waiting until the Frenchman had finished reading. 'So, Jean-François - what do you think?'

The Frenchman shrugged. He didn't really think anything.

Glenn pressed home the point. 'I mean about the obituary. The last paragraph.' The American was raising his voice.

Jean-François still didn't understand Glenn's point. Heike-Ann also looked confused.

Frustrated, the American took back his phone, and brought up the final sentences on Stolz so the words filled the screen.

... The cause of Stolz's death – at the age of one hundred and three - is yet to be confirmed by Berlin medical authorities. But it is understood that certain peculiarities surrounding Werner Stolz's life have generated international interest. All Stolz's pre-war papers are to be reviewed by a team drawn from The United States, Russia, France and the United Kingdom. Their work investigating this Nazi-turned-philanthropist has already begun.

Glenn pointed at the device. 'See? Who do you think they've been talking to?'

Jean-François seemed innocent. 'You think these journalists spoke to someone?'

'Of course they have. They wouldn't print that unless they knew.' Glenn began quoting the last sentence, his irritation obvious. 'It says, "Their work investigating this Nazi-turned-philanthropist has already begun".'

Finally Jean-François was beginning to understand. 'Well, I'm sure it was none of our team. It could have been someone at the care home – or the police ...'

Glenn was unconvinced. He looked accusingly at Zenyalena. 'Did you make this public?'

Before Zenyalena had a chance to answer, Heike-Ann finally spoke up. 'It was me.'

Glenn and Zenyalena both turned to her. Jean-François' face invited the German policewoman to explain.

Heike-Ann lifted her palms as she spoke, as if she had nothing to hide. 'A man from the newspaper called me yesterday. They asked me to confirm that the international team had arrived. All I said was "yes".'

Glenn and Jean-François looked at each other, uncertain what to do next.

Glenn followed up with questions. 'How did the journalist know about our investigation, Heike-Ann?'

'He said he'd been told by the Berlin police.' Heike-Ann's answer was straightforward. It was hard to believe she was lying.

'Come on – that's a trick from Journalism 101,' sneered Glenn. 'Make something up, pretend you had it from someone else, and ask for "confirmation". You thought he was telling the truth?'

'Yes, I did. He sounded truthful. Why should he lie?'

Jean-François held Heike-Ann's hand. He squeezed it, as if to emphasise that she had done nothing wrong.

But Glenn was still angry. 'Can we all agree: no more publicity? No speaking to journalists – or emailing, or any contact with them. Right?'

Jean-François looked uncertain.

Zenyalena volunteered a compromise. 'No publicity unless at least three of us want it. Agreed?'

Glenn thought then slowly nodded his acceptance. 'We'll have to get Myles Munro's agreement, when we get back to him.'

The American stared down at the obituary again. The consequence of it was clear. It meant the team's work was no longer secret. Anybody reading the newspaper, or anybody who did a simple internet search for Werner Stolz, would find out that the dead German's affairs – as well as his body – were the subject of research. Research which had been ordered at the highest level.

Eventually the door opened. A prim secretary appeared, holding the door handle. 'Gentlemen, ladies. You may come through now,' she said with a haughty tone.

Zenyalena allowed Jean-François to lead the way, then followed on. Glenn and Heike-Ann trailed behind.

They were being invited into a wood-panelled office. Books were carefully arranged on the shelves, cataloguing German court cases over many years. They looked neat and probably unread.

Wearing thick-rimmed glasses, an austere-looking man pointed to the furniture without making eye contact. 'Good morning. Please ...'

Jean-François, Zenyalena, Glenn and Heike-Ann were offered leather-bound seats. As they sat, it became clear their seats were lower than the lawyer's, forcing them to look up at him

The German lawyer repositioned a paperweight on his desk, then took off his glasses to polish them, paying more attention to imaginary dust on the lens than to the four people in his room. '... Now, I understand you have come to me in connection with the late Mr Werner Stolz.' His English was weighed down by a thick accent.

Jean-François nodded. He sat forward, keen to make his point. 'That's right. You are the custodian of some of Mr Stolz's files?' The Frenchman said it as a question.

The lawyer remained silent.

Uneasy at the lawyer's failure to respond, Jean-François continued. 'Well, we are an investigation team representing the four Allied war powers – France, Great Britain, the United States and the Soviet Union.'

'Does the Soviet Union still exist?' The lawyer started chuckling to himself.

Zenyalena rolled her eyes. 'The Soviet Union's legal rights and obligations passed to the Russian Federation in December 1991.' She turned to Jean-François, encouraging him to continue.

'Yes, and we would like to examine all the papers placed in your keeping by Mr Stolz.'

The lawyer remained silent. Jean-François remained silent also, determined to make the lawyer answer this time.

Finally, the old German spoke. 'You are correct that, before Mr Stolz died, he authorised me to safeguard some of his possessions.'

More silence. Jean-François was becoming infuriated. 'So, can we see them?'

'No, you cannot.'

'And why is that, exactly?'

'Because Mr Stolz was very clear about who was allowed to see them, and you are not that person.'

CHAPTER 18

Stolz's Old Apartment,
Am Krusenick, East Berlin
Noon CET (11 a.m. GMT)

The room was closing around him. His breathing became even more difficult. Myles looked up again at the air filter, and the black carbon stain darkening in the centre. The whirr of the lift motor vibrated in his ears.

Then he understood: carbon monoxide poisoning.

He tried to remember the symptoms: nausea, blurred vision, vertigo, exhaustion ... He had them all. Were there others? He didn't know, but he could feel consciousness fading away from him.

Fresh air – he was gasping for fresh air.

Still lying on the floor, he jolted his head towards the door, hoping to suck oxygen from under it. He tried to stretch, dragging his damaged leg behind him and pushed with his elbows and thighs, the only parts of his body still strong enough to take him to safety.

He was getting closer. But the gas was closing in too.

Then he felt the presence of someone else in the room. Someone behind him, a man standing beside Stolz's papers.

Desperately he tried to turn his head, but his muscles had stiffened too much. He couldn't quite twist his body enough to see ...

Then Myles felt a boot on his neck. The weight began pressing him firmly to the floor, and the sensation of total blackness took over him completely.

CHAPTER 19

The Lawyer's Office,
Berlin
12.05 p.m. CET (11.05 a.m. GMT)

Glenn was fuming. 'And who is that person that Stolz gave his papers to, Mr Lawyer, Sir?' He said the words 'Mr Lawyer' with a sneer.

'I'm not allowed to say.'

Glenn stood up. For a moment, it seemed he might throw a punch.

The lawyer felt the need to explain himself. 'You may not be acquainted with German law. But the position concerning an individual's last will and testament is very clear. Mr Stolz stipulated his papers were not to be given out, other than to a specific individual. He also stipulated that I was not to divulge that individual's identity.'

None of the team knew what to do next. Zenyalena thought she'd try. 'So, what legal means can we use to change your position?'

The lawyer lifted his head up and looked down his nose at the Russian. 'There are no legal means to change my position. Not even the Supreme Court of Germany can force me to divulge the information I safeguard for the late Mr Stolz. A German federal court could ask whether Werner Stolz was of sound mind, and whether he made his will voluntarily. It is easy for me to prove that both of those conditions were met.' The lawyer concluded with a shrug.

Glenn snarled at him again, but didn't know how to respond. Zenyalena and Jean-François both looked blank.

Eventually Heike-Ann spoke up. 'Sir, I believe that the German Supreme Court was established by the Basic Law, with the Federal Republic of Germany in 1949.'

'The constitution, yes.'

'Good. And Article 25 of the Basic Law makes German law subservient to certain international laws, correct?'

The lawyer didn't answer immediately. Heike-Ann was straying into constitutional law, an area which clearly left the man uncomfortable.

Heike-Ann didn't allow the lawyer's silence to stop her. 'Sir, I believe that this commission of investigation, which I have been mandated to facilitate, has a legal basis which overrules provisions of the German Basic Law.'

The lawyer looked nervous, as though he'd been humbled by an amateur but was trying to hide it.

Heike-Ann rammed her point home. 'You see, this team does not just have diplomatic immunity. It has a mandate which originates in the Treaty of Yalta. That means it comes from international law, which overrides Germany's *Grundgesetz*. So if this team make a request, you have a legal obligation to comply.'

Jean-François rallied behind her. '... And we request all your papers on Werner Stolz, including information about whom you should give them to.'

It was almost half a minute before the lawyer offered an answer. 'You must put your case in writing,' he said, dryly.

Glenn slammed his fist on the table. 'Damn that! We've already got it in writing.' He pulled out his printed emails and thrust them in the lawyer's face.

The lawyer peered down his nose at the American. 'So you have a copy of the Treaty of Yalta. Good for you. You must still make your case in writing.'

Zenyalena squared her eyes to the lawyer's. 'No. Under the authority granted to our governments in 1945, you must submit your papers to us immediately. If you do not then you are obstructing international law, which underpins the German constitution.'

Zenyalena, Glenn, Heike-Ann and Jean-François all focussed on the lawyer, watching him weigh his options.

The old German lawyer could tell Zenyalena and the motley foreigners in his office were partly bluffing. None of them were legal experts. If he tried, he could delay them in the courts. Perhaps humiliate them, as they were humiliating him now. But he knew that was unlikely. The Great Powers would never allow it. Instead, they'd crush him. The foreigners only needed to hire a semi-competent lawyer and they'd easily get what they wanted. The legal point was clear: certain aspects of international law *did* trump the German constitution, even after all these years.

It was just a question of time: surrender Werner Stolz's papers now, or be forced to later, by the courts.

The lawyer looked again at the four people in front of him. 'Without confirming I accept your legal position, I am willing to comply with your request,' he acknowledged.

Jean-François looked at Zenyalena and Glenn, not sure whether to believe their luck, while Heike-Ann smiled shyly.

The lawyer said something in German to his secretary, who nodded discreetly, scurried into a side office, and returned a few seconds later with a single box file.

Zenyalena looked disappointed. 'Is that all?'

The lawyer smirked, slightly surprised that he was having the last laugh. 'Yes, that's all.'

Glenn, Zenyalena and Heike-Ann also rose to their feet, all keen to leave the lawyer as fast as they could. Heike-Ann and Jean-François shook hands with the man as they left; Zenyalena refused.

Last to leave was Glenn. 'One question.'

'Yes?'

'Who was the person Stolz authorised you to give these papers to?'

The lawyer paused before he answered, wondering again whether to hold back the secret. But he knew the same logic applied: *tell now or be forced to tell later.* He looked through his thick glasses at the American. He would at least gain pleasure from answering the foreigner correctly, without satisfying him at all. 'The papers say "These are for a foreign man about to die, at the start of a trial by air, fire, earth and water".'

Glenn frowned. 'And who's that?'

The lawyer shrugged, 'I do not know,' he said. Then his face contorted into an artificial smile, gloating openly. 'Goodbye.'

CHAPTER 20

Berlin

12.20 p.m. CET (11.20 a.m. GMT)

Driving back to Stolz's old apartment in Am Krusenick Street, the team celebrated.

Jean-François seemed happiest. 'That lawyer – what a, a …' he searched for the words in English, '… a stuff-ball!'

Zenyalena and Heike-Ann laughed.

It took them a quarter of an hour to reach Stolz's flat. As the car pulled up in the drive, the four people inside climbed out casually. Zenyalena and Jean-François were still smiling as they approached the building. They had no thoughts about what might lie inside.

Glenn unlocked the outer door, went through the lobby, then entered Stolz's ground-floor apartment.

A body lay on the floor. It was Myles, frozen in place.

Glenn bent down to him, shaking Myles' shoulders in panic. 'Myles? Myles, you alive?'

Myles didn't move. The American shook him even harder. He searched Myles' body for signs of life. Nothing.

The others arrived. Jean-François called out, unsure how to react. 'Myles?'

Zenyalena looked around, alert to danger.

Then, very slowly, muscles on Myles' face began to twitch. He opened his eyes and tried to focus, and started spluttering on the floor, only half conscious.

Glenn shouted at him. 'Myles, what happened?'

Myles was too dazed to reply. Glenn realised, and pulled him up into a sitting position.

Myles finally started to remember where he was. He called out, gasping. 'Air …' He was desperate for breath.

Heike-Ann pushed the door to the apartment wide open. A fresh breeze blew through the building – a through draft. A window was open somewhere in the apartment.

Glenn enlisted Jean-François' help, and together the two men hauled Myles outside. There, Glenn encouraged the Oxford lecturer to take some deep breaths.

Myles gradually felt his head begin to clear. '… Has he gone?'

'Who?' asked Glenn.

Myles didn't know who, but he could still feel the boot marks on his neck.

Then Myles remembered the gas. He remembered the lift motor running far longer than it should. He remembered the vent, and the filter. He remembered the sickness. Carbon monoxide sickness.

The four others stood around him, all confused.

'Are you OK, Myles?' Heike-Ann sounded genuinely concerned.

Slowly Myles began to explain. 'I think they tried to gas me. Carbon monoxide poisoning - from the lift motor …'

Zenyalena and Jean-François scoffed. Even Heike-Ann was sceptical. Only Glenn went back to inspect the lift machinery in the lobby.

Heike-Ann checked Myles' pulse. She took a small bottle of water from her bag and offered it to him.

Myles brought the bottle to his lips, spilling some as he drank. 'Thank you …' Sitting outside the apartment while he recovered, Myles realised the people around him still didn't understand what had happened to him. He tried to explain it all. '… Just after you left, someone turned on the motor to the lift in the building. But it didn't just work the lift. It pumped carbon-monoxide gas into the apartment.' He could tell they all seemed shocked.

Zenyalena was still trying to grasp the order of events. 'Is that why you opened the window? To clear the air in the apartment? Why didn't you just open the door, or walk outside?' There was a barb in the Russian woman's voice. It was hostile questioning.

Myles tried to be as honest as he could. 'I didn't open the window. It must have been opened by someone else.'

'But why didn't you just leave the building?'

'I couldn't – the poisoning stopped my muscles. And someone put a boot on my neck.' Myles rubbed his collar as he spoke.

Finally Jean-François gripped the seriousness of the danger. 'You think you could have died?'

Myles nodded.

Jean-François put his hand on Myles' shoulder. 'Then, Mr Munro, we need to take you to a hospital.'

'Thank you, but I'm alright.'

'You sure?'

Myles nodded again, not wanting to leave, and trying to work out who had almost killed him. 'Which of you was the last to leave?' he asked. 'When you went to the lawyer, which of you was the last one to get into the car?'

Jean-François, Zenyalena and Heike-Ann looked blankly at each other.

Then an American voice spoke from behind. 'Me. I was the last to leave,' admitted Glenn. 'And I've just checked out the pipework in the building: something's been done to it …'

Glenn led the whole team back to the entrance lobby. Myles walked with Heike-Ann's arm supporting him, propping up both his ruptured knee and his recovering lungs.

The American took them to the lift machinery, housed behind a wire-framed door. It was old technology – probably Communist-era, from before the Berlin Wall came down. Most of the metal had darkened from age and dirty grease. It all made the green plastic pipe, which bent round from the exhaust of the motor, instantly out of place.

Glenn's finger pointed to where the pipe led. 'Look,' he said. 'Someone recently attached the pipe, so it pumps the fumes straight into Stolz's old apartment.' He gripped the pipe hard and pulled at it. It came away in his hands.

'Leave that,' called Heike-Ann.

Glenn obeyed, confused.

'Fingerprints,' explained Heike-Ann. 'We must get this checked out.'

Zenyalena frowned. 'It'll have Glenn's fingerprints on it now ... If it didn't have them already ...'

Glenn's face fumed with anger. The accusation was obvious. 'If you're saying I would do something like try to kill ...'

Myles tried to calm them both. 'Nobody thinks Glenn tried to gas me. Zenyalena's just trying to understand what happened.'

'We need the police for that,' volunteered Heike-Ann.

Silence.

Heike-Ann was surprised the team didn't welcome her suggestion. She made her point again. 'It was attempted murder, right? So we should contact the police.'

Zenyalena spoke firmly. 'We can contact the police. But their work must be limited to this incident. They are not to investigate Stolz. The attempted murder of Myles and the Stolz investigation are separate. OK?'

Heike-Ann turned to the Englishman, asking her query in a very reasonable tone. 'Myles – you want the police to investigate this, right?'

Myles nodded. 'Yes, they should. But they have to tell us everything they discover. Does German law allow for that?'

Heike-Ann tipped her face to one side. 'The police can tell us some things.'

With Myles back on his feet, slowly he was able to lead the team back into the room. The others followed, all keen to know more about what had happened.

Once they were all inside, Myles leaned on a crutch and pointed to a chair. 'This is where I was sitting. I had the papers in my hand …'

Heike-Ann, Glenn and Jean-François observed the scene from the doorway.

Zenyalena picked up the file Myles had been reading. 'What do you think of Stolz's papers?'

'Interesting. He liked dates.' Myles put out his hand and the Russian returned the file to him. He started looking through it, trying to find the papers he'd been reading before he was gassed. 'There was one piece … Dates when the way the world traded across borders had changed …' Myles kept trying to find it. '… The page was dated *Juli 1940*, which means July, right? It was written at the bottom of the page – although that date must have been added later …'

Zenyalena's eyes narrowed in suspicion. 'Why must the "1940" date have been added later?'

'Because it was so accurate. The paper described events since then,' said Myles, still searching. 'Things which couldn't have been known back in 1940.'

'Well, where is it?'

No matter how hard Myles looked, he couldn't find it. The page he had been reading was gone.

CHAPTER 21

Langley,
Virginia, USA
8.39 a.m. Eastern Standard Time (1.39 p.m. GMT)

Sally Wotton shook the rain from her hair and threw her broken umbrella in the bin. *Damn thing …*

Trying not to spill her morning *venti* latte, she put her security pass between her teeth and took off her coat. Her arm caught in the sleeve. She fumbled, tried to yank it and coffee leapt out of the cardboard cup onto her black trousers. She was examining the stain when the door opened for her – from the inside.

It was her boss. 'Hello Sally – caught in the rain?'

'Yes, Sir.'

The man only half-acknowledged her, then retreated inside.

Sally cursed again. She tried to brush the stain clean, finished with her coat, and hung it up. Finally, she swiped in and walked into the secure area, looking up at the clock: nine minutes late.

Walking through the open-plan office, she tried to ignore the other analysts – most, like her, had just got in. Their computers were still powering up. But she knew they'd arrived on time. The only person who had been late was her.

She put down her latte, and pressed the 'on' button while she adjusted her chair.

Sally typed in her username code, A439, and reminded herself of this week's passwords, ready for the prompts she knew were coming. She typed the first sixteen-character code using just one hand:

EB9A-W33H-JQ9H-JHHX

Then the second code, typed with the other hand:

RTKK-SBNN

She pressed 'enter', and the machine seemed satisfied.

She sipped her latte again, knowing she had several minutes before her computer would be fully ready to use. The delay was deliberate, like a time lock on a bank vault. It was an extra precaution to protect the information inside.

She stretched the fabric on her trousers to check the coffee stain. *So annoying …* And the Central Intelligence Agency didn't offer much in the way of laundry facilities. The stain would have to wait until lunchtime.

She checked her watch, looking again at the other analysts – none of whom made eye contact. Eventually her gaze returned to her sterile desk.

Slowly, her computer yawned to life. She watched the screen as the colours changed.

Beep.

A small box of text had appeared. Sally clicked on 'Proceed', then – at last – the morning's summary came up.

Special Sites Report (24 hours)

She scrolled down through all the jihadist stuff. Al-Qaeda and ISIS belonged to other teams. Most of the time, like today, she ignored it.

Far more interesting were the other sites. Usually oddballs, cranks and students experimenting with the internet. Some were computer hackers testing the security – trying to upload an untraceable website, filling it with terrorist stuff just to make sure Langley was watching. Almost always they were easy to trace – and the CIA *did* trace them. It was just that the agency couldn't be bothered to react.

Drug-traffickers, people-traffickers and the mafia who ran the 'dark web' weren't for Sally either. Sally reported them, passing them on to whoever needed to know. But rarely did they impact directly on America's strategic security interests.

And she didn't bother with electronic espionage, either. Everybody knew China was spying on America. Cyber systems from the rising superpower had penetrated US strategic infrastructure already. But China was what they called a 'rational actor'. It was predictable, and measures to deal with it were already in place.

She was looking for that very rare thing: a web-based threat to US interests which was credible, and which wasn't linked to radical Islam or any nation state.

Her eye stopped at an unusual-sounding site.

File name: Mein Kampf Now
Threat level: three
Original IP location: unknown.

She glowered at the screen, annoyed that a new site with a level-three security threat had come up as untraceable.

She sipped her coffee again, and decided to look at the site itself.

As she clicked her mouse, the screen filled with a photograph of Hitler saluting. She'd seen the picture before – it was a common library stock image of the dictator. Nothing new there. Probably just another sick Hitler fansite, posted by an American teenager spending too much time in their bedroom.

She scrolled down to check the words. They were in English.

> *In January and November 2024, I will destroy the traditions of trade so that America is forced to use technology to save its commerce with the world. World organisations will face a crisis.*

She raised her eyebrows - this was more interesting. She remembered all those accounts of 9/11: some said Al Qaeda had attacked New York's World Trade Centre because they really believed all the world's trade was coordinated from inside the building. Was this threat similar?

And more unusually, it was so specific. It gave a date, several years off – why 2024? It was too far away to be threatening. When eventually the date had come and gone, the threat would seem redundant. Silly even. Unless, of course, it was accurate …

She scrolled down the screen.

> *… and in March 2043, I will undermine your technology and throw all your international trade into confusion. You may stop me in September 2043, but by January 2044 I will have succeeded. Your trade will have become like an ocean that is everywhere and nowhere.*

Sally sipped her latte once more. What sort of whack-job made threats – predictions, even – thirty years out?

She shook her head, dismissing it all. *Oh well, one for the tech boys …*

She pointed the mouse to an icon at the top. A drop-down list appeared:

Ignore
Add to Watchlist one (low priority)
Add to Watchlist two (medium priority)
Add to Watchlist three (high priority)
Request further technical services (tracing)

Sally drew the cursor down until the last option was highlighted. She clicked it, then watched as the grainy image vanished from her computer screen.

CHAPTER 22

Schlosshotel Cecilienhof
Potsdam, near Berlin
6.15 p.m. CET (5.15 p.m. GMT)

Back at the hotel, Myles wondered how close to death he had been. Whoever had pumped carbon monoxide into the room had certainly meant harm. But had they tried to kill him and failed, or just tried to scare him – and succeeded?

He picked up the phone and began to dial. After two rings, a familiar voice answered.

'Helen Bridle speaking.'

'It's me,' said Myles, noticing her voice picked up when she recognised him. 'I've missed you,' he said. 'How have you been?'

'I'm still looking into Corporal Bradley - looks like he's had quite an unusual life ...'

'How's Berlin?'

'Interesting, and the team I'm with is even more interesting,' he said. Gradually Myles got round to telling her about the carbon monoxide attack. Helen's voice became agitated and he tried to calm her down. 'It's alright, honey. Whoever it was: if they had wanted to kill me, they would have done it.'

Helen wasn't persuaded. 'Or they'll just try again. Who do you think it was?'

'I don't know,' he admitted. Myles tried to recall the vague presence he felt in the room while he was losing consciousness. Even when they had placed a boot on his neck, they had stayed calm. Myles thought they might have been wearing a gas mask, although he hadn't been able to see them properly. 'They might have just wanted Stolz's papers.'

'Which means it wasn't one of your team, right?' Helen's logic was sharp. Zenyalena, Jean-François, Heike-Ann and Glenn all had access to Stolz's documents, so they didn't need to steal them.

'Yes, and they were with a lawyer at the time,' he said.

'So, they have an alibi,' she added. 'Someone else broke in to steal Stolz's files, and they could do something similar again. Stay safe, you understand? Don't risk your life for bits of paper. OK?'

'Love you, Helen.'

Myles replaced the receiver, and immediately regretted doing so. He missed her deeply, and wondered if he should take more of her advice.

The team had arranged to meet back in their private meeting room of the Cecilienhof Hotel. Jean-François was reading a book about Nazis and their interest in the occult when Myles arrived, hobbling up the stairs to meet him, still hampered by his bad knee. As Myles laid his crutches by his seat, Jean-François jumped to his feet and offered to pour Myles a coffee. Myles accepted gratefully.

Glenn arrived, looking more rested than before. He explained he had found a good running route around the lake. Heike-Ann arrived perfectly on time, followed only a minute later by Zenyalena, who was wearing a purple power-suit. Myles guessed her clothes were meant to be fashionable. They were certainly hard to ignore.

Jean-François produced a folder and placed it on the table. Inside was a list of all the files they had from Stolz. As he spread the papers out, it became clear there were three lists. Jean-François had been working hard, typing up the lists in his hotel room. 'This is what we have,' he explained. 'This first list sets out all the files from the official 1945 archive. The second is of the files we found in Stolz's room, both in the care home and at his apartment. The third describes the papers given to us by Stolz's lawyer.' He paused. 'We could divide the papers between us - but all of us would have to agree ...' The Frenchman lifted his palms. He wanted someone else in the team to make the next suggestion.

Zenyalena responded quickly. 'How would we decide who gets what?'

Glenn gently pushed the list towards her. 'Which files would you like to look through?'

Zenyalena wasn't sure how to react. Then she scowled. 'If I choose, does that mean I won't get to see the others?'

Myles tried to defuse the issue. 'We could photocopy all the papers. We all get a copy of everything. Then we divide up the workload.'

Only Glenn was hostile. 'Do we really have to photocopy them *all*?' He said the word 'all' in an American drawl, as if photocopying large quantities of paper was a European fetish.

Jean-François raised his eyebrows towards Heike-Ann. 'Heike-Ann – can you handle the copying?'

Heike-Ann didn't feel humbled by the request at all. 'I can get everything photocopied within a day. It is no problem,' she said.

The team split up for several hours, until Heike-Ann called them back together in the early evening. They returned to the hotel's executive meeting room to find several stacks of paper. 'There were just 230 sheets in total,' she declared. 'Not too many.'

Jean-François was gracious. 'I hope you didn't have trouble carrying them,' he apologised, referring to her pregnancy, as he flicked through the pile of papers. They were neatly ordered, almost perfectly so. Numbered stickers on cardboard separator files divided each subject. Different translations were on different coloured paper: white for the German original, green for English, pink for Russian and light blue for French.

Glenn and Zenyalena eyed the stacks around the room, checking they were identical. They certainly looked the same. Zenyalena, though, wanted to be sure. 'This looks very good – thank you, Heike-Ann. And you're sure this is a copy of *all* the papers we have?'

'Correct – yes. It was easier than it looks: the computer which did all the translations also did the photocopying.'

Glenn followed up on Zenyalena's theme. 'But, Heike-Ann, do you think there could be any others?'

Heike-Ann looked confused by the question. She thought for a moment, then shrugged. 'I suppose so. I don't know.'

Myles was the only one of the team who found the computer translations awkward – and not just because they would be hard to carry with his injured leg. To him, they seemed too neat. *Too bureaucratic.* It was an odd way to summarise the lifetime's work of Werner Stolz – the grey man had become a set of multi-coloured papers.

Heike-Ann raised another sheet in the air, waving it for the team to see. 'I also had this translated for you. It's the police report about Stolz's apartment.'

She was about to put the paper down, but Zenyalena peered closer. 'What else does the police report say about the property?'

Heike-Ann scanned it again, half-shaking her head, as though it was all trivial. 'Dates of previous incidents.' She pointed to a small table on the paper. 'Three break-ins, all reported by Mr Stolz. Here are the dates, and the action taken by the police.'

Myles realised these were probably the most significant facts in the document. 'Well, how did the police respond?'

'Er …' Heike-Ann was reading from the list. 'First time … they interviewed the occupant – Mr Stolz. Stolz confirmed nothing had been taken. They advised the occupant on household security. Second time … the same. Third time … they interviewed Mr Stolz, again. This time, Stolz said he had to leave his apartment while the burglar was there.' Heike-Ann scanned the document to make certain there was nothing else. 'Yes. That's all.'

Myles tried to understand what they had just learned. 'So here's Stolz. Very rich, but living in a ground floor apartment that gets broken into. Did he put on new locks after the first break-in, as the police recommended?'

Heike-Ann couldn't find the answer on in the police report.

Jean-François tried to help. 'I noticed the locks on that apartment. There were several. All different. Looked pretty strong to me. Most of them must have been new … The main one on the front door was very shiny.'

Myles absorbed the information. 'So it can't have been a normal burglary. The thief or thieves were looking for something, and they probably knew what it was. And they came back – twice. So they didn't get what they were looking for.'

Heike-Ann checked the dates on the police report. 'I think it was about a week after this third break-in that Stolz left for the nursing home.'

Myles tried to put his thoughts together. Stolz was able to escape from a determined burglar, then two weeks later he checks in to a nursing home.

'Stolz didn't go to the nursing home to be looked after. He went there for protection,' he said. Now it made sense. Myles was beginning to understand what Stolz had been thinking. The old man wasn't senile at all. Quite the opposite. He was trying to protect himself – and whatever it was the burglar had tried to find.

Myles looked at the others around the table. Zenyalena and Jean-François were wondering the same thing. Glenn obviously seemed to think it was less significant. He had already started reading through his papers.

Jean-François decided to call time on the meeting. 'Again, thank you, Heike-Ann. This is excellent. Glenn, Myles, Zenyalena: let's all read through our files, and meet again tomorrow morning. Each of us will report on what we've learned. Is that accepted by us all?'

Myles, Glenn and Zenyalena all indicated it was fine. All three were now looking at their files. It was already too interesting for them to put down.

Myles had quickly become absorbed in the documents. The first file was a translation of a government brief. Dated May 1940, it had been written for one of the top Nazis at the time - probably Himmler or Hess.

> All human civilisations have searched for meaning in the sky. This search has taken many forms. It has led science and generated many 'myths of the heavens', myths which feature in almost all religions. The fact that these have survived so long indicates one of two things: either they contain an essential truth, or humans are naturally inclined to believe them. Both possibilities create important opportunities for the Third Reich ...

Myles remembered Himmler's obsession with the 'Holy Lance' – the spear thought to have pierced Jesus' side when he was on the cross. The artefact – or at least, a piece of wood sanctified as the relic by a medieval Pope – was recovered from Nuremberg after the war.

> ... Our Führer has already decreed that the Reich shall defend itself by controlling the resources of Europe – both natural and super-natural. This means we must study whether the state of the heavens really does impact on human affairs. If it does, we must find and understand this link before our enemies do.

He scratched his head. Could this really be true?

He read some more. The next page was entitled, 'Interrogation of Karl Ernst Krafft, November-December 1939'.

> Reichsminister Hess,
>
> You are aware of the written prediction from Karl Ernst Krafft, that our Führer was vulnerable to 'assassination by explosive material' between 7th and 10th November 1939. Following the fatal bombing on 9th November, when Providence saved our Führer by the tiniest of chances, Krafft was interviewed nine times over the coming six weeks. The Gestapo is confident that Krafft had no direct knowledge of the bomb plot, and no association with the bombers. Krafft was able to explain his prediction through other means.

> We are now employing Krafft to make further predictions about the course of the war.

Myles was suspicious. Krafft may have anticipated things. But did that mean he really predicted them?

People had been trying to predict the future since civilisation began. Shamen, wizards, and holy men - they all claimed to know what was about to happen. It gave them power. Some of them were right, but they could have been right by accident.

Maybe there had been ten Nazis like Krafft. They could have made ten different predictions. If only Krafft's came true, the other nine would be forgotten. It doesn't mean Krafft did anything special.

Myles turned the page. The next paper was a graph. The bottom axis was labelled 'Jahre', which a post-war clerk had translated as 'years'. The timeline seemed to run from 1620 to the year 2000. But what were the two wavy lines above it, rising and falling together? Myles turned the paper, trying to understand, but it still made no sense.

He read the box of text on the side:

> By checking more than three centuries of data, we identified a natural event which rises and falls tightly with the number of war deaths. We calculated the probability this correlation was pure chance as less than one-in-a-million-trillion. It enables us to anticipate the future course of this war, and how much blood will be spilt in the coming battles ...

Both lines on the graph plunged down for the bloody War of the Spanish Succession, around 1700, and there were other falls for the Seven Years war of the 1750s and during the bloodiest years of the Napoleonic era. Then there was a huge drop between 1914 and 1919, for the Great War, and another fall, in the early 1940s, until one of the lines stopped. From about 1944 to 2000, there was just one line on the graph.

He realised one line must be war deaths over the last centuries – the line which ran through until 1944, the last year for which the Nazis had data. But what was the other line? What 'natural event' had the Nazis found which correlated so accurately with casualty rates over all those decades?

Myles suddenly became aware of himself. He looked up: Glenn, Jean-François, Zenyalena and Heike-Ann had all gone to their rooms. Awkwardly, he gathered his papers back into the cardboard box, and lifted it. His knee still restricted by the brace, he manoeuvred the limb out from under the table and hobbled towards the steps. His mind still swirling with thoughts about Krafft and the lines on the graph, Myles made it into his room, slumped onto the bed, and fell swiftly asleep.

CHAPTER 23

11.55 p.m. CET (10.55 p.m. GMT)

Dieter allowed himself to smirk, knowing it would humiliate his prey. 'Now, try to think if there's anything else I might want ...'

By tilting his head, Dieter was able to maintain complete eye-contact with the person he was watching. He slowly moved his face towards his victim's, drawing out his tongue to slurp blood from the man's chin. 'Hmmm. Salty – like rare beef,' he said, smacking his lips as though he was savouring a fine wine.

He sauntered back to his original position, still grinning, and began strolling around the room. As he circled, he mocked the man with his footwork. 'I'm guessing you used to like dancing,' he said. 'Go on – try it now. Don't feel shy,' he offered, looking at his own feet. 'Try to … *relish* this experience.'

He read the man's expression. There was something there, something besides pain and the other side-effects of a drawn-out death. 'You're thinking,' he said. 'That's good – keep doing that.'

Dieter took out his smartphone, checking the in-built flash was enabled. He lifted it up, and framed the image in front of him. '… Smile, now …'

He waited for the man to react, but it was clear he wasn't going to cooperate. So Dieter took the picture anyway, then checked it. *A good image – perhaps even good enough for the webpage …*

Dieter polished the smart phone with his thumb, wiping away a smear as he admired the technology. Drawing out the moment, he turned the device over, examined the back of it, and felt the weight in his hand. 'They make them very well nowadays,' he remarked. 'All sorts of clever apps – some of them cleverer than you, even,' he said to the man before him. Very carefully, he slipped the smartphone back into his pocket, and tapped it.

Dieter pondered as the man dangled. Persuading the man to wear a noose of piano wire had been fun. All achieved so simply, just by holding the man at gunpoint. *How easily people could be fooled into cooperating with their own demise …*

'You're wondering about the wire, aren't you,' he mused. 'I don't think it will slice *completely* through your neck. But someone did a test with a guillotine in 1905, and found heads can remain conscious for half-a-minute without their bodies. So if you are decapitated, you'll know. For thirty seconds. That's nice, isn't it?' Then Dieter thrust his face forward again, staring into the man's popping eyes. 'So, is it *just* these papers? There are no more?'

There was some reaction – a little twitching, and an attempt to speak from behind the tape. The man was trying to say 'yes,' and it was convincing.

For Dieter, it meant there was no more reason to keep him alive. He observed how the wire cut into the man's neck, and how the interrupted blood flow gave the man an involuntary erection. The man's pulse rate had been quickening fast but was now starting to fall away. He waited a few moments. Firing the bullet through Stolz's head had given Dieter a surge of euphoria. But this killing was a disappointment – except for the thrill of beating the hotel's CCTV system.

Dieter turned to look at the papers. He flicked through the stack, deciding where to start. He was beginning to understand what Stolz's secret might be, and why his paymaster thought it was so valuable. It might be valuable to him, too.

Dieter's plan allowed him two-and-a-half hours to read through the documents – when he had scheduled another disturbance to the digital CCTV recording, which would give him a ninety-nine-second window to leave.

He sensed the hanging man was trying to communicate.

Finally ...

Dieter went towards him and ripped the tape from the man's mouth. But only saliva mixed with blood oozed out. The man's tongue, like the rest of his body, soon fixed in place.

Dieter pushed the corpse to watch it swing, to-and-fro, above the hotel bed. Then he swaggered away to concentrate on the secrets.

DAY THREE

CHAPTER 24

Smolenskaya Square
Moscow
6.15 a.m. Moscow Standard Time (3.15 a.m. GMT)

Even though his new line manager was away, Ludochovic didn't conceive of altering the disciplined routine which guided his every working day. Perhaps because he was approaching retirement from the Russian Foreign Service, he now respected his responsibilities earnestly, taking them much more seriously than he had in middle age. What were once chores had since become the rituals which gave purpose to his life.

And so, just before the sun rose on a foggy Moscow dawn, Ludochovic completed the complicated processes which readied the Russian Foreign Ministry's Department of European Affairs for the day ahead. He scanned the overnight security sheet for incidents – there were none – checked the seals on the main cabinets, wafted the electronic surveillance monitor around a few of the desks to detect any eavesdropping devices – none of those, either – and cranked up the mainframe computer to which all the personal terminals were connected. Then he completed the checklist of tasks near the door, finishing it off with a very precise signature, and checked his watch while he started the coffee percolator.

Finally, still alone in the office, Ludochovic prepared to gather the information he would need for the day ahead. As ever, his in-tray contained envelopes from the Foreign Ministry night team and the intelligence analysts: the usual reports. He opened his desktop terminal and set it to download emails, and walked over to check the fax machine. His last check was little more than a habit; hardly anyone in the Russian Foreign Ministry used faxes anymore as the technology was slow, cumbersome, and much less secure than properly encrypted email, so Ludochovic was perturbed when the machine suddenly switched itself on. Even more surprising was the covernote: a page scrawled in large handwriting, directing him to keep safe the 230 sheets which were to follow.

Instead of a signature, there were just two letters at the bottom of the sheet: ZA, the initials of his line manager, Zenyalena Androvsky.

CHAPTER 25

Schlosshotel Cecilienhof
Potsdam, near Berlin
6.30 a.m. CET (5.30 a.m. GMT)

Sunlight began streaming in through the bedroom window. Blearily, Myles woke, realising he had gone to sleep without closing the curtains. He was still wearing yesterday's clothes, and papers were sprawled across the bed – some floated onto the floor as he stirred and sat up. He tried to gather them together, checking what they said as he put them back in the file.

Reichsminister Hess,

Krafft reports that the war will proceed excellently for Germany throughout 1940 and most of 1941. However, he believes the prospects for the Reich look much worse from 1943 onwards. He advises, therefore, that the Reich should seek a peace with Great Britain in 1941, once the easy gains have been made ...

Myles scratched his head. Could Rudolf Hess – Hitler's deputy at the time – *really* have believed this stuff?

Myles knew that Hess flew to Scotland in a Messerschmitt Bf110 in May 1941, on a one-man peace mission. But Winston

Churchill refused to negotiate, so Hess was interrogated by British intelligence. They concluded Hess believed all sorts of 'mumbo-jumbo', and that he had been deluded by Nazi fortune tellers. The whole episode was bizarre, and was never properly explained – other than that Hess was mad, which was Hitler's official line too.

Myles looked at the other files. Most of them were self-explanatory, but a single page they had received from Stolz's lawyer was peculiar. Simply called 'Locations', it contained just four lines:

Location One: Schoolmate's Tract. ONB (where the empire began, 15.III.38)

Location Two: See Location One.

Location Three: See Location Two.

Location Four: sealed

He checked the back of the sheet. Nothing – that was it. It was as if Stolz was presenting a riddle of some sort, but with clues No one could solve. Perhaps they had just been reminders to himself, in case his memory failed with his extreme old age.

Frowning, Myles put the 'Locations' page to one side, and turned to the three files marked 'Nuclear'. Myles guessed they would be about Nazi plans for a wonder-weapon – after all, if Hitler had developed an atomic bomb, he could have dropped it on London and Moscow and won the war. The files might contain something secret, maybe stolen from the Russians – or Americans. But instead, he found what seemed to be notes from an enthusiast.

The first page of 'Nuclear' was about the Manhattan Project. There was a picture of the site in Los Alamos, then the time, latitude and longitude of the first nuclear reaction:

Event: December 2nd, 1942, at 15.25 (GMT-5 hours)
Location: Chicago, USA
41 degrees and 51 minutes north;
87 degrees and 39 minutes west

Nothing secret here: anyone with an internet browser and a search engine could find it with just a few clicks. The Nazis probably even knew about it before the end of the war, through their US spy network. So why had Stolz kept it?

Then Myles noticed some numbers at the bottom. Numbers which didn't seem to relate to anything. He furrowed his brow, confused.

9 Gem – 10 Sag.

Below it was a series of dates, each with a short description. It was a set of predictions, some for events which had already happened. Myles started at the top:

August 1945: Nuclear used for show of power

Myles found himself nodding – it was the month when bombs were dropped on Hiroshima and Nagasaki to force the Japanese surrender.

He read further.

January 1961: Nuclear event causes death

Another accurate forecast: Myles recognised the date of the world's first fatal nuclear accident, when three power station workers had been killed at Idaho Falls in the USA.

Myles' eyes rushed further down the list, skimming over predictions for the Chernobyl and Fukushima nuclear disasters. Every date was correct.

Myles squinted at the page, still bleary, wondering if he could be reading it correctly. Again: Stolz's predictions seemed to have come true.

Myles looked at the rest of the list:

2015-2016:	Faith in old nuclear myths changes profoundly.
December 2015/ July-Sept 2016	Major Nuclear event (as in September-October 1957 and April 1986).
August 2016:	Danger of military nuclear loss
September-October 2027:	Shocking nuclear news, then great powers seek to contain significant and fatal nuclear event.
2049-2052:	Nuclear power used for war: time of increased threat/tension

Did it mean those events were sure to happen? Or had Stolz just got lucky in the past – very lucky?

Myles checked the date again. In the corner, in small writing:

2nd Oct. 1949

So – Stolz *had* carried on making predictions, even once the war was over.

Myles closed the file, bewildered by all the information he had read.

His thoughts were disturbed by a loud knock behind him. Myles called out, 'Yes, who is it?'

The door opened. It was Glenn. 'You should keep your room locked,' he said.

Myles nodded, accepting the point. He'd gone straight to bed, and been too absorbed in Stolz's mysterious papers to think about locking it since he woke up. 'Sorry.'

'Not a problem. You coming down to join us?'

Myles looked up at the clock. 7.15 a.m. Fifteen minutes late for the meeting.

Glenn tipped his head forward with his eyebrows raised, his face confirming, *yes, you are late.*

Myles scooped up his papers, then limped out of the room. He locked the door in front of Glenn before he followed the bald American downstairs.

Myles was expecting the whole team to be waiting for him in their executive meeting room. But just Heike-Anne was there. 'Zenyalena and Jean-François late too?' he asked.

'Just Jean-François,' explained the German, as if she was apologising on the Frenchman's behalf. 'Zenyalena went to look for him.'

Glenn left to order coffees for the team, then Zenyalena appeared. 'Still no Jean-François,' she said, looking flustered. 'His door's locked, and he's not inside.'

Myles and Heike-Ann looked at each other. Myles asked the obvious question. 'If his door's locked, how do you know he's not inside?'

'I banged his door, and called out,' said Zenyalena. 'If he's still inside, he must have become deaf overnight.'

Myles could imagine just how loudly Zenyalena would have thumped on the door. 'He's probably out. For a jog, or at breakfast or something.'

Glenn returned and sat down at the table. 'So Jean-François isn't here. Let's make a start without him.' Glenn's posture made clear he was taking charge again. 'Pigou can join us when he's ready.'

Myles and Heike-Ann shrugged their agreement. Even Zenyalena – for once – accepted the American's lead.

'Good.' Glenn opened up his file, and placed it on the table. 'I read through the files I was given. They were interesting. There was stuff about the V1 and V2 rockets, but most of it was public information from the internet or textbooks. All stuff we could find out ourselves if we had an hour in a good library. Except …' Glenn pulled out one of the papers and spun it on the table for the others to see. It was some sort of map of north-eastern France, with lots of dots, lines and dates laid over the top. '… I found this.'

Heike-Ann was stumped. 'What is it?' she asked.

'I thought it showed launch sites for the V1 and V2 rockets,' said Glenn. 'Hitler fired them from France into England in 1944 and early '45 …'

Myles, Zenyalena and Heike-Ann began to nod, prompting Glenn to carry on.

Then Glenn used a pen to highlight a line on the page. '... Except these lines here.' The line ran almost vertically, north-south down the page, and seemed slightly curved. 'These lines look like satellite tracks,' explained Glenn. 'But the Nazis didn't have satellites. The first satellite went up in 1957. So why did Stolz plot them? This paper claims to have been written in 1943. It doesn't make sense.'

Myles could see the team look puzzled - it *didn't* make sense.

The American turned to the next file. 'Then I found this.' It was from the file labelled, 'Sarin'. Glenn had circled the date: December 1944. 'Ladies and gentlemen, this paper seems to confirm what before was only suspected – that the Nazis had developed Sarin, and they were planning to use it.'

'Excuse me,' asked Heike-Ann, unafraid to admit her ignorance. 'What is "Sarin"?'

'It's a toxic liquid. Super-toxic, a nerve agent – the chemical weapon used on civilians in Damascus in 2013 which turned Syria into a real international crisis ...' Glenn pointed at the paper. '... This paper shows that the Nazis had discovered it, tested it successfully – probably on Jews or prisoners – and were planning to use it if Germany was invaded. Nobody knows how far their plans got. There were searches after the war, but nobody found any stockpiles. To use Sarin effectively you need to disperse it ...'

Myles watched – Glenn was talking about something he knew quite a lot about. It confirmed his suspicions: the clean-shaven American had a military background. Either that, or he was something with the intelligence services.

'... The best way,' continued Glenn, 'is to spray it from a plane, or strap it to a bomb which explodes high-up ...' Glenn used hand gestures to show something exploding. 'Explode a half-litre bottle of Sarin, from the top of Big Ben, say, and you'll kill tens of thousands of Londoners. Except, during the war, all the people in London were carrying gas masks, as a precaution against exactly this sort of attack. Now, from these papers, it looks like the Nazis really did have this stuff.'

Myles took Glenn's point further. '... But when the Allies came in 1945, they found neither the papers nor the Sarin. Which means Stolz must have hidden them somehow.'

Zenyalena suddenly looked concerned. 'And maybe hidden the Sarin, too. Do the maps show where it is?'

Myles and Glenn shrugged.

Zenyalena decided it was time for her to present. 'Well, I read my papers too. Some were about the British Empire - mostly just facts from an encyclopedia. But this was the most interesting page.' She pulled out a paper and put it on the table. It was entitled simply 'End of British Empire'.

Glenn pulled a face, not sure what to make of it. 'Looks like it's just some dates, right?'

'Yes, three of them,' confirmed the Russian. 'But they seem important. The first, October–November 1956, it says "Hubris then humiliation – Empire loses its confidence".'

She looked at Myles, who understood the date. 'The Suez crisis, right?'

'Yes, Myles - when the United Kingdom made a secret deal with France and Israel,' said Zenyalena, clearly enjoying the chance to shame Britain. 'They attacked the Suez Canal, but President Eisenhower refused to support it. Britain was forced to withdraw, and the Prime Minister resigned in disgrace.'

Zenyalena and Myles both looked to Glenn for a reaction. The American looked sheepish. 'Hey – don't blame me. I just follow the President's orders.'

Myles shook his head. 'That's not the point, Glenn. In 1956, your President made Stolz's prediction come true.'

'He was trying to get re-elected at the time. I don't think Stolz would have mattered all that much to him.'

'Agreed, Glenn. But it means, somehow, Stolz made yet another accurate prediction.' Myles turned back to Zenyalena. 'What else does it say about the British Empire?'

'Well, there's something about 2024 and 2025, saying a "challenge will rip out national confidence" ...' She pulled a face, as if to say she couldn't possibly know what that meant. '... Then this one: October 1984. He writes "UK power is suddenly undermined by a military shock."'

Glenn looked confused, raking his memory. Then he began to smile. 'Ah – he got one wrong. If he means the surprise attack on the Falklands, that was 1982. The UK wasn't attacked in October 1984, right?' Finally, Glenn thought he had one over on the dead Nazi.

But Myles shook his head. 'Correct, the UK *wasn't* attacked in 1984. The prediction still came true, though. In October 1984, a terrorist bomb destroyed the hotel being used by Prime Minister Margaret Thatcher. "Suddenly undermined" is a good description: the building was literally blasted away from under her.'

No one answered. Instead, the whole team just stopped and fell silent, as they realised what they had in front of them. Unless he had been using some sort of trick, Stolz really had been predicting the future.

And whether it was a clever hoax, or Stolz had actually made accurate predictions and was genuine, they had to work out how he had done it.

CHAPTER 26

St Simon's Monastery
Israel
8.20 a.m. IST (6.20 a.m. GMT)

Father Samuel switched off his alarm clock. The alert was unnecessary: he was already awake, thinking through all that might happen following the peculiar events triggered by Werner Stolz's death. Slowly, he swung his legs out of bed, gathered himself, and picked up his encrypted communicator. One new message. He clicked it open:

Full surveillance of international investigation team in place. See attachment: this is what they have.

Then he clicked on the attachment, to open a very long file made up of 230 pages of information. It was an electronic intercept, taken from a photocopier in the Headquarters of the German Diplomatic Police.

Quickly, he typed a reply.

Good work, My Ally. Keep watching.

Father Samuel felt his heartbeat quicken as he checked the papers as fast as he could.

Krafft, the German mystic ...
V2 bombers ...
Economic cycles ...

Nothing he didn't yet know – although he suspected it would be news to many people who read it. Would it satiate their curiosity, or fascinate them to find out more? Father Samuel didn't know, but at least he knew what the international team had.

Until he noticed an obscure one-page document towards the end of the attachment – a sheet which didn't seem to relate to any of the others. From the single word title, Father Samuel realised it could be more important than all the other information in the attachment put together.

Swiftly, he began his morning prayer, and called on God to make the international team pass over that single page.

CHAPTER 27

Schlosshotel Cecilienhof
Potsdam, near Berlin
8.30 a.m. CET (7.30 a.m. GMT)

Three loud raps on the door broke the silence. Heike-Ann dutifully sprung to her feet to pull open the heavy door. It was a man from the hotel staff carrying a tray of coffees. Silently, they watched him serve beverages. Only once the waiter had gone, and the soundproof door had settled back in place, did the conversation resume.

Glenn volunteered the first reaction. 'So, Stolz thought he could predict the future.'

Zenyalena shot back. 'More than "thought". He *did* predict the future.'

'Oh come on.' Glenn was pulling his chin back into his face, looking sceptical. 'Nobody really believes all this. There's always a better explanation. It's just that people love voodoo stuff.'

Heike-Ann seemed to be agreeing with the American, tilting her head as she sipped her water.

Glenn realised the others were only half-convinced. 'Look,' he said. 'Stolz's "predictions" were probably written by a bunch of flunkies – just Nazis trying to impress their beloved Führer.'

Zenyalena shook her head. 'Then explain how they're so accurate.'

'Most likely they were written after the event. Maybe Stolz wrote lots of predictions and just kept the ones which turned out to be true. There are lots of ways he could have done it.'

Zenyalena started to lean her head back and look down at the American. 'So how do you explain Stolz getting so rich?'

'Lots of people get rich ...' Glenn seemed to suddenly become aware he was talking to a Russian brought up in the Communist era. '... Well, lots of people get rich in the *West*, anyway. It doesn't mean they have special powers to predict the future.'

Glenn tried to laugh it away, but the others all looked unsure - as though they wanted to believe Glenn, but the evidence they'd seen in Stolz's papers was just too compelling.

Still hoping the Englishman was his most reliable ally, Glenn turned to Myles. 'You teach at Oxford University, one of the world's top academic establishments, right?'

'I'm only a lecturer there,' said Myles.

Glenn made his point. 'Look at the evidence. People have been trying to predict the future for years. It's never been done. It's far more likely Stolz was doing some sort of fast-and-loose magic trick. Maybe he got money for it or something. He couldn't have really been predicting the future. How could he?'

'You may be right,' said Myles, answering slowly. 'Perhaps this is one big trick. But what if the Nazis really *had* cracked some ancient science which allowed them to predict the future? They'd keep it secret, wouldn't they – just like Stolz. A very small number of people would have protected it – perhaps just him. And if they could, they'd make their fortunes from it after the war, just like Stolz.'

'He must have written his predictions afterwards,' huffed Glenn.

'Then we have to test his predictions another way.' Myles picked up the papers. He turned to Heike-Ann. 'We've got the originals from Stolz, right?'

Heike-Ann nodded.

'Then we send them for carbon dating,' announced Myles. 'If papers have the date "1942" on them, then we can take a sample and see whether they really were written around that time.'

Zenyalena took up the theme. 'Is carbon dating accurate?'

'It's not perfect,' accepted Myles. 'But it's accurate enough. We should know whether they were written in the 1940s. We just need to check whether they were written before the events they predict. We'll have to get them sent to a laboratory. It usually takes a few weeks ...'

Glenn, Zenyalena and Heike-Ann were silent, absorbing Myles' suggestion.

Then, Myles remembered: Frank.

'...although I know someone who could speed it up for us – someone at the Imperial War Museum in London. Is everyone happy with me sending some of the papers to be tested?'

Zenyalena replied stiffly. 'Russia objects to Britain's Imperial Wars, but we are OK with the museum testing these papers.'

'Thank you, Zenyalena. Glenn?'

Glenn rubbed his fingers on his forehead, thinking. 'I agree, but we need Jean-François' consent before we send off papers. And we've already agreed our work needs to be kept secret. We can't spread it to too many people.'

Myles nodded, picking up a pen. He started writing a note on the back of one of the photocopied sheets.

Frank - can you have these papers carbon dated, please? Quickly if possible.

This work to be kept secret.

Thanks - Myles.

He allowed Glenn, Zenyalena and Heike-Ann to see the note. All three seemed content. Heike-Ann produced a large envelope for him and offered an array of Stolz's original papers.

Myles thanked her, selected some of the papers at random, then placed them in the envelope. He sealed it, then wrote Frank's name and the Imperial War Museum address on the front. 'We'll post this when we get the say-so from Jean-François,' he explained.

Glenn started shaking his head, as though he was answering questions to himself. 'You know, this just doesn't feel right. If the Nazis had a secret method for predicting future events, how come they lost the war?'

Nobody answered. Not even Zenyalena, who just sipped her coffee.

Myles, meanwhile, turned to Heike-Ann, his mind elsewhere. 'What does "ONB" stand for, in German?'

Heike-Ann looked blank. 'Where's it from?'

Myles pulled out the paper titled 'Locations'. He laid it in front of the other three, and pointed to three capitalised letters.

> Location One: Schoolmate's Tract. ONB (where the empire began, 15.III.38)

'We know Stolz hid some of his papers – probably after his flat was raided,' recounted Myles. 'If we find the rest of his papers, we'll know how he did it ...' He began directing his words to Glenn. '... And whether it was a parlour trick or whether Stolz really had found some sort of correlation which allowed him to make accurate predictions.'

Glenn looked at the 'Locations' page. 'So "Where the Empire Began - 15.III.38". It looks like a date, and I know you Europeans put the month in the middle, right? So, March 1938. Stolz would have been in his twenties. Where was he on the 15th of March 1938?'

Zenyalena threw up her hands. 'Where Stolz was on a random day almost eighty years ago? We can never know that.'

'We might,' said Myles. 'Anybody got a smartphone? What was happening on 15th March 1938?'

Glenn pulled a slick mobile device from his pocket. Myles sensed he was showing off the new-looking gadget. Within a few seconds the American had found the Wikipedia webpage listing dates from the year mentioned in Stolz's clue. 'Here's what there is for 15th March 1938,' said the American, as he began reading. 'Soviet Union announces that one-time leading communist Bukharin has been executed. French Premier Blum reassures Czechoslovakia. Hitler makes a speech in Heldenplatz, Vienna, Austria, proclaiming the "Anschluss", or Union, of Germany and Austria.'

Myles leapt forward. '"Where the Empire Began" – Stolz was from Austria, right? So for Stolz, the Empire was the Third Reich, and it only *became* an empire when his country, Austria, united with Nazi Germany - following Hitler's speech in Vienna.'

Glenn tried to understand. 'So you're saying Stolz hid his papers where Hitler made his speech in Vienna – this "Heldenplatz" place?'

Heike-Ann was dismissive. 'Nice idea, Myles, but "Heldenplatz" means "Place of Heroes".' She was shaking her head as she spoke. 'It's a huge, open square. You can't hide papers in a square like that and keep them secret.'

'You've been there?'

'Yes. As a schoolgirl. The clue doesn't make sense.'

Myles accepted her point. 'You're right – it doesn't make sense. But if we want to find out how Stolz did it, we have to go to this "Heldenplatz" square. Somewhere in "Heldenplatz" is where he hid his secret …' Myles looked around at Glenn, Zenyalena and Heike-Ann, silently asking them whether they wanted to travel south. '… So, what do you think? This is probably the best clue we have.'

Zenyalena was clear. 'Simple – we go to Vienna.'

'Thank you, Zenyalena. Heike-Ann?'

Heike-Ann shrugged her shoulders. 'I don't get a vote. I'm here to assist you. If the team wants to go to Vienna, I'll come along.'

'Good. Thank you, Heike-Ann. And Glenn?'

Glenn was more uncertain. 'I don't know. We go to some huge square in Vienna. Then what?'

'We look for clues,' replied Myles straightforwardly. 'And if we don't find any, we come back here.' Myles was about to say more when he was interrupted by the sealed door being opened and the receptionist poking her head inside.

'I know you asked not to be disturbed, but are you able to take a call? We've had a call from the French Foreign Ministry asking for you,' she explained. 'Should I put it through?'

Glenn nodded to the receptionist, who acknowledged him and left. A few seconds later, the phone began to ring.

Cautiously, the American picked it up. 'Hello?' He frowned with his eyebrows, concentrating on the faraway voice. 'My name's Glenn. I'm the United States representative on this team. And you are?'

After a short pause, Glenn nodded, seemingly satisfied by the answer. 'Hello, Carine.' He listened some more, then looked surprised. 'Well, he didn't ask us!' Glenn's eyes scanned around the rest of the group.

'These things happen,' continued the American. 'Apology accepted. When's he coming?' Glenn's face widened again, as he turned his wrist to check his watch. '… Well that's probably going to be before Jean-François himself gets out of bed this fine morning…'

He leaned forward. '… And thank *you.* The team will discuss it with Jean-François. Until we agree to it, we haven't agreed. We'll probably send this Pascal guy straight home again. Understood …? Yes, *Merci* to you, too.' Thank you.'

Glenn took the phone from his ear and pressed a button on it, checking it was off before he placed it back on the stand. Then he shook his head, dismissing the telephone conversation. 'French Foreign Ministry,' he explained. 'Sounds like Jean-François has invited someone else to join the team. Why not have a party and just invite people from the street?'

Zenyalena kept her gaze fixed on the American. 'Why do you ridicule him, Glenn? Jean-François probably has a good reason.'

Glenn paused some more. 'I'll tell you what,' he said, with the look of a man about to cut a deal. 'We'll put all this to Jean-François. If he can persuade us to take on another person, then we will. And if he's up for Vienna, then we all go. Otherwise, we stay here and the team stays as it is. Agreed?'

Zenyalena began to grin, as though she had just won a small victory. It was the first time in the whole investigation that Glenn had conceded something. She decided to cash in her winnings. 'Let's go up to Jean-François now, and ask him. All of us. He must be in – back from his run or whatever.' She stood up.

Heike-Ann started gathering the papers on the table while Glenn reluctantly also came to his feet. Myles lifted himself on his bad leg. Zenyalena waited until everyone was with her, then led the party of four upstairs to the bedrooms.

On the upper floor, Glenn, Myles, with Heike-Ann bringing up the rear, checked the door numbers as they walked down the corridor.

Zenyalena was already ahead of them, pointing to the end. 'It's this one.' She rapped her knuckles sharply on the door. She called through the door, her tone slightly embarrassed. 'Mr Jean-François. Wake up time!' Zenyalena smirked, imagining what Jean-François might be doing, and why he might not want to answer.

The team looked at each other silently. The room was silent too.

'Jean-François.' Zenyalena's voice was sterner this time.

Again, nothing.

Myles bent down to look through the keyhole. He closed one eye and squinted inside with the other. 'I can't see anything in there. It's too dark – he hasn't opened the curtains.'

Glenn started to look concerned. He gestured for the others to make space. Then he knocked very loudly. 'Jean-François.' He was almost shouting though the door. 'Wake up now. Are you alright?'

Still there was still no answer.

Looking reluctant, the American took two steps back, and rushed towards the door. His shoulder slammed into the wood, which stayed in place. Glenn recoiled. Then he turned accusingly to Myles. 'You gonna help me, or just stand there?'

'Let's just get the spare key from reception,' suggested Myles.

Glenn dismissed the idea. 'No,' he said. 'Let's just barge it open.'

Myles sized up the door frame. It was robust. Then he looked back at Glenn, and down at his own injured leg. 'OK, let's get inside.'

Together, they pushed again. The lock buckled, and the door swung open. Myles stumbled forward, unable to see into the darkness.

Zenyalena flicked a light switch.

Aghast, the four intruders – Zenyalena, Glenn, Heike-Ann and Myles – stood in silence at what they saw: in the middle of the room, Jean-François dangled from piano wire which cut tightly into his neck. Pale and lifeless, his face was frozen in an expression of terror.

CHAPTER 28

10.14 a.m. CET (9.14 a.m. GMT)

Myles rushed to the hanging body. He grabbed the Frenchman's legs, which were cold and felt like pre-cooked meat, to push the body upwards – if there was any chance Jean-François was still alive, the weight needed to be taken from his neck. But the movement only forced the blood which had pooled in the man's mouth to spew out. Myles felt the liquid soak onto his back.

Looking up at Jean-François' neck, Myles could see how deeply the wire had cut. Exposed flesh glistened with half-dried body fluids. The skin was bruised blue, and distorted muscles bulged out on one side. Jean-François' tongue was poking from his mouth, and his lips were discoloured.

Quickly, Glenn grabbed the chair from the desk and stood on it. The American unwound the piano wire from the light socket, so that all of Jean-François' weight transferred to Myles who, still holding the man's legs, manoeuvred the body onto the bed.

The Frenchman's cadaver was stiff, and his face fixed in an expression of extreme fear. His eyeballs gazed out as if he had seen pure evil, the blood vessels inside them had burst. It was clear that the wire had not just cut into his throat, but also choked his jugular artery, severing the blood supply to his head for however long the Frenchman had been hanging.

Myles bent down, daring to peer straight into Jean-François' last moments. There was something about the dead man's face, his eyes and his jaw. Myles tried to see beneath the red saliva oozing out of Jean-François' mouth to wonder what the man's last words might have been. The torture evident in his eyes was not just physical, but also psychological; it seemed his death had come in the midst of absolute terror.

Heike-Ann pushed two fingers onto an unbloodied part of Jean-François' neck to check for a pulse. She shut her eyes while she waited the few seconds it took to be absolutely certain the man was dead. Eyes still closed, she shook her head and withdrew her hand. There was no need for her to announce that Jean-François had no pulse. All four of them had already concluded the Frenchman died several hours ago.

While Heike-Ann and Zenyalena moved away, Heike-Ann with her hand to her mouth in shock, Glenn pointed to Jean-François' wrists. 'Look …' he whispered. Without touching the body, the American drew Myles' attention to two narrow red lines. '… His hands had been tied. And now they're free. Someone cut the binding after he died. Someone watched him die.'

Myles understood. 'And piano wire. It's meant to be one of the cruellest ways to die. You know, when the Stauffenberg bomb plot failed to kill Hitler in July 1944, the dictator ordered the conspirators to be hung from piano wire.' Myles kept trying to read Jean-François' expression. 'It's as though whoever did this was trying to ... they weren't just trying to kill Jean-François. Right?'

Glenn acknowledged the point, while Heike-Ann supressed an audible reaction.

Zenyalena was distracting herself from the corpse by examining the Frenchman's desk. Papers from Stolz were still out, as though Jean-François had been reading them when he was disturbed by his killer. Also, his laptop computer was still on, showing a screen saver. Zenyalena clicked on the mouse. A webpage came up, probably the last webpage Jean-François had read. Zenyalena turned the screen around so they could all read it.

Gauquelin

Zenyalena scrolled down.

Michel Gauquelin (1928-1991) was a French statistician and writer ...

She spoke to the others without looking up. 'It's a biography. About another dead Frenchman ...' The Russian pulled out one of the papers, '... And it matches what he'd been reading from Stolz. Look – a paper from Stolz on this "Mr Gauquelin".' Then she noticed Jean-François' email system was open too. Zenyalena guided the cursor on to the 'sent' folder and clicked. There was a single, fairly long message sent just before midnight. Zenyalena brought it up. 'It looks like he was emailing the Quai D'Orsay, the French Foreign Ministry.'

Glenn exhaled demonstrably, making clear he thought it was bad taste for Zenyalena to be reading their colleague's emails so soon after he had been murdered.

Zenyalena ignored him, and carried on reading. 'The email's in French,' she said. 'There's a whole bunch of stuff here about ... us. He says, "Glenn, United States, probably military intelligence, obstructive at times, secretive ..."'

Glenn raised his eyebrows, but didn't say anything. He looked across at Jean-François' body, deciding not to challenge the dead man's assessment.

'Er, "Myles Munro, Great Britain",' continued Zenyalena. '"Cooperative, unusual and exceptionally intelligent ... Zenyalena

Androvsky, Russia, prepared to cause disruption within team but determined to understand Stolz …"' She skimmed on through the text, deliberately leaving out some of Jean-François' words on her. 'Then he goes on to describe Stolz's papers. He says, "Stolz's papers seem to describe future events. It seems the Nazis made predictions which have later proven to be correct. The question is, *how*? Stolz may have found some link between human events and predictable natural phenomena. This would have allowed him to forecast future natural events, and then make accurate conjectures about human affairs – all with very precise timings for when they would happen …' Then Zenyalena skipped to the end. '"… I suggest you send someone else to join the team here – we need someone who understands both statistics and history. Lieutenant Colonel Pascal would be ideal, if he's available. Otherwise, try someone at the French Defence Academy."'

There was silence in the room. Myles and Glenn's eyes naturally reverted to Jean-François' body. They were trying to understand the man's final moments, and – like amateur sleuths – studying the horrific corpse to deduce whatever they could about who killed their friend and colleague.

Finally, Heike-Ann spoke up, her voice now flat and authoritative. 'Gentlemen, Zenyalena. We are in a room where a murder happened, and we are contaminating evidence. Please, can we all leave?' Myles sensed that Heike-Ann's request was motivated by more than just a professional need to help a police forensic team - she was also reacting to the corpse, her hands on her swollen belly, as if she was calming her unborn baby.

Zenyalena reminded her who was in charge. 'Thank you, Heike-Ann. But we have already established that the authority of this team to investigate Werner Stolz is above the normal laws of Germany. And that includes any laws you have about evidence at crime scenes. Agreed?'

'Yes, but,' Heike-Ann gulped, preparing to answer back quietly. 'This is now the second unlawful killing in Berlin, after Stolz himself. Three, if we include the attempted murder with carbon monoxide …' She gestured towards Myles. 'I have no idea who did this to Jean-François. And I don't think any of you do, either …'

Glenn, Myles and Zenyalena all looked blank. None of them even had any suspicions.

'… OK,' concluded Heike-Ann. 'We need to bring in the German police. This needs a proper investigation. Before anything else bad happens.'

Glenn's posture seemed to be agreeing with Heike-Ann. 'She's right. We have all of Stolz's papers. We can take them back to our capitals, and each of us can examine them there.'

But Zenyalena wasn't having it. 'No, Glenn. We *don't* have all of Stolz's papers. We know he hid some more – probably in Vienna.'

'In Heldenplatz? Come on …' Glenn said the words mockingly, ridiculing the idea that Stolz had managed to stow some papers secretly in a large, popular piazza in the centre of the Austrian capital. He squared up to Zenyalena. 'Anyway, without Jean-François, we have to end this investigation.'

'No, Glenn. If we stop examining Stolz now, we can be sure his secret will be lost.' Then she caught something in the American's eye. 'Or is that what you want? Do you want Stolz to keep his secret?'

'No. I want to find it as much as you do. But look, Zenyalena.' He pointed at Jean-François' body, still lying on the bed. 'That could have been any of us. You, me, Heike-Ann or Myles. And who knew what Jean-François was researching? Not many people.' Glenn was scanning the others for a reaction. 'Jean-François' death needs to be investigated as much as Stolz's papers. And until we know who did this, there's a chance that someone else gets killed. It could be you next, Zenyalena.'

Glenn's last comments were met by quiet shock. He had gone too far –almost as if it was a threat. There was no need for the Russian to reply.

The four of them stood still, all eyes fixed on Jean-François' corpse.

Finally, after more than a minute, Heike-Ann spoke very quietly. 'Come on. I think it's time for us to leave the room, now.'

Without words, they all accepted she was right. Together, the team shuffled back out, acutely aware that their former leader was no longer with them.

CHAPTER 29

10.35 a.m. CET (9.35 a.m. GMT)

Myles, Glenn and Zenyalena walked back down to the hotel lobby, still silenced by what they had seen.

Heike-Ann used her mobile to contact the Berlin police, then informed the concierge with a quiet explanation. Hotel staff swiftly made sure nobody else went upstairs until the emergency services had arrived.

The first police units came within minutes. Others followed, including a medic and forensic teams. Only once they were well-established did Heike-Ann return to Glenn, Zenyalena and Myles, who had found seats within sight of the reception. Nobody felt able to return to the team's executive meeting room, except the Russian who had gone back to retrieve her half-drunk coffee.

'The Berlin police want us to write statements about last night,' instructed Heike-Ann. She turned to Myles and Glenn. 'English is fine. And Zenyalena – you can write in Russian. We can translate.'

One of the officers came over and gave Myles, Zenyalena and Glenn two sheets of paper each and a pen. Still sombre, the three of them started writing. Heike-Ann caught the attention of the officer before he left and indicated she should write something, too. The officer duly returned with pen and paper for her.

After a few minutes, Glenn leaned back and handed his sheets back to one of the police officers. He looked over at the others. 'Did any of you hear anything – in the night?'

Myles shook his head, still writing.

Only Zenyalena looked up to answer. 'I don't think we should share our evidence. That would be corrupt,' she said curtly.

Glenn mused the point over in his mind, wondering if Zenyalena was accusing him of something. But he didn't react.

Zenyalena finished her statement and handed it in. Heike-Ann did the same.

They turned to Myles, watching his hand struggle across the paper. His fingers gripped the pen in an odd way, seeming to push the pen rather than pull it, and his words looked clumsy on the page. Only after several more minutes did he sit back like the others, his statement finally completed.

Myles sensed the others had been watching him, intrigued by his messy handwriting. He tried to guess what they were thinking. 'You're right,' he said. 'They didn't choose me for my pen work.'

The smallest smile appeared on Glenn's face. 'Dyslexic?'

Myles shrugged. 'I don't know.' He raised his eyebrows to show he didn't care either.

It was as Myles handed in his papers to a member of the crime investigation unit, which was rapidly taking over the hotel, that he noticed a man who had just arrived – someone not with the police. With a military bearing and a shoulder bag, the man went to the hotel's main desk. He spoke to the receptionist and there seemed to be a brief conversation. After some uncertainty, the visitor looked shocked. Then he was pointed towards Myles, Glenn, Zenyalena and Heike-Ann, sitting quietly in the lobby.

The man approached, his face uncertain. 'Good afternoon. Do you speak English?' He spoke with a noticeable French accent, similar to Jean-François'.

Myles pulled himself up with his crutches. 'Lieutenant Colonel Pascal?'

The Frenchman looked puzzled. He hadn't expected to be recognised.

Myles smiled as they shook hands. 'Good to meet you. I'm Myles Munro, from Britain.'

Zenyalena stood up also, extending her hand to the French Colonel. 'Zenyalena, Russian Federation.'

Glenn remained seated, and just waved his hand in mock welcome. 'Glenn. United States.'

Heike-Ann stood up to offer the Frenchman a chair. But the man just seemed confused. Carefully he placed his shoulder bag onto the floor. 'At reception they said "Condolences" when I asked for Jean-François. He's… he's dead?' He said it in disbelief, not ready to accept it could be true.

But the four faces in front of him confirmed it. Heike-Ann put her hand on the man's shoulder and encouraged him to take a seat.

Pascal duly sat down. Still not sure where to begin – the French Colonel seemed to have too many questions in his mind. 'But… how?' he spluttered. 'When did this happen? He emailed me last night …' The colonel seemed to be assuming it had been an accident. Finally, he realised the presence of so many policemen in the hotel was no coincidence. 'Murdered?'

Zenyalena started nodding.

Heike-Ann felt the need to qualify the Russian woman's answer. '*Probably* murdered. An investigation has started.' She tried to console the Frenchman with her eyes

'But he told me there was an international investigation team,' said Pascal. 'All about … Er, Mr Werner Stolz. Is that right?'

Glenn looked up, resigned. '*Was* is correct. We no longer have the whole team. The investigation is with the Berlin police now.'

Zenyalena exploded. 'No. This investigation is *not* over.' She stamped her foot on the word 'not'. It made the coffee table rattle, and some of the police team waiting in the lobby looked over. Zenyalena hunched forward, keen to make her points more quietly but with just as much force. 'Look. This investigation has been mandated at the highest level …'

Zenyalena's words were interrupted by Glenn scoffing, but he let her continue.

'… It's only over when we say it's over,' she said. 'And if we let this German police investigation take over the Stolz papers, we all know what's going to happen.'

'Tell me, what'll happen, Zenyalena?' taunted Glenn.

Zenyalena took the bait. 'I'll tell you what's going to happen, Glenn. Jean-François' computer will go to some scientist who works for a German court. Everything Stolz wrote will go to some great warehouse where it never gets looked at again. Whatever secret he had, it will always stay a secret.'

'But Zenyalena, we can't go on. We've lost our team – unless you haven't noticed, one of us got killed last night. He was our team leader, for Christ's sake …' Glenn was getting exasperated. '… And that means it's not safe for us to continue. It's with the police now. It has to be. Hell, it was all nonsense anyway.'

Zenyalena stood up. She lifted her half-drunk cup of coffee and flicked it towards the American. Glenn reacted swiftly, standing to dodge the flying liquid, but some of it still landed on his sleeves.

Glenn brushed off his clothes. 'I think I should fly back to the States.'

He turned to leave, but Zenyalena called after him. 'Wait. Wait— there is a way we could continue.'

'Explain.'

'We have a replacement for Jean-François – here.' She pointed at the Frenchman. 'Colonel Pascal, your ID, please.'

Pascal was now doubly confused – still digesting the news about his friend's death, and also trying to understand the mad Russian woman. He pulled out a diplomatic passport and a military identity badge, and offered them to whoever was interested.

Glenn accepted them both, checked them, then handed them back with a nod.

'So Pascal's on the team?' pressed Zenyalena.

'No,' insisted Glenn. 'Under the deal reached by our respective foreign ministries, it has to be nominees from each of the four governments. Not just – no offence, Colonel – the "friend" of a nominee. And it's still too dangerous.'

Myles watched them argue. Glenn definitely had a point – whatever value this investigation might bring, Jean-François' death changed things. Myles knew he'd been lucky to survive the carbon monoxide attack. Whoever was trying to harm them would try to do it again.

Zenyalena could tell she was losing the argument. She looked around for support. 'Lieutenant Colonel Pascal – surely you'll come with me?'

Pascal looked uneasy. He was shaking his head. 'I don't know what this investigation is about. But I'm sure it wasn't so important that Jean-François should die for it.'

'But Colonel Pascal – to continue is what your friend would have wanted.'

The Frenchman could tell Zenyalena's appeal was a little desperate. He wasn't budging.

Zenyalena turned to Myles. 'Myles – will you join me? We only have to travel to Vienna. Otherwise, all these papers – whatever secret Stolz had discovered - it'll all go to bureaucrats.'

That word – 'bureaucrats'. Myles thought of the mindless paper pushers who had plagued him for so long. The people who always wanted to control things, and who destroyed the things they controlled. He remembered the note from Corporal Bradley, written way back in 1945. Bradley had warned them about the bureaucrats.

Myles began to nod. 'Yes, Zenyalena. We should go to Vienna. You, me, and whoever wants to join.'

Glenn cursed. 'Damn it, Myles. That goes against the whole international protocol.'

'I know – so?' said Myles. 'Maybe protocols have to be ignored sometimes. You coming?'

Glenn shook his head, still disgusted the Englishman had sided with the Russian.

Myles understood. He spoke to Pascal. 'I know you're upset. You're probably still in shock. But we'd like it if you came with us, if you can.'

Pascal studied Myles' face, then Zenyalena's. He could tell the two of them were determined to go. Slowly, he seemed to acquiesce. 'OK, but just to Vienna.'

Myles turned back to the bald American. 'You know, Glenn, you may not want to come, but I'd feel safer knowing you were with us.'

Glenn glanced sideways at Myles, wondering if the Oxford academic had some clever plan. Myles just raised his eyebrows, open-faced: he wasn't hiding anything.

Glenn turned to Heike-Ann. 'Will the Berlin police allow us to take off to Austria?'

'Yes, Glenn, in a few hours. We can all be traced if they want to follow up. It's not a problem.'

'Then if we travel, we have to do it quickly,' concluded Glenn. 'We have to wrong-foot whoever did this to Jean-François. The police must let us take the overnight train to Vienna. Tonight.' Glenn looked up at the others, his face still uncertain.

Zenyalena gloated. 'Good – so America *can* be persuaded after all.'

The five of them stood up, preparing to pack their things and decamp from Potsdam's Schlosshotel Cecilienhof.

Then Zenyalena stopped, 'One more thing,' she said, jerking her head towards Myles. 'Jean-François was our chairman. Although Lieutenant Colonel Pascal can represent France, our team still needs a new leader.'

Myles didn't respond, but he saw Glenn's expression. He could tell what the American was thinking. *Glenn would not allow Zenyalena to be leader, and Zenyalena would not accept Glenn.* Myles felt the faces of the two superpower representatives turn towards him.

It was Zenyalena who made the suggestion. 'Myles, would you … be our leader?'

Myles realised he didn't have much choice. Involuntarily, he found himself nodding.

He was about to lead the team south – to Vienna.

Just a few metres from the room where Jean-François's body had been discovered, a man was breathing through his mouth to remain as quiet as he could. He was still trying to listen to all that was happening in the hotel, while remaining unseen.

Just as Dieter had expected, the police had come. Also, as expected, the police had presumed the killer was far away. After all, the Frenchman's body was several hours old; he checked his watch to calculate exactly how old. Reliable, German police – they were so predictable, it made him smile …

Less expected was that the so-called 'international team' were travelling to Vienna. Did they know what they were looking for, or just hoping to find something? Whichever was true, there was a chance they could find out more.

He took out his communicator, and typed a message with his thumbs.

International team suspect more Stolz papers hidden in Austria.

Dieter pressed 'send', wondering how his paymaster would receive the news.

He didn't wait for an instruction to follow the team; he would do that anyway.

And he would remain unseen.

CHAPTER 30

Berlin Hauptbahnhof 'Berlin Central Station', Central Berlin

9.04 p.m. CET (8.04 p.m. GMT)

As Heike-Ann anticipated, the Berlin police forced the team to wait several hours in the hotel. Finally, when they were allowed to leave, they had just a few minutes to collect clothes, personal items and their copies of Stolz's papers from their rooms. Then they shared two taxis to Berlin's Central Station, and managed to board a train to Vienna at sunset.

Myles sat alongside Pascal for the rail journey south, and watched the German countryside swish by as the twilight turned to darkness. Illuminated buildings would flash out of the gloom, then whizz past as the train journeyed on. He would glimpse farms, level crossings and the silhouette of trees, each for just a second before they disappeared from view. Spotlights shone up at a faraway church, turning it into an eerie beacon of something sinister.

He thought about Helen. He was anxious to know what she had discovered about Corporal Bradley. Then he wondered whether she would hear about Jean-François' murder somehow – with all her sources in the media, it was likely. He would have to tell her about the death first, so he could justify why he still needed to find Stolz's secret, even though the stakes were now so much higher. He resolved to call her as soon as he had a quiet moment in Vienna.

Myles felt the movement of the wheels on the track and remembered all those histories about the First World War: it was the rail network, they said, which had tripped Europe into war. Back in the ill-fated summer of 1914, each of the imperial powers had sent its troops to the front according to train timetables. When they heard that rival empires had mobilised, they were forced to do the same for fear of being left unguarded. And once the mobilise-by-rail plan had been put into effect, there was no way to stop it.

Myles also used to lecture on how railways ensured a defensive war: it meant troops could be sent fast to plug any 'breakthrough' in the trenches, while the attackers could never advance faster than marching pace. Defenders always had the advantage, leading to the long, slow, and bloody attrition of World War One.

Some of his students had trouble accepting such a simple explanation: that so many deaths could be blamed on the movement of railway vehicles. Human affairs explained by physics. Myles was uncomfortable with it, too. But the facts fitted: life and death in the 'Great War' had been determined more often by train tracks than by the decisions people took.

It was hard to guess what the others were thinking. Pascal still seemed numbed by Jean-François' murder. The impact of the news was only hitting him now, a half-day after he had heard about his friend's terrible demise.

Zenyalena, sitting opposite, was more upbeat. She was enthralled by the night-time scenes through the window – dimly lit farms, some roads which ran alongside the railway line, and an occasional castle, floodlit for tourists. It was as if she was still searching for clues about Stolz. She seemed like some of the better students Myles taught back in Oxford: always keen to learn, and fearless to take a gamble on being wrong for the prize of extra knowledge.

Glenn was slumped with his arms folded, as if he didn't care. But he was still reading through Stolz's papers. Myles sensed a determination about him, and a quiet professionalism hidden behind his difficult manner.

Heike-Ann also said nothing. Like Pascal and Zenyalena, her eyes were directed out of the window. But instead of trying to spot things in the darkness outside, she seemed hypnotised by the movement.

Pascal nudged her. 'Hey. You were there when they found Jean-François. What was he reading before he died?'

Heike-Ann looked surprised by the question. Then she remembered – the computer screen. 'Gauquelin. Michel Guaquelin. The biography of a Frenchman who died in 1991.'

Pascal's face looked blank. He didn't recognise the name. 'And do you think he asked for me because of this "Gauquelin", or something else?'

Heike-Ann lifted her shoulders. 'I don't know,' she admitted.

Like Myles and Glenn, Zenyalena had been listening in. 'There was a page about Gauquelin in Stolz's papers.' She started flicking through the files, trying to be helpful. Then she pulled something out and handed it to him. 'Here.'

Pascal turned the page toward him and read it.

> Michel Gauquelin started as a sceptic of all things mystical, and tried to use maths to prove there was no basis for many traditional beliefs. But when he investigated the birth dates and times of thousands of people, he established that the position of the planets Mars, Jupiter and Saturn at the time of birth really did influence their future career. His results were verified by several respected sources and have been repeated in many independent

> studies since. Gauquelin became most famous for the so-called 'Mars effect': people born when the planet Mars is on the horizon or directly overhead are more likely to excel in the military or at sport than people born at other times. Since Mars is a planet traditionally associated with war and sport, Gauquelin's findings confirmed an ancient tradition. Gauquelin's conclusions have split the scientific community between those who accept his work but can't explain it, and those who insist it must be fraudulent.

Pascal turned the paper over. There was nothing on the other side. 'That's all?' he asked.

'That's all,' confirmed the Russian. 'Which is why we need to find out more.'

Pascal looked at the paper again, then slumped back in his seat, silent.

It was a few seconds later before Glenn spoke, his eyes still fixed on his papers. 'So, Pascal, if you're wondering how you got yourself into this mobile madhouse, Michel Gauquelin is the crazy Frenchman you should thank.'

Pascal just looked blank, unsure how to respond. 'You mean this "crazy Frenchman" is somehow responsible for Jean-François' death? Even though he's dead?'

Zenyalena butted in. 'No, Pascal, you should blame a different Frenchman. One from four hundred years ago: Nostradamus,' she explained. 'He was a famous mystic who used ancient "science", like astrology, to predict lots of things. Even the rise of Hitler.'

Glenn turned away, an expression of contempt on his face.

Zenyalena ignored him. She began to recite from memory.

'From the depths of the West of Europe,
A young child will be born of poor people,
By his tongue he will seduce a great troop;
His fame will increase towards the realm of the East.
The edicts of the Pope will be overruled
By Hitler, and Italy is a fascist republic.

'Wild men ferocious with anger, cross over rivers,
The greater part of the battlefield will be against Hitler;
In armour of steel they will make the great assault,
When the child of Germany will heed No one.'

Zenyalena looked around, expecting the rest of the team to be amazed by the accuracy of the prophecy. Instead, they just looked mystified.

Myles spoke with a puzzled frown. 'Did Nostradamus *really* write the name "Hitler", back in the 1500s?'

'He wrote "Hister" – just one letter out,' answered the Russian. 'And everything else he got right – Hitler's alliances with the "realm of the East", Japan and fascist Italy. And how the Allies turned the battlefield against him. There's even a line about how Hitler's fate would remain a mystery – which it did. The Allies were never sure the Nazi dictator really killed himself.'

Heike-Ann leaned forward, her body language most sceptical of all. 'You know, Nostradamus' poems could be read in other ways.'

Zenyalena accepted the point, but only partly. 'True, but the Nazis used them,' she said. 'Stolz might have been ordered to research how Nostradamus made his predictions. And perhaps he actually found out.'

CHAPTER 31

Langley,
Virginia USA
5.44 p.m. EST (10.44 p.m. GMT)

Sally Wotton wondered whether she should really be doing her job at all. Perhaps her PhD was wasted. It certainly felt that way when she was just browsing websites. Special websites, for sure, but most of the sites she checked for the CIA were too amateurish to be threatening.

In the last fortnight, only one website had really impressed her boss. It was that *Mein Kampf Now* page, the Hitler fansite with library images of the dead dictator and the nutty predictions far off in the future. Crazy stuff, but not yet proved to be nonsense. And whoever was behind it had protected it with multi-layer defences. It was the high quality of those cyber-walls, added to the very odd nature of the threats, which made it so intriguing.

Noticing the site had earned her two words of praise from her boss. 'Thanks, Sally,' he had said. It was the only truly positive feedback she'd received since she started her job.

Sally re-read the report from the tech boys. They confirmed they couldn't locate the site because it wasn't really located anywhere. Instead, they described it as 'transient' with 'multiple uploading paths'. It meant there was very little chance of finding out who was behind the site, or – just as important – where they were based. From the data traces, somewhere in Europe seemed the most likely source, but that was little more than a guess.

An alert at the bottom of her computer screen changed colour, indicating something new had just been uploaded onto one of her listed 'watch sites'. Sally clicked on the icon.

Mein Kampf Now

Sally leaned forward in anticipation. She waited, while her computer connected itself to the page. Then she leapt back in horror, recoiling from the screen as fast as she could.

The image which repelled her was a grotesque photo of someone hanging in a hotel room. Dead, or nearly dead, the man was suspended by thin wire which gouged into his neck. The picture had been taken with a flash, making his face look especially pale and drained. Crimson fluid dribbled from the victim's tongue, which protruded from his mouth as though it was trying to escape. From the man's horrific expression, he was dying in terrible pain.

Now she knew this website was serious. Photos of someone being murdered in one of the cruellest ways possible automatically made *Mein Kampf Now* a priority.

As she began to overcome her initial revulsion, Sally scrolled down the page. The terrifying image shifted up and out of her sight. It was replaced by recently-added text.

In August 2016, I will prove my power with a nuclear device. Your military will be very scared! Then, in the autumn of 2027, I will use atomic power to cause destruction and death. But even this will be nothing compared to my nuclear activities in the years 2049, 2050 and 2051...

Sally's heart quickened.

> ***... And I will strike the United Kingdom in 2024 and 2025, ripping out its confidence as a nation.***

Did that mean a nuclear attack against the UK? Sally thought not – it was another sort of strike. These were two different threats. And like the others, they were disturbingly precise.

What worried Sally most was the pathological determination behind it all. Murdering someone to make a point? Making bizarre boasts long in advance? Super-tight webhosting which not even the CIA could crack? It all pointed to a committed psychopath. *Mein Kampf Now* was masterminded by someone who would use extraordinary means to carry out their extraordinary threats.

She scrolled back up to the ghastly photo, tagged it 'For Immediate Analysis' and sent it to the tech boys – they may have failed to find out where the website was coming from, but if the picture was genuine it would contain clues, perhaps in the background.

Then she printed out the latest version of the website, impatiently looming over the machine as the pages came out.

As she was running down the corridor, rushing the print-out to her boss, Sally wondered what they could do about the nuclear threat, and the danger to the USA.

And she knew, whoever was behind *Mein Kampf Now*, they would make sure their terrible predictions came true.

DAY FOUR

CHAPTER 32

Heldenplatz
Vienna, Austria
7.53 a.m. CET (6.53 a.m. GMT)

All five of the team managed to get some sleep on the train. It meant that when they arrived at Vienna's Central Station, they had all been oddly refreshed by the overnight journey.

They climbed out, and took in the modern design of the terminal building – clean glass and iron. Like Berlin, it must have changed enormously over the century of Stolz's life. Myles caught sight of a large digital clock: if there was a rush hour in Vienna, then this was it. But the commuters seemed too poised to be rushing. This was, after all, a city famous for its waltzes – everything moved at a pace which was measured and sedate.

From Vienna's Central Station, it was a short taxi ride to the central square – the 'Heldenplatz'. The three men and two women just squeezed into a single vehicle, Myles the most cramped of all, with his head bent over to fit inside. But he could still see the great sights of the city as they drove by – the Opera House, museum and grand shopping arcades – mixed with the normal scenes of modern Europe: small cars, mothers with children, and a rubbish collection truck.

Myles watched Glenn survey the architecture – one thing about Europe that the American seemed to respect. Heike-Ann and Pascal were awestruck. Only Zenyalena seemed slightly resentful. Myles shot her a queried expression. She just raised her eyebrows in response.

The taxi pulled up near an ornate building.

Heike-Ann helped Myles with his crutches, making it easier for him to swing his injured leg out of the vehicle. Like an impromptu tour-guide, she pointed to the space behind them. 'Here we are: Heldenplatz. It means "Place of Heroes".'

Glenn looked around them, disappointed. 'So this is it? This is the square?'

Heike-Ann nodded.

Glenn seemed unconvinced. 'It's not the best place to hide a bunch of papers, is it?'

He was right. The piazza was almost barren, the surface made of hard concrete and paving stones. The only obvious landmarks were two statues of men on horses: Prince Eugene of Savoy and Archduke Charles of Austria.

Myles read out Stolz's description again:

'"Schoolmate's Tract. ONB (where the empire began, 15.III.38)."'

Zenyalena looked up at the statues. 'Could Stolz have gone to school with Prince Eugene or Archduke Charles?'

Pascal's face lightened up for perhaps the first time since he had been told of Jean-François' death. 'I doubt it,' he said. 'Not unless he was much older than we think.' The Frenchman gestured towards the cast iron plates on the bottom of each statue. Their dates were 1663–1736 and 1771–1847. Zenyalena accepted the point.

Glenn started looking at the paved surface. 'Where exactly did Hitler speak from in 1938?'

Zenyalena and Pascal started searching for plaques or marks in the ground – anything which might show where the dictator stood to make his famous 'Anschluss' speech.

But Heike-Ann was quick to stop them looking. 'There won't be any signs. De-Nazification: any marking would count as a "monument" to Hitler, and the laws forbid that.'

Glenn started shaking his head. 'So, we can't even know where he stood? And even if we did know, it would just be a spot on the pavement.' He was looking despondent. 'Ridiculous. This whole thing is ridiculous. We ain't finding anything to do with Stolz here. Come on, Myles – you've got to admit. It's not looking good, is it?'

But Myles wasn't giving up. 'If these papers are not hidden in the square, could they still have a "Heldenplatz" address?'

Heike-Ann weighed up her answer. 'I suppose so, yes. Some of these buildings around the edge could count.'

'And what are the buildings?'

Heike-Ann glanced around, squinting in concentration as she tried to recall what they all were from her visit as a schoolgirl. Standing in the centre of the square, she began to turn a full 360 degrees, labelling off the sights as she saw them. 'There's the Hofburg Palace, the Conference Centre, the city's ring road, the outer castle gate, the national library, the parliament, the town hall … Austria's unknown soldier …'

As she spoke, Myles realised: Heldenplatz didn't offer too few places for Stolz to hide his papers. It offered too many.

Glenn picked up the theme. 'Austria's unknown soldier. Did Stolz see himself as an unknown soldier?'

Zenyalena answered with sarcasm. 'You mean a secret behind-the-scenes bureaucrat type of soldier?'

Then Myles made the connection. 'But Hitler did. That was how he promoted himself. He made himself out to be an "everyman" – the voice of the trenches. The unknown soldier betrayed by the politicians in Berlin.'

Pascal was puzzled. 'So we look at the tomb of the unknown soldier?' he asked.

'No,' explained Myles. 'Stolz's clue was "Schoolmate's Tract". It means we look for schoolmates of Hitler.'

Something Myles said seemed to resonate with Heike-Ann. She took out her smart phone and found a webpage. The search term, 'Hitler Schoolmate' yielded several thousand results, but one name was clearly at the top. '"Wittgenstein", she read out. 'Anyone heard of someone called "Wittgenstein"?' She said it oddly, like she was tasting strange food.

Myles could see none of the others knew the name, apart from perhaps Pascal who was trying to recall. 'Ludwig Wittgenstein was either mad or a genius, probably both,' he told them. 'He was an Austrian who fought on the same side as Hitler in the First World War. But unlike Hitler, instead of using his spare moments to refine fascism, Wittgenstein developed a philosophy – a completely different way of thinking about the world. You've heard of "I think therefore I am"?'

Glenn spoke tentatively. 'The foundation of Western philosophy? Is that right, Myles?'

'Yes – it used to be. Until Wittgenstein proved it was wrong. Some say the mad Austrian – Wittgenstein, not Hitler that is – destroyed Western thinking. Philosophy has never been the same since. While Hitler was threatening Western civilisation, Wittgenstein was destroying its ideas. And if they were at school together, we may have broken into Stolz's clue.'

Heike-Ann had found a webpage showing the two of them in the same photo – an annual school photograph from Linz Realschule, 1901. In neat rows, a class of eleven- and twelve-year old schoolboys was posing for the camera. Wittgenstein was near the middle, with the junior Hitler just one row above. Heike-Ann held the phone where the others could see. Hitler's unmistakable eyes seemed to drill out towards the camera. Just from the image, they could tell the future dictator was a strange boy.

Heike-Ann scrolled down. 'It says here they were born in the same week, both in April 1889. Wittgenstein on the 26th, Hitler on the 20th.'

Pascal tried to think it through again. 'So, how is Wittgenstein connected with Heldenplatz? Was he here when Hitler spoke in 1938?'

Myles knew he couldn't have been. Wittgenstein was probably teaching at Cambridge University at the time, and the philosopher was never a fan of Hitler. Then it hit him. 'But Wittgenstein *did* write some famous papers,' he said. 'And his first book was called the "*Tractatus*". "Schoolmate's Tract" - it must mean "Wittgenstein's *Tractatus*".'

Then, like a light illuminating her face, Heike-Ann suddenly understood another part of the clue. '"ONB" – I thought it was something translated into English,' she said. 'But the automatic translator didn't change the letters, because it's an abbreviation. It's ONB in German. ONB means *Österreichische Nationalbibliothek* – the National Library of Austria ...' She pointed. '... And it's just over there.'

CHAPTER 33

Heldenplatz
Vienna, Austria
8.30 a.m. CET (7.30 a.m. GMT)

As Myles saw the words, in English under the German, 'National Library of Austria – Heldenplatz Entrance', he knew they'd come to the right place. He hobbled towards the door of the building as quickly as he could, his ruptured knee slowing him down when he wanted to rush. The rest of the team followed behind, then Glenn, Zenyalena and Pascal overtook him as they realised, like Myles, that this must be where Stolz had hidden his papers. Only Heike-Ann walked more slowly, careful not to strain herself while she was pregnant.

Glenn started quizzing a receptionist. 'Do you have all the books written by Ludwig Wittgenstein?'

An intelligent-looking woman in her mid-thirties, the receptionist nodded. She quickly saw her reaction was good news to the bald American and his friends and obviously felt the need to bring him down a little. 'But you know he really only wrote one book, the '*Tractatus*'. All the other things he wrote were just papers, articles for academic journals – that sort of thing…' The woman seemed familiar with Wittgenstein's work.

Zenyalena decided she couldn't let the American lead the questioning. She elbowed Glenn out of the way and spoke to the receptionist herself. 'So are all his books— er, sorry, his one book. Is it on display?'

The receptionist shook her head. 'Only copies - the original manuscript is in an American University. But since Wittgenstein wrote it in the trenches, there's not much left, just a few soggy notes.' She checked on her computer. 'Er, we have twelve copies – in the Upper Reading Room.'

Zenyalena looked around at the others. Twelve copies of a very public library book. It wasn't a promising way to hide secret papers.

But Myles knew they had to check. 'And which way is the Upper Reading Room?'

The woman stood up to point around a corner to some stairs. Myles thanked her as he took her directions. The others followed, then Zenyalena began half-running, trying to get to the books before anyone else in the team. Myles heard Glenn mutter curses as he ran after her, with Pascal closely behind. Only Heike-Ann stayed with Myles, both of them moving at walking pace.

After two steep flights of stairs, Myles and Heike-Ann followed a corridor into the Upper Reading Room, which was vaguely eerie. The air inside was cold and still, and No one was inside, except Glenn, Pascal and Zenyalena, who had just found the right shelf.

'But they're paperbacks,' Zenyalena complained. Disappointed, the Russian pulled down the first of the identical books. 'Where inside do we look?' She started flicking through the pages, realising there was too much to read.

Finally Myles caught up, calling across to Zenyalena as he arrived. 'Find the contents page. Then find where Wittgenstein explains how we deceive ourselves when we think we're making free choices.'

The five of them huddled around the Russian. It was Heike-Ann who saw the contents page first. 'Section Five. Turn to Section Five,' she said.

Zenyalena quickly rifled through the pages until she was on Section Five.

Nothing – just a normal chapter.

'Try the other books,' instructed Myles.

Zenyalena picked up the next copy. Glenn took one too. Pascal and Heike-Ann did the same.

It was Heike-Ann who found some thin pen marks scribbled in the margin. Someone had notated the book, as if a student was making notes to themselves. But something about the handwriting – it was jagged and deliberate – suggested it had been written by an old person with an infirm grip. Heike-Ann held out the notes for the others to see:

Schauen Sie in die Ablage der Wiener Polizeiakten von 1913 - WS

Myles pointed at the last two letters. 'WS – Werner Stolz, right? What does the rest of it say – can you translate?'

'It says, "See the file of official records from the Vienna police from 1913."'

Myles acknowledged the clue, then gave an instruction to the team. 'OK, let's split up. Everybody look for old Austrian files.'

Glenn and Zenyalena immediately started looking in opposite parts of the Upper Reading Room. Pascal went back towards the door, obviously looking for someone to help.

Heike-Ann turned to Myles, who started searching around the room, wondering where the files might be. His eyes soon gazed upwards: the Upper Reading Room had a small raised level which seemed more promising. The only way up seemed to be via an old cast-iron staircase. Together, Myles and Heike-Ann started to climb, Myles careful to ease the weight on his bad knee.

At the top, they split in opposite directions, and took several minutes to check the tall ranks of shelves for anything which might look like old Vienna police records. Myles sensed this part of the library was rarely visited. It was also quite enclosed, almost hidden, making it the ideal place to store sensitive papers, or – if Stolz had more sinister intentions – to set a trap.

'Hey,' Heike-Ann beckoned Myles over.

Myles limped towards her, and the German woman pointed to something beyond her reach. Myles stretched up and took the little-used box file from the shelf. Heike-Ann checked the label on the side and confirmed it was the one Stolz had meant, then, with a sense of ceremony, slowly opened the lid.

On top was an inventory: the list of papers the file contained. She lifted it up and passed it to Myles.

Underneath was a formal certificate of some sort. 'It looks like an official document,' whispered Heike-Ann, as she touched it with her fingers, unsure whether to handle it. The paper was faded and the ink pale. The old Germanic typeface confirmed it was from another age – from before the First World War.

Myles stared at the rubber stamp in the corner. 'Police?'

Heike-Ann began reading the German and nodded. It was a copy of a police report from 1913. Underneath were near-identical reports from 1912, 1911 and 1910. She began to go through them. 'Er, these are from the Vienna police ...' She scanned through them. Apart from being very old, they seemed unremarkable - detritus of a long-gone imperial bureaucracy. '... Something about conscription – "all Austrian men are required to register for military service". These are reports about someone who didn't turn up as they were required.'

Myles made sure he understood. 'You mean it's about a draft dodger?'

'Yes . . .' Then something she read struck her. She pulled back. In an instant of revulsion, she put the papers back down.

Myles tried to console her. 'What is it? Are you alright?'

She was, but she seemed shaken. 'This isn't a normal record. Look at the name . . .' Heike-Ann pointed back towards the sheet, drawing Myles' attention to two words near the bottom but refusing to touch them. '. . . Adolf . . . Hitler. This is a summons for him . . .'

Heike-Ann's eyes up gazed up at Myles for a reaction. 'That's why this is so important,' he said. 'This is evidence that the dictator – a man who often boasted about his military record as a young man, a man who forced millions of others to fight – tried to avoid serving in the army himself. It's proof that Hitler was a draft dodger. The Gestapo tried to get hold of these documents in 1938, when Hitler took control of Austria. Looks like they managed it. They must have been given to Stolz for safe keeping.' Then Myles saw another document underneath. 'What does this one say?'

Composing herself, Heike-Ann took a short pause to translate, then started pointing at the page. 'It's another police report, again from 1913. It logs a "Mr Adolf Hitler" as guilty of the minor crime of vagrancy. In Vienna, 1913.' She frowned, not sure what to make of the report.

She was about to reach for the next page when they heard metallic clangs: someone was climbing the iron staircase. She glanced at Myles, wondering whether to hide the papers.

Myles said nothing, but just raised his hand: they would wait silently to see who it was.

More sounds; then they saw a bald scalp come up to their level, and relaxed as they greeted Glenn. 'Have you found it?' he called out.

'Depends what "it" might be,' replied Myles. 'Can you fetch the others?'

Glenn accepted, and went back down to find Zenyalena and Pascal. A few minutes later all five of them were back together, in the most enclosed and isolated part of the building. They all stared down at the box file.

The next paper in the box was a page torn from a book – page number 113 on one side and 114 on the other, with printing in a gothic font. Someone – presumably Stolz – had underlined a few sentences.

Heike-Ann lifted it out, hesitantly. 'So, er, I'll translate …' She started reading. 'It reads, "The longer I lived in that city, the stronger became my hatred for the promiscuous scum of foreign peoples, and the bacillus of human society, the Jews. I hoped I could devote my talents to the service of my country, so I left Vienna in Spring 1912."'

Heike-Ann put the page down, glad to be rid of it. She turned to her team leader. 'Myles, you know what this is from, don't you?'

Myles checked his assumption was right. 'Bestselling book of the 1930s?'

Heike-Ann nodded, but Zenyalena, Glenn and Pascal still needed her to explain. 'It's from *Mein Kampf*,' she revealed. 'Hitler's manifesto and autobiography.'

Pascal still looked confused. 'I thought that book had been banned.'

'You're right,' said Myles. 'But, there are still lots of copies of *Mein Kampf* around. The Nazis printed millions of them. Newlyweds got them as a "wedding present" from the state, which allowed Hitler to skim off millions in royalty payments. But the question is: what's so special about this page?'

Glenn picked up the single sheet, and checked both sides. A normal page from a book, it looked completely ordinary. He tried to see a pattern in the sentences which had been underlined. 'Myles? Can you make sense of it?'

Myles wasn't sure. He turned to Heike-Ann. 'So in *Mein Kampf*, Hitler writes, "I left Vienna in Spring 1912" – but it contradicts the police report.' Then he worked it out. 'It means Hitler lied in *Mein Kampf*, and Stolz had the evidence.'

Glenn was still puzzled. 'But Stolz was a Nazi, right? He loved Hitler. Adored him. So why offer proof that Hitler lied?'

Myles acknowledged the point – something didn't make sense. 'Is there anything else in the box?'

Heike-Ann turned over another sheet of old text. Underneath she saw some much fresher paper. 'This isn't from 1913.'

It wasn't. Printed on bright white paper, probably using a modern computer, was a single line of text. The words were simple:

Zweiter Ort: wo es geschrieben und er fett wurde – minus 32 Meter

Heike-Ann scowled as she translated. 'It says, "Location Two: Where it was written – and he grew fat - minus thirty-two metres". Does that make any sense?'

Myles peered over. 'It must mean "Location Two". It's directions to Stolz's next hiding place …' Then he became confused. '… But Wittgenstein wrote his book all over – in trenches all over the Eastern Front, in a military hospital after an injury, then in a prisoner of war camp in Italy. The *Tractatus* wasn't written in a single place.'

Zenyalena smirked. 'And was Wittgenstein fat?'

'No. In all the photos I've seen, he looks very thin. He was always thin.'

Glenn turned the paper towards him. 'Is that really all it says? Is that it - exactly?'

Heike-Ann was sure. She pointed at the letters. ' Minus 32 Metre' – you see, minus thirty-two metres, or thirty-two metres below. That's what it says. Those are the exact words.'

Pascal tried to be logical. 'So if Wittgenstein wrote only one book, and he wrote it in lots of places …?'

Glenn rattled through some ideas. 'Where he started writing it? Where he finished writing it? Did he always write it in bed, or at a desk – so we look for the desk? But "minus thirty-two metres" … What could it mean?' The American was running dry.

Myles tried a new tack. 'Are we sure Stolz means the *Tractatus*? Could he mean another book?'

Zenyalena was starting to get frustrated. 'Well, what other book could it be? Come on – we'll try to crack that one later. What else is in the folder?'

She leaned over and removed the page about 'Location Two' to reveal an older sheet. It looked like one of Stolz's papers from the lawyer's office – some predictions made during the Second World War. The date confirmed it: 1942. And the title of this one needed no translation.

USA.

Glenn grabbed it quickly. 'Let me see that.' Glenn scanned it, half-hoping he could stop himself if he found something he wanted kept secret. But it was no use. He soon realised he could only understand the dates and numbers. The words were still in German.

USA – 4. Juli 1776, 17.10 Uhr (WEZ-5),
Philadelphia, USA
(39 Grad 57 min. Nord, 75 Grad 10 min. West)

Glenn held the paper where Heike-Ann could see, and invited her to translate.

Heike-Ann's eyes took in the words and tried to summarise. 'It's more predictions. It says, "War undermines US Power in the following months". Then it lists August 1814; April 1968; May 2004; and then also April 2059, September 2059, February 2060 and December 2060 ...'

Myles recognised some of the dates. August 1814 was when the British burned down the White House. In April 1968, America was tied down in Vietnam, and in Iraq in 2004.

Heike-Ann was translating to herself, coming towards the end of the page. '... The conclusion is "The next anniversary in this 83-year cycle comes in the first week of June, 1944. Within this week, the moon cycle suggests the most likely date for a large-scale, seaborne assault on Reich-territory is on the 5th or 6th of June 1944."'

Myles and Glenn shared a glance. They both understood what they had before them. *One of the greatest secrets of the war – the timing of D-Day – had been predicted by Stolz.*

Pascal, Zenyalena and Heike-Ann looked at each other. Like the perfect magician, Stolz had left them amazed.

Glenn held the paper, stunned. 'How did he do it? How did he predict these things?'

Nobody had an answer.

Pascal pointed at the file box. 'Is there anything else in there?'

Glenn pulled back the USA paper. Underneath was a thin set of papers in a cardboard cover. He looked at the title, unable to read the German, then passed it to Heike-Ann for a translation.

Heike-Ann took hold of the file and immediately began nodding. 'This is it. It explains it – how he made his predictions. The title reads "Ein Ratgeber über den Mechanismus für das

Voraussagen der Zukunft" – which means "A practical guide to the mechanism for predicting the future."'

All eyes watched as she began to open the pages.

But it was Myles who sensed something beyond the paper itself. 'Does anybody else smell that?'

Zenyalena and Pascal both sniffed the air. 'Smoke?'

Myles turned around: flames had burst from one of the book racks. The library records were burning fast. He tried frantically to locate a fire hose or spray canister, but there was nothing in sight.

Pascal advanced towards the fire. Covering his fingers in his sleeve, he pulled out one of the burning racks and let it fall onto the floor. Then he tried to stamp out the flames. It worked, but the rest of the bookshelf continued to burn. 'This fire's spreading,' he shouted.

Glenn and Heike-Ann checked the exits. There only seemed to be one escape, which was back down the stairs. Glenn called to the others. 'Come on – it's not safe to stay here.'

Pascal ignored him, still battling the fire, while Zenyalena was trying to protect the documents. She'd gathered all the papers and squashed them back into the box file.

Finally Myles found a fire alarm: a square of glass surrounded by red plastic. He took a book from a nearby shelf and jabbed it in. The glass shattered.

An alarm started ringing, and water started falling down from sprinklers in the roof. But the moment it showered onto the flames Myles realised it wasn't water at all – the liquid caught fire.

Almost instantly, the whole room exploded into a fireball.

CHAPTER 34

St Simon's Monastery,
Israel
11.15 a.m. IST (9.45 a.m. GMT)

Father Samuel allowed his fingers to trace the mosaic embedded in the oldest wall of the monastery. He marvelled at the bright yellow and orange tesserae, crafted by some long-dead artisan, and arranged in the shape of a comet. Heathens on the edge of the artwork all gazed at the heavenly body, their mouths open in fear and foreboding. Only the saintly figure in the middle remained unperturbed by the display above. Father Samuel tracked the saint's halo, which was aligned with the comet's tail … It was a message from the past which he needed to remember now.

Then he let his fingers move down to his belt and gripped his secure receiver hard, making his fingers turned pale. Slowly, he lifted it to type out the next message.

This international investigation must stop.

But as he pressed 'send' he realised it wasn't enough. Not even close.

He typed again.

Their information goes to me, No one else. Confirm this.

Again, he pressed 'send'.

There was no reply from his handheld machine. He couldn't even be sure it was working. Even if it was, he had lost all faith in his accomplice. The man he had hired was adept at technology, and his ruthlessness was useful – sometimes. But he was far too unstable to be trusted, and Samuel now accepted it was a mistake to think he could control the man through money.

Furious, he hurled the device at the mosaic. Metal and plastic parts exploded off the communicator, showering around the chamber and onto the floor. But the mosaic was undamaged, and the hallowed saint remained as beatific as ever, still gazing up at the comet. Then he saw the communicator was intact, too – damaged, but still serviceable.

Father Samuel understood fate was against him, now. He needed something else to preserve the secret. This matter wouldn't be determined by men with guns, secure receivers or spy equipment. It was about something much, much bigger. Huge forces might be unleashed, which meant huge pressures would be needed to contain them.

He fixed his eyes on the mosaic: this was not the first time the heresy had challenged his creed. Christianity had survived before. The same methods might even work now, in these godless times …

Father Samuel realised he needed some very powerful allies. It was time for him to fly back to Europe and establish an unlikely friendship, all for the greater good.

CHAPTER 35

National Library of Austria, Heldenplatz, Vienna

8.50 a.m. CET (7.50 a.m. GMT)

Myles called out over the blaze and the piercing sound of the alarm. 'Someone's put gasoline in the sprinklers.'

The team tried to protect themselves as heat exploded all around them. Glenn shouted to them over the noise. 'All of you: get out – now!'

He directed Heike-Ann to the stairs, then called back to the Russian. 'Zenyalena – come on!' Glenn tugged her by the arm, trying to haul her to safety. But this made her drop the box of papers, which splattered open on the floor. 'We've got to go.'

Zenyalena was drawn back to the documents, but Glenn heaved her down the stairs.

Pascal tried to see Myles through the smoke which was rapidly filling the room. 'Myles?'

No answer.

The Frenchman called again. 'Myles – where are you?'

Myles emerged, and noticed Pascal's jacket was wet with liquid from the sprinklers. Petrol – if he got too near the flames he could catch light. 'Pascal, you need to get down.'

Pascal understood. He moved towards the stairs, with Myles close behind. Quickly they descended back to the lower floor of the Reading Room – Myles hobbling with his limp as fast as he could – where they met up with Glenn, Zenyalena and Heike-Ann.

Glenn immediately started asking questions, shouting above the noise of the fire. 'What happened?'

Heike-Ann shook her head, concerned that everybody was safe and trying to remain calm for the sake of her unborn baby.

But it was Zenyalena who was most shocked. 'The papers. Where are they?' She looked at Pascal, expecting the Frenchman to have brought them down, but he hadn't. Stolz's documents were still upstairs, about to burn.

The team members looked at each other, realising the confusion.

Pascal immediately started taking off his wet jacket. 'We've got to get them.'

Glenn squinted in disbelief. 'You're going back?'

'Someone's got to.'

Glenn, Zenyalena and Heike-Ann stood aghast while the Frenchman started climbing back up the stairs. He bent his forearm to cover his face, coughed, then took in a deep breath.

Only Myles – ignoring his injured knee – was brave enough to follow. 'I'm coming with you,' he shouted.

Pascal turned back with a grateful smile as he reached the top.

The smoke was now much thicker, making it hard to see which way to go. As Myles reached the upper level, he tried to point over to the Frenchman. 'Over there – the papers. They're over there ...'

Pascal was already edging towards them.

Then Myles felt a sudden rush of air. A tall shelf was falling towards him. Instinctively, he tried to dodge it and the shelf crashed down just behind him, but books, files and papers had scattered everywhere, making it even harder to get around. Some started to smoke and burn. Myles realised that the fallen shelf had landed over the stairs, blocking their way down. Their exit was gone.

He tried to see through the smoke, wafting it from his face. 'Pascal – have you got the papers?'

The Frenchman came back with the box file under his arm. 'They're here. But how do we get out?'

Myles and Pascal crouched down, trying to shield themselves from the heat. Pascal kicked at the fallen shelf, but the flames seemed to strike back. Every kick sent a new flare bursting out. 'It's no good,' he yelled.

Myles started looking elsewhere. The combustible liquid was still raining from the sprinkler system, making the flames roar, and the blaze was getting stronger. They didn't have long.

Myles shouted over the noise. 'Pascal – we can't go down. We need another way out.' He retreated back into the room – away from the stairs.

Pascal followed, trying to protect the precious box file. 'Myles, can you see a window?'

Neither of them could. The smoke was too thick

Then, as they reached one of the book-lined walls, Myles looked up to see in the ceiling, a skylight. 'Come on – we can climb out.'

He barged into one of the few shelves which wasn't alight. It tilted more easily than he expected, then crashed sideways, until it hit another and stopped. It was left leaning at an angle. Myles began to use the fallen shelves as rungs on a ladder and scrambled up, dragging his weakened leg as he climbed. At the top, he could reach the skylight. It wasn't locked. He bashed it hard with the side of his fist and forced it open.

Pascal was coming up behind and lifted the boxfile to Myles, who passed it through the hole above them. Then the two men climbed up, and out. They felt the wind, and smoke-free air: they had made it onto the roof.

Standing on Austria's National Library, they could see smoke coming out from below. Already parts of the rooftop were beginning to smoulder from the fire underneath. One section had fallen through. They both knew the rest was probably unstable.

Pascal wiped soot from his face. 'We can't stay up here for long,' he shouted.

'Agreed.'

He and Myles looked around for a way off.

Pascal gazed down. 'We could jump,' he suggested. But as he said it, he already knew they couldn't. It was too far down.

Myles tapped his knee. 'There must be another way.' Desperately he looked around. Then he saw a cable – probably a phone line. It came out of a higher part of the roof and ran over the Heldenplatz, sagging only a little. 'Do you think it'll take our weight?'

'Don't know. We can try.' Pascal suggested, urging Myles to go first.

Myles approached the wire. He grabbed it with both hands, then leaned forward. Gently, he allowed the cable to take his weight. Finally, he lifted up his legs. The cable tensed, but held.

He slid his front hand along, then his trailing hand. Quickly, he was able to progress several metres – high above the hard surface of Heldenplatz.

But as he pulled himself away from the building, the cable started to sag. He felt himself pulling on the metal – the telephone line was stretching.

He called over to Pascal. 'Stay back – don't come on yet.'

Pascal understood, hunkering down as flames started to burn through the roof below him.

Myles kept going – sliding his front hand forward, and following up with his rear.

Then he heard a shout from below. A familiar American voice – it was Glenn. 'Munro: jump ...'

He looked down. Firemen were pumping air into a giant yellow cushion below him.

Myles stayed hanging for a little while longer, waiting for the emergency landing pad to inflate fully.

'It's safe, Myles. Jump!'

Myles let go. He felt himself drop, then land gradually as the inflatable swallowed him up and took his weight. All completely painless - even for his knee.

He looked back up. Still carrying the box file, Pascal took a long run up then launched himself from the building. His legs kept running as he travelled through the air. The Frenchman arced forward, then down, landing just next to Myles. And just like Myles, he landed smoothly in the giant inflatable.

Both men tried to find their bearings again. They were confused, disorientated and covered in black marks from the fire. But they were both safe. And so were the papers.

CHAPTER 36

9.30 a.m. CET (8.30 a.m. GMT)

Myles and Pascal were helped to their feet by Austrian firemen. A paramedic covered them in a reflective blanket and huddled them into an ambulance, where they were checked over for injuries. One of the crew took off the flexi-brace to examine Myles' knee. Pascal's shirt was stripped off, the flammable liquid was wiped from his skin, and a stethoscope placed on his chest. Both of them made sure the boxfile from the library was always in their sight.

A cordon had been set up around the building and police were holding back a growing mass of people. Journalists and tourists were crowding round. With flashing lights everywhere, and emergency vehicles now dousing the flames with hoses from several directions, Myles guessed the historic building would survive. But the fire engines had arrived too late for most of the books and records in the Upper Reading Room.

Pascal wiped sweat and dirt from his face. Still exhausted from his efforts, he tried to speak calmly to Myles. 'How did they do it? It can't be a coincidence. I mean – gasoline in the sprinkler system?'

Both of them were almost too shocked for words. Myles put his hand on Pascal's shoulder. 'Thank you for what you did up there.'

'We saved Stolz's papers. I hope they're worth it.' The Frenchman tapped the box. Myles could see he was tempted to open it.

The paramedics pronounced both of them healthy. The authorities asked for contact details, in case there was any follow up, but Myles simply ignored the request. Instead, he limped slowly back to the cordon, with Pascal closely behind him. There they met up with Glenn and Zenyalena, who had watched the whole of their escape from the library's fire evacuation point – a spot in the middle of Heldenplatz. Heike-Ann reunited Myles with his aluminium crutches.

Zenyalena grinned with glee when she saw Pascal still carried the box file. She was about to take it when Glenn stopped her. 'Wait,' he said, firmly. 'First we need to know what happened.'

Pascal was still recovering from the fire. 'Someone set fire to the place. Deliberately. That's what happened ...' The Frenchman's voice was controlled but tense.

'You don't think Stolz set the trap himself?' asked Myles.

Pascal shook his head. 'He couldn't have ignited it."

'Whoever killed Jean-François – they're following us.'

Myles accepted Pascal's words, then realised the arsonist might still be there. Perhaps in the crowd, or pretending to be one of the journalists on the scene. He had read that some serial killers loved to watch as their crimes were discovered – joining the audience gave them a sense of power. But as he tried to spot anything unusual amongst the people standing around the ONB, nothing seemed to stand out. Apart from a small boy who had pointed to Pascal's sooty face, No one seemed to be watching them. Also, No one had tried to take the boxfile.

Soon, all five of them were scanning the faces of the people in Heldenplatz – studying the firemen, police and library staff just evacuated from the building for anyone suspicious.

Myles wondered about a strange-looking tourist, a large Scandinavian-looking man who didn't seem as interested in the fire as the others. But then the Scandinavian was joined by a woman, probably his wife, and a young girl –he was probably innocent.

It was Zenyalena who offered an alternative explanation. 'We don't know for sure that someone's following us. The fire could have been set off by a device. Either a timer, or something remote controlled.'

Myles accepted she had a point. 'True. But we know someone killed Jean-François. It wasn't suicide.'

The Russian pointed to the boxfile. 'Come on. We need to read through the papers. Now.'

Heike-Ann and Glenn seemed unsure.

Zenyalena's voice became stern. 'Look, we have to be fast. It's the only way to keep ahead of whoever is doing all this.'

Myles and Pascal relented and with little enthusiasm, Heike-Ann and Glenn did too. Pascal handed the boxfile to the Russian, and the five of them retreated to a café where they could read through it.

Finally, away from the smoke of the building, the noise and crowds, the team of five sat down. Pascal hailed a waiter from his seat and ordered water. Myles rested his healing leg. Glenn and Heike-Ann kept their eyes fixed on the boxfile, noticing it was slightly charred from the flames and smoke, but otherwise intact.

With a sense of ceremony, Zenyalena slowly reopened the lid. Seeing the text in German, she passed it over to Heike-Ann for translation.

Heike-Ann understood her responsibility. 'It reads, "Mechanism for predicting the future"', she announced. 'It's a report of some sort.'

Glenn frowned. 'Who's it written for?'

Heike-Ann scanned the paper, her face open. 'Er, it doesn't say …' Then she looked at the core of the text and began translating. '… It says: "The methods we have found most effective come from Ancient Babylon, Egypt and Greece – pioneers who suspected the universe was more connected than people realised. They tested their assumptions, keeping those which held true and discarding the rest. It took many hundreds of years for the true connections to be distilled in this way …"'

Glenn shook his head, distracting everyone. 'So Stolz was doing mumbo-jumbo shit!'

Zenyalena slapped the air, telling him to shut up and allow Heike-Ann to continue.

The German policewoman duly carried on, pointing her finger beneath the words as she read them. 'The Christian Church tried to co-opt this growing body of belief – the three wise men who followed a star were accepted into the Gospels, and festivals like Christmas and Easter were set according to the calendars of the sun and moon. By medieval times, this "science" …' she paused, as if the word science was inappropriate, '… was becoming more accurate and so was outlawed, in 1542, to remove its threat. The ban forced the knowledge underground for more than three centuries. However, the legislation became difficult to enforce when, in 1903 and again in 1914, two different courts in New York State accepted predictions based on the planets were both scientific and very accurate …'

Glenn looked at Myles, who didn't know what to make of it all.

Heike-Ann carried on, absorbed by what she was reading. '… In 1936, a US court decided to allow newspapers to make predictions as long as they divided people into just twelve groups. That is how the USA and other western countries came to adopt the least accurate form of astrology and scientific astrology was lost.'

Zenyalena interrupted. 'So an American court allowed horoscopes just because they couldn't be true, while accurate predictions stayed illegal?'

Heike-Ann nodded, continuing with the translation. 'This gives the Third Reich a golden chance to perfect the ancient science, unrivalled by the West.' She turned the page. 'We collected details about the planets and information about human affairs, then looked for a link. One of the first patterns we found concerned Pluto: whenever Pluto progressed into a new sign of the zodiac, it brought a new system for administering sovereign states and their money. Each new system was linked to the symbolism of the zodiac sign it entered. By knowing what had happened for the times Pluto changed zodiac sign up until 1939, we have predicted what will happen in the future:'

She took a table from the file, probably typed during the war. The team stared at it. Myles recognised it from somewhere: he'd seen this before ... It listed the dates when borders were set throughout Africa, when the US Federal Reserve was established, and for the 1939 Pact of Steel. Then it predicted the start of the European Union, the World Trade Organisation and the Credit Crunch, all with the exact month, perfectly precise.

Then he remembered – this was the page he'd been reading in Stolz's flat before being knocked out by the carbon monoxide.

Heike-Ann could see the team were silenced by her information. She carried on reading from Stolz. 'We then looked for patterns between the planets. The orbits of Saturn and Neptune mean they align every thirty-six years. These times coincide with subversive revolutionary activity: the Boston Tea Party in 1773; South American revolutions in 1809; European Communist Committees set up in 1846; Marxist political parties in 1882; and the communist revolution in Russia in 1917. They will come together again in 1953 when we expect major "rebalancing" in the Soviet world, and three times in 1989 (March, June and November) – the last of these dates, in the second week of November 1989, coincides with other planetary events, making it particularly notable.'

Myles remembered Helen reading these dates on the museum's stolen papers. And he could see Heike-Ann knew all about the Berlin Wall. After the first hammer cracks on the evening of 9th November, the wall was taken apart with vigour on the 10th, 11th and 12th, and by the middle of that month it was history: destroyed in the second week of November 1989, just as Stolz predicted. The collapse of the Berlin Wall was probably the most important political event in Heike-Ann's life, and in the life of most Europeans alive. And yet it had been foreseen with such accuracy, all those years ago by Stolz.

Heike-Ann looked sullen. 'I studied science at university. This should not be possible.'

'Too damn right,' scoffed Glenn. '"Hogwash" is the word you're looking for.'

But Zenyalena encouraged their translator to keep working. 'Well, I studied literature. Old classics – Shakespeare, Chaucer – they're full of this stuff.'

Heike-Ann raised her eyebrows – Zenyalena seemed to be an expert in a bizarre field. The translator's eyes turned back down to the page and she continued to read out loud.

'"We soon found other planetary cycles were linked to different human affairs. The forty-two-year cycle between Uranus and Saturn correlated with scientific discoveries and inventions. The much longer cycle between Uranus and Neptune was linked to mass communication – and we expect humans to exchange information differently after these two planets come together in the early 1990s."'

Zenyalena interrupted. 'The internet?'

'That's just a coincidence,' scoffed Glenn.

Heike-Ann ignored them both and carried on with the text. '"We found that since all the cycles between the planets seemed to affect people, when they were added together, it gave us a measure for stability in human affairs. Instability led to war and death. We checked three centuries of warfare, and found there were sixty-one times more war deaths when the planets, Jupiter-to-Pluto, were closing in than when then they were separating. This correlation was so unlikely to have occurred by pure chance – about one in a million-billion – that even sceptics accepted we had found the link. By charting the planets, we could forecast how many people would die in future conflicts."'

Myles remembered Stolz's graph with the two lines. So that's how he did it: the angle between each pair of planets, all added together, allowed him to predict the number of war deaths. *And all with astonishing accuracy.*

Heike-Ann lifted the police reports on Hitler out of the boxfile and put them to one side. Somehow the official documents proving the dictator was a draft dodger had become unimportant. The pages from Stolz which predicted the future so accurately were what mattered now.

'Come on, Heike-Ann,' said Pascal, trying to steady her. 'We don't know how much to believe it, not yet. There must be more.'

Heike-Ann looked in the file. There were just two pages left, paper-clipped together. She lifted them out. 'There's this,' she said. 'It's called "Nuclear".'

Pascal urged her to read it.

Heike-Ann took a deep breath, then began translating again. '"We learned the date of the first nuclear reaction in December 1942, and saw the date was marked by planets opposing each other in the sky on an axis of nine degrees Gemini to ten degrees Sagittarius. We found this position in the sky was linked to nuclear events in the past, such as the discovery of uranium in 1789, of radioactivity in 1896, and the cluster of advances made in 1932, including the discovery of the neutron. Then we calculated when planets would strike this axis again, adding the traditional meaning of each planet to make our predictions."'

Heike-Ann had reached the second page, which was a table. It contained a list of twelve dates, the earliest being 1945 and the last 2052.

Myles found himself recognising the dates; even though he couldn't read the German, he knew what had happened on each occasion which had already occurred. 'That's how he did it,' he said Myles. 'The dates all match up.'

Zenyalena was nodding. 'Chernobyl, Three Mile Island, Fukishima – even the Cuban missile crisis,' she added. 'It all ties in.'

Pascal checked the box for any secret compartments. There were none. 'So there are no more papers? That's all?'

Heike-Ann looked again, confirming Pascal was right.

Zenyalena seemed to concentrate, then kicked her head back, staring at Heike-Ann. 'Location Two. What was the clue, again?'

Heike-Ann was still too stunned to speak. Myles answered for her. '"Location Two: Where it was written, and he grew fat, minus thirty-two metres".'

No one seemed to have an answer. Myles tried to solve it for them. '"It" – if we can work out what "it" is, we'll get the answer.'

Glenn flicked through the rest of the papers again – the police reports on Hitler, the page from *Mein Kampf*, and Stolz's history of the science of prediction. 'Could it be something here?' he wondered. 'Where '"it" was written – could Stolz mean where he wrote this stuff?'

Then Myles got it. He smiled, scratching his head to wonder why he hadn't got it sooner. He took the papers from Glenn, then spread them out in front of them. 'This is the order we found the papers in the boxfile, yes?'

The others agreed. Then Myles began pointing to the documents in turn:

Police reports on Hitler
The page from *Mein Kampf*
The clue about Location Two
Stolz's history of the science of prediction

'So the page immediately before this paper about "Location Two" was the one torn from *Mein Kampf.* Right?'

Glenn started to show he understood. 'So the clue, "Where it was written" means where *Mein Kampf* was written? So, Myles, where did Hitler write *Mein Kampf*?'

'Near Munich, southern Germany, when he was in prison in 1924,' said Myles. 'Location Two must be thirty-two metres from Hitler's jail cell.'

Zenyalena stood up. 'So, we go to Munich.'

'OK,' said Pascal, 'but we need to be much more professional. Whoever is doing this – starting the fire, killing Jean-François – we've made it easy for them. If just a single one of us is reporting back to our national capitals, it's easy to see how someone could be on our trail.'

He stopped, realising from the reactions around the table that he had said something significant. 'What did I say? *Is* someone reporting back to their capital?'

Silence. After a few moments Glenn held up his hand, as if pleading in court, and said, 'Fifth Amendment.'

Pascal's face relaxed. 'OK - no more phone calls from now on, and all phones turned off.'

Glenn nodded. '… And we better take the SIM chips from our phones too – just to make sure they're not tracked.'

The whole table understood: some mobile phones could be tracked even when they were switched off.

As the four team members started to take out their mobiles and extract the chips, it was Heike-Ann who was left to order a taxi.

Within minutes a Viennese cab adorned in the latest advertisements had appeared. The team knocked back their drinks and climbed aboard for the four-and-a-half hour drive to Landsberg prison.

They were glad to have survived Vienna, but also aware even greater dangers lay ahead.

CHAPTER 37

To Landsberg, near Munich
Southern Germany
4 p.m. CET (3 p.m. GMT)

The taxi soon found its way to the autobahn – the high-speed motorway link between the historic cities of Vienna and Munich, laid down during Hitler's heyday. Famously, there were no speed limits on these roads – it was one of the few areas of public life the dictator had not tried to control. Contemporary newsreels about them portrayed Hitler as the master of new technology, which the *Autobahnen* were at the time. Myles and the team were travelling along an avenue of Nazi propaganda.

But just as the Nazis had tried to lead the new 'science' of fast roads, they had also been busy trying to forecast the future. To control the future. Myles realised: Stolz's work gave the Nazis a bizarre authority over people's lives. Like shamen and witchdoctors, if the Nazis had been able to predict what was to happen, it would make them enormously powerful.

Myles imagined how Hitler's regime would have used their knowledge. They would have built a bureaucracy around it – perhaps a 'Ministry of the Future'. He pictured a little man with an artificial expression on his face, welcoming him into an office. Myles would sit down to be told what he was going to do. He might complain, but he would have no choice, because Stolz's science of prediction had squeezed choice out of people's lives. Myles would be interviewed, interrogated, forced to sign …

The image vanished as Myles was jolted awake. He looked up. The taxi was slowing down, as it came to their destination. They had arrived.

Myles recognised the building immediately. It wasn't like a normal prison. Instead of the usual grey concrete, the facade was Art Nouveau, from 1910. Inside, the four main cell blocks formed a cross, allowing a single guard in the centre to keep track of all the inmates. And the most celebrated 'inmate' of all was Adolf Hitler.

Myles remembered how the judge in Hitler's trial had been sympathetic to the Nazi firebrand. The prisoner was let out after just 264 days, despite a charge of treason for trying to overthrow Germany's democratic government. The future dictator would go on to sentence many Germans to much worse punishments for much smaller offences.

Myles recognised the building from one of the most haunting photographs of the Hitler story. It showed Hitler standing outside the prison the day he left, at the end of 1924. Even though the man had put on weight – just as in Stolz's clue – Hitler's eyes were still determined, and yet somehow dead looking, too.

Glenn was also staring up at the green copper turrets and latticed windows as if it was familiar, a wry expression on his face. 'So this is where we put 'em, huh?' said the American, half admiring, half gloating.

Myles realised the American had heard of the building from a slightly later time in history. 'Yes, Glenn. In 1945 it became known as "War Criminal Prison Number One". All the top Nazis who'd been caught were locked up here until the Nuremberg trials.'

Zenyalena and Heike-Ann also gazed at the building. Like Myles and Glenn, they reacted with a mixture of awe and disdain.

This was where Mein Kampf *was written: a place so historic, and yet so evil, too.*

Pascal was last out of the taxi. He looked up like the others, then asked a more practical question. 'So, do you think they'll let us in?'

He turned to Heike-Ann, who understood the cue. She stepped forward, and walked towards the reception area. Her eyes met an official – an older man with heavy glasses sitting behind a transparent partition. The official seemed intrigued by the pregnant lady and the foreigners accompanying her as Heike-Ann politely introduced herself. 'Heike-Ann Hassenbacker.'

The official silently raised his eyebrows, as if to ask, 'and what do you want?'

Heike-Ann pulled out a folding license holder and showed the man her police identification card. The man asked for it to be handed to him under the glass. Heike-Ann passed it through. Only after he had inspected it for several seconds did the official concede it was genuine. '*Wie kann ich Ihnen helfen?*' he asked in a gruff voice.

Heike-Ann paused before she responded. 'Do you speak English? I would like to talk to you in English please – so these four people can understand me.'

The official scowled at Zenyalena, Pascal, Glenn and Myles. 'Alright, then. We can speak English.'

'Thank you,' said Heike-Ann. 'This is the prison where *Mein Kampf* was written?'

The official's face reacted immediately. He'd seen Hitler tourists before. Several of them came by the prison every month. Some to mock, some to wonder, a disturbing few to worship. Widespread fascination with Hitler, and the huge efforts to wipe away everything which could be a shrine to Nazism, meant this was one of the small number of places which still had a clear link to the dead mass murderer. 'It is,' conceded the official.

'Do you have a record of visitors to the prison?' Heike-Ann eyed the man's computer. 'Can you tell me when a man called Werner Stolz visited?'

The official turned to his keyboard and typed in the surname. A list appeared on the screen.

K. Stolz – August 15.
M. Stolz – August 15.
O. Stolz – March 5.
I. Stolz – February 1.

He scrolled down the list, starting to shake his head before he reached the end. 'No. No "Werner Stolz" came here.'

Heike-Ann halted, puzzled.

Zenyalena pushed her way to the window. 'How far back do your records go?'

'On the computer, back to 1989.'

Myles could tell Zenyalena was thinking of asking the man to go back before then, through the paper records. But the official was anticipating the request, and his face already told them the answer: if they asked, he would say no.

Myles started to think aloud, knowing there must be another way around the problem. 'We don't need to go back before 1989. We know Stolz hid the papers recently, in the last few weeks – since the break-ins at his flat.'

Heike-Ann started to look confused. 'So he didn't come here?'

Myles shook his head. 'He didn't enter the prison as a visitor, no. But that doesn't mean he wasn't here …' Myles turned to the official. 'Do you have a … a basement, or underground section or a cellar?'

'Just a store room.'

'How far down is it?'

The official shrugged. 'One floor. A few meters down, maybe.'

'Could someone have tunnelled down from there?'

The official shook his head. 'No way. This is a prison. When it was built they made sure No one could tunnel out.' The uniformed man checked the faces of the people in front of him, confirming to himself that Myles and Heike-Ann were genuine. Then he opened a drawer, pulled out a sheet of paper, and unfolded it to his visitors. 'This is a map of the prison.'

Myles and the team stared at the simplified blueprint. It was obvious that several details had been missed off so the illustration couldn't be used to help prisoners escape.

The official pointed to a large rectangle around the main buildings. 'This line here shows the borders of a plinth,' he said. 'Before they started building the prison, they laid down foundations. The prison stands on a layer of concrete twelve meters thick. No one could tunnel under here.'

Disappointment washed over the whole team. They must have misunderstood Stolz's clue.

Where it was written – and he grew fat – minus 32 metres

Stolz couldn't have buried something thirty meters below where *Mein Kampf* was written.

Glenn started shaking his head. 'Looks like Stolz has been yanking our tails.' The American didn't need to say they should give up. His tone made that obvious.

Zenyalena was frustrated. She tried to peer at the map in more detail, as though if she looked hard enough she might find something.

Pascal leaned back. 'Don't forget, Stolz was more than a hundred years of age, and frail,' he suggested. 'Even if the old man could slip into the prison unnoticed somehow, there was no way he could dig through twelve meters of concrete. He'd need help, and they'd make a huge amount of noise.' Pascal was shrugging. Like Glenn, he seemed ready to stop the search.

Heike-Ann was waiting for orders from the team. Only Zenyalena seemed intent on breaking the code. But, like the others, she could see no way it could be true.

Then Myles realised. He clutched the paper, and turned it over, checking it was blank on the other side. He pointed to the rectangle of concrete. 'What's outside here?'

The official looked confused by the question and simply pointed around. 'Streets. It's the outside of the prison.'

'Yes, but what's below it?'

The man shrugged again.

It was the answer Myles had expected. He turned to the team. 'Looks to me like Stolz found the perfect hiding place. Nobody's going to start digging thirty-two meters below a prison – because the prison authorities won't let them.'

Glenn's face still looked bemused. 'So how did he dig?'

'He didn't,' answered Myles. 'Remember – as Pascal said, he was an old man. He just climbed down. Down, then across. There must be some other entrance to a place thirty-two meters below the prison. And that entrance must lie outside the prison perimeter.'

Pascal started to come alive at the idea. 'You mean, a secret trap door?'

'Something like that. It would cover steps leading down to under the prison. And that's what we have to find.'

The team started to spread out, moving away from the bemused official and into the well-tended gardens between the prison and the main road.

Pascal was the first to see something promising. 'This could be it ...' he declared, peering down at a plate on the ground.

The team came over, with Myles vaulting on his crutches behind them, and Heike-Ann walking at a more deliberate pace than the others.

Pascal had found a folding metal cover surrounded by weeds and long-grass. It was half-hidden, and sited in a triangle of turf behind a bus-stop. The plate looked old – slightly rusted, and covered in a pattern of small squares which Myles had seen before on the floor of German tanks from World War II. It was fixed in place with a modern padlock. Pascal gripped the shiny lock, sizing it up. 'It's heavy, but we can probably break it open.'

Zenyalena found a nearby drain cover. She lifted out the thick grill with both hands – it was obviously a strain - then hauled it over to Pascal. 'Will this do?'

Pascal raised his eyebrows – he didn't know, but he'd try. Swinging the drain cover, he tried to knock the padlock off.

Clunk.

Nothing.

He tried again. This time the lock sprang open. He tossed the drain cover away, allowing it to clatter on the ground, then peeled off the broken padlock and heaved up the rusted cover to the manhole.

The whole team peered down, staring into a deep, black hole.

Myles pulled a small coin from his pocket and tossed it down. It took more than two seconds of silence before a few faint 'tings' echoed back up, as though the coin was bouncing around the inside of a giant slot machine. 'Well, it's deep. And there's probably a solid floor down there.'

Pascal knelt on the ground and poked his head into the darkness. The team waited while his eyes adjusted to the light. Then the Frenchman re-appeared, a new expression on his face. 'There's a ladder, leading down,' he said, excitedly.

Zenyalena pushed herself towards the hole. 'Can I go first?'

No one answered. They all knew the Russian would go forward anyway.

Pascal helped Zenyalena swing her legs into the space where the metal cover had been and pointed towards the ladder. She looked pleased as her feet found the rungs, then began climbing down, into the darkness.

After several seconds, the team heard her voice call back. It sounded as though she was inside a cavern. 'It's definitely very deep…'

Glenn prepared to climb down after her, but Myles stopped him. 'Wait, Glenn, it's an old ladder. Wait until she's at the bottom.'

Glenn accepted the Englishman's advice. The four waiting above ground lingered, looking at each other nervously.

Finally Zenyalena emerged again, breathing heavily from the climb, but exhilarated. 'It's a vertical tunnel – probably about thirty metres deep,' she said, 'although I didn't go all the way down.'

'Can you see down there?'

Zenyalena nodded, still catching her breath. 'Yes – as long as you let your eyes adjust. It takes a few seconds.'

Glenn fished out his key chain, and the small flashlight attached to it. He pressed a button, and the light turned on. 'And what's down there?'

The Russian smiled. 'You'll have to see for yourselves.' And she disappeared again.

Glenn took the cue, and approached the edge of the hole. He peered into the darkness, waiting until Zenyalena had stepped off the ladder at the bottom, then followed her down. Heike-Ann did the same, determined to prove that, even though she was pregnant, she could still cope with adventure. Myles followed – his ruptured knee ligament making him the slowest to descend. Pascal was the last of the five to step onto the ladder, and begin the long climb down.

CHAPTER 38

7.36 p.m. CET (6.36 p.m. GMT)

Dieter watched, calm and still. Hidden from view, he watched as one by one, the international team stepped into the hole. *Down they go …*

He waited, enjoying the moment. Just being so close to them gave him an adolescent thrill. He even felt the urge to giggle, but managed to supress it. *They were all so dumb …*

Instead, he just kept watching, listening as the last footsteps clanged down the metal rungs.

He didn't know what the motley international team would find down there, but he knew it would make things much easier for him. After all, they'd got him the stuff from Vienna. Useful stuff. Papers he wouldn't have found on his own.

Information which confirmed he was close to Stolz's secret.

He lifted out his smartphone. With a smirk, he replied to Father Samuel.

Confirmed: the information goes to you, and only you.

Then he switched to his own webpage, and began to type.

In the year 2059 and 2060 I will cripple the USA through war. This war will be the climax of my other attacks, which I am just about to begin.

He checked the message – was 2059 too far away to be scary? Maybe, but the date was accurate. Stolz's predictions were always precise.

Briefly, he wondered whether Father Samuel might stumble across the page, and realise what he was doing. But it was unlikely. And so what if he did? Samuel's money mattered less now. Dieter had seen a much greater prize.

He pressed 'send', knowing the obstacle course of fake IP addresses, proxy sites and multiple web chains made his submission completely untraceable. Not even the CIA would be able to track him down.

It meant he could attack without being attacked himself. Just like Hitler in the early days …

Dieter also knew he had developed the perfect form of warfare – his strikes were invisible because they were never really made. He was just claiming credit for the inevitable, and letting people assume he commanded a great force.

He leaned his head over the manhole. Near the bottom of the ladder was the last of the international team, just going down the final rungs.

No time to do anything as clever as put gasoline in the sprinkler system now. That had been a masterpiece.

He needed something quicker – much quicker.

Casually, he bent down, and inspected the old Nazi ladder. A few metres below the surface, there was a join where two parts of the metal were held together by just four rusted steel bolts. Weak bolts. And with just a single kick, he was able to knock two of the bolts away.

He checked down below. None of the team had noticed the loose bolts clanging onto the concrete floor.

Then Dieter grinned: the team may have been able to descend into the cavern. But they would never climb out …

CHAPTER 39

Underneath Landsberg Prison
Near Munich, Southern Germany
7.38 p.m. CET (6.38 p.m. GMT)

The descent was through what seemed to be a wide chimney, lined on all four sides with brick, until it opened out into a much wider space near the bottom. Myles sensed a musty smell in the air – the space had probably been sealed for many years.

About halfway down he saw a flashlight switch on below him. 'Watch out for the junk,' Glenn called out, shining a small light at the bottom of the ladder. Directly below Myles was a decayed mattress, and part of an old vehicle chassis. Both must have been thrown down – or fallen into the space – several decades ago. 'Stay to the left, Myles, and you can get round them,' directed the American.

Myles took the cue from Glenn and lifted his immobile leg around the obstacles. He was soon standing on a firm concrete surface.

Glenn swung the light around, gradually tracing the edge of the floor. The wall was mostly intact, with only some water damage where it met the flat concrete they were standing on. Then something shone back – two small circles, glowing in the dark. Glenn fixed the beam at them, pointing it straight in their direction, The reflections froze in place. Then a squeak, and a rodent scampered into the darkness.

'Rats!' exclaimed Zenyalena. She shivered. 'I'm cold. Glenn – give me the torch…' Glenn didn't respond immediately, but kept pointing the beam around. It was several seconds before he offered to hand it over.

Zenyalena tugged it out of his hands. '… Thank you.' She stepped out, away from the ladder, and pointed the small flashlight upwards. Although the beam wasn't really powerful enough, it was clear that they were in a huge cavern. She shone the light at joints in the concrete slabs which formed the ceiling several metres above them. 'Man-made. Probably by the Nazis.'

Glenn disagreed. 'We know the prison was built *before* the Nazis came to power.'

'Yes, Glenn, but the Nazis converted this place into … into …' Zenyalena didn't know what they had converted it into.

Myles called over to her. 'There's probably a lighting system. See if you can find a bulb somewhere.'

Zenyalena swung the beam above them until she found a very old lightbulb, probably manufactured during the war, judging by the design – dangling from a cable. Then she traced the cable back with the flashlight. It ran down the wall, into a metal box near the floor.

Pascal walked over to the metal switching box, with Zenyalena – and her torch – close behind. For a few moments Pascal peered inside, and swapped some fuses around, muttering in frustration. 'The fuses have blown – maybe all of them,' he complained.

'Do you think the Nazis vandalised it before they left?'

'No, just abandoned ...' Pascal pressed something and looked up, optimistic. For a moment the lights blinked on, then they went out again. '… And this thing's rusted. Stolz couldn't have used it recently.' Angry, Pascal kicked the metal. There was crackle and some sparks, and finally the lights hummed on again – permanently this time.

The whole, huge cavern was illuminated around them. The team stared at it, eyes wide with awe and bewilderment.

There was desk in the middle of the room, next to a table covered in papers. Boxes were piled in a far corner. Maps lined the walls, many titles printed in Gothic typeface, and embossed with swastikas in the corner. Some had lines and other markings drawn on them.

Myles peered back up. He could see the ceiling clearly now. It was the underside of the concrete plinth beneath the prison. Oddly, bolted onto it were several small upside-down railway tracks – nine concentric circles - and from each one hung a wire with a globe attached.

He remembered the clue: 'Where it was written – and he grew fat - minus 32 metres.'

Myles got his bearings and tried to work out exactly where in the vast underground space would be exactly below Hitler's cell. 'It's somewhere in the middle of this space.' He limped towards the table in the centre of the cavern. On top of it, half buried in papers, was a book. Myles picked it up and read the cover.

Ephemeris

Strange. 'Anyone know what an "ephemeris" is?' he called out, the words echoing from the concrete walls.

He was greeted by blank faces, as Glenn, Heike-Ann, Zenyalena and Pascal drew near.

Myles began flicking through. It was a book of timetables, just like the one he'd found in Stolz's East Berlin apartment just before he'd been gassed with carbon monoxide. With a different month on each page, there were several columns with a different symbol at the top of each.

Zenyalena pointed at the page. 'Look – the crescent symbol. That must mean the moon …'

Then Glenn noticed the last column was topped with the letters PL. 'And this must be Pluto …'

Myles understood: it was a timetable for the planets. He checked the first page and the last.

On the first page: January 1st 1900 – and on the last: December 31st 2099.

Someone had calculated the position of the planets on every day for the whole of two centuries.

Then an idea came to him. He turned to the middle of the book, then back a few pages to 1989 – November. He ran his finger down the column next to Pluto, and the column three away from it. 'We can test Stolz: Saturn and Neptune …' As Myles looked down the columns, he realised it confirmed what Stolz had written: Saturn and Neptune appeared together in the sky exactly when the Berlin Wall came down, both at ten-and-a-third degrees of longitude. The ephemeris was precise to the day.

Quickly Myles turned to 1917, to see where Saturn and Neptune were during the Russian Revolution. The planets crossed – both at four degrees this time – in exactly the month that Czar Nicholas and his royal family were kicked out by the masses. He was about to check on Stalin's death thirty-six years later, but he was distracted.

It was Zenyalena, calling out from a corner of the cavern. 'I think it's a control panel.' She had found a corroded metal desk, and was pointing to the dials and lettering. 'I'm freezing – does this control the heat, do you think?'

Myles directed Heike-Ann towards the device. 'Can you make sense of it?'

Heike-Ann went to join Zenyalena and nervously reached out at the dial. 'I think it's … it's some sort of calculating machine …' Heike-Ann slowly turned the knob, experimenting as numbers rotated behind a glass display. '… Not a number calculating machine. This is a calendar.' She pointed to the dials. Each was inscribed with a single word. 'Look – this means "Uranus, Jupiter, Neptune …" It's a calendar for calculating the position of the planets.'

Zenyalena tried turning one of the dials. There was a clunk from the ceiling as something lurched along the rail. The globe beneath it followed, swinging slightly as it juddered into a new position. Zenyalena's jaw dropped. 'Amazing. The Nazis must have used it to work out where the planets were.' She turned the dial again, causing another clunk on the rail above. A different hanging ball shifted this time.

Myles shook his head, still not understanding. 'But why? The ephemeris told them where the planets were. So, how did this help them? It just shows them what they already knew.' He pointed again at the control panel. 'There must be something we're missing. Some other button or … something.'

Heike-Ann started checking out the desk for any other buttons or switches; something they hadn't found yet. She looked all around the sides, then at the bottom of the desk. Suddenly she reacted to something. She bent down and flicked a switch. The globes lit up, projecting light onto one of the spheres near the centre.

Zenyalena ran over to it, marvelling upwards at a spectacle of 1940s engineering. 'Look – this one's the Earth,' she shouted, excited. 'It's got the continents painted on it. And there are dots for major cities.'

Glenn squinted up. 'It's kind of an odd way to light up the Earth, wouldn't you say?'

But it was Pascal who realised more. 'The lights from the planets: they cast a shadow. It allowed the Nazis to calculate where each planet would rise in the sky, and where it would set. See this: the red light …' Pascal was pointing to the red sphere next to the 'Earth' globe. '… It must be Mars. The light from it hits half of the Earth – the other half is in shadow.'

Realising Zenyalena was still baffled, the Frenchman tried to explain. 'There's a line all around Earth where the light becomes shadow,' he said, turning his finger in a circle. 'The line joins all the places where Mars would appear on the horizon – either rising or setting. This model allowed them to calculate the places where the planet would be on the horizon, as viewed from Earth.'

Myles, Zenyalena, and Heike-Ann gazed up, wondering at the bizarre, antiquated invention slowly revolving above them. Then Glenn called out from the back of the cavern. While the others had been distracted by the metal control desk and the hanging spheres, the American had been rummaging through the papers on the tables behind them. 'Hey, you guys,' he called. He was holding up some large maps of the world. Heavy curved lines had been drawn on them. 'Could these be Nazi satellite tracks?'

'Not for man-made satellites,' Myles called back, 'Because the Nazis didn't have them ...' Then he got it. '... But if you put these lines on a globe they'd divide it into two halves. Each line must show all the places on Earth where a planet was on the horizon.'

The team understood. But they were no wiser – why had the Nazis done it? And why build such a huge facility to make the calculations?

Glenn noticed one of the maps had been copied several times. First he saw the birth date and time.

18.30 Uhr, 20 April 1889, 48.15 N, 13.04 E,
(Branau am Inn, Österreich).

Then, underneath, in gothic script, two words which provoked both disgust and fascination.

Adolf Hitler

Zenyalena lifted it out, and held it flat with Glenn's help. Heike-Ann, Pascal and Myles crowded around.

It showed several lines flowing like satellite tracks over a map of the world, each labelled with the name of a planet, written in German: Mars, Jupiter, Saturn, Uranus …

Heike-Ann pointed to places which had been circled. 'Look: important places in Hitler's life: Stalingrad in Russia, the Western Front in France, Warsaw …'

But Zenyalena saw them differently. 'They're also places with lines going through them. That line shows almost exactly how Hitler divided Poland with Stalin, and look at Hawaii – when the Japanese attacked Pearl Harbour it undermined his authority.' The she noticed another line, which cut through the Ardennes and ran up into Norway. 'And look: this is where Hitler did his Blitzkrieg – his "lightning war" which surprised the Western Allies – twice, when he attacked there in 1940 and again, in 1944.'

Glenn was cynical. 'You mean where he lost the Battle of the Bulge?'

But Zenyalena refused to concede. 'Don't you see?' She thrust her face towards Glenn to make her point. 'His 1944 offensive was almost brilliant. If he hadn't squandered his army in the East, it would have broken through. It was a real shock.'

Myles acknowledged the point. 'She's right, Glenn. Those places in France and Belgium were important to Hitler. It's also where Hitler won his reputation in the First World War.'

Zenyalena was already pointing at another line. 'And again: look, Mercury. You must have studied Greek mythology at school, didn't you? Remember: Mercury was the "winged messenger" of the Gods. And when Hitler was born, Mercury was on the horizon in a line running up through Munich, Nuremberg and Berlin – the places where he made his greatest speeches, and where propaganda gave him power.' Her finger darted to yet another line. 'And another – Mars, planet of war: it was just setting, just going below the horizon, over both Stalingrad and

El Alamein – the two most important places where the "God of War" abandoned him.'

'Oh come on,' huffed Glenn, letting go of the paper. 'This is getting ridiculous. You can't say Hitler lost at Stalingrad because at the moment he was born in 1889, fifty years before the battle, the planet Mars happened to be setting over the city.'

'Look at the facts, Glenn: this Mars tracks the limits of Nazi military forces …' Zenyalena's voice was quiet as she spoke in awe. '… And it's amazingly accurate.'

'So you're saying if Hitler had been born an hour later,' – Glenn could barely bring himself to say it, it sounded so ludicrous – 'his armies would have been stopped hundreds of miles further west?'

Zenyalena didn't answer. Instead, she began sifting through the rest of the papers on the desk. She pulled out three more maps and read the titles. 'We have, er … 7· October 1900; 15.30 Uhr, 48.08 Nord, 11.34 Ost (München). Who's that?'

Heike-Ann looked at the gothic script in the bottom corner of the sheet. 'Himmler. The man who set up Hitler's killing factories.' She pointed to a place which had been circled in South-East Poland. 'Look, they've circled Auschwitz.' Auschwitz was on the intersection of two lines labelled 'Uranus' and 'Jupiter'.

Zenyalena answered without looking up. 'According to the legends and literature I've read, Uranus is associated with brutal surprises, and Jupiter just exaggerates everything – which sums up Auschwitz.'

Myles noticed another line, running through western Germany. 'And that's Mars, setting on the horizon where Himmler surrendered to the Allies in 1945,' he said, looking up at the others. 'There was an old prophecy that he'd betray Hitler, and he did. With this map the Führer knew exactly where.'

Zenyalena had already picked up the next chart. 'This one is 30th November 1874, 01.30 (51:52 North, 01:21 West Oxfordshire,

England). Winston Churchill ...' She was taking in the map and the places which had been circled. '... So Churchill had Mars rising in Italy – where he tried to get the Allies to launch the second front. Uranus directly over Moscow – he sent shock troops to attack the Soviet Union in 1919, and Mars setting over Washington DC.'

Glenn chuckled slightly. 'Churchill surrendered to the Yanks, huh?'

'Yes, Glenn, in a way he did,' admitted Myles. 'When he was in charge, the British Empire gave way to American leadership in the world.'

Heike-Ann had the last chart. 'Here's Emperor Hirohito, of Japan. 29th April 1901, 22.00, Tokyo, 35 degrees 2 minutes North; 139 degrees 46 East. He has Uranus directly over Hawaii, and on the horizon where they did their Far East attacks, along with Mars, Jupiter and Saturn.' Then she looked slightly confused. 'And, Neptune is directly over Moscow. What does that mean?'

'Confusion and illusion,' explained Zenyalena. 'Neptune is the God of the Sea – you can never see what's underneath. It means Hirohito was successfully deceived by Moscow.' She said it with patriotic pride. 'If Japan had attacked the Soviet Union in 1941, we would have been forced to fight on two fronts and lost. But Stalin fooled the Japanese. Germany was forced to fight on two fronts, instead.'

Pascal eagerly started looking around. 'There must be more than just Hitler, Himmler, Churchill, and Hirohito. Let's look: they can't have built all this for just four people.'

They all searched for more maps. Lifting up papers, Heike-Ann asked if there could be a chart on the Soviet leader. But Zenyalena, double-checking all the Hitler maps, explained that Stalin was born a peasant, and nobody was ever sure of his real birthday. Pascal checked under the desk, Glenn went to the other tables and Myles began looking along the edges of the room.

Myles came across a wooden crate. There was some old German writing on it, and an industrial serial number of some sort, with a large letter 'K' – aged, as though it was from the war. Myles wiped off a layer of dust. He lifted up one side, surprised by how heavy it was, and as he tilted it, a gentle rolling sound came from within. Myles peered through a crack in the wood to see metallic lumps inside. Then he realised it didn't contain maps, but grenades. Very gently, he replaced the crate on the ground, aware just how close he had been to setting them off.

'Guys, be careful when you're looking. If there are any more old explosives here, they could be volatile,' he warned. 'One touch and … the five second fuses will probably have gone already.'

Glenn answered with a call from the other side of the cavern. 'Hey. When did the Nazis invent highlighter pens?' The American was holding another of the Hitler maps, printed with lines just like the others. But this one had been scribbled on – in fluorescent orange. He summoned Heike-Ann over to translate.

Heike-Ann looked at the bright ink. 'It says, "Location Three: 500 metres south of the railway carriage, close to where he …"' Heike-Ann hesitated, as though the translation had become difficult. Her face turned up, half in apology. 'The words – in German it means literally "swapped his vision". I don't know the English. "Where he swapped his vision, but didn't serve".'

Myles and Glenn looked at each other, unsure of the meaning. Then Heike-Ann turned the map over. A single word was scrawled on the back in the same deliberate handwriting they'd seen in the Vienna library.

Stolz.

She showed it to the international team, who all understood. It was Stolz's third clue. But where was the dead Nazi sending them?

Glenn started shaking his head. 'Typical Nazi. He writes something strange on a map, when he could have just put an X. What the hell does "swapping vision" mean?'

Myles tried to decode it for a moment, then realised he wasn't meant to. 'Stolz didn't want us to know. Not us. These clues were meant for someone else. Someone who would understand them easily.' Myles had a suspicion who the clues were for, but he didn't say. 'Come on. We need to get out of here.'

The team agreed: it was time to leave. Zenyalena made sure they collected the maps, while Heike-Ann checked they had switched off the metal control panel. Myles took a last look at the planets hanging from the ceiling, then turned to join Glenn and Pascal, who were preparing to go back up the ladder.

Pascal began to climb, but the ladder started to spin under his weight. The metal creaked, then a joint near the surface snapped apart. Pascal tumbled back onto the floor, the rusty ladder clattering down onto him.

Myles rushed over to help as fast as he could with his bad knee. 'You hurt?'

The Frenchman blinked, half-dazed from the fall. 'No, I'm … OK.' Myles and Glenn lifted off the broken metal. Slowly Pascal sat up, dusting off his hands.

Myles inspected the ladder, wondering how it could have broken. There were fresh marks on the rust, as if a bolt had just fallen out.

Pascal had recovered, and was standing back on his feet. 'I am lucky to fall from only a low height, but not lucky enough to be up there when the ladder broke …' He was pointing upwards.

Myles stared up, too – at the faraway daylight some thirty metres above them, and wondered how the hell they were going to get out.

CHAPTER 40

8.10 p.m. CET (7.10 p.m. GMT)

Zenyalena was first to react. ‘Come on – we have to hold the ladder while someone climbs up.’

Heike-Ann and Glenn lifted the broken metal frame, and tried to put it back in place. But the break made it useless: no matter how high they lifted it, it wouldn’t reach the top of the shaft. Anyone who climbed up would still be well below the entrance. The brick-lined vertical tunnel was too smooth to finish the climb without help.

Glenn allowed the ladder to fall back down again. ‘Anyone got any other ideas?’ he asked.

Heike-Ann and Zenyalena looked blank.

Even Pascal seemed uncertain, offering a suggestion he wasn’t sure of himself. ‘Er, could we wait?’

Myles shook his head. ‘No. Nobody knows we’re here – not even the prison official who showed us the blueprint. We only found the manhole because we were searching for it.’

Zenyalena shouted upwards, trying to call through the hole, ‘Anybody up there?’ But her words just echoed around the chamber. Above ground, No one would hear a thing. She called again, trying to disguise the fear in her voice. ‘HELLO …?’

Still no answer. They were trapped, and they all knew it.

Zenyalena crossed her arms and rubbed her shoulders. 'So what do we do now?' She looked at the three men, expecting one of them to have an answer. 'Myles? Glenn? Come on.'

Glenn turned his face down to the ground, and scratched his exposed scalp. 'Maybe, Zenyalena, the trouble is that we came down here too quickly. If we'd taken the time to do it right – like tying a rope up there – we would be in the clear. So let's not rush next time. Agreed?'

She shook her head sharply, then flung her hands in the air and stamped on the concrete floor. 'Don't you get it, Glenn? If we don't get out of here, there won't be a "next time". We're trapped. See?' Zenyalena rapped her knuckles on the concrete wall, which broke the skin on her fist. She turned her fingers towards the American to show him the damage.

Pascal saw Glenn was about to say something sarcastic, but raised his hand to stop him. 'Wait. Both of you. We have plenty of time. We're not short of air. We can survive three days without water, easily …' He pointed at a small pool of water at the base of one of the walls. '… And there's even water to drink if we have to.'

Zenyalena exploded in fury. 'You want us to drink rat piss? I'd rather die of thirst.' Then she remembered something. 'Hey. What was it the lawyer said? The "Stuff Ball" in Berlin. He said the papers were for "A Foreign Man about to die …" That was Jean-François, right? He said, "A Foreign Man about to die – before the trial by Air, Fire and Water". The trial by air was the carbon monoxide gas attack on Myles. We had the fire in Vienna. So this is the test by water. The final test.' She looked accusingly at Pascal. 'So you're right, Pascal. We are going to die of thirst.'

Glenn was shaking his head. 'Wrong again, Zenyalena. You missed out Earth. The lawyer said, "Air, Fire, Earth – then water". This has got to be the test by Earth.'

'OK, Glenn,' Zenyalena was barely covering her anger. 'So you mean this place is going to cave in on us instead? Buried alive, huh? Oh, that makes me much happier.'

Pascal stretched out his arms, trying to keep Glenn and Zenyalena away from each other. 'Stop. It's not helping.' Not sure how to solve it, the Frenchman turned to Myles. 'Myles – what do you think?'

But Myles had already left.

'Myles?' Pascal scanned around the cavern to see where their team leader had disappeared to.

Myles had limped into the main chamber, then around the edges, checking the walls for anything which might help.

Glenn realised what he was doing. 'Come on – our team leader's right,' he called to the others. 'There must be another way out.'

Zenyalena and Heike-Ann rushed over while Pascal hobbled. The fall from the ladder had hurt the Frenchman more than it first seemed.

With his fingers spread wide open, Myles silently waved his hands over the walls.

Glenn watched him for a moment, curiously, then called out from behind. 'What are you doing?'

'Trying to find air currents,' explained Myles. 'The Nazis must have put in a ventilation system. It could be our way out.'

The American understood, and started doing the same. He directed the others to copy. Soon they were all feeling around the wall, desperately trying to find any sort of breeze.

Heike-Ann hesitated, then called out. 'I think I've found it.' She had found a metal grill – hard to see because it had been painted the same grey as the concrete inside the cavern. The edges had been sealed with strips of paper.

Glenn immediately took out a pen and started to poke through the seal. Soon the whole of the plate had been revealed. It was about one metre square.

Then Glenn stepped back. 'Can we get this off?' he asked.

Heike-Ann, Pascal and Zenyalena simply stared at it. Zenyalena tried to kick it, but it didn't make an impression.

Then Myles called out from behind. 'Can someone help me with this?' He was holding part of the broken ladder and Pascal rushed over to lift the other end. Together, they wedged part of the metal into the edge of the grill and, like a giant crowbar, managed to lever the plate from the wall. It tumbled to the ground with a clang.

Zenyalena rushed into the hole, ducking her head inside. She looked up, then called out. 'It leads upwards, and there are rungs on the wall.'

Heike-Ann and Glenn shared a look of relief as the Russian started to climb up the ventilation shaft. 'Can we get out at the top?' called Pascal.

Zenyalena answered with the noise of footsteps ascending the ladder, each clank on metal echoing further away each time.

Myles counted: fifty-five steps in total. But after the footsteps there was silence. Myles tried hard to listen – hearing only perhaps a faint rattling noise. There was nothing more. Then came the much faster sound of descending footsteps.

Zenyalena emerged, frustrated and sweating. 'It's blocked,' she said. 'It's an air vent, and it's at ground level. But we can't get out that way.'

Heike-Ann queried the Russian's statement, confused. 'Could we get up there and call for help?'

'It wouldn't work,' replied Zenyalena, shaking her head. 'The Nazi's put an armoured hood over the vent. It means that, even at the top, you can't shout to the prison or the road. If you tried, nobody would hear.'

Pascal stepped into the vent and looked upwards, then came out again. Like Zenyalena, he had no idea how they might ever get out. Glenn tried to supress his frustration, while Heike-Ann sat down by the wall, dejected. She started stroking her pregnant belly, trying to calm her unborn baby.'

Myles scratched his head, thinking about what else there might be in the room – something to help them escape. Then he remembered: the grenades. 'Could we blow our way out?'

The others looked at each other, uncertain.

'The explosives.' Myles gestured at the crate he had lifted earlier. 'If we can get them up there, we could blast away whatever's blocking the air vent.'

Pascal picked up the theme, nodding as he thought through Myles' idea. 'Even if it doesn't clear the way out, the explosion will raise the alarm, and we'll get help.'

'Fine, gentlemen,' it was Zenyalena, still with a hostile tone in her voice. 'Blow up the roof and it could come down on us. And whoever triggers the explosives up there will definitely die.' Come on, Myles – you said it yourself. Those old grenades will be volatile.' Her eyes wide, she stared accusingly at the men. 'Not ready for a suicide mission? Thought not. Neither am I.' With that, Zenyalena sat down on the ground, leaning her back against the wall with her arms folded.

Nobody said anything for more than a minute. Myles took a measure of the people around him. Pascal and Glenn were weighing up odds while Heike-Ann still looked shaken. Even Zenyalena seemed quiet for once. Myles knew what had to be said. 'Well, even though it's dangerous, it looks like one of us has to try. Anyone got any better ideas?'

Glenn cast a sideways look at Myles to confirm he was serious. Then, after a few more moments to think it over, Glenn turned to the others. 'Myles is right. We could sit here and wait for Christmas. But I don't think Santa Claus is going to come down that chimney and save us.'

Still the others said nothing. Glenn took it as acceptance. 'Shall we draw lots to decide who goes up?'

Nervously, the three others in the chamber began looking at each other. Their expressions confirmed they were prepared to take the chance, as long as the others would too.

Glenn turned to Heike-Ann. 'Do you have some business cards?'

The German nodded, looking perplexed. When Glenn stretched out his palm, she passed him some small cardboard rectangles.

Glenn checked them on both sides. Satisfied they were identical, he marked a large cross on the front of one of them, then counted out three more. 'Heike-Ann, you're not in this because you're pregnant,' he said, looking at the cards, which he turned over, shuffled, and fanned out under his thumb. Then he wafted the four-card spread towards the middle of the group. 'Who wants to go first?' For once Glenn was speaking solemnly, aware that this card game could mean both survival and death.

Pascal looked at Myles, his eyes asking permission to step forward. Myles nodded his consent. Cautiously, the Frenchman advanced, checked Glenn's face, then picked the bottom of the four cards. He pulled it free, then turned it over.

No cross.

He allowed it to drop to the floor, exhaling in relief.

Myles and Zenyalena looked at each other, not sure which of them should choose next. 'Just you and me, Zenyalena.'

'You, me and the American,' she corrected.

'Yes, and Glenn. Do you want to pick?'

Zenyalena tried to make a joke of it. 'Usually I'd insist on ladies first, but I think this time a man should take the lead.'

Myles understood. Like Pascal before him, he faced up to Glenn, examined the three remaining cards, then picked the top one.

Carefully, he slid it out then turned it over, showing it to the others before looking at it himself. From their reactions, he knew. In the middle of the front: a cross. Myles had picked the marked card.

Glenn's eyes widened as he realised the card he marked may have condemned the Englishman to death. Heike-Ann and Pascal immediately looked sympathetic. Only Zenyalena seemed vaguely satisfied by her reprieve, relaxing her shoulders in relief it wasn't her.

Myles tried to gauge what he had to do. He lifted his head upwards, wondering how he would manage it. Then he glanced back down at his knee brace, and bent to loosen it slightly.

Heike-Ann put her hand on his shoulder. 'Is there any way we can assist you?'

Myles didn't know – he wasn't sure whether he could manage it at all.

Then Pascal slapped his palm on Myles' back. 'Your bad knee means you need help, Myles.' He paused. 'I'll help you carry the explosives,' he offered.

Myles nodded in gratitude. With the Frenchman, he hobbled over to the box of grenades and together the two men carried it to the bottom of the air shaft. Heike-Ann, Glenn and Zenyalena all stepped back – half fearful, half out of respect.

Myles ripped open the box, explaining as he looked inside. 'These are old German grenades – they used to be called potato mashers. The "K" on the box means "kalt", that's the German word for "cold". Right, Heike-Ann?'

Heike-Ann confirmed Myles was correct, keeping well away.

Myles gently picked one up, and unscrewed a cap at the bottom of the handle. A small porcelain ball dropped out, attached to a thin string. 'In case I don't make it and you need to set off more, pull this string. There's a friction mechanism inside, which sets off the fuse – five seconds, usually.'

Glenn was frowning. 'But why is the box labelled "cold"?'

'Because these were for the Russian front,' said Myles. 'The Nazis found their normal grenades often failed in the freezing temperatures, so they made ones which were especially sensitive, like these ...' After all these years, Myles accepted the chemicals inside would have changed. '... But now, who knows. They could have become even more unpredictable, or this whole box might be duds.'

He pulled out two, delicately placing them in his pocket. Then he ducked his head into the air vent where the metal plate had been. From the bottom of the shaft he looked up at his target.

Myles placed his hands on the rungs, then his good foot, then carefully bent his damaged knee to drag his other foot up, too. Hand-foot-hand-foot ... Slowly he hauled himself up the vertical tunnel. His injury made it hard – he had only three limbs, not four, to pull himself up. But he kept going, dragging himself upwards, careful to make sure the old grenades stayed safely in his pocket. *Twenty-one, twenty-two, twenty-three* ... He examined the rungs as he went, wondering whether there would be any quick way down, apart from falling.

He kept climbing. *Forty-five, forty-six, forty-seven ...*

The top was coming into sight. He understood now what Zenyalena had described. The Germans had built a steel and concrete hood at the top of the vent. It was bomb-proof, designed to protect the ventilation shaft from an Allied air raid. But the steel was now rusted, and the whole structure fixed in place. Myles could just see daylight and the outside world, and his ears detected the faint whoosh of cars driving nearby.

He tried calling through the gap. 'Help ...' But his words just echoed back to him. There was no way anyone would hear.

Myles' feet reached the nearest thing there was to a platform and he crouched down to keep his head from clanging against the roof.

Carefully, he drew the two grenades from his pocket and started searching for places to put them. The first he poked towards the daylight, pushing it as far in as it would go. The second he placed on the floor, wedging it tightly in a fissure in the concrete.

He called down the air vent to the team. 'Grenades in place. Take cover.'

Myles heard a faint scrambling below him as the team found safety within the chamber. Then, silently thinking of Helen for one last time, he twisted the bottom caps of both grenades at the same time, and gently fished out the cords inside from the small porcelain beads attached to each one. Holding both beads in one hand, he tugged them sharply, half expecting them to explode instantly. Then he began climbing back down the shaft as quickly as his limbs could manage.

Five …

The relief that the grenades hadn't exploded immediately was lost in the rush. Furiously he hobbled down the air vent as fast as he could.

Four …

Foot-hand-foot-hand … His injury made it hard to place his right foot on the rung each time he tried.

Three …

Myles kept climbing down, knowing these could be his last seconds alive. He was now almost five metres down from the grenades …

Two …

There was no time to reach the bottom. He pulled himself into the wall for protection from the blast, clutching hard and ducking his head down into his shoulders.

One …

CHAPTER 41

Heritage Hotel
Oxford, England
7.14 p.m. GMT

Father Samuel handed his passport to the receptionist, and placed his travel bag beside him on the floor. Although he was only moderately overweight, it was enough for long trips to be an exertion – the overnight flight from Israel and the convoluted rail journey from London's Heathrow airport to Oxford had both been harder than expected.

'You are just here for two nights, today and tomorrow?' asked the receptionist. When Father Samuel confirmed her information was correct, she pressed a button on her computer and passed him a short printed card. 'Please just fill out your contact details here and sign here,' she directed, pointing to different boxes on the form.

Father Samuel feigned gratitude, then shuffled to one side of the main reception desk, where a pen was chained to a leaflet dispenser. But instead of taking the pen to sign the form, he was drawn to one of the tourist leaflets. It was promoting a university event which was open to the public, and it was happening tonight.

He lifted out the flyer, disgusted that such material was openly available in the city, while he desperately tried to learn more about the event. What did it mean if discussions like this were already happening – publicly and seriously – and in Oxford of all places, a city overflowing with academic respectability? It meant his mission was even more vital than he had imagined. Even without Stolz's papers, it seemed as though, in Oxford at least, the secret was barely a secret any more.

He would have to find out what was said – to discover what information was already out there, and who knew about it.

Samuel filled out the form, handed it in, then took his key card and accepted the directions up to his room.

Before he left reception, he folded one of the promotional leaflets and placed it in his pocket. Then he lifted out all the others, scrunched them up, and stuffed them in his travel bag for disposal in the seclusion of his room.

It was just a small gesture, but one Father Samuel hoped would help prevent the Oxford Astrology Association's speaker meeting on 'War and the Natural World' from having *too* large an audience.

CHAPTER 42

Beneath Landsberg Prison
Near Munich, Germany
8.25 p.m. CET (7.25 p.m. GMT)

Myles waited.

Silence.

He didn't know whether to be relieved he hadn't been killed, or depressed that the grenades hadn't exploded. He kept clutching the wall, his head tightly tucked in and his grip firm, still expecting the blast at any moment. But it didn't come.

Slowly, he poked his head out, instinctively looking up. Was there any clue which might indicate whether the grenades were duds? Old explosives – they were like fireworks: not be returned to once they'd been set off, whatever happened. But he *needed* them to go off.

He would need more grenades. He had to repeat the whole thing: more grenades, another attempt.

His thoughts were disturbed by a sound below him. *Footsteps on the rungs.*

He looked down: Pascal was climbing up towards him. 'Stay there, team leader,' called the Frenchman. Pascal was approaching with speed, coming fast up the shaft.

'Careful – they could still go off,' warned Myles.'

The Frenchman didn't respond. He obviously knew. Then Myles saw he was carrying two more grenades, one in each hand, as he pulled himself up the rungs. Myles winced as Pascal allowed the grenades to brush against the ladder.

Myles shifted to the side, allowing Pascal to squeeze through. The Frenchman called as he climbed up past Myles. 'It's my turn now,' he said. 'You should get down.'

Myles briefly wondered why the Frenchman was volunteering, but Pascal made clear Myles had no time to think. 'Myles, climb down. Now!' he instructed.

Quickly, Myles hobbled down the rungs as fast as he could, leaving Pascal to climb up above him. *Hand-foot-hand-foot …*

As Myles approached the bottom, he heard the Frenchman reach the top.

Pascal called down. 'Now get clear …'

As Myles reached the last step, he let go of the rungs and clambered back into the underground cavern.

Pascal's voice called down again, much fainter now, echoing through the vertical tunnel. 'I'm setting them off …'

Myles listened: silence, then the quick clang of steps and hands on metal rungs, rushing down the air vent. He pictured Pascal coming down as fast as he could go. Myles covered his ears, and positioned himself flat against the wall. Heike-Ann did the same, while Glenn and Zenyalena lay flat on the floor.

They were looking at each other when the blast came. Myles felt his whole body judder. The cavern shook as a rush of air shot into the underground space. Dust filled the room, and the hanging spheres swayed on the ceiling.

Then the inevitable clatter of an object. It was a body, tumbling from halfway down the vertical shaft. Myles, Heike-Ann, Glenn and Zenyalena rushed back towards the bottom of the air tunnel. There they saw the Frenchman's body, lying in blood on the floor.

CHAPTER 43

8.33 p.m. CET (7.33 p.m. GMT)

Pascal's face was bloodied, and his torso covered in dust from the explosion and fall. Myles grabbed his shoulder and tried to turn him.

Glenn shouted into his ear. 'Pascal – Pascal – you alive?'

Myles put his fingers on the French colonel's neck and found his pulse. It was racing.

Slowly, the Frenchman started to rouse. He opened his eyes. Myles noticed the man's pupils were dilated in shock.

Pascal put his hand out, looking for something to grab hold of. 'I'm alive?'

Zenyalena and Heike-Ann took hold and pulled him up. 'Yes, you're alive,' answered the Russian. 'But you shouldn't be.'

Myles was particularly grateful – Pascal's heroism had probably saved his life. 'Do you feel OK?' he asked.

Pascal clutched his head. He tried to explain himself, but the combination of the fall and his poor English made it hard. 'I think I have "visions",' he muttered.

'You see two of everything? Double vision?'

The Frenchman nodded.

Zenyalena turned her head upwards. Sunlight was coming down from the top of the shaft – the concrete cover had been blasted away. 'You've done it. You cleared the exit,' she said. Her face began to smile for the first time since they had gone below ground. 'We can escape!'

Heike-Ann looked at Pascal's leg. Although there was no wound, except for some cuts to his face and arms, the Frenchman would clearly need help getting up the ladder. Myles started to lift him, and Glenn came to assist.

But Pascal brushed them off. 'It's fine. I can climb …' The French colonel staggered to his feet and, almost drunk with concussion, grabbed hold of the rungs. He started to haul himself up, taking each rung slowly. Glenn and Myles watched closely, following him up the ladder, aware he could fall again, but he eventually made it up all fifty-five rungs. Finally, at the top of the vent, Pascal stepped onto the concrete top of the air shaft, stumbled over the debris from the explosion, and collapsed onto the grass outside the prison. Myles followed, careful to lift his leg over the rusted metal that was now twisted into odd shapes.

There were already three prison staff standing around them, alerted by the explosion. One of them was holding handcuffs, ready to lock up any prisoners who had just tried to escape. But when they saw Myles' knee brace, they bent down to help. Very politely, they asked to see his ID. Myles obliged.

Glenn, Heike-Ann and Zenyalena came up, one after the other. Zenyalena inhaled the fresh air deeply and turned her face to the bright sunshine, clutching Stolz's papers from the cavern. Soon, all five of the team were sitting on the grass, glad to be out of the underground complex.

It was Glenn who spoke first, still catching his breath from the climb. 'Pascal – you need to see a doctor.'

Pascal's expression seemed to agree – he was still recovering.

But Zenyalena was resolute. 'No,' she said, firmly.' 'If we lose Pascal, our mission could fail.'

Glenn shook his head. 'This man's just been a hero. Our mission must pause so he can have medical treatment.'

Myles could tell what Glenn was thinking – they had only just survived, and they should quit while they still could.

Zenyalena was resolute. 'I think we can all agree on two things. First, that we need to carry on finding out Stolz's secret. Second, we need Pascal. That means we go on. Tonight. Pascal, I'm sorry, but you'll have to get treatment later.'

Glenn dismissed her with a huff. 'Sorry Little Miss Russia, but we don't even know where the trail leads next. We can't go on tonight, because we don't know where to go. We have to treat Pascal first,' he said. Still shaking his head, he started turning the dial on his watch and conspicuously pulled a long wire from inside it which he held up, still attached.

Heike-Ann looked at him, bemused. 'What's that?' she asked.

Glenn kept concentrating on his watch as he answered. 'I'm calling in a medical chopper,' he explained.

Pascal and Myles looked at each other, unsure how to react. But 'Zenyalena exploded. 'What?' she demanded.

'I'm calling in air support,' replied the American. 'To take Pascal to the nearest US military hospital.'

'No, you will not,' Zenyalena insisted.

Glenn ignored her, still adjusting his watch. Finally, when he was satisfied, he looked up at her. 'Too late,' he gloated. 'The helicopter will be here in about eight minutes.'

For a moment Zenyalena seemed outmanoeuvred. She stared at the other members of the team, aghast. Then she became confident again. 'Then we all go with him,' she stated, as if it were an unquestionable fact. 'The team will stay united.'

Glenn raised his eyebrows, feigning indifference.

Myles decided that he ought to step in. 'Is that OK, Glenn, if we all go in the helicopter?'

'If there's space, then yes,' acknowledged Glenn. 'They'll probably send a Chinook CH-47, so we should be fine.'

'And at the other end – this US military hospital,' probed Myles. 'Will we all be allowed in?'

Glenn didn't reply immediately. Then he shrugged, and simply offered, 'That's up to them. If not, I'm sure you can stay nearby.'

Zenyalena was still furious. 'If we do go into this secret US military base, or whatever it is, this is the maximum number of nights we will stay there.' She thrust a single finger, her middle finger, towards the American.

Glenn shook his head dismissively. 'You can stay just one night if you want to. I'll be staying until Pascal's had his emergency care.'

'Don't think the Americans can stop this,' Zenyalena shot back. 'And if your watch can transmit signals, why didn't you disable it when we all disabled our phones in Vienna? And why didn't you get help when we were trapped underground a few minutes ago?'

'I couldn't get a signal underground,' explained Glenn. He was about to say more when they were all distracted by a low-pitch fluttering noise above them. The whole team craned upwards to see a huge twin-engined helicopter manoeuvring through the sky. The Chinook buzzed close towards them, blasting a strong downdraft onto them which made them shield their faces, then began circling for a place to land. After a few moments when it seemed to dangle in the air, the helicopter started to move directly towards the sports stadium beside the prison.

'Come on,' said Myles, lifting up Pascal. Glenn and Heike-Ann accepted his lead while Zenyalena made sure she had the papers.

One of the prison officials guided them towards the sports stadium, and onto the grass football pitch. The Chinook had landed on the centre circle, its rotor blades still spinning fast and blasting air throughout the arena. Aircrew beckoned them towards the rear-ramp, urging them to run.

Briefly, the prison official stopped them, making a point of checking all of their IDs. But he was swiftly satisfied and seemed particularly impressed by Heike-Ann's police card.

Heads down, Glenn, Zenyalena and Heike-Ann ran between the jets at the back of the aircraft to climb aboard – Heike-Ann cradling her abdomen as she went, instinctively protecting her unborn baby from the noise and juddering. Once inside, they quickly found seats and began buckling themselves in. Helping Pascal, Myles moved more slowly, but soon they were both aboard. The Frenchman was taken by a team of three paramedics in military fatigues who strapped him onto a treatment tray for take-off. Myles was handed ear protectors and instructed to sit down.

There was a hand gesture from the aircrew, and within seconds the rotors had cranked back to full speed. The whole machine began to shudder. Then the rescue helicopter jolted upwards, nose first before lifting completely into the air. The Chinook rose quickly, and banked. Myles caught one last glimpse of Hitler's prison, and the small grenade-scarred crater around the air vent, as the machine roared away.

CHAPTER 44

Above Southern Germany

8.48 p.m. CET (7.48 p.m. GMT)

It took less than a minute for the Chinook to reach its chosen altitude and begin a steady course for wherever it was heading. The rear ramp was only partially closed, allowing Myles to survey roads, rivers, farmhouses and Bavarian woodland as it flew. The sun had set in the western sky and, from the twilight shadows, Myles reckoned they were flying south.

His attention turned to the paramedics. They had already cut off Pascal's shredded clothes to reveal cuts and scars, mainly on one side of the Frenchman's legs and torso. One of the men was concentrating on Pascal's head and neck, while another was checking for internal injuries. A drip had been fitted into the Frenchman's arm.

Although he couldn't hear what they were saying, Myles thought their body language was encouraging: Pascal's injuries were not life-threatening.

The head paramedic moved towards Glenn and shouted something in his ear. Glenn shouted a short reply, confirming something and pointing back at Pascal.

The twin-engined helicopter flew on for less than ten minutes before it banked again, and then started to descend steeply. Zenyalena and Heike-Ann both grabbed their seat straps tightly as it swooped down. Within moments, the Chinook had levelled off just a few metres above an enclosed landing site. Then it lowered itself vertically for a smooth and surprisingly gentle landing.

Ground crew scampered onto the machine and rushed out with Pascal, the three paramedics following closely behind. Then two other men came aboard, both wearing smart US army uniforms and calm in their demeanour. One, an African-American who was clearly in charge, gestured for the international team to stay in their seats. They all waited for the rotor blades to slow and the noise to die, which took almost a minute. Finally, the leading officer mimed for people to lift off their ear defenders, which the team did, almost in unison.

'Welcome to the US Army Garrison Garmisch-Partenkirchen,' announced the soldier, 'otherwise known as the Edelweiss Hotel.' He said it with a twang, then started handing out folded glossy leaflets to Heike-Ann, Zenyalena, Glenn and, finally, Myles. 'During your stay in the resort …'

Suddenly the man became alert. He spun round, ready to strike, then caught something thrown at him by Zenyalena. It was one of the glossy leaflets, screwed up into a ball.

'Thank you, Ma'am,' he volunteered, sarcastically.

'Edelweiss, like the movies?' she shouted. 'Is this a medical centre or a holiday camp?'

'It's both, ma'am. When there's an emergency medivac, the choppers just fly to the nearest facility – which for you was here. And I think that makes you lucky, ma'am. Believe me, there are worse places. You're welcome to stay here as VIPs while your colleague is treated, and even more welcome to walk out of the front entrance, if you prefer. Just take some ID with you, or you won't be allowed back in.'

Zenyalena shook her head in disbelief. 'Decadence,' she said.

'Just trying to keep our soldiers happy,' retorted the American officer.

'Myles could tell from Zenyalena's face that she was about to respond, but something else came into her mind. 'Did you say, "Army Garrison Garmisch-Partenkirchen"?

'Yes Ma'am,'

She nodded to herself. 'That's why it sounded familiar.'

'This is where Stolz was questioned, and Kirov was killed, seventy years ago, isn't it?' she asked. 'Hmm? And who killed him?' Then, without waiting for a reply or asking permission, she unbuckled herself and marched off the helicopter.

The official welcoming party raised his eyebrows. He clearly had never heard of Kirov before, and decided to ignore her. He turned to address his comments to his remaining guests. 'For those of you who want to stay, there's food, a bar, telephone and video-conferencing facilities, and family entertainment. Each of you will have a suite. Ma'am, if you're pregnant, skiing may not be for you, but gentlemen ...'

'Is the telephone secure?' interrupted Myles.

'Yes, sir, it is,' confirmed the officer.

'Good,' said Myles. 'I need to call my partner, back in the UK.'

Glenn nodded his approval. 'Let's all meet up later,' he said. 'Breakfast at seven a.m.'

Heike-Ann and Myles agreed as Myles was guided out of the Chinook and away from the helicopter landing site.

Passing buildings mostly made of brick and concrete, Myles was led towards the main part of the complex. An athletic-looking woman with a very American smile noticed his leg and held the door open for him. Inside, there were families enjoying precious rest and relaxation together, off-duty soldiers checking out a gift shop, and children seated around a flat-screen TV which was showing cartoons. The hotel rooms were clearly upstairs, and his guide pointed out the restaurant as they walked by – it looked more functional than fancy. Then, through a wooden door, Myles was led down concrete steps, past two underground car-park levels, and into a smaller basement area.

'I'll need your mobile and any other communication equipment you have, Sir', Myles was told. He obliged, emptying his pockets into a tray. Then, a soundproof cubicle was unlocked for him, he was guided in, and the door politely closed behind him. Myles was alone.

A speakerphone, handset and computer keypad were on the desk in front of him, with a computer screen integrated into the wall. Hesitantly, he pressed what he thought was the 'on' button, to see the screen come to life with a live video-feed of himself. Then, experimenting with the unfamiliar system, Myles clicked on an icon at the bottom of the screen. A list of options appeared. He typed in Helen's Skype name, and waited for the video-call to go through. After about a second the image switched to the familiar inside of their shared flat in Oxford's Pembroke Street. Helen was pulling her chin away from her laptop in mock surprise.

'Hey Helen,' said Myles, relieved to see her. He had interrupted her eating toast, her evening snack.

Helen finished her mouthful, still off guard. 'Myles – where are you?'

'I can't say, but I'm glad you're safe.'

'You've been worried about *me*?' she joked. 'I tried getting hold of you, but the Government refused to say where you were. Simon Charfield at the Foreign Office said they couldn't tell me because I wasn't a relative … anyway, how's your knee?'

'Getting better. I'm managing without crutches.' He didn't want to admit he'd forgotten them outside Landsberg prison in the rush to climb aboard the helicopter. 'How are you?'

She brushed her hair behind her ear. 'Well, I've missed you,' she said, blowing him a kiss. 'Enjoying the sights of Berlin?'

Myles paused, wondering how much to divulge. He knew he could trust Helen. But he worried that confiding in her – telling her about Stolz and the Nazi secrets – would put her in danger.

She sensed what he was thinking. 'Go on. Tell me.'

'What if … You know ...' his voice trailed off.

'I thought it might, put me in danger? Come on – I'm a big girl now.' She said boldly.

Myles exhaled. 'So … I went to Berlin. It turns out Werner Stolz must have been really loyal to Hitler, because they gave him very important documents. Stolz probably stayed a Nazi all his life. The team of us – the Russian woman Zenyalena, an American who uses the name "Glenn", and a French Colonel called Pascal, all helped by a German woman from their diplomatic police service, Heike-Ann – we all looked through his papers, including some we got from his lawyers office. And we think we discovered his secret.' Myles stopped abruptly.

'So what is it?'

Myles looked at her image on the screen, wondering how to phrase it. Would she think he was mad or just mistaken?

'Come on,' she pressed. 'You gotta tell me. What was Stolz's secret?'

'The planets,' confessed Myles. 'They seem to be connected with human events.'

Helen looked confused. 'Huh?'

'Astrology,' Myles explained. 'It works.'

She frowned. 'Really?' Her face was contorted, as if Myles was telling a silly joke. 'Come on. You mean, *I'm an Aquarius, you're a Gemini*, that sort of stuff?'

Myles found himself nodding. 'That's the way it looks. From Stolz's papers, the ones we've seen.'

'And you believe it? Come on, Myles – how can you believe this crap?' She emphasised the word 'crap' with her hands, as if something was exploding between them. 'You're an academic at Oxford, believing in – I don't know what? How can the position of, say, Jupiter make me choose sausages rather than bacon in the morning?'

Myles tried to calm her down. 'I know. It sounds crazy. But the evidence points that way.'

Helen took another bite of toast while she chewed over Myles' bizarre news.

Myles felt the need to explain more. 'I don't know how it works either. But that wasn't what Stolz had found. He didn't know *how* astrology worked. All he knew was that it *did* work. Somehow.'

She kept at him. 'OK, so what's the evidence?'

Myles leaned back in his chair, trying to remember the papers. 'Well, first of all, the patterns between the planets. Take Saturn and Neptune. Since ancient times, Saturn has symbolised order and structures, while Neptune is linked with dissolving things away, and the ideals of the masses. The two planets orbit at different speeds, which means they come together in the sky every thirty-six years.'

'As we view them from Earth?'

'Yes. And the last time they came together was the second week of November 1989, when the Berlin Wall came down. The timing's exact. Every thirty-six years, when the two planets come together, something big happens to do with revolutions. The next one is February 2026 – perhaps China will give up on Communism then, or the Communists will be returned to power in Russia, or something. Stolz thought there would be conflict on that date somehow.'

Helen sipped from a mug which was out of view of the laptop camera. Now I get it,' she said. 'That was on one of the

Stolz papers I read while you were in hospital. Did Stolz have anything else?'

'Yes. Lots.' Myles could tell she was intrigued, but still far from persuaded. 'The old Nazi had a chart predicting the number of people who would be killed in wars each year, and it was extremely precise. One-in-a-million-trillion precise,' he said. 'Hey, Helen - you know Pluto is associated with power and wealth?'

'As in "Plutocracy" - government by big money – you mean?'

'That's right. Pluto: it's the slowest planet, and when it goes into a different sign of the zodiac, there seems to be a big deal to do with governments and money.' Myles listed the dates he remembered. 'Er … 1884, 1913, 1939 ... the dates when the EU and the World Trade Organisations were set up … even the credit crunch. The next one's in 2023. Stolz reckoned something about technology and world organisations on that date.'

Helen's face became sceptical again. Myles knew that, as a journalist, she'd come across lots of people who were convinced of nonsense. Cures for cancer, mind-reading machines, even voodoo. Usually it was hokum. When there really was something to it, it was only because people expected there to be. It was the belief, not the cure itself, which did the curing. The 'placebo' effect. Helen paused before she spoke. Myles guessed she was trying to find a tone of voice which didn't condemn him. 'You know, scientists can explain why people believe in ghosts,' she said, 'even though they don't exist. Could there be another explanation for all this?'

Myles didn't answer immediately. It was a difficult question. 'I'm not sure. It really looks like there's something in it. But if there is, I don't know how it works. And I'm not about to look at the planets before I make decisions, if that's what you mean.'

Helen relaxed. 'So how do the Nazis fit in?'

'Well, it looks like the Nazis worked this out, and more. Stolz had papers predicting events in the USA and UK, and he had maps predicting Hitler would be vulnerable around Stalingrad. Then there's stuff about when nuclear accidents are likely. And statistical work, too – data connecting future careers with the position of Mars when people are born. We think he's got more – much more. We've only found half of it so far.'

'You know where the rest is?'

'No, not yet. We've only got clues,' he admitted. 'And the trouble is, we're not the only ones looking for it.'

As he said the words, he thought he heard a noise behind him. He checked, but the door to the soundproof cubicle was firmly closed.

CHAPTER 45

Russian Foreign Ministry
Moscow
11.13p.m. MST (8.13p.m. GMT)

Ludochovic pulled the receiver away from his head - it was the only way to save his ears from his line manager's ranting. He had heard enough about Zenyalena's travails underground, the rats and the brutish Glenn, whom the woman was convinced was a CIA spy. He just waited until she stopped screaming down the phone at him, which he hoped would be soon.

It was several more minutes before Ludochovic was able to say, 'Thank you, Ms Androvsky,' and ask, 'So what exactly do you want me to do from here?'

After another few minutes of high-volume hysteria, Zenyalena's voice became more reasonable. He listened patiently while she explained how the Americans were probably listening in, even though she had taken the precaution of calling from a mobile outside the US army base. And although it was definitely peculiar, what she was saying made sense. Ludochovic found his pale head nodding silently in understanding.

'So,' he concluded. 'I will check the data. This means I will check the birthtimes and places of Hitler, Himmler and Churchill...'

'...And Hirohito,' demanded Zenyalena's voice through the phone.

'...*And Hirohito*. And I will use the NASA website to calculate where the planets were when these people were born. And then?'

Ludochovic listened to Zenyalena's detailed instructions, making notes with his pencil, and trying not to demonstrate any surprise in his ever-calm voice.

'I will do that, Ms Androvky. And I will let you know whether the lines really do match up,' he confirmed.

Zenyalena's single word response – 'Da' – was enough for him to start work. He accepted he was there to follow orders, however bizarre those orders may sound.

CHAPTER 46

US Army Garrison Garmisch, aka 'Hotel Edelweiss' Garmisch-Partikirchen, Southern Germany

9.17p.m. CET (8.17p.m. GMT)

Myles' eyes were drawn to a public information notice on the back of the cubicle door. Under the title 'Far From Home?' was the silhouette of an American soldier with a rifle on his shoulder and a phone to his ear. The phone cable led to a woman and two children standing beneath the Stars and Stripes. A sinister figure in a balaclava loomed nearby, planning some sort of ambush. 'If you tell them,' ran the strapline, 'you could put them in danger.'

'Myles!' Helen was shouting at him from the computer screen. 'Are you still there?'

'Sure, I'm here,' said Myles pulling himself back into view of the video feed.

'Come on,' she complained. 'Tell me who else is looking for Stolz's secret.'

Myles scratched his head. 'We don't know exactly. In Berlin, someone piped carbon monoxide into our room, and the Frenchman in our team was murdered and had to be replaced. Then in Vienna there was a suspicious fire, and in Munich we were trapped in an underground cavern.

'An accident?'

'Maybe,' conceded Myles. 'Being trapped could have been bad luck, but there was nothing accidental about the rest.'

Helen was momentarily silenced, shaking her head while she absorbed the facts. After a long pause, she asked, 'You sure you want to continue with this?'

Myles was sure. 'Yes,' he said, firmly. 'I have to – it's too important.'

'Don't tell me you're still trying to clear your name from all that "Myles Munro is a terrorist" nonsense.'

Myles shook his head. 'I don't care about that. It's that Stolz's papers could explain why Hitler took some really dumb decisions, like invade Russia,' Myles explained. 'The dictator could have been following bad advice from an astrologer, who told him he could win...'

Myles could see from her face that Helen was beginning to understand why it mattered so much to him.

'...And then there's the other possibility,' he added. 'Even more important – that somehow planets really *do* influence people. If that's true, Stolz's work could change everything we know – more, even, than the discoveries of the greatest scientists.'

Now Helen looked sceptical again. 'Really? Even more than, say, Isaac Newton?'

'Isaac Newton also did lots of work on astrology himself – he was convinced there was something in it,' remembered Myles. 'When Halley – the man who discovered the comet – mocked Newton for it, Newton famously replied "Sir, I have studied the matter".'

Myles pondered for a few more moments as a thought struck him. 'I wonder what happened to his research?' he mused. Then he lightened up. 'Hey – remember Corporal Bradley? From the papers we read in the hospital? Well, Helen, he was right. If all this stuff – all these unexplained facts – get buried, or just given to a bureaucrat, they'll be wasted. Like Bradley, I think there's something here, and it could change science for ever.'

'I tracked the Corporal down,' announced Helen.

Myles laughed. 'I knew you would.'

'He went to live in Alaska after the war, where he worked in a government job. He got married, and settled near Mount St Helens – quite close to where the volcano was in 1980. It destroyed his house, and he would have died, but he had sold up several months before.'

'So he's still alive?'

Helen shook her head. 'I'm afraid not. He died, back in 1980, aged 62.'

'Old age?'

'No – a road traffic accident. In the same week that his former house was buried by volcano lava, his car was crushed by a truck.'

Myles raised his eyebrows. Bradley's death was several decades ago, but it was still sad to hear of the man's demise. 'I guess, when it's your time to go, it's time to go.'

Then Myles thought some more. 'Hey – did you find out why Bradley sold his house? Did he know the volcano was going to erupt before anybody else? It's like he knew something huge was going to crush him, so he tried to escape, but fate still got him anyway. It just happened to be a truck rather than a volcano.'

Helen shrugged. 'That was all I could find out. But I could keep looking. I might be able to persuade my editor there's a news item here. A human interest story, at least ... We could link it with Stolz, if that's not too secret. Where are you going next? I could meet you there.'

Myles slumped. 'We don't know where we're going next,' he admitted. 'Stolz's next clue was about a railway carriage. We don't know which railway carriage. But something like 500 metres south of it - near where he swapped his vision but didn't "serve".'

Helen frowned. 'Who's "He"?'

'Probably Hitler – it's been Hitler in the other clues so far,' explained Myles.

'Who do you think Stolz left these clues for?' asked Helen.

Myles paused before he answered. 'For the Nazis, I think,' he suggested. 'Clue One referred to Wittgenstein, whom Hitler met at school, the second to where the dictator wrote Mein Kampf. It's as if the old man Stolz tried to code his secret so only a true Nazi would be able to follow.'

'Except, you've followed him so far,' said Helen. 'So Stolz did a bad job.'

Myles nodded – either Stolz had done his job badly, or there was something else the team hadn't worked out yet.

'Or,' added Helen, 'you're on the wrong track...'

Track. The word triggered Myles' memory. He recalled a newsreel of the dictator in 1940, cocky and triumphant. Suddenly it came to him: Hitler was next to a railway carriage in France. *Hitler's railway carriage...*

'Looks like you've thought of something,' said Helen.

'It's the special train – in eastern France,' announced Myles.

Helen asked him to explain, so Myles told her about Hitler's theatrical show of vengeance after his first proper Blitzkrieg. 'In June 1940, Hitler made the French sign their surrender in a railway carriage. It was the same carriage used by the Germans for their surrender in 1918, which ended World War One.'

Helen was impressed. 'That has to be the railway carriage in the clue. Where is it now?'

'Nobody knows – it was destroyed in 1945,' conceded Myles. 'It could have been lost in an air raid, or the Nazis might have blown it up, afraid they might be forced to sign another German surrender inside,' explained Myles. 'But there's a replica. In a French museum. The next clue must be 500 metres south of it.'

Helen was nodding, impressed by Myles' puzzle-solving skills. 'That all makes sense. But what about the 'vision swapping' thing?'

Myles pulled a face, admitting he was guessing. 'I'm not sure,' he said. 'But I know Hitler was blinded in a gas attack on the Western Front. It could have been nearby. He lost his sight for several weeks. According to *Mein Kampf*, it was also when he was in the trenches that he discovered his vision for a "New Germany".'

'You mean, when Stolz said Hitler "swapped his vision", he was trying to be funny?'

'It's the best I can think of,' admitted Myles.

Helen smiled. 'Well, you've convinced me,' she said. 'The most important thing is that you stay safe, OK?' Her eyebrows were furrowed in concern.

'You too, Helen. Seriously – be careful. It could put you in danger.'

Helen seemed to dismiss the threat. 'I love you, Myles,' she said, blowing him another kiss.

'I mean it, Helen,' he insisted. 'Whoever's been sabotaging our team, if they find out you're researching this too…'

'Tell me you love me,' she interrupted.

'You know I do,' he said. He winked at her through the video-feed. 'And let's make sure we're together again soon.'

She nodded and smiled, then leaned forward to turn off her laptop.

'Stay safe,' repeated Myles, but Helen's image had already disappeared.

'Er, you finished in there?' called an American accent. Myles spun round to see an acne-faced serviceman poking his head into the cubicle. 'It's just, I've got this one booked,' explained the young soldier.

'Sorry, yes,' Myles apologised. He checked he hadn't left anything behind, and vacated the small room. The soldier thanked him.

Back in the underground corridor, Myles hobbled back up to the main part of the garrison complex, looking for the rest of the team. It was almost deserted. The gift shop had closed, the big children's TV was switched off, and the only people in the large reception area were a burly soldier and an infant asleep in a pram.

Myles tried to find the medical area, hoping to check up on Pascal. But instead, he only found a part of the base which was off-limits. He peered passed a uniformed guard, who was protecting the entrance to a long corridor, but he couldn't tell what was inside. Politely but firmly, the guard told him he couldn't enter.

He retreated to the restaurant, where, although they were closing up, the female manager took pity on him and got him an all-American T-bone steak with fries and milkshake. Myles ate it gratefully – alone, but with the restaurant manager popping by several times to ask if he needed anything.

Back at reception he found he had been allocated a room – one of the largest, and with a mountain view, the receptionist explained. She also pointed him towards the 'elevator', noting that English people usually called it a lift. He limped into it, found his room, and swiftly went to bed.

But he found it hard to sleep. He was unnerved, and couldn't expel the last image of Helen from his mind. She was now as intrigued as he was. Like him she'd take risks to find out Stolz's secrets. That meant she might be targeted, too.

His call to check she was safe had, in fact, made her less safe. Just like Corporal Bradley, it seemed Helen's fate was to be in danger. By trying to protect her from that fate, Myles had had only made it more likely.

CHAPTER 47

Heritage Hotel
Oxford, England
10.05p.m. GMT

Father Samuel double-locked his hotel door, and pulled the laptop from his bag. It took a few moments to turn on – time for Father Samuel to calm himself in silence. He pulled out the flyer from the 'War and the Natural World' event, and laid it next to the keyboard, hoping the technology would work.

Exactly as Dieter had shown him, he double-clicked on his 'CCTV' icon, then, when the prompt came up, filled in the time, date and location of the event. The computer programme began to search, then came back with:

Frank Wellesley, speaking to Oxford Astrology Association, (Hosted by University of Oxford)?

Samuel clicked 'Yes', and the machine began to search some more.

A few moments later, four images came up, each showing a different CCTV image related to the event. Screenshots One, Three and Four were all from outside – either of people entering the venue, or the street outside. But Screenshot Two was perfect: a recording from inside the room. The camera was even centred on the main stage. And, just as he had hoped, there was a green tick in the corner beside the words 'Audio Available.' Father Samuel clicked on the image, and prepared to watch the show. He would have to thank Dieter for this.

To his dismay, the audience was not made up of the hippies and mystics he had expected. Instead, all the people looked respectable, intelligent and engaged. At the designated start time, the room was almost full.

'...Our speaker has already made news by explaining how celestial bodies impact on human affairs,' explained a blonde woman who seemed to be introducing the event. 'Indeed, his recent exhibition is in danger of making astrology respectable....' More laughter. '...So, Ladies and Gentlemen, let's welcome the curator of the Imperial War Museum, Frank Wellesley.'

Father Samuel fast-forwarded through the applause. The main speaker needed a walking stick to stand up. Samuel smiled: God had punished the man already.

'Every major civilisation has studied it - from Babylon, to ancient China, the Arab world and the Mayans of Central America,' lectured the speaker. 'And though their discoveries were far apart, their astrology was very close. So why is astrology today regarded as so unusual? Because it's consigned to entertainment magazines. In the mind of the public, it's alongside fortune cookies and water divining...'

'And a good thing too,' chuckled Father Samuel to himself. He fast-forwarded some more, until the speaker was gesticulating with two fingers.

'Two big institutions have deliberately tried to discredit astrology,' said Frank.

'First,' he counted, 'The Christian church.'

Father Samuel slumped in his chair, while Frank explained how Christianity had tried to absorb astrology. 'Christmas Day on the solstice, even though Jesus wasn't born that day. Jesus on the cross during a solar eclipse. It's all astrology. When the Roman Emperor Constantine took on Christianity, he made these things part of his new religion. And the three wise men who followed a star – Constantine made them kings. He was trying to buy astrologers with a crown.'

'But later, when the Church was firmly in power,' continued Frank, 'It saw astrology as a threat - an alternative source of ideas and prophecy which had to be crushed. They did this through a Papal edict in 1586: all astrologers were to be excommunicated. Even reading about astrology was officially made a sin,' he explained. 'It was a decision taken by the same Pope who banned contraception…' There were a few laughs.

Father Samuel silently shook his head. The secret work of his Church had been exposed. He watched as Frank moved on to the second big institution he was accusing of a cover-up.

'…But the even greater force to discredit astrology has been science. Science used to be about proving things through experiments. It was about seeing what really happened, and then trying to explain it. But now, science is the religion of our times, and men in white coats are its priests. Nobody dares say when science is wrong…' The audience was listening eagerly. '…That's why, in my exhibition, I showed things which scientists pretend can't be true…'

At last, something Father Samuel could agree with. Just like him, Frank Wellesley understood that science had got too big for itself.

'Like the relationship between wars and eclipses. Alexander the Great, the Crusades, the First World War, the Korean War, even Kosovo and Ukraine – the link with eclipses is stronger than one-in-a-trillion. The evidence is right there, on the NASA website. And I think some scientists must have realised astrology had some truth in it,' speculated Frank. 'They knew they'd have to rethink their theories, and they'd be discredited. So they discredited the facts about astrology first. They made it fashionable for people to assume – without checking the data – that astrology was nonsense. Applying the scientific method to the correlation between planets and people was labelled 'unscientific'. Committees didn't just refuse to fund research on it, but destroyed the academic reputations of everyone who exposed the evidence. A French statistician by the name of Gauquelin was even assassinated for going public with the facts...'

Father Samuel cursed. He spooled forward to the end.

'... So the challenge for us is not to show the relationship between the planets and human events. That's easy,' concluded the museum curator. 'Most people know astrology is true, just as they have for thousands of years. The challenge is to use this knowledge for good purposes, and to keep it from people who would use it for evil.'

Father Samuel thumped the desk with his fist. This had gone way too far.

He delved in his bag for his communicator, switched it on, and hastily typed a new message to Dieter.

All means now valid. Destroy all Stolz papers. Call me.

He pressed 'send' and waited, hoping for a reply within a minute, as before. But there was none. A full ten minutes passed. Still nothing. *What had happened to Dieter?*

And while he waited, Father Samuel's eyes wandered back to the CCTV footage, which he had allowed to run on. The speaker was dealing with questions, and one of the questioners looked familiar. A woman; poised and confident and with television hair. Samuel recognised her now: that American TV journalist. He turned up the volume to hear her question.

'Helen Bridle, CNN. If astrology's true, how come nobody's noticed it yet?'

Father Samuel froze. *Was a major broadcaster about to bring this heresy to the general public?*

It was too much: he'd need a way to silence them all.

And for some, there was only one way to be sure of their silence.

DAY FIVE

CHAPTER 48

Outside Landsberg Prison,
Southern Germany
3.19a.m. CET (2.19a.m. GMT)

Dieter had become invisible.

No one could see him. No one realised he was there. No one knew who he was. His disguise was working.

But it also meant he had been forgotten. No one had remembered what he'd done. No one apart from Dieter himself, of course.

It was almost ten years ago, now. Throwing pink paint over the leader of the far right group in the European parliament had been only part of it. It was hitting the politician with the tin which had landed him in jail.

If Dieter had been attacking the politician because he was too extreme, like everybody else, he might have got off. But Dieter had assaulted the man because he wasn't extreme enough.

Perhaps Dieter should have lied in court. His lawyer told him to stay calm, and pretend he was making a political statement against the far-right leader because the man was racist. But Dieter detested the man - the politician offered no protection at all to the Germans who were, forced to live under French rule because their land had been surrendered as 'war compensation' decades earlier.

Like Hitler, Dieter's single year in prison had been easy. He'd learned useful things: a thief had taught him how to beat a CCTV system. A murderer had taught him what it felt like to kill someone, including how to overcome the instinct to offer mercy in the closing seconds. Both had been useful when he'd broke into the Berlin Hotel to kill Jean-François…

Dieter was glad his most recent victim had been a Frenchman. He would make that other Frenchman, Pascal, disappear soon too…

The year in prison also made him focus. It wasn't enough just to attack the metropolitan culture, the silly 'live-and-let-live' mentality of his childhood city, Strasbourg, and all the Euro-nonsense that went with it.

Stolz's secret would enable him to reverse the humiliation. No longer would Germans, like him, be ashamed of their past. Dieter would soon be able to shame the French. And wasn't it the purest poetry that he'd be able to do it at the Compiègne railway carriage? Just like Hitler.

Dieter looked up at the prison. He tried to pick out cell number seven. Hitler's old cell. What would the brilliant dictator have made of the international team?

Dieter knew: Hitler himself had predicted the Cold War. It was in his writings. Dismissed now, of course, but the once-great man had seen it all. Hitler knew the alliance between the Americans and the Soviets was phoney. Just as the international team was phoney now. Perhaps Hitler had been informed by forecasts from Stolz. Perhaps Stolz was just a genius, much like Dieter himself.

Now, he realised, his mission to uncover Stolz's secret had given him the chance to be much more. What had started as paid work, hired by the fat Christian from Israel to gather some papers, had given Dieter a chance to win the stature of a world statesman. It was just as Hitler himself had promised:

'No matter how weak an individual may be, the minute that he acts in accordance with the hand of Fate, he becomes more powerful than you could possibly imagine.'

Dieter wondered whether he could really pull it off. Surely he could. After all, he had already with 'lived one prediction - that he was virtually indestructible, and that was due to hold true for another two days. Using Stolz's secret, Dieter would scramble up the pile of excrement called society to win the human race.

Now only plastic tape was preventing Dieter from going inside – tape set up by all the municipal officials and prison staff, all the useless people. Calmly, Dieter walked towards the blast hole. He stepped over the broken concrete where Pascal's grenade had blown off the cover and he bent down, under the cordon. Then he took hold of the ladder, and climbed down. *Invisible.*

In the cavern below he went straight to the metal desk and the machine with the dials. He quickly found the switch, and waited while it hummed and buzzed into life.

Then he set the dials, one by one.

January…
29th…
Dusk…

It was Dieter's own birthday, his birth year, his time of birth.

He lifted his head to watch the hanging globes sway, revolve and settle in their new positions. The coloured lights started to shine on the third sphere from the sun. Dieter stared up, trying to make out what would happen to him in northern France. Mars was active there – but did that mean action or violence? And he was going to be surprised there, too - an unexpected role reversal, a sudden loss of power. A twin threat of some sort.

Dieter knew he had to prepare himself. If he was facing a trap, then he wanted to lay the trap himself.

But then he saw, in the eastern half of Germany, so, so many lines converging on Berlin.

Uranus, Mars, Neptune, and Saturn: all four were active in the German capital. All active for him.

Uranus: surprises
Mars: violence
Neptune: illusion
Saturn: authority

Perfect: the place where he could *surprise* the world with *violence*, and become an *illusion* of *authority*.

So it was to be Berlin. Berlin would be where he would transform himself. In Berlin he would cease to be Dieter-who-threw-paint-at-the-fascist. He would become Dieter, new leader of the world.

He knew the old phrase: he who controls Berlin controls Germany, he who controls Germany controls Europe. He who controls Europe controls the World. *Very soon that person would be him.*

Quietly, Dieter turned off the machine, stepped back, and slowly climbed up and out of the cavern beneath Landsberg prison.

Back on the patch of grass, he turned his smartphone back on, and waited while it found a signal. There was a new message from Father Samuel:

All means now valid. Destroy all Stolz papers. Call me.

He smirked, relishing the feeble panic of his paymaster. Then he pressed 'call'.

Father Samuel answered almost immediately. 'My friend,' he said. 'Did you understand my message?'

'Yes,' replied Dieter. 'Would you like the whole team to be… concluded?'

Father Samuel paused, but only briefly, before he answered, 'I would.'

'Then you need to deliver something for me,' said Dieter, coolly. 'I need one device, fully operational and set exactly as we discussed, and it needs to be old.'

'How old?' asked Father Samuel.

'A century would be perfect,' replied Dieter. 'German manufacture, please – they're the best, usually. And by noon at the latest, it needs to be precisely five hundred metres south of this location: 49 degrees, 25 minutes, 38 seconds north; 2 degrees, 54 minutes 23 seconds east.'

Dieter could hear Samuel inhale, shocked by the demand as he scribbled down the longitude and latitude. After a few seconds, the query came back. 'But my Friend, that is in northern France. And I do not even have the device yet.'

'Correct. But just as I have delivered for you, I know you will deliver for me.' Dieter ended the call without waiting for another excuse, then he walked away – back to the taxi rank.

There was an extra guard on duty at the prison – probably because of the explosion earlier – and someone walking their dog on the other side of the main road. But neither of them noticed him.

No one had noticed him at all.

CHAPTER 49

US Army Garrison Garmisch, aka 'Hotel Edelwiess'
Garmisch-Partikirchen, Southern Germany
6.30a.m. CET (5.30a.m. GMT)

Myles' hotel telephone rang, waking him from sleep - someone had set an alarm for him, although he didn't know who. He slumped out of bed to pull back the curtains. The Alps looked stunning: brightly lit by the dawn sun. The almost-full moon was about to set behind them. For ancient peoples – with no televisions or street lights – these heavenly bodies would have been natural marvels. No wonder they struggled to understand the passage of the moon and planets above them. No wonder they searched for a mysterious connection between the state of the sky and their own lives. What had they found, exactly? Myles wondered whether he was close to discovering it again.

As he gazed at the view, Myles understood the real puzzle of the planets was not whether there was a connection. There definitely *was* a connection. The evidence was clear – to everybody except the scientists and religious fundamentalists who had a motive to deny it. Planets could be used for predictions, and those predictions could be good or bad, useful or harmful. The real puzzle of the planets was: how could the power to make accurate predictions be kept from people like the Nazis, and used only for good? That puzzle was far harder to solve.

He remembered Glenn had called for a rendezvous in the restaurant at seven a.m. Not wanting to be late again, he dressed quickly and hurried down.

Glenn was the only team member to be there before Myles. The American was already halfway through a breakfast of pancakes and maple syrup.

'Did you have a good rest?' Myles asked.

Glenn huffed. 'No, but then I didn't really expect to.' He passed his hand over his perfectly clean-shaven scalp, as if he had spent his whole break agonising about Stolz. There was almost a minute's silence before Glenn spoke again. 'So what do you think about all this horoscope shit?'

Myles knew a loaded question when he heard one. But he decided to be honest. 'You know, I'm not sure.' He tried to explain. 'The thing is this, there *is* a correlation. Stolz has found clear patterns between the planets and human events.'

'Oh, come on,' scoffed Glenn, swigging coffee. 'You're meant to be an academic.'

'Yes, and that means accepting evidence. If the evidence isn't what you expected, you have to go with the evidence. You heard of quantum physics?'

Glenn raised his eyebrows, chewing.

'You see Glenn, quantum physics doesn't make sense either,' explained Myles, leaning forward to avoid other people in the restaurant listening in. 'It says electrons can influence each other without any sort of connection between them. It sounds like so much nonsense, but it's been proven as true.'

'So you're saying Stolz proves astrology to be true?' Glenn put the question like a dare. 'Really?'

Myles looked down, shaking his head. But he wasn't saying no. He was about to explain when he felt a pair of hands on his shoulders.

It was Zenyalena, wide-eyed as ever, wearing bright green this time, and clearly re-energised. 'Gentlemen. Myles – Glenn.'

Myles and Glenn returned the greeting.

Zenyalena sat down beside the American and lifted a pancake from his plate. 'Any news on Pascal?' she asked, lifting a piece of pancake into her mouth chewing rapidly.

Myles and Glenn both shook their heads.

Zenyalena shrugged, then pulled a face. 'So, have you two learned anything interesting overnight?' she asked.

Myles was about to answer when he noticed Heike-Ann at the entrance to the restaurant. She hadn't seen them yet, so Myles stood up and beckoned her over.

'Well, I found out about this place,' announced Zenyalena, unconcerned that nobody seemed to be listening. 'It was a German army base before the Americans took it, and it held out for a whole month after the end of the war.'

'And your point is?' asked Glenn.

'We know Stolz took one of the last planes out of Berlin in April 1945. He came here, for some reason,' Zenyalena explained. 'Then the Americans insisted on interviewing him here – not one of the interrogation centres they had already set up. Very odd.'

'Nothing odd about that,' retorted Glenn. 'Stolz flew to southern Germany to escape the Red Army. He probably preferred surrendering to the Americans, which makes perfect sense, given how the communists were treating people.'

'So how did you treat Lieutenant Kirov? There's no memorial to him here. No record of him at all.'

Glenn clattered his knife and fork onto the table, exasperated. 'Of course there's no record of him, Zenyalena. It was seventy years ago, soldiers had been dying every day, and he wasn't even American. What do you expect?'

'Well, I say we find out more,' insisted Zenyalena.

Furious, Glenn stood up. Myles wondered whether he was about to hit the Russian, but suddenly his face broadened into a smile. Heike-Ann's did too, then Zenyalena's. They had all seen Pascal.

Pascal joined them at the table, wearing fresh clothes and looking relaxed. Apart from a small wound on his jaw, which was covered by a surgical dressing, he seemed completely unharmed.

'Looks like you got the medical treatment,' said Glenn.

Pascal tipped his head to one side. 'I was expecting something huge and American,' he joked, gesticulating with his hands. 'But it was just a First Aid station!'

'What can you expect from a place called 'Hotel Edelweiss'?' mocked Glenn. 'You OK?'

'Yes – it was all minor. They released me after an hour.'

'Enough,' said Zenyalena. 'We are all here. We need to keep ahead of whoever is following us.'

Myles saw the others eye each other. Another argument was looming – perhaps one which threatened to pull the team apart. 'I know where Stolz's next clue leads,' he interjected. They all looked at him.

'Where?' asked Pascal.

'France,' Myles explained. 'About five hundred miles west of here.'

Glenn pulled Stolz's paper from his pocket, and unfolded it to reveal the clue, written out in garish highlighter pen. 'You sure?' he asked.

Myles nodded. 'I am. The only question is, how do we get there?'

'There's a vehicle rental place in the town,' proposed Zenyalena.

Pascal acknowledged her suggestion, but dismissed it. 'Too slow,' he said. 'We need to be faster than whoever's following us.' Then a thought struck him and he turned to Glenn. 'Could we fly?'

'Another helicopter? I don't know,' said the American. 'It's not a medical emergency this time. But I can try for you.' He stood up from the table, and began looking for someone to ask.

As soon as he was gone, Zenyalena turned to Myles. 'This place – it's 500 metres south of a railway carriage, is it?'

Myles indicated she was correct. 'Yes, in Compèigne,'

'Then, I say we fly to the carriage,' continued the Russian, 'but we travel the last half-kilometre by ourselves. We don't want an American army helicopter crew barging in on whatever we might find there.' Without waiting for a reaction from the others, she turned her mobile phone back on and started to book a rental vehicle – a minibus – to meet them in France. She passed her phone over to Myles so he could give the exact location.

Glenn returned, and, looking surprised himself, announced that there was indeed a helicopter which could take them, leaving in forty minutes. It was another Chinook, flying to the NATO Headquarters in Belgium, with space for passengers and time for a minor detour. It could complete the journey in less than three hours. Heike-Ann, Zenyalena, Pascal, Glenn and Myles made sure they were on board. Soon, they were thundering into the sky above the United States Army Garrison Garmisch-Partenkirchen, and soaring away.

CHAPTER 50

Langley, Virginia,
USA
5.10a.m. EST (10.10a.m. GMT)

Sally Wotton's desk was quiet again.

The last upload to *Mein Kampf Now* had caused quite a stir. She had been asked to give 'emergency briefings', presentations to the top management group and one-to-ones with various deputy directors. It was the first time senior types at the CIA had taken a real interest in her work. A few of them even seemed interested in her, and she'd been asked – ordered – to come into work especially early, just in case there was anything new. But with no updates on the terror-group website for a while, and no breakthroughs from the tech boys trying to trace the uploads, the trail had gone cold. Even the photograph of a dead man hanging in a hotel room had been a tease – some analysts reckoned it was taken in northern Europe because of the furniture, but the background was too out-of-focus for anything more precise.

It meant Sally was back to browsing the web. Or, more accurately, browsing those websites which a CIA computer algorithm had identified as 'suspect', and which belonged to the category assigned to her.

There was the usual dross. 'Death sites', crazy protestor sites, and obscene stuff which tried to frighten but didn't. Sally paid special attention to all the Hitler sites which came up, just in case any were connected to *Mein Kampf Now*. When she'd suspected one yesterday, she'd raised the alert immediately and within minutes a lonely teenager in rural Tennessee had his bedroom invaded by a swarm of Federal agents. Even though the agents soon found the youth wasn't connected to the terror group, the teenager's mother still took away his computer privileges and grounded him for a month as a punishment.

It made Sally wonder even more about her job. She was trying to do what the CIA was meant to do – to protect the USA from threats. Yet, when it had actually happened, Sally's role seemed to have amounted to giving a few PowerPoint presentations and getting some deputy directors to nod their heads in concern. She was fairly sure others had begun working on *Mein Kampf Now* without telling her, making her feel left out.

She scrolled down today's list of highlighted sites.

Death to the Yankees...

Capitalism is piracy....

Humanitarian Pursuit...

She squinted, checking the words again. *'Humanitarian Pursuit'?*

She scratched her head. Why was something humanitarian a threat? Surely pursing humanitarian goals was a good thing, wasn't it?

She clicked on it, and instantly realised why the algorithm had selected it. The website was linked directly to *Mein Kampf Now.*

Humanitarian Pursuit ***believes the threats made by Mein Kampf Now are horrendous. We believe in the Universal Declaration of Human Rights, and that all people should be allowed to thrive in peace and prosperity in every part of the world...***

> **Mein Kampf Now** *and* **Humanitarian Pursuit** *have opposite goals...*

She scrolled down. There were pictures of starving African children eating from tins of food aid, and a poverty-stricken farmer trying to take in a failed harvest. Library images? She didn't know. She guided her cursor to read the text at the bottom.

> **Humanitarian Pursuit** *would like to meet the instigators of* **Mein Kampf Now.** *We want to talk to you, to understand you and – yes, we are self-confident enough to use the word – negotiate with you...*
>
> *We believe* **Humanitarian Pursuit** *and* **Mein Kampf Now** *can agree a peace deal.*

Sally raised her eyebrows.

'Humanitarian Pursuit' – she'd never heard of it before. She typed the phrase into a search engine, and the only page to come up was the one already on her screen. She checked whether this 'Humanitarian Pursuit' was registered with any Federal authority. It wasn't.

She didn't know whether to praise it or be suspicious. Was trying to negotiate with *Mein Kampf Now* a good idea or a very stupid one?

She knew her seniors wouldn't be interested in this one. There were thousands of do-good organisations all across the world. Even though this one was trying to 'do good' with *Mein Kampf Now*, it wouldn't be a priority for the CIA.

But it was a priority for her. Sally sent a request to the tech boys – she wanted the site traced and monitored, just like the original Hitler site.

Then she realised something very odd about the site indeed, and she smiled to herself. Something so simple, so easy to overlook. *Now that would definitely interest her boss…*

At last, her over-trained brain had been useful after all…

CHAPTER 51

Northern France

11.15a.m. CET (10.15a.m. GMT)

The flight was punctuated only by a brief refuelling stop just before the twin-engined helicopter passed out of German air-space. The team stayed on board. As they flew on, into France, Myles could make out the tell-tale ditches which had marked out the First World War trenches from a century earlier. Most had grassed over, and some of the shell holes had been filled in, but the undulating surface of the fields was still scarred by the Great War.

As promised, the international team were dropped exactly where Myles had specified: in Compiègne, on a well-tended patch of grass and pavings in the middle of a wooded area. The Chinook had evidently called ahead – the site had been roped off, and tourists moved away so that the helicopter, was able to descend safely. The team rushed out, thanking the helicopter crew as they left.

Only as the Chinook departed, rising away with its shuddering noise and squall, did Myles realise what a peaceful place they had come to. Like some sort of ornamental garden, there were solemn monuments and flagpoles, as well as the two-room museum and railway carriage he was expecting.

'You're the historian,' said Zenyalena, turning to Myles. 'Do we need to know about this railway carriage, or can we just follow Stolz's directions?'

Myles lifted his shoulders, unsure. 'It may be important. I don't know.' They moved towards it. The paintwork on the outside had been polished to a high shine, and the inside was preserved like a crime scene. Peering in through a window, Myles pointed to the table in the centre of the carriage. 'This is a copy of Field Marshall Foch's private train – commander of British and French troops towards the end of World War One. When a German delegation crossed the front lines to discuss peace terms, this is where they were taken. The Allies bugged their communications with Berlin, so they knew they could demand an unconditional surrender, and they got it. It was at that table that the Armistice was signed, and the Great War ended.'

Zenyalena didn't want the team to dwell on the history too much. 'And then, later?'

'Well, the First World War was known as the "War to End All Wars",' recounted Myles. 'But the treaty which followed soon became the "Peace to End All Peace". Hitler believed the Germans had been tricked. He thought they could have fought on to win, blaming Jews in Berlin for giving up early. That's why, in 1940, when his armies had beaten France, he made the French surrender in this same railway carriage. He was trying to undo the humiliation of 1918. Or rather, pass that humiliation onto the French....'

Pascal, Heike-Ann and Glenn listened carefully to Myles' words. Just as he did in Oxford's lecture halls, Myles captivated his audience.

'... The Free French liberated this place from the Nazis in September 1944, just two weeks after the last train had taken people from here to the death camps...'

They were all fascinated - except Zenyalena. 'Thank you, Myles. I think that is enough. Now let's follow Stolz's directions.'

Glenn held up his hand. 'Wait. Surely there's a reason Stolz sent us here. We need to know why? Pascal nodded.'

'Could we at least check out the museum?' asked Heike-Ann.

Zenyalena shook her head. 'No time. Stolz hid his secret files south of here, and that's where we need to go before anyone else does. If there is a reason why Stolz hid them near here, we'll be much closer to finding it when we find those papers.'

Pascal, Heike-Ann and Glenn accepted they would have to leave the carriage and go with the Russian – she couldn't be allowed to find Stolz's next hiding place alone.

Zenyalena marched to the car park, leading the team as she went. Myles tried to keep up with the pace, but the sharp pain in his leg forced him to limp along behind.

The vehicle Zenyalena had hired was easy to find – it was the only minibus there. As she had arranged with the rental company, the keys were underneath one of the back tyres. Reaching for them, she spoke to the team, 'Stolz said we needed to go five hundred metres south of here. No need to measure the distance – this has GPS. Easy.' She clutched the keys in her palm, and opened the driver's door.

Myles followed Heike-Ann and Pascal into the back of the minibus. Glenn, last in, made a point of riding shot-gun, sitting next to Zenyalena, who was in the driving seat. The American wanted to watch the GPS.

Zenyalena spoke without looking at him. 'Set it for five hundred metres - due south.'

Glenn played with the controls, pausing to check it was right before he gave her the go-ahead. 'Done.'

Zenyalena turned on the ignition and let the engine rumble for a few seconds before putting the vehicle in gear and driving out.

The computerised voice from the GPS – a woman with a mid-Atlantic accent which reminded Myles of Helen - was unambiguous. 'At the next turning, take the first right…' The first right was a small, gravel lane. It led away from the railway carriage and the ceremonial space around it, into the forest. '…200 metres…'

The team eagerly watched out of the windows. They were driving into the wood. The spot chosen by Stolz was somewhere amongst the trees.

'…100 metres…' declared the GPS.

Zenyalena allowed the vehicle to slow as they approached. Gravel crunched under the tyres. Myles sensed this road was not used very much.

' …. You have now reached your destination.'

Zenyalena stopped the minibus.

Without a word, Glenn jumped out, then opened the door for the other passengers. 'We're here – wherever "here" is. Let me know if you see something.'

Myles, Pascal and Heike-Ann stepped down onto the track. Zenyalena turned off the engine and lifted the handbrake, subtly pocketing the keys.

Silence. Not even the leaves in the trees made a sound.

Myles glanced around. They were on a rough roadway – small stones on mud - in the middle of a dense forest. Undergrowth covered most of the ground to both sides of them. There were no other people between here and the museum in Compiègne. It was a good place to hide something, although the seclusion also made it sinister.

Myles saw a pattern on the ground at one side of the small road; the undergrowth was missing. He hobbled towards the brambles to make sure. As his suspicions proved correct, he advanced more slowly – partly out of respect, partly out of fear of unexploded munitions. It was a trench, from the First World War. 'Be careful,' he called back to the others. 'This place could still be dangerous.'

While Pascal, Glenn and Zenyalena began to follow, Heike-Ann remained where she was. 'Well, if it isn't safe, shouldn't we stop?' she asked.

But Myles was already out of earshot. He examined the earthworks. Corrugated iron still held up the walls – rusted in places and defaced by recent spray-can graffiti. Wooden duckboards on the bottom of the trench had been buried by a century of autumn leaves and other detritus. One side of the trench stopped where it had been filled in, in order to make the track where the minibus was parked. The other side led into the unknown, turning at a right-angle. The dense tree cover made it much darker in that direction.

As carefully as he could, Myles slid down into the trench, keeping the weight off his healing leg. Soil scraped onto his elbows. Weeds rubbed against his clothes.

Glenn jumped down beside him. 'So this was the Western Front, huh?'

Myles nodded. 'Part of it. The trees would have protected this part from artillery, which is probably why it's still here.'

'But Myles, I thought Stolz's clue said 'where He didn't serve'. Does that mean Hitler served in the trenches somewhere else?'

Still gauging his surroundings, Myles shook his head. 'Hitler never really spent much time in the trenches at all – just a few weeks out of the whole four years. His war record was mostly propaganda. Nazi fiction. He lied about it in Mein Kampf, too. Hitler spent his First World War comfortable in regimental HQ, a safe distance behind the front...'

Glenn kicked one of the sides. A small volume of earth tumbled down. 'So you reckon we have to search this whole trench? Stolz could have hidden his stuff anywhere.'

'No - remember: Stolz was an old man when he hid those papers, and he hid them recently,' said Myles, as he started limping along the trench. 'We just need to look for signs of someone hiding something.'

He remembered explaining to his students how trenches zig-zagged: to limit the damage from artillery shells, and to stop a single gun being placed along the length. The international team would have to turn at each corner until they found whatever Stolz had buried.

Pascal and Zenyalena came down to join Myles and Glenn in the trench. Only Heike-Ann stayed near the minibus, too afraid to leave the gravel track.

Myles started to limp along the narrow passage. 'Look for anything unusual. And watch out for booby traps,' he warned. 'Armies left lots of them whenever they retreated. Some didn't get cleaned up afterwards.'

They turned the first corner. Part of the wall had collapsed, but grass was growing where it had fallen away. It was an old slippage. Myles stepped over it and continued, to the second corner, with the others following behind.

Myles noticed a white surface on the side near his feet. He bent down to inspect it. It was old - part of a skull buried many years ago. Then some beetles began crawling out of the earth beside them. Zenyalena winced. They left it and continued forward.

They reached the third corner and Myles stopped. There, in the middle of the pathway, was an old ammunition box. It looked as though it had just fallen from the side of the trench. But something about the hole it had come from made Myles wonder: the exposed soil was fresh, with spade marks, as though it had been dug out recently. Myles bent towards it without touching. Paint on the metal cover had flaked off, and the rim where the lid joined the main part of the box was rusted. But there was much less rust than on other steel artefacts he had seen dug up from the trenches.

Zenyalena called from behind. 'Do you think it's from Stolz?'

Without answering, Myles tried to look closer still. Then he saw it: a swastika. It was the confirmation he needed. 'Yes. It must be. We're in a First World War trench, and that's a Second World War ammunition box. The swastika – it's from the Nazis.'

Still without touching, as they all knew it could be deadly, the four of them positioned themselves until they were all standing above it. Glenn pulled a utility knife from his pocket, flicked open one of the blades, and offered it to Myles who took it gratefully.

Myles knelt down and slid the blade into the rust, between the lid and the main box. It was looser than he expected. 'Do you want to stand back, just in case?'

Zenyalena frowned. 'Of course not – we want to see what's inside.'

Nobody else tried to protect themselves either – curiosity drew them all in. If the tin was booby trapped, Heike-Ann, still standing by the minbus, would be the only survivor.

CHAPTER 52

Compiègne
Eastern France
11.35a.m. CET (10.35a.m. GMT)

Gently Myles placed pressure on the handle of the knife. The metal ammunition box flexed, like a spring being compressed and the rust started to crack. Myles eased the knife along. He felt it move then, suddenly, the lid flung open, spraying dirt onto his face.

Inside they saw a transparent plastic bag sealed with tape. 'Now this isn't from the world wars,' said Myles, lifting it out of the metal tin, and carefully turning it in his hands.

The bag contained a weighty bundle of papers and a bottle. Clear liquid inside the bottle glugged from side to side as Myles tilted it. Then he noticed the label: something in German. 'We're going to need Heike-Ann to translate this before we open it.' He looked up at the faces of Glenn, Pascal and Zenyalena. They all nodded. Finally, something they could all agreed upon.

After checking there was nothing else in the metal box, Myles carried the plastic bag out of the trench as carefully as he could. They all returned to the gravel track and clustered around Heike-Ann, who pulled some latex gloves on her hands before taking the bag from Myles. Then she placed the bag on the gravel, in clear view of the whole team, and delicately started to unpick the seal.

The plastic opened easily enough. Heike-Ann extracted the papers. There were lots of them: perhaps a hundred sheets. Most had yellowed with age, and had type-written text on them.

Zenyalena urged her to translate. 'Well, what do they say?'

Heike-Ann squinted at the papers. This first one – it's a medical report. From Pasewalk military hospital, dated 1918.

The original?' asked Myles, 'If it is then Stolz was even better connected than we thought.'

The others looked baffled. 'Explain,' demanded Zenyalena.

'Young Adolf Hitler's medical file,' said Myles. 'It'll show he wasn't really blinded by mustard gas in October 1918, as he claimed. He lost his vision because of a mental collapse. A former Chancellor of Germany tried to blackmail Hitler with the file, but the dictator had him murdered, and the medical report disappeared.'

'Until now,' said Pascal, awestruck.

Heike-Ann nodded. 'Yes, it is on private Adolf Hitler,' she confirmed. 'And I'd guess it was the original.'

Zenyalena grabbed the historic document without looking at it. 'What's next?' she urged.

'The title, it's 'Eid' in German – it means 'the passing of an oath or solemn promise'.'

The others stood bemused, waiting for Heike-Ann to explain the main text.

Heike-Ann started to read and translate at the main time. "Im April 1945 versprach ich ihm dass ich als Teil der Operation Werwolf auch weiterhin für Deutschland kämpfen würde. Diese Flasche mit einer konzentrierten Mischung aus Sarin und Tebum war die Waffe, die ich erhielt...' '*In April 1945, I promised Him I would continue to fight for Germany, as part of Operation Werewolf. This bottle of concentrated Sarin and Tebum mixture was the weapon I was given.*"

She looked down at the liquid inside the glass container. 'Tebum?' she queried, glancing up at Myles.

'Tebum is a nerve agent, like Sarin,' Myles explained. 'Chemical weapons developed by the Nazis. Lethal – even in tiny doses.'

Heike-Ann made sure she was clear of the bottle. She turned to the next page. 'Between April 1945 and May 1990, I could not access the Bunker Am Krusenick ....'

Myles and Glenn looked at each other. *Am Krusenick.*

It was the road where Stolz had his basement flat. The place where Myles had been gassed.

Heike-Ann kept reading, translating as she went. '... So for the main part of my life I was forced to do without the knowledge we had rediscovered. These notes explain the method I developed in the absence of that science and our equipment.'

Heike-Ann turned the paper over to check there was nothing on the other side. It was blank.

Zenyalena urged her to look at the next pack of paper. 'Well, what was his method?'

Heike-Ann started again. The page was thick with text. 'It's, er, a set of principles for – for predicting things. How to foretell life events, that sort of thing,' she said, trying to summarise it.

The others exchanged glances, urgently wanting Heike-Ann to translate more. Heike-Ann just leafed through the pages, realising there was too much to go through. 'This page is all about how to get the timing of an event... this one is all about how different angles have a different impact...' She was becoming overwhelmed.

'Come on. This is just more hogwash,' said Glenn, shaking his head to dismiss it all.

Heike-Ann looked sceptical too. She turned the page, to reveal something from the office of Joseph Goebbels. 'It's a propaganda plan,' she offered. 'Operation Blinker, it's called.' She scanned it. 'Looks like a set of seven instructions for covering up the secret.'

Zenyalena snatched the 'Operation Blinker' page. Heike-Ann let her take it while she picked out the next set of papers – two sheets held together with a paperclip. The headline on the front page read simply 'Nixon'. She held the page up for Glenn, who instantly recognised the disgraced President's name.

Glenn's face reacted with surprise. Without saying anything, he invited her to read it out.

'It starts "Richard Milhous" Nixon, born 9.35p.m. PST 9th Jan 1913. 33:53 North, 17:49 West (Yorba Linda, California, "USA")'….' Heike-Ann began scanning through the text. 'It says "Low chance of winning Presidential election in November 1960 because on Inauguration Day in January 1961, Nixon has both Jupiter and Saturn at the lowest point in the chart, opposing point of career success... 1968 election is much better, because then Jupiter on the rising horizon makes for popular Presidency with foreign policy focus. Saturn on setting horizon indicates confrontation with Congress."

Myles could see the others absorbing the information. 'Well, it's right so far – Nixon lost the 1960 election, then won in 1968. What else does it say, Heike-Ann?'

'Er… '1972: Jupiter allows for criticism to be brushed off' then, it says 'April 30th 1973: Uranus at 90 degrees to Sun – shock challenge to public image…" Heike-Ann turned the page. '… And on the next sheet, it says '20th October 1973… something more about planets. Nixon to issue shock instruction, over-reach his power and respond in anger to achieve deception. Failure likely..." She looked up. 'Myles: what was that about?'

Myles remembered his US history. 'It was called the "Saturday Night Massacre". Nixon tried to be bold. He dismissed the special prosecutor into Watergate, and also his Attorney General. It backfired on him, though.'

Heike-Ann turned to the last page on Nixon. 'Then it concludes: "Neptune, Moon, Venus, Mars", and Uranus – total difference from exact angles reaches zero on 8th August 1974 at 2105 "Eastern Standard Time."

Myles recognised the date and time. 'Middle of the evening... The precise moment of Nixon's resignation, live on TV. Stolz got it exactly right.'

'I'm still not convinced,' said Glenn, frowning. 'Did he write that before Nixon resigned, or afterwards?'

Heike-Ann scoured the page. 'It doesn't say. It's not dated...'

She turned the page, trying to find more. '...There doesn't seem to be anything else on Nixon. But it does have this. It says "We were able to apply these methods to countries as well as people. 5.10p.m. on July 4th, 1776, counts as the USA's birthday, when the colony launched a broadside over water against the British Empire. We realised that the planet Uranus returned to where it was on that first Independence Day in April 1861, exactly when Union troops fired cannons across Charleston Harbour to start the US Civil War. Uranus returned there again in early June 1944 for D-Day, when the Americans again launched a momentous attack over water, and we can expect something similar next time, in May 2026, or during the first three months of 2027".'

Myles remembered the papers from Vienna. 'The 83-year cycle. It was the Uranus cycle – that's how long it takes the planet to go round the sun. Combining it with the moon – that's how Stolz predicted D-Day.'

Heike-Ann read on. ' "We also applied these methods for the United Kingdom, using the Act of Union, which took effect on midnight on 1st January 1801. This warned us of Neptune causing problems of arrogance and deception in October 1956, and Pluto undermining the leadership through destructive power in October 1984.' " Underneath the page, Heike-Ann found a more recent sheet – dated just three months ago. She showed it to the others as she translated. "As a final proof, I have applied my methods to predict the forthcoming events ..."

She held up the list – a couple of US senators were named, with dates in the near future next to each one. Stolz had also thrown in the names of a US Supreme Court Justice, a European Prime Minister and a well-known pop star. Beside each one, next to a month and year, were the words 'to die': Stolz was foretelling the death of each one.

None of the team knew what to make of their discoveries. Pascal seemed transfixed by the liquid, Glenn's body language was trying to convince the others it was all nonsense, while Zenyalena was running her finger over one of the papers, trying to absorb Stolz's principles for prediction.

It was Myles who drew them back to what could have been the most important reference in the whole box. 'What did he mean by "his equipment" in "Am Krusenick"? and "The main part of the knowledge we rediscovered"?'

Pascal tipped his head, scowling at the others. 'You must have missed something when you checked out his basement flat.'

Glenn wasn't so sure. 'We checked it pretty thoroughly,' he replied. 'So did your friend Jean-François. And the German police.'

Heike-Ann looked back at the words. 'Bunker Am Krusenick. It says "Bunker". Could there be a bunker somewhere in Am Krusenick – under where Stolz used to live?'

'It could make sense,' suggested Myles, 'if the place was only accessible through Stolz's old basement flat. That would explain why the old man went there as soon as he could, after the Berlin Wall came down... And why he left a mansion outside Nuremberg for a damp inner city flat.'

Heike-Ann was about to reply when a crack exploded in their ears. Myles instinctively felt himself diving to the ground, almost hitting the bottle of nerve agent. He felt air rush past him and splinters of wood fly around as more bullets whizzed nearby. Exposed on the gravel road, Myles tried desperately to work out where the firing was coming from.

Pascal was next to him, also looking like he was trying to make sense of what had happened. Zenyalena and Glenn had dived towards the trenches. The American was trying to crawl into the ditch for cover.

Then Myles saw Heike-Ann fall to the ground.

CHAPTER 53

Compiègne
Eastern France
11.55a.m. CET (10.55a.m. GMT)

Myles saw Heike-Ann had been hit near her elbow of her right arm. Pascal made eye-contact with Myles, indicating they needed to help the woman towards the trench and quickly lifted her legs while Myles grabbed the German's good arm, staying low. Together, they carried her towards the undergrowth, and passed her down to Glenn. Myles and Pascal slid into the ditch after her.

The firing continued over their heads. Zenyalena started to check Heike-Ann's wounds while Glenn and Myles tried to understand who was attacking them.

'It's coming from at least two places,' said Myles, cowering. 'There must be two guns.'

He saw Pascal bend down to their wounded German translator. Then the Frenchman lifted himself out of the trench and started crawling back to the road.

'What the hell's he doing?' Glenn shouted across to Myles.

Staying within the trench, Myles and Glenn could see Pascal crawl forward, his weight on his forearms. Then they glimpsed what he was crawling towards: a machine gun – *which was firing by itself.*

Myles and Glenn crouched low, covering their ears from the horrendous noise, feeling their whole bodies shake with the clatter of the gun. Glenn slung himself tight into the protection of the trench. Myles felt splatters of mud and other debris showering them, kicked up by the arc of bullets.

Pascal poked his head up to check how the gun was positioned – it was hidden under a camouflage net and mounted on a tripod, sweeping one way then the other. But its elevation was fixed: it was not firing down. There was just enough space for Pascal to crawl underneath the torrent of bullets.

The Frenchman rushed towards it as quickly as he could, then knocked the gun upwards from below. It took him just a moment more to stop it firing.

With one weapon down, it was much easier to locate the other. Like the first, it was hidden and mounted, with No one at the controls. Myles saw Pascal crawl off towards it.

Myles and Glenn ducked again as the bullets swept towards them. They waited for the stream of metal to pass, then Myles called out above the clatter of the automatic gunfire. 'Pascal?'

No reply.

Glenn stared nervously at Myles: had the Frenchman been hit? Myles shouted up, 'Pascal. Are you there?'

Still no reply.

Neither of them wanted to lift their heads out of the trench to look.

Then they heard movement – a noise above the racket of the machine gun, something rushing through the undergrowth, and a body slamming onto the earth with a grunt.

'Pascal?'

Nothing. The bullets swept close again.

Unable to work out what was happening above them, Myles and Glenn looked down to Heike-Ann and Zenyalena. Zenyalena had improvised a bandage around their translator's upper arm.

Heike-Ann was still alert, but she looked pale and sweaty, and was clearly in pain.

Rat-a-tat-a-tat-a-tat-a...

The bullets swept overhead once more, skimming the top of the trench and sending splatters of earth flying into the air. Myles' head recoiled, ducking into his shoulders. He saw Glenn trying to protect his ears from the racket.

Then it stopped. Silence – finally.

Myles looked at the American, who raised his eyebrows in surprise. Had Pascal disabled the second gun?

Myles called out again. 'Pascal? Are you there?'

After a long moment, the reply came back. Pascal's words were breathless and exhausted. 'Yes. I'm here. And it's safe now.'

Myles poked his head up, and saw Pascal recovering: the Frenchman was sitting on the second gun, relieved but drained.

Myles called out. 'What happened?'

Pascal was too out of breath to answer immediately. Instead he just patted the gun metal. 'I knocked it down.'

Myles and Glenn started climbing out of the trenches. Glenn approached the first gun, checking it was safe while Myles walked towards Pascal and the gun he was sitting on. He recognised it from pictures he'd seen: a Vickers .303 heavy machine gun. Once one of the most common automatic weapons from the Western Front, but now old and rare. He wondered if it could have come from the Imperial War Museum.

Then he saw something next to it – a small black plastic box.

Pascal lifted it for him to see. 'It was attached to the firing button...' The Frenchman pulled out an aerial, still catching his breath. '...Radio-controlled.'

Glenn called over from the first gun. 'Same here - this thing's been set on automatic,' The American was running back towards them.

Zenyalena emerged from the trench, with Heike-Ann's arm over her shoulder. Heike-Ann was conscious, but in pain. Myles, Glenn and Pascal saw the Russian woman was struggling, and rushed over to help. All four of them – their ears still recovering from the clatter of the machine gun – carried Heike-Ann back to the gravel track, near to where she'd been hit, and laid her down. Blood had already seeped through the bandage.

Myles held her hand and lifted the injured limb in the air. 'We'll keep it up – you'll lose less blood that way.'

'Thank you.' Heike-Ann was wincing, holding back the intense agony of a gunshot wound, and clearly worried about her pregnancy.

Pascal put his hand on her forehead, trying to calm her.

Glenn was still livid. 'What was that? We've just been attacked. By…by…' He didn't know what to say.

Pascal completed the sentence for him. 'By a ghost.'

Myles could tell something crossed Zenyalena's mind as she ran swiftly towards the first gun determined to inspect it for herself. It was just a few seconds later when she called out from where the first gun had been. 'We've been betrayed.'

Glenn shouted back, angry that Zenyalena was stating the obvious. 'Of course we've been betrayed. Hell, we've almost been killed.'

'No, Glenn. It's one of us,' said Zenyalena, her eyes fixed and with a deadly tone in her voice. 'One of the five of us must have done this.' She ran back over to the group, a furious look on her face. She was clutching one of the black boxes which had been attached to the machine gun. 'Look….' She held up the device, gripping it so tightly her fingers had turned white. '…This is a short-range receiver. Someone must have set it off from very close by. She threw it down then smashed it with her heel. 'One of us.'

'You're talking nonsense, Zenyalena,' said Glenn, still shaking his head. 'Whoever it was could still be hiding round here - so *not* one of us.'

Heike-Ann called up from the ground, where she was still resting with her wound. 'They used those things guarding the East German border – automatic machine guns. It could have been set off when we picked up the ammunition box.'

Zenyalena was having none of it. 'You're saying Stolz set those guns up? Some sort of trap to hide his precious papers?' She pointed at the machine guns. 'Those guns couldn't have stayed hidden for any length of time. Not for even for a few days. Someone would have found them. And if they were there for a long time, they would have stopped working. Guns – especially vintage machine guns – need constant maintenance.'

Myles realised Zenyalena had a point. But it led to a terrible conclusion: one of the five of them was somehow involved in setting the trap.

Calmly, Pascal tried to mediate. 'So we know those guns were put there recently, probably to hit whoever found Stolz's papers. But it can't be someone from our team, because any one of us could have been killed. It must be someone who had worked with Stolz.' His logic was clear: someone else was trying to keep them from Stolz's secret - someone prepared to use deadly force.

But Zenyalena still wasn't accepting it. 'No. Jean-François' murder, the fire in Vienna, the ladder breaking in Munich, even Myles being gassed in Berlin. Whoever's trying to stop us finding Stolz's secret - they must be getting help from someone on this team.'

Myles looked at the other team members. If there was a traitor, who could it be? He wondered about each of the four people beside him.

Heike-Ann was still nursing her wounded arm. Surely she wouldn't have set the gun to fire on herself?

Not Pascal, either. In the most heroic way possible, the Frenchman had just proved he was trying to help the team. And he had risked his life underground in Munich, and during the fire in Vienna, too.

Glenn? Glenn was still a mystery. Myles knew he was connected with some murky part of the US Government machine. Glenn had always been the most sceptical of Stolz's material. But surely the American would have easier ways of disrupting the mission than setting up ancient machine guns?

That just left Zenyalena. Certainly, she was volatile. But could she be mad enough to set up the guns and start the fire in Vienna? Unlikely. And Zenyalena was the most keen to find the traitor - she didn't seem like the sort of woman who could bluff like that.

Myles reckoned none of them could be a traitor – unless he was missing something. There had to be some other explanation.

Myles raised his voice. 'When we left Munich, we all agreed to keep this place secret, so we couldn't be followed. Yes?'

All four of the others agreed.

'So, did anyone mention this location to anyone else?'

Pascal shook this head, looking straight back at Myles.

'I told the helicopter we were going to Compiègne,' admitted Glenn, 'but not about the last 500 metres.'

'Heike-Ann? Zenyalena?'

'No,' explained Heike-Ann. 'At the army base I told my husband I'd be flying to France, but I didn't say where.'

Zenyalena gave a fuller answer. 'I gave a report to Moscow, but that was about what we found in Munich. Not about this.' She saw Glenn was still sceptical. 'There's no way Moscow could do this… even if someone intercepted my report, they wouldn't know about this place.'

Myles tried something else. 'So, maybe someone has found a way to follow us.'

Pascal raised a query. 'But setting up the machine guns would take time. We'd see them do it. And if they did, why use remote controls?'

Myles accepted Pascal was right. Even if someone was tracking them, it wouldn't explain what had been happening. He was about to ask what they do next, when the quiet of the forest was interrupted by a faint noise. Something was coming down the gravel path. Footsteps.

Myles' eyes alerted the rest of the team to the danger. Without words, he pointed to the trees, urging them to leave the track. Silently, Pascal and Glenn carried Heike-Ann into the undergrowth while Zenyalena ran back towards one of the machine guns. Myles crouched behind a tree, resting his supported leg on the ground as silently as he could.

He listened carefully. The footsteps were getting closer. It sounded like a single set of footsteps: just one person? Zenyalena also guessed whoever was coming was alone, and indicated to Myles she was ready with the gun.

But Myles recognised something odd about the steps. It wasn't the sound of a normal person walking. The footsteps came in pairs - someone walking with an uneven gait.

Myles allowed his head to emerge from behind the tree. He could see the silhouette, and recognised it instantly. A familiar voice call out.

'Myles? Myles, are you here?'

Myles allowed himself to stand up. In full view, he stepped out and walked back to the main track. Then he approached the man he had known for twenty years. He went to shake hands with his old pal. 'Frank – Frank, why on earth are you here?'

As ever, Frank was sweating, but his face opened up when he saw his university friend. 'Myles. Good to find you.' The museum curator let his walking stick rest on his hip while he searched for an envelope in his bag. 'I came to give you the carbon-dating results – you said they were urgent,' he explained.

Then he realised Myles was not alone. First Pascal appeared, then Glenn. Heike-Ann sat herself up, wincing in pain as she did so. They looked at him, accusingly. Frank obviously couldn't understand why.

Glenn made the first comment, his tone hostile. 'So, Myles: was it *you* who told someone about this location?'

Glenn and Pascal stared at Frank, blaming him for the machine guns.

Myles knew he had to stand up for his old friend. 'Yes, I did. I told my partner, Helen.'

Frank gathered Myles was in some kind of trouble and tried to back him up. 'Er, yes, that's right. And it was Helen who told me.' Nervously he felt the need to say more, trying to sound positive. 'Helen Bridle – she's with CNN, you know.' The museum curator held up the envelope. 'I came to give Myles these - carbon-dating results.'

Glenn snatched it away.

Quickly, Pascal grabbed Frank's walking stick. 'Is this a real walking stick? Or is your limp just an act?'

'It's childhood polio, Pascal,' said Myles, defending his colleague again. 'Frank's had a limp for years. And in case you're wondering - could Frank have set up those machine guns? The answer's no.'

Frank's eyes looked scared, as if the danger he sensed in the people around him was suddenly very real. 'Machine guns? We had two stolen from the museum over night. But how did they get here?'

Myles was about to point to them when he felt his body recoil again.

Rat-a-tat-a-tat-a-tat...

They all ducked as another explosive clatter of gunfire burst around them.

The bullets stopped. Myles turned to see what had happened. It was Zenyalena: she was holding the German machine gun, and had just fired a burst of bullets above their heads. 'All of you: stay there. Myles: you lied. You told someone about this place, then tried to keep it secret.' The Russian stood up, her hands still on the firing mechanism. 'And in Vienna – that fire. You were behind it.'

'No.'

'Come on. It all points to you. The gas attack in Berlin – you did that yourself, didn't you …' Zenyalena's voice had a sarcastic tone to it. '…And Munich. Now I understand. The grenade didn't go off because you didn't want it to. That's why Pascal had to do it.'

'Oh, Zenyalena, come on.'

'Be quiet. Traitor.' Zenyalena was lifting up the gun, pointing it towards him. It was heavy – she could only just manage, and she was keeping her fingers away from the barrel, probably because the recent shots had made it too hot. Myles saw the belt of ammunition was almost finished. If she did shoot, she'd only manage one or two bursts of fire. But then, that was probably all she'd need to kill him – perhaps to kill them all.

Zenyalena staggered back to the gravel track, her eyes warily scanning Frank, Glenn, Myles, Pascal and Heike-Ann in turn. 'We've worked out there must be a traitor. Now we know that the traitor is the Englishman. And he was working with this man.' She eyed Frank, sceptically looking at his weak leg. 'What I don't know is whether any of you were also involved. Pascal, Heike-Ann, Glenn: do any of you want to admit something?'

Glenn, Pascal and Heike-Ann looked at each other – confused and defenceless.

Glenn tried to calm the Russian. 'Zenyalena, I think you're wrong.'

'Well, I think I'm right,' she replied, curtly. 'Myles has a past which he has refused to mention: his involvement with terrorists from Africa. Any denials, Mr Munro?'

'The newspapers had bad information,' offered Myles.

'Not good enough, Myles,' dismissed Zenyalena. 'We've always known you're a misfit. Now, you've tried to kill us. To kill me. Which means, I should kill you.'

She steadied the heavy gun on her hip, preparing to fire.

Pascal shook his head. 'Zenyalena, don't do this. There must be some explanation.'

'No.' She stared back at Myles. 'Myles: go over there.'

She was directing him to stand apart from the others. To stand next to the trench, where his body would tumble after he'd been shot.

Myles stared at the gun. Obey or resist?

Zenyalena shook the weapon in her hands, making sure the ammunition belt was hanging loose, ready to feed into the firing mechanism. Her eyes were open wider than ever. Myles knew she wasn't bluffing.

The Russian spoke deeply and firmly, giving directions he had to obey. 'Go. Now.'

Very slowly, palms open and pointing downwards to show he was following her instructions, Myles started to walk.

Then Glenn called out. He had opened Frank's envelope. 'Wait. Zenyalena.'

'What?'

'The carbon-dating stuff. It looks genuine.'

Zenyalena didn't seem convinced. Muscles on her face twitched: she was deciding between asking for more details and shooting Myles immediately.

Frank called out. 'Yes, they're genuine. I checked all the papers.'

'And who are you?'

'I'm the curator of the Imperial War Museum in London.'

'Prove it,' Zenyalena demanded.

Frank looked at her gun. 'Er, that weapon. It's an MG 08/15 air-cooled German machine gun. Nicknamed a "Spandau gun", because it was manufactured in Spandau, near Berlin. The model you have dates from 1917. Check the serial number – it'll prove I'm right.'

But Zenyalena refused to check. Instead she just curled her lip. 'That just proves you know something about this ambush.'

She prepared to fire on Myles. 'Mr Munro. You're about to die. Anything we should know before I kill you?'

Myles thought about rushing her. Knocking her over, pushing the gun into the air... It might work, but she'd probably pull the trigger before he even got close.

Instead, he'd have to convince her. 'I told my partner, Helen, where we'd be, and I shouldn't have, Zenyalena. I'm sorry.'

'Sorry for setting up the machine guns?'

'No, that wasn't me. But there's one more place we have to look. Maybe it'll explain everything.'

Zenyalena's eyes narrowed. 'Where? We've checked out all of Stolz's locations. Vienna, Munich, now here. Where else is there?'

'There were four locations, remember.' Myles breathed out. He started talking to the others as much as Zenyalena. 'And the fourth location must be in Berlin.'

'Berlin? Come on, we've already been there.'

'No. The bunker in Am Krusenick street. Stolz's last location - it must be underneath his old basement flat.' Myles looked at Pascal. 'Pascal: would you come?'

Pascal's eyebrows rose. For a moment he looked open-minded, then he seemed to make up his mind. 'Yes, Myles, I will come.'

'Good. Thanks Pascal. Glenn?'

Glenn paused thoughtfully before he replied. 'No, Myles. We've looked enough. This search has got crazy. I say we call it off now…' The American turned to Zenyalena. He didn't have a weapon, but he spoke as if he did. 'And Zenyalena, put down that gun. Nobody gets killed. Heike-Ann needs to go to hospital. We should all just leave.'

Zenyalena swivelled her gun towards Glenn. 'Glenn: get in that vehicle. Take the driving seat, please.'

Glenn raised his hands above his head, in an 'if you really want me to' gesture. He opened the door to the minibus and climbed inside. 'Where are the keys?'

Zenyalena gestured with her eyes to her pocket. 'Pascal, Heike-Ann, Myles and you, Mr Imperial Curator…'

'Er, Frank. My name's Frank.'

Zenyalena just waved the Spandau gun towards him. 'All of you. Get in the back.'

Pascal helped Heike-Ann into the minibus. Frank limped in after them, with Myles helping his old friend on board. Myles followed them in.

Zenyalena waited until they were all inside. Then, still clutching the heavy machine gun to her waist, she strained with the weight of the passenger door and heaved it shut. Leaving her captives in the vehicle, she walked back into the road. With one hand, she picked up the bottle of nerve agent liquid. Carefully, she placed it through the open window onto the seat next to the driver.

Glenn glanced at the bottle of nerve agent, a scared look on his face. Myles saw the danger, too. If Zenyalena fired at the bottle, they'd all die within seconds.

Zenyalena was several metres away from the bus now, standing in front of it, and ready to shatter the glass with a bullet.

Instead, the Russian quickly searched the area. She collected the bundle of papers which had been in Stolz' ammunition box. Then, checking around her again, she ran back towards the minibus, and climbed into the seat next to Glenn.

Glenn pointed to the glass bottle. 'You be careful with that.'

Zenyalena nodded. She manoeuvred the machine gun onto the floor – there was barely enough space for it – then picked up the bottle. 'I'm going to carry this…' She turned round to make eye-contact with Myles, Pascal, Frank and Heike-Ann, all sitting in the back. Her eyes sized them up. '…So if I die, we all die.'

Then she pulled out the keys for the minibus and handed them to Glenn. 'Drive. Back to Berlin,' she ordered. 'Back to Stolz's apartment block in "Am Krusenick" Street. We're going to discover what the old Nazi was hiding once-and-for-all, even if every one of us dies finding it.'

Glenn understood. He turned on the ignition, and started the vehicle rolling along the track, away from the forest and towards the highway.

CHAPTER 54

1.20p.m. CET (12.20p.m GMT)

Dieter lifted out his smart phone with one hand, turned it on, waited, and kept it low.

There was a new message from Father Samuel.

Twin devices, not one. Sorry. Still alive?

So the fat man had set him up – two machine guns not one. Dieter smirked – it was just as the globes in the underground cavern had predicted for him.

No need to reply - better to play dead, he thought. He already had the money. He wouldn't need to contact his old paymaster again.

Instead, without looking at the screen, he began to type.

The world is about to change. This change will start in Berlin.

He pressed his thumb on the bottom of the screen.

'Send'

Hiding the glow of the phone with his jacket, Dieter typed on.

...This change will be broadcast live on CNN...

He supressed a grin.

> ***There will be no talks. Humanitarian Pursuit – the answer is 'no'.***
> ***Prepare for terror! Prepare for the return of the Reich!***

He remembered Stolz's list – the two US Senators, the European Prime Minister and the pop star – and the dates they were due to die.

> ***On these dates I will kill these people...***

In a single motion, Dieter pressed 'send' again, as he palmed the phone into his hand.

Then he bent down to slip the device back into the strap on his ankle, as if he was tying his shoelaces.

Dieter settled back in his seat, and turned to look at the scenery of eastern France as it passed his window. The international team were so, so dumb... they still hadn't worked out how their prize information was leaking to the *Mein Kampf Now* website...

He was still invisible. Still unnoticed. Still in disguise...

And he knew his latest upload– specific individuals with clear dates when they would die – was his best yet.

Within seconds, his upload appeared on a computer screen three thousand miles away.

Sally Wotton jolted up in her seat. It was another message.

Frantically, she scanned through the names of the people being threatened, then she hovered her cursor over the names, copied the list, and pasted it into a new email.

> ***Urgent: Immediate Federal Protection required for named individuals....***

Sally knew she had to act fast. She hoped her email would save some of the people named on the website. Perhaps the psychopath behind *Mein Kampf Now* would be caught as he tried to murder the people he had just condemned.

And she also saw: the tech boys were finally making progress. The latest upload had come from the east of France, somewhere near the historical town of Compiègne.

But it made Sally wonder. Was this really a lone psychopath, as she suspected, or was there a group behind the *Mein Kampf Now* website? How was someone in France or Germany going to kill senators based in the US?

She had always imagined a single loner was behind the threats – a common terrorist profile: male, educated, and with a motive to hate. But this suggested there might be a network.

What sort of conspiracy was Sally dealing with?

She didn't know, but she knew she was close to cracking it.

CHAPTER 55

Driving to Berlin
3.50p.m. CET (2.50p.m. GMT)

Myles knew going to Am Krusenick had only bought time. Just a few hours, nothing more, before Zenyalena killed them. Nothing more. They would never find Stolz's secret – certainly not in the old Nazi's Am Krusenick flat, because there couldn't be a bunker hidden under Stolz's apartment in East Berlin.

It was well-known that Hitler had built huge tunnel systems, mostly dug by slaves. These subterranean caves had stored stolen art and protected Nazis like Stolz from the Allied bombing campaign. But Myles remembered the newsreels of Soviet soldiers in May 1945 – the victorious Red Army in a destroyed Berlin, which hunted down snipers left fighting after their Führer had killed himself. When the Red Army had doubted Hitler was really dead, they had searched every room in every building. They had found thousands of German girls and women hiding underground, terrified of being raped, but not the Nazi dictator. Myles recalled the famous picture of Churchill from July of 1945: the British warlord inspecting Hitler's bunker during a break from the Potsdam Conference, trying not to gloat. Then during the Cold War, and especially after 1961 when the Berlin Wall sealed off half the population, everywhere had been surveyed again. Berlin's unique history meant the city had been searched for underground spaces many times over several years – and by very committed Communists. How could any remain secret?

Myles reckoned that whatever had been in the Am Krusenick bunker, it would have been ransacked by Red Army soldiers in 1945. The 'scientific equipment' Stolz wrote about was probably destroyed. And that meant, when they got to Berlin, when they searched Stolz's flat again, they would find nothing. They would be back where they had just been: to Zenyalena making accusations, to Myles being accused, and to the Spandau gun being pointed at him again.

He thought of Helen, wishing he could escape to be with her.

He looked around the minibus. Pascal was tending to Heike-Ann's wounded arm - their German translator was still losing blood. Myles sensed the Frenchman was eager to strike back. Glenn was driving, carefully and silently, still very self-contained but Myles could tell the American was wondering whether to call Zenyalena's bluff. Myles tried to make eye-contact with Glenn through the rear-view mirror, but the man didn't want to engage. Myles wondered: if Zenyalena held him at gunpoint again, would Glenn allow him to be shot?

Myles didn't trust the American. He sensed Glenn had some other agenda, although he couldn't yet work out what it was.

Then there was Zenyalena. As the minibus chuntered along the highway, from France into Germany, she was still cradling the nerve agent in her hands. The Russian woman would peer down at it, then glance at the GPS device on the dashboard. Sometimes she would turn to the back of the vehicle, checking on the four passengers who had become her prisoners - at least until they uncovered the last part of Stolz's puzzle in Berlin. The minibus ride had not calmed Zenyalena. Myles could see the woman still feared for her life, and was prepared to kill.

That left Frank. Like a schoolboy who'd tried to please but got everything wrong, Myles' old university friend seemed the most nervous of all. Myles could tell Frank was still confused: the museum curator had come to hand-deliver some carbon-dating results. How had he ended up being held at gunpoint by a mad Russian woman? And driven to Berlin? If Frank had been less of a friend, he would have blamed Myles. Instead, Frank stayed silent. He just looked out of the window, watching as the scenery passed by and the minibus slowly travelled east.

Myles remembered Frank's envelope. 'The carbon dating – can I see the results?'

Zenyalena's head spun round, alert to any sort of trick Myles might pull. For a second she froze, glaring straight at Myles and Frank. Then she relaxed slightly. 'Yes. Read them out for all of us, please.'

Slowly and deliberately, careful not to alarm Zenyalena, Myles drew the papers from the envelope. Inside were three sheets of computer print-outs, with columns of numbers on each page. He tried to understand them. 'Frank, can you explain?'

Frank looked over at the papers. 'Certainly. I tested all the samples you posted from Berlin. This first column,' he pointed to the left-hand margin, 'that's the item reference number. Each page tested was given a different code by the laboratory.'

Myles looked down the list: he had given Frank forty pages from Stolz's file, and the carbon-dating lab had numbered each of them, from B1 to B40. 'What does the 'B' stand for?'

'Berlin. The second column shows the percentage confidence we have in the result.'

Myles skimmed the column: on all three sheets it was either ninty-eight per cent or ninty-nine per cent, with a single ninty-seven per cent.

'You see, Myles, all the data is at least ninty-seven per cent certain,' continued Frank. 'The third column show the range of dates when the paper was probably written.'

Myles turned through the report. Through most of the first two pages of computer print-out, the dates were listed as between 1939 and 1943, with a few 1944s and 1945s creeping in towards the bottom. Then, on the last page, there were anomalies: three of Stolz's papers were more recent. 'So everything really was written during the war, except these last three papers, from 1959?'

'That's right Myles. For all of them except those three, the date on the paper itself was probably accurate,' said Frank. 'Those last three – they must be fakes. They looked like the other Stolz papers, and had dates from 1942 on them, but they were written later.'

Myles tried to absorb the information: someone had been doctoring Stolz's papers. He wondered why. 'Tell me: what did these three papers say – the fake ones? What was on them?'

'Well, you see, that's the funny thing. One was about China attacking Soviet Russia in the 1950s, one was about Germany rising again in 1957, and the other was about Cuba – saying it would be destroyed by a volcano.'

Myles squinted in disbelief. He checked again with Frank. 'But ... but that's all nonsense. None of that happened.'

'Correct, Myles. You would think that someone who falsified a prediction – to write something after it happened – they'd write something true, to make themselves look wise after the event, right?' Frank was explaining the results as if he was about to deliver a big punchline. 'But, whoever tried to fake Stolz's papers in 1959 was doing the opposite. They were trying to make predictions which were false.'

Zenyalena's hand swiped out. She grabbed the computer print-outs from Myles. Then she stared at him, checking his face for any signs of resistance. Once it was clear Myles was letting her take them, she checked the numbers for herself. After a few seconds she turned back to Frank. 'How do I know these figures are genuine?'

Frank shrugged. 'I don't know. I suppose you have to ask the lab which did the testing. There could have been some sort of mix-up, but it's unlikely.'

Zenyalena's face screwed up with suspicion again. 'Mix-up? Well isn't that a quaint English word for all this …' She threw the papers into the back of the minibus. They fluttered towards Heike-Ann, whose face was looking pale. Pascal brushed them aside, careful to keep Heike-Ann's wounded arm high in the air.

Although the Frenchman was obviously angry, he didn't retaliate. Just like Glenn, who kept driving, Heike-Ann who lay semi-conscious on the floor of the minibus, and Frank, who was still terrified.

'Wait,' demanded Zenyalena suddenly, directing her words to the American. 'Stop here – pull over.'

The others watched as Glenn gently slowed the bus into a rest-stop. There were no other vehicles in the large layby – just a picnic bench and a postbox. None of them knew what Zenyalena had in mind.

Zenyalena waited until the vehicle had come to a complete rest, then gestured towards Frank for the envelope which had contained the carbon-dating results. Frank duly handed it over, still bemused.

'Stay still, everybody,' ordered Zenyalena. She lifted up the gun and carefully placed the glass bottle of liquid back in her seat. Once she was outside, she took some of Stolz's papers, and scribbled something on the top sheet – Myles couldn't see what it was, only that the words were in Russian. Then she wrote an address on the envelope, stuffed the papers inside, sealed it, and pushed it into the post box. Careful to keep the machine gun she was carrying low, so none of the fast-moving cars on the highway would notice it, she climbed back into the minibus. 'Now drive, Glenn – to Berlin.'

Once more, the vehicle accelerated onto the main road, heading east.

Myles wondered whether he'd just missed a chance to disarm Zenyalena. Perhaps. But if he had tried, it might have been messy.

Then, like the rest of the team, he slumped into his thoughts, half-hypnotised by the movement of the vehicle, while his mind tried to solve the puzzle of Werner Stolz.

CHAPTER 56

Oxford
England
8.10p.m. GMT

Helen ended her call to the States, thrilled that her editor had given her pitch the go-ahead. Proof of a link between the planets and human affairs would make an amazing news story, and she hoped the personal angle, tracing Bradley's work from Germany to Alaska, was just right for TV. Although she also accepted it was going to be difficult – and not just because so many people would try to rubbish her work…

To start the piece, she needed to link up with Myles and his international team. She looked forward to seeing him again – she knew he'd love a surprise visit. But Myles had refused to carry any sort of mobile - it was important No one could track where he was, he had told her. It meant the only way she could reach them was in person. She'd have to travel to eastern France, to get as close as she could to Compiègne – and the railway carriage they'd discussed in their video call twenty-four hours earlier.

Her taxi soon pulled up outside the flat in Pembroke Street.

'Yes, Heathrow Airport, please,' she confirmed to the cab driver.

'Which terminal, Miss?'

'I don't know, yet,' she admitted.

But she did know she wanted to get there fast. It wasn't the TV package. Something deep in her gut told her Myles was in trouble.

CHAPTER 57

Oxford University
England
8.20p.m. GMT

Father Samuel thanked the college porter for the directions, and lumbered into the quad. He watched his footing on the uneven stone slabs, and barely registered the undergraduates he passed, some of them giggling, as he counted off the staircases to number twelve. In normal times, he would have stopped to admire the Renaissance masonry, and seek out religious symbolism in the gargoyles. He would have visited the chapel to absorb the incantations, or read the inscriptions.

But these were not normal times, and Father Samuel was not here for his own pleasure. There was no way he could enjoy himself when his whole belief system was under threat. And it wasn't just his worldview: the shared understanding of Christianity, delicately constructed over centuries, often in the face of persecution, was in danger. The Church was imperilled by a revelation which questioned faith around the globe. Samuel was in Oxford to prevent a shock which could be as crippling as Pope Pius's failure to oppose the holocaust, the recent child sex abuse scandals, or even the Enlightenment. Indeed, faith had never recovered from what he once preached was 'the decent into rationality'.

Father Samuel confirmed he had reached staircase twelve, and heaved himself up the wooden steps. He found the door at the top was already open.

'Come on in, Sam,' invited the familiar voice, smug as ever.

Father Samuel duly entered. 'Thank you for seeing me, Professor,' he said, bowing his head. He sat in the only available chair, which he guessed was used to humiliate undergraduates every weekday during term time.

'So you've seen the light, then Father Samuel?' teased the professor, turning to greet Samuel with a gloating expression. Even though he was past sixty, the academic still seemed juvenile much of the time.

'I've come to make peace, if that's what you mean,' offered Samuel.

'Peace? You mean a compromise?' dismissed the professor. 'So we agree that God "half-exists", or something like that?' He shook his head. 'I think we both know that's a bad idea.' The professor laughed to himself.

Father Samuel nodded in understanding. Professor Cromhall had certainly done well from his 'outspoken' critique of the Church, and defence of science. It had made the man a television celebrity. The professor could even pretend to be a rebel, which was absurd given his place in the establishment.

'Perhaps reconciliation is a bad idea, Professor,' said Father Samuel. 'But there are some ideas we should discredit *together*.'

The professor did not respond immediately. Instead, he tried to gauge Father Samuel's face and eventually spoke with a more measured tone.

'What sort of ideas do you have in mind?'

'Ideas which – were they widely believed – would make us both fools. For example, that there could be a link between the position of the planets and human affairs,' offered Father Samuel, testing the professor with a hint of a smile.

'Astrology? That's all nonsense,' retorted Professor Cromhall. He sounded confident again. 'No intelligent person looks at the evidence for that. Being intelligent means considering other evidence, while refusing to consider how planetary cycles match up with people's lives.' He said the words with a sneer, reciting the mantra he knew was false.

Their eyes met, and silently they acknowledged the truth. They both had to *say* astrology was nonsense, since everybody in authority said that. Their status would be in jeopardy if they said anything else.

'Your pride in never having applied the scientific method to the link is well-placed, Professor,' taunted Father Samuel, softly. 'After all, in a battle between the traditional scientific method and astrology, I'm not sure who would win.' He let the words float off into the air.

'OK,' suggested the professor, negotiating. 'I'm prepared to say "the evidence for astrology is no greater than the evidence for the existence of God." Would that help?'

Father Samuel wasn't buying. 'It's not enough,' he explained. 'The Nazis found evidence which goes much further. There's a real danger it leaks – *to the public...*'

Finally, Professor Cromhall's expression changed. He became ashen as he realised what the public revelation would mean. The myth that science could explain everything would be shattered. Faith in people like him would disappear. His credibility, his book sales, his television appearances – all would be lost if the link between the planets and human affairs was accepted.

'...Professor, two centuries ago, scientists like you displaced churchmen like me to become the most trusted authority in society,' continued Father Samuel. 'Now you risk being displaced yourself by a new field of understanding. Science, like the Church, will belong only to yesterday.'

The professor sized up his guest, wondering how much he could trust Father Samuel. Finally, he decided it was probably worth taking the risk. 'Well can't you…' The professor drew a single finger across his neck, miming a guillotine.

'It worked in the past. The French statistician who publicised this before, Michel Gauquelin – when he died in 1991, it wasn't from natural causes,' said Father Samuel, raising his eyebrows to make sure the professor understood the euphemism. 'And just this morning, in France, one of my most diligent volunteers sacrificed himself for the greater good. But now there are too many people to silence.'

The professor gulped. 'So you have another plan?'

'I do,' said Father Samuel, finally nodding. 'Let me explain…'

CHAPTER 58

Germany

10.40p.m. CET (9.40p.m. GMT)

After ten-and-a-half hours of driving the minibus had reached the outskirts of Berlin. They were back in the land of tidy streets, perfectly kept green spaces, and architecture from the city's so very mixed history.

Glenn pointed to the fuel gauge. It was almost empty. 'We really need gas.'

But Zenyalena shook her head. 'No. Keep going.'

'Can we just drop Heike-Ann at a hospital, to make sure her baby's OK?'

'No. We keep going.' Zenyalena's tone was firm. Her eyes flashed, wide and intense, making clear to all she was mad enough to use the machine gun – perhaps even the nerve agent.

Glenn did as he was told, his eyes fixed on the road. Then, finally, he caught Myles' glance in the mirror. Myles exchanged looks with him; it was an, 'I'll trust you if you trust me', expression. Within a second, it was gone. But it was enough to give Myles hope. Or at least, *some* hope.

The minibus slowed as it reached its first traffic light. Myles wondered about trying to jump out, but he knew he couldn't - not with his bad leg. He'd never escape alive.

The lights turned green, and the vehicle rumbled forward again, boxed in by traffic, as it drove towards the centre of Berlin.

They continued down more streets, through the famous parts of the city – along the Kurfürstendamm, within sight of the Reichstag, and through the Brandenburg Gate. The oversized Russian embassy was nearby – the only building which really caught Zenyalena's attention. Soon they were approaching Stolz's old neighbourhood.

Finally, the minibus turned into Am Krusenick. Glenn rolled on to number 38. He parked up and put on the handbrake, then turned to Zenyalena for his next instructions.

Zenyalena's eyes stared down at the American's pockets. 'You've still got the keys to this flat, haven't you?'

Glenn paused before he replied. Myles could tell he was wondering whether he could get away with a lie; but the Russian woman was watching him too closely. Slowly, Glenn nodded. He delved in and pulled out the keys, letting them jingle in his fingers.

Zenyalena carefully placed the bottle of nerve agent on her seat. She bent down to pick up the First World War machine gun again, then turned to the passengers in the back. 'Everybody out.'

Pascal slid open the minibus door, then placed Heike-Ann's healthy arm around his shoulder. Myles helped the Frenchman lift her down.

Zenyalena kept her distance, worried one of the team was going to rush at her to grab the gun. She scanned around, checking she wasn't being watched from the street, then glanced up at windows in the buildings opposite. It was almost dark – even if there had been someone, they probably wouldn't have seen the four men and one wounded woman being herded from the minibus at gunpoint. 'Glenn: unlock Stolz's flat,' she ordered.

Glenn slotted the key into the first lock and turned it. The door to the block of flats swung open. He led the way into the lobby area then unlocked Stolz's basement flat. It too opened, and Myles remembered the musty river smell which ran through the building.

Zenyalena's face instructed the American to walk in. He obeyed, followed by Frank, with Myles and Pascal helping Heike-Ann. Zenyalena kept the gun on them all, silently watching them enter. 'Gentlemen. I want you to take up this carpet and show me what's underneath.'

Myles and Pascal rested Heike-Ann in one of the seats while Glenn kneeled down. He peeled back the edge of the carpet to reveal wooden floorboards.

Zenyalena pointed at them, her brow sweating with fear. 'Pull them up.'

Glenn looked back at her, his face asking 'how?' The floorboards were nailed in place.

Zenyalena eyed Glenn suspiciously, then grabbed a pillow, which she held to the end of the gun: an improvised silencer. 'Stay back,' she said, aiming at the floor.

Glenn jumped away.

Zenyalena pulled the trigger, unleashing a short burst of bullets. Myles felt his ears pop while splinters flew into the air. Vibrations shook the room.

The Russian kept a tight grip on her gun, even though the barrel would have become scalding hot. She checked the ammunition belt: just a few rounds left, but it was all she needed to keep giving orders. She looked down at the shattered floorboards. 'Now, take them up.'

This time Glenn obeyed, and began lifting the broken timber. Myles offered to help, but Zenyalena motioned with the gun barrel, instructing him to keep away.

As Glenn tugged at the broken wood, a dark space began to appear underneath. Myles peered into the hole. Concrete steps were leading down, into some sort of void.

Glenn looked back up to Zenyalena: as long as she held the gun, the American knew she was in control. 'You want me to go down?'

Zenyalena considered the idea, then shook her head. 'No. Myles: your turn.'

'Down there?'

'Yes, Englishman. Lead on.'

Myles tipped his head to one side, accepting the command but not sure how he was going to do it. Glenn shuffled aside, letting Myles through.

Still hobbling from his ruptured knee ligament, Myles edged towards the hole. He stepped down onto the first step, then the second, slowly descending into the dark. He had to duck his head to climb below the hole in the floorboards.

Downstairs was a basement like any other: the walls were damp and bare, there was a power socket and a cable, but nothing unusual. Then Myles noticed a hole in the concrete floor. It hadn't been cut smoothly, probably just made by someone attacking the floor with a pickaxe. Stolz must have done it soon after he bought the flat, back in 1990. He would have been younger and fitter then. But he hadn't needed to be strong: the concrete was thin, and – unusually for war concrete – it hadn't been reinforced with steel.

Suddenly Myles realised why. It was a double floor...

Now Myles understood how Stolz had kept the bunker secret. In March or April 1945, when the Nazis knew the Russians were coming, they must have sealed the bunker with concrete. It had been done quickly – which was why there was no steel. But it was enough to fool the Soviets – they would have found only the basement with a concrete floor. Stolz's secret would have remained hidden through the four decades of the Cold War. Then, in 1990, Stolz returned to break it open again. But to keep the bunker secret, he sealed off the whole basement with the floorboards at ground level. Not since the time of the Nazis would anybody but Stolz have seen whatever lay below.

Myles wondered what to do. He could go down, into the bunker - perhaps even try to escape. But would there be another exit? Unlikely: if there was, the bunker would have been discovered many years ago. Myles was probably standing over the only way in and the only way out.

He edged towards the cable and turned on the power at the socket. Electricity began to hum, and Myles saw light emerge from the void beneath him.

'What's going on down there?' It was Zenyalena, calling from above.

Myles knew now wasn't the time to lie. 'There's another level down, something below the basement.'

'A bunker?'

'I guess so,' answered Myles, peering at vertical steps which led into whatever was beneath, a fixed ladder down through a manhole.

Zenyalena started to approach, still carrying the gun, and looking suspicious. 'Find out what's down there,' she ordered, tapping his side with the gun barrel.

Myles looked back at Zenyalena's paranoid eyes. She had given up all pretence of being calm. Now she was pathological. There was no way Myles could refuse.

Careful to avoid sudden movements, Myles placed his good foot on the first rung, then lowered himself to allow his braced leg to take a lower rung. One step at a time, he kept descending until his whole body was inside the brightly lit bunker.

Zenyalena shouted down to him. 'What's inside?'

Myles tried to make it out. The first thing he saw was a bright yellow handle bearing the word 'Vorsicht' in Nazi-era lettering. He peered closer: it was the handle to some sort of emergency escape hatch. The small door had rusted, and had probably never been used.

The rest of the bunker was piled high with stacks of papers. There were reams and reams, some filed between cardboard covers, others just stacked in rough piles towering up to the ceiling. It was accompanied by the smell of old newspapers which had been allowed to become damp.

'.... Looks like... just papers.... I think... Myles shouted up to Zenyalena and the others.' He shook his head in disbelief. *A storehouse for bureaucrats...*

He stepped off at the bottom and saw one of the cardboard covers. He wiped off the dust to reveal a swastika. *Nazi bureaucrats...*

Zenyalena's head was poking down from above. Her voice was edgy. 'Well, what do the papers say?'

Myles picked up a file and opened it. The first sheet was titled 'Hauptmann Gerhard Schnitzer, geb. 24. Februar 1910.' Then there was a list of dates with a few words scribbled in German by each one. By the last date, 24, Dezember 1942, was simply a '†' symbol, and the single word 'Stalingrad'.

'Myles, can you hear me? What do the papers say?'

'Er, looks like old personnel records,' he suggested. 'German.'

He heard Zenyalena scuffle above him, but ignored it. He was too fascinated. What did these records mean? Why hadn't the Nazis burned them, with all their other papers? And why had Stolz needed them so much?

He picked up the next file. Like the first, there was a large swastika on the front. Inside were papers for several soldiers – one page on each.

Leutnant Heinz Bruen, geb. 4.Dez 1919
4.März 1935 – registriert Hitler-Jugend
30. Juni 1939 – registriert Panzerdivision
10. Juni 1940 – verwundet, Frankreich

5. Juli 1940 – ausgezeichnet mit dem Eisernen Kreuz 2. Klasse
27. Juli 1943 – † Kursk

He rifled through the papers. Each page was a list of dates for a different soldier. Different birthdays, but always the same date of death. The file was a collection of people killed on 23rd of July 1943, at Kursk - the largest tank battle in history.

Myles stared at one of the rough piles of paper. No cardboard cover on this, just a box to hold the sheets together. The top page had decayed too much to read, so he lifted it to read the one below.

Hannah P. Rosenberg, geb. 4 Januar 1905, 9.30 Uhr, Hamburg.
21. Juli 1926 – Hochzeit
1. Juni 1927 – Geburt der ersten Tochter
28. September 1928 – Geburt der zweiten Tochter
13. September 1930 – Geburt des Sohnes
3. Mai 1941 – Ehemann im Krieg getötet
27 Januar 1944 – †

The page had been signed with an illegible scribble and the time '14.18 Uhr' next to it. Different handwriting had added at the bottom:

† 14.35 Uhr

Myles wondered what the German text might mean. He lifted the next sheet.

Maryam Gold, geb 10. Juni 1910, 22.30 Uhr, Lüdenscheid
22. Juni 1932, Hochzeit

15. October 1932, Anstellung in Metzgerei
12. November 1938, Italienreise
27. Januar 1944 † (Existenz des Ehemannes beendet)

It had the same illegible signature with the time two minutes later – '14.20 Uhr' .

And underneath, again:

† 14.35 Uhr

He flicked through the next page, and the next. All ended with exactly the same date, and the same time.

What happened to all these people on the 27th of January 1944, at two-thirty-five in the afternoon?

Then he noticed the '†' symbol. The same symbol as on the Kursk and Stalingrad files of German soldiers.

Suddenly the realisation hit him. Myles felt his whole body judder, as he tried to contain his reaction to the pages he was holding.

Of course: all the people died. More precisely, they were executed. Myles was looking at interview notes taken minutes before these people were stampeded into gas chambers.

Part of him wanted to drop the pages in disgust – to get rid of them - but he knew he shouldn't. There was something special about these records. All other records of the holocaust had been systematically destroyed. So why had a Nazi kept these?

Footsteps started clanging down from above. Glenn was descending the ladder to join him, followed by Frank and Pascal, who was helping Heike-Ann with the difficult steps. Heike-Ann was barely able to find her footing – she looked drowsy, and was paler than ever. Myles thought she might stumble or collapse at any moment.

Then he saw Zenyalena above them all, herding them down with her gun.

Glenn reached the bottom first. 'What is it, Myles?'

Myles showed one of the papers to Glenn. 'Death records.'

'Death records?'

'Yeah,' said Myles, disgusted. 'From the Nazis.'

Frank helped settle Heike-Ann on the floor, then leaned towards one of the stacks of papers. 'Well, what do they say?'

Myles waited until Zenyalena's feet were on the ground before he explained. 'They're records from people who died. Some of them Nazis killed in battles, from Kursk and Stalingrad. But most from interviews with Jews just before they were….' He didn't say the last word – murdered. Somehow using normal words to describe the holocaust wasn't right. All of them knew about the industrialised killing of so many millions of people. It couldn't be described in any normal way.

The team gazed in awe at the musty room. The papers on all sides made it feel claustrophobic. Glenn checked two piles, then a third. Frank looked at one of the covers. Pascal tried to count how many columns of paper there were.

But Zenyalena refused to accept it. 'Just papers?' she grunted. 'Is that all?' She lifted her boot and kicked a stack in frustration. It tumbled down, collapsing beside her. Dust lifted up into the air, and the smell of damp mould grew stronger.

As the papers fell, they revealed part of a machine, which had been hidden behind. With dials and numbers on the front, it looked like the mechanical desk from the underground cavern near Munich.

The team gazed closer.

Zenyalena sensed the others coming towards her. 'Stay back.'

They obeyed: since firing at the floorboards, Zenyalena had seemed trigger-happy.

She gestured with the gun towards Pascal. 'Well, don't just wait: take off the papers. Show us what it is.'

Pascal duly began to peel away the stacks of loose files. He revealed a dull metal desk with a basic keyboard. There were several dials with arrows on each, and an automated teleprinter attached to one side. The whole machine was mechanical, looking just like an Enigma code-making machine. It was a primitive computer. A Nazi computer.

Pascal lifted his head up. 'I've found a switch.' Pascal pressed the button, and lights appeared from the behind the keyboard. It began to buzz. Still looking down at the machine, the French colonel spoke, hesitant and unsure. 'I… I think we have to enter data….'

'What sort of data?'

'I don't know. Looks like… dates. Dates and times.'

Zenyalena's fingers rippled around the gun barrel while she pondered what she would do next. 'OK. Enter this: 5th September 1974.'

Pascal typed in the details, then waited. The machine seemed to want more data before it could work. 'There's still a light on for time and location.'

'Then put in 0830 in the morning. Location: St Petersburg.'

Pascal queried it. 'There are only pre-set options,' he said, still trying to master it. 'There's a "Leningrad" – the old name for St Petersburg.'

Zenyalena nodded her approval, and Pascal entered the city name.

Then, as if the machine were alive, it started whirring. Cogs and contraptions hummed inside, clicking and connecting. For almost a minute, the mechanical computer made loud, clockwork noises as small pieces of metal buzzed, rotated and settled inside.

Then the tone changed. It was the hammer of the teleprinter. A page was being typed out.

Zenyalena's eyes flickered nervously between the machine and the people in the room. Myles, Pascal, Frank, and Glenn watched transfixed while the most primitive computer any of them could imagine began to generate its result. Only Heike-Ann ignored it, lying semi-conscious on the floor.

Zenyalena waited for the teleprinter to finish, then lurched towards it and snatched off the paper with one hand, the other still clasping the machine gun. She held the page close, not letting anyone else read it. She read it twice, seeming as if she didn't believe it the first time. She stared at it for several seconds more, as her grip on the gun seemed to loosen.

Then Zenyalena looked up. Her eyes were different now. She looked less angry, but also subdued, as though she had been confronted with a terrible reality.

Myles wondered if he had even seen tears in the Russian woman's eyes. He tried to speak as softly as he could. 'What does it say, Zenyalena?'

'Predictions,' she replied.

'5th September 1974 – that's your birthday?'

'Yes,' she said, turning the page to show them all.

Geb.5.Sept 1974
August-Oktober 1998 – Reise (80% Wahrscheinlichkeit)
Juni 2003 – Verwundet (60% Wahrscheinlichkeit)

Myles recognised the dates, but not the other words written in German. 'What does it say?'

'It says I travelled in 1998, and was injured in June 2003. The percentages are probabilities – 80% and 60% likely.'

'And were you?'

Zenyalena nodded.

Myles scanned through the rest of the page. On the bottom line was today's date. Beside it was a familiar symbol. A single symbol, all on its own.

†

Underneath, the words:

Plötzlich – 66% Wahrscheinlichkeit

Zenyalena and Myles looked at each other. Both of them understood what the machine was predicting.

Zenyalena wiped her face, clearing her eyes of any sadness. "Plötzlich" means "sudden", she explained.

Glenn tried to sidle close to her. 'Oh, come on. This is just a fairground show. You don't really believe it, do you?'

Zenyalena clutched the gun barrel tight in her hands. 'Stay back.' More calmly, she motioned to Myles. 'Myles. Do you believe it?'

Myles wondered whether to lie, but decided it was better not to. 'Yes, Zenyalena. I do. I do now. And I see how they did it.' He gestured towards the paper stacked all around him. 'These records. The Nazis gathered information from all these people. Soldiers who died, Jews they murdered – all of them. There could be more than a million sheets here. Then they found out which planets were significant when they died, identified a statistical link, and used it to make predictions.'

'Predictions like mine?'

'Yes, Zenyalena, I reckon so.'

Glenn was still shaking his head. 'It doesn't make the prediction right, though.'

Zenyalena was still on edge. She turned the Spandau gun back to Glenn. 'When were you born, Glenn?'

Glenn pulled his passport from his back pocket and showed the birthdate to Zenyalena.

Zenyalena acknowledged it. 'Good. What time?'

'I don't know. About eleven in the morning I think.'

'Where?'

'Maine.'

Zenyalena shot a look over to Pascal. Pascal understood, and dutifully entered the data.

Suddenly the machine was active again. It whirred and whizzed, as gears and cogs clunked together inside. They listened to the noise of little beads being shunted along an internal abacus, of circuits being formed, then broken, then connected again, and of life-decisions being calculated.

Then, as before, the tone changed as the printer started. Rippling her fingers on the air-cooling shaft of the gun barrel, Zenyalena invited Glenn to step forward.

Trying to pretend he didn't care, Glenn extended his hand towards the paper. He picked it up and glanced at it. 'I can't read it. It's in German.'

'Well, show it to Heike-Ann.'

Glenn kneeled down and put the paper in front of Heike-Ann's face. Heike-Ann – groggy and only half-awake – translated the paper. 'It says the year you were born… a seventy per cent chance of getting married in the year 2001. Then travel in May 2005 and November 2010. Some mention of travel for work this year. Then more stuff for 2018, 2028. Something about you retiring in 2030…'

Zenyalena called over to her. 'Nothing for now?'

'Just travel for work. That's all.'

Zenyalena nodded, accepting the point. She gestured with the gun. 'You.'

Frank looked round. 'Me?'

'Yes, you. Mr Museum Curator, or whatever it is you do. Tell me your birthday, place and time.'

Frank raised his eyebrows. 'Er, right then. I was born in Birmingham, England. Born at 5.10 p.m., on the 21st of March.'

Pascal entered the data, by now familiar with the dials and controls. Again, the machine crunched the information and the wheels inside began to rotate and tumble.

Frank peered round, sweat collecting on his forehead, while he waited for the noise to change.

Then the teleprinter started. Careful to make sure No one could approach her gun, Zenyalena ripped the paper from the machine.

She took time to study the page, as a slight grin spread on her face. 'Were you injured when you were six-and-a-half?'

Frank frowned, puzzled. 'Well, yes. If you'd call it an injury. That was when I contracted polio.' He tapped his weak leg.

Zenyalena accepted the answer. 'Heike-Ann,' she called over. 'What does "Wassertod" mean?'

'It means, literally "water-death" - drowning,' murmured Heike-Ann from the floor.

'I'm going to drown?' Frank seemed scared. Then a flicker of laughter appeared on his face, as if the prediction might be a joke. 'Well, the machine's half-right and half-wrong. You see, my house boat sunk just a while ago. I almost did drown, actually…' Frank looked for support from the other faces in the bunker. 'The machine probably got the dates a little wrong.'

But Zenyalena shook her head, her voice still deadly. 'There's no mistake. According to this machine, you're going to die the same day as me. Today. So don't think you've escaped.'

Frank clutched his collar and loosened the shirt around his neck. 'Does it really say that?'

Zenyalena threw the paper towards him.

Frank tried to grab it as it fluttered towards the floor. He stared at it, confirming that the last date was today, with the '†' symbol next to it. Frank turned to his friend. 'Myles, do you think this is true?'

Myles put his hand on Frank's shoulder. 'I don't know.'

'Well, do you think I have a choice?'

'Yes, we all have a choice. You escaped when your boat sank, didn't you? Just don't take a bath today. Whatever these predictions say, we can still stay safe.' Myles began directing his words at Zenyalena. 'Come on, Zenyalena. Can't we all go, now? None of us wants to die.'

'No. One of us is a traitor. And at the moment, Mr Myles Munro, the most likely person is you.' She pointed down toward Heike-Ann. 'Her identity pass is in her purse. Glenn: take it out please.'

Glenn bent down to their wounded assistant and, careful not to cause her any more pain than she was already experiencing, lifted her handbag away. It was easy for him to find her German police identity card. He checked it, then passed it to Pascal, who typed in the details.

Again, the machine whirred and clanked. Then the teleprinter began typing and a page of details spewed out. Glenn stepped forward to take it, then crouched down to the floor to pass it to Heike-Ann.

The German policewoman read through it, not reacting. Then finally, as she reached the bottom, her eyes smiled. 'It says next year I'll have another baby.'

Zenyalena darted forward. 'Show it to me.'

Lamely, Heike-Ann lifted the page for the Russian. Zenyalena scanned down the list of dates. The last line, with the ominous † beside it, was way off in 2041. Heike-Ann would survive.

Zenyalena called to her side. 'Pascal – where were you born?'

'Paris. Do you want me to enter my details?' Pascal seemed to be the only member of the team keen to know his future. The Frenchman eagerly turned the dials, setting up the machine to predict what was to come.

They waited in silence while the mechanisms inside did their work. Another full minute of clockwork clanking. Then the page printed out. Pascal went to take it but Zenyalena stopped him. 'No, leave it Pascal,' she ordered.

Pascal looked unsure but knew, at gunpoint, he had no choice but to obey.

Zenyalena turned to Myles. 'Englishman - carry it to Heike-Ann, please.'

Myles glanced an apology to Pascal, then picked up the page. It seemed much longer than the other predictions. Myles handed the sheet to Heike-Ann, who scanned the page. 'It says lots of things. It says you were dishonoured… received new wealth… Then travels this year. Also, this month, lots of extra courage and good luck. Then – tomorrow – disillusionment and…' Heike-Ann's words trailed off. The German didn't want to read out the conclusion.

Myles took the sheet back and studied it himself.

The last line was tomorrow's date, some words in German, and the ominous symbol:

†

Myles looked across at Pascal. He didn't need words.

Pascal understood. The Frenchman just looked down at the paper to confirm the date. 'Tomorrow?'

'Yes, Pascal. That's what it says. "Death from multiple causes".'

Zenyalena tossed her head back. She let her hair brush on her shoulders, as if she was beginning to care about things much less. 'Seems like dying's about to become quite popular.'

Myles pointed down at Heike-Ann. 'Look, Heike-Ann needs treatment. And she's pregnant. Forget this machine and let's get her some help.'

'That's not what the machine says,' said Zenyalena coldly. 'The machine reckons Heike-Ann doesn't need any help. Her and Glenn are the only ones who are going to get out of here. You should help Frank, Pascal and me instead – we have only hours to live.'

'Nonsense, Zenyalena. We can all get out of here alive. We just have to climb out.'

'Don't you even think about it, Myles. No one gets out of here until I say they do.' She pitched the gun towards him. 'Myles - when were you born?'

Myles was about to answer when Zenyalena interrupted him. 'No. Wait. I don't trust you. Show me your passport.'

Myles conceded, trying to be calm. From his back pocket, he lifted out his passport and handed it to Zenyalena.

Zenyalena looked at it, frowning in scepticism. 'This is you?'

'Yes. Of course it is.'

'You're older than you look.' She checked the details again, half-smiling to herself. Still holding the machine gun, she gestured towards him. 'Show me that – the page of predictions for Pascal. Pass it to me.' Zenyalena received the teleprinted paper on Pascal and held it in the same hand as Myles' passport. 'Well, well. Looks like you've got a twin.'

'A twin?'

'Yes. You and Pascal. Both born on 29th January, same year.'

Myles and Pascal looked at each other. Pascal asked first. 'What time?'

'Ten-to-five in the evening, in Britain. You?'

'Ten-to-six. Evening also. But Paris is an hour ahead. So it's the same time. Exactly.'

Zenyalena called out to Pascal, reading from Myles' passport. 'It says here he was born in Southampton.'

Pascal's eyes turned down in sympathy. He knew what the machine was about to say: Myles would share the same fate as him.

The cogs and wheels whirred again. Myles heard metal grind and tumble, imagining the complicated mechanics inside.

The teleprinter switched on, hammering letters onto the page. Even though the type was in German, Myles could understand the dates, reading line by line as the machine printed.

Myles scanned through it, realising he had led a life almost identical to Pascal's.

It showed the date he had been dishonoured – *correctly.*

It showed the date he had found 'new wealth' – *correct again, when he was given the Oxford lectureship in military history.*

Then tomorrow's date, with the same deathly symbol next to it.

†

The only difference between his record and Pascal's seemed to be words printed below the '†'.

Aus grosser Höhe,
Existenz der Freundin hört zwei Tage später auch auf

Myles focussed on it, trying to distract himself from the prediction that he only had twenty-four hours to live. He concentrated, as if somehow he could crack the German. But he couldn't. 'What does this mean?' he asked.

Pascal didn't know. Zenyalena gestured towards Heike-Ann, urging Myles to check the words with her. So Myles bent down, and passed the paper to their wounded translator.

Heike-Ann read it, then looked up at Myles. 'It says, "Death from a great height".'

Myles refused to react. He could tell she was holding something back. 'Is that all?'

Heike-Ann paused, before asking, 'Do you have a girlfriend or partner?'

'Yes.'

She was speaking softly. 'What's her name?'

'Helen. Helen Bridle.'

Heike-Ann nodded, pausing again before she broke the news. 'Well, I'm afraid this says "Girlfriend also ceases to be, two days later". According to the predictions, Helen's going to die two days after you.'

CHAPTER 59

East Berlin

11.05p.m. CET (10.05p.m. GMT)

Myles tried to absorb the prediction about Helen, desperately wondering what he could do to protect her. If she just stayed in a safe place, could she avoid her fate? Myles knew he had to call her, or find some way to get a warning to her. It would be his last chance to communicate with her, if the predictions were accurate.

Zenyalena weighed the gun barrel in her hands. 'So two of us will die today, two tomorrow, and two will survive,' she said, eyeing the five people in front of her while she decided what to do.

Myles tried to reason with her. 'Only if you believe the machine, Zenyalena. It doesn't have to happen. You can still live. And the fact you're holding that Spandau gun, means you're more likely to survive than any of us, I'd say.'

'Shut up. This isn't about survival. It's about the Nazi's greatest secret…' Zenyalena's voice was shrill. She edged towards Myles. '… You see, someone has been trying to keep us from this secret. That's why they killed Jean-François. That's why they started the fire in Vienna, and trapped us underground in Munich. They even set-up machine guns against us in France. And if Stolz's secret is worth protecting, it means the predictions are true. Which means I'm about to die…' Zenyalena was now speaking just a few inches from Myles' face. '… And I know one of you here has been trying to stop us finding this secret. Which means one of you is about to kill me.' Zenyalena looked straight at Myles.

Myles stared back without flinching. He watched as the Russian woman flexed her hand near the trigger. Was she about to shoot? Myles couldn't tell. But he knew she was about to do something…

Suddenly the Russian turned the gun barrel towards Glenn. 'Glenn: on your knees.'

Glenn was shocked. 'Me?'

'Yes, Mr American, you. Do it now.'

Glenn submitted, kneeling down on the floor. 'Zenyalena, I'm…'

'Quiet. Put your hands on your head.'

Glenn obeyed.

'Who do you work for?'

'The American government.'

'Which part?'

Glenn paused before responding. 'A government agency.'

'Which one?'

Glenn didn't answer. Myles guessed he *couldn't* answer. He probably wasn't allowed to, even under duress.

Zenyalena shook the gun as she pointed it at him, her voice rising as she spoke. 'CIA?'

Still Glenn didn't answer, but his body language seemed to confirm it. Some sort of intelligence agency. Zenyalena relaxed slightly. She had the response she wanted.

Then Glenn began to shake his head. 'Actually, no. I'm not with the CIA.'

'Really? Then why all the macho-spy stuff, Glenn?'

Still on his knees, Glenn sounded apologetic. 'I'm only an advisor. I'm a Federal Government employee, but my job is to write reports about stuff.'

'What sort of stuff?'

'Agricultural outputs, job numbers, trade ratios, statistics.'

Zenyalena leant back and laughed. 'Ha! The great Glenn. Just a bureaucrat after all!'

'I was sent here by my government. We all were.'

'I know. There's nothing wrong with being a bureaucrat, Glenn.' Zenyalena was trying to sound polite. Nice, even. But it was insincere. 'Nothing wrong with being an "advisor" at all. The problem is that you've been trying to stop us finding this place, haven't you…'

Glenn contorted his face. Without words, he was accusing her of talking nonesense.

Zenyalena started addressing her words to the others. 'I assume you've all noticed, too. Haven't you? Every chance he had, this man tried to make us think Stolz's work was false. He always tried to slow us down and stop us. I got you on the helicopter to France, didn't I?' said Glenn.

'Right into the ambush with this,' she replied, tapping the firearm. And now we've found the secret, the machine predicts that he's going to get out alive and keep it for himself.'

Slowly she walked around the confined space, careful to step over the tumbled stacks of paper, until she was standing immediately behind him. Then she lowered the gun barrel until it levelled with the back of Glenn's head. One press on the trigger and the American would die instantly.

There was sweat on her face, and a wry grin. Zenyalena looked up at the others for a reaction. 'Now, I have a puzzle for you all,' she declared, amusing herself. 'If Glenn is about to die, it means the predictions are false, which means there was no secret to protect, so he must be innocent. But if Glenn lives, then the predictions are true, and he's guilty. Innocent if he dies, guilty if he lives. Should I pull the trigger?' She lifted her eyes to Myles. 'Myles: should I pull the trigger?'

Myles shook his head firmly.

'Why not, Myles? Don't you want Glenn to be innocent?'

'Because I don't want Glenn to die. Zenyalena, we can all still live,' he pleaded. 'You can be stronger than the predictions.'

Zenyalena smirked. 'Nice try, Myles.'

'No, Zenyalena. If you kill Glenn then you prove the predictions false. You may even destroy the accuracy of the machine.'

'Now you're getting desperate. We know that at least one person here is not who they say they are. And I know: that person is about to kill me, unless I kill him – or her – first.' She positioned her finger on the trigger, aiming at Glenn's tightly-shaven scalp. Myles saw the muscles in the American's neck tense up. Glenn knew he was probably about to die….

Suddenly, there was an interruption.

'Wait.' It was Pascal.

Zenyalena looked up, her eyes suspicious.

The Frenchman paused, trying to measure his words before he spoke them. 'The person who is not just who they say they are is… is me.'

Zenyalena jolted. She pivoted on her feet and turned the gun barrel towards Pascal, squinting sceptically. 'Explain.'

Pascal showed his empty palms in surrender. 'Some terrorists are trying to get hold of Stolz's secrets.'

'And you're a terrorist?'

'No. I'm with a humanitarian group. I'm here to negotiate with them.'

Zenyalena's eyes narrowed. 'The French government sent you here to negotiate with terrorists?'

Slowly, Pascal nodded, shame-faced. His cover had been blown. He tried to explain. 'When Jean-François was murdered, there was a terrorist website which claimed responsibility for it.

They made other threats, too. The French government sent me here to find them and cut a deal.'

'But they didn't want to be seen to be talking with terrorists?'

'Correct. If people knew the French government negotiated with such people, it would encourage more of them. We'd be forever held to ransom.'

Glenn piped up, still kneeling. 'So the French really do talk with the bad guys…' There was sarcasm in his voice.

Pascal responded with sincerity. 'I was sent here by the French, but I don't work for them. I work for an organisation committed to peace. It's called "Humanitarian Pursuit".'

Zenyalena was nodding subtly to herself. Pascal's story rang true. 'So that's why you took such risks? Saving the papers from the fire in Vienna, placing the grenades underground in Munich, taking out the machine guns in France.'

'Correct. I knew that we had to keep searching for Stolz's secret. Otherwise we'd never find the terrorist.'

Suddenly Zenyalena became optimistic. 'So you know who the terrorist is then?'

Pascal let the question hang in the air. Myles sensed there was a reason why he couldn't answer.

Zenyalena kept on. 'Is it someone in this room?'

Still no response from Pascal.

Finally, the Frenchman stepped out from behind the machine. 'Zenyalena, it's like this. I know something but not everything. I know someone here is not who they say they are. That person is linked to the terrorist group – they've been sending things to the terrorist website. And I know it's not you.'

'How do you know that?'

'I can't say, Zenyalena.'

'So who is it?'

Again, Pascal didn't answer, but his eyes were sweeping over Frank, Myles, Heike-Ann and Glenn. The accusation was obvious: it was one of the four of them.

Zenyalena turned towards them. She studied their faces, searching for any sign of tension: something which would reveal who was guilty. Slowly she allowed the MG 08/15 to sway in her hands, hoping one of them would admit something when the gun-barrel pointed their way.

But nobody reacted. She still couldn't spot the traitor.

Pascal studied the four faces: Myles, Frank, Glenn and Heike-Ann. Only after a long pause did he return a glance to Zenyalena. 'There is a way we can identify the terrorist, but it's not something my organisation could support.'

'What is it?' Zenyalena was getting frustrated.

Pascal's tone was sombre. 'The terrorist has killed before. I think they will only reveal themselves when the alternative is death.... Which means, we must threaten death.' Pascal exhaled, and looked down as he spoke. He hated his words as he said them.

But Zenyalena was encouraged - she seemed to have the advantage again. She jerked the weapon in her hands, pointing it back towards Myles. 'Myles. Is it you?'

Myles shook his head in denial.

But before Myles could speak, Pascal interrupted again. 'No, Zenyalena. Each of them will deny it. They have to be threatened together...' He scanned the room for ideas, then saw some coiled power cables, and turned to the American. 'Glenn – give me your utility tool, please...'

Glenn checked with Zenyalena. Her stance was underwriting Pascal's request. Glenn duly passed his utility tool to the Frenchman.

Pascal collected the tool and flicked out the main blade. Then he measured lengths of power cable and began to cut them, talking quickly. 'To the three of you who are innocent, please accept my apologies in advance for what I am about to do.'

He turned to face Glenn. 'Glenn, please put out your hands.'

'Come on Pascal - is this really necessary?'

Zenyalena levelled the gun at him. 'Yes, Glenn, it is "really necessary". Do as he says.'

Glenn put out his wrists. Pascal wrapped a length of power cord around them, then pulled it taut. He fixed it in place with a double-knot. 'Glenn, if you're innocent, then I'm sorry.'

'Well, I am innocent, so I hope you *are* sorry.'

Pascal gave a half-smile, then went on to Myles. 'The same, please: your wrists.'

Myles checked with Zenyalena: the Russian was pointing the gun at him. There was no way he could refuse. Reluctantly, Myles held out his hands.

'Thank you, Myles…' Again, Pascal wrapped a cord tightly Round them and knotted it. He pulled it hard to test it was secure. It was.

Next Pascal bent down to Heike-Ann. He tried to engage her eyes as he bound her wrists, one of them now dark red with blood. '…I'm sorry, but I have to do this.'

Heike-Ann managed only a groggy reply. It was inaudible.

Finally, Pascal reached Frank. 'Come on, Frank. If you've done nothing wrong, you've got nothing to fear.'

Frank was refusing to put out his hands, keeping his arms folded. The museum curator shook his head. He was incensed.

Zenyalena tried to cajole him, pointing the gun barrel towards him as she spoke. 'Frank, do as the others. Allow yourself to be tied up.'

'No.'

'Frank, you must.'

'No. I know what you're going to do.'

Zenyalena looked surprised. She genuinely didn't know what they were about to do. She kicked him. 'Well, Frank - What are we going to do?'

'You're going to let the water in,' replied Frank, gesturing towards the emergency hatch with the yellow handle. 'Come on. It's obvious. We're next to the River Spree, and we must be below the water level down here. You expect one of us to confess as the water's rising. Except I've just been told I'm going to die today, and that it's "death by water". So I hope you understand why I'm reluctant to have my hands tied.'

Pascal tried to make Frank relax, 'Nobody's going to drown, if you do as you should.'

'Good. Then don't tie me up.'

Zenyalena's face tightened. She hadn't expected anyone to refuse. She gripped the gun firmly and toyed with her finger near the trigger. 'Frank. This is your last chance.'

Frank sensed Zenyalena was serious. He tried to control his rage, looking around, as if to find another reason not to have his hands tied. Then, very slowly, he relaxed his arms and pushed his wrists out, towards Pascal.

'Thank you, Frank. This won't take long....' Pascal tied the cable around Frank's wrists, checked it was firm, then turned back to the machine. 'OK, Zenyalena. I'm going to need your help with this.'

'What are you planning?'

Pascal was too focussed on the Nazi prediction machine to respond. He delved his hands into the inner workings, feeling his way around the device. After a few moments his expression changed. 'This. This is what the terrorists want.'

Zenyalena squinted, unsure. 'The whole machine?'

'No. We wouldn't be able to take it out of here,' conceded Pascal. 'It's too big. But there must be a small part inside that runs the programme.' Using Glenn's utility knife, Pascal had managed to unscrew a heavy cover plate from the top of the machine. He peered down inside. 'I can see it. The mechanism. And we can lift it out.'

Zenyalena glanced across at her captives. They all glanced back, as Pascal called over. 'Zenyalena, I need you to help me extract it.'

Checking again that No one was going to rush for her weapon, Zenyalena hauled the gun onto her shoulder so she could lend Pascal a hand. Together they managed to pull out a suitcase-sized mechanism. The core of the Nazi computer was surprisingly light. Mostly gears and wheels - like the inner workings of a clock, but also with beads on rods like a small abacus, and sockets where cables plugged in.

'Thanks, Zenyalena.' Pascal gathered his breath. He stared at the delicate device in front of him. 'This machine is the greatest of the Nazi wonderweapons.'

Zenyalena frowned, unsure. 'But, can it kill?'

'It's far more powerful than that. It can predict the future. It is the product of a truly massive research programme. More than a million deaths were involved in gathering the information it contains. SS Captain Werner Stolz might even have killed people to test it. It was refined and honed until it was the perfect prediction device – perhaps one of the first real computers. Unfortunately for the Nazis, it must have predicted a future in which they were defeated....' Pascal turned to the four people on the floor, all with their hands bound. '... And we can see why it's so valuable. It's already cost many, many lives. Most recently, my good friend Jean-François. It may be about to cost more...' Pascal's voice was even. He spoke his ultimatum with strength. '... So, Frank, Heike-Ann, Glenn and Myles - whoever is the terrorist collaborator in this room, reveal yourself now. Or I will destroy this machine.'

There was silence.

Pascal looked around at the four people with their wrists bound. Still nobody spoke.

Pascal tried again. He held up the heavy metal plate he had taken off to extract the inner core of the machine's workings, and pointed a corner towards the delicate device. 'I can smash this machine so easily – and the greatest scientific advancement of the Nazis will be lost forever.'

'It's not, actually.'

Glenn turned to see the person who had interrupted Pascal's speech.

Heike-Ann lifted her head up from the floor to look.

Zenyalena scanned her hostages.

But Myles knew already. It was a voice he'd known since university.

It was Frank. Pascal looked down at him. Zenyalena slung the gun barrel back into her hands, levelling the weapon at him.

Frank was unfazed. 'Whatever you say, it's not the Nazi's greatest scientific achievement.'

Pascal squinted in suspicion. 'No? What was, then?'

'I don't know. Rockets. Jets, maybe.'

'Why not this?'

'Because it doesn't belong to the Nazis. The ancient Greeks built machines which could predict the position of the planets. And the prediction part – lots of civilisations have done that.'

'But this Nazi machine is so precise…'

'So are modern computers. There are programmes online which give predictions and dates like that machine has just done.'

Pascal and Zenyalena didn't know how to respond. Zenyalena's fingers tightened around the trigger, ready to fire at Frank in an instant. Silence gripped the room.

The museum curator was eventually answered by Glenn. 'Frank's right. Whereas the Nazis took years to gather the data for this machine, the internet can gather data in seconds. Now people are just a single click away from hokum about the planets...'

'It's not hokum,' Frank was getting frustrated again. He turned to Glenn, angry that the American was belittling his theories. 'Not nonsense at all. Predicting things from the planets is more accurate than predicting the weather. And there are lots of websites which can do it – most of them better than that Nazi clockwork thing.' Frank could tell Glenn was still a sceptic. 'Look, Glenn, I can prove it to you. We need to go online. Has one of you got a smartphone?'

Glenn shook his head. 'No. We all got rid of them in Vienna, when we realised we were being followed.

'Well, I've got one. In my trousers, if we can get a signal down here.' Frank started wriggling. He was struggling to stretch his tied hands into his back pocket, as if he was trying to reach something.

Bang

The vibration of the Spandau gun shook the whole underground room, deafening everyone. Zenyalena jerked backwards, shocked by what had just happened, as her gun recoiled.

Heike-Ann, Pascal and Glenn stared at the Russian, wondering how her weapon had fired.

But not Myles. He had seen where the bullet had gone. 'Frank?'

Frank was bent double, looking confused. He tried to shake his head. 'I think I'm not too hurt...' But blood was spreading on his shirt.

Zenyalena's face froze in shock. She really hadn't expected the Spandau gun to fire. She dropped it and rushed towards Frank, lifting him up. 'I'm sorry. I'm so sorry.' She cradled him, then realised it was doing no good, so she pulled up his shirt instead.

A single bullet wound, in the chest.

Frank wheezed out a few words. 'Is it… is it bad?' He tried to inhale, but air wasn't coming into his mouth. Instead, the wound was taking blood into his lungs.

Myles called over to Zenyalena. 'Put pressure on it.'

Zenyalena tried, working desperately. She ripped cloth from Frank's shirt and pressed it into the wound.

Myles tried to shuffle towards his old friend. 'Frank, we're going to help you, OK?'

Frank gave as much of a nod as he could. Myles could tell Frank was overcome by pain.

Zenyalena became frantic, pushing the fragment of cloth harder into the wound. Frank was beginning to lean over, collapsing on the floor.

Glenn came across and began to help too. 'It's a lung wound. We mustn't let air into it.'

The American snapped into action, a trained first-aider. Even though his hands were tied, he managed to push them into the wound hard. Frank seemed to revive a little.

Myles tried again. 'Frank, Frank – can you hear me?'

Frank started spluttering. Myles knew he had to help his friend immediately. Frank probably had only minutes left.

Then Myles saw someone grinning down and pointing the gun towards him. It was the person he had least expected to be the traitor.

CHAPTER 60

Randolph Hotel
Oxford
10.15p.m GMT

Father Samuel and Professor Cromhall were guided through to the private dining room by the most courteous restaurant staff either of them had ever experienced. Sparkling cutlery on a crisp white table cloth awaited them, along with Philip Ford, Executive Chairman of one of London's richest financial institutions.

'Father Samuel, Professor Cromhall,' said the chubby banker, straining to shake hands with his guests. 'So good to have the time for a proper conversation.'

Father Samuel bowed his head with humility. 'Thank you for agreeing to see us, Philip.'

The banker gestured to their seats, then to the menu. He made sure his dining partners ordered their food before the real business started. 'So, how can I help you?'

'It's how we can help each other, really,' began Father Samuel. 'You see, some information is at risk of becoming public. Information which might impose, er, "unnecessary costs" on all of us…'

The banker pulled a face, wondering whether he was about to be blackmailed. Silently his expression urged Father Samuel to continue.

'… It's to do with the planets,' continued Samuel. 'The correlation with human behaviour: the secret is leaking out.'

'Financial astrology?' scoffed the banker, straightening his knife and fork, which were already perfectly positioned. 'Does anybody still believe that?'

'Yes, I thought *you* did, Mr Ford,' answered the professor, half accusing, half taunting his host. 'At least, that's why my university has invested so much of our endowment through your bank. How else were you generating such excellent returns?'

'If you mean the link between Venus and the gold price,' mocked Ford, 'that stopped more than a decade ago. When people heard about it, and used it for deals, the correlation was traded away. Market forces.'

'Not just Venus,' pressed home the professor. 'All the correlations. They are how you earn your bonuses, aren't they? Market-beating returns, year-after-year – you can only do that with special knowledge. Knowledge which is rare, perhaps because few people trust it.'

The conversation shut down as the door to their private dining area swung open. Three waiting staff brought three magnificent-looking plates of food, which they made a show of presenting before gently resting them before the diners. Eventually the staff left and privacy was restored.

Father Samuel made sure the banker understood. 'You see, Philip, if this information gets out, all your competitive advantage will be lost - just like betting gold on Venus lost its lustre when others joined in.'

'And not just your bonuses,' added the professor. 'Profits in the insurance industry would collapse if more people knew about their future. Mortgage dealers wouldn't be able to charge a risk premium. Pension providers, too – the whole financial industry stands to lose billions if this gets out.'

Philip Ford decapitated a prawn. Without words, he let his guests know he didn't like being pushed around.

Father Samuel sensed the banker's mood, and tried to offer reassurance. 'Please don't feel you are alone, Philip. We too are deeply concerned about this.' He tried to make a joke of it. 'You're dining with two people who have even more at stake than you. We would all be impoverished.'

Professor Cromhall tried to underwrite the point. 'The father is right. Faith in science would be shattered if this gets out.'

Philip Ford digested the pleas with his food. So they all wanted the information supressed. This wasn't a hijack, it was a business proposition. 'So what do you want from me – money?'

Father Samuel and the professor nodded.

'How much – a few million?'

'That's too much,' demurred Father Samuel. 'Half a million would be plenty, Philip, for what we have in mind. But we must be quick....'

CHAPTER 61

East Berlin

11.19p.m CET (10.19p.m GMT)

Myles looked up at the Frenchman, 'Pascal – can you untie me? To help him?'

There was no answer. Instead of trying to help, alongside Zenyalena, Pascal had picked up the weapon.

'Pascal?'

Pascal was pointing the Spandau gun towards Myles. 'Stay there.'

Myles froze.

Zenyalena's eyes widened. 'Pascal. You?'

Pascal didn't answer. Instead, he just tilted his head slightly. He fired, and the bullet killed Zenyalena in an instant. Zenyalena's body slumped down onto Frank's legs. Frank yelped in shock.

Glenn and Myles turned their gaze to Pascal, trying to understand what had just happened. It made no sense.

Glenn grabbed Zenyalena's chin and turned her face towards him. Zenyalena's head flopped sideways, expressionless. Glenn let go, and the dead Russian collapsed. 'So Zenyalena was the terrorist?'

Pascal didn't respond.

Myles turned to see Frank still suffering. Blood was filling his lungs. Just as the machine had predicted, the curator was drowning. Myles tried to shuffle towards his friend, but the Frenchman turned and pointed the gun at him.

'Freeze,' ordered Pascal.

Myles knew he had to obey. 'Pascal, we've got to save Frank.'

'Why?' Pascal threw the word into the air without wanting an answer. He was glancing through some of the papers, deciding which ones to collect.

'So, Pascal – you're the terrorist?'

'Not according to the website.'

Myles and Glenn stared at each other, still trying to understand. Myles was completely baffled. 'The 'website'?'

Pascal bent down and pulled a smartphone from his ankle – it had been strapped to his leg, hidden. 'Yes, the website. It's where the "terrorists" are.' He said 'terrorists' with a sneer. 'You guys and – sorry, Heike-Ann, ladies too – wouldn't get it. I've been uploading predictions from Stolz to a website. Then, when they happen, claiming credit for the events.'

Myles glanced back at his old friend, dying in front of him. 'But why did you save us – in Vienna and Munich? And in the forest in France?'

'Because I could – it was a thrill. And the predictions said I was almost invincible…'

Myles was more puzzled than ever.

Pascal mused on, talking to himself as if he was the only person in the bunker. '…And taking out those old machine guns felt… amazing. It made me feel like a real soldier. Some people would pay a lot of money for excitement like that.' The old Pascal had gone.

Myles realised the helpful French Colonel had just been an act. 'But - if those predictions made you "invincible", how come you're due to die tomorrow?'

Pascal looked at his watch. 'If the predictions are true, then yes. But I'll die the most respected man in the world.'

'Most respected? You won't even save Frank from drowning in his own blood…'

'Only we know that. And soon the world will think Frank was killed by you, Myles.' He held out the smartphone again. 'It's easy. I've already gone online to predict that the world will soon be transformed from Berlin. A new Reich – starting where Hitler started. All I have to do is put your name to it.' He glanced across at Glenn, pulling a face of mock sympathy. 'Oh - don't feel left out. I'll name you, too. There are lots of people willing to believe the plot to destroy the world, or whatever they call it, was inspired by Brits and Americans working together.'

Myles still couldn't make sense of it. He tried to absorb it all. 'And you, Pascal?'

'I will name myself as the head of the humanitarian mediation group trying to sort out this mess. I just put my name on the 'Humanitarian Pursuit' site. Easy.'

'But Pascal…'

'Call me Dieter, please. That's my real name. And that's the name people will soon be praising all over the world. You really believed I was a French Lieutenant Colonel, didn't you?'

Glenn shook his head, still not understanding. 'Dieter – Pascal – I don't know what you are.'

Dieter laughed. 'Well I'm not French, at least.'

'But that call from the French Foreign Ministry, asking us to let you join the team. It was a woman's voice.'

'Yes. I paid her to do that. An actress – I said it was for a TV show. She's dead now.'

'And the email from Jean-François?'

'I wrote that, while he was hanging. And I'm glad you were impressed by my fake ID, Glenn – they were expensive. Paid for by someone who thought they could order me around, just as Germany used to be ordered around.' Dieter leant towards Frank, bending down to examine the curator's wound.

Frank was already gasping, his lungs flooding quickly.

Dieter sneered. 'Well, the prediction said water, but it looks to me like your friend might drown in his own blood. It is liquid, I suppose.' Dieter left Frank, and instead shifted towards the emergency water hatch. He kicked it, and the yellow lever jerked across.

Myles watched in horror as the metal plate buckled. Rust started to darken as it grew damp. Water was seeping through from the River Spree behind. 'You, you can't…'

Just seconds later the hatch burst open. Water began pouring into the secret bunker.

Myles looked across at Frank: the predictions were coming true. His old university friend *would* drown.

Myles had a choice, and only an instant to make it: try to save Frank, or take on Dieter – with his hands tied.

Dieter guessed what Myles was thinking, and trained the machine gun on him. 'Stay where you are, please, gentlemen…' The Frenchman had stepped over them, back to the prediction machine. For Glenn and Myles, he was out of reach – for now.

Myles felt the water reach him. It was cold, and quickly spread across the room. Heike-Ann tried to lift her head as the water gushed in, and formed a rising layer on the ground. Gushing in, it filled the room quickly. The stacks of paper were getting wet. Myles looked again at Frank. The man seemed confused as much as he was in pain. 'Frank – Frank?'

Frank's eyes rose toward Myles. He seemed apologetic again – *sorry for dying…*

Myles watched as Frank's eyes seemed to switch off, and knew he had to help his old friend. Ignoring Dieter, he shuffled across to Frank and slammed his bound hands on the man's chest.

Dieter caressed his finger on the trigger, tilting his head as he spoke. 'Myles, leave him.'

Myles refused to obey the instruction. He was determined to save his old friend.

Glenn replied for him. 'Are you so hung up on the predictions that you're trying to make them come true?'

Dieter didn't answer.

Glenn kept taunting, calling up at him. 'You want Frank to die just so the machine is correct? That's nuts.'

Dieter turned to the American. Glenn's eyes widened in horror – Dieter was about to shoot.

Then, without words, the Frenchman just pulled the trigger.

Clunk.

Dieter looked down at the gun to see what had happened. The ammunition belt was exhausted.

Dieter edged back, then he let his gun fall into the water, but grabbed the utility knife instead. He held it down towards the two of them.

Realising they had a chance to overpower him, Myles and Glenn both rushed to their feet.

Dieter stabbed out at Myles. Myles dodged the blow but lost his balance. He stumbled down into the rising water.

Then Dieter lurched towards Glenn. Glenn rocked back, lifting his forearms in self-protection.

Dieter grinned. He leapt back to grab the innards of the Nazi prediction machine, hauling out the suitcase-sized device in a single motion. Quickly he darted towards the steps. Then he checked again behind him.

Myles stared up at him, defiant. Even though Myles was sitting with his hands bound in water now well-above his ankles, he was refusing to give up.

But Dieter knew he had them. 'I'm not going far….'

He started to climb, still holding the knife and hauling the core of the Nazi computer as he clambered up the ladder.

Glenn looked to Myles, who had already turned back to Frank. The Englishman was applying pressure to his friend's wound again.

Myles glanced up at the steps where Dieter had just gone. There was no chance of them stopping the man from escaping. He called over to Glenn, 'Keep Heike-Ann's face out of the water.'

Glenn turned to the woman, who was lying on the floor, almost completely covered in water. She was barely conscious. The American put his bound wrists behind her head and hauled her up. Heike-Ann seemed to revive a little.

Frank, though, had grown pale. His face was contorted from trying to hold his remaining breath. Then the muscles on his forehead eased a little, as if he had a joke to share. He tried to speak, but could only mouth the words. 'The machine's wrong – not death by water…'

Myles slammed more pressure on to Frank's chest. 'Stay alive, Frank. Damn it – stay alive…'

But it was no use. Frank's lungs were almost completely full. Frank swung his head from side-to-side. He obviously knew he was about to die.

'Frank…'

Frank tried to say something more, but blood started to choke him. It began dribbling out through his teeth.

A look of alarm cast over his features. He glanced towards the exit – the way Dieter had climbed out just moments before – knowing he would never follow. Then Frank's eyes started to lock in place.

Myles rammed more pressure against the chest wound with his hands, pushing as hard as he could. He tried to tip Frank's head forward, hoping to clear the blood from his mouth.

But the more he tried, the less difference it seemed to make. He tried again, and again, and again…

Glenn called over. 'He's dead, Munro.'

Myles knew it, but still couldn't abandon his friend. He kept the pressure on Frank's entry wound, even though Frank's lungs were already full. He checked Frank's neck: no pulse. His old friend's body had gone limp. In a last effort, he lifted his hands to grab Frank's hair and shake it, but it made no difference.

Frank was gone.

Finally Myles paused, then let go, exhausted. Frank's dark blood oozed into the water. The body slumped down with it.

Glenn called over again, straining. 'Come on – help me with Heike-Ann.'

Glenn was still holding up their German translator, who was conscious again but sagging in his arms. The American tried to heave her towards the exit hampered by the cord still around his wrists.

Water was rising fast. It had come level with the top of the emergency hatch. Some of the old Nazi papers were beginning to float on the surface. Picking up dirt and dust, and mixed with blood from Zenyalena and Frank's bodies, some of the liquid had turned maroon.

As Myles stood up, the water came to his knees. With his hands tied, and one leg injured, he had trouble with his balance – just walking towards Glenn was difficult. 'We've got to get out of here.'

'Agreed,' said Glenn, pulling Heike-Ann with him. Myles took the woman's legs and they began to carry her.

They took her to the bottom of the rungs which led back up to Stolz's apartment. Myles stared up. It was a ten metre climb – with tied hands, not easy to do while carrying Heike-Ann...

Glenn saw his concern. 'Do you think we can do it, Myles?'

'We've got to try...' Myles lifted his foot onto the bottom rung, which was hidden below the water, whilst still holding Heike-Ann. Then he realised he couldn't hold the rungs and Heike-Ann at the same time. Not with his hands tied. '...Can you untie me?'

Glenn nodded. He tried to unpick the knotted cable, but it wasn't loosening. He kept at it, trying different ways to free the knot, but there was no way it was going to slacken.

As Myles desperately tried to loosen the bindings on his wrist, he didn't notice the stack of papers next to him start to sway. The water was making it unstable. Suddenly, the column collapsed, hitting Myles on the side and knocking him into the water. They were submerged.

Myles struggled to find air again, pushing up through the sheets of paper which covered the surface like lily pads. He had to regain his footing, then pushed up. Eventually he broke free, and shook the water from his head. Sheets of wet paper stuck to his body.

The water was now up to their waists. Glenn was finding Heike-Ann even harder to carry.

Myles looked at Glenn's face and sensed what the American was thinking: with the rising water, the thick wads of paper floating on top of it, Heike-Ann's semi-conscious body and their hands tied, could they really escape?

CHAPTER 62

11.30p.m CET (10.30p.m GMT)

Glenn struggled with Heike-Ann in his arms, trying to lift her. 'Well, Myles – you gonna help me carry her up?'

'No. Not up,' Myles replied quickly. With his eyes, he indicated sharply downwards.

Glenn looked confused. 'Down? You crazy?'

'It's the only way, Glenn. If we go up, Dieter will take us out one at a time – with your knife.'

Glenn began to realise Myles was serious. He watched while Myles delved down, through the paper floating on the water, and found Heike-Ann's legs. Then he lifted. Together with Glenn, Myles placed her on the empty shell of the prediction machine – safely out of the water.

Glenn cast a 'you first' look at Myles, who nodded in acknowledgment, as he waded back towards the emergency hatch.

Myles took a deep breath, then ducked his head down. The water was too murky to see through, but he knew where the hatch was. He felt his way in. It was a narrow tunnel. The sides were smooth, Nazi-era concrete, part covered in algae. The water became clearer as he swam out of the bunker, but it was flowing against him.

He pulled himself along, trying to beat the current. The tunnel went along, then down. He kept hauling himself through, following it for a metre or so, until it started to rise again. Myles felt the weakness in his knee as he moved forward, and a deep pain in his lungs – he needed to breathe. But he ignored the instinct to turn back. Then, through the cold, clear water, he could see some sort of light. The tunnel led straight to the river Spree.

His instinct told him to continue – to swim up for oxygen. He was about to allow himself to float to the surface, up into the clear air above the river. But then he realised: if he escaped now, he'd never be able to get down to the hatch again. He had to go back.

Myles pulled his legs into his chest and manoeuvred his tall body around in the tunnel, trying to shut out the intense sensation in his chest. Swimming in this direction he could allow the flow to push him along, back towards Stolz's secret bunker. He reached the open emergency hatch, squeezed through, then burst up through the surface of the water.

He spluttered for air, peeling a wet sheet of paper from his face. At last, he could breathe again.

Glenn shouted over. 'Can we do it?'

Myles nodded, still catching his breath.

Glenn saw Myles needed to get oxygen back into his body, but the water was still rising. They had to leave fast. 'Time to go, Myles.'

Myles understood. 'Glenn: I'll lead, you push Heike-Ann down after me, then follow. And Heike-Ann – can you hear me?'

Heike-Ann roused, trying to respond.

'Heike-Ann, I want you to breathe, now - as deeply as you can. Understand? You'll need to hold your breath.' Myles prepared himself again – a deep breath, an exhale, another deep breath to fill his body with air, then he ducked down.

It was harder this time. The water was higher – meaning there was more paper to push through, and further to go down before they reached the emergency escape hatch.

When Myles was finally in the tunnel, he wedged his feet against the sides and bent back to take Heike-Ann.

Through the water, he felt Glenn passing him the woman's hands. Fumbling in the cold liquid, Myles only just managed to grab them. He hauled her along with him, and pushed on.

The extra resistance from Heike-Ann's body made it difficult to advance along the tunnel. He was progressing at only half the speed he had gone before. Could he make it this time?

Then he felt Heike-Ann's body come with him. Glenn was pushing from behind.

Myles kept on, along the horizontal part of the tunnel, feeling where the concrete was still smooth. He pushed against decayed joints and girders, trying to get traction against the current.

Then he came to the downward part. He kept pulling, hoping Heike-Ann's body wouldn't get stuck. He dragged the body down, down and… eventually - through.

Finally, he was at the outlet, where the tunnel fed into the River Spree. He pulled Heike-Ann once more. Nothing. She seemed stuck.

He yanked again. Still no movement…

His lungs were piercing from the dive but Myles tried to ignore the agony. He knew he probably had only one last chance… Then he felt Heike-Ann's body loosen. It was coming free. Glenn had pushed her again.

As quickly as he could, Myles kicked with both his legs, ignoring the twinges in his bad knee. He swam up towards the surface, lifting Heike-Ann with him. At last, he broke into the air, and gasped as his mouth became clear.

He dragged up Heike-Ann, who bobbed to the surface, followed closely by Glenn. Glenn burst for breath too, inhaling suddenly and deeply.

Myles checked on Heike-Ann , and shouted to the American over the noise of the water. 'She's still unconscious.'

Glenn tried to shake the water from their interpreter's face, then hold her up so she could breathe. But she didn't seem to be responding. Myles knew they had to get to the riverbank fast.

The access tunnel had opened into the middle of the river, where it was deep. Half covered in algae and green underwater plants, it was easy to see how it had remained hidden throughout the Cold War. It meant Myles and Glenn had to swim about ten metres to the side, dragging Heike-Ann with them, both with their hands still tied. 'Keep her head out of the water…' Myles shouted over the rush of the water.

They swam as quickly as they could, still holding Heike-Ann with their bound wrists and kicking with their legs. As they neared the edge, Myles realised there'd be no way up: this part of the river had been lined with concrete.

He scanned the riverbank. A short distance downstream there were some metal stairs leading up to the pavement. With a tilt of his head, he pointed them out to Glenn, who understood. They changed course, and allowed the flow of the river to wash them along. Eventually, they reached the steps, Myles crashing into them first.

Together they hauled Heike-Ann out and dragged her clear. With her lying down on the flat surface, Myles turned her pale body to the side, and then pumped her chest, careful not to press on her swollen abdomen. Water surged out. He repeated the motion. More liquid came out of her. This time, though, she seemed to react; she was woozy and looked to be in pain – but alive.

Still recovering and breathing heavily, Glenn allowed himself a small sigh of relief. 'You know, Myles – I didn't think we'd get out of there.'

Myles put Heike-Ann in the recovery position. 'So you didn't believe the prediction you'd survive?'

Glenn didn't answer. Myles wondered if he still had something to hide.

CHAPTER 63

East Berlin

11.42p.m CET (10.42p.m GMT)

It was late evening in the centre of Berlin, Myles could see his breath in the air.

He bent down to check on Heike-Ann. Her face was blanched and cold, her body sodden. 'We've got to get her some proper treatment,' he said, checking her gunshot wound and the improvised bandage. She needed treatment fast.

Glenn looked down at his wrists, frustrated they were still tied. 'Any ideas?'

Myles glanced around for something which could free his hands, and fixed upon the concrete along the river bank. He rubbed the electrical cable on the edge - the plastic coating tore, and gradually the metal strands inside began to fray. As they severed, the binding became looser. Back and forth, he pressed hard on the sharpest part of the concrete, until the cord was loose enough to slip his hands out. He rubbed his wrists where the cable had been.

Then he saw, about a hundred metres away, two people - a man and a woman enjoying a late evening stroll. He darted off towards them, calling out. 'Hey – hey…' Waving his hands as high as he could raise them, Myles got the man to turn his head. Then he stumbled on the pavement stones, and had to break his fall with his shoulder.

The man rushed over, and placed a hand on his back. 'Ist alles in Ordnung?'

Myles gasped in reply.

The woman realised he wasn't local. 'English?'

Myles nodded. He pointed to the man's jacket, still catching his breath. 'Do you have a phone? We need an ambulance…' He turned to show them Glenn and Heike-Ann – two silhouettes by the riverbank. One standing, one lying flat.

The man pulled out a mobile phone, slowly dialling the number but Myles urged him towards Glenn and Heike-Ann. 'Go – go there.'

Although the man was uncertain, Myles directed the couple again. The woman led the way towards Glenn and Heike-Ann, and the man began to follow, his phone clutched to his ear as he went. Myles stayed where he was, still recovering, watching as the man and woman reached his friends. He knew Glenn and Heike-Ann would alert the Berlin Police.

Briefly, Myles wondered about going to the authorities himself. They might let him warn Helen, but he wasn't sure. He certainly couldn't trust them. Just trying to explain everything would take too long. If Dieter had put Myles' name on some terrorist website, he'd be arrested before he could warn anyone. They'd never believe what he now knew about the planets, and without that they wouldn't take the threat of Dieter seriously. Helen would die.

No, he needed to find the man who fooled them into calling him 'Pascal'. Dieter had to be stopped by Myles himself, and he needed to do it fast. He was fighting the worst prediction from Stolz's machine: that Dieter would cause Helen to die in two days' time. The thought of Helen drove him on even faster. He *had* to save her.

Myles gauged his bearings: the underwater tunnel was only a few metres long. Stolz's place in Am Krusenick must still be close. But he realised they'd come out on the other side of the river.

He searched along the footpath, scanning for some way to get back over. Upstream there was a small road bridge. He started hobbling towards it, limping as fast as his legs would allow, as the night air felt even colder on his wet clothes and knee brace, which was stiff and waterlogged. He stumbled again, and crashed down on the hard surface. Ignoring the injury, he pushed himself back up and carried on.

He reached the bridge and staggered up the raised part, his gait uneven. Would he really be able to confront Dieter like this? He imagined the psychopath was waiting in Stolz's basement, ready to strike him and Glenn as they emerged, with the rising water, from the chamber below. The narrow entrance meant only one of them would have been able to climb out at a time. For Dieter, it would make the perfect ambush. But Myles could surprise him from above. He could knock him out or lock him in. As long as Dieter hadn't predicted what he would do.

Myles' shoes were clipping loudly on the pavement. Still going forward, he bent down to prise them off. It didn't work. He accepted he had to stop, then fumbled with the laces, before he could toss each one into the water. He continued on again, his socks now much quieter on the concrete.

He looked at his watch – a quarter to midnight. The machine had predicted he would die tomorrow. Did that mean he should attack Dieter immediately, in the last fifteen minutes of the day?

Myles kept hobbling forward, trying to solve the puzzle as he ran. Could he trust a prediction machine? Even though it had been accurate in the past, would it come true again?

He thought again of Helen, and wondered how she could die in two days' time if Dieter himself was due to die tomorrow. He tried to force the predictions out of his mind. He had to concentrate.

He turned onto Am Krusenick - the minibus was still there, but no sign of anyone.

He limped along as swiftly as he could, his wet socks padding along the pavement. He was watching for any signs of Dieter as he went. A few bedroom lights were on behind curtains, but they were far away. Myles was still alone.

He approached Stolz's apartment block. Wet footprints were on the ground, leading out. Myles stared down at them: Dieter seemed to have come out, gone to the minibus, then run away.

Myles' first thought was to follow them, to chase Dieter while the trail was still hot. Had Dieter doubled-back? Was it a trick?

Myles charged up the steps, ignoring the pain surge in his knee. At the top he opened the entrance to the lobby, and rushed to the door of Stolz's flat. It was unlocked: he barged in, and checked the room.

No one around, and no place to hide.

He gazed down at the hole in the floorboards. Was Dieter waiting below? He froze and listened, wondering in the silence whether he had already made too much noise.

Nothing.

Then he crept through the broken floorboards, carefully stepping into the hole and down the steps.

The basement was flooded. Sodden sheets of paper covered the surface of the water, which had stopped rising. But no sign of Dieter. Myles cursed. The man had escaped.

One of the pages washed against his foot. Myles fished it out. It was the life story of 'Person Number 1006220', their ethnicity confirmed by a small Star of David. Life events were summarised in German words which Myles couldn't translate - born in December 1912, with something in May 1930, August 1935, and January 1939. The last date was 3rd August 1943.

Myles held the paper with two hands as it dripped. He didn't know whether to preserve it out of respect or screw it up in frustration.

Person 1006220: another victim of the bureaucrats.

Then he saw a form slowly turning in the water. He peered closer, trying to make it out. Slowly he identified a boot, then realised it was attached to a body. It was Zenyalena, her face staring down to the bunker. Zenyalena, Jean-François, even Frank… Dieter had killed them all.

He pulled the dead woman towards him, feeling its weight in the water, and delved into her pockets. The keys to the minibus were there – he fished them out, then flicked the dirty water from his hands as he limped back out.

Myles dashed upstairs, back to the lobby, and outside, where the air felt even colder.

He opened the door to the minibus and peered inside. There were wet footprints by the pedals, and the wiring had been pulled down from under the dashboard. Dieter had tried to hotwire the vehicle, but failed.

Then he realised: the bottle of nerve agent was gone. Dieter must have taken it.

So that was Dieter's plan: to set off one of Hitler's 'wonder-weapons' – seventy years late.

Myles looked at his watch: one minute to midnight.

Would he die from Sarin poisoning tomorrow?
Would thousands of others?
Would Sarin kill Helen too, making his partner 'cease to be' two days later than Myles?

Angry, he slammed the door shut, and ran as fast as he could, following the wet footprints on the pavement.

He knew he must be ten minutes behind Dieter, but not much more. If he ran, there was a chance he could still catch him.

Myles sprinted along Am Krusenick, his feet in wet socks feeling every piece of grit on the road. But he ignored the pain, and ran on. The neoprene bandage which supported his healing knee seemed to be slowing him down. Quickly he reached down, ripped apart the Velcro, and tossed it away.

He limped on – faster now. Dieter's footprints turned. Myles turned with them. Then, round the corner, they seemed to disappear.

It didn't make sense. There was nowhere for the Frenchman to go. No patch of grass to hide his footprints. No surface which wouldn't show the water. It was as if Dieter had flown into the air.

Myles desperately scanned around. No clues anywhere – nothing which seemed out of place.

Then he noticed, thrown into a kerb some metres away, a jumble of footwear. Myles rushed closer: it was Dieter's socks and shoes, all sodden with water. Dieter must have realised he was leaving a trail, so he took them off, dried his feet somehow, then continued on barefoot.

With no wet footprints to follow, Myles didn't know where to look. He checked his watch again. Just past midnight...*on the day he was due to die.*

DAY SIX

CHAPTER 64

East Berlin

12.02a.m. CET (11.02p.m. -1 GMT)

Myles felt the crisp night air again – his wet clothes were freezing more than ever, and clinging to his body, making it difficult for him to move. He was in no condition to attack Dieter.

Myles turned, and started jogging back to the minibus, gripping the keys he had just taken from Zenyalena's body. He jumped into the driver's seat, poked the keys into the ignition, and turned them. Then he drove away, leaving Stolz's apartment for good.

Confused by the small streets of Berlin, Myles decided to turn onto whichever street was larger at each junction he found. That way, he knew, he'd soon find a street with directions. The roads were deserted. Certainly no sirens or screaming ambulances. Dieter hadn't set off his wonderweapon yet….

Myles soon reached the autobahn, and then accelerated, speeding towards Potsdam - the only place near Berlin that he knew.

After twenty minutes he recognised his surroundings – he had been driven this way by Glenn when he first arrived in Germany. Once he found the signposts, the Cecilienhof was easy to reach.

The minibus's tyres screamed as he swerved into the hotel carpark, then parked up and jumped out, losing his balance on his weak leg. Only as an afterthought did he turn off the headlights and the engine. He'd need the vehicle again.

He headed straight to reception.

Fortunately, there was a familiar face on duty: it was the brunette. She was shocked to see Myles – so late at night, breathless, and desperate. She was obviously perturbed by Myles' appearance, tilting her head warily as if she wanted to comment on Myles' wet clothes and lack of footwear. 'Mr Munro – how can I help?' she said, her voice unsteady.

Myles ignored her. Instead, he grabbed the hotel's courtesy phone and dialled a familiar number as fast as he could.

00… 44… 7788…

It was Helen's number – her CNN mobile. The number rang.

No answer, then a recorded message.

'Hi, you've reached Helen Bridle. Please leave a message and I'll get back to you as soon as I can.'

Beep

Myles wondered what to say. 'Er, Helen. Are you there? Sorry to call you so late. You're probably asleep… But this is important. Please pick up the phone….' Myles realised his voice was sounding a little desperate, as the receptionist caught his eye. '… Er, Helen. When you get this message, please stay somewhere safe - far away from Berlin. Understand? Nowhere near. If you do, you'll die – probably from concentrated Sarin or some other Nazi chemical. I don't know exactly, and I can't say how I know. Not over the phone, not 'til we're face-to-face again. I'm looking forward to seeing you face-to-face again soon. So please trust me, don't go to Berlin… er, thank you. And, er, love you, too.'

He put down the phone. Had he done enough to keep Helen out of danger? Would his message save her life, two days from now? He thought of calling again, but realised it wouldn't help. There was no more he could say.

'Clothes. Do you have any spare clothes?'

The woman sized Myles up, her eyes still alarmed. Myles wondered if she saw blood from Heike-Ann's wound on his trousers. She turned to fetch something from an office behind her, then came back with a pressed white business shirt. 'I have this… Sir?'

But Myles had already gone over to the internet terminal next to the front desk, determined to find the terrorist website. He found a search engine and typed in: *'Mein Kampf Now'*, then pressed enter. Ten of 134,000 results came up. Myles scrolled through the first screen, then the second, then the third, then the fourth. None of them seemed right.

Next he tried *'Humanitarian Pursuit'*. Pages appeared on peace negotiations, food aid, even mountain climbing. But still no sign of the website he needed. He searched his own name – something he hated doing, since the inevitable headlines came up – 'Myles Munro: Oxford terrorist', 'University Lecturer linked to bomber'. But they were all old. There was nothing new, or from Dieter. He slumped back in his chair.

Myles' mind drifted to the predictions about himself: that he would die today, too, and that Helen would somehow 'cease to be' two days later.

He began typing.

'A-S-T-R-O-L-O-G-Y… P-R-E-D-I-C-T-I-O-N-S'

A selection of sites appeared. He wondered: would they confirm the verdict of the Nazi prediction machine? Of course they wouldn't. It didn't matter which of the sites he picked: none of them would predict someone was about to die on a certain day, especially if that day was today.

'Mr Munro, Sir…?'

Myles turned. The receptionist was pushing a trolley towards him: coffee, orange juice and warm toast.

'Early for breakfast, I know, Sir,' she smiled. 'But you look like you could do with something to eat.'

Then she offered him a bag of clothes. Myles peeked inside: a whole business suit, with shirt, underwear, a tie, and a pair of smart shoes.

'I guessed your size, Sir – we have others if you need them. And feel free to take a shower.' She pointed to the door of a luxury suite behind reception, beaming sympathetically.

Distracted, Myles thanked her with his eyes, and picked up the toast. Only as he began eating did he realise how hungry he was.

But his mind was still focussed on Helen. He had to save her.

He remembered Dieter's words: 'The world will soon be transformed from Berlin – a new Reich starting from where Hitler started…'

Dieter had to set off the lethal liquid from somewhere high-up, so it could spread through the air.

But where had Hitler started his Reich? Not in Vienna in 1938, as Stolz had thought. Hitler had destroyed Germany as soon as he came to power. Myles went back to the keyboard.

H-I-T-L-E-R 1-9-3-3

Straightaway an image came up: the Reichstag, Germany's parliament building, in flames. Of course. Myles remembered how Hitler had hired a stooge to set it on fire a month after coming into office. It gave the dictator a perfect excuse for 'emergency measures' which shut down democracy. The Reichstag didn't re-open properly until after the war.

Myles clicked on the image, and saw the new glass roof to the building. It was high. Sarin released from the top into the wind could blow over the whole city. The ideal place to set off the wonderweapon.

Myles rushed back to the receptionist. 'Do you have any tourist leaflets?'

'Certainly Sir…' She pointed to a whole stand full of promotional flyers and brochures, trying her best to be helpful, even though she was still obviously unnerved by Myles' appearance. 'Do you want any particular one, Mr Munro, Sir?'

'The Reichstag. Do they have a tourist programme?'

She nodded, and picked out the leaflet. 'Yes – visits from eight in the morning, I think.' She looked back at the clock behind her as she handed him the paper. 'Five-and-a-half hours away. You've still got time to have a shower….'

Myles was already engrossed in the leaflet, trying to work out where Dieter could set of the bomb.

'Er, Mr Munro. You really should freshen up, if you want to visit. Otherwise, they might not let you in…'

Myles looked up and accepted the point.

He picked up the clean clothes and wandered towards the shower room. He had to be ready for what the machine had predicted would be his last morning alive.

And he hoped Helen picked up his warning.

Exactly 588 miles due west of Berlin, as Helen was taking out her phone to pass through airport security, she noticed she had a missed call. No number had been left, but there was a message. Stepping out of the line, she pressed 'play' and listened.

Then, without a moment's hesitation, she hurried back through 'Departures', to the long line of ticket desks within Heathrow's Terminal Two. 'I need to change my flight,' she explained, remaining professionally calm. 'To Berlin – whichever airport is closest to the city centre. The next flight, please.'

CHAPTER 65

Schlosshotel Cecilienhof
Potsdam, near Berlin
4.50a.m. CET (3.50a.m. GMT)

Fed, washed and dressed, Myles thanked the receptionist as he left the hotel.

'No problem, Sir,' said the brunette.

Myles wondered whether the woman would call the police – he could tell his bloodied late night appearance had alarmed her. She may even have overheard his warning to Helen. So, as soon as he was in the minibus, he turned the ignition, barely allowed the engine to settle, and pulled out of the carpark. Then he noticed the fuel gauge – was almost empty.

To the east, the sky was beginning to lighten. In an hour or so the sun would rise. His last sunrise?

Myles wondered about driving away. Driving to Helen. Anywhere – just to escape, so they both had a chance of surviving the Sarin attack. But would that make them safe? He didn't know. It would certainly leave the people of Berlin in danger.

He looked at the fuel gauge again – if he tried to drive anywhere but the centre of Berlin, he wouldn't get there.

He realised that whatever the prediction said, there were some things Myles had to do. Danger mattered less than his duty. He just *had* to stop Dieter. He didn't have a choice. Not because of the prediction, but because of who he was.

Onto the autobahn, he checked his watch again. Ten minutes past four: whatever was going to kill him had less than twenty hours left.

He drove towards the centre of Berlin. Still no wailing police sirens. Still no sign of panic. Still most people asleep, although he did notice some early morning buses carrying a few drowsy commuters to work.

He knew Dieter would be on his guard, and would recognise the minibus if he saw it, so he couldn't risk parking near the Reichstag. Instead, he drove near the building, then found a sidestreet about a kilometre away. He pulled up, took out the key, and locked the vehicle behind him.

Trying not to put more pressure on his recovering knee joint than was necessary, he walked towards the Reichstag. He stopped in the Platz der Republik, the green space outside the modern parliament building, where he found a bench.

From there, he had a distant view of the entrance to the Reichstag. He could see anybody who entered, but was far enough away that he wouldn't be noticed himself. Myles was tall, certainly, but dressed in a fresh business suit, Dieter was unlikely to spot him.

Then he waited.

The first rays of sun lit up the park. Myles noticed a municipal cleaner amble around, emptying the bins. He saw an early morning commuter rushing somewhere with a coffee cup, a couple of disorientated tourists, and eventually a tour group from the Far East.

As the time passed six forty-five, he saw security men enter the Reichstag, relaxed as they clocked in for their morning shift. Roughly a quarter of an hour later, the night shift clocked off, leaving the building calmly, either alone or in pairs.

The sun was becoming stronger now. As it rose over the Reichstag, it shone straight into his eyes. Myles shaded his face with his hand, determined to keep watching.

It got to half-past seven, and tourists started to gather near the entrance. parliamentary staff with ID badges ignored them as they swiped into the building, their mind on other things. A quarter-to-eight, and the crowd was swelling. Was Dieter amongst them? There was certainly No one dressed like Dieter, and nobody wearing wet clothes.

Five minutes to eight. Still no sign.

The security man in charge of the door was looking up at the clock. Then the entrance opened. The compliant tourists were counted in. None of them could have been Dieter. Myles had been wrong.

Still more people were nearby: a politician with an aide, comparing notes on the day ahead. A secretary in uncomfortable heels. A huddle of journalists. Almost by coincidence, Myles saw a well-dressed man with body language he recognised from somewhere. Like Myles, the man was checking his watch, rushing to some sort of meeting…

Then Myles sat stiff, as the shock electrified his whole body: it was Dieter.

Myles stood, started to jog, then ran across the grass towards the Reichstag, ignoring the weakness in his knee. He reached the entrance just as the main door was closing.

'Verzeihung, mein Herr,' said a security official.

'Sorry?'

'I'm sorry, Sir, no entry.'

Myles peered over the heads of the people in front of him. He could see Dieter had been checked off some sort of list and allowed to wander freely within the building. 'But I need to go in,' Myles pleaded.

'Have you arranged with us in advance?' The guard could tell Myles looked confused. He'd met many tourists like him before. The official spoke with a firm tone – respectful, but closing off the option. 'Visitors are welcome, Sir, but you have to register with us beforehand.'

Myles searched the man's face. Head tipped forward and lips pursed, the man had an 'I'm sure you understand' expression.

Myles thought about explaining, but knew it would be no use. If he told them Dieter was about to unleash Sarin, the bureaucrat would arrest him, not the real terrorist.

Myles gestured towards the guard's papers. 'Well, can you put me on the list now, please?'

'I'm afraid not, Sir – we only accept reservations by email.'

'I can email you now if you like. Do you have internet access, somewhere?'

'We do, Sir. But I'd need to see your ID to let you use it.'

Myles checked his pockets and eventually found his passport – which was still wet – and handed it over.

The guard paused, wondering whether to accept the soggy document. But he did, checked it, then raised his eyebrows as he glanced back at his list. 'Munro, Myles… Mr Munro, we already have you on the list. For the 0800 tour.'

Myles couldn't understand how his name had been put on. The hotel receptionist? Helen back in Oxford? Glenn, even? Someone had done it for him. He decided now was not the time to wonder who or how. He had to catch Dieter, and stop him doing whatever he was planning.

'Thank you, Sir.' Myles nodded to the guard as he took back his passport, and hobbled through the security gate.

He shuffled towards the pack of visitors, joining the group just as it left the entrance area to begin the tour. He scanned over their heads to see Dieter near the front, about ten metres away.

Again, he thought of calling out, of trying to get both himself and Dieter arrested. But he still couldn't trust the guards. They'd just arrest him. Dieter could run and set off his wonderweapon. No, Myles had to do this another way.

Gently, he tried to manoeuvre through the people. He passed an Italian couple, bumping the woman as she read from a guidebook. Myles went round an American adjusting his camera-straps, and overtook two students gazing up at the new architecture. He was getting closer to Dieter…

Then a stout woman came to the front, the ID card dangling from her neck indicating she was some sort of official guide. 'Good morning, and welcome to the Reichstag building….' The woman clapped as if she was bringing a classroom of juniors to order.

Myles tried to pay attention, but his mind was on Dieter. The woman caught his eye. Myles felt duty-bound to smile back, pretending he was vitally interested in what she had to say.

'…This is the building that most famously was destroyed in February 1933. The fire that night….' The tour-guide started directing her words elsewhere in the crowd.

Myles checked on Dieter. The Frenchman was bending down to tie his laces. Myles still needed to get closer. He tried to ease his way past a man in a wheelchair, then a mother with her teenage daughter. But he knocked the girl's digital camera, which clattered to the floor.

The tour official glared at him, then pointed at the wall. Her outstretched arm was blocking his way. '… And this is actual graffiti from Russian soldiers in May 1945. The Soviets lost about 70,000 soldiers fighting for Berlin at the end of World War Two, and this historic writing, drawn with coal on sandstone, was preserved as a memorial to those deaths…'

Myles raised his eyebrows in mock-interest, forcing himself to turn and admire the Russian lettering high-up on the inside walls. He turned back to look for Dieter, but the woman was obscuring his view.

Now the guide was beaming her eyes at him – the woman was trying to flick her hair back. Was she *flirting* with him? She raised her voice. '… And when this building was renovated for reunited Germany, in the 1990s, a decision was made to be sensitive to history. At the base of the large, spiral ramp to the ceiling, you will see photographs from the past – such as President Truman, Prime Minister Winston Churchill and Soviet Premier Josef Stalin, meeting in Potsdam to discuss the fate of Europe after the War. There's also a picture of US President Ronald Reagan, when he made a famous speech here in the summer of 1987…'

Myles allowed the woman's gaze to swing away. Finally, he could walk forwards again.

He limped on, towards where Dieter had been. But the man wasn't where Myles was expecting. Myles turned around to look properly. Where had he gone? Myles checked the entrance again. No sign of him there…

'Sir, you look as though your child has just run off.' The tour guide's humour roused a small laugh from the crowd.

'I… I don't have a child.'

'Well, whatever you're missing, I can help you find it later.' The corners of the woman's mouth rose, locking into a professional smile. Myles returned the gesture feebly, still concentrating on Dieter. He allowed himself to drift with the herd as the tour guide led them on – into the centre of the building.

Myles knew Dieter must have peeled off somewhere. Into a toilet? Or a side-corridor? Somewhere… but where?

'Now, ladies and gentlemen, would you all please look upwards…' The guide's instructions were unnecessary since they were all gazing upwards anyway. Above them was a huge dome, made of glass panels in a metal frame. A ramp spiralled down from the very top, allowing people to walk up to the highest point in the building, viewing all of Berlin on the way up. '… You will see glass, which symbolises the transparency and openness of the new Germany…'

Myles noticed a curved cone hanging down from the centre of the dome above. Mirrors had been placed on the sides. Reflections of tourists as they climbed to the top appeared then disappeared, as the people shuffled out of view.

'… And by climbing up to the top of the glass dome, people can look down on their elected representatives working in the parliament below them. This is the opposite of the discredited dictatorship of Adolf Hitler, when the politicians looked down on their people…'

Then, in one of the mirrors, Myles glimpsed a reflection of Dieter climbing up the ramp. Within an instant, it was gone again. But it was enough for Myles to know the psychopath was walking to the top of the glass dome.

'… And we hope this new German parliament will survive much longer than the last…' But the guide's words were lost on Myles. He'd already started racing up the ramp, hobbling as fast as he could, desperate to catch Dieter before the man ended this newest vision of Germany.

Myles sprinted upwards, forcing the muscle around his wounded knee to compensate for his weakened ligaments. He ignored the guide, who made some sort of joke about her audience running away. He began to spiral up, grabbing the rail with his hand to pull himself faster – knowing it was probably his last chance to catch Dieter.

He passed the pictures of Berlin through the ages: the horror of World War One, the rise of the Nazis, the Reichstag burning down in 1933, Hitler controlling Europe, then the city in ruins. Myles ignored them all. He had to climb higher.

He overtook a crowd of foreigners bunched around another guide. He limped past a security guard, a very old woman who had probably known Germany during the war, and an old man with grey skin in a wheelchair, who was being pushed slowly to the top.

Myles didn't register any of them. As he reached the halfway point, he began to see the panorama of the city – the offices, the old buildings, the open spaces. All in danger, if Dieter released the liquid from Stolz's wonderweapon.

Myles raced on, refusing to be distracted by a small chunk of the Berlin Wall visible on the ground below, preserved as a monument to the Cold War. He tried to look ahead, desperately seeking out Dieter. But he still couldn't see him. He had to keep going.

Myles was approaching the top, now. He ignored the pain in his lungs, and the twinges in his ruptured knee. An attendant frowned at him for running. Myles nodded – he understood – but kept on anyway. He just had to catch Dieter before the Sarin liquid was released.

Only as he approached the top viewing platform did he allow himself to slow. He looked around. Surely this was where Dieter must be… Myles scanned a full 360 degrees, but there was still no sign.

He studied the tourists around him: a family group, some teenagers, workmen in overalls… none of them looked like Dieter. Where had the man disappeared to?

Myles paused, and finally stopped. He bent down, his hands on his knees to catch his breath. He looked up and stared around again. He was at the top, now. Such a small place – how had Dieter vanished?

He knew he had to think. To stop Dieter meant thinking like him. Myles had to understand what Dieter was planning.

Myles knew Dieter had the bottle of nerve agent – taken from Stolz's tin in the trench. He could have pretended it was water to bypass the guards at the Reichstag entrance. So where would he have taken it?

Myles scanned around again. He looked down at the spiral ramp, checking Dieter hadn't run down again. No sign of him.

He checked the lower viewing platform, and the ground-floor of the Reichstag building. Still no sign.

In desperation, Myles looked outside, checking the panorama of Berlin in case Dieter had managed to leave the building. Dieter was nowhere.

Myles spun around, beaten, drawing confused looks from the tourists on the viewing platform beside him.

Suddenly, he felt his knee buckle. The joint collapsed beneath him, and he tumbled to the floor in agony. Pain was surging back. His ligament had ruptured again. Resisting the urge to cry out, Myles cursed himself for removing the neoprene support, and for pushing himself so hard.

The intense pain made him look up. And only then, noticing the glass above him, did he spot the opening in the dome. Workmen had removed one of the transparent panels. Myles couldn't tell whether it was to clean the glass or do repairs, but there was now an access to the outside. It was a space large enough for someone to crawl through, and to get onto the roof. It was the only way that Dieter could have gone.

Myles pushed himself off the floor, just managing to stand on his one good leg. He edged towards the hole and grabbed the sides with his hands, then lifted himself up. Some of the tourists took photos, imagining Myles was performing a stunt or making a protest. Myles ignored them, concentrating on getting up. He squeezed out, suddenly feeling the wind blast against his skin, then clambered round the slippery glass dome at the top of the building, until he saw the man he had expected to see.

Holding the bottle of clear liquid high, with his arm outstretched, Dieter was about to release the nerve agent.

CHAPTER 66

Central Berlin
8.23a.m. CET (7.23a.m. GMT)

Myles tried to edge closer, pulling himself along a rail with his arms, his weight on his one good foot as he dragged his useless leg behind him. He felt the wind blow hard against him as he tried to circle round the top of the dome. He wondered if he could catch Dieter unaware. Perhaps to grab his liquid, perhaps to push him off. Anything to stop the man setting off the wonderweapon.

Clumsy as ever, Myles gripped tightly to the steel frame. He heaved his leg around a metal bar trying to approach quietly.

Dieter was just a few metres away. The Frenchman's back was turned. Myles had a chance.

'...Don't get blown off, now... that's not your fate...' It was Dieter's voice.

Slowly, Dieter's head turned to face him, raising the clear liquid toward Myles as if he was making a toast. 'Good morning, Myles. Glad you could make it...'

Myles froze in place. He didn't know how to react.

'...Don't worry about being blown off the top of the dome. You can come closer if you want...' Dieter saw Myles wasn't moving. The Frenchman shrugged and began to smirk. '... Or you can stay where you are. Up here, we're both close to the heavens. That's why I added your name to the guest list for the Reichstag. I knew you'd come. Even though you'd been told you were about to die, I knew you'd come to the most dangerous place there could be.'

Myles kept gripping tightly to the metal frame. He tried to keep his voice calm and reasonable. 'It doesn't have to be dangerous, Dieter. We can both get out of this. Just because the machine said we'd both die today, it doesn't mean we have to.'

Dieter grinned again. 'You think? You really think that? Is that why you telephoned someone due to die in two days' time, to warn them away?'

'Helen?'

'Yes. You did call her, didn't you?'

Myles didn't want to satisfy Dieter by confirming he was right. He remained silent, just tipping his head forward, encouraging Dieter to say more.

'You're wondering how I know, aren't you, Myles? Shall I tell you how I know you called Helen?'

'Go on.'

'Because she's there. Look.' Dieter turned his head, pointing out towards the Platz der Republik – the large green space where Myles had waited just a few minutes before. There was Helen, directing a cameraman who was setting up his equipment. Helen hadn't seen them. Myles' call last night, telling her not to come, must have encouraged her. And when he said Berlin, she had naturally come to the city's centre of government – to the Reichstag. Trying to make her safe had put her in danger. He kicked himself for not predicting how she would react. Even if he warned her away now, she'd only come closer. Typical Helen – always heading towards trouble...

Dieter saw Myles' face and began to laugh. 'You see - even when we try to cheat our fate, fate still wins. You know, Myles, after we all climbed out of the cavern in Landsberg, I climbed back in. The globes said Berlin was the place I'd change the world.'

Myles' eyes fixed on the bottle of clear liquid in Dieter's hand. 'What do you want your fate to be, Dieter? You could still walk away from all this…'

'Not anymore. Not with the websites, remember? I'm the humanitarian, you're the terrorist.' Dieter lifted the bottle up, pinching it between his thumb and forefinger, and letting it sway in the wind. 'If you try to take this liquid, my funeral will draw many more people than yours - probably even more than Helen's, when she dies of Sarin poisoning the day after tomorrow.' The man was still keeping himself a few metres clear from Myles. 'You *are* trying to take this liquid from me, aren't you, Myles?'

Myles paused before he answered, then decided to be honest. 'Yes, I am.'

'You see, Myles? You might say it's your character, or because you want to save people – perhaps just to save Helen. But you're completely predictable, too. Just as the machine assumed you were.' Dieter began to smirk. Intellectually superior and he knew it. 'You can't leave here either…'

Myles refused to respond.

Dieter began to ponder. '… So let me predict, Myles. You'll ask me to come down again. I'll refuse. Then you'll go for the Sarin. We'll both fall all the way down there.' He peered down. 'You die from a great height. The bottle smashes, releasing the Sarin, so I die from multiple causes. The Sarin kills thousands, and when Helen examines your dead body, she inhales this stuff and dies tomorrow evening. All the machine's predictions come true – every single one. I die a martyr, you die a terrorist, and Helen's death means CNN runs the story for a whole week.'

Myles tried to shake his head, still gripping the metal. 'Why are you so keen to know what's going to happen, Dieter?'

'We all are. It's human nature.'

Myles thought about making a lunge for the liquid. It was exactly what Dieter was expecting, but what else could he do? In his mind, he calculated how far he was from Dieter – close enough for it to be worth a try.

Myles looked down: the surface of the glass dome curved away from him, down to a mid-level viewing platform. Some of the tourists were already gazing up, realising that Dieter and Myles were not on the top of the dome for any normal purpose.

Could Myles drag Dieter down to the rooftop without the glass bottle breaking? Unlikely: if they slid down the glass dome, he wouldn't be able to keep hold of the liquid.

Dieter lowered the bottle slightly, holding it straight in front of Myles, taunting him. 'I'm ready to die, Myles. I've found Stolz's secret. And my death will help make Germany strong again.'

'Is that why you did it all?'

'No. I did this because Stolz's secret belonged to Hitler. The Führer left it for the German people. When they hear I died trying to stop you releasing the Sarin, I'll become a hero. They'll respect the things I stood for.'

Now Myles understood: Dieter *wanted* him to attack.

Dieter grinned once more, gripping the neck of the bottle as if it was an old stick hand-grenade. 'No, Myles? Not coming towards me?' Myles saw Dieter's eyes pick out Helen on the green space below. The psychopath pulled his arm back, aiming, preparing to throw…

Something in Myles removed his capacity to choose. A deep instinct thrust him from the metal frame, lunging the small distance towards Dieter.

Dieter turned to meet him. As Myles' body slammed into the Frenchman, Myles felt the bottle of liquid smash against his shoulder. Within an instant, liquid burst out, soaking his shirt and splashing onto his face.

Myles knew he was covered. He knew he had no chance of surviving the nerve agent. And, as he lost his footing on the roof, it was his character which made him grab Dieter on the way down.

Together, they began to slide off the glass dome. Faster and faster, Dieter and Myles accelerated as the curve of the dome became steeper. They began to freefall. Down towards the hard surface below.

Myles gripped Dieter as tightly as he could. He saw the viewing platform rushing up, towards his head. He knew both of them would die.

In the last moment before his skull smashed against the concrete, Myles got satisfaction from hoping he had saved Helen.

Hoping that, in one small way, he had managed to beat the predictions.

CHAPTER 67

Langley, Virginia,
USA
5.25p.m EST (10.25p.m GMT)

As Sally Wotton prepared to close down her computer, she took one last look at the image of Myles Munro. He had been quite good looking…

And he had been to so many places: Afghanistan, Libya, Iran… And that was just recently.

The Oxford University lecturer in military history had obviously lived an exciting life. Such a pity - that life was now over.

Her fingers touched the screen, wishing she could have saved him from the deadly fall. But she'd seen the live feed from the satellite. There was no way he could have survived. The paramedics had carried away two completely motionless bodies.

The public reports about him from several years ago, when he was sacked over a scandal involving terrorists from Africa, didn't ring true to Sally. She could tell he had been a scapegoat. They always try to blame the misfits…

The fact that Myles had been a misfit was obvious. Myles had clearly suffered from some sort of high-performing learning disability, a diagnosis confirmed by the CIA psychological assessment of him. Sally had found the file so interesting she had read it twice. And from what she, could tell about his popular lectures at Oxford, his radical theory about Clausewitz was one of the greatest advances in military theory in almost two centuries. He had certainly been very bright. Very bright indeed.

Sally sometimes felt a bit like a misfit herself, although she guessed she'd been luckier in life than poor old Myles Munro.

But at least there was one thing she could do for this man – although it seemed a bit late: she could prove he'd been made a scapegoat *again*.

Sally's logic was simple. Myles Munro had been named as a terrorist on the *Mein Kampf Now* website – alongside some federal employee called 'Glenn'. Sally knew both were innocent. She knew because she had quarantined the site, alongside the *Humanitarian Pursuit* site which had tried to negotiate with them. Both sites had been isolated from the World Wide Web, so the psychopath's threats had been read by No one. Or rather, No one outside the CIA.

It meant whoever was behind *Humanitarian Pursuit* must also have been behind *Mein Kampf Now*. There was no other way the humanitarians could have known about the terrorist threats.

And by uploading Myles Munro's details onto the *Mein Kampf Now* webpage, the psychopath had given Sally an important lead. It meant she had a name, so she could order a bug on Mr Munro's home phone, in Oxford, England, and all the numbers associated with it. When Myles Munro himself had made a desperate call to his partner's CNN mobile, warning her to stay away from the Reichstag in Berlin, it had given them just enough time to get the message where it needed to go. Enough time to send agents to central Berlin, although sadly not enough time to save Myles Munro himself.

And the other guy? It looked like the psychopath uploading the threats had been someone called Dieter. An easy news search had revealed who this Dieter person was: a radical fascist, brought up as a German in Strasbourg half a century after the town was given to France as compensation for World War One. He was an agitator, a rebel, an ideologue who had been jailed for throwing pink paint at a far-right Euro-politician. Dieter had tried to become a new Hitler, but failed.

Dieter had uploaded his own picture to the *Humanitarian Pursuit* website. He'd tried to claim credit for making peace with a terrorist organisation responsible for all sorts of bad things – from the deaths of senators, to nuclear accidents, to economic depressions and even wars.

So why hadn't this Dieter guy put it all behind him? Why the terrorist website? Why the bizarre threats, most of them way off in the future? Sally understood: because Dieter believed he could predict the future. It allowed him to claim credit for bad things which happened. So why not try to claim credit for bringing peace?

It was all nonsense. It must be. Nobody could predict the future – it was impossible. *Wasn't it?*

What if this dead Dieter person really *had* found a way to predict the future? Now the technical analysts had found the real IP address and the location traces, she knew exactly where in Berlin this man had been. If Dieter had left paperwork – perhaps a machine or something - she could fly over, find it, and try to predict the future herself.

It would be far more interesting than her day job. She had just finished with the most interesting case her job would ever bring. She would close down her computer, only to power it up again tomorrow, and the day after that, and the day after that. Sally was about to leave the office, dissatisfied as ever, only to return the next day…

She went back to the computer screen to re-read the tech boys' report on locations, but she couldn't open it any more.

Her security status didn't allow it. Someone had changed the classification – it was now officially too sensitive for her to read. Even the traces from Dieter to contacts in Israel and England had gone. She slumped. No trip to Berlin. She wouldn't be able to escape her job. She would have to leave the office, and be ready for another day there tomorrow.

As Sally Wotton left her computer and put on her coat, she finally understood how predictable her life was after all.

CHAPTER 68

Berlin
Germany
11.35p.m CET (10.35p.m GMT)

Dieter tried to tense his neck muscles to lift up his head, but blood in his hair had congealed, sticking him to whatever he was lying on. He ignored the pain, and tugged several times until his scalp was free. As his vision cleared, he realised he must have been concussed from the fall.

Blearily, he looked around him. To one side, a paramedic in a yellow bio-chemical protection suit was preparing Myles Munro's cadaver. Myles' skin was grey, except for the ugly head wound from which his life had drained away. The paramedic was calmly removing the Englishman's clothes and wiping the man's tall body. Dieter allowed himself to smirk. He may have failed to save the last great secret of the Nazis, but he had at least killed the Englishman. And in doing so, he had proved Stolz's wartime prediction computer – that triumph of Nazi science - was accurate.

He wobbled his head around to survey his own body, which was fixed in place on a medical bed. He realised he couldn't move his legs. Worse, he couldn't feel them. He reached his hand down to his pelvis, but there was no sensation at all.

Towards the far end of the sterile white room in which he lay, two men, also wearing full protective suits, stared at him.

'Help me,' Dieter uttered. One of the men lumbered towards him.

Dieter hoped the man would treat him, even honour him – after all, he had just saved Germany. But instead of helping Dieter, the man produced a sidearm. Dieter knew the weapon: a SIG-Sauer P229, a handgun favoured by various parts of the US Federal government. Then he recognised the face inside the bio-mask: it was Glenn.

Glenn peered down, and pushed himself right up to Dieter. 'Where's the Sarin?' he snarled.

Dieter glared back, refusing to answer. Then he motioned towards Myles. 'Death from a great height,' he boasted.

Dieter saw Glenn's non-reaction and laughed. 'You believed the machine too, didn't you…'

He grinned. Eyes still fixed on Glenn, Dieter's fingers delved towards his pocket and found the old enamelled pillbox he had stolen from Stolz. Reassuringly, he felt the famous crooked cross on the cover, and marvelled at the German craftsmanship which had miniaturised the swastika so perfectly. He flicked the box open.

Glenn saw the movement and thrust his gun against Dieter's temple. 'Don't think you can still release it - you'll be dead before you try.'

But Dieter just smiled. Gently, he lifted the clouded capsule from his pocket into his mouth, carefully positioning it between his teeth.

'Last chance,' threatened Glenn.

Dieter replied with just a single word, 'Führoxia.'

Dieter was just able to bite down on the cyanide pill before a bullet from Glenn's pistol blasted through his brain.

Death from multiple causes.

And just as Dieter had managed to die like Hitler, he was also remembered like the Nazi-dictator: with no grave, no glory, and no monuments ever built in his honour.

DAY SEVEN

CHAPTER 69

Russian Embassy,
Berlin, Germany
2p.m. CET (1p.m. GMT)

Even though it disturbed his regular daily schedule, Ludochovic did not hesitate to obey the first half of Zenyalena's handwritten command:

> *Bring all the Stolz papers to the Berlin embassy immediately, where I will meet you...*

The instant he had received the note – contained within a package sent in an 'Imperial War Museum' envelope from a postbox on the French-German border – Ludochovic had booked himself on a flight, and made his way to the German capital. An official car met him at the airport, and drove him straight to the Russian embassy. Police cordons and 'bio-hazard decontamination' barriers, which had surrounded part of the nearby Reichstag for some twenty hours, delayed the last part of his journey only by a few minutes.

His trouble was: what to do about the second part of Zenyalena's instructions?

> *... but if I don't appear, then publish everything from Stolz.*

The problem was Zenyalena *had* appeared, but not as Ludochovic had expected. Indeed, it was Ludochovic himself who had to sign for receipt of the sodden body from the German diplomatic police, identify Ms Androvsky formally, and ensure the death was handled as a consular matter under international protocols, rather than by the national authorities of Germany.

The whole affair seemed very unorthodox to Ludochovic. Just like his now deceased line manager, and the unorthodox international mission she had set up to investigate Stolz. He was sure there was more to all this than he knew – just as there had been when a predecessor of his had received Kirov's dead body, the Soviet liaison officer who interviewed the last Nazi, back in 1945. Like Kirov, Zenyalena had been killed by a single bullet while working with 'allies' to investigate Stolz. And why was Zenyalena's body so wet? It was more than suspicious. As Zenyalena herself would have said, 'this one smells'.

Briefly, he considered visiting the East Berlin apartment where Zenyalena's body was reported to have been found. He wondered about re-starting the international team with new members, or sending out another demarche to provoke a revealing reaction from the United States, as Zenyalena would have done.

But, as a dutiful servant of the Russian Foreign Ministry, Ludochovic understood his job was solely to obey. That meant he had three tasks. First, to repatriate the body of Ms Zenyalena Androvsky for cremation. The service would take place in Moscow, just in case there were any friends, family or loved ones who might want to attend, although Ludovic suspected there would be none.

Secondly, he should put all the facts he knew on file, by writing a complete report about the whole affair. It would be as detailed as the reports from 1945, and archived, just in case it might be needed seventy years from now, as the report on Kirov had been.

And third, out of respect to his deceased line manager, he would carry out the last request he had received from her: he *would* publish online the material from Stolz.

Meticulously, Ludochovic gathered all the papers he had, including the latest papers in the War Museum envelope and the documents Zenyalena had faxed through earlier. Even though some had been annotated by Ms Androvsky, and initialled 'ZA', he reckoned her handwriting was anonymous enough as to be untraceable. He crossed out the word 'Secret', then passed them on to the Information Management Officer at the Russian Embassy in Berlin, alongside the routine request that they be released – without attribution.

The Russian Information Management Officer counted the pages rather than read them. There was far too much for a clever leak, or for the items to be placed somewhere significant. Instead, he just passed them on to the tech team, who in turn posted some of the pages on their ghost blog sites – webpages with small readerships, masquerading as normal blogs, but used for the dissemination of official propaganda.

The instant Stolz's papers went online, keywords within the documents were picked up by web monitoring software. That, in turn, triggered the automatic publication of other material. Philip Ford's half-a-million pounds had been put to good use.

In fact, some of the money the banker had provided had been offered as a prize: Father Samuel and the professor had united to offer a reward to whoever could provide evidence for the most unexpected correlation. Entrants had compared the divorce rate in South Carolina with the American bee population. Links had been found between the number of space missions and sociology degrees awarded. There was even a correlation between the marriage rate in Alabama and the annual death toll from electrical accidents.

Of course, No one took any of the correlations seriously. They were 'just for entertainment', as the press release announced. Father Samuel said they showed that God had a sense of humour. It meant anyone who found Stolz's papers online would have thought they were a joke too, which was exactly what Father Samuel intended.

Professor Cromhall continued to preach science, now confident he could pretend there was no mystery to the universe. The most dangerous mystery – the bizarre but powerful correlation between the planets and human affairs – had been buried. If necessary, the professor could discredit and ridicule the link, which would save Cromhall from being discredited and ridiculed himself.

The banker, Philip Ford, could eat his prawns in peace, very content with the return on his small investment of half a million pounds. It had safeguarded a lifetime of financial gains.

And Father Samuel flew back to his monastery, finally satisfied that Stolz's secret had been hidden again as much as it ever could be – under piles of spurious information, alongside false predictions and fabrications of the original papers, on a remote part of the internet. Even though Stolz's big secret was secret no more, Father Samuel had discovered the perfect way to hide the truth.

CHAPTER 70

Somewhere in Berlin
Germany
10.30p.m. CET (9.30p.m. GMT)

The machine whirred, then buzzed, then started hammering out loud clicks. Mechanical and electrical parts inside, connected by a tangle of wires, did their work. The experts sat beside it, waiting for the machine to spew out its information. They waited on its verdict, and waited, and waited…

Click … Click … Click …

It was the clicking which woke him. Myles found himself inside the large white tube of a full-body scanner. 'Hello? Is anybody there?'

'Bleiben Sie bitte still liegen.'

'Excuse me?'

'Remain still, please, Sir,' replied the voice. It sounded official.

Myles waited, until the machine whirred again and his body was rolled out onto a trolley-bed.

One of the experts approached. 'Mr Munro, you'll be pleased to know everything seems fine,' the man smiled, his hands relaxed in the pockets of his white coat. 'Your head, Mr Munro. Specifically, your brain. No problems at all.'

Myles squinted, confused. 'You mean… normal?'

'We wouldn't use that word, Sir. No damage, and everything else seems healthy. Within the range we would expect.'

Myles frowned. 'But… another doctor told me I had… part of my brain was the wrong shape, or unusual. Something like that. He said it made me different.'

The medics looked at each other, one of them chuckling slightly. They reacted as if they'd heard the comment before. 'We're all different, Mr Munro.'

'But, my brain…?'

'Yes, it's different too,' confirmed the expert. 'But nobody knows how the shape of brains affects people. There's research going on into that.'

'Yes, they asked me to take part.'

'Good, Mr Munro. But even if the research allows people with brain scanners to predict what people will be like, we don't want to label people. Sounds a bit like … what the Nazis used to do, don't you think?'

'But isn't that what you medics do,' suggested Myles. 'Don't you label things?'

'Not brains. We don't label brains, Sir. It would be too much like trying to predict how people were going to live. And we wouldn't want to do that. People should decide their own lives for themselves. Don't you think so, Mr Munro?'

Myles thought through what the medical expert had said.

He was still wondering about it when a man appeared. The figure sauntered over, confident and composed. The man's face gazed down at Myles, blocking out the lights in the ceiling.

'Glenn?'

Glenn rocked his head forwards with a grin. For the first time since Myles had known him, the American had allowed fine stubble to sprout through the toned skin on his scalp. The two medics who'd been viewing Myles' MRI scan acknowledged Glenn and his senior rank. They left Myles and Glenn alone together.

'Good to see you again, Myles. You feeling OK?'

Myles wasn't sure. He looked around, realised he was in a hospital, and surmised correctly he wasn't well. 'So what's wrong with me? Sarin poisoning?'

'There was no Sarin. Stolz left only water in that bottle. It's just your head got smashed and your knee – usual stuff.'

'My knee? My knee - again?'

'Other one this time,' said Glenn, gesturing to his legs. 'Although they both need to be fixed.'

Myles gazed down to see both his lower limbs were now in plaster. He was immobile again. 'How long to heal this time?'

'Longer than last time …' Glenn smirked, and checked No one else was within earshot. '… The difference is – now you can work out exactly when you'll be fit again.'

'So it's real? Stolz – he really had worked out how to predict things?'

'Of course,' admitted Glenn. 'Greatest secret of the Cold War.'

Myles was perplexed. 'You mean, you were pretending all along not to believe it?'

Glenn shook his head. 'It's not something to believe or not believe. It just *is*. And let's face it – some of it does sound pretty crazy. Hirohito didn't declare war on Russia because he was born when Neptune was over Moscow? No one can believe that. You just have to notice it's true and live with it.'

Myles frowned, determined to argue the point. He tried to sit up, pulling on his headboard. But the movement sent pain through his newly broken leg, which was attached to a wire suspended above the bed. He winced, then kept quiet as he realised one of the medical orderlies was looking towards him.

'Try to lie still,' insisted Glenn. 'Let me know if you want me to get you some pain killers.'

'No, it's alright. How do you mean, it just "is"?'

'Planets make patterns in the sky, human affairs make patterns on earth, and some of the patterns match up. We've dumped billions into NASA, but we still don't understand how it works. All we know is that it just does. It's accurate enough to make predictions which are much better than, say, weather forecasts.'

'Predictions like when the Berlin Wall's going to come down?'

'Exactly.' Glenn gently eased the trolley-bed along, wheeling it towards a wall. His mouth spoke close to Myles' ear so that he couldn't be overheard. 'Ronald Reagan was the president who used it most. Like the eclipse over Iceland in 1986 – eclipses are linked to military victories, so he held the summit in the eclipse zone – to win the Cold War through a deal with Gorbachev.'

'Just Reagan?'

'He was the only president to use it knowingly, although it's public knowledge that we've also advised more than one First Lady. For the others, our advice was given through "forecasting agencies" – one of them in Alaska.'

'Corporal Bradley?'

Glenn nodded. 'Bradley set it up. With help from Stolz, of course. All our forecasts have to be sanitised, so they seem based on computer models, statistics, agricultural output figures, that sort of thing. It means presidents always have deniability. We wouldn't want the public to know their officials were basing decisions on the position of the planets, would we?'

Myles still didn't understand. 'But what about Dieter? Wasn't he putting all this stuff on the web – and making you and I out to be terrorists?'

Glenn grinned again. 'Yes… sort of… And also, no.'

Myles cocked his head in disbelief.

Glenn felt the need to explain some more. 'Dieter was using Stolz's predictions to claim credit for things,' he said. 'But they were things which were going to happen anyway. So his terror website predicted nuclear accidents and the death of a senator. When those things actually happened, he hoped people would blame the terror group.'

'So why didn't they?'

'They didn't see his website. We quarantined it. It was only accessible to a few folks in Langley, and Dieter himself.'

'And I guess Dieter is now dead?'

Glenn didn't answer with words, but his face reacted in a way which confirmed Myles' suspicion.

'Your guys killed him?'

'He tried to kill himself, actually.' Glenn answered with his eyebrows raised. 'He took a suicide pill – same type as Stolz. He probably stole it during one of the times he burgled the old man's Berlin apartment… although I put a bullet in him, too – just in case his cyanide capsule was some sort of chemical weapon.'

Myles could only vaguely remember fighting with Dieter on the glass dome of the Reichstag.

'You got concussed.' Glenn pointed at Myles' forehead. 'Then we sedated you as a precaution. You've been out cold for almost forty hours. Hence the brain scan.'

Myles lifted his fingers to feel bandages on his forehead. 'Worse than in Vienna?'

'Much worse. No inflatable this time. Both you and Dieter were pretty wasted when you fell down – into the authority of Berlin's American military police.'

Myles looked around. He began to realise he wasn't in a normal hospital. A doctor in fatigues, signs in English, an information poster telling people about veterans' benefits. He was in a *military* hospital. 'I'm under the authority of the American military police, too?'

Glenn winked, confirming Myles was right. 'Allied War Powers Act. You're in the old American sector of the city.'

'You know, quite frankly Glenn, I'm glad to be anywhere. I thought I was going to die. And that's what the machine predicted, too.'

'The machine was wrong.'

Myles was puzzled. 'You mean Stolz's computer doesn't work?'

'Oh it works. We're testing it right now. Pretty accurate so far. No, it was wrong because you gave it the wrong information.'

'But I only put in the time and day I was born, didn't I?'

'Not quite, Myles. When you were born, you Brits were trying some Euro-experiment – living with the clocks one hour forward in winter time. It means the birth time entered into the machine for you was out by sixty minutes.'

While Myles digested the information, and wondered whether being born an hour earlier had really saved his life, Glenn sighed. 'Of course, this stuff isn't secret anymore – when the Russians got Zenyalena's body, they posted Stolz's papers on the web.'

'So now everybody "knows"?' asked Myles, amazed that the Americans could let the secret out so easily.

'Not exactly "knows",' laughed Glenn. 'The information is public now, which is new. But our guys have directed search engines towards false predictions rather what the Russians put up. And all the statistical evidence about the connection between the planets and what people do: there are respected scientists and statisticians rubbishing that right now, because the whole scientific community knows this could blow their intellectual worlds apart. Some experts are dismissing it as a coincidence; others say it's a joke. There's even a prize being offered for the most bizarre coincidence people can find. The fact that astrology can make accurate predictions has been buried in the noise. People won't take astrology any more seriously than they did before, so we're safe.'

Glenn's tone became more serious. 'You know, Myles, Heike-Ann's not going to talk – she's signed all sort of confidentiality agreements and is just looking forward to her new baby now. The French thought was everything finished when Jean-François was killed. And all the public saw about the international team was a fire in Vienna and a rooftop accident in Berlin – they didn't know we were chasing Stolz's secrets.'

'Accident? You mean people thought Dieter and I just slipped off the Reichstag?'

Glenn nodded. 'And it means you can go back to teaching Oxford students about the past, not telling them how to predict the future. Right, Myles?'

Myles understood the obvious threat in Glenn's suggestion. 'Or?'

'Or, Myles, some very respected people will say you've fallen for hogwash.'

Myles relaxed, dismissing Glenn with a shrug and a turn of his face. 'Threats don't do it for me, Glenn. I don't care about my reputation.'

Glenn wasn't surprised by Myles' response. He certainly didn't seem angry. 'I know. But you will keep it secret, Myles. You've seen how dangerous it is. If people knew their future, they'd stop trying. They'd think they were invincible, like Dieter. Or go round doing stupid things. If people in America didn't believe they could control their own lives, we would have lost the Cold War, and probably the Second World War, too. If you let this secret out, you'll hurt every human being who ever wanted to make a decision for themselves. You'll be taking their futures away from them. I know you're a good man, Myles – you're not going to do that to people.'

Myles absorbed Glenn's words. Perhaps the American was right: like nuclear weapons, the power to know the future was just too dangerous to be out there. It had to be controlled, so people could enjoy the freedom to live as they wanted – even if that freedom was an illusion.

'That's why you think I'll keep it secret?'

Glenn grinned. For a moment, Myles wondered if the American was about to pull out a gun, or inject him with a syringe full of poison. 'Glenn?'

'I've done your predictions, Myles Munro. You'll be going on another mission in a few months. Probably when your legs are better, because there's quite a bit of running, the machine said. More military history I think, terrorists with gold, something like that – I don't know ...'

Myles still didn't understand. Why did accepting one more assignment – and a bizarre-sounding one at that – mean he wouldn't reveal Stolz's secrets?

'... And between now and then, you'll have other things on your mind.'

'Glenn?' Myles frowned, demanding an answer from the enigmatic American, but Glenn just strolled away. He gave Myles a casual salute from the end of the corridor, nodding his head in respect to the Englishman who had saved his life in Stolz's bunker two days ago. Then he disappeared.

Myles lay on the trolley-bed, wondering about it all. He was distracted by a commotion – far off in another part of the hospital, but loud enough for Myles to hear.

'... But I am a relative.'

'No media, ma'am.'

'Under US Federal law you have to let me through ... look it up ...' It was a familiar voice. A few moments later, flanked by two US marine guards who seemed to be restraining her, Myles saw the television hair he had grown to love being marched towards him. Truly flustered for perhaps the first time since he had known her, Helen was standing beside his hospital trolley. 'Myles, these men don't believe we're engaged to be married ...'

One of the marines was about to say something when Myles noticed a ring sparkling on Helen's hand. It was the first time he'd seen it. 'That looks nice on you,' he said.

The military men relaxed a little when they realised Myles really *did* know Helen Bridle – the woman from CNN wasn't just there for an interview.

The taller marine tipped his camouflaged hat to Myles, who was still lying down. 'Sir, this hospital is regulated by federal laws which only allow guests if they are related to the patient. Miss Helen Bridle claims to be your fiancée. Is that true, Sir?'

Myles paused, but only for a moment, looking at Helen as he answered. 'Yes. It's true.'

'Thank you, Sir. Ma'am, my apologies.' The marines left.

Helen bent down and kissed him. 'Thank you, Myles.'

'For saying you were my fiancée, or for agreeing to marry you?'

'Both.' She kissed him again, then looked at his bandaged head, and his plastered legs.

'I love you, Helen,' he whispered, relieved.

'You won't be chasing old Nazis anymore, now, I hope?'

'He wasn't a Nazi. Stolz was just trying to make sure his secret didn't go to bad people. That's why he swapped the Sarin for water, and why he left insulting clues about Hitler. All his life, he kept those records about Hitler dodging the draft and to his medical file. He could have destroyed them, but Stolz's second secret was that he hated what the Nazis stood for. Perhaps he did during the war, too.'

'And his other secret was about the planets?'

Myles nodded.

Helen frowned, concerned. 'You know, I told my editors to do a story on it – on all the amazing coincidences between planets and human events. None of them took it. It's not going to run.' She looked baffled, as if a bizarre editorial process had decided to miss out on one of the greatest scoops of the century.

But Myles knew why – he remembered what Glenn had said. Helen's editors probably understood what would happen to their reputations if they told the truth. 'Helen, it means people won't learn how to predict their future from the planets. But is that really bad?'

'Well, what did Stolz predict for you?'

'Two days ago, his machine said that, today, my girlfriend would "cease to be".'

Light glinted into Helen's eyes from the ring on her finger – a ring she had bought for herself, knowing Myles was too much of a misfit to buy it for her. 'Then, Myles, I guess it came true. I *have* ceased to be your girlfriend. I'm your fiancée now.' She smiled, tucking her hair behind her ear. Then emotion burst all over her face as she realised she was with the man she was going to marry.

Myles put his hand through her hair, letting it rest on her neck. His future was standing beside him, and it was the only part of the future he wanted to know.

EPILOGUE

Oxford, UK
Seven months later

Helen was about to press 'confirm' when the doorbell rang. She frowned as she checked her watch, not sure who it could be. Standing up, she leaned towards the window, and peered down onto Pembroke Street. There, beaming up at her, sweating and recovering his breath, stood her fiancé.

She smiled back, then shouted down to him, 'Did you do the whole route?'

He nodded. She raised her eyebrows in admiration, then turned to press the entry buzzer, and listened to his footsteps bound up the stairs, two at a time.

She kissed him as he came in through the door, then made a show of wiping his sweat from her cheeks. 'Still OK with the leg?' she asked, noticing a graze on his shin as she said it.

'That's just from where I tripped near the lecture hall,' he explained. 'They're both fine.' He squatted down on his haunches, proving he could stand up again without pain.

'Good,' she said, beckoning him over to her computer. 'So how about trekking through the mid-West for our honeymoon?'

Myles smiled again. 'Shouldn't we plan our wedding first?'

Helen opened her mouth to speak but was interrupted by the phone. She pulled a face, then picked up the receiver. 'Hello?'

She slumped a little when she recognised the voice. 'OK – he's right here,' she said. 'Simon Charfield,' she mouthed silently, as she passed the phone over.

Myles took the phone, slightly fazed. 'Er, hello?' he said before a pause.

After a few moments he began to concentrate on Simon Charfield's questions. 'Ah, well,' he began answering, 'It certainly had a great impact. A forerunner to modern chemistry, it led to the discovery of oxygen, explosives… it also caused the death of King Charles the Second, who experimented with it – if he hadn't died, Britain might not be a democracy.'

Then she saw him frown.

'Really? Are you sure? They might be faking, you know,' cautioned Myles.

Helen gesticulated at him, silently, asking him what it was about.

Myles put his hand over the receiver. 'Terrorists performing alchemy,' he whispered in reply, before concentrating back on the phone call.

Then she saw him nodding.

'Of course, I'm very curious. If someone really can turn mercury into gold then…' Another pause, then, 'So what exactly to do you want me to investigate?'

Myles looked at her admiringly as he waited for the answer. Their eyes connected. He winked lovingly. But she knew what would happen next.

'OK, Simon,' he said. 'Tell me more …'

LETTER FROM IAIN

Thank you so much for reading *Secrets of the Last Nazi*. I really hope you enjoyed it.

And, if you've got this far, you've probably realised both secrets are true. They are.

Hitler really was a coward in World War One - he managed to spend less time in the trenches than almost any other private in his regiment. And, despite all his rhetoric, he ducked out of military service for Imperial Austria at least three times. The Nazis managed to hide these facts for years. Many people were hoodwinked, and some respected journalists in the West even colluded in the myth.

It's also true that planets can be used to make accurate predictions about human affairs. Like Glenn, I don't know how or why, but they can. In February 1988, I saw someone use the Saturn-Neptune cycle to explain exactly what would happen to communism the following year – including the precise week that the Berlin Wall would come down. If you say 'that should be impossible', then I agree with you, but that doesn't stop it being true.

Several top Nazis knew this truth, including Himmler, Hess and Goebbels – probably others, too. Unfortunately, my investigation ran dry when I tried to discover more about Nazi research programmes, and what they had found out – the evidence had been destroyed or hidden. I hope the fiction parts of *Secrets of the Last Nazi* give you some idea about the intrigue around all this. I'm still expecting the evidence in this book to be distorted, and to be attacked and ridiculed personally for presenting it – statistician Michel Gauquelin really was harried to his death for exposing some of it.

Writing can be lonely, and connecting with my readers when the story is told is both enjoyable and important. If you did enjoy *Secrets of the Last Nazi* and have an opinion on the story, I'd be delighted to read it in a review, no matter how short. I love reading reviews and always appreciate the fact that people take the time to write them – even if you only put down a few nice words. They also help other readers discover my books for the first time, especially if you are kind enough to give me lots of 'stars'.

As for Myles Munro, he has more 'impossible' truths to discover, and more adventures – ***The Last Prophecy of Rome* is coming soon**. If you'd like to **keep up-to-date with all my latest releases,** just sign up here:

www.bookouture.com/iain-king

Thank you so much for your support – until next time.

Iain King

@iainbking

www.iainbking.com

STOLZ'S PAPERS

The papers which follow were made public on the internet, on the instructions of Ludochovic.

Handwritten annotations are from Zenyalena Androvsky, and initialled 'ZA'.

SECRET

Mechanism for Predicting the Future – History

5 July 1940

The methods we have found most effective came from ancient Babylon and Egypt, where they were pioneered along with other branches of science still in use today. They were developed by the ancient Greek philosophers, who suspected the universe was more connected than people realised. Aristotle made assumptions then tested them, keeping those which held true and discarding the rest. It took many hundreds of years for the true connections to be distilled in this way.

The Christian Church tried to co-opt this growing body of belief – the three wise men who followed a star were accepted into the Gospels, and festivals like Christmas and Easter were set according to the sun and moon. But by medieval times, as this science became more accurate, it threatened the official Church, and so was outlawed. In England, the 1542 Witchcraft Act banned all studies which linked human affairs with the position of the planets. This legislation was updated several times, and spread throughout Europe and to the USA. The ban forced the knowledge underground for more than three centuries, preventing pioneers - including Sir Isaac Newton - from publishing their discoveries. However, the legislation became difficult to enforce when, in 1903 and again in 1914, two different courts in New York State upheld predictions based on the planets as both scientific and very accurate, and a new strategy was needed to hide the link between the planets and human affairs.

It was done through a special sort of 'bad' prediction, first published in a US newspaper. When the publishers were tried under the Witchcraft Act (in the 1936 Barbanell v Naylor case), the court ruled newspapers could make public predictions as long as they were written as public entertainment, and people were divided into just twelve groups. It meant horoscopes fell outside the Witchcraft Acts because they were too vague to tell the fortune of any individual. That is how the USA and other western countries came to adopt the least accurate form of astrology, and scientific astrology was hidden.

However, it created an opportunity for the Third Reich. On orders from SS Reichsführer Heinrich Himmler, we followed the method of the ancient Greeks: we looked for a link between the planets and human affairs. When we found one, we tested it. Links which were reliable and repeatable we kept, others we cast aside, until we had refined a large body of knowledge.

One of the first patterns we found concerned Pluto. This planet was named after the God of the Underworld and was discovered in 1930 – a time of power politics and economic turmoil. We soon found patterns about wealth, power and national borders: whenever Pluto moved into a new sign of the zodiac, it brought a new system for administering sovereign states and their money. Each time, the new system was linked to the symbolism of Pluto's new zodiac. By knowing what had happened for the times Pluto changed zodiac sign up until 1939, we have predicted what will happen in the future:

Date Pluto changed signs	Zodiac sign Pluto moves into	Event
October 1823 and February 1824	Aries (traditionally associated with military threats and war)	Monroe Doctrine: US President threatens war with any power which intervenes in the Americas.
December 1852	Taurus (associated with farming)	Napoleon III becomes French Emperor and promotes free trade in agricultural goods.

April 1884	Gemini (associated with communications and measurement of time)	Berlin Conference sets borders in Africa and international conference agrees on time zones.
December 1913	Cancer (associated with homeland, protection and family values)	Federal Reserve established in USA – local banks are protected at a national level.
May-June 1939	Leo (associated with leadership)	Pact of Steel unites economies of Germany and Italy.
January 1957 – April 1958	Virgo (associated with bureaucracy and efficiency)	Bureaucracy and organisation to determine cross-border economy. *ZA: European Union set up.*
October 1971	Libra (associated with diplomacy and negotiation)	International economic organisation will be replaced by negotiation. *ZA: Nixon abandons gold standard*

August 1984	Scorpio (associated with evolution and renewal)	Economic protection will be abandoned. *ZA: Widespread deregulation*
January 1995	Sagittarius (associated with travel, trade and exploration)	The way of trade across the world will be transformed. *ZA: World trade Organisation set up.*
November 2008	Capricorn (associated with banking, conservatism and austerity)	Lending will become strict and banking will change. *ZA: Credit crunch after banking crash.*
January 2024 and November 2024	Aquarius (associated with new technology, and world organisations)	Technology will replace tradition as the basis for trade; crisis for international organisations. *ZA: ???*
March 2043 and January 2044	Pisces (associated with religion and confusion)	Technology of world trade will be abandoned in confusion (efforts to save it in Sept 2043) *ZA: ???*

May 2066 to January 2068:	Aries (associated with military threats and war)	War and power will settle cross-border economy (as with the Monroe doctrine) *ZA: ???*

ZA: I checked these dates on the NASA 'Horizons' website - http://ssd.jpl.nasa.gov/horizons.cgi

We then looked for patterns between the planets. The ancient Greeks associated Saturn with structures and natural limits. Neptune, discovered in 1846, is about ideals and the aspirations of the masses, but also the sea into which those ideals dissolve. The orbits of Saturn and Neptune mean they come together every thirty-six years, and these times mark major events in how the romantic ideals of Neptune are made real by Saturn. In 1773, they sparked the Boston Tea Party. In 1809 they triggered revolutions throughout South America. April 1846, and Karl Marx set up his first Communist Committee in Brussels. May 1882 was when the Communist Manifesto was translated into Russian, and Marxist political parties appeared in Europe. In 1917, Saturn and Neptune coincided with the communist revolution in Russia.

They will come together again in 1953 when we expect major 'rebalancing' in the Soviet world, and three times in 1989 (March, June and November) – the last of these dates, in the second week of November 1989, coincides with other planetary events, making it particularly notable.

ZA: Stalin died in March 1953 causing big change throughout communist world.
1989 - March: first free elections in Russia.
1989 - June: Tiananmen Square massacre, China.
1989 - November: Berlin wall down.

We soon found all the planetary cycles were linked to different human affairs. The forty-two year cycle between Uranus and Saturn correlated with scientific discoveries and inventions. The longer cycle between Uranus and Neptune was linked to mass communication – and we expect humans to exchange information differently after these two planets come together in the early 1990s. *ZA: internet.*

Since all these cycles seemed to affect people, we found that, when they were added together, we had a measure for stability in human affairs. Instability led to war and death. We checked three centuries of warfare, and found there were many more wars deaths when outer planets were coming together in the sky rather than separating. We developed an index which predicted war deaths far more accurately than conventional means based on morale, weaponry, and battlefield terrain etc. The correlation we found was a one-in-a-million-billion possibility (1 in 1,000,000,000,000,000). Even sceptics accepted we had a link. Then we charted the planets to forecast how many people would die in the world's future conflicts.

SS Capt. Werner Stolz, 5 July 1940

~~SECRET~~

War Eclipses

October 20th, 1985

The Office of the President of the United States (POTUS) has asked for advice regarding the Soviet Union. This note suggests where and when POTUS should meet Premier Gorbachev for a deal most likely to end the Cold War on favourable terms.

We examined eclipses, which have long been associated with wars. Our research also confirmed the truth in astrology beyond reasonable doubt: the possibility of these events happening by chance is less than a one-in-two-trillion (one in two million million).

ZA: I checked this, and its true.

Alexander the Great

Alexander the Great's victories were famously attributed to eclipses. The solar eclipse of 4th July 335BC, just before Alexander invaded Persia, occurred only 223 miles from Tyre – a city he captured in a defining moment of his campaign. The solar eclipse was centred closer to Tyre than 99.92 % of the places that it could have been.

The Crusades
In September 1093, Byzantine Emperor Alexios asked for help fighting the Muslims. Pope Urban II, in turn, urged all Christians to capture Jerusalem – sparking the Crusades, which lasted two centuries. The solar eclipse of 23rd September 1093 was centred just 164 miles from Jerusalem, closer than 99.96% of places on the earth's surface that it could have fallen - a one-in-2,300 chance.

World War One
British and German troops first clashed about two days before the crucial Battle of Mons, which was on 23rd August. Meanwhile, the war's most significant battle on the Eastern Front was at Tannenberg, which began on 26th August. The solar eclipse at 12.34p.m. on 21st August 1914 was centred just 281 miles from Tannenberg, closer than 99.87% of the earth's surface.

Korean War
Voting monitored by the United Nations took place on 10th May 1948 - but only in South Korea, leading to the Korean War two years later. The solar eclipse the day before the elections was centred only 277 miles from Seoul, closer than 99.88% of the earth's surface.

Recommendation to End the Cold War: a Reykjavik Summit in October 1986

There is an eclipse in the evening of 3rd October 1986 centred just 569 miles from the capital of Iceland. Therefore, we recommend a summit in Reykjavik in October 1986, during which President Reagan can press Premier Gorbachev to eradicate nuclear weapons and end the Cold War.

Stolz, October 20th, 1985

ZA: NASA has maps of all these eclipses online - copy and paste these links into your browser:

Alexander the Great's battle: http://eclipse.gsfc.nasa.gov/SEsearch/SEsearchmap.php?Ecl=-03350704

The Crusade eclipse near Jerusalem: http://eclipse.gsfc.nasa.gov/SEsearch/SEsearchmap.php?Ecl=10930923

The Great War eclipse: http://eclipse.gsfc.nasa.gov/SEsearch/SEsearchmap.php?Ecl=19140821

The Korean War eclipse: http://eclipse.gsfc.nasa.gov/SEsearch/SEsearchmap.php?Ecl=19480509

Reykyavik summit was held 11th-12th October 1986 - the key superpower summit leading to end of the Cold War. The eclipse is here: http://eclipse.gsfc.nasa.gov/SEsearch/SEsearchmap.php?Ecl=19861003

The chance of this happening being random really is less than one in two thousand billion.

PS - President Putin was selected as Premier of Russia one day after the intense August 1999 eclipse. The eclipse explains how the Kosovo crisis almost became World War Three, and anticipates war in Ukraine: http://eclipse.gsfc.nasa.gov/SEsearch/SEsearchmap.php?Ecl=19990811

SECRET

Nuclear

19 March 1943

American Nazis have informed us of the secret US nuclear programme. We have learned the date of the first nuclear reaction in December 1942, and saw the date was marked by planets opposing each other in the sky – from nine degrees of Gemini to ten degrees of Sagittarius. A little research proved that this position in the sky was linked to nuclear events in the past, such as the discovery of uranium in 1789, of radioactivity in 1896, and the cluster of nuclear advances made in 1932, when the nucleus was first disintegrated. Then we calculated when outer planets would strike this axis again, and found these dates. Adding the meaning of the planet allowed us to make these predictions:

Date	Event and Prediction
5-10 August 1945	Pluto at trine (120 degrees), Mars crosses axis: nuclear used for show of power. *ZA: Nuclear bombs on Hiroshima (6th) and Nagasaki (9th) force Japanese surrender.*

1960-1963:	Pluto at right angles - Nuclear power threatens war: time of increased threat/tension. *ZA: Height of the Cold War - when Khruschev and Kennedy squared off in the Cuban missile crisis.*
January 1961:	Pluto at right angles and lunar eclipse cycle - nuclear event causes death. *ZA: Worlds first fatal nuclear accident at Idaho Falls in the USA. Three workers at the power station were killed.*
1973-5:	Neptune crosses axis - nuclear tension eased with ideals. *ZA: When the Strategic Arms Limitation Talks (SALT) led to a deal between the USA and USSR.*
March 1979:	Saturn at right angles to axis - major nuclear event. *ZA: Three Mile Island accident in Pennsylvania.*
April 1986:	Saturn crosses axis with Jupiter at right angles - major fatal nuclear event. *ZA: Chernobyl accident in the Soviet Union leads to many deaths.*
1998-1999:	Pluto crosses axis - nuclear power threatens war: time of increased threat/tension. *ZA: India and Pakistan become nuclear rivals for the first time.*

March 2011:	Mars at right angles but Jupiter at third-of-a-circle (120 degrees) - fatal nuclear event with worst effects prevented. *ZA: The Fukushima nuclear accident in Japan, triggered by a tsunami.*
2015-2016:	Neptune at right angles to axis – hidden threat of nuclear loss; discoveries from disintegration or fusing of nuclei, similar to 1932; faith in old nuclear myths changes profoundly. *ZA: ???*
December 2015 or July – Sept 2016:	Saturn crosses axis – major nuclear event (as in September-October 1957 and April 1986). *ZA: ???*
August 2016:	Mars, Neptune and lunar eclipse cycle at right angles to axis and Saturn - danger of military nuclear loss. *ZA: ???*
September-October 2027:	Uranus crosses axis with Jupiter and Mars at right angles but Neptune and Pluto at third-of-a-circle (120 degrees) - shocking nuclear news, then great powers seek to contain significant and fatal nuclear event. *ZA: ???*
2049-2052:	Pluto at right angles to axis - nuclear power threatens war: time of increased threat/tension. *ZA: ???*

SS Capt. Werner Stolz, 19 March 1943

~~SECRET~~

Nixon

January 12th 1959

We have been hired to consider the future of Vice-President Richard Milhous Nixon, born at 9.35p.m. Pacific Standard Time on 9th January, 1913, in Yorba Linda, California, USA. This is our analysis.

Nixon has a low chance of winning the Presidential election in November 1960 because on Inauguration Day in January 1961, Nixon has both Jupiter and Saturn at the lowest point in his chart, opposing the point of career success. The 1968 election is much more promising, because Jupiter is on the rising horizon, making for a popular Presidency with a foreign policy focus. Hence, we recommend he runs for President in 1968. But he should be aware that Saturn on setting horizon indicates confrontation with Congress.

ZA: Nixon did lose the 1960 election, then won in 1968. Stolz was right.

If he seeks re-election in 1972, the prominence of Jupiter allows for criticism to be 'brushed off' and any success to be exaggerated. Saturn directly overhead indicates a high-point of career goals in 1972.

ZA: in 1972, Nixon cut his big deal with China and was re-elected on a landslide.

On April 30th 1973, he has Uranus at 90 degrees to the Sun, indicating a shock challenge to his public image.

ZA: when the Watergate crisis got hot - the day three of his Watergate conspirators resigned unexpectedly. Another accurate prediction.

On October 20th 1973: crunch aspects between Uranus, the Sun, Neptune, Jupiter and Mars mean Nixon may issue shock instruction, over-reach his power and respond in anger to achieve deception. He is likely to fail. Temperance advised.

ZA: The 'Saturday Night Massacre', when Nixon sacked his attorney general and the special prosecutor into Watergate, but it backfired on him, though.

Finally, we note that the total difference of the planets active and challenging in Nixon's chart – Neptune, Moon, Venus, Mars, and Uranus – to the chart itself reaches zero on 8th August 1974 at 2105 Eastern Standard Time. His Presidency may lose credibility at this moment, never to recover.

ZA: The exact moment of Nixon's resignation, live on TV. Extremely accurate.

Stolz/Bradley, January 12th 1959

~~SECRET~~

USA

12th January 1942

The Declaration of Independence was made at 5.10p.m. on July 4th, 1776, and counts as the USA's 'birthday' - when the American colonies launched a broadside against the British Empire, across the ocean. We realised that the planet Uranus returned to where it was on that first Independence Day in April 1861, exactly when Union troops fired cannons across Charleston Harbour in the first battle of the US Civil War. Uranus returns there again in early June 1944, and – when factoring in the position of the moon, which determines the tides - we can expect a similar American broadside across an expanse of water on 5th of 6th June 1944. We should also anticipate something similar in May 2026, or the first three months of 2027.

ZA: This is how Stolz predicted D-Day so accurately.

From the USA chart, we also note that war challenged American Power (because Pluto was 90 or 180 degrees to the position of Mars on 4th July 1776) in August 1814, when the British burned

Washington DC and the White House. A similar challenge to US power happens on these dates: April 1968; May 2004; April 2059; September 2059; February 2060 and December 2060.

ZA: In April 1968, America was tied down in Vietnam. The 2004 date was the US losing Iraq. 2059 and 2060 - who knows?

~~SECRET~~

United Kingdom and British Empire

20th June 1941

The United Kingdom was established by the Act of Union, dated as midnight on 1st January 1801. This warns us of Neptune causing problems of arrogance and deception in October 1956, and Pluto undermining UK leadership through destructive power in October 1984.

ZA: Stolz predicted the Suez crisis of October 1956 and the Brighton bomb in October 1984 which almost killed Prime Minister Margaret Thatcher. Very accurate for both.

Note that Former Reichsleiter and Deputy Führer Rudolf Hess has stolen our predictions for the UK, including predictions for the outcome of the current war. We believe Hess flew with these papers to Scotland on his unauthorised mission for peace negotiations. On orders from SS Reichsführer Himmler, we will not reproduce the other predictions relating to the British Empire.

~~SECRET~~

Discrediting Gauquelin

30 May 1991

ZA: All this on Gauquelin is confirmed by several public sources available online.

Summary: Michel Gauquelin (1928-1991) was the French statistician who made public the link between people's career and their planets at birth. His death this month will be accepted as suicide, successfully concluding our operation to discredit him and his work.

Detail: In 1955, Gauquelin published his research which revealed the one-in-a-million correlation between the position of planets when people were born and their future career. His so-called 'Mars Effect' demonstrated that people born with Mars on the horizon or directly overhead were statistically more likely to prosper in martial fields, such as sports or the military. He found similar links for Saturn, Jupiter and the Moon, in each case supporting traditional astrological interpretations. Gauquelin also made public the one-in-a-million correlation between the planetary positions of children and their parents.

Gauquelin's proof risked encouraging further research which might expose our work, so we discredited him. This involved:

Disputing Gauquelin's Methods: Using respected academic committees, we forced Gauquelin to use larger sets of data, data from different countries and new research. Gauquelin did, and each time he was still able to show the correlation. Unfortunately, one of our tests (proposed by Harvard Professor Zelen and named the 'Zelen' test,) strengthened Gauquelin's findings.

Blocking Verification: We prevented the publication of independent tests from a respected scientific body which confirmed Gauquelin's results.

Appeal to Authority: In 1975, we gathered the signatures of 186 scientists, including 18 Nobel Prize winners, to sign a public letter. The letter highlighted the least accurate forms of astrology, and asserted there was no 'verified scientific basis' for a link between human affairs and the planets. This claim was easy to make, since the signatories themselves controlled the means by which the link could be verified.

Contaminating Data: We were able to pretend there was no correlation by using selective data. We publicised this bogus version of Gauquelin's research widely. (Regrettably one of our respected scientists discovered we were doctoring the data and resigned to expose this.)

Direct Harassment: By distorting Gauquelin's published replies to our criticisms, we were able to intimidate the statistician from further work. Gauquelin was also subject to abuse and [REDACTED].

We have ensured that Gauquelin is blamed for his own death: his body will not be discovered until nineteen days after his termination. Forensic traces will have degraded, and a verdict of suicide will be recorded.

Stolz, May 1991

~~SECRET~~

Geography

February 3rd, 1948

SS Reichsführer Himmler instructed us to apply our discoveries to geography. By positioning lights to shine on a globe, we calculated where and when planets crossed the horizon, as viewed from Earth. We discovered the following:

Reichsführer Adolf Hitler
(Born 20th April 1889, 6.30p.m., Branau Am Inn, Austria).

When Hitler was born, Mercury was on the horizon in a line joining Munich, Nuremberg and Berlin - the places where our Führer made his greatest speeches, and where propaganda gave him power. Mercury is traditionally the 'winged messenger' of the Gods, associated with words and communication.

The line tracing the points where Saturn, the planet of authority, was directly overhead was used to partition Poland with Stalin in 1939. When the Japanese attacked Pearl Harbour in Hawaii – the place where Saturn was directly underneath – it undermined his authority.

Mars, the war planet, was setting below the horizon along a line linking Stalingrad in Russia, with El Alamein in Libya - where the 'God of War' abandoned him.

Uranus cut through the Ardennes and ran up into Norway: where Hitler launched his Blitzkrieg, war' which surprised the Western Allies twice - in 1940 and again, in 1944. They were also the places in France and Belgium where Hitler won his reputation in the First World War.

SS Reichsführer Heinrich Himmler
(Born 7th October 1900 at 3:30 p.m., Munich, Germany)

For Himmler, we found that lines for Uranus (sudden shocks and new technology) and Jupiter (exaggeration) intersected over Auschwitz, the place he created of mass, sudden slaughter by new technology.

Mars was setting on the horizon over the place in northern Germany where Himmler surrendered to the Allies in 1945. There was an old prophecy that he'd betray Hitler, and he did. With this map we could warn the Führer exactly where.

British Prime Minister Sir Winston Churchill
(Born 30th November 1874, 01.30 a.m., Oxfordshire, England).

Mars, the war planet, was directly below Washington DC when Churchill was born: the British P.M. effectively surrendered to the USA – under his rule, the British Empire gave way to American leadership in the world. But Churchill had Mars rising in Italy, where he tried to get the Allies to launch their second front. Uranus was directly over Moscow – he sent shock troops to attack the Soviet Union in 1919, and almost bombed them in 1945. Jupiter, the planet of hype and good luck, was rising on the horizon over El Alamein, where he scored a much-publicised victory over the Nazis; and on South Africa, too, where he famously escaped from a prisoner of war camp as a young man.

Emperor Hirohito

Born 29th April 1901, 10.00 p.m., Tokyo, Japan).

Neptune was directly over Moscow when Hirohito was born, correctly anticipating that the Emperor would be deceived from the Russian capital. The Nazis encouraged the Japanese to attack the Russians, to force the Soviets to fight on two fronts. But the Emperor was tricked by Stalin. He did not attack, and Germany had to fight on two fronts instead. Hirohito was born with Uranus directly over Hawaii – where the Japanese troops did the surprise attack from the sky. Mars was setting over Midway – where a fateful sea battle turned the war against the Japanese.

Stolz/Bradley, February 3rd, 1948

ZA: I checked all this information through the NASA site (http://ssd.jpl.nasa.gov/horizons.cgi) – it's all true. But much easier to check it with one of the many free online services which do the same.

~~TOP SECRET~~

Operation Blinker

(From the Reichs Ministry of Public Enlightenment and Propaganda – Office of Joseph Goebbels)

20th July 1942

ZA: Operation Blinker was the plan created by Dr Goebbels' Ministry of Propaganda for keeping this information secret. Most of these seven points have already been put into effect. When will they reach point seven?

Upon seeing the correct information, reasonable people conclude there is a link between celestial bodies and human affairs. **We cannot let this happen**, because it would challenge faith in science, religion, key parts of the economy and the government. To prevent this, we have developed a seven-step disinformation campaign:

1. <u>Use authority figures to ridicule the search for a link</u>

Authority figures must state 'Of course it's nonsense' whenever this topic is raised. The population must be encouraged to conform: people should be praised when they repeat 'of course it's nonsense'. Scientists must say 'No intelligent person would apply the scientific method to this.' Anyone who searches for a link must be regarded as stupid or disturbed, and denied research funding.

2. Assert that no link is possible

Assertions that something is impossible are usually accepted, even when made without evidence. Such assertions have slowed many other discoveries including plate tectonics, powered flight, and quantum physics.

We must create a similar superstition for this, that there can be no link.

3. Use the law to maintain secrecy

This tactic has already succeeded for many centuries, and must continue.

4. Destroy all who make links public

Any individual who makes public the link being human affairs and celestial bodies must be discredited. Ridicule is the best means for this, since it also discourages people from taking their evidence seriously. We must discredit the motives, reputation and academic pedigree of all who reveal the evidence. Their status in society, their friends, family and their life can all be threatened. Publishers must also be intimidated into silence.

5. Discredit the evidence presented

Any error or imperfection in evidence presented for the link between human affairs and celestial bodies must be exaggerated. Debate must become focussed on the error or imperfection in the evidence, not the evidence itself. All evidence must be labelled 'unscientific', or deliberately misinterpreted as fiction for entertainment.

6. Contaminate evidence presented

Strong evidence of a link must be contaminated by spurious data which suggests there is no link. The two sets of information must be mixed, and the spurious data must become more readily available. Bad practitioners of the science of prediction must be encouraged, since their abundance hides the link still further.

7. Subsume any evidence into conventional belief systems (e.g. religion, science)

If evidence of a link between human affairs and the position of the planets is made public, we must incorporate the new knowledge into our current belief system. The Christian Church adopted astrology at the Council of Nicea in 325AD, and can do so again. Modern science may seek to use quantum physics – which has already demonstrated distant particles can influence each other without being connected – to adopt some evidence as it emerges.

If all other attempts to conceal the truth about the link between the planets and human affairs fail, then authority figures must say they believed it all along. Suggested line is: **'This evidence was generated by the scientific method. It is a method we have always supported, generating a conclusion we have always suspected. We have disproved the superstition that there is no link between the planets and human affairs. Now we can apply this evidence for the common good.'**

THE LAST PROPHECY OF ROME EXCLUSIVE EXTRACT

Chapter 1

Rome, Italy

It was the wrong place for a holiday.

The crowds, the hassle, the noise….

Worst of all: the constant reminders of war.

Myles wanted a break, but knew he wasn't going to get one here.

He had read about Rome as an undergraduate: just one term to cover the whole Roman Empire. He'd forgotten most of it now. The lectures, the lecturer and that old history book – it all seemed so long ago.

What he remembered most were the other students. Some of them were very unusual, one of them more than the rest. The one he would never forget…

He looked around and tried to be impressed.

So this was Rome.

He gazed at the magnificent statues: gods, emperors and senators. He saw the Coliseum, where gladiators brawled and died. He studied the city walls which tried but ultimately failed to keep out the enemy. He even visited the old grain stores, Rome's strategic stockpile of food which kept its citizens plump. Stores once filled by harvests from across the sea, until barbarians overran the land which is now Libya...

Myles tried to let the monuments change his mind, but they couldn't. Everything about the greatest empire the world had ever known was shaded by one single truth: that it was brought down.

Rome declined and fell: everybody knew that. But that most famous fact hid an enigma. Perhaps the city's greatest puzzle – the riddle of Rome.

How was the world's greatest superpower - the most sophisticated civilisation of its age, an empire for more than a thousand years – defeated by a bunch of homeless barbarians?

Rome's wonders would always be overshadowed by the mystery of how they were lost.

Helen grabbed his arm. 'Shall we see the Pantheon?' she suggested. She was still trying to lift his mood, and he could tell. 'You ought to teach this stuff to your students, Myles…'

Myles shrugged. She was right: Rome was an empire built on war and conquest. Perfect material for a military historian. He should teach it.

But he knew he couldn't. And the reason why was something he could never explain to Helen.

They passed a fast-food outlet, an ice-cream seller and a man hawking plastic sunglasses for five euros a pair. School groups trampled over the ancient squares. Great artefacts were being smothered by chewing gum. Will our civilisation end this way?

They crossed a piazza towards the Pantheon. Myles looked up at the sandstone columns guarding the entrance, then hauled open the over-sized wooden doors to go inside. Helen followed close behind.

Their eyes adjusted to the gloom. The only light came from the single window in the centre of the ceiling. They moved towards the middle of the patterned marble floor, directly below the window. Then their gaze slowly fell down to the alcoves and statues around the side of the circular building. Constructed in 126AD, Rome's heyday, this was a church built for the worship of all the gods - long before Emperor Constantine converted to Christianity and tried to bring the whole Roman Empire with him.

Bang

Myles crouched down, hunching his head into his shoulders. He scanned around.

He couldn't tell, but No one else had reacted. A few people even looked at him as if he was odd – which he knew he was.

Helen saw it first. She motioned with her eyes: the huge doors to the Pantheon had been slammed shut, and the domed ceiling amplified the sound.

Myles calmed himself.

Helen put her hand on his face, and asked 'Are you OK?'

He was. It was just instinctive. His body had adapted to behave that way in Helmand. It would take time to unlearn.

The army thought it had cracked Post-Traumatic Stress Disorder. In a change since Vietnam and the Second World War, troops were now flown from the frontline in groups. They were given time in an isolated place where they could drink away their memories – together, with people who had experienced similar things. By the time they returned home they had already half-forgotten their wars.

Not Myles. He had been a lone civilian advisor. His experiences had been unique, and nobody but Helen had any idea what he had been through. When he saw a street, his first thought was still to wonder where someone would place a machine-gun to control movement. When he saw a patch of grass, he feared an improvised explosive device – a deadly IED - could be buried underneath.

The symptoms would be obvious in anybody else, and therefore treatable. But for Myles, an unorthodox specialist in war and a misfit by any standard, it was hard to say what behaviour was normal.

Afghanistan hadn't made him violent. Myles would never be that. Nor had his experiences made him hateful, which was a common expression of combat trauma. But Afghanistan had turned his imagination against him. He used to dream up solutions. Now he dreamed up enemies.

'Myles, you need to get back to the hotel,' said Helen.

Helen was right.

They turned around. Away from the spectacles of the long-gone empire, into the commercialised narrow streets and the crowds.

They passed a homeless man in one of the alleyways. He looked tired and hungry. Myles could tell the young man didn't have much - unshaven and with ruffled hair, he'd probably been sleeping rough for weeks. So Myles found some change and threw it towards him. The man thanked him with a nod.

Outside a Hard Rock Café they saw men and women in business suits. They were standing about and chatting nervously, like they didn't belong there. Obviously foreign. Myles picked up their accents: American.

Some of them recognised Helen, but none of them reacted. Myles guessed they were used to dealing with famous people.

Then he realised: these people worked in the American Embassy, which was opposite. He could faintly hear a fire alarm, which explained why they were all outside.

Just routine - it was only a drill.

Myles smiled at them. Some of them smiled back, others just ignored him. None of them were worried.

Then he looked up to see a very large cardboard box suspended from a rope. A man in dark glasses was manoeuvring it near a second-floor window.

The man lifted his glasses.

Myles caught his eye and saw a sinister look. He grabbed Helen's arm and pointed. 'A bomb,' he whispered. 'It's got to be a bomb…'

Helen tried to work out how Myles could know the dangling box contained explosives. But Myles was already amongst the crowd. 'Move away – quickly,' he warned. 'It's a bomb.'

The Embassy workers took time to react.

'Quick. It's a bomb,' Myles insisted. He was flapping them away with his long arms. A few started to move slowly, until two or three started to run. Then everybody began to run with them. 'Helen – run away!' Myles could see this was the perfect terrorist trap: set off the Embassy fire alarm then blow up all the staff as they muster outside.

'But Myles…' queried Helen.

'Quick!'

Senior executives, mid-level diplomats and all their support staff: everyone hurried away. Helen reluctantly moved back with them.

They started to gather at the far end of the street. From there they could see what would happen - but not a safe distance if the Englishman's warning was right. They all watched: half-curious, half-alarmed.

Myles had become alone in the street. He looked up at the window. The man holding the cardboard box was looking nervous now.

Suddenly he left the box to swing on the rope and darted into the building.

Myles rushed over to the apartment block where the box was hanging. *Damn the consequences.*

This was one terrorist he was determined to catch…

Lightning Source UK Ltd.
Milton Keynes UK
UKOW05f0605060317
295973UK00015B/315/P

9 781910 751107

The Assassin and the Pianist

Book 4 in the Dan Stone Series

A Novel

David Nees

The Pianist and the Assassin, Book 4 of the Dan Stone, series is a work of fiction and should be construed as nothing but. All characters, locales, and incidents portrayed in the novel are products of the author's imagination or have been used fictitiously. Any resemblance to any person, living or dead, is entirely coincidental.

To keep up with my new releases, please visit my website at www.davidnees.com._Scroll down to the bottom of the landing page to the section titled, "Follow the Adventure".

You can visit my author page and click the "Follow" button under my picture on the Amazon book page to get notices about any new releases.

.

Manufactured in the United States
ISBN 9798618930659

For Carla

You are there; you listen tirelessly; you strengthen me.

Many thanks go to my beta readers, Eric and Chris. You both contribute so much through your thoughts and insights. Eric, your tireless efforts to make me write my best are valuable beyond words to express. Without your help this story would remain much less polished. Thank you both for the generous amount of time you gave to my endeavor.

Thank you, Carla and Catherine for your sharp-eyed proofreading. You both find so many things I always miss.

I owe a large debt of gratitude to Mark Irchai, an upcoming concert pianist of great skill. He generously spent time with me over the phone and in emails to help me understand the nuances of playing the piano at a world-class level. I recommend going to see him perform. You can visit his website at www.markirchai.com

Thanks go to Rolf Kyburz for his permission to use the photo you see on the cover. He is an insightful music blogger and takes wonderful pictures. Visit his site at www.rolf-musicblog.net.

And my grateful thanks to Alina Bercu who generously allowed her visage to appear in my work. She is the pianist in Rolf's picture. Her performance of a Beethoven concerto was the inspiration for my description of the piece. Visit her website at www.alinabercu.com.

Thanks also to Onur Aksoy for his great cover design. He is talented and works diligently with sometimes conflicting directions to produce great covers. Visit his website at www.onegraphica.com/

The Assassin and the Pianist

"What we have once we can never lose. All that we love deeply becomes a part of us."—Helen Keller

"Love is all we have, the only way that each can help the other."—Euripides

"This will be our reply to violence: to make music more intensely, more beautifully, more devotedly than ever before."—Leonard Bernstein

Chapter 1

He sat in the upstairs room looking out at the hedges lining the gravel drive. The pale winter light softly illuminated the room. The south-facing bank of the driveway hungrily drank in the weak warmth from the sun, eager to leave behind the hard freeze of winter. Downstairs a Chopin Étude was being played on a piano.

The precise cadence of the notes was only slightly tattered on their journey from the piano to his room upstairs. As he absorbed the music, the vise that held his mind in its painful grip, slowly, almost imperceptibly, began to relax. The music had its restorative effect on him, as it always did.

It was during these times, when his brain was released from the fierce clamp of pain, that he could go over the events, as best as he could remember them, that had occurred to bring him to this stone house with a woman playing the piano downstairs.

He remembered again the car journey on the icy roads, through the hills. He was in the back seat with his hands tied. Next to him sat a large man. The man's partner was driving. They were hurrying to...where? He didn't know.

The car sped around a turn and started to slide on the frozen road. The man in the backseat said something in Russian. Dan could understand most of it.

"Slow down or you'll kill us." The man's voice was low and thick.

"We were told to hurry. Not let anything distract us. The boss is eager to talk with him," the driver replied.

He assumed they were talking about him, but he had no idea why someone would want to talk with him, let alone tie him up. His head throbbed with a fierce pounding. His vision alternated between blurry and clear. Nothing made sense. Why was he bound? Who wanted to talk to him? Who were these men?

He was vaguely aware that the men had been with him for some time, holding him captive. They had asked questions. They had beaten him. They had injected him with chemicals that had made him confused and disoriented, sometimes causing him to lose consciousness. Now he could barely function and only in the present. And the present was a confusing puzzle.

On the next turn the car hit black ice and slewed sideways. The driver flailed away at the steering wheel trying to control the vehicle, but there was no traction. The captive instinctively ducked his head between his legs and the car slammed into the guard rail, spun back onto the pavement, and flipped on its side.

The burly man sitting next to him was thrown against the side window, smashing it with his head. The driver flew against the steering wheel and slammed his forehead into the car's windshield.

The bound man sat back up. For the moment the other two were stunned from the blows they had received. He reached for the man's pocket. The man had pulled a folding knife from it earlier to pick at his nails. He grabbed the knife and cut his wrists free. He pushed against the door. It was jammed. Panic rose like a black cloud to engulf him. He slammed his shoulder into the door again and again. The blows only ignited the pain from his other wounds. He leaned back and brought his legs up and kicked against the window until it cracked open.

He threw himself out of the now broken window and rolled onto the icy ground. The shock of the frigid air convulsed his chest causing him to almost choke. Looking back into the car, he saw his two captors stirring. Without hesitation, the man climbed over the guardrail and skidded down the frozen slope to the river below. It was shallow and moving fast over the boulders as the water sped down out of the mountains.

He didn't hesitate. The terror he felt came from above. He needed to get far away from it. He splashed into the frigid waters, straining for the other shore and the cover of the trees. Half way across, he slipped on a rock and fell into the water. Coming up he gasped for breath. There was a shout from above and a shot rang out. He heard the bullet strike the water to his right. The shot sent him scrambling to the shore and into the trees.

More shouts came from above. More shots flew into the woods after him. There was splashing from behind. They were coming.

He ran; now without thought, like a wounded animal. He dodged through the trees, falling, getting up to run again, not stopping. His only desire was to outrace the sounds of the men pursuing. His legs were weak and he stumbled repeatedly. His lungs burned from the sharp, winter air but he kept going, panic driving him.

He burst out into a field and stumbled towards the trees on the far side. Out in the open the wind hit him with a fierce blow. It came from the north, cold and hard, almost knocking him off his feet. Then the shouts came again, behind him. More shots rang out. One slammed into his shoulder and threw him to the ground. The dirt was rock-hard, frozen by the unrelenting wind which had sucked all the heat from the soil.

A short cry escaped his lips, but he got up and stumbled forward. His body was operating automatically, fleeing from the terror and pain that pursued him. More shots came, thrown off by the wind, then he was back in the cover of trees. Still he stumbled on. He was a mindless beast, desperate to escape no matter the cost to his body, like the wolf that would chew off his paw to escape the trapper's deadly tool.

Time passed as he lurched through the forest, over the frozen, rocky ground. He couldn't tell how long, but the pale daylight faded. There were no sounds of pursuit now. He slowed to a walk. He was moving in an unsteady manner on feet now frozen beyond feeling. There was a sharp pain in his shoulder, joining his other injuries. Every part of his body protested his movement, but he kept going, his ears alert to any evidence of pursuit.

Where was he? Where could he go for shelter, for safety? His thoughts came in jumbled clumps. He couldn't sort them out and didn't have answers. He could only go on, with an animal's instinct to survive. To get away from the ones chasing him was his only concern. He couldn't recall anything except that he had been a captive, beaten and tortured, and was now free and in danger of freezing to death in this deadly wind. He also did not know who he was.

Chapter 2

Ahead he could barely see a light shining through the trees. He came to a stone wall and climbed over it, falling to the ground on the other side. Was it safe? He shuffled towards the low, stone house. Suddenly a dog began to bark, loud and aggressive. The man stopped. A door opened and a dark figure stood there in the light spilling out from the room, looking into the yard. Looking for him?

"Who's there? came the voice in a thick, rural French accent.

The man bolted to the left, across the yard, through a gate, and into a field, straining to reach the safety of the forest again. The dog kept up its barking, but thankfully, was not released.

Again, when the sounds behind him faded, he slowed his pace. He wore a medium-weight jacket, now wet from the river, that offered little protection from the wind which remained strong as the evening progressed. In addition, the temperature was dropping. His mind, even in its ravaged state, registered the harsh reality that he needed to find shelter in order to survive the night.

He kept moving, downwind, not fighting the wind's relentless pressure. Again, he saw a light. Should he risk approaching? His weakening state and the increasing cold drove him to try. This time he circled the cottage, aiming for the barn on one side. Maybe he could find shelter there?

He approached as carefully as he could. His numbed feet were unreliable. He feared a stumble would expose him to the occupants of the house. When he got to the door, he grabbed it and lifted the latch. The cold metal gave a sharp screech. Without waiting he pulled on the door, forcing it against the wind until it finally opened enough for him to slip through.

Inside, the dark was more intense. For a moment he stood with his back to the wall, sheltered from the wind. It was still cold, but there was some relief in the stillness. There were animals in the barn. A horse started to snort nervously. There was more noise as the other animals stirred from sleep to stamp in their stalls, nervous of this strange intruder.

Then a dog began to bark. Again, from the farmhouse. Panic began to rise again. The man lurched forward to the wall of one of the stalls. The horse inside shied back and slammed against the wood. The man grabbed a blanket from the wall as the horse whinnied its alarm. The dog was now in full cry.

The man ran for the door and bolted through it as he heard a voice call out again, asking who was there. He hobbled out of the farmyard on unsteady feet clutching the blanket and lurched forward in an awkward gait for the safety of the woods. A shot was fired in his direction, but the bullet went wide. The man sensed he couldn't be easily seen, but still kept up his quickened and unsteady pace. Ten minutes later he stopped and wrapped the blanket around him. He was panting from the effort and felt his strength draining. The blanket helped but it would not keep him alive out in the wind. He needed shelter, yet there was none that didn't seem to come with a dog and a suspicious farmer.

A farmer who would turn him over to authorities.

In his confused state, how could he explain himself? They would put him in a cell. He let out a reflexive groan at the thought of being confined again. The torture would start. The beatings and drugs until he didn't know day from night. Until he couldn't answer the insistent questions even if he wanted to; questions he could now not even remember. He was just a body in the present, hardly able to think, let alone understand who he was and how he came to be in his situation. He functioned only through a desire to survive.

More groans escaped him; he started again, with unsteady steps, walking downwind. There had to be shelter for him. There was nothing else to do but to keep moving. Now not so much to escape his pursuers, but to find shelter.

He began to stumble more frequently. Each fall resulted in more blows to his already battered and bruised body. After each fall it took longer for him to get back on his frozen feet which felt like stumps. He began to think about lying down behind a boulder; there were many in these foothills. He could get out of the wind, curl up in the blanket, and go to sleep.

Something deep inside of him recoiled at this treasonous thought. There lay death. He couldn't let that happen. He would die on his feet. With each fall, he wrestled with himself, but each time he forced himself erect to continue.

He was now moving in slow motion. Lurching from tree to boulder, banging into them, using them to keep from falling, but moving, always downwind. The wind, still had strength but was not the overpowering force it had been earlier.

Then he heard something—music, notes being played on a piano. How in this wilderness of wind, woods, and stone? He stopped and turned his ear to catch the faint sounds as they came and went, carried by the wind. Was he hallucinating? It made no sense to be hearing music in the forest, on such a winter night. But nothing made sense except the fact that he was steadily freezing to death. To his clouded mind, the sound seemed to hold hope for succor. At least it was something other than angry dogs and farmers with rifles. Hallucination or not, he decided to aim for the sound.

He turned in the direction of the music. He was now walking sideways to the wind. It found every gap in his blanket to assault him with more cold. He stopped often, when the notes disappeared, and waited for the wind to bring them back. The wind, which seemed to be trying to kill him, also carried a hope for survival in the notes that blew past him.

After a half hour of stumbling along, he had hardly gone more than three hundred yards, but the music was stronger. He was making progress. He willed his body forward. He was almost spent and going, now more upwind, made his progress slower. Could he reach the place from where the music came? In his mind he began imaging a warm refuge with soothing music that never ended, flowing over his damaged body.

What if there's nothing there? The terrible thought crossed his mind and caused him to stop. But the music was stronger now, and clearer. Surely it was real. He had no alternative but to follow the sound. He came to the edge of the woods. There was a stone wall, like the one's he had crossed earlier. But now it looked impassable in his depleted condition. Ahead there was a large cottage, substantial, built of stone with its back to the wind. There were lights inside, glowing, inviting, promising warmth.

Get over the wall. It was four feet high. He leaned over it and tried to raise one leg. It wouldn't go high enough. He scraped at the stones with a frozen foot, until it jammed on a purchase. With a great heave, he pushed off and twisted his torso over the rocks. A cry escaped him as pain seared through his body. The blanket slipped free and he fell forward into the field.

He was over the wall. Slowly he regained his feet, pulling himself erect with the stones. Where was the blanket? He looked around. The wind now was attacking him with a renewed strength out in the open, away from the protection of the trees. Looking back over the wall, he could see the blanket on the ground, out of reach. It was as lost to him as if it were in a different world. He did not have the strength to climb back to retrieve it.

The man turned. *Get to the light. Get to the warmth. Get to the music.* He stumbled across the open field. The wind seemed to attack him, as if trying knock him off his feet, to keep him out in the open where it could freeze him solid. Then he was against the south-facing wall of the cottage. The wind now could only assault him in gasps as it swirled around the sheltering wall. He made it to the door. The music was now louder, more welcoming, holding more promise.

His body slammed against the door and with one last effort he banged his fist on it before collapsing. Darkness overwhelmed him.

Chapter 3

Jane Tanner sat in Henry Mason's office. Henry had formed a small team that operated within the CIA. It was unknown to all but a few, and charged with clandestine missions that would not be looked upon favorably by any oversight committee.

"Still no word from Dan?" Henry asked without much hope. Dan Stone was his agent who had gone missing. He was the tip of the spear in Henry's war against the terrorists.

Jane shook her head. "Not for the past five weeks. After the shootout in Marseille. He wasn't among the bodies, but we've heard nothing since."

Henry waved his hand in irritation. He knew the story; he had read the report. What he needed was new information.

"No one found the briefcase?"

Again, Jane shook her head. "We're still looking. We haven't found Pavlovich yet either. I have to assume that he's still in possession of the case."

"And he's gone to ground. I would think with all our assets we could unearth where he's hiding."

Jane gave Henry a cold smile. "He's nondescript, a nobody. One who can hide himself quite well. He managed to be obscure enough to stay out of harm's way during the Soviet breakup, *and* maintain a job. Then he managed to steal the briefcase and disappear. And he's kept out of sight for the last five years while he tried to figure out how and where to sell it."

"And that blew up in his face. You think he's going to try again?"

"Maybe...eventually. He seems to be a patient man. But this doesn't help us find Dan."

"I don't like losing an asset, but I like less the idea of a briefcase full of weaponized anthrax floating around somewhere."

The briefcase had been taken by Roman Pavlovich. He had been a minor Soviet bureaucrat working in an obscure warehouse. When the communist country broke apart, money was offered by the west to secure nuclear weapons so they wouldn't fall into the wrong hands. Bio weapons were also included and arranged to be warehoused safely. Some of them found their way to Pavlovich's warehouse. Years passed and authorities turned to other issues. Pavlovich realized that no one was paying much attention to the dangerous items stored under his care and control.

His wife had left him; he had little hope of making a mark in the new Russia and little hope of more than stagnation in his life. Alone and resentful, he decided that he would use his position and his anonymity to give himself a large payout.

What was stored was a strain of inhalation anthrax. It was the deadliest form of the disease. Released in an urban area thousands of people would be infected before it could be identified. The early symptoms were identical to a cold or the flu. Once it was identified it would be too late; so many people would be carriers that the disease would be hard to stop.

The delivery method was absurdly simple if one didn't care about their own health. One could simply walk the city streets letting the spores drift out of a backpack, perhaps accelerated by a small squeeze pump. Nothing would seem amiss. The mission would be fatal, like that of a suicide bomber, but there would be enough true believers to volunteer for the task. A car or motorcycle driven through the city could accomplish the same results only more quickly.

"How can we be sure it hasn't already wound up in the terrorist's hands?" Henry asked.

"We can't be sure of anything right now," Jane said. "But I still stand by my report that the shootout at the exchange interrupted everything. Since we didn't find Pavlovich's body, we can assume he's alive. There was no time for any of the parties to hide bodies."

"Yeah. It was a mess for sure."

Jane nodded. "And Dan wasn't found at the site either, so I'm guessing he's alive as well." She paused for a moment. "If Pavlovich is still alive, it's a good guess that he has the briefcase."

"He runs like a mouse, back into the woodwork when the two cats started fighting."

"Something like that."

"But if Dan's alive, why hasn't he checked in?"

"Maybe he's been captured. If so, we have to find him."

"We have to find the briefcase," Henry replied. "I know you have a special relationship with him, but the briefcase comes first."

"Maybe for you, but I'm not willing to walk away from the best asset we have in this fight." She paused to point her finger at him. "And that's not because of our 'special relationship', as you call it."

Henry sighed. "Just don't let your feelings compromise your judgment."

"Have I ever?" Jane stood up. "So, I can assume that I have permission to keep working on finding Dan?"

"*And* the briefcase."

The men saw their captive fall to the ground. They watched him get up and stagger forward, towards the cover of the trees. They fired more shots, but the wind took the bullets wide of the mark. Then he disappeared into the woods. They ran through the field to the edge of the forest.

Ahead they could barely hear the sounds of the man's fleeing over the roaring of the wind. They plunged into the dark. The trees snagged at their coats; dead branches tripped them. Their path was twisted as they wove through the forest. The sound coming from their quarry grew fainter. Their more careful pace seemed to be slower than the man they pursued. After ten minutes, they could hear nothing ahead, but they kept going.

At the next clearing they stopped. There was no one in sight. There was no trail to follow. They could only hear the wind. They looked at one another.

"You want to go on?" the driver asked.

"No, but do you want to tell the boss that we lost him? Especially since it was your fault?"

"*Chert s toboy*, to hell with you," the man said in Russian. "It was the ice. I couldn't see it and when we hit it the car went out of control. It could have happened to you."

"I would have been going slower," the larger man said. "You were driving too fast."

"If I had gone slower, we might not have made it up the mountain. Too slow and you get stuck."

"Too fast and you crash, *durachit*."

"Who do you call a fool?" If you had been more careful with the drugs, we would have gotten what we needed and wouldn't have been transporting him. We'd have just killed him and reported back to the boss."

"The boss wanted him no matter what we learned. But what do we do now? Keep going?"

"I'm freezing," the driver said.

"Me as well. But I don't want to tell the boss we lost him. Maybe we go back. He will die out here tonight. And if he finds help, he'll be turned in to the local *gendarmes*. He'll seem to be crazy to everyone.

"Let's go back then and wait, my friend. He will either die tonight or show up in a day or two in the village."

"Then we try again. Once we get the car righted."

The men turned and retraced their steps.

The crash at the door intruded upon Christina's playing. There were two thumps which might have been the wind or something blown by it hitting the door. She finished the short Franz Liszt piece she was playing and stood up. It must be the wind, she told herself. Who would be at her door this time of night?

Her cottage was ample in size, two stories with a large country kitchen and cozy living room incorporating a generous stone fireplace and hearth. Beyond the living room was her music room. It was well insulated and had a humidifier to keep her instrument from drying out. The house had steam heat, updated and improved at great expense and trouble. The fireplace added additional warmth during the fierce *mistrals* that blew in the fall and winter. The heat generated was fed into the music room, moderated by the humidifier that was kept hard at work this time of year.

Christina walked to the front door. She opened it and there, lying on her front step was the crumpled figure of a man. She cried out in shock and stepped back, closing the door. What was going on? *Is he dead? On my doorstep?* She took a breath and pulled the door open again. The wind charged inside blowing past her, flooding the cottage with its chill. She ignored the cold and bent down to the man. A faint plume of vapor came out of his mouth. He was breathing but unconscious.

She grabbed at his coat and started to pull him inside. It took many tugs, each one yielding a few inches of progress to move his body across the threshold. Finally, he was inside and Christina slammed the door shut against the wind and cold. She leaned back and caught her breath. The man didn't move.

Her mind was filled with questions. How could she revive him, warm him up? Was he dangerous? What if he tried to harm her after she saved him? She shook her head. First things first. *Get him close to the fire*. She took a deep breath and started to drag him into the living room. Rugs got in the way. When the body was half way into the room, Christina stopped and moved the carpeting aside. It was easier to drag him along the wooden floor.

Then she placed one of the rugs near the hearth. She would lay him on it and stoke the fire. The added radiant heat from the flames would help amplify the warmth of the room. When she had a place ready by the fire, Christina began to drag the still-unconscious body across the room. After some minutes she pushed him onto the rug, parallel to the fireplace. Next, she put more logs on the fire. The flames grew higher and she could feel their warmth projecting into the room. She went upstairs, where the bedrooms were located, and grabbed extra blankets and brought them down. Before she spread them out, she stepped to the rear of the cottage and opened the door. The wind blasted straight inside. She quickly grabbed an armful of firewood and brought it inside, using her back to force the door closed against the wind.

There was enough wood inside now for hours. She realized she would have to keep watch, not only to stoke the fire, but to make sure an errant spark didn't jump out, catch a blanket on fire and burn down the cottage, killing them both in the process. *That certainly won't do.*

Before covering the man in blankets, Christina realized that she would have to remove his wet clothes. All her work would be for naught if he stayed wrapped in those icy garments. She shuddered at the thought of touching him further. Still it had to be done. Starting with his shoes, sturdy hiking boots, she began. When she got the boots and socks off, she saw his feet. They were white, ice cold to the touch. Were they frost bitten? She didn't know, but she knew they had to be warmed.

She went to his torso and pulled off his jacket and shirt. There was blood. He was wounded. *Oh my God.* She found the wound in his right shoulder. Even to her untrained eye, it looked like it might be from a gunshot. There was no tearing or laceration as might be expected with some type of accident. There was a puncture wound on the rear part of his shoulder. The entire area was swollen and purple indicating internal bleeding. She lifted his shoulder and didn't see any other wound. The man let out a groan and Christina dropped the shoulder back to the floor.

The injured area was not bleeding at the moment, so Christina turned her attention to the rest of his clothes. She undid his belt and unzipped his pants. It felt wrong, somehow, for her to be doing this with him unconscious. Nevertheless, it had to be done. She began to pull and finally wrestled his legs out of the trousers. Faced with his underpants and exposing his genitals, she decided not to remove them. He'd have to warm up without her invading his privacy, or offending her sensibilities any further.

Next, she covered the man with her blankets, tucking them in carefully to cocoon him and trap the heat. He didn't stir except to groan occasionally, which startled her. When finished, she stood up, her mind going over what else could be done.

Water bottles! There were two of them in the cottage. She immediately turned to retrieve them and fill them with hot water. She would put these against his feet and his chest. When she had finished with this last effort, she made herself a cup of tea and sat down to watch over the man.

She took out her cell phone to call the authorities, but there was no service. The wind must have damaged one of the towers. It happened regularly when the *mistral* blew. She looked back at the man. He was too heavy to drag outside and into her car. Besides, he might not make the journey, having to go back out in the cold.

She sighed. She would have to stay up tonight, feeding the fire, replacing the water bottles, and wondering who her strange visitor was. He not only seemed to have been shot, but his body bore the scars of old wounds along with signs of fresh traumas. She was no nurse, but it looked like he had been severely beaten. Tomorrow, she hoped, would bring some answers but not, danger.

Chapter 4

It was deep into the night. The wind had finally quieted down to a moderate breeze. It would regain its strength with the new day, but for now the relative calm stilled the night. The man groaned at intervals without regaining consciousness. His body had begun to shiver, violently. Christina put her hand under the blankets and felt his back, legs and feet. They were still cold. After putting fresh hot water in the bottles, she sat back. What else could she do?

She remembered reading about using another's body heat to warm people suffering from hypothermia. Was it an old wives' tale? She didn't know. Should she try it? The man was still unconscious and didn't show any signs of awakening. She could strip to her underwear and slide in behind him. With his front to the fire, and his back against her body, and all wrapped in a blanket cocoon, he might recover and warm up. She shuddered at the thought but there was nothing else to try.

She took a deep breath, got up, and stoked the fire. Then with a deep breath she began to take off her clothes. Her instincts said "no" but her sense of duty said she should do what was necessary to help this person. *Besides*, she thought, *he's unconscious*. She knelt down and worked her way under the cover and up against the man's back. Her body wanted to recoil from the chill, but she resisted. She forced herself tight against his back, letting her legs wrap over his. She was six feet, two inches tall. Her body stretched out the full length of the man's. She put her right arm over his side and across his torso. Her arm pressed against his chest, but she kept her hand closed in a fist, unable to force herself to touch his body with her fingers. It seemed to be too intimate a gesture, even if he couldn't recognize it.

The rest of the night was spent with Christina hugging the man, getting up to replenish the hot water bottles, and add wood to the fire. The man's shivering quieted through the night. He was getting warmer. He would not die. By dawn, Christina got out of the blankets and put her clothes back on.

The man began to stir. Groans escaped his mouth as he became conscious. Christina got up and went into the kitchen. She made some hot chocolate, put it in a glass with a straw, and came back into the living room. He was sitting up, facing the fire. When he heard her steps, he turned. There was fear in his face. His eyes had a wild look to them. Christina stopped and stood still, as one would when confronted by a startled animal in the forest.

She held out the glass. "Hot chocolate. It will warm you and give you some strength." She spoke in French.

The man just stared at her, as if not understanding.

"*Comprenez-vous le français?*"

He slowly nodded his head.

"Do you want the chocolate?" she asked.

He nodded again.

Christina stepped forward and held out the glass. The man extended his uninjured arm and took it in his trembling hand. He put the straw to his lips.

"*Fais attention*, careful, it's hot."

Christina watched him as he drank the warm chocolate. In between sips through the straw, he put the warm glass to his face and chest, trying to absorb all of its heat in every way possible.

When he had finished, he put the glass on the floor. Christina sat down on the couch. He began to groan louder and put his left hand to his head. The groans became cries. His hand grasped his head and his body twisted with a pain that he could not extinguish. He lay back down and pulled the blankets over him, curling into a ball, now whimpering from the hurt that seemed to attack him.

Christina sat, frozen by what she had seen. There seemed to be more pain than what was caused by the wounds on his body. Something in his head, she guessed from the way his body reacted. She got up and took the glass back to the kitchen. She would leave him alone. He needed more rest. She would help with his wounds later. The shoulder injury was the important one. The others did not seem dangerous, even though they looked painful.

Maybe later she would get some explanation from her mysterious stranger. There was still no cell reception. Her call for help would have to wait.

Christina watched for the next hour. When the man had stopped writhing, seeming to have gone to sleep, she got up and went into the music room, to her piano. She was a world-class concert pianist. Saving a stranger's life was one thing. Missing a day of practice was another.

She lived what one might describe as a monastic existence. Constant practice was the price one paid to remain at the top levels in the performance field. Even with a prodigious amount of natural talent, honed over many years of teaching and development, one still had to submit to a rigorous schedule of practice to remain in the top ranks.

Still young and early in her career, Christina had realized that she needed a hideaway. Somewhere to go in between performances. A place of beauty, but secluded so she could get away from the crowds and distraction.

She was tall with naturally light brown hair, her figure slim but well endowed—something which, she learned early on, was a distraction to men. She had a thin face with a long, aquiline nose that gave her a regal look. Her brown eyes were large, like a doe's, and very expressive. They caught you and held you in their gaze. Even with all her obvious beauty, she was a shy person. And there were many fans, some bordering on being frightening with their insistence on their love for and devotion to her.

They had given her an extra incentive to find this cottage. It was located in the Provence region of France, nestled in the *Maison du Parc Naturel Régional du Luberon,* near the village of Vachères. It was northeast of Avignon, but off the regular path of tourists. And in the winter, the whole region was left alone by the flocks of visitors that came during the summer months.

She put her strange visitor out of her mind and sat down at the piano. She started with some scales, playing them in ascending and descending runs. Her fingers moved fluidly over the keyboard. Her mind quieted and relaxed. The runs increased in speed until they were a rippling cascade of notes going up and down. She modulated the key and continued, going through all twelve keys. Next, she played the scales, this time hitting four notes simultaneously with each hand, moving up and down the keyboard in ever more aggressive strikes and going through all the keys again.

After twenty minutes, Christina began a Chopin Étude, Opus 10, Number 3. It started light and reflective, relaxing her from the aggressive scales she had been playing. The piece built to a strong climax, faster, more aggressive, then softened into a revisit of the opening theme. The études were all short so she played them over more than once before moving on.

In the living room, the man regained consciousness. The terrible pain that had attacked him, like a vise squeezing his head, was gone. He could feel his other injuries now with his mind calm, not tortured, and his head not screaming in such pain as to drive out all rational thought. The music from the next room flowed over him. He marveled at the rippling notes. *Was it the music that gave him relief?* It sounded so refreshing, so clean and the pain faded as the music enveloped him.

He took a physical inventory of his body. He noted the bruises and categorized each one according to its severity, how it impacted his movement, and how vulnerable it would make him in a physical conflict.

The bullet wound (he knew exactly what it was) gave him some concern, but he was able to determine that the joint was not damaged. The bullet would have to come out. He marveled at how calmly he could come to and accept that diagnosis, confident of its accuracy. Where did this ability come from?

Even now, more relaxed, and without the terrible pain in his head, he found only a black void when he reached into his memory for clues to his situation. He didn't even know his name. Would this person (she almost seemed like an angel to him in his desperate state) send him away? Where would he go? Even when he recovered physically, how could he go forward not knowing who he was and what had caused his terrible situation?

He relaxed back in the blankets. For now, he'd rest and absorb the music. That was enough.

Chapter 5

Christina practiced for two more hours. The man dozed off and on without the pain in his head returning. When awake, he focused on the music coming from the adjoining room, marveling at it and the clarity of the sound; its cleanliness and crispness sometimes delicate, sometimes strong and bold, but always sharp and clean. Then he would fall back asleep, grateful for the respite from the pain that attacked him.

When she had finished practicing, she went back into the living room. The man was sitting up, blankets wrapped around him. His left arm was across his knees which were pulled up to his chest, while his right arm, the one with the shoulder injury, lay in his lap. He turned towards her when she came in. Again, there was the fearful look in his face.

"Are you thirsty? Hungry?"

He nodded.

"Both?"

"*Oui.*"

She pulled a chair up close to the fire and put more logs on the blaze. The day was sunny but sharply cold. The wind had returned in force with the new day.

"Sit here," she said, "I'll get you some water and make something to eat for both of us."

She stepped back and watched the man slowly uncoil himself and rise. He fought to remain steady and Christina resisted the urge to lend him her arm. Dragging the covers with him he shuffled to the chair and sat down heavily in it.

"Better?" she asked.

He nodded.

She brought him a glass of water and then went into the kitchen to prepare something for them to eat.

Fifteen minutes later, Christina came out with a tray. On it was a bean and pasta soup she had made earlier in the week, an assortment of cheeses, a salad of greens, cherry tomatoes, and hard-boiled eggs sliced in half. There was also some roast beef slices and fresh bread.

The man stared at the food and swallowed. It seemed to Christina that he may not have eaten much recently. He looked at the tray with eyes full of hunger.

"*Allez-y, mangez* go ahead, eat."

He looked up at her and then tentatively began to try the food. Soon he was devouring what she had prepared. Christina went back to the kitchen and brought back a plate for herself along with some wine, leaving the tray for the man to consume.

When he had finished, he looked over at her. "*Merci.* I didn't realize how hungry I was. I think I made a pig out of myself." His face had a look of, if not fear, now, then worry.

She smiled. "*Ce n'est rien*, it's nothing."

"My name is Christina, Christina Aubergh. What is your name?"

His face showed confusion.

"What's your name?" she now asked more forcefully.

He shook his head and looked down at the floor. "This will sound strange, but I don't know my name."

"You don't know your name? How can that be?"

He shook his head again. "I don't know how it can be, I just know that I don't know." He looked up at her, directly into her eyes. "I don't know who I am."

She stared at him. His eyes locked on to her with a startling intensity, but without the earlier fear showing in his face. It was an intense look that backed up his outrageous statement.

Christina took a deep breath. Things were getting complicated. Her neatly arranged afternoon of practice, reading and relaxing was disappearing into a confusion she hadn't anticipated.

"You don't know who you are. Do you know how you got here, to this cottage? Do you know how you got your wounds?"

"I was running away from some men who held me captive. They shot me while I ran. I didn't plan to come here. I needed shelter and this cottage, your house, didn't have a dog or a man with a gun."

Questions rose up in Christina's mind. She tried to sort them out; to come up with what was relevant.

"You speak French, but you're not a native. Where are you from?"

He shrugged. "That's just it. I don't know where I'm from." Then he switched to English. "Do you speak English? *Parlez-vous Anglaise?*"

"I do."

He continued. "I'm more comfortable in English so that must be my native language."

"You sound American."

He seemed to think about that for a moment and then nodded. "Probably right."

"So, you're an American who was captured...can we assume by some bad people?"

He nodded.

"And you escaped," she continued. "They shot you as you ran and you wound up on my doorstep."

He nodded.

She stood up. "We must go to the police. They will help you. There is no cell reception, but I can drive you to the village."

The man stood as well, now with panic in his eyes. "No, no." His voice was strong. "No police. I don't know who I am. They'll put me in a jail to find out. I can't get put back into a cell. The ones chasing me will find me and kill me."

"You don't know that. You said they were bad people. The police wouldn't tell them."

He shook his head. "No, no. The police won't have to tell them. They'll be able to find me. If they think I've survived the night, they'll be waiting for me. They know I'm confused and can't say who I am. They'll know I'll wind up with the police. I can sense it."

He looked at her now, pleading with his eyes. "Don't call the police."

Christina stopped. "But what do I do with you?"

He now looked confused again. "I don't know. Let me stay and recover my strength? Then I'll go away. I won't be a burden and the men chasing me won't have any idea I'm here."

She paused. "Let me think about it," she said. "First, let's tend to your wound. You need a doctor, so we should at least do that."

Again, he shook his head. "I can tell you what to do. The bones are not broken, the joint will work. We need to clean and sterilize the wound and remove the bullet. I can tell you how to do it."

"What?" Now Christina had panic in her voice. "I can't do that. I don't know how. I'll hurt you."

"I know what to do. Don't ask me how I know, but I know. You won't hurt me. I'll guide you." He hurried on. "Boil some water and get some clean towels or rags. You'll need alcohol, a knife, a tweezer, and some tape to cover a bandage." He gave her a pleading look with his piercing gaze. "You can do this."

The intensity of his pleading, the look in his face won her over. She gave in and got up without another word to gather what he asked for. The man went into the kitchen to wait for her.

He was sitting at the kitchen table when she returned.

"Pour some of the alcohol on the entrance wound."

He let out a small groan as she did as he instructed. Along with the supplies he had told her to get, she had found some latex gloves which she put on.

"Now reach into the channel the bullet made and find the bullet. All the tissue is soft and the bullet is hard, so you'll know it when you feel it."

"I can't stick my finger in your shoulder," she said. The thought made her stomach turn.

"You have to. Close your eyes if necessary. It has to be done by feel anyway."

She slowly pushed her finger into his wound.

He let out a grunt and she quickly pulled back out.

"I'm going to grunt and groan but don't stop. It's just a way to handle the discomfort. I don't mind any pain. I mind not getting the bullet out."

She started again. Her eyes were shut tight and she unsuccessfully tried to close her ears to his grunts. Then she felt it. It was hard, with a ragged edge.

"I found it," she exclaimed.

"Good. Look how far your finger is in the wound. If you can get your finger around the bullet, you can try to pull it back with you. If not, you'll have to go in with the tweezers. That's why I want you to see how deep it is."

"I can't get it to come. I don't want to hurt you further."

"Okay. The tweezers are boiled clean. Use them. Just go slow and when you grasp it, don't let it loose.

Five agonizing minutes later, the bullet emerged along with a fresh supply of blood.

"Oh my God, it's bleeding," Christina said with alarm.

"Press a towel against the opening to staunch the flow. It'll stop soon. It couldn't be helped."

When the bleeding slowed, the man had Christina put more alcohol on the wound and then wrap a clean towel around his shoulder and upper arm. She closed this tightly with tape.

"I need a drink," she announced as she stood up.

"So do I," he said. She stopped and looked back at him. He smiled at her. "You did a good job. Thank you."

She brought back two glasses and a bottle of cognac.

He raised his glass in a toast. "Here's to you. Florence Nightingale."

Christina looked confused.

"The woman who tended the wounded in the Crimean War. She founded modern nursing."

Christina took a deep drink and shuddered. "I'm no nurse."

She put her glass down and looked at the man.

"If I'm going to let you stay for a while...to heal...I can't call you 'man' or 'stranger'." She paused for a moment and thought. Then her face lit up. "I'll call you 'Rossignol' since you mentioned the nurse. It's French for nightingale. You also came to me in the night so it fits."

"I came in the night and in a gale. You made a pun in English. That's very clever of you." He smiled now. His smile lit up his face and took away some of the fierceness of his gaze.

"It also can mean 'picklock'. Don't try to emulate that part of the meaning since I'm trusting you in my house."

Christina gave up any thoughts of practice as they made small talk and basked in the momentary glow of the brandy and their successful operation.

Chapter 6

They sat in the kitchen with the sun shining through the south-facing windows. They could both feel the warmth it brought, even with the wind roaring outside. Christina watched this stranger—Rossignol, as she had named him. He was polite. She couldn't help but notice he was good looking even with his wounds. She wondered at his past and what events had occurred, for his body to show so many scars.

The rational part of her, the one which usually predominated in her life, told her to send this stranger away. But she saw how injured he was. She had seen how pain attacked him. It was something beyond his physical injuries. And where would he go? He would be vulnerable and, if he were telling the truth, easily captured by the men from whom he had escaped. Against the part of her that was shouting to send him away, a quiet part said that she should not do this. It would be wrong. Her routine was not so sacrosanct, so important, that she should turn away someone in such need.

Where would things lead if she allowed him to remain? She didn't know, but consoled herself with the thought that he would just be staying a few days perhaps a week. And his memory would return, or he would figure out how he was going to live without it. That was his burden. Then he would depart and her life could go back to its routine again.

She made up her mind.

"You can stay. I have a spare bedroom. But you must not interfere with my practice routine. It is important."

His face broke out in a broad smile. "You are kind...and I am grateful. I have a strong sense that this is a safe place. I have not been in a safe place for some time. I'll try to make myself useful and stay out of your way."

"Staying out of my way is most important. I don't know how useful you can be in your state."

"The soup you served me, it's called *soupe au pistou*, is it not? A bean and vegetable mix, like minestrone?"

"Yes. How do you know this?"

"I don't know, but I think I know something about food, about cooking. Perhaps I can cook for you."

"We'll see. Let me show you to your room. You should rest and I need to clean up the kitchen and living room and practice some more."

Nikolai and Maxim went back to their overturned car after abandoning their pursuit of the captive. They called a tow truck which righted their car and then retraced their route. It was dark now. They stopped at the first village they came to, figuring this was the most likely place to hear of a confused stranger being discovered, assuming their captive had survived the night.

They had held him for weeks in a small hideout in Marseille. Repeated interrogation along with beatings had not delivered the information they were seeking. They knew he was an assassin, probably working freelance. He had been involved in the Milan shootout, where he had been captured.

After the debacle in Milan, they had fled to Marseille with their captive. The Italian police were swarming all over northern Italy in the wake of the killings. Their boss, Yevgeni Kuznetsov, was head of a Russian mafia gang. His son had been killed in the Milan gunfight and Yevgeni was sure this assassin was responsible.

What the two soldiers of Kuznetsov's gang needed to find out, and what their boss wanted to know, was the identity of the little man with the briefcase. The nondescript man held one of the most mobile and lethal weapons in the world in his possession. He seemed to have scurried away when the deal blew up. After getting that information out of their captive, they were to kill him, slowly and painfully.

They took their captive to a rented house in the suburbs of Marseille and began to work on him.

"We must try the drugs," Maxim said.

"They're dangerous to use. They could destroy his mind," Nikolai said.

"You worry about his mind? We're going to kill him."

"I don't want to ruin it. If we do, we never get the information."

"We aren't getting it now. We may kill him with these beatings before we do."

Nikolai looked thoughtful. "Maybe he doesn't know what happened to *malen'kaya mysh'*, our little mouse."

Maxim let out a harsh laugh. "That would be convenient, my friend. He knew about the transfer. He was there."

"So were the others, those damned Chechens."

"Zhenya will take care of them. We are to take care of this American."

The car was damaged but drivable. When they reached the closest village, Nikolai and Maxim rented a room in a *maisonette.* It was a small establishment near the center of the village with eight rooms to let. There they would wait for word of the missing man.

"When we get him back, we take him to Kuznetsov. Then he can do what he wants," Maxim's voice was harsh. He wanted to be done with this man and let his boss handle him. He was also fearful of any fallout from their lack of success.

The man ended his reverie. Christina finished the étude she was playing. No matter how many times he went over what he could remember, he could only recount the events from the ride in the car, just before the crash up to the present. When his mind was free from the vise of pain, he would go over it again and again, trying to reach further back, but there was only emptiness—a blank wall he couldn't penetrate.

He slipped back under the covers of the bed. Christina had brought up the down comforter from the living room and he could feel its insulation working to keep his body heat contained. Soon he was drifting off to sleep. The throbbing in his arm began to subside. The soothing sound of the music came up the stairs into his room. He had purposefully left the door open to allow the music in.

Hours later, he awoke. It was getting dark outside. He sat up. A sharp pain shot through his right shoulder when he tried to move his arm. *This will take a while.* He hoped Christina would give him the time to heal. After that, he didn't know. Without a past, he had no direction forward. His mind went over the steps he had to take. *Avoid the two men chasing him. Find a weapon. Find money. Search for someone who could tell him who he was and what he was involved with.* It all seemed too complex. One thing was certain: he did not have an ordinary job nor did he do ordinary things.

He got up and went to the window. He stared out at the property, assessing its defensive possibilities as well as any danger points. He noted the stone wall marking the edge of the open field. He looked at the small barn, which was more like a shed or garage. *Probably yard tools in there, maybe a car.*

Putting on his trousers, he went to the other rooms to assess their views. When he was done, he had a sense of the strengths and weaknesses of the cottage from a defensive perspective; where an aggressor would hide and vulnerable places where one could sneak up on the main building. He didn't know why he did those things, except that it seemed to be important.

The music stopped. He went back to his room and put on his boots. He came downstairs in his pants and shirt. Christina was in the kitchen. The daylight was disappearing and he could feel the chill growing.

"You need a sweater," she announced. "You don't want to wear your coat inside. I have some large sweaters—too large, really. I use them for snuggling on a winter evening. Since I'm actually a bit taller than you, they might fit you fine. A little tight, but they'll keep you warm."

She ran upstairs and returned in a minute with a bulky wool sweater.

"Let me help you," she said. She held it while the man slipped his injured arm through the sleeve, then the other arm, and then she gently pulled it over his head. Their bodies bumped together in the process. She could smell his scent, not unpleasant, but strong. She stepped back.

"That should be warmer."

He looked at her for a moment, then said, "Thank you."

She felt her face grow hot with a blush.

"I'm making a *Brandade De Morue*. Do you know of it?"

He thought for a moment. "Cod and potatoes?"

"Correct. So, you can remember some things."

"I'd let go of all my food memories if I could remember *who* I am."

"Perhaps that will come, as you heal."

She began to prepare the meal and the man helped as he saw a need and as she allowed. She could tell he knew his way around a kitchen and cooking. When they had finished, they went into the living room with glasses of wine. Christina relit the fire which she had allowed to die out earlier in the afternoon. The large stones, heated over the previous night and through much of the day, still radiated their stored energy into the room. The steam radiators clanked as they performed their duty directed by the thermostat. The noise they made when heating had shocked the man at first. Now he relaxed in the cozy ambience the room projected, the radiator's clanking offering only the promise of warmth.

"What will you do when you leave?"

He looked at her, concern now replacing his relaxed countenance.

"I'm not hurrying you out. I mean after you're healed."

"I don't know. If I don't know who I am, I can't figure a way forward. I know I must have gotten involved with something bad to wind up with those two men after me."

"You seem too polite to be a bad person. People can't hide their natures, especially if they don't know what they're hiding."

"I'm glad you don't think I'm a bad person. I'm not sure how I would know."

"Well, you don't think about doing bad things, do you?"

He shook his head. "I don't think about much except to keep trying to recall something that will give me a clue to my identity."

Christina clapped her hands. "I didn't think to ask, or check. Do you have any ID on you?"

"I'm sorry. I already looked earlier, when I went upstairs to lie down. Nothing."

She finished her glass of wine and got up. "I've got to practice a new piece for a little while. I've gotten behind on my schedule. You should try to get some sleep. I'll close the door to the music room and if you close your bedroom door, you may not hear me."

"I'd like to hear you. It seems to help me. I get terrible headaches. I was having them even before escaping. My head feels like it's in a vise, being squeezed. I think your playing soothes my head."

"If you think it helps, I'll leave the door open."

She got up and went to her piano. The man got up and took the glasses into the kitchen. He began to clean up with one arm as best he could as the music started. Then he went upstairs to his room and lay down to listen.

This playing was different. He could tell she was playing passages, parts of a larger piece over and over. It didn't bore him or make him frustrated to listen. Instead he tried to submerge himself in what he was hearing. He listened for the differences. Why she played a section repeatedly? What was she looking for? His mind tried to engage in the process that was going on. And slowly he relaxed and fell asleep.

Chapter 7

Roman Pavlovich stood outside of his car. He was nervous. He had just arrived and exited the vehicle. Now, standing there, with his briefcase, all alone, he began to doubt the wisdom of his actions.

He was in the courtyard of an abandoned factory. It was along *Via Achille Grandi*, which was not very grand and didn't go anywhere. The complex was located off the SP14, a four-lane roadway leading out from downtown Milan through the industrial area.

A man had approached with another briefcase, which Pavlovich expected to be full of money. They would exchange briefcases and Pavlovich would walk away with five million Euros. He started to imagine, again, the sun-soaked beaches, the women.

The man approaching him was large. That gave Roman some concern. But he trusted they would abide by the deal. The money was small change to acquire such a massively lethal weapon. The man stopped two paces away and opened his briefcase to give Pavlovich a view. In it was neat stacks of one-hundred euros. Roman had already figured out how many it would take to make up five million. A 100-euro note was .11mm thick. There were 50,000 of them in five million, so they would total 5,500 mm when stacked. That would result in eighteen stacks of notes, 300 mm high or roughly one foot. He tentatively reached out to the briefcase. There were eighteen stacks. He fanned a bound stack at random. There was no blank filler paper.

The man's dark eyes bore into him. Roman started to sweat. The man nodded, indicating Roman should open his case. He set it on the ground and took out a key. The case was made of aluminum with a sturdy lock. He turned the key and lifted the case back up, opening the lid to show the man its contents. There were three stainless steel canisters inside. They had lead seals attached to wires that ran through the lids. The lid could not come off without breaking the lead seal. On the side of the canisters was the symbol for bio-hazard. The man nodded and indicated for him to close the case.

When it had clicked shut, the man stepped forward and grabbed Roman by the neck with a huge hand. The hand squeezed his neck but stopped short of choking his air off completely. Roman tried to step back but couldn't move against the man's powerful grip. The man pulled Roman forward and started to drag him and the metal case back to the warehouse from where he had emerged.

A shot rang out and the large Russian's head opened up. He fell backwards to the ground. The hand gripping Roman went limp. More shooting erupted. Roman dropped to the pavement, clutching the briefcase as the shots flew overhead. Soon men were dashing across the courtyard. Roman began to crawl while the battle raged over his head. When he reached a wall, he slithered around it and began to run. A stray shot flew past him and he turned a corner.

A man shouted for him to stop. It only spurred him forward. He had a sense that no one wanted to hit the briefcase, which he kept clutched to his chest. The adrenalin propelled him far beyond what his body would normally be capable of. He sprinted across the broken pavement of the parking lot, past a half-drained settlement pond, through a field of scrub vegetation and into the cover of some trees.

He only stopped for a few breaths and then started again. He ran across grass fields now, throwing himself over fences. Then he headed south, back towards the highway. He crossed the road and slid down the grassy berm onto the feeder road, *Via Rivoltana*. No cars were coming. He kept running away from direction of the shooting. Whoever survived would come looking. They would be in cars. He couldn't outrun them. Ahead there was a culvert, a drainage ditch. It went into a pipe to cross under the divided highway, but it also went in the opposite direction, underground in a pipe, deep beneath some warehouses. Who knew how long it was and where it came out?

Roman took deep breath and entered the dark pipe.

Sometime after the Milan episode, Bulat Zakayev's phone rang.

"*Da.*" The man spoke in a thick, husky voice.

"Do you have the briefcase?" This voice spoke in cultured English with a hint of a British accent.

Bulat, the Chechen arms merchant, knew he was speaking to Rashid al-Din Said. Said was a billionaire Saudi merchant. He kept his hands clean but was able to cause large sums of money to flow where he wanted. In this case, he had fronted Zakayev a considerably large sum of money, two million dollars, to capture the briefcase for him. When delivered, the package would be worth an additional eight million.

"*Nyet*. The mouse slipped away. But we will find him."

"The buy was set up. The man was going to meet with Kuznetsov to make the sale and you were to jump in and take the package. You had enough men to make this happen. What went wrong? I only get confused information from the *polizia* and press."

"We are on your secure phone?"

"Of course. Do not change the subject. I have spent two million dollars. That is enough for me to know exactly what is going on."

"The exchange was taking place. We were ready. Then one of Kuznetsov's men grabbed the mouse and started to take him with them. Someone, I don't know who, shot, and killed the man. There were other shots. My men opened fire. We didn't target the mouse. He had the briefcase. No one wanted to puncture it and release its contents."

"Then the gunfight started?"

"*Da*. It was bloody. My men charged, trying to get to the briefcase. Many were killed."

"And the man escaped...with the briefcase."

"*Samom dele*, indeed."

There was a sigh on the other end. "Your men didn't shoot first? They hate Kuznetsov."

"No. They were disciplined. Lecha Maskhadov would like nothing less than to kill Russians, but he understood the larger prize—a chance to wage war on another level. It was a third party. Only one person as far as we can tell, but we don't know who."

"Do you know who the man with the briefcase is?"

"*Da*. Roman Pavlovich. He was an invisible bureaucrat in the Soviet era. He was assigned to catalog weapons after the breakup. Looks like he found the briefcase and stole it. It was easy. He just wouldn't catalog it and no one would even know it existed."

Zakayev paused. It sounded like he was taking a long pull on a cigarette. "He sat on it for a long time. The danger comes when one has to reach out. One has to connect with people to sell, to turn the briefcase into money. That's what he discovered."

"So, he'll hide again."

"He will hide. But now others will look for him. Us, Kuznetsov, Interpol, and who knows what other agencies."

"Then you must find it first. Does anyone but you and Kuznetsov know the contents of the briefcase?" Rashid was concerned as to how big the search would get. He couldn't operate if too many agencies were also out looking for this man.

"Who knows? But they're not fools. They know something important was going on to cause such a killing."

"Can this be traced back to you?" It was a loaded question. Rashid was not above cutting ties and retreating if his connection was compromised. He'd done it before. He would find another group to search for the briefcase.

He could almost hear Zakayev shaking his head. "*Nyet, nyet*. They will think it was a battle between two factions of Russian mafia, maybe over drugs. They will not have the sense to figure out that Chechens were involved. None of the dead we left behind can be linked to me."

"But maybe Lecha? I assume they were all from his clan?"

Bulat did not answer.

For now, Rashid would not worry about him. He was a layer of insulation between the Chechen mobsters and himself. They were coarse, profane, and not very subtle. But Bulat understood jihad and the need for weapons. He could be relied upon to be effective, even if those he used were not very delicate or stealthy. He would wait for now and let Bulat Zakayev try to find this man.

"So, you will find him? He is an amateur, after all."

"He is an inconspicuous, little man. A government worker, used to keeping his head down. They make a fine art out of being unseen, unnoticed. While many look for him, he will know how to remain inconspicuous. It will not be easy, but we will find him...and the briefcase."

"See that you do. I paid you two million and have gotten nothing so far. The briefcase is now more out of my grasp than before I paid you all that money."

"You will get your money's worth. Remember, I lost good men in this process. Their brothers and cousins want to know why and what I'm going to do about it. Blood is serious to us Chechens."

Chapter 8

The next day, Rossignol awoke. The pain in his head threatened to explode. He lay still, not wanting to trigger the eruption. He could hear Christina in the kitchen. Soon the smell of coffee and eggs reached him. His stomach responded with some growls telling him to get up. He moved carefully, getting dressed and headed downstairs.

"You're up," she said with a bright smile. The morning sun backlit her face and hair, causing a halo to surround her countenance.

"Yes," he said.

He moved carefully towards the table.

"You are still in pain?"

"My head. I don't want that pain to start again. It's almost too much to bear. The other injuries are not so difficult for me."

She frowned. "Do you know what causes the pain, the headaches?"

"No." He refrained from shaking his head.

Christina went back to the stove. "Sit down, I'll bring you some eggs and coffee."

After eating, the man felt better. There was a knock on the door. It startled both of them.

"Are you expecting someone?" the man asked.

"*Non.* Few come to visit. That's what I like about it here." She stood up. "Go upstairs. I will answer the door."

The man went to the staircase and waited. He was out of sight, but wanted to listen to the conversation.

Christina opened the door. Standing there was Émile Geroux, Christina's neighbor. He lived with his wife, Henrietta, a half mile away by the country lane and many fields apart. He felt a fatherly sense of duty to check on Christina since they had become neighbors. In addition, they shared a business relationship whereby she leased her fields to him to plant a vineyard. After the harvest and winemaking, Émile shared the fruits of his labor with her, keeping her in a good quantity of decent, if immature, local wine—mostly rosés and reds with a few bottles of white.

"Christina, *Je suis désolé de vous déranger*, I'm sorry to bother you, but there was a disturbance the other night and I wanted to make sure you were okay, *da'accord?*"

"What happened?"

"Someone stole a blanket from Jacques Bisset's barn. I think he was in my yard as well. The dog barked and I stepped out and saw a figure running into the woods. Yesterday I went out and tried to see if there was a trail to follow. I came across Jacques's blanket on the far side of the stone wall across your field. I was worried that whoever stole the blanket may have come here. Henrietta insisted I come by to check on you."

Christina smiled. "I'm fine. I didn't hear anyone. Between the wind and my playing, I doubt I would have heard any disturbance. But thank you for checking on me."

Émile sniffed the air. "Ah you have made a fine aroma in the kitchen. Eggs and coffee." He shrugged his shoulders as if to indicate that it was cold and he could use some sustenance before beginning his trek back home."

"Would you like a cup of coffee before you head back home?"

He smiled broadly. "*Oui, merci.*" And he stepped inside as Christina stepped back.

They walked into the kitchen. Christina noted with some alarm the two empty, but obviously used, plates sitting on the counter. She quickly stepped in front of them and put them into the sink. Then she got a fresh plate and served up a scoop of eggs from the pan along with a large mug of coffee.

Émile dug into the food with relish and then took large sips of the hot, rich coffee.

"Ah, Christina, you are a good cook as well as a great musician and beauty. Any man would be overjoyed to have you for his wife. I am always surprised that there are not lines of men along your driveway, waiting for an audience with you."

Christina gave a light laugh. "You know the answer to that. It is precisely why I live here, to avoid such scenes. I have no time for marriage and do *not* want to be tied to a man."

"So, we are the beneficiaries. We get to visit your beauty, your music, and," he raised an empty fork, "your cooking." Then he frowned. "But it is so sad for the men in the world."

"Émile, you are a rogue. A nice one to be sure. I appreciate your concern and help, but I will handle my personal life on my own."

She gave him a large smile which he reflected back to her.

"Now, I must practice. I have much work to do."

"Ah *oui*. Always the practice. You sacrifice much for your music." He stood up and started for the door. "Make sure you lock the door each night."

Christina followed him to the entrance.

"Are the police looking for him? Did Jacques report anything?"

"*Non*. The police can't do anything. We watch out for ourselves."

"I'll be careful." She closed the door after him and leaned against it.

The man came into the hall. "No one called the police. That's good."

She nodded and looked up at him. "I don't like keeping secrets, especially from good people like Émile." She started for the music room. "And you have a lot of secrets. I'm going to practice. You should lie down and rest. You need to heal."

Three weeks later, Rossignol sat on his bed listening to the Chopin Étude. The music coming up the stairs, continued to soothe his headaches, like a healing balm spread over his wounds. His reveries still only went back to the car, the accident on the icy road and the event that triggered his escape and his flight to this sanctuary.

Christina, in spite of her pronouncement that he had to go in a week, had not sent him away. She could see the healing that still needed to be done. As his shoulder healed, he became more helpful, cooking and cleaning and, tending to the fire when she asked for it. He even fixed some leaks around her windows making the cottage less drafty.

He took to sitting in on some of her practice sessions—something she was not sure about at first. But he was an attentive audience, especially when she was playing whole pieces, whether études or working on upcoming concert music.

He began to ask why she played certain pieces the way she did. She showed him how to look at the music and the dynamics. Without his knowing how to read music, or play the piano, she discovered that he could follow a score from listening, relating what he heard to the notes written on the pages. He got lost often, at first, but soon he was able to follow along without missing a measure. It surprised her that his ear could connect what he heard to what he saw on the page, especially since it must have seemed to him to be a foreign language.

"How do you connect so well? You can't actually read the music."

"You've shown me how the notes work together, the half steps, whole steps and larger jumps, the timing of the notes. I can see how two notes together, a whole or half step apart, will sound dissonant. I can understand and hear. If they are thirds or higher apart, you get harmony. It sounds pleasant to the ear."

"But I play so many notes."

"And I can't follow them exactly, but I know that when I see a storm of notes on the page, I will hear that storm. And you showed me the way to tell how fast or slow it is. I'm just going along for the ride when you get going."

She laughed. "I've never heard one describe listening as 'going on a ride'."

"But it is in a way. I'm the one riding—the listener. You—the player—are the one driving the car, or the piano in this case."

That night they sat at the kitchen table. A particularly strong mistral had blown itself out over the past three days and the night was quiet and still.

Christina looked at the table top. The conversation had died down to mirror the quiet of the night. Rossignol seemed to savor the peacefulness. Christina was reluctant, but she knew they had to discuss his stay with her. A routine had been established. She had found herself comfortable with his presence. He was helpful, unobtrusive when she needed privacy, and an ardent listener to her music with astonishingly insightful questions about the profession of music at the level she played. She had begun to enjoy his presence and that bothered her. Part of her wanted to go back to her solitary existence but part of her enjoyed him being there, in different ways.

His presence had been disclosed to Émile. The man had a nose for investigation and it had become increasingly hard to keep Rossignol hidden. After some discussion Émile had accepted the man's presence. He had acted like a concerned father, looking out for the welfare of his precious daughter.

Rossignol convinced Émile that he had no bad intentions. The presence of two unsavory Russians in the local village convinced Émile that Rossignol was telling the truth and that he was probably one of the good guys, since the Russians were obviously not.

"Why do we not go to the police?" he had asked.

"I can't. I don't know who I am. There are bad people out there looking for me. I have to recover my memory so that I know what I'm up against."

"And if you don't?"

Rossignol looked at him with fierce eyes. "If I don't, then I doubt I'll survive for very long."

In the end, Émile, gave his blessing and agreed that he and Henrietta would keep Christina's secret. No one was talking to the Russians and Émile had the feeling they would soon leave as the locals became more questioning of their presence.

"Christina's safety is paramount," Émile said grandly. "When the men leave, it will be safer and you will have time to find your memories. But," he wagged a finger at the man, "when she says you must go, you must do as she says. *Comprenez vous*?

Rossignol, nodded.

Chapter 9

A month had gone by since his conversation with Émile. He and Christina had settled into a comfortable routine. He was finding ways to be ever more helpful. He kept the cottage clean and repaired things as they broke. He would call on Émile when there were larger problems.

The steam heat sometimes became reluctant to perform. Rossignol would go to Émile and bring him back. Émile would take the lead with Rossignol becoming the assistant. Much sweating and cursing would occur but Émile always managed to get the problem solved, with at least a band-aid applied, if not the ill cured.

It started innocently enough. Rossignol would massage Christina's neck and shoulders after hours of practicing. He knew how to knead the tightness out of her muscles. From watching her, he could see that she had some issues with her hands as well. Arthritis would be crippling for a concert pianist. She had to be too young for that, yet how she held her hands and rubbed them together worried him. It also struck him as odd that he was worried.

One night after they had eaten, Christina was on the couch with a glass of fresh red from Émile's grape harvest. It was full and fruity, but not harsh. Not what would be called a great wine, but an honest one. Rossignol sat down at the other end of the couch. Christina had taken off her shoes and now put her feet in his lap.

Without a word between them, he began to massage her feet through the soft wool socks. She let out a sigh and sipped her wine. He slowly began to work his fingers deeper into her soles, touching and triggering all the stress points in her feet. After a while he slid off her socks and continued with his hands in direct contact with her skin.

Christina felt a sense of relaxation flow over her. Tension began to drain from her body. She was amazed at how massaging her feet could have such a soothing effect on all her stress. A warmth began to spread over her, rising in her abdomen and flowing out through her body.

I should not let this go on. Part of her wanted to step back. This seemed too intimate even though he was only touching her feet. The other part of her insisted on enjoying the feeling without worrying about where it might lead.

He switched from one foot to the other and back. Then he gently moved up and began kneading her calves. A tingle spread through her body, now more centered in her mid-section. She knew this. A sexual arousal. Her breathing intensified. She hoped it wouldn't give away her growing excitement.

While he did not go above her knee, Christina wasn't sure if she would have stopped him. When he did stop, he kissed the instep of her foot. She opened her eyes and looked at him. He was staring at her, intensely but not in a harsh manner. He lifted her legs and slid towards her.

"Let me have your hand." His voice was quiet but firm.

She reached out her left hand and he began to gently massage it, working his way around her palm and then beginning down each finger. He wrapped a strong hand around each finger and gently squeezed as he slid downward, as if milking a cow, pulling all the tension out to the tips and away.

When he was done, he switched hands and began again. The intimacy of it struck Christina. Their hands so closely connected. It was almost as if she were coupling with him in a bed. Her breath came in increasingly strong gasps. When he was done, he looked again at her. Without thinking she reached up and took his face in her hands and pulled him close. They kissed. Softly at first, then with more intensity. He lurched forward to loom over her. When they broke, she lay back panting.

"We should stop," she declared. Her protective instincts reasserted themselves against the passion of the moment.

He looked calmly at her and then nodded. Without a word, he sat back down at the end of the couch.

"I don't know if we should go further," Christina said. Her words sounded weak, evasive. "I still don't know you. You don't know who you are. Maybe we should wait until your memory recovers."

He sat quiet for a long time.

"I'm much better now. Should I leave?"

"No, no," she said with concern in her voice.

She sat upright.

"I like having you around. I just think we should not go too fast. This is all new for me."

"For me as well." He turned to look at her. "With no memory, almost everything I do is new." He smiled.

"For someone who got caught up with bad people, you are a sweet man."

"Thank you for that. And thank you for not sending me away. My headaches are fewer now. I know it's due to your playing. It's healing me. I think I'm your biggest fan."

"My secret fan." She got up and went into the kitchen to pour herself another glass of wine.

The next day Christina announced that her secretary and scheduler, Chloé Bergman, was coming to visit.

"I put her off as long as I could, but she insists. And she is right. We have much to work on for the next year." She looked Rossignol in the eyes. "I cannot keep you a secret from her any longer. She'll not be amused and you may have a hard time winning her over, but you must try. I can't have such conflict in my life."

"I should go, then."

Christina shook her head. “I don’t want you to go. But I want Chloé to understand why you’re here. She’s important to me.” She paused. “And you, oddly enough, are becoming important to me. I know that sounds crazy, but I have to admit it.”

He stared at her without speaking.

“You have nothing to say? A woman says you’re important to her and you just sit there?”

“I’m stunned. You are overwhelmingly important to me. You saved my life. Your music is healing my brain.” His face now took on a look of great concern. “You are the most important thing in my life. With my memory gone, I don’t know anyone else except you and Émile. And being here seems to be the best way to regain it.”

He reached across the kitchen table and took her hands in his.

“Whatever I was out there in the world, I’m safe from it here. Here I can be healed, be your audience, learn from you, and, I hope, give you something in return.”

“And someday you will leave.”

“Someday you will probably make me leave. I may not want to go until you do.”

He smiled.

“I remember Émile’s edict. To leave when you say to go.”

Chapter 10

Two days later a car pulled into the driveway on a crisp, cold but sunny day. Rossignol was up in his bedroom; Christina was in the music room. The woman got out and grabbed her briefcase and suitcase from the trunk. She made her way to the door with the bags and a portfolio stuck under one arm. After fumbling with the door, she burst into the cottage.

"Christina, I'm here," she announced in a loud voice.

She entered the living room and dropped her assembled baggage on the floor as Christina came out of the music room.

"There you are," Chloé Bergman said.

"Chloé," Christina said as she kissed the woman's cheeks. "How was your drive?"

"The same as always, long. But at least the weather was clear."

"Shall I make you a cup of tea?"

"My usual, thank you."

They both went into the kitchen. Chloé put her briefcase on the table and began to spread out some papers.

"Relax from your trip," Christina said. "You just got here and I still need to practice."

"I know you do," Chloé replied as she shuffled papers on the table, "but we have much to do. You've been avoiding me and now we're behind in scheduling."

Christina brought over two cups of tea. Chloé poured two heaping spoonsful of sugar into her cup and went back to her papers.

"We have to nail down the travel details for the Buenos Aires and Rio concerts. Then there's next year's schedule. I'm still trying to line up a Paris concert. It will be such a hit. The papers all talk about you and where you hide out. Many guess it's somewhere in France which only increases the French public's interest. We have to capitalize on that. Then there's America. I think this next year you should go. And we've got to decide on London, Barcelona, Budapest, Vienna, Berlin, and Milan. Venice would also be a good venue for you. More intimate."

"Chloé, slow down. You make me dizzy. Did you remember that I want to stop in Asunción when we're in Argentina? I want to hear one of the works of Flores...one of his *symphonic guarania* pieces."

"There's so little time, but I'm working on it. Now about the travel..." Chloé stopped as her eye caught sight of the man standing in the doorway of the kitchen.

"Hello, who's this?"

Chloé turned to look at Christina.

"Are you going to introduce me to this stranger?"

She began to restack her papers, her tea now ignored, glancing alternately at Christina and the man standing in her cottage.

"You're not alone? Christina, what's going on?"

"I'll tell you if you give me a moment," Christina replied.

"This is Rossignol. It's the name I've given him, "Nightingale. Rossignol," she gestured towards Chloé, "this is Chloé. She is my assistant and secretary...and friend."

The man dipped his head. "How do you do?"

Chloé sat there, her face reflecting something between stunned and confused. Then she turned back to Christina.

"So, tell me."

"Tell you what?"

"Christina." She sounded exasperated. "tell me who is this man and why is he here? You said you call him Rossignol. Is that his first or last name?"

"I said it's the name I've given him."

"*You've* given him? What the hell does that mean?"

"I don't know my name," the man said.

"Don't interrupt," she snapped. Then she turned back to look at the man, "What? You don't know your name?"

Chloé looked back and forth between Christina and the stranger.

"Christina," she began now in a calmer voice, "you moved here to be alone. Now there's a stranger in your house and he says he doesn't know his name. So, you name him. This doesn't make sense. How long has he been here? Is this why you've been avoiding me?"

Christina motioned to Rossignol to come in and sit down.

"Let me tell you what has happened," Christina said.

"Please do," Chloé said in a not-too-friendly voice.

Christina recounted the recent events to Chloé. She told her of his lack of memory, how he had fled his captors, and how he needed time to heal and recover.

"You really don't know who you are?" Chloé asked, turning to the man.

He gently shook his head, all the while staring at Chloé with his piercing gaze. "I can go back to being in the car and then there's just a black wall."

"From what Christina said, it sounds like the men who held you captive were criminals. That makes you suspect of being a criminal."

She turned back to Christina. "Can we talk in private?"

Rossignol stood up. "I'll leave you two alone." He grabbed his coat in the hall and went outside for a walk.

Chloé leaned towards Christina after he closed the door. "You can't let him stay here. This could be dangerous for you, personally...and it could ruin your career. How would it look if it came out that you were hiding a fugitive from justice, some major criminal? I can just imagine the cancellations in bookings."

"No one knows he's here."

"No one? Émile doesn't know? How did you keep this from him?"

Christina smiled ruefully. "Well...he knows. It's hard to keep anything from him. But he's sworn to secrecy."

Chloé put a hand to her forehead. "Why? Why risk so much? On a stranger no less."

Christina stared at the table for a while, thinking. "He was hurt, like a wounded animal. I couldn't send him away. He's right. If I had called the authorities, they would have locked him up. He doesn't know who he is. Then the men chasing him would have been able to get to him."

"And that's your problem?"

"Chloé, he was so hurt. They hurt him. He needed help."

"He looks okay now. Why don't you send him packing?"

Christina paused.

"Is there something you're not telling me?" Chloé asked.

"He's...he's...nice to have around."

Chloé's face reflected her exasperation with her employer and friend.

"Okay, dear. You are going to have to explain that to me."

Christina toyed with her tea cup.

"He's a good audience. He loves my playing. He says it heals him. He used to get terrible headaches. They would put him on the floor in agony. Now they come less often and are less severe. My music apparently soothes him."

She smiled at her friend.

"There is something else going on as well. He listens so intently. I am actually getting good feedback from him. I didn't expect that, since he's not a musician, but he has an ear. He hears my music the way a musician would hear it. He hears nuances that I'm sometimes not fully aware of."

She paused for a moment, then continued.

"He asks questions that make me think about a piece. He'll point out that in a certain passage I may have missed what the composer was aiming at. He's reading and learning about the composers I'm playing and connecting what he learns about their lives to their music. It's uncanny how insightful he is. I think my practices are getting better with him around."

There was an awkward silence. Then Chloé spoke up.

"Are you...are you two...?"

"Are we lovers? That's a very personal question, don't you think?"

"It's one I think I have a right to ask. I've been with you for six years. I'm totally loyal to you and have busted my butt to help your career advance. We're a team, you and I. I want to know if you're going to throw all that off for...for what? A strange man who doesn't know his name? You sound like the damsel in a romance novel."

"That's not fair. I'm still focused on my music, my career. You're still important to me. We *are* a team. But he's here for now. I don't want to argue with you about it. Maybe in the spring, but I won't send him away in the winter."

Chloé sighed. "Okay. Let's do some work on your upcoming schedule."

Chapter 11

After a week, the two men looking for their escaped captive were feeling distinctly uncomfortable. The *hôtelière* was asking ever more pointed questions about who they were. She was always polite but she dug for information from the unlikely duo staying in her *petit hôtel.* There were questions in the two restaurants gracing the village as well.

"We have to leave. We are attracting too much attention," Nikolai said.

They had reported the escape to their boss, Yevgeni Kuznetsov. He was not happy but accepted the assessment of the two men that the assassin had died in the woods somewhere, his body by now probably eaten by wild boar. He might never be found in the foothills of the *Luberon.*

When Émile heard of their departure, he breathed a sigh of relief. Christina would be safe now. He could see her reluctance to make the stranger leave, especially in the winter. He commiserated with Chloé about her concern regarding Rossignol. She was part of Christina's small support team, something Émile, in his own way, felt he played a role in as well. But he counseled patience. Christina would send the man away in the spring and all would return to normal, as before his intrusion.

After Chloé's visit, the new routine re-established itself in the cottage. Christina would spend the morning practicing with Rossignol listening intently. If he needed to repair something, he would forego the listening for the repair work. They would eat a lunch together and after, if the day was pleasant, would go for a walk. In the afternoon Christina would put in another three to four hours of practice.

She loved the walks. Sometimes they carried-on long conversations. He asked many questions about her life, but there was little he could offer about his own.

"You've been playing the piano since you were four?"

Rossignol sounded amazed that someone could start so young with such a large instrument.

"Yes. And I gave my first public recital concert at twelve. I've been playing professionally for twelve years."

"And all that time, you've been practicing. How many hours do you think you've practiced on the piano?"

She laughed. "I don't think I want to count them."

"And it doesn't get tiring for you? Doing the same thing over and over?"

"It's what I love doing, what I have a gift for—so, no."

Rossignol was quiet as they walked along.

"It's the principle of diminishing returns," he said suddenly.

"What are you talking about?"

"In any endeavor, the more refined one's skills become, the more one gets closer to perfection, the smaller the gains are."

She gave him a confused look.

"When one begins pursuing a skill, one makes gains in large chunks. The curve of the rise in skill over time is quite steep."

"If one has some natural gift in the area one is pursuing."

"Of course. A person could try to learn something for which they have no natural ability. That person would not get far before becoming frustrated, realizing the futility of their efforts. But," he went on, "if one has some skill, that learning curve reflects large gains initially. I think that later in the process, the curve flattens out. You spend more and more time, working on smaller and smaller refinements."

He could see Christina's brow furrow. "I can see that. It's what I've experienced. But how do you know this? Without your memory?"

Rossignol shook his head. "I don't know. The thought—the principle if you will—came to me while I was thinking about the hours of practice you put in. It seemed to make sense to me."

"For someone with no past, you seem to make a lot of sense."

"Something I don't understand though, is how you don't get bored. It seems like you play the same pieces, over and over. And all by mostly-dead composers. It doesn't seem repetitious to you?"

"All those dead composers left us a massive amount of wonderful music, so there is much to explore—a lifetime's worth. And the music is not dead. It lives in each musician who attempts to play the pieces, who puts their stamp on a piece."

"How is that? The pieces are played differently?"

"Of course. The music notation is a guide if you will, a roadmap. It may be more or less detailed according to the composer and his markings and notes. For example, Beethoven, in a sonata he wrote, Opus 110, put a note in one section. It reads, 'little by little returning to life'. Now what does that mean?"

He shrugged. "How would anyone know?"

"Precisely! Some think it means to get louder, some think sharper, or brighter, and some think it means to speed up. The music leaves itself open to interpretation. The music is alive."

"But each musician plays it the same way, for years, don't they?"

"Not necessarily. People change over time. They grow, they develop different perspectives, they mature. All this comes out in our music."

She stopped and turned to him. "Look, even without your memory, you've probably changed. Certainly, our connection has made changes in you. I know it has in me."

Rossignol stared intently at her as they stood in the lane.

"Meeting you, you saving my life, introducing me to your music. That certainly has changed me. I think for the better.

Christina reached up and touched his cheek.

"I think so as well."

He bent down to her and they kissed in the cold, bright day.

The massaging of her feet and hands had become an evening ritual. One night, when he had finished, Christina got up from the couch and reached out her hand to him. After taking his hand, without a word, she led him to her bedroom. They embraced and fell back into the bed. Somewhat awkwardly, each helped the other take off their clothes. He began kissing her face and neck as she lay back. Then he worked his way down to her breasts. Jolts of intense pleasure shot through her body. Her belly tingled in anticipation.

She ran her hands over his muscled torso, touching his wounds, old and new, now without fear. Then she opened herself to him.

"Gentle," she whispered.

He grunted in reply but entered her with care, moving slowly. Christina sighed and pulled him into her, wanting to engulf all of him.

The first episode didn't last long before he exploded inside of her. He lay back, panting, without words. She rolled over to him and kissed his lips, his face, and chest.

"I didn't hurt you, did I?" he asked.

"No. It's just been a long time."

It had been five years since she had given herself to a man. That moment had been the first time for her. A traumatic affair with an older conductor when she was nineteen. It had ended badly with the wife finding out and threatening exposure. He had dropped Christina without warning or hesitation. In her *naïveté* she had thought they were meant for each other and that their affair would somehow become permanent. Shocked and hurt, Christina had closed up and immersed herself in the music. Love and companionship were for others she had concluded. Her music was what mattered. She would dedicate herself to it.

Now this man had come into her life. A wounded soul that needed healing. A stray, Chole would say. Christina smiled at the thought. Still a small voice spoke a warning to her. She was making herself vulnerable. To open her heart meant that her heart could be broken. But it seemed so natural, so right. *And anyway, I'm older now, and not so naïve.*

Later they made love again; this time more slowly with less urgency. Christina felt herself carried away in a climax of physical surging, their two bodies responding to the most primal of urges, and their giving themselves to it without reservation.

Afterward they made themselves something to eat and sat back sipping some of Émile's wine. Little was said. Little needed to be said. Their bodies had directed them and were now quiet, satiated. Their minds held no questions, accepting what they had experienced together without regret.

The winter wound on. Chloé came to a grudging acceptance of Rossignol's presence. She could see how well he treated Christina but still retained the hope that he would be gone in the spring. When Christina and Chloé left for the South American concerts, Rossignol stayed alone in the cottage. Émile would come over and drink the wine he had made. Henrietta took to inviting him over for meals which were a treat for him. Being alone, he often ate improvised, half prepared meals. Henrietta's ample feasts were a great treat and provided him with generous leftovers that he could eat from for two days following.

The hunting season was past, but Rossignol and Émile often tramped through the woods, exercising the dog and enjoying the sharp, winter air. When the mistral blew, everyone huddled inside. Although he did not venture there often, the village had accepted Rossignol. Émile's vouchsafe and his relationship with Christina were enough to win over the villagers. He became, if not a native, less than an outsider.

Chapter 12

Yevgeni Kuznetsov was pleased. One of his men had been contacted by an anonymous source with a message offering to complete the sale of "the item you tried unsuccessfully to acquire." His IT experts could not track the origin of the cleverly masked message. The best they could come up with was that it was sent from a computer in a networking café in Amsterdam. Kuznetsov was sure the computer would no longer be used. He was also sure that his *malen'kaya mysh'*, his little mouse, wanted to try again to sell the briefcase. He only needed to keep those damned Chechens out of the picture and this formidable weapon would be in his possession.

He had no intention of using it. He was not interested in mass murder, a terrorist activity. He was interested in money and power. The briefcase, with its contents, would give him much of that. He would offer it to his government. It would bring much money, far more than the five million he had promised the mouse. And he would be seen as a protector of Russia.

Yevgeni decreed a total blackout on the information. He could not afford to have this next encounter go awry. Once he had the weapon, he could unleash his anger on the Chechen gang.

They were despised by him for good reason. They continually tried to muscle in on his business which consisted of the drug and sex trades as well as legitimate importing and exporting, always, of course, with favorable tariffs. It didn't hurt his profits that many items were smuggled amidst the legal goods. Friendly politicians and authorities, well paid by him, helped smooth his business dealings. As Yevgeni profited, so did they. When the briefcase was in his hands, he would exact his revenge for the Chechen's ambushing the exchange in Milan.

Back in Washington, DC, Jane Tanner, while not losing hope, was frustrated. She had made little progress on finding Dan. The most she had been able to establish was that he had not been killed. Listening in on Kuznetsov had not uncovered any firm clues except that they had captured him and then lost him, somewhere in France. Further investigation had turned up nothing.

Henry, her boss, was impatient. His main concern was the briefcase and the canisters of weaponized anthrax it contained. The thought of multiple containers of the Tier 1 biological agent on the loose gave him fitful nights. Its ease of delivery and the fact that multiple large cities could be hit simultaneously was unnerving. It had caused enough havoc in 2001 when it was sent through the mail. Releasing in the air would be many times more disastrous. Whole populations of the country could be infected and health care facilities overwhelmed. The economic fallout could trigger a recession.

"Who knows how many kilos are in that briefcase," said Henry. "It's probably enough to decimate multiple large cities. It keeps me awake at night."

"Roman Pavlovich. He's the key. He survived the shootout but hasn't been seen or heard from since."

Just then Fred Burke, Jane's research assistant, burst into Henry's office.

"Don't you believe in knocking?" Henry said with some irritation.

"Sorry. Warren, just got something. An email intercepted by the NSA. They passed it over to the agency and Warren picked it up. It originated in Amsterdam and was about trying to complete the sale for something. It said an item, and I quote, 'you tried unsuccessfully to acquire'. That might be our guy."

Henry looked at him. "That's pretty thin. Anything else?"

"We don't know who sent it but we know who received it. It was someone in Kuznetsov's gang."

Henry raised his eyebrows. "That's something. Tell Warren to focus on monitoring everyone we know of who's working for Kuznetsov."

"We don't have the capacity to monitor everyone," Warren replied.

"And we can't go wide on this, even within the agency," Henry said.

"I'll give you a list of the top players," Jane said. Her voice evidenced her frustration, but this was a step forward. Pavlovich probably could only be found when he reached out to try to sell the briefcase.

"He must be getting panicked about holding on to it. I figured he'd go dark for a year at least," she said.

"He knows a lot of people are looking for him," Henry said. "If the Chechens find him, he'll be killed. No big payout and luxury retirement. The briefcase has become as much a danger as an opportunity now. But he's still got to try to monetize it like he planned."

"His problem is he doesn't know how to set up the exchange. He could steal the briefcase and hide it for years, but he has no idea of how to sell it safely," Jane said.

As spring approached, Rossignol began to go for long runs—five to ten miles. These were mixed with aggressive hikes in the mountains. Émile offered his favorite dog so Rossignol could exercise him. Émile was not interested in such intense activity. Soon enough he would be working hard in the fields he owned and leased.

Rossignol didn't have a specific reason for exercising, but deep inside him, he knew that he needed to get his body fit again. *Fit for what?* The question came to mind often, but it didn't deter him from his expanded training routine.

The winter concerts went well, especially in South America. Christina was lauded for her technical brilliance, but still suffered some critical comments regarding her interpretation of pieces. The critics were agreed that she was too cool, her precision not enhanced by enough passion. They stated that more emotion brought to her performances along with her obvious technical skills would bring her playing to a new level. Still they praised her. She was not that upset by these criticisms. She'd heard them for years.

Christina was sitting with Chloé one afternoon in February. They had come back from a performance in Mexico. She had performed a set consisting of a mix of Liszt's Hungarian Rhapsodies and Manuel de Falla dances. The unlikely combination was well received, the Liszt pieces having a slightly similar feel to the de Falla dances. The lack of emotion showed more clearly in the Spanish pieces as the critics had pointed out.

"I wouldn't worry about the reviews," Chloé said.

"That's what you always say, and I don't," Christina replied.

They were sitting in the living room. The fireplace was unlit; not much needed in these late winter days.

"Still I wonder what made you put the de Falla pieces in? You must have known they were outside your comfort zone."

Christina shrugged. "I don't know. I like them and wanted to try something new. It seemed like Mexico City might be the place to see how it would go."

"A sympathetic audience?"

"I guess. The audience seemed to like them, even if the critics were less enthused." She got up from the couch. "Do you want a cup of tea, or some wine?"

"A glass of wine, please."

When Christina came back, Chloé leaned forward to speak.

"Spring is nearly here. Your schedule is going to get very busy. Don't you think it's time to send Rossignol, or whatever his real name is, away?"

Christina stared at her long-time friend over the rim of her glass.

"You still don't like him?"

"I've come to terms with him. I don't dislike him. I can see that he cares much for you and is helpful. But he *is* still a mystery and that worries me."

"He's more than helpful. My practices are getting better with him." She looked away in thought for a moment. "There is something about how he reacts, how he hears my music." She shook her head. "I don't know. He's untutored, but very insightful. He has become my muse in a way."

"But he's not a musician, Christina. Is your sense colored by your affair?"

Christina looked sharply at her friend.

"Don't look at me that way. I can see what's going on. There's an intimacy between the two of you. It's been growing over the winter, slowly, but steadily. I can guess what is driving that. Nothing good can come out of this. He's a mystery man, probably with a bad past."

She looked pleadingly at her friend.

"Chloé," Christina began slowly, "are you jealous?"

Chloé dropped her eyes. "Maybe...a little. It gets very confusing in my mind. I love you. I want the best for you, and I worry this man may not bring that."

Christina reached over and took Chloé's hands in hers. "My dear Chloé. He will never displace you. I value your love, your friendship, your loyalty. But he brings something new, something different and I'm getting inspiration from the relationship."

"But it can't go on...can it? You *will* send him away this spring? Like you promised?"

Christina released Chloé's hands. "First, I never promised you that. You promised yourself that. Second, I'm not sure I'm ready. We'll be away a great deal of the time, so he won't be around so much. Let's see how it goes."

Chapter 13

Christina did not tell Rossignol to leave when spring arrived. He was now strong and energetic. His headaches came less frequently. He still didn't know who he was but the veil seemed to be lifting. He remembered being held captive in Marseille, but not why or where. From some intense conversations with Émile, Rossignol had come to the conclusion that he had been given drugs to pry a secret from him; something he couldn't remember. These were details he didn't want to discuss with Christina,

Chloé visited every couple of weeks to work on scheduling and logistics with Christina. Much of the work could have been done over the phone, but Rossignol guessed she wanted to keep checking up on him and his relationship with Christina. Chloé seemed to accept their situation with a modicum of good grace, while retaining her reservations.

Rossignol seemed to be preparing for something, but when Christina asked, he couldn't say what it was.

"Are you getting ready to leave?" she asked him one day.

"No, why do you ask?"

"You exercise like you're preparing for a contest, some kind of event. You run, you hike, you do hours of calisthenics. It doesn't seem normal. You're getting to an extreme level of fitness."

"Maybe I'm inspired by your dedication to your art, your practice routine. I don't play an instrument, I don't paint, but I seem to be experienced in fitness. Maybe I had a fitness background. Maybe I was an athlete." He smiled.

"Don't toy with me. There's definitely something serious about your routine. It's more than just wanting to get in shape and recover from your injuries."

Rossignol looked thoughtful. "You're right. I feel a compulsion. Maybe it's the result of being held captive, being hurt. I want to make myself stronger so that doesn't happen again."

"But you don't want to leave?"

He shook his head.

"You're not bored with this simple life? Watching me practice, go off to concerts while you stay here? Émile's company cannot be too stimulating for you."

"I don't get bored. I miss you when you're away, but I am never bored with you around, even when you practice hours a day. I enjoy it."

Later that week, Christina went to Vachères. Rossignol would accompany her occasionally, but they both felt it best to not have him be seen too much in the village. As much as the people supported her and kept her presence to themselves, tongues liked to wag, and her having a man with her, was much too juicy a piece of gossip for the locals not to discuss. Within the town it was fine, but talking with friends and relatives outside of the village could spread the knowledge of this stranger and bring the wrong attention.

The day was still chilly, around fifty degrees, but the sun was bright and the mistral was not blowing for the moment. As she walked past the larger restaurant in the village, she noticed a priest, staring at her. He stood across the street, in front of the small church. His purple shirt, under his jacket indicated that he was more than a priest. *A Monseigneur?* One didn't often see bishops in the village. The parish was small and the priest old. It seemed as though he was posted here as part of a retirement plan.

Still, she guessed, bishops had to check up on their parishes once in a while.

His stare was unnerving. She ducked into the bakery and dropped him from her mind as she delighted in the scent of fresh-baked bread. She purchased two loaves and some croissants, those as a treat, and stepped back outside.

There he was—the bishop. He had crossed the street and now stood in front of her as she left the bakery. He had an intense stare, not completely unlike Rossignol, but darker, more mysterious.

"*Pardonne-moi*," he said in a deep baritone voice. "I apologize for interrupting your shopping."

Christina stared at him. She waited for him to continue.

"You are the pianist, are you not? The one Father Lucien told me about."

"I play the piano, if that is what you mean. But why would the Father talk about me?" Some concern came into her voice.

"I asked him who was the concert pianist that lived nearby. He told me it was you and from his description, when I saw you moments ago, I guessed it must be you."

"Why would you ask Father Lucien about a pianist? And how did you know there was a pianist in the village? Maybe lots of people play the piano here. I'm not so special."

The bishop smiled. "I am forgetting my manners. Let me introduce myself. I am Monseigneur Louis-Marie Cochin."

"*Comment allez-vous*, how do you do?" Christina said. She held out her hand, but didn't give the bishop her name.

"I am well, *merci*." He took her hand in his. It was a gentle grasp. "Your name is Christina Aubergh, is it not?"

"How did you know?"

"Father Lucien, again." He smiled at his weak attempt at a joke. The intensity, however, never left his eyes.

"What is it you want?" she asked. Her mind was racing. Why would a Monseigneur be interested in her? Why would he seek out her name?

"If I could have a few moments of your time, *s'il vous pluît*? We can have a cup of coffee perhaps and I will explain."

His dark eyes bore into her in sharp contrast to his mellow voice and words. She nodded and he led them back to the restaurant where they sat at one of the tables back in the corner. When the waiter came, he ordered them two coffees.

"Unless you would prefer tea?"

Christina shook her head.

"*Mademoiselle*, I have been a priest for thirty-five years. I am dedicated to the church and my duties in it. But," he raised a finger, "I discovered in my twenties, shortly after entering the priesthood, that I had a gift. I wrestled with it for many years, first wondering about it, then trying to deny it, thinking it was incompatible with my calling, maybe of the devil. I finally came to accept it for what it was. A gift. Maybe a quirk of nature, maybe from God. I've learned not worry about its origin, but determined to use it for good."

He paused as the waiter returned with two coffees.

"You speak very mysteriously Monseigneur, but what you say doesn't answer my question."

"I will come to that, give me a moment. The background is necessary to understand."

He sipped his coffee.

"What I am about to tell you is known only to me and my confessor. This gift that I have..." he paused. "The best way to describe it is that I can see things most cannot. I, and others like me, sense what is not readily seen."

"You are a fortune teller? You can see the future? Like the gypsies in the marketplace and carnivals?" To Christina that seemed very much incompatible with being a priest, let alone a Monseigneur.

He shook his head. "*Non, non*. I cannot see the future. I can see what is and understand patterns to give me a hint about what might come...but no visions of the future. This sense I have, this gift, indicated that I should come to visit Father Lucien. That there would be a pianist here whom I needed to talk with."

"And that pianist is me? I mean no disrespect, but this is all too fantastical. Father Lucien didn't talk about me at some point earlier?"

He shook his head. "I know it's hard to accept. It took me years and I experienced it."

"Even if I accept what you say, why do you need to see me? To speak with me?"

A kernel of concern began to grow inside of her.

"It is about the man who is staying with you."

A chill now spread from that kernel and flowed through her body.

"Did Father Lucien tell you? Did he put you up to this? My personal life is no concern of his."

"Be calm, *mademoiselle*, Father Lucien did not tell me about the man. I saw that he was here." He paused and pointed to his head. "The gift."

"There are two things of import to tell you. First, this man has a dangerous past. He also has a dangerous future—"

"I thought you couldn't read the future," Christina said in a sharp voice.

"I told you I can see patterns. There are also others like me. We can share things without seeing or speaking to one another."

He paused as the waiter went by.

"The man has lost his memory. He doesn't know who he is. But he will regain it. How or when I don't know. But it will set him on a dangerous journey. One that will take him away from you. That is the other thing I want to tell you. You could be hurt in the process. Not physically, but emotionally. I felt I needed to warn you to guard your heart."

"You do sound like a fortune teller now. All full of generalizations, with no specifics so people can read what they want into your words. How can you do things like this?"

Christina was now getting angry at this man, a high official of the church who came and disturbed her tranquility and spoke like some hustler in a carnival. What did he know? She stood up.

"I don't put much stock in your ramblings. But you have succeeded in disturbing my peace of mind. If that was your intention, you achieved it. But," she pointed her finger at him, her eyes now narrowed in anger, "you should be ashamed."

With that she turned and stomped out of the restaurant.

Monseigneur Louis-Marie Cochin sighed and finished his coffee.

Chapter 14

When Christina got back to the cottage, she was still upset. Rossignol sensed it immediately. "What happened?" he asked.

"Nothing," she answered. She busied herself with putting away the food she had purchased.

"It *is* something. I can sense it."

She finished her task, poured, a glass of wine, and sat down in the kitchen.

"Tell me," he said.

Christina looked at him. There was an innocence about him. His body indicated he had led a violent life and his eyes were those of a hunter, a predator. Yet he was gentle with no guile. She didn't want to break that spell, to ruin it with the words of the Monseigneur. They were words that threatened disruption to the joy she now felt with this man.

She shook her head. "It's nothing. Someone spoke badly to me and it upset me. I must let it go. It is nothing for you to be bothered about."

She finished her wine and got up.

"I have to go practice now for a little while. Can you get something together for dinner later?"

Christina put the Monseigneur's comments and warning behind her. Rossignol was now an ever more important part of her life. Their nights of love making brought great pleasure to her. She often found herself anticipating the evening and their time in bed together, imagining the various delights he would visit upon her. She discovered a strong appetite for the delicious orgasms she experienced. There was an exciting sense of indulgence and guilty pleasure at the gratification she felt from it all. She could tell that she was pleasing Rossignol in turn.

Without discussing it, they would pause in their love making when Chloé came to visit. The cottage was small and lacked a certain amount of privacy.

Christina was sitting in the kitchen one morning after breakfast. The day was going to be warm. They would open the windows after the morning chill had burned off. The wind, which had blown strongly for two days was now gentle.

“This will be a special Provence day,” Christina announced.

“What do you mean?”

“The light. It will be special today. The mistral blows away all the dust and pollen in the air and the light becomes so bright and luminous. It’s as if everything is glowing. I think it’s why van Gogh, Cézanne and the others came here to paint. Not just for the number of sunny days, but for the clarity of the sky and the light.”

“Too bad you have to spend the day practicing. We should take a walk in this special light.”

“Maybe.” She shifted in her chair. “I have to decide on a piece for my Paris concert in September. I have to include it in my practice along with the other pieces I’m preparing.”

“No rest for the weary artist.” He reached over and took her hand. “I noticed something about your playing in the last month.”

She looked at him. He had insights that were unexpected. He noticed things. Often, he would point out where she was being dismissive of a passage. Technically correct, but not treating it with respect, not trying to pull the latent emotion out of the notes. He could hear that in her playing.

"You've been letting more feeling into your pieces. I can hear it. I have no idea how that comes about, the piano being a percussive instrument, but it's there. Do you recognize it?"

Surprise showed on her face. He had heard what she had begun to notice. A subtle change in her playing. Was her style changing, evolving? Was it due to this strange affair of theirs?

"I *have* noticed it. It's nothing intentional, but my style is changing."

"How does that happen?"

"Subtle changes in how the fingers strike the keys, the wrist action, how one's arms come into play...even the torso. Then there's how far into the note one plays—"

"What does that mean?"

"The pressure I use on the keys, how sharply or slowly I strike, how long I hold the key down—how far I play into it. In addition, there is the interplay between the pedals and all of the rest."

He shook his head. "So many variables, so many subtleties. How do you control all of that?"

She smiled. "In this case, it's happening by itself. Something coming out through those variables, maybe giving expression to how I'm changing."

His eyes now fixed her with their intensity. "And how are you changing?"

She stared back at him. Her past instinct of caution raised its head. *Don't show your feelings, don't show you heart.* But it was too late for that. She overrode the voice.

"I don't know...maybe it's our relationship. My world seems brighter—newer now, with you." She paused and smiled coyly with her large, doe-like eyes locking onto his sharp gaze. "Have I given away too much?"

The intensity of the moment crashed like a wave on the shore and was broken. He looked away and smiled. "No, no. I feel the same, except that everything is still new to me. To be here, now with you, in this relationship, compared with my situation that frozen night…it's unbelievable to me. I treasure every moment with you."

He turned back to her.

"And I find I have this enhanced sense—an ability to read others, you, Chloé, even Émile. And then there's your music. How do I understand it so well? How do I follow along with the score? I have no idea of how I acquired this gift. Have I always had it? I don't know how to read music. Who knows if I've spent much time listening to classical music. And yet, here I am, understanding what you play, and more…being able to help you get more emotion, more expression into what you play."

He shook his head.

"This increased sensitivity. Maybe from my amnesia? I wonder sometimes if something changed in my brain."

Christina smiled at him over the table. They joined hands. Her fear, her caution melted away with his declaration.

"I must go practice," she declared, now energized by her renewed confidence in their affair.

"I want to listen," he said getting up with her.

Rossignol faithfully attended Christina's practice sessions. She was working on bringing Beethoven's 5th Concerto, the Emperor, back to performance level, while introducing a new piece, Ravel's Piano Concerto in G Major. Both pieces were challenging and both had achingly beautiful middle sections, the *adagio* or slow part.

"I've shied away from these pieces," she said after one session. They were preparing some food to eat for the evening. "There is so much emotion in them. I've performed the Beethoven and received mixed reviews due to how I handled the middle movement."

"I'm hearing more emotion when you practice. I don't know what it was like before, but it sounds as though you are reaching for the beauty in the pieces. Both bring tears to my eyes sometimes."

She glanced at him, while washing vegetables in the sink.

"I do that?"

He nodded. You don't see me."

Work went on through the spring. Practice for Christina consisted of working with various pieces for upcoming concerts, all in various states of readiness. As a concert approached, she would spend more time on that piece. A few days before, she eased her practice routine and spent most of the reduced time on the soon-to-be-performed piece.

Then Christina would leave, usually with Chloé, bidding Rossignol goodbye, and heading off. If the concert was on the continent, she would be back in a few days. Smaller venues required only a day working with the accompanying orchestra. Larger events would require her to spend two or three days practicing with the musicians.

Little seemed changed in her concerts. Her practices, which had been getting more expressive, had not translated into her playing. She still kept her emotions in check, holding back and allowing her technical brilliance to carry the evening's performance. For the critics it was the typical Aubergh concert, full of technical wonder and precision, but short on emotion.

Spring flowed into summer. The tourists flooded into Provence. Émile griped about the traffic they brought as well as the clutter they represented in the village. His previous year's wine had been sold to the local businesses and they seemed happy with the results of their investment. His complaints about the tourists glossed over the fact that they provided some of the sales stimulus for his winemaking efforts.

Rossignol helped Émile with the preparation of Christina's fields. Émile had added, with her approval, the establishment of asparagus beds. These would be planted but they would provide only a minimal harvest for another two years.

"Investment in the future," he had said, trying his best to look like a wise sage. "One must allow the plants to feed their own root systems. With patience, we will have green and white asparagus. Only the best, for the local chefs. They will come to prize not only Émile's wine, but his produce, as well."

The shared labor was a distraction for Rossignol who had begun to experience some restiveness as his health and strength returned. He expanded his exercising during Christina's absences, doing longer, harder runs, not just on the lanes, but through the woods and hills. He had made a pull-up bar and slant board that augmented his calisthenics.

When she was back at the cottage, they would take up their routine again. His days then were filled with his wonder at her music and the enjoyment they shared in their daily routines together, not to mention their steamy nights of love making—sometimes out in the yard on a blanket, under the stars, during the warm summer nights.

As the summer progressed, Christina's playing opened up emotionally. With Rossignol as her audience, she played ever more expressively. The Ravel piece, Concerto in G Major, was becoming ever more interesting to Rossignol's ear.

"I read that your Paris concert is part of a celebration of Ravel and the eightieth anniversary of this piece. I want to be there for it."

They were sitting in the courtyard of the cottage on a soft summer evening.

"Is it safe? To go out to a big city? Do you think people are still looking for you?"

"I don't know. I think it's safe." He paused for a moment. "Do you not want me to be seen? To remain a secret here?"

"*Non, non,*" she said hurriedly. "I just want you to be safe."

"It will start some gossip, though. Unless I attend anonymously and not be with you. I would do that if it's better, but I'd rather be with you...before and after."

She looked over at him with her large eyes and smiled. "I confess that gives me some worry, but I don't want to hide you." She looked away for a moment. "I'm just not sure how to explain you."

"Maybe don't. Let me be a mystery. It should just increase the public's interest."

"Chloé would probably agree."

She reached over and gave him a kiss.

"I would love to have you with me. We'll make a holiday of it and I'll show you Paris."

"I may have been there before, but it will be all new now, especially with you."

Chapter 15

Yevgeni Kuznetsov was depressed. He knew he wasn't keeping it from his wife, Duscha. They both still mourned the loss of Vasilij, their only son. It had hit Duscha especially hard. The loss burned like a consuming fire between them, taking away their peace.

He generally kept Duscha isolated from his enterprise. It was not her concern. Her name meant 'happy' and he wanted her to be so.

They had a daughter, Nadyuska, who was twelve. Yevgeni wanted to keep her separate from his world of criminal activity. He hoped Duscha would increase the amount of attention she paid to her daughter as a way to overcome her grief.

He kept her in the dark, letting her concentrate on being a good wife, managing their social activities which he did little to involve himself in. She also was adept at spending the money he took in. The loss of their son threatened to undermine this separation he had established. The grief played out. For Yevgeni, it found expression in a cold determination to exact revenge. For Duscha it was expressed in a critique of Yevgeni's work, his gangster life, which had taken their son.

Yevgeni had grown up in the *bratva*, the brotherhood. He had lived in Stalingrad (or Volgograd, as it was now called). His father had left the family and his mother abandoned him early on. He was left to the streets and the *bratva* took him in. They had become his family and had remained so ever since. It was a point Duscha harped on when they fought, accusing him of being more faithful to his brotherhood than his wife and children. It hadn't helped that Vasilij's participation in Yegveni's dealings had resulted in his death.

Yevgeni was a powerfully built man. He stood about five feet ten inches tall with a thick, muscular body. Few would want to take him on, but he went around with even more intimidating bodyguards. He had schemed and fought his way to the top of one of the more powerful gangs in Moscow. They all participated in a loose coalition and generally tried to keep the peace between them, not invading each other's territories or activities.

As critical of his activities as she was, Duscha enjoyed the luxuries his profession provided. They were fabulously wealthy, allowing her to indulge herself in luxuries and even bring Yevgeni to partake of some. He availed himself of the typical luxuries—a mansion outside of Moscow; expensive cars; chauffeurs; nights out at one of his clubs with one of his favorite girls. In this last, he was not so different from other mob bosses. If he were forced to, he had to admit he enjoyed partaking of some of the luxuries Duscha indulged in.

They also owned a dacha outside of Moscow where they both enjoyed spending time. The Russian connection to the soil would come out in Yevgeni then and he'd spend a couple of happy days working in the garden, splitting wood for the fireplace, and generally reconnecting with nature. During his absence a caretaker saw that all remained in order. In the winter, the dacha was generally closed up.

An unusual luxury for Yevgeni was classical music. He could play no instrument and was not cultured in the sense that he had a large grasp of the arts or could pontificate on them among intellectuals. But he had a love for the music, as well as a good, if untutored, ear for it. Of course, being Russian, he favored the Russian composers,

He steeped himself for years in Russian music. There was Mussorgsky (the stately Pictures at an Exhibition) and the incomparable Tchaikovsky with his grand piano concertos, the Nutcracker Suite, and the bombastic 1812 Overture. Rimsky Korsakov was a favorite; his Russian Easter Overture painting a picture of a spring dawn with the melting of winter's frozen grip, a dawn of resurrection in a long, grand crescendo. The piano was Yevgeni's favorite instrument and so Rachmaninoff also claimed a spot in his heart.

But he had enlarged his interest to more modern composers and had discovered Ravel. Not Russian, but so interesting, with his rhythms and nods to jazz music which was in full swing when he had been composing.

Duscha had learned over the years to read her husband's moods. She understood their loss was going to eat at their relationship. As much as she was angry with her *Zhenya's* work, she knew this was who they were, what they were. She decided to take action to break the dark spell that seemed to surround them. One day she made a proposition to her husband, not something she did lightly or often.

"*Zhenya,* I have an idea," she said on one of the rare evenings they were home together. "There is a concert in Paris this fall, honoring Ravel. I know you listen to some of his music. Why don't we go there for a short vacation? We can go to the concert and I can shop for some of the latest fall fashions."

Yevgeni looked at her, almost in wonder. Usually she would just say that she wanted to go to Paris and travel on her own, realizing that he rarely put business aside. But he was depressed. The fact that his men had allowed his son's killer to escape, probably to his death, but nevertheless out of Yevgeni's reach, meant he would not be able to exact his revenge. Maybe Duscha had a good idea, he thought with some surprise.

Taking his feelings of loss out on his men was not helping. And there had been no further contact with Pavlovich who seemed to have gone into hiding. *A frightened cow is afraid of a bush.* It would be good to change his venue, his view. With it might come new perspectives to help net his man with the briefcase, while avoiding the Chechens, whom he knew were still hunting for the *malen'kaya mysh'*.

"Yes, *dorogaya*, my love. Let's do it."

Duscha clapped her hands. "I will plan everything. We will have a wonderful time, you will see."

A wonderful time spending my money, thought Yevgeni, but he only smiled.

Concerts came and went. The Ravel celebration in Paris grew closer. Christina's practice sessions became more intense and more closely focused on Ravel's Concerto. The emotion that crept into her playing was now more clearly on display. She dug into the second movement, deceptively simple in sound, but it was not easy to bring out the romance and the love that was embedded in the movement.

"Christina," Rossignol said one day after practice, "you must show this new side of your playing in this concert. From what I read in the papers you've been hiding this new dynamic. They still talk about the Ice Queen."

"It is easy with you here, in this room. It's intimate and you are such an insightful listener. I can feel your support as I play. I trust you. I feel your connection to me, so it's easy to open myself up. With the larger audiences I become reserved again. I don't want to show my heart, my feelings. What if they don't like me?"

She looked away, out of the window to the field shining in the late afternoon light.

"I feel safer, being reserved, being technically correct."

He reached for her and put his arm around her shoulders. "But they will love you, even more, for showing them the emotion of the piece. The second movement sounds like a love story the way the composer wrote it. There are moments of doubt, as all lovers sometimes must feel, but the affection, the tenderness returns. Let them see more of that."

She shook her head. "I don't know..."

"Look, I'll be with you. I'll even attend all the practices. And I'll be sitting up front when you perform. Play to me, if that will help. The audience will hear and receive what you say to me in your music. They'll love you for it as I do."

Finally, the day of their departure to Paris arrived. Chloé had driven down the day before to take them to the city. They went a week early so that Christina could not only show Rossignol the city, but purchase some clothes for him including a tuxedo for the evening's concert.

"You must look the part," she said.

"And what part is that my dear?"

"The consort of the queen," Chloé replied.

"Chloé," Christina said in a sharp voice. "Be nice." Turning to Rossignol, she said. "It is to look like a proper suitor, companion, or lover." She paused. "There, I said it. If we're to be seen and talked about, you can't be some vagabond I picked up because that is not what you are." She pointed her finger at him. "You are a man of substance."

"Even if I don't know what that is?"

"*N'a pas d'importance*. Doesn't matter. There is no denying you are a serious man. Other's must see that in how you look since they won't have the good fortune to get to know you."

"The clothes make the man, is that it?" He smiled back at her.

"No, the clothes *represent* the man."

There were three days of practice. Some of it spent on the other Ravel pieces, so Christina played a smaller part in each day's routine. The performance menu led off with "Daphnis et Chloé," a ballet in one act with three separate scenes. There were to be no dancers. The piece was generally performed with the orchestra only. This was followed by an intermission.

In the second half, the orchestra played "La Valse," written just after World War I. It was to be a score for a ballet, but the impresario, Daighilev, had refused to stage the work. The evening concluded with the Piano Concerto in G Major, since the concert was marking the eightieth anniversary of its publication.

The concert was to be held at the *Salle Pleyel* the home of the *Orchestre de Paris*. The 3,000-seat concert hall had opened in 1927 and had undergone a renovation between 2002 and 2006, improving the acoustics and lowering the seating to 1,913. The hall was located near the *Arc de Triomphe* in the *Quartier du Faubourg du Roule* which was where the luxury fashion shops of Paris were located.

Rossignol and Chloé usually stood or sat together during the rehearsals. They had many moments to fill, often with small talk.

"This," Chloé said spreading her hand around the concert hall, "represents an escalation in your relationship with Christina. It will bring new pressures on you, and on her."

Rossignol looked at Chloé. They were standing in the wings of the stage watching the concert master work through some sections with the orchestra. Christina sat patiently at the piano.

"I'm not sure what you are saying."

Chloé took a breath and leaned closer to Rossignol. "I'm saying that showing you in public makes Christina more vulnerable. I don't want to see her hurt or her reputation ruined."

"You care a lot for her, I can see. Are you in love with her? I get a sense of jealousy from you."

Chloé looked at him. There was anger in her eyes. "You don't know me and what I feel is none of your business."

"Chloé," Rossignol said with much tenderness in his voice, "I know you more than you think. You're in love with Christina. I can sense it."

He could see in her face that his remark had hit home.

"It's all right. I'm in love with her as well. But you should understand she doesn't love you in the same way. She probably never will."

"That's fine for you to say, but we were doing just fine before you came along. You've changed everything." She looked at him, her face angry.

"And we're all doing well now. You know I would never do anything to hurt her...or you. But," he paused for emphasis, "I won't give up what the two of us have created. I'm not trying to shut you out, but you should not try to come between us. That will ruin everything, for you as well as for Christina and me."

"Are you threatening me?"

He shook his head. "I'm not threatening you. I like you and I can see Christina's affection for you. I just hope we can get along...for Christina's sake."

Chloé's expression softened. "Just don't drive me out...please."

"I won't. We're her inner circle, so to speak. I want us to get along."

He reached out his hand to shake and Chloé, after some hesitation, took it.

The three were staying in the *Hotêl Lancaster Champs Elysees*. The building had been built in 1889 as a mansion by a Spanish nobleman. It now ranked as a five-star establishment and had been favored since its conversion by artists and celebrities. The rooms had retained their turn-of-the-century luxurious flavor. They had dark hardwood floors and twelve-foot high ceilings. These were accompanied by floor to ceiling windows, elaborate crown molding, and paneled walls showing original artwork. Staying in the hotel was taking a step back into a period of luxury not matched by more modern hotels, no matter how finely they were finished.

The night before the concert, they enjoyed an exceptional dinner in the hotel's restaurant, *Monsieur*.

The restaurant was bathed in a soft golden light from the indirect fixtures built into the valence at the joining of the walls and ceiling. Elaborate chandeliers complemented each section of the main dining room. The signature of the restaurant was the chef's featuring the food from different regions of France which changed each month.

Following the dinner, they retired to their rooms. Christina was hungry for Rossignol and they made love in the large, high-ceilinged room with decadent abandonment. Chloé spent a restless night in her room worrying about the upcoming concert.

Chapter 16

The day of the concert, Christina, Chloé, and Rossignol went to the hall just after lunch. Christina immediately shut herself in a practice room, one of the many off the main hall. Rossignol came in to listen. She warmed up and then went into the piece, playing it with a full range of emotion and passion.

After two passes through the piece, stopping to hone a particular section she sat back and sighed.

"I'm ready."

"Do you play with the orchestra before tonight?"

"Yes. This afternoon, with the conductor. It's like our dress rehearsal. Then everyone goes to get something to eat and we reconvene about 7 pm."

"The concert starts at eight?"

She nodded.

"Christina, you must show the audience this range of emotion. It will make for a remarkable evening."

She let out a long breath. "I'll try. I would like to lie down for a while and then we must get a bite to eat before this afternoon's practice."

Christina went to her dressing room. Rossignol wandered around the hall until he found the concert master, the first violinist. He took the man aside.

"Miss Aubergh is going to be playing a bit differently this evening. I want you to spread the word to the orchestra, and the conductor. Her technique has evolved and she's going to let the public see her new style."

The man looked at Rossignol. He'd seen him sitting in the hall the past few days. He knew he and Christina were a couple but he had no idea what this man knew of music. The doubt showed on his face.

"What are you talking about?"

"I'm not a musical expert, but I've been listening to Christina for months. She is changing. You need to be prepared to go where she leads."

"Do you know anything about music? She has shown nothing new in our practices. One doesn't spring surprises on the conductor and his orchestra at the last minute. I think you are being a bit melodramatic. Why I don't know."

He paused to look down the hallway for a moment in thought.

"Tell Ms. Aubergh to just play the concerto as we practiced and the concert will be a success."

"I'm just asking you to be prepared. Tell the conductor she is not the Ice Queen anymore. Not after tonight."

The man turned to look at Rossignol.

He smiled. "Trust me on this."

The dressing room was a flurry of action. Rossignol kept to one side as Chloé fussed over Christina's gown while a hairdresser worked on her hair. Finally, everyone but Chloé and Rossignol were shooed out. Christina put on her make up. Her large eyes, accentuated with the makeup, gave her a striking look. Those eyes could capture you with a glance.

Then she put on a pair of soft, fuzzy gloves and began walking about the room, gently kneading her hands. Then she sat down at a keyboard which not attached to anything, and began to do silent runs up and down the keys.

They heard the applause for Daphne et Chloé and then it was intermission. There was a gentle knock on her door. Chloé opened it and in stepped the conductor, Herbert Michaud. He had taken over the *Orchestre de Paris* five years ago and had molded it into one of the finest orchestras in Europe.

"Ms. Augergh, we will be ready for you soon. It is a very appreciative audience. Everyone is looking forward to the concerto. It will be a grand finish."

He paused as if uncertain what to say next. Christina looked at him. He was in charge, even though she was the soloist. Monsieur Michaud was the master of the evening.

"Philip, my concert master, said that we should be ready for something new, something we didn't practice? Is this true?"

"*Non*, maestro. I play the piece as it is written."

"As we practiced?"

She nodded.

"*Excusez-moi.*" Rossignol interjected. "I may be able to shed light on what Philip related to you. He went on to explain about Christina's new style of playing and how she had been holding back in practice.

"And you have not shown this, to me? And you want to show it to me tonight?"

Christina said nothing.

"It will be a memorable performance, believe me. I have heard it. I trust you are capable of joining her where she leads and bringing the orchestra along?" Rossignol asked.

"Who are you?" Michaud demanded, now in a somewhat irritated tone.

"Someone who listens well."

"He has the ear," Christina said. "He's untutored, but he has a gift. That gift has helped me unlock another range in my music. One I'm ready to show to the public."

"But without showing me, or the orchestra. This is unheard of—"

"Before you insist," Christina said. "I am not going to violate the music. I'm finding new depths to it...and to me. I think you will see right away where I am going and will be able to communicate that to the musicians."

"Think of this as a great adventure," Chloé offered from the corner of the room.

Michaud looked over at her. His face now a mix of irritation and confusion.

"You are all mad. You especially, Ms. Aubergh." He shook his head. "Do not ignore me out there. Do not ruin this evening for me, for the orchestra, and for all who came to celebrate this eightieth anniversary of the concerto."

He turned on his heels and went out of the door.

"What did you say to him?" Christina asked after he had left.

"I spoke to Philip, the concert master. My instinct is that they should be ready for something a bit different. I know you can do this and I didn't want the orchestra to be unprepared. They have heard the Ice Queen these past three days. Tonight, they will here Christina Aubergh without a mask. In her full splendor."

Christina put her hands to her head and groaned. Chloé went over and put her arms around her.

"Put this out of you mind. You go play the piece, as you feel inspired to play it. Don't worry about this." She looked over at Rossignol who now looked sheepish at the reactions he had triggered. "Rossignol meant well and the conductor will be fine." She smiled at him.

They heard the clapping as the curtain opened to start the second half. Christina got up. Chloé opened the door and the two went out to the wings of the stage. Rossignol followed. Now Christina started to pace, slowly, quietly, calmly. She held her hands together, gently working them. Chole gestured for silence. Neither spoke to her.

Then she kissed Christina on the cheek and said, in a low voice, "I'll watch from here."

Rossignol went up and kissed her on the cheek. "Play for me. They will hear, but play for me. I'll be in my seat listening."

He quickly went around to the side stairs and entered the main hall to take his seat near the front just as the applause died down.

Christina watched him go and then went into her private space.

Chapter 17

The applause for the La Valse had died down when Christina stepped out from the wings. The clapping rose again as she walked across the stage to the piano. After shaking hands with the conductor, she sat down and the audience became silent.

The first movement, *Allegamente*, began with a whip crack from the percussion section, which started the piano and piccolo out to lead the orchestra in an enthusiastic opening romp that quickly moved into a bluesy statement echoing Gershwin's Rhapsody in Blue.

The jazz age was in high swing when Ravel wrote the piece. Jazz musicians had long given consideration to classical composers, but the reverse wasn't so true. When the concerto was written however, in the, early thirties, many composers were giving a nod to jazz themes. Ravel certainly did this through much of the concerto.

The piece moved into a gentle melody played in short solo passages before an echo of the blues emerged. There were sudden shifts from the rapid, syncopated sections to more contemplative parts where Christina pulled everything out of the score. She stretched time in subtle ways, leaning on certain notes to accentuate the emotion of the score.

Ravel wrote only one cadenza in this concerto, coming approximately half way through the first movement. Her playing was marked by originality. While staying within the confines of what Ravel wrote and not violating his authorship, she pushed and pulled at what he had composed as her feelings directed. When the cadenza came to a close, Christina looked up and her eyes met with Michaud.

She nodded as she closed the section and the orchestra filled in. She sensed they were together now. He had seen what she was doing, what she was expressing, and had adjusted his directing immediately. He would bring the orchestra along.

The movement ended with a furious run of the piano from the bass notes, rhythmically pounded out and punctuated by the orchestra. From there her fingers climbed up the keyboard with furious arpeggios in a sprint to the final note. Christina brushed back her hair after striking the final chord with the orchestra. She glanced at the audience and was met with Rossignol's enthusiastic gaze.

The conductor turned to her, waiting for her to begin the *Adagio assai*, the beautiful middle movement. In this movement, the left hand played a one-two-three waltz beat. This three-chord sequence would carry on through the entire movement. It challenged the soloist to keep the two parts together because the melody line, played with the right hand, often didn't match downbeats with the underpinning chord sequence. This seeming occasional misstep kept the listener a little off balance.

Rossignol had described the movement as a love song, played by the right hand. Christina performed it that way for him. She let her emotions flow through the music, moving it forward.

Ravel had written long, single notes in the melody for the right hand. This was challenging for the pianist, since, once struck, the note could not be worked or shaped. The sound stayed out there, by itself, as the artist had played it, without vibrato, or shaping, or swelling, or softening. Christina's emotions, while guiding her now, were accompanied by her considerable technical skills. The notes came out with all the tenderness she aimed for and hung beautifully in the air until she moved on.

Part of the way through the movement, the flute came in, followed by an oboe and then a clarinet, to pick up her song. The piano now played a gentle accompaniment. After a major chord resolution, Christina took over the melody with the larger orchestra now filling in. Hints of doubts showed up in the music; the clouds that can accompany lovers, marked with minor notes slipped into the melody, giving the listener a subtle jarring. But the composer, and Christina, kept the love story going, moving the melody back to the positive. Again, the minor theme came in, but it was followed this time by a warm resolution in the strings.

The theme became more complex as the orchestra backed away and Christina began a virtuosic run of assent expressing passion, fear, worry and then passion again. The orchestra under Michaud's guidance, followed Christina in the rise to the movement's moment of climax.

Then came the duet between the English horn and the piano. The horn took up the love song with Christina playing runs behind him like crystalline water trickling over pebbles in a stream bed. The horn player seemed to be transported. Christina looked up at him for the briefest moment and their eyes met. He now participated in her shaping of the melody, following her liquid runs. The two instruments danced together until the flute and oboe came in to join the story being told.

The strings now filled in as Christina ended the movement with a perfect, measures-long trill by her right hand while her left completed the three waltz-like chords underneath. She slowed the trill down in a steady manner, maintaining a mathematical precision, never letting the *ritardando* stumble. Her precision never faltered even as she slowed down to the final few notes and the gentlest of stops with the last chord from her left hand.

The note died away as Christina looked up at Michaud with a shy, half-smile on her face. He had both hands across his chest as if trying to capture the beauty of that moment and hold it close to him. He turned to her, his eyes glistening with threatened tears, his face full of affection.

After gathering himself, Michaud began the *Presto*. It was bright and Michaud began it just the slightest bit faster in tempo. He seemed to know where Christina was headed. After the opening notes, she bent her head to the piano and her fingers flew across the keyboard

A prancing dance of sound came from the piano as the orchestra applied staccato punctuations to her playing. A sharp energy came from the orchestra as the piano led the way. Christina pushed, alternately attacking the keys and then being gentle with them. Her runs up and down the keyboard involved cross-hand fingering, with her hands flying. A smile broke out on her face as she reveled in the excitement of the piece.

She now bent low over the keyboard, looking up only at the end of each flourish. Her hair came loose, strands hanging down in her face. She ignored them. She was immersed in the runs and arpeggios from Ravel that she so loved. She would have as much fun with his brilliance as she could. She pushed the pace ever so subtly until, with the last chords struck by her and the orchestra, the piece ended with the bass drum's loud report.

There was a moment of silence and then the audience erupted. Shouts of acclimation along with wild clapping broke out. Christina looked up, spent from the exertion. Michaud smiled at her. She stood and he reached down to shake her hand. She turned to bow to the audience who were now on their feet. The director stepped down and took her hand and kissed it. She raised their hands to the crowd which clapped even louder.

The orchestra was also in full cheer as well. Michaud directed them to stand and, after they had taken their bow, he and Christina walked off the stage. When they reached the wings, Chloé reached out and embraced her with a fierce hug.

"That was wonderful. I have no words to describe it except that you can no longer be called the 'Ice Queen'."

"My dear," Michaud said, taking her hands in his. "You have made my year. What a surprise and joy. You pulled more out of Ravel than anyone I know. This was a triumph!"

He turned as the audience would not stop clapping. "We must go back. They want more of you."

They walked back out.

There were three more curtain calls. The audience did not want the night to end. They sensed that something special had taken place. They saw how Christina had immersed herself in the music: her body language, not being an affectation, but a reflection of the energy and passion with which she played. They had heard the passion and the pleasure with which she performed and had seen how the orchestra had been brought along.

Those who knew the music well, realized that this night's performance would become the benchmark for the concerto: a measure for any artist who would subsequently play the piece. And this from an artist only in her twenties.

By this time Rossignol had joined Chloé in the wings and, after the last curtain call, they went back to the dressing room. Attendants were bringing bouquets of roses back to her room. Inside was a bottle of Krug Grande Cuvee Brut Champagne in an ice bucket.

Rossignol opened the bottle with a loud pop of the cork and poured three flutes.

"A drink of water first," Christina said.

Chloé handed her a glass of mineral water which she drank thirstily.

"To the new Christina," Rossignol said raising his glass.

The three took sips.

"To a new era," Chloé said. "I see new music to conquer. Your playing will become the standard for so many pieces."

Christina blushed and pushed back a strand of her hair. There was a gentle knock on the door. Rossignol opened it and Michaud stepped inside. He greeted Christina with three kisses on her cheeks.

"When I was told you were doing something different, I practically had a heart attack. This was such a noteworthy concert, being a Ravel celebration. I would have been ruined if it went wrong. I wanted to insist on playing it safe, just as we had practiced. It would have resulted in a good performance: one the critics would laud, but would also cast some faint aspersion on, for missing the emotion of the piece."

He smiled and held her hands again.

"But thankfully I didn't insist. My dear, you broke out and did something unheard of in concert performances. After the cadenza in the *Allegramente*, I understood that you were going to bring this piece to life in a way not seen before."

"I appreciate your indulgence," Christina said.

"Indulgence! *Non, ma chérie.* I was carried away by you, as were the audience. The *Adagio assai* was so beautiful—the most beautiful I have heard. And I was able to participate in that. From there it was a fun romp all the way to the end."

There were more knocks on the door.

"Thank you, Christina, for this gift tonight."

He bowed and started for the door.

"Will we see you at *Chez Bourret*?" Michaud asked before he left.

Christina looked at Rossignol who's face reflected his ignorance of what *Chez Bourret* was. Chloé nodded and Christina said yes.

"*Bien*," said Michaud and left. Outside the door reporters had gathered. They surrounded Michaud and peppered him with questions.

"*Chez Bourret* is a restaurant where all the musicians go to relax and wait the early editions with their reviews," Chloé said to Dan.

She turned back to Christina. "You should probably go out and say something to the reporters as well. This is a special moment. Many of them understand and the rest go along with the herd."

Christina rolled her eyes and took a sip of the champagne.

"Don't be like that," Chloé said. "This is the new you. Open, showing your emotion and passion. You have to say something."

Christina sighed and got out of her chair. She stepped out and the questioners turned to her, letting Michaud slip away.

Amid the questions more people showed up. Yevgeni Kuznetsov was among them. He had brought with him a huge bouquet of roses. He shouldered his way forward and presented them to Christina. Chloé was now at her side and took the bouquet. Christina smiled and nodded to him.

"Mademoiselle, you have made my visit to Paris more memorable than I ever could expect. Tonight will be a night all who were here will recall to their children and their grandchildren. The night Ravel was played with such force, such beauty, such delight. We are blessed to have heard you tonight."

"You are too kind, sir," Christina replied.

She held out her hand and he took it and brushed it with his lips in the way of a proper gentleman. Raising his head, he noticed Rossignol standing to one side and a little behind Christina. Their eyes met. Yevgeni was caught off guard. The man's gaze was intense, almost predator-like. He'd seen it many times before, but never in such a gentile context. The man looked away and the moment passed. *I wonder who that is*? After another glance he turned to go as others pressed forward to gain a moment of Christina's attention.

Chapter 18

The next morning Yevgeni was sitting in his hotel suite with a glass of orange juice, coffee, and *Le Figaro*. He turned to the arts section to find reviews of the previous night's concert. There he saw the picture. It was of Christina, along with others including the director, Herbert Michaud, and the man whose eye he'd caught last night. Yevgeni stared at the picture for a long time.

Duscha came in and poured herself a cup of coffee with cream and sugar.

"Last night was very nice," she remarked. "I think I still prefer our Russian composers to this more modern stuff."

Yevgeni didn't answer. He just kept staring at the photo.

"Zhenya, are you listening?" She stepped around behind her husband. "Oh, there she is. She's very pretty." She reached over and pointed to the older man in the photo. "Who's that?"

"That's the director."

"And that man?" She pointed now to Rossignol.

"I'm not sure. He had a strange look about him."

"What do you mean? Do you think he's her lover?"

Yevgeni didn't answer.

"That would be interesting if she had a secret lover," Duscha said with a smile.

He put the paper down and now looked at his wife. "So, what are your plans for today?"

"I know you don't like sightseeing...or shopping...so I thought I would go out by myself to visit some of the shops. See the fall fashions."

"And spend all of my money?"

Duscha gave him a pretend serious look. “Zhenya, I could never do that. You have so much.”

He smiled.

“Besides, she said with a glint in her eye, “you want me to look my best this fall and winter at our parties. After all, a well-dressed wife is an honor to her husband.”

“Did you make that up?”

“Maybe.” She smiled and sat back down. “What will you do today? Wait, I know. You will sit here and do business with your phone.”

“You know me well, *moya lyubov’*, my love.” He turned his attention back to the picture, then to the article underneath.

Along with an accolade of the performance, which Yevgeni already knew was outstanding, the columnists speculated as to who Christina’s mystery man might be. The press had observed a certain affection, even intimacy between them but no one could figure out who the man was. Her secret lover was all they could guess. She called him Rossignol, ‘nightingale’, which seemed like a strange name to everyone and did nothing to lessen the intrigue surrounding the two.

By the time Duscha had dressed and gone out, Yevgeni was starting think the mystery man might be the one he was looking for. Christina was known to have a hideaway somewhere in France, probably in the south. His men had lost their captive in Provence, in southern France. Could this be the assassin that he was seeking? The man who had killed his son?

He had made connections before with less evidence than he had now. A grim smile played across his face. He would follow up on this idea. Maybe the assassin had survived his escape. If so, he must have found refuge that night. Somewhere nearby. He had never shown up in the village. Could it be that Christina lived in that area? That he had found refuge with her? He knew of the stories. No one knew where she went. But perhaps he knew. And maybe he would find the man he sought in the same place. He picked up his phone and called Moscow.

The next day Christina and Rossignol slept in. When they awoke, they ordered breakfast in their room. Coffee, orange juice, and a selection of croissants and pastries, along with some eggs for Rossignol.

"Do you want to spend some time seeing more of Paris?" she asked.

He shook his head. His mind had been going over the face he had seen outside of the dressing room. He couldn't place it, but it concerned him. He didn't know why, but a strong sense of caution had come over him.

"I think I've had enough for now. This is all so new to me and I'm not used to the crowds and the noise."

"It is fine, *mon amour*, we can come back another day. Having you with me was such a treat, I want to do it again." She leaned towards him with a coquettish look on her face. "Do you want to travel more with me?"

"I do. The increased stimulation may help me recover my memory."

"*Excellente*. I will call Chloé and we'll depart this morning."

A day later, Yevgeni and Duscha flew back to Moscow where Yevgeni immediately met with his lieutenants.

"I think our assassin is alive," he announced when they had gathered in his offices.

Yevgeni's office was upstairs at one of his nightclubs. Below was a bar and disco with topless dancers spread throughout the floor. Small rooms were set off from the main one. They were for more intimate connections between the dancers and customers. The nightclub did a lively business most nights with weekends being packed. Kuznetsov's gang owned three similar clubs around the city along with others in St. Petersburg, Volgograd, Belarus, and Ukraine.

"How do you know?" his cousin, Pyotr, asked.

"I saw him. In Paris."

"How can you be sure?"

"Get Nikolai in here," Kuznetsov said. "I'll ask him about this." He held up the picture in the newspaper.

After Nikolai confirmed the man in the picture was the assassin a commotion arose in the room. Yevgeni held up his hand for silence.

"He's with a pianist, Christina Aubergh."

"It's hard to believe he survived the night," Pyotr said. "He was shot, injured, and should have frozen to death."

"Yet there he was. I saw him."

He went on. "Nikolai and Maxim did not see the body. They only guessed he must be dead. There was no mention of him in the local village." He pointed to his cousin. "But what if he didn't go to the local village? Maybe he found shelter at a farmhouse? Maybe this pianist took him in?"

He got up and started walking around the room.

"They seemed to be lovers. At least that is what the press reports. He could have given her a story and then seduced her. From what I know of her life, she's young...and unattached."

He continued his pacing.

"He feels that the search for him has died. He thinks he is now safe. He leaves the hideout and accompanies her to Paris. Only I'm there. Something he would never guess could happen."

He sat back down at the head of the table.

"Now I know he is alive and he does not know that I know. Now I will get my revenge. We have the upper hand."

"But where is he hiding?"

"Somewhere in Provence."

Chapter 19

It was October. The air was crisp and clear. It was cooler than in the fullness of summer, but the sun still remained strong enough to warm the days. The lavender had mostly been harvested, but the flowers, freshly dried could be found in all the villages. Their scent was everywhere, filling the air with a lovely perfume.

The vineyards were turning golden in hue as the leaves changed. The locals were out in the fields, harvesting the precious grapes. This activity was especially intense in Avignon where wineries abounded. But even in the lesser known villages, people were working the harvest which, while not making its way to large markets, was destined to become some of the enticing local wines found throughout the region.

Thankfully, the hordes of tourists were gone along with the traffic they brought. The narrow country roads now were often jammed with slow moving tractors pulling wagons of grapes to the local winery. The local markets overflowed with produce from the surrounding countryside providing a cornucopia of fresh food to the local kitchens and restaurants.

In short it was a special season among all the four seasons that seemed so special in Provence.

One day Émile came around to visit. He was excited. Wild boar season had arrived. He sat with Christina and Rossignol as they shared some wine and Émile consumed the leftover parts of their lunch, even though his Henrietta had fed him well before walking over to Christina's cottage.

"We must go into the woods tomorrow," he said emphatically to Rossignol. "We will seek out the fierce boar. We'll locate the herds and next month we can use the dogs to drive them and bring home a fine haul."

He smacked his lips at the thought of roast boar and boar stew on a cold winter night with a glass of full-bodied red wine. He had just such a bottle waiting in his house.

"You are going to go murder some animals, are you?" Christina asked, partly in jest, partly in concern.

"Indeed, we are. And I'm sure you will enjoy the repast. Henrietta will have you over for a feast from our quest."

She shook her head. "As long as I don't have to clean it."

Émile turned to Rossignol. "Shall we go? Tomorrow?"

"Yes. It sounds interesting. They're dangerous are they not?"

"Very," Émile said with much drama in his voice. "We must be careful and brave. I will bring my rifle."

The next morning the two men set out. The day dawned clear and cold. There was a slight frost on the ground in the low places where the cold, dense air had settled. Their breaths formed clouds of steam that trailed off behind them as they tramped into the rocky foothills of the *Luberon*. Rossignol was energized by being out in the woods. Each man carried a satchel of food and water. Émile had included a bottle of wine in his for their lunch, such as it would be.

The dogs had been left behind much to their disappointment. They looked forward this time of year, not only to a romp in the woods but to the chasing of the boar. That was the big event for the dogs. It was the climax of their year to exercise their pack-driven blood lust in pursuit of herds of boar. The only down part was the humans would not let them ravage the carcasses after a kill. Still, the dogs seemed to enjoy this season best of all.

"Will we shoot today?" Rossignol asked.

"Probably not. We probably won't get close enough. But we'll learn where the herds are and where they congregate, and next month, with the help of the dogs, we'll go shoot some. The dogs drive them to us. On our own, the herds can just keep moving away from us, more easily than we can close for a shot."

"But you never know?"

"You never know," Émile admitted.

They hiked in silence through the morning without spotting any herds. They came across signs—hoof prints, disturbed ground where the boar had been rooting for food—but no animals. After lunch, Emile packed away the food and wine and they started out again. Rossignol had begun to despair of seeing any of these renowned animals.

As they came to the top of a ridge, Émile put out his hand and sank to the ground. Rossignol instinctively did the same. He crept up to Émile and looked to where the man pointed. There, down from the ridge, on an open flat area, was a herd of boar. They were a good distance away, hardly visible, sometimes disappearing in the grass where it grew taller.

Émile put his rifle to his shoulder to sight through the scope.

"Are you going to shoot?" Rossignol asked in a whisper.

He shook his head. "Just look. They're too far away. I bet they come here regularly though. We can set up a drive to get them next month."

Émile's rifle was an antique—a Mauser 98 with a 4-power Zeiss scope. It had belonged to his grandfather who had taken it from a dead German in World War II and kept it. Emile's father had used it for hunting, as did Émile. There were more modern weapons but the 98 was accurate and, even with outdated optics, the shots Emile usually took with the dogs driving a herd were well within the scope's range.

"Do you want to see?" Émile asked.

"Yes. Is the rifle loaded?"

Émile nodded.

Rossignol took the rifle. A chill went through him as his hands closed over the stock and grip. He settled the stock on a rock and looked through the scope. The animals jumped into clearer view, still small with the limited magnification, but now seen more clearly. Without thinking about it, he noticed the wind movement in the field. He lifted his eyes from the scope and checked the wind in the sight line to the field.

"What distance is the scope zeroed in for?" Rossignol didn't know why he had asked such a question. Somewhere in his mind, it made sense to ask it, even if he was not sure of what to do with the answer.

Émile gave him a questioning look. "One hundred meters."

"How much correction do you get with each click?"

Now Émile looked harder at Rossignol. "About twenty-five meters with each mark. How do you know about this?"

Rossignol put his eye back to the scope. "I don't know. These just seem to be the right questions to ask."

He turned the adjustments on the scope and then looked downrange at the herd. "What do you think? Three hundred meters?"

"That's a good guess. It's too far for this old rifle, though. We can't shoot. We'll spook the herd and they may not come back to the area."

Rossignol didn't answer. He turned back and dialed in the elevation adjustment on the scope. Then he settled back to the rifle to study the herd. A quiet came over him. A calm. Émile and the rest of the world faded. He watched, like a voyeur, spying on the herd, looking for a large sow. He remembered that Émile had said the sows tasted better than the males.

He was only faintly aware of Émile beside him. He worked the bolt action of the rifle and chambered a round. Émile said nothing. Rossignol's world narrowed. He focused the rifle on a particularly sizeable sow. She looked healthy with no young ones clamoring around her. There were no conscious thoughts in his mind.

A line seemed to stretch between him and the sow—strange, but also somehow familiar. He could see the trajectory of the bullet, its path from muzzle to heart. It all seemed so complete. His finger tightened on the trigger. Gently he closed his hand. The gun barked and gave him a familiar and satisfying kick in the shoulder. The sow tipped over and the herd scattered into the brush.

"Mon dieu! Incroyable!" Emile said in a shocked voice.

Rossignol rolled away from the rifle, leaving it propped against the edge of the rock outcropping. His head was swimming. Lights flashed in his eyes, blurring his vision. He could not see Émile standing, looking down at the field in amazement. He could barely hear Émile's voice through a ringing in his ears.

Images began to flash in his mind like a movie projector run wild. They were disconnected. Men shooting, a man running through a field. A blow on the head. Being tied up, the questions. And then, seemingly out of time, a sense of a mission and a woman, strong, authoritative, giving him orders. A name emerged out of the kaleidoscope of pictures running in his mind. Dan. Dan Stone.

Slowly he emerged from a mist that seemed to have engulfed him. He must have looked dazed. He certainly felt dazed.

"Are you okay?" Émile asked. "You look odd. I was talking to you just now and it was like you didn't hear. Your eyes were not focusing."

Rossignol didn't answer. He knew his name now. It was Dan Stone. More information was tumbling back into his consciousness. Some of it unwelcome. He couldn't stop the flow; he could only watch it unfold in his mind.

"That was a shot!" Émile exclaimed. "You have shot before, no? I could not make that shot, nor could my father."

Dan didn't answer. Images were still tumbling through his brain.

"Can you hear me? Rossignol?" Émile asked as he sat down next to him and put his beefy hand on Dan's arm.

"I can hear you," Dan said in a strained voice. "I think my memory is coming back. So many images." He paused. "In fact, I know it is."

"*Lourange dieu,* praise god."

"My name is Dan, Dan Stone. I remember that now." He stopped for a moment. "There's more, but it's confusing."

"Dan is it? I think I prefer Rossignol. Dan is so simple and now I see you are not a simple man. You are a man with shooting skills...of a very high level." This last, Émile said with a serious note in his voice.

Dan got lost again in the images flashing in his mind, trying to make sense of them as they appeared. They were still disjointed and confusing. It disoriented him. The two sat there quietly for some time. Émile seemed to understand that Dan was sorting impressions, memories that had just erupted in his brain. Dan drifted in and out of awareness, hardly conscious of the Frenchman.

Finally, he sighed. He reached for his pack and grabbed a water bottle, taking a long drink.

"Has it all come back? Do you remember who you are and how you are so skilled with a rifle?"

"Not all of it. There's still confusion. It's like my brain is downloading what had been hidden for all this time, but it's out of order, or so it seems."

He rubbed his face and head. Émile reached into his pack and offered Dan the bottle of wine. Dan took a drink.

"I hope I can make sense of it over time."

"What do you remember about yourself, this Daniel Stone person? Where does this skill with a rifle come from?"

"I was a sniper in the army. I remember that."

"Do you remember why you were captured, who pursued you?"

"It has to do with a mission I was on. An assignment, I think."

He stood up. "Let's go see about the sow I shot. I need to let the memories sort themselves out a bit."

They hiked down to the field. The shot had penetrated just behind the ear, hitting the sow's brain and killing her almost instantly.

"That was perfect placement. I know I told you about where to aim, but from that distance, to try for the brain?" Émile shook his head in wonder.

He took out his hunting knife and quickly went to work field dressing the carcass. After gutting it, he told Dan to find a six-foot pole strong enough to hold the boar. Émile tied the legs together and when Dan returned, they slid the pole through the legs and hoisted the animal on their shoulders.

An hour later, they walked into Émile's farmyard. He called out to Henrietta as he hoisted the carcass up on a rope over a tree limb so he could go to work on it. Henrietta came out and exclaimed at their catch.

"I didn't think you would be so fortunate. You told me not to expect any game today."

"I know," Émile replied, "but Dan, Rossignol, made an incredible shot. We have a fine sow here. It will be delicious eating."

"Rossignol? You called him Dan. Is that your name?" She now turned to Dan.

He nodded. "My memory has started to come back."

"It was when he shot the rifle. That seemed to trigger his memory," Émile said. "Now I have to get busy skinning this beast."

He went into the barn to get a sturdy table which he carried back into the yard. Meanwhile, Henrietta went back into the house and returned with a collection of knives used for skinning and butchering. She set them on the table and then went back inside to get a plastic cooler and partly fill it with ice.

Émile stood back to look at the carcass. "You can stay and watch if you like. When you get back are you going to talk with Christina?"

"I'll have to, yes."

"What will you tell her?"

"Who I am, for a start."

Émile turned to him and looked Dan straight in the eye. "And who are you? Now that you remember."

Dan stared back at the man. He knew the question came from a protective attitude towards Christina. Émile had grown comfortable with Rossignol as he had observed how affectionate the two had become. But Dan was a new person to him now. Émile probably wanted to know the full story.

"I'm not fully sure who I am, but I think it will all come back."

"You spoke of a mission. What was it? Did it have to do with you being captured?" Émile spoke to Dan while he continued to cut away at the carcass.

"I think so. You want to know if I represent a threat to Christina. I don't think I do. The men chasing me have gone. It seems as though I've disappeared...from everyone."

"But now you know what that business was all about?"

"It had to do with getting something. A briefcase. One filled with a dangerous material, a weapon of some kind."

"That was your mission?"

Dan nodded.

"And these other men, the ones who captured you? They were looking for the briefcase as well?"

Again, Dan nodded.

Émile stopped to look at Dan. "Where is this briefcase now?"

"I don't know." He shook his head.

"So, you still need to find it. And that will lead to more danger, possibly danger for Christina."

"If I go looking for it."

"You won't? You said it was dangerous. Who gave you this mission? Will they let you just decide to not pursue it?"

"Émile, I don't have all the answers yet. But no one knows where I am. I seem to be lost to everyone. Things can stay that way, at least for now, maybe for the future as well."

Émile snorted and turned back to the boar strung up on a tree limb. "I think you are a dangerous man. I think you need to tell Christina all you know. It may make her sad, but I don't want to see her in any danger."

He returned his attention to the carcass.

Chapter 20

Dan slowly walked back to Christina's cottage. His mind was working furiously to sort out the flood of memories. Émile was right. He needed to tell Christina about himself, but first he needed to sort out exactly who he was. The facts were slowly coming into place. He was a sniper. He worked for a clandestine organization. The woman...her name stayed just out of reach of his memory, but he could see her face...she gave him his orders, his missions.

He was not on his first mission. Others started coming back into his mind: the sniping, the shooting, the disruption. He had killed many times in the past. It was always related to a mission, some endeavor that had a higher purpose. Killing bad men. Men who wanted to harm the world, harm civilians. He was still a soldier, only now in a civilian army.

When he entered the house, Christina came out from the practice room to greet him.

"How did your tramp in the woods go...are you all right?"

She could see the distraction and worry in his face.

"You're pale. You look unsettled and confused. Is everything okay? Did you get another headache?"

He shook his head and reached out his hand to her. She came into his arms and hugged him.

"Tell me what's wrong. You don't look right. Did something go wrong in the woods today? Did Émile get hurt?"

Dan led her to the couch. “No, he’s fine. I recovered my memory today. At least, some of it.”

Christina gasped. She secretly had hoped for and dreaded this day. What change would it bring to their relationship?

“That’s wonderful,” she said with as much enthusiasm as she could muster. “Does that make you happy?”

“Yes and no.”

“I don’t understand.” She paused for a moment, then voiced one of her fears. “You’re not married, are you?”

He smiled. “No. I’m single. I *was* married. Some of that is coming back now. I think she died...or was killed.”

“Oh no. I’m so sorry for you.”

She reached out to hug him again, but he held her off,

“I found out that I’m very good at shooting. I shot a boar at very long range.”

“Are you in the army? Are you a *tireur d’élite*...what do they call it...a sniper?”

Dan took a long breath. “They call it that when you are in the military. I’m not.”

She looked at him. She felt the questioning in her mind reflected in her face.

“Outside of the military, one is called an assassin.”

There was silence. It hung like a curtain between them. Christina’s eyes remained open, staring at Dan. He met her gaze.

“And my name is Dan...Dan Stone.”

“Daniel? Like in the lion’s den? Daniel was a prophet and a visionary. He walked through fire and tamed wild lions.” She paused. “It is a good name, but I like Rossignol better.”

“Christina, I have a violent—”

“We don’t have to speak of your past. I don’t know of that. That is not you, not the man I have come to love.”

She got up to pace around the room. The fire was lit and burning low, keeping the room cozy against the evening’s coming chill.

"You have disappeared. No one is looking for you. You said so yourself. You can stay with me. We can have a life together."

She reached down to take Dan's face in her hands, her long fingers caressing his cheeks.

"You do love me, don't you?"

There was a plaintiff tone in her voice.

He looked up into her eyes. "I do. You saved my life. You gave me a new life and opened a new world of music to me."

"And you opened up my world. You unleashed a range of expression in me that's made my life and music more complete."

She sat back down next to him.

"We belong together. We are good for each other. The past is coming back to you, but you have the choice to adopt it again and make it yours, or go in a new path. The one we are on, the one we have set up without your memories. We can still do that, can't we?"

He pulled her close to himself. They just held on to one another. One, trying to still sort out the jumble of pictures that were still tumbling forth in his mind, the other holding the man she loved, fearfully, not wanting to lose him to his past, wanting to keep him with her in their new life together.

The afternoon slipped into evening and the sky filled with red in the west as the sun set behind the high cirrus clouds.

Nikolai and Maxim stood in Kuznetsov's office nervously wondering why they had been summoned.

"I have found our assassin. No thanks to you," Yevgeni said. "It seems you cannot find anyone, neither the mouse nor the assassin. I'm going to give you a chance to redeem yourselves. If you fail me this time, it will be your last failure."

He chose the same two men because he wanted men who knew that not only their jobs, but their lives were on the line. That understanding would make them very focused and very ruthless. He wanted such men now.

The two didn't answer but looked fearfully at their boss.

"He is in Provence. Probably near the village where you stayed."

Nikolai chanced a comment. "But we got no sign of him while we were there."

"No, you didn't. He probably has the local people covering for him. I think he's staying with a pianist. She probably has a hideaway near there and the locals protect her privacy. That could include our assassin."

"How did you find out?" Maxim now risked asking.

"Never mind how I found out. You concentrate on what I tell you to do. You are to go back to the village. Start applying some pressure. Not too much, but some. Find out where the pianist is staying. Her name is Christina Aubergh. If the villagers know of her, you can bet our man is nearby. Find him. If you can, bring him to me. But he doesn't get away again. You bring him to me or you kill him."

Chapter 21

Dan and Christina had long conversations during the following evenings. She kept to her practice schedule and they both worked to maintain the routine they had set up, but spent much time talking about his memories. He told her about his past as it came back to him: His wife, Rita, the killing of her and the baby, his revenge, and then new life with an organization that sent him out to kill terrorists and those who helped them.

He mentioned Jane Tanner, his boss. However, he kept back from Christina that he now remembered a deeper emotional connection between the two of them. It seemed so far away now, living in the cottage, in the Provence countryside, alongside this beautiful woman with whom he had fallen in love.

"You fight against bad people. Monsters that would kill innocents and destroy lives. I knew you were a good man. That doesn't change."

She seemed satisfied that her Rossignol was not a man who had crossed a line between good and evil. Though he had lived a violent life, he was on the side of the righteous.

"But now you can retire from this life, no? We can have a new life. Your past does not have to define your future."

Dan stared at the fire, deep in thought.

"You can step away?" Christina persisted.

"Maybe. If the past doesn't catch up with me. But I feel a bit like a soldier leaving the battle before it's over."

"The battle will never be over. You've done your part, in and out of uniform. Now you've stumbled onto a new life...and so have I. One we found together." She paused as if afraid to go on. "You don't want to give up that new life, do you?"

He turned to her, seeing the pleading in her eyes. "No, I don't want to give up our life together. But it seems less certain, now that I know my past."

"It's not," she exclaimed in a loud voice. "It's solid. It's real. We are not children having a summer affair. I retreated into myself for five years. You opened me up again, to you, to the world. Our relationship has substance."

He pulled her close to him.

"Now I am afraid," she said, "that your past will seek you out, find you, and take you away from me."

"Don't fear," he said softly. "We will find a way to live with my past. To leave it where it is, behind me."

Suddenly he sat upright. "I have the house in Venice, but I can't go back there. People I work for know about that place."

He had told her about where he lived, the house in the Venetian suburbs. There were items hidden there that he would need in order to function outside of his Provence hideaway.

"I have to go to Paris."

"What's there?"

"I have funds, credit cards, and identity cards stored there. I kept them in a separate storage unit that no one but me knows about. I should go tomorrow."

"So quickly?"

"Better now than later." He didn't mention the weapons stored there. With his memory back, he now felt vulnerable being unarmed.

The next morning Dan was up at dawn. Christina helped with some breakfast and packed him a lunch to eat on the road. When he was ready to leave, she grabbed him in a fierce embrace.

"You will come back, won't you? Promise me."

"Yes, I promise."

"Collect what you need and come back quickly."

"I'll stay one or two nights. I have to scout the storage location before I go in and retrieve what I need."

"Scout it?"

"Make sure it isn't being watched."

"But you said no one knows about this."

"They don't. Or, more accurately, they didn't when I set it up. I'm remembering that one of the keys to survival is to not take anything for granted."

Christina shuddered. "Don't talk about surviving. That's your past. We're setting up a new future."

"True, but I need a few things from my past before I can turn from it."

He headed out to her car.

It was a seven-hour drive to Paris. Dan entered the City of Lights after sunset. He drove to a repair garage in the twelfth *arrondissement* located to the northeast, just outside the *Périphérique*, the ring road around the city. The garage was grandly titled *L'Art de L'Automobile*. The name hung over a dingy storefront with a garage-style door to one side, wide enough for cars to enter. The neighborhood was a mix of two-story, run-down buildings, some abandoned with graffiti painted on them and six story, ornate structures that spoke of a more refined era, now serving as apartment buildings.

Dan got out and pounded on the door. Deep inside the building, he could see a glimmer of light. After a minute of non-stop knocking a short figure approached.

"*Sommes fermer*, we're closed," a hoarse voice shouted out.

"Luc, open up."

"Victor, is that you?" Luc knew Dan only by one of his aliases.

The door opened. Inside was a swarthy, dark-haired man in mechanic's overalls. He reached out a thick hand, which seemed to have a permanent coating of grime on it, and pulled Dan inside. After looking up and down the street he closed the door and locked it.

"Where have you been *mon ami*? I haven't seen you for nearly a year."

"Busy."

"With things you cannot speak about, I'm sure." He looked Dan up and down with a critical eye. "*Allon*," he said.

Luc turned and walked through the garage, filled with cars in various states of repair or disrepair, to a back office. He closed the door after Dan entered and adjusted the blind on the window before turning up the light.

"I can't let *la canaille* see any lights inside. Don't need to be bothered by them.

"I hope you don't consider me riff raff."

"*Non, mon ami*. You are...*spécial*."

"I noticed you had to think for a moment."

Luc shrugged. He took a bottle of brandy from his drawer along with two glasses and poured two drinks. He handed one to Dan and raised it in a toast.

"Here is to your health and well-being. Why do you come to see me late at night?"

"I need to park the car I'm driving for a day or two. I have to retrieve something and need to make sure I'm not being watched."

"Contraband? I can get some boys to retrieve it if you're worried. If they are pinched, they can beg ignorance to the *gendarmes*. They will get off and no one will find you."

Luc Tsiganes was a very good mechanic. He was a gypsy who had settled down in Paris and found his niche fixing automobiles. He also was very good at building secret compartments into any vehicle. This skill served smugglers well and greatly helped to augment his legitimate income from repairs. The extra money also never had to be reported and so he enjoyed the double satisfaction of not only defying the law, but avoiding taxes, something of an art form in much of France.

Dan had discovered Luc a few years earlier when he made a compartment for Dan in his Peugeot 607 to hold his weapons when he traveled. Luc enjoyed the sense of being part of some dark, international intrigue, something more grand than smuggling cigarettes or liquor.

"I appreciate the offer, but I think it's best for me to personally see about this. If anyone is watching, I want to identify them."

Luc shrugged. "Suit yourself. You can park here inside for a couple of days."

Dan had rented a two-and-a-half-meter storage cubby at the *Shurgard Port de Charenton* self-storage facility near Luc's repair shop. The next day he took a bus to a point two blocks away from the storage facility. He had told no one about this place, but Dan couldn't take a chance that someone had discovered it. Especially someone on the CIA team for which he worked.

If he was going to stay with Christina, he had to stay lost. And, in the back of his mind was the nagging doubt about how he had been captured. He needed to figure out what had gone wrong. Mistakes like that would kill him. Had he been compromised? Like in Mexico? He shook his head. Those were the thoughts of someone still in the game. If he was going to be out, he didn't have to worry about that. Still, the thought nagged at him.

He slowly walked the two blocks to the facility, carefully checking to be sure he was not being followed. There was no need to check in at a counter. Each customer had a separate security code to let them into the building and then into the area in which their locker was located.

The management relied on security cameras, which were all over the place. Dan had dressed with that fact in mind. He wore a jacket with a large hoodie sweatshirt underneath, and had on a pair of dark sunglasses. The look was threatening, but he didn't expect to meet any of the limited security staff that worked at the building. The cameras would capture his picture, but he expected that and by keeping his head down, there would be little to see.

Once inside his storage area, Dan turned on his light and opened the duffel bags. Inside were passports and fifty thousand euros in cash. Another bag held an M4 carbine broken down along with a 9mm handgun. In addition, there were multiple magazines, two suppressors, and a couple of hundred rounds of ammunition for each weapon. A third bag held multiple license plates and auto registrations. After going through everything, Dan packed up the weapon bag, stuffing it with the passports and cash along with a pair of license plates and their corresponding registration. There were two sets, one for the Peugeot 607 and one for the Land Rover. Both were titled in the name of Victor James, a security analyst working for an American firm.

With his bag in hand, he turned out the light and left the locker, keeping his head down. Outside, he began a circuitous route back to the repair shop.

Chapter 22

Dan had been back for a week. He had hidden his duffel bag in the barn. Christina never went there; she didn't have any livestock. It was used as rough storage which suited Dan's purposes just fine. He didn't like keeping a secret from her but saw no value in alarming her with the presence of weapons and the alternate ID, all of which spoke of his violent past.

Émile had come over to check on things. Dan guessed it was to check on him. They sat in the living room. It was a chilly November afternoon. Christina was practicing in the music room. Dan opened a bottle of wine for him and Émile.

"I was in the village yesterday," Émile said as he took a long swallow of the red that Dan poured. "It seems the two men that were here last year have returned. They're being more open, asking now about Christina by name. They say they're fans and know she lives nearby. They say they want to meet her, get her autograph."

He snorted in disgust.

"They do not fool anyone. They do not know anything about music. Everyone is suspicious of them."

Dan studied the fire. A sense of dread crept through his body. His brow furrowed in concern.

"This isn't a good sign," Émile continued. "How do they know about her? You and I know they are looking for you. How do they connect the two of you?"

His voice carried his grave concern. Dan understood this was precisely what Émile had been worried about: his past catching up with him and ensnaring Christina.

"I don't know how they make that connection. We've never been anywhere together beyond the village, except for Paris. Could someone have seen us together?"

He stared at the fire for a moment. Then he slapped his hands together.

"Damn!" he exclaimed.

"What is it?"

"Our picture, with us together, was in the papers the next day...multiple papers, after the concert. There was even an article wondering who I was. The mystery man they called me."

"*Merde*," Émile said in almost a growl. "You have too many eyes searching for you. You can't be seen anywhere with Christina."

"I'm beginning to wonder."

"No wonder to it. This is what I worried about from the first."

"Don't tell Christina," Dan said. He gave Émile a sharp look.

"Then *you* must."

"I will but first I need to think about what to do. I can't just let these two men hang around until they stumble upon our whereabouts. When I tell Christina, I want to have a plan ready."

"A plan? How to get them to go away?"

"Maybe." Dan thought for a moment. "I need your help."

He looked at Émile who nodded. "What do you need?"

"I need a weapon. Not just any weapon." He went on to explain the carbine and 9mm hidden in the barn. "I need a stealth weapon. A .22 caliber pistol with a silencer."

Émile gave him a long questioning stare. "That is an assassin's weapon, no?"

Dan nodded. "Can you help?"

Émile looked thoughtful. "I don't know people like that." He paused to think some more. "But I have a cousin in Marseille. He knows some people of ill repute. He may be able to help."

"He can't ask a lot of questions."

"He knows when to ask and when not to ask. I will call him tonight."

"The sooner the better."

Émile finished his wine in a final gulp and got up. "I should go now. I will help you but you must tell me what you are going to do to protect Christina."

"I will. I've got an idea. It has to do with why these men are looking for me. But first I need the weapon."

Just then Christina came out. "Émile, what brings you here?"

"Just to see you and make sure your mystery man is being good to you."

"You know about his memories? He told you about his past, no?"

Émile nodded.

"Well, we're going to leave that behind. He can start anew, a new life with me."

Émile smiled. "That would be good." He turned back to Dan. "I must go now. I'll be in touch."

When he left Christina sat down on the couch. "What will he be in touch about?"

"Boar hunting. The season for hunting with the dogs is getting close. He's anxious to go out. Maybe he thinks my shooting will get him a record harvest."

"I think I prefer to not think about your shooting skills."

"The skills don't go away, even with a change of life. My skills and instincts will remain. They are part of who I am."

She leaned against him. "I know. But I prefer not to dwell on that...your habits from your old life. Think about your new habits and your new skills, such as your astounding insights to music."

"That seems to be part of an ability to read people, a sensitivity. From what I've remembered someone far away, an old man—an ancient man in many ways—gave me that gift. Apparently, it applies to music as well as people."

She sat back up and looked him in the eye. Now very alert, her large eyes grabbed his full attention. "So, you can read me? All that I think?"

Dan smiled and reached out his hand to brush her hair and cheek. "You, my dear, are an open book to me."

"*Ce n'est pas juste*, that's not right." She tried to look angry. "A woman must have some secrets."

"You have no secrets from me, *mademoiselle*. And right now, I sense you want me to give you a foot massage and then make passionate love to you."

She smiled and held out her hands to him. "I am defenseless against you."

She lay back on the couch and put her feet on Dan's lap. Later, he picked her up and carried her to their bedroom where he undressed her, carefully and slowly, savoring every inch of her body as it revealed itself to him. Then he began to kiss and touch her, patiently building her excitement until she was fully inflamed.

"Come now, take me," she said in almost a growl of lust. "Don't play with me. I want to feel you inside of me. I want to feel the release, yours and mine."

He mounted her but moved slowly, savoring the steady, building pressure in his body. He knew she was experiencing something similar, a tingling that would begin in her abdomen, travel down her belly, inflame her nether regions and even reach her toes.

When it was over, they lay back beside each other, spent and relaxed.

"Isn't this better than your old life? Than your memories? I can make you happy. You will never want for anything with me."

Dan smiled at her renewed offer. This doe-eyed woman who was so shy, so beautiful and pristine-looking, yet who could unleash such passion and abandon. She made beautiful music and now, with Dan's improbable help, had brought her music to a new level. Perhaps they *were* made for each other.

Along with those thoughts though, was the image of the two men looking for Christina, looking for him, in the village. The men who had almost killed him, almost destroyed his mind. They had returned and they would drag him back into his old life, unless he could put some of those parts to rest and shut them down.

Or could he?

Chapter 23

The next day Émile came over in the morning. He happily accepted a cup of strong coffee and some of the local pastries Christina had purchased in the village.

"Ummm," he exclaimed with his mouth full. "Don't tell Henrietta. She will chastise me for eating your treats."

"*L'absurdité*, you do so much around here, I'm happy to feed you."

"I am taking your man with me. I need his help on an errand. I have to go visit my cousin in Marseille. We will be gone all day."

"You never told me about this," Christina said looking at Dan. There was a hint of concern in her face.

"I didn't know he planned to go today. Émile wanted company and I would enjoy the trip. I hope you don't mind?"

She paused before answering. "No. I don't mind. I have to practice. The Florence concert is in six weeks and I have much to do." She seemed to have made a decision. She reached up to touch his cheek, oblivious to Émile's presence. "I know it can get boring for you here with me always practicing. You need to do other things sometimes. I'll be waiting for you with a fine dinner and some good wine."

She gave him a not-very subtle wink and turned to clean up the dishes.

Dan grabbed his jacket, gave her a kiss on the cheek, and followed Émile out of the door. Then he stopped and turned back to the cottage.

"Christina," he called out as he came through the door. "Don't go into the village today."

She turned to him. "I'm not, but why do you say that?"

Dan's mind raced. "Two reasons. One it doesn't feel right. Two I would like to go with you. I haven't been there for a while. If I'm to not get bored, I should go on these outings with you...or do them myself."

"*D'accord*," she said turning back to the sink.

Dan ran to join Émile in his pickup truck.

"What's your cousin's name?" Dan asked as they drove towards Marseille.

"Jean Geroux. He works in a shipping office. With all the smuggling going on, he gets to know some of *les criminels*. He is not one of them. He never involves himself in smuggling, but he knows who the players are."

"I hope this doesn't compromise him. You don't want to ask favors of criminals. They will expect favors in return."

Émile laughed. "He's way ahead on that count. He does favors by looking the other way, by not getting involved. He doesn't take money for that even though his boss does. He's just fitting in. It's the way of such things."

"You told him what I need?"

"Yes. He says he can get one for you. He wondered why such a weapon. I told him to be smart and not wonder."

They drove on in silence. Émile drove like many Frenchmen, especially those from the countryside. They could be calm and relaxed people until they were behind the steering wheel. Then they seemed to turn into road warriors, neither giving not expecting quarter in a seeming battle of wills with any other car in their vicinity. Dan could only tighten his seat belt as Émile careened the old pickup down the narrow backroads, honking oncoming traffic aside while tailgating and looking to pass anyone who got in his way. Often the passes were made with a prayer of no oncoming vehicles, since neither Dan nor Émile could see far enough ahead to guarantee success in the maneuver. When they got to the A51, Dan could relax some as the wider, busier road forced Émile to behave more discreetly.

"I think you need to tell me exactly what happened to you, why these men are back looking for you, and why you need an assassin's weapon."

"I really can't. It's a military secret and not something you want to get involved with. I certainly don't want to burden Christina with any disturbing stories."

"Ah, so they are disturbing? All the more reason to tell me. Don't worry, I won't tell Christina, but I should not be in the dark about what is going on. I may have to protect her, or myself, at some point."

Dan just stared ahead and didn't answer.

"And don't worry," Émile said looking over at him, "I won't tell any of your military secrets. I'm just a simple country *paysan*."

Now Dan looked back at him. "I don't think you are a *paysan*. You are too clever."

"You owe it to me since I was responsible for you recovering your memory."

"And I paid you with a larder full of boar meat. Now watch the road. You scare me with your driving."

"It is a sport, *non*? Now tell me what you know. I will drive like a woman if that helps."

"We don't all have to try to prove our masculinity behind a steering wheel."

"I am the master of my vehicle. Now tell me what you know."

Dan sighed. How far could his tale go? It would provide gossip far too delicious for Émile to resist. The stories he could relate would provide many a round of free drinks in the village. Such stories would eventually find their way outside of the local area and to higher authorities.

"You realize that if I tell you everything, that will get out and other people will come around. They will make your life miserable...and Christina's, as well. They will find me because of your stories."

"*Tu as raison, peut-être,* maybe you are right. Leave out what you must but tell me what is going on."

"*D'accord.*"

Dan slipped into his memories. The road faded as Émile drove along, thankfully in a more placid manner. The scene opened in his mind and he began his story.

"I was...am...on a mission. Someone stole a very dangerous weapon from the Soviet Union. They were trying to sell it. My job was to find the person and the weapon and recover it. It could not fall into the wrong hands."

"What hands would those be?"

"Terrorists, or the mafia."

Émile concentrated on the road. Dan continued.

"My problem was that I couldn't find the man who had the item. Our sources suggested that he had contacted the Russian mafia. We identified a *pakhan* or boss and I settled in to follow his operation.

"When he sent a *Brigadier* and his crew to Italy, I followed. It seemed probable that this group was to make an exchange for the weapon. The son of the *pakhan* went along with the group so I knew it was an important trip.

"I had no way of knowing where a meeting would take place...or even if there was one. I trailed them to an abandoned warehouse complex just outside of Milan. I hid behind a dumpster and an old, concrete block wall. A single car drove into the complex and parked in the empty lot between two buildings.

"I guessed it was the man with the weapon. At that point I had no idea how I was going to get it, or keep the exchange from taking place. If the mafia got the weapon it would just be that much harder to get it back."

Dan painted the scene of the transfer and the two men who approached each other, one with the metal briefcase—the weapon—and one with a briefcase full of money.

"When the exchange took place the mafia soldier grabbed the man. I shot the *boyevik* in the head. I couldn't let the exchange be completed. As soon as he dropped a man ran out from the warehouse followed by others. He was shot—this time by someone firing from the opposing building. Then a gun battle erupted with men charging into the courtyard."

Dan described how the man selling the weapon grabbed the case and scurried on his belly away from the firefight.

"He was headed for a field with some tree cover on the other side of it. Once there, he could disappear with the weapon. No one dared to shoot at him for fear of hitting the weapon."

"What is this weapon that makes them so afraid?"

Dan shook his head. "I'll tell you what I can, but not more."

He closed his eyes again to recapture the scene.

"Just as I set out after him, I got shot. The impact dropped me to the ground. Before I could return fire or crawl to cover, someone hit me over the head and that's all I remember of the scene."

He opened his eyes. They were on the outskirts of Marseille. Émile had pulled over at a rest area and parked.

"The next thing I remember is being tied up in a chair with those two men who are now in the village. They tortured me and injected me with drugs, all the time wanting to know where the *malen'kaya mysh'*, the little mouse, was." He paused for a moment. "I think they thought I was the man's backup and was trying to escape with him."

"I remember reading about that. A major gang shootout in Milan. It made all the papers. Everyone said it was related to drugs."

"But now you know different."

"Yes. This is very serious. How do you...we...protect Christina?"

"The first step is to neutralize the two men in the village. Quietly, if I can."

Émile started the truck and pulled back out on the highway.

"Does neutralize mean what I think it means?"

"Not necessarily. But I have to get control over them. Frankly I want them alive so I can ask them some questions. There are things I still need to know. What is the status of the search and whether or not their group is still a threat to me."

"And if they are?"

"Then I have to deal with that threat."

Chapter 24

They entered Marseille and parked near the *Gare Marseille-Saint-Charles* train station. From there it was a five block walk to Émile's cousin's apartment. He lived on the fourth floor on a narrow side street. It was near the docks and an easy bus ride to work. He was married and had one child in *L'Ecole Primaire*, the fifth-grade level.

They knocked on the door. Jean answered.

"Émile," he said with a big grin on his face and reached out to give him a hug. Émile turned and introduced Dan using Rossignol as his name.

"Where is your family?" Émile asked.

"Nicole is in her room studying, or probably texting a girlfriend, and Margot hasn't come home from work yet."

"Can we talk here?" Émile asked.

Jean shook his head. "We can go out. Nicole is fine alone. Let me tell her."

He disappeared for a moment and then came back and grabbed his coat.

"Let's go. You can buy me a drink and tell me more about this favor you need."

They sat down at a corner bar in a back booth.

"You're asking for a very special handgun. It is an odd choice. More like for an assassin than for house defense."

"Can you get me one?" Dan asked.

"I can. I shouldn't ask, but I'm curious as to why."

"Don't be curious. It won't help and could be bad for you," Dan responded.

"He's told me enough to know this is important and not for any bad purpose," Émile said.

Jean was not a large person like Émile. He didn't have that French peasant build, solid and stocky. He was slim, with dark hair which he kept slicked back to look like a gangster. Dan sensed Jean's excitement at being near danger but not getting involved. He was a voyeur, looking in on the underworld of crime and gangsters. *Playing with fire.*

"Sometimes there is safety in not knowing. Safety for you and your family," Dan said. "If you can get me what I need, I disappear from your life and you never hear from me again. That's best. The gun will never come into the hands of the authorities. It will disappear with me."

The waiter came with their drinks. Jean had a pastis, Émile, a glass of red wine, and Dan a beer, *Bières de la Plain*, a local brand that had become well known not only in Marseille, but throughout France.

After taking a deep drink of his pastis, Jean told of his efforts to find what Émile had requested. When he had finished reciting his story, all designed to make him appear to be a man with powerful, and dangerous connections, he sat back looking satisfied.

"What exactly did your connections come up with?" Dan asked.

Jean leaned across the booth table with a conspiratorial air. "A CZ Kadet...with a threaded barrel. The supplier has the silencer to go with it."

Dan noted the incorrect use of the word "silencer" not "suppressor".

"That will work," he said.

Jean smiled at his success.

"How much, where and when?" Dan asked.

"Tonight. I will take you there. It will cost you two thousand Euros."

"*Woah! C'est trop cher*, that's too expensive!" Émile exclaimed.

Dan ignored him. He looked Jean in the eyes.

"Does that include your cut?"

Jean shook his head. "Five hundred Euros, for me."

Émile whistled, even more taken aback.

"You will take me there tonight?"

"*Oui*. We will have dinner first. We can bring some food back to the apartment. Margot will appreciate that. After the meal I'll say I'm taking you around to see someone about work."

Dan nodded. "Two thousand for the gun and suppressor, cash when I get the goods. Five hundred for you, after the deal is done. I'll need a box of bullets with that."

"*Bien*," Jean said and finished his drink.

They stopped at a restaurant that offered take-away meals. Jean ordered and twenty minutes later they were back at his apartment with the food.

Jean's wife, Margo, was a plain yet attractive looking woman. She was a bit shy and retiring which also described the daughter. Margot had little to say during the meal after making a polite fuss over Émile. When dinner was over, the three men departed.

They walked through the streets towards the train station. In a dark back alley, they met two men. Even with little light Dan could see the men were armed. They looked to be North African, which didn't surprise him. There were a lot of North Africans in France and many resided in Marseille. Like all groups, they had their own criminal element, involved in smuggling people and drugs into the country.

Dan sized them up. They were slight of build, but tough. He concluded they could take care of themselves. One of them had a scar running along his cheek from his ear to his jaw, the result of a knife fight.

"This is the man I told you about over the phone. The one who came to purchase the gun," Jean announced in a self-important manner.

"You have the money?" one asked in heavily accented French. Dan could tell he was the leader of the two.

Dan nodded without speaking, making direct eye contact with the man. He put his hand on Jean's arm as if to tell him to stand aside and not speak. It was important to let the two gangsters know his group were not easy marks to be ripped off. Next to these men, Jean, looked like the poseur Dan had sized him up to be. Émile, while big and burly, looked out of place in the city. Someone who could be stopped by a show of force, especially with a gun. Dan instinctively knew the leader had to see him as a hard man, one not to mess with.

"Let's see the pistol," he said.

The man took it out of his pocket and held it up. Dan took the money out of his pocket and held it up.

"The suppressor?"

The man took the tube out and screwed it onto the barrel.

Dan held out his hand. The man locked eyes with him. He stared back unblinking. After a moment's hesitation, the man handed the weapon to Dan. It was bruised and beat up. The serial numbers were filed off, something Dan knew would be futile if the gun ever needed to be traced. He ejected the magazine, checked the chamber, cocked the weapon, and, pointing it down the alley, dry fired it. After checking it over, he nodded.

"You have bullets? I need a box."

The man looked at his companion who took a box of .22 long rifle ammunition out of his pocket. Dan held out his hand with one finger in the air. The man looked at his boss who nodded. He took one bullet out of the box and handed it to Dan.

Dan put it in the magazine and pulled the slide back, chambering the round. He pointed the gun down the alley again, at a large bag of trash and pulled the trigger. The gun made a muffled pop that could not be heard outside of the alleyway.

Dan nodded in satisfaction and pulled the two thousand euros out of his pocket and handed it to the man.

After counting the money, the man finally smiled and seemed to relax bit.

"One has to wonder why you need such a special weapon. It is not good in a shootout. Not good for killing except at close range."

"One can wonder," Dan replied, not adding more to the conversation.

"Shall we get a drink to celebrate a successful deal?" Jean now said with some forced enthusiasm.

"We should go," Dan said. "I think these men have better things to do." His answer did not give any room for discussion or dissent.

"We leave together," the first gangster said. "At the end of the alley, we go different directions on the street."

After the two men had departed, Dan reached into his pocket and gave Jean the agreed-to five hundred euros.

"Émile and I will head back to his truck. We have a long drive ahead.

"I understand," Jean said. "You need anything else, you let me know, through Émile. As you can see, I have my connections."

"I see you do." Dan paused for a moment as they shook hands. "A word of advice?"

Jean looked at him.

"Don't play the tough guy. The real tough ones see right through it."

He turned to go as Émile and Jean embraced and said goodbye.

"Why did you say that?" Émile said when he caught up to Dan.

"Those two guys in the alley, they don't respect Jean. They know he's a phony. Jean plays a dangerous game with men like that. If he ever makes a mistake and crosses a line, they'll cut him up. They might even harm his wife or daughter."

"He got you what you needed, didn't he?" Émile was now coming to the defense of his cousin.

"He did. I'm thankful for that. But I saw how he acted. This is a big game he's playing. He doesn't realize how easily he could get hurt. You should tell him to be careful."

"He takes a risk to help you and you talk him down?"

"Émile, I don't talk him down. I know this type of people. I've killed some of them and had some of them try to kill me. He doesn't understand he's playing around the edges of a dangerous world. If he's going to do that, he needs to be what he is., a bureaucrat, a manager. To pretend he's more, a tough guy, will only get him hurt."

Émile shook his head and they walked on in silence.

Chapter 25

"What are you going to do with the gun?" Émile asked as they drove back to the village.

"I'm going to use it to take control of the two Russians, as I told you."

"If you kill them, you will be put into prison."

"I'm not going to kill them...at least not near here. I need some information from them."

Émile thought about that for a few miles.

"Before you do anything, you must talk to Christina. It sounds like you'll be going away, so you'll have to explain that."

Dan stared out of the side window for some time. "You're right. But I'll have to leave out the details."

"*Bien*. That will do."

When they got to Christina's cottage, Dan got out of the truck.

"Émile. Thank you for doing this. And tell Jean to be careful. I don't want to see him or his family get hurt. You can let him know I have a lot of experience with the kind of men we did business with."

Émile nodded.

"Look in on Christina when I'm gone to make sure she's safe."

"As before, only now more frequently. Don't worry about her. Worry about being able to return after you do what you must do."

Dan turned and walk to the cottage. It was late at night. Christina was asleep in the bedroom. He took off his jacket, which held the CZ pistol along with the suppressor and bullets, and hung it in the front closet. He crept up the stairs with no sound and slipped into the bedroom.

Inside, he stopped and looked at Christina asleep in the bed. A half-moon had come out from behind the clouds and bathed her in a pale light. Her hair was spread out over the pillow like a dark thunderstorm. The faint outline of her breasts and hips could be seen on the covers. He drank in the moment. Her lying there, serene, soft, full of innocence. She was a startling mix of ingénue and lustful lover. The dichotomy kept him always a little off balance.

Taking his clothes off, he gently slipped under the covers and nestled his body up to hers. She didn't wake, but instinctively drew close to him. He relaxed with the touch of her body and slid into a deep slumber.

The next morning over coffee and some croissants, Dan and Christina talked.

"The two men who captured me are back in the village."

"*Mon Dieu*!" She put down her cup. "Can they find us?"

Dan nodded. "Eventually. They don't seem to be worried about being noticed this time. Someone will let slip something about the two of us."

"How did they know to come back, to come here?"

"The village is the nearest place to where they lost me. Why they are here, I don't know." He paused to look out of the window. "There were photos taken of you and me together in Paris, after the concert. Maybe their boss saw them."

"Who is their boss? Is he looking for you?" Her voice was full of her growing stress. She had a sinking feeling that this problem was not going to go away easily; that it would disturb their relationship, their plans in a fundamental way.

"Their boss is a member of the Russian mafia. He is after the same thing as I am."

"What is that?"

"A dangerous weapon. I'm trying to find it so it doesn't fall into the hands of terrorists or gangsters, like him."

"You have to do this? What about our plans? You said you would put your past life behind you."

"I would...I will, if I can. But it has found me and I can't ignore that. It's too dangerous to ignore. I have to finish this out in order to put things behind me—in order to come back."

Her large brown eyes began to glisten as tears started to form. "In order to come back? You're going away?"

She could see the sadness in his face. At the same time, she could see the determination in his eyes. It was a new look. One harder than she had seen before.

"I don't want to—"

"But you will. I can see it in your eyes."

"It's the only way to keep you safe. To make a safe place for us, for our future together."

The tears now started to trickle down her cheeks. She kept staring at the man who had opened her heart. And because of that, he now possessed the power to break it. The man who was now going to leave her. Fear began to engulf her. If he went away, would he ever come back? There was so much she didn't know. What dangers would he face? What people from his past would he encounter? And would they pull him back into his old life, away from her...forever? It was too much.

In spite of her efforts not to, she began to cry.

Dan jumped up and rushed to her. He knelt down and wrapped his arms around her as she buried her head in his chest.

"I fear you won't return. I'll lose you, just when you..." She couldn't say it. "It's too cruel, too hard."

"I'll return. You gave me life. I owe my life to you. I love you, not only for that, but for so many other reasons. Your music, your laughter, your beauty, your seriousness... You've made me a better man. I can see an innocence in you, the singleness of your purpose. And now you've let me share in that purpose."

He pulled back to take her head in his hands and looked into her eyes. She saw the intensity, now fueled with his passion.

"I will return."

"Promise me?"

"I promise."

Later, at the door, Christina grabbed him.

"You won my heart. Now don't break it. You come back like you promised. You won't be cruel to me and leave me alone? Now that you've taken my heart, my love?"

"I won't. I may be gone for a while. I don't know what I face, but I'll put it behind me, behind us, and come back."

"Will I hear from you?"

Dan shook his head.

"Will you think about me?"

"When I can. When it's safe to do so."

"I don't understand."

"You should not understand. I have to go do things that are part of my past. Things I don't want to talk about with you. Better to leave them unsaid."

He kissed her with a deep, long kiss and turned to walk down the drive to the village.

Christina stood in the doorway watching until he disappeared. Then she closed the door and sat down to weep.

Chapter 26

Dan walked the five miles to the village. There was little traffic on the road. He had his duffel bag with him. It contained a change of clothes, a 9mm, his newly acquired .22 caliber CZ, and his M4 carbine broken down to fit inside. He needed to find where the men were staying and ambush them without any shooting. He needed them alive. That meant finding a place to observe without being seen.

The village was not large, but big enough to have two restaurants, a small grocery store, a greengrocer, and *charcuterie*. In addition, there was a farmer's market that ebbed and flowed as produce came into harvest. The men would be moving about asking questions as well as eating. Dan expected they would be found in the restaurant that had a well-stocked bar, especially in vodka. Nighttime drinking would most likely be part of their routine.

As he walked down a street approaching the center of town, a priest stepped out from an alleyway. Dan stopped. He had an intense stare and he was looking straight at Dan. He'd seen that look before. With his memory now intact, he knew the man was a Watcher, one of a very special group of people who had skills in perception that went well beyond what would be considered normal. He had discovered them in Mexico and they had proven to be helpful in his mission. *They're even in the priesthood?*

The priest nodded at Dan and started off for the church on the corner. Dan understood he was being asked to follow. Watchers had always been helpful in the past and he could use some help. There was no reason to not follow the priest.

They walked through the dark sanctuary and into a side corridor with offices running along it. The man entered one of the offices. Dan followed and the priest closed the door.

"You know who I am." It was not so much a question as a statement of fact.

Dan nodded, waiting. The priest would tell him whatever he had to tell him in his own time. Questions, he had learned before, were not necessary.

"Sit down," the priest said. "I am the area *Monseigneur*, but as you know, I am more than that."

"I never expected to find one of your kind in the church."

"As you have been told, we're everywhere."

"You have something for me? Some information?"

"I became aware of you a year ago. I was aware that you had lost your memory and were hiding out near the village. That's why you came to my attention." He glanced at the duffel bag Dan carried. "I know about the two men you seek. They are staying in *Maisonette du Provence*. They are on the third floor, sharing a room."

He sat down at his desk and continued. "You must not kill them here in the village. They have information to give you." He paused. "I would prefer you not kill them at all, but I understand what you do."

"Will they help me find the man with the briefcase, the weapon?"

The *Monseigneur* shook his head. "Sadly, no. You will be able to see that with your enhanced perception. It has come back has it not?"

Dan nodded.

"What information do I need to get from these men?"

"They will lead you into Russia. It is a dark place with much hidden from us. You will be in great danger if you go there, but it is the only path we see for you."

"What is that path, if not to find the briefcase?"

The priest looked intently at Dan. "It is that, but it is also more. You seek to put this life behind you. That will be hard to do. To have any chance of that, you have to give life to your enemy. That will be the only way if you want to find any peace."

"I don't understand. Who is my enemy and how do I 'give life' to them?"

"Serge Kuznetsov. How you do that will only become clear when the moment comes. I don't see the future in any detail, only possibilities—what must or should be done."

"The Russian gangster. He sent these men. He thinks I know where the weapon is."

"He is not sure of that. He's been contacted again by the *malen'kaya mysh'*. He will try again to acquire the briefcase. The man holding it is now very afraid. He knows now that it represents either great wealth for him or death. He will be careless in his fear."

"I'm to retrieve the weapon *and* make peace with Kuznetsov? That sounds impossible, or foolish."

The priest held Dan with his intense gaze and a thin smile crept into his face. "It is more difficult than you imagine. There is another party, Chechens. Led by a very dark man. Lecha Maskhadov. We can't see him clearly. He's surrounded by much darkness. He is a warlord, a man of much power in Chechnya. He will try to intercept the transaction. It was his presence in Milan that triggered the gun battle there."

Dan nodded. Now the chaos of that day made some sense. Another ambushing party. One that had arrived before anyone else—certainly before Dan.

"They must have an inside informant in Kuznetsov's organization...or an insider from my organization talked."

The priest's smile grew broader. "You understand more quickly now."

"So many moving parts. Where do I begin?"

"Many moving parts, but your path will unfold as you follow it, like a trail in the woods that keeps opening before you. Start with the two men."

Dan nodded.

"And remember, you need to give life to your enemy. That will be key to your success."

"Will I know how to do that?"

"When the moment comes, you should be able to recognize it. You now have the gift the shaman in Mexico gave to you. Someday you may equal us."

"I doubt that. It seems as though killing limits one's contemplative senses."

"Strive for balance."

The priest stood up.

"You will keep an eye on Christina? I would like to know she's safe while I'm gone."

"I will, along with Émile."

"Will I make it back to her? Do we have a future together?"

The *Monseigneur* shook his head. "No foolish questions now. You know we don't see the future in any detail. Our futures always depend on our actions. And even then, we can't always be sure of the outcome."

He grabbed Dan by the shoulders and looked deep into his eyes. "Be careful. You are going into a heart of darkness. One of many in the world. This one is especially dangerous for you. Learn as much as you can from these two men and then proceed carefully, but with courage."

He opened the door of the office.

"The men will probably go to the tavern tonight to eat and drink. The *hôtelière* will not be on duty. They are in the first room on the left at the top of the stairs...third floor."

Dan nodded and went out.

He went to the small café on the edge of town to sit and get something to eat. It was out of the way, did not have much of a bar, and wouldn't be visited by the two Russians. He waited out the afternoon pondering what the *Monseigneur* had said. Suddenly he felt overwhelmed. He had been away from this level of intrigue for almost a year, and now it came crashing down on him in the most complicated manner. He didn't feel up to the task. How could he unravel all the complexity the *Monseigneur* talked about and get back to Christina? Could he even survive this mission?

He felt a desire to call Jane, his handler and contact, but the threat of a spy in the group held him back. Someone had given out information about the rendezvous in Milan. At this point he could only trust himself. The hope of getting any outside help was unrealistic. He was on his own, as he had been so many times before.

"But not really," he said aloud. The Watchers were out there. Were there any in Russia? If there were, they'd find him. He wouldn't have to look.

It grew dark. At 9 pm, Dan left and made his way to the *maisonette*. As the priest said, no one was at the desk by the stairs. He took out his .22 pistol and carefully climbed to the third floor. At the first door, he stooped to pick the lock and, with the pistol leading, gently pushed it open. A quick scan showed no one inside. There were two beds, one dresser, and a small desk with a straight-back chair. A TV was along one wall with a stuffed chair in front of it. The rooms on each floor used a common bathroom at the end of the hall.

Dan put his duffel bag on the floor, pulled the easy chair to the wall, turned it to face the door, and sat down. He put his pistol in his lap and waited.

Chapter 27

Lecha Maskhadov was a dangerous man. He had fought and killed his way to be a recognized warlord, ruling a clan of Chechens that held much sway in the country. He and his soldiers had fought viciously against the Soviets during the Yeltsin era struggles and his country's failed struggle for independence.

Maskhadov's fighters were instrumental in defeating the Russians in the town of Vedeno located in the mountains to the south of Grozny, near the border with Dagestan. He later fought in the battles to free Grozny from Russian troops which brought him greater visibility and respect among Chechens outside of his clan.

When the tide turned, Maskhadov was smart enough to recognize it and mended his relations with the mother country. In the end, he was not tried by Putin in the new Russia, but became an ally, helping to maintain control over his country. The resultant peace and semi-independence helped to quash any resentment by other Chechens towards his alliances. Now he enjoyed the power he had gained over his region of the country and his clan.

He aligned himself with the larger Chechen mafia, becoming one of its bosses. His militia were now absorbed into the mafia structure. They brought a singular brutal discipline to the organization already known for its brutality. The connection cemented Lecha's power.

He was a large man with a beard, now beginning to be flecked with grey. His body was thick and solid. His eyes were dark, almost black, fierce and without compassion. His face, leathery and lined, showed the effects of a hard life as a fighter. Lecha had no respect for softness, either in his personal life, his family life, or among his fighters.

He had taken three wives, the latest being just eighteen years old. Russian law didn't allow more than one wife, but the leader of Chechnya had ruled that only applied to civil marriages, licensed by the state. Muslim marriages, he stated, allowed for up to four wives in accordance with the Koran and so he would follow that tradition. The president's support of Putin allowed him certain dispensations regarding local customs

Lecha, as the dominant warlord of his clan, enforced clan justice, often without waiting for approval from the clan elders. They supported him because he brought money and influence to the clan. Even though he was wealthy, he presented a modest appearance to the public. Rather than appearing to enrich himself from his activities, he made a big show of spreading his gains to his clan.

This morning he was dealing with petitioners. He sat in his rough office in Vedeno while clan members lined up outside for their moment with this fearsome man.

A young man came in with his hat in hand, bowing as he approached Lecha's desk.

"What is your problem?" Lecha growled. These sessions irked him, but were a necessary part of his leadership.

"My sister is going with a man. Someone outside of our clan." He mentioned the name. It came from a group that had feuded with Lecha's clan in the past; the origin of which went back hundreds of years.

"You have told her to stop?"

"She doesn't listen to me. Our father is dead, killed by the Russians, so I am responsible for my family and her behavior."

"You've told her and she doesn't listen."

The man nodded. "She is also dressing immodestly in short skirts and is not covering her hair.

"How long has this been going on?"

"For six months. I've tried and tried to talk sense to her. To show her that she is bringing shame on our family. She says that such things are outdated. She is a western person. She says she has a good job in Grozny, and will live as she sees fit."

"She plays the whore, running around with men you don't approve of, dressing provocatively, and ignoring you." Lecha fixed the young man with his dark eyes. "You have my permission to deal with this as is customary. She has ignored you and won't behave. You must not let that continue."

"I know. But how can I take action? She is in Grozny."

"Get her to come home for a family gathering and feast. If she doesn't respond to your invitation, go and kidnap her. Bring her to Vedeno and put her to death. That is the only way since she has brought dishonor to your family."

"I must do this?"

Lecha gave him a withering look. "Your father is dead. It falls to you. To not do this will only increase your family's shame." He paused for a moment. "And then I will have to deal with you as well as your sister."

Lecha handed the man two thousand rubles for his trip and sent him on his way.

The telephone rang and Lecha called a halt to petitioners before he answered the call.

He hung up the phone after talking with Bulat Zakayev, the arms dealer who had hired him. The man had offered a half million euros to find a Russian with a briefcase full of something deadly. Two hundred and fifty thousand had been paid with the other half due upon delivery. Now Bulat was not happy. Lecha figured it was because someone else was also not happy: the person Bulat would sell the briefcase to.

How much was Bulat getting out of this transaction? Lecha scowled. A lot more than he was, he guessed. And all the risk was on him. He had lost good men in Milan.

Men from his clan. The losses had caused criticism and tarnished his reputation. He couldn't allow that.

When he had returned to Chechnya, he had taken action against some of the hotheads. They were members of his clan, so he didn't execute them. Instead he kidnapped them. He took them to a remote cabin in the mountains where he beat them for two days. In the process he showed them pictures of their families, their wives and children. He told them in great detail what would happen to the women, the molestation and shame that would be visited upon them, some by him personally, some by his soldiers. The boys would be killed, so the men's seed would be wiped from existence. It was enough to ensure obedience and quash any thoughts of usurpation.

During the call Lecha negotiated an additional one hundred thousand euros for the loss of his men. Bulat swore, but in the end agreed to pay. That fact confirmed to Lecha there was much more money involved in this transaction than Zakayev had let on.

After he had hung up the phone, his lieutenant looked at him warily. When Lecha got in a dark mood, one had to be careful.

"The call went well?" He had heard from his end that more money had been agreed to. How that would get passed down through the ranks was always unsure, but he expected to reap some benefits.

"Send out seventy thousand rubles to all the wives and mothers of those killed in Milan."

The amount was less than a thousand euros, which left a large amount of cash for Lecha, his senior officers, and clan elders.

The lieutenant nodded.

"Do you have any more information from our mole?" Lecha asked.

Earlier Maskhadov had managed to bribe someone in Kuznetsov's gang, a man who had been close to Kuznetsov but had fallen out of favor with him and had been moved to a lowlier position with much lower earnings prospects. Maskhadov had offered a sizeable amount of money which would allow the man to build up enough to leave and start a new life in some small manner of luxury outside of the country. As a result of that decision, he didn't spend his treasonous earnings but stashed them for his eventual departure.

It was because of this reluctance to spend the money that Lecha's informant hadn't come to the attention of the *Obshchak*, the security group in Kuznetsov's organization. They were in charge of uncovering turncoats, spies and others who might hurt the organization. If caught, retribution was swift and thorough, often spreading to the unfortunate individual's family if the transgression was deemed serious enough. It sent a message to anyone else contemplating breaking their oath of loyalty.

"He says the *malen'kaya mysh'* has again made contact but he doesn't know if an exchange has been arranged."

"So, we do it again. This time there should be no third party. Whoever that man was, he gave away our presence with his shot. That gun battle allowed the mouse to get away. If we learn of the meeting point, we can kill the mouse on the way and take what we need."

"The mole thinks the exchange will take place in Russia this time. Kuznetsov won't agree to any other country. He wants to be close to his support."

"That puts us close to ours as well," Lecha said.

Chapter 28

The two men Dan waited for came back to the hotel just before midnight. Dan could hear them on the stairs. They sounded tipsy. *All the better*. The key turned in the door and the men entered. Before they could turn on a light, Dan spoke in Russian.

"Don't move or you're dead men."

They froze in surprise.

"I have you covered with a silenced pistol. I can kill both of you and no one will hear the shot. Slide off your coats and drop them to the floor."

When they had done as he commanded, he told them to sit on the floor in front of their coats. Then Dan switched on a floor lamp next to the chair. He tilted the shade towards the men. They stared at him, not seeing him clearly with the light in their eyes. There was a mixture of surprise and anger on their faces.

"I see you have returned. Only this time we meet on different terms. I could kill you both now and remove your bodies from the room. No one would look very hard for you since you are not well liked by the villagers. But someone asked me to not do this." He waited for a moment to continue. "I also need some information. So, we will take a ride. Unlike the last time, my hands won't be tied and it isn't snowing."

Dan stood up He pointed to the man on the right.

"Take out your pistol, slowly and lay it on the floor in front of you." When the man had done that, Dan instructed the other one to do the same.

"Now stand up," he told the man on the right. "Turn your back to me and step backwards in my direction." He instructed the man on the floor to put his hands on his head. "If I see your hands drop, I'll shoot you without warning, *ty ponimayesh'*, do you understand?" The man nodded.

Dan had the man who was standing put his hands behind his back. Dan set about tying them with a section of short cord.

"If you make it hard, the pistol may go off and strike you in the spine. You could be paralyzed for the rest of your life, although that would probably be short."

When he was finished, he had the man sit on the floor again and did the same with the second. After securing the men, Dan pulled out their bags and stuffed their personal effects into them.

"Now we go for a ride. Who has the keys?"

The first man responded. "I have them."

"Okay. You will drive when we get to the car. I will bring the bags. We go out front door on my command and then around to the car. It is in the back?"

The man nodded. "*Da*."

The driver got in with the second man sitting beside him. Dan got into the back seat to keep an eye on both men. He cut the driver' hands loose, but left the second man tied.

"What's your name?" Dan asked the driver.

"Nikolai."

"And you?" He turned to the passenger.

The man didn't respond. Dan poked his head with the CZ.

"Answer me."

"Maxim," the man said in a low, growl.

"Good. Now drive," he told Nikolai.

"Where?"

"I'll tell you later. Right now, head north on D14."

Dan did not use the obvious route, south and west to Avignon. He wanted to drive through the more remote parts of the *Luberon* before heading west to the A7 and north to Lyon. He would use the time on the back roads to learn what he could from his two captives.

"What brought you back to Vachères?"

"How do you know we've been here before?" Maxim asked. Dan decided he was going to be the problem. His voice was full of anger and resentment at being tied up.

"Don't play dumb. Word gets around. You two are not much for blending in."

"We were told to find you," Nikolai offered.

"After you stopped looking before? That was nine months ago. I'm betting you didn't think I'd survive the night."

"Too bad for you that you did," Maxim said. His voice remained harsh with a surly tone to it.

"And here you are, tied up with me in control. Maybe I'll be taking you to a nice, remote cabin where I can interrogate you the way you did me. How would that be for you?"

"You don't have to do that," Nikolai said. His voice reflected a distinct concern for his well-being.

"I'm asking again. What brought you back to Vachères?"

"Don't tell him nothing," Maxim said. "You caused this problem when you slid off the road. Don't make it worse."

"We have time," Dan said. "I want you to think about how much I'll enjoy questioning you. I have some getting even to do. Call it revenge. My memory has returned, including of those days you held me captive. You have much to pay back."

They drove in silence. Dan let the thought sink in, of enacting revenge on the two men that had so brutally tortured him.

"I know you work for Yevgeni Kuznetsov. I assume he sent you back. I want to know why. You must have thought I was dead. What changed?"

"I don't know anything," Maxim said, still with his angry voice.

"*Krutoy paren'*, tough guy, eh? We'll see how tough you are when I go to work on you."

"How about you?" Dan leaned over to the driver.

"Don't answer," Maxim said in almost a snarl.

Dan whacked him on the side of his head with the pistol. "Open your mouth when I don't ask you and I'll shoot an ear off. Keep your mouth shut unless you want to give me any useful information."

"Nikolai, why did Kuznetsov send you back? I can get this without causing pain, or I can get what I need after causing a lot of pain. *Tvoy vybor*, you choose."

Nikolai hesitated a moment. Maxim slouched in the seat and glared over at him but didn't speak.

"The boss said he knew you were alive. He saw you in Paris, at a concert. He likes classical music."

"French as well as Russian composers it seems," Dan said.

He wondered at the vagaries of how chance or fate worked. If Christina had decided to use the Beethoven piece, Kuznetsov might never have discovered him. He put that thought out of his head. He would have found him out sooner or later. Dan was going to be accompanying Christina on many more concerts. It would have happened at some point.

But now he had a momentary advantage. Kuznetsov didn't know that he had captured his men. Didn't know Dan was aware of him. He had to use that to his advantage. What he needed was more information.

"What does Kuznetsov want from me? Why send you back?"

"We don't know. We just do what he says to do," Maxim replied.

"I didn't ask you," Dan said. He turned again to the driver. "You tell me why."

"Like he said, we just do what he asks."

They drove on in silence. Dan realized he would have to escalate the situation if he was going to get any useful information. Kuznetsov was interested enough in him to send two of his men back. He must have been told by these men that Dan didn't know where the man with the briefcase was. If Dan could not help him get the briefcase, why bother with him?

"Pull down that road," Dan said.

They were down in a valley. A small, dirt two-track ran off to the right into the woods. It could barely qualify as a road. Nikolai turned and gave Dan a questioning look.

"Do it," Dan said.

The road was rough and barely passable. It wound into the forest and began to snake its way up the hillside. It probably connected with other two-tracks and was used by hunters to access the more remote parts of the park.

Twenty minutes later and about a mile in, Dan told the driver to stop. He ordered him to get out and then opened the door for Maxim. The two men stood together facing Dan at the edge of the trail.

"I'm going to ask more questions. You're both going to answer me. You're going to tell me everything you know about your assignment, about your boss, and about what he knows of the briefcase and the man who stole it. If I don't like your answers, or if I think you're lying or holding back, I'll start shooting parts of you. You won't die, but you'll feel a lot of pain."

Maxim glared back at Dan. Nikolai gave him a wary look.

"Let's start with you, Maxim. Why did Kuznetsov send you back to find me?"

Maxim didn't answer.

"It will only hurt to not answer," Dan said. He stared hard at Maxim.

"I don't know. Ask him. I only do what I'm told."

"Does Kuznetsov know where the briefcase is? Is he in contact with Roman Pavlovich?"

"I don't know anything about that," Maxim answered.

"Why does Kuznetsov want me? Does he still think I know where the briefcase is?"

"I don't know. I only follow orders. I don't ask questions."

"Where's Kuznetsov now? If I want to visit him, where do I go?"

Maxim gave out a short laugh. "That would not be healthy."

"It doesn't matter. Where would I go?"

"I don't know. He moves around a lot."

"Last question. Can you take me to Kuznetsov?"

Maxim shook his head. "I told you, I don't know where he is. He regularly changes his location."

"Seems to me you don't know much."

Maxim sneered at Dan.

"Since you don't seem to be able to help me, I have no use for you."

He took out his CZ pistol. Maxim's sneer faded into concern and then fear.

Without another word, Dan aimed the CZ at Maxim and put a bullet into his forehead. The man collapsed to the ground. Dan stepped up and, putting the weapon near his chest, fired another bullet into his heart, tearing it apart, but the man was already dead.

Nikolai gasped at the quickness of the execution.

Dan turned to him. "I hope you can be more useful to me," he said.

"I have a wife and a daughter," Nikolai said. The tattooed gangster now looked frightened.

"You are in the wrong line of work for raising a family."

"I've been a member since a teenager. You don't get to quit. You just follow orders, stay out of trouble and hope you survive."

"All the while doing what your boss says." He paused to give Nikolai a long look. "You're a *boyevik*, a soldier, right?"

Nikolai nodded, giving Dan a wary look but didn't say anything.

"So, you do what your *brigadier*, your captain tells you to do."

Again, Nikolai nodded without saying anything.

"And if he tells you to kill someone, you do it, *korrekthyy*, right?"

Nikolai nodded.

"This is just business between you and me. Killing you if you won't help is just business. Your family has nothing to do with my decision. If you're helpful, you can live. If you are not, you're just extra baggage...and I have to travel light. *Ponimayu*, understand?"

Without waiting for a reply, Dan proceeded.

"For the last time, I'm going to ask why did Kuznetsov send you back to the village?"

Nikolai took a deep breath. "If I tell you things, my brigadier will kill me. If he doesn't Mister Kuznetsov will."

"And if you don't tell me, I'll kill you right here, tonight. It is more certain you will die from me than from your bosses."

"But they will take their time."

"I can do that for you as well. No one will find you here in the forest. You can die slowly or eaten by wolves or boar, whichever finds you first."

Nikolai sighed. "I have no way out."

"Now you understand. But I can let you escape if you serve me well. That is your only hope."

The man seemed to make a decision. He sat down on the side of the trail and stared at Maxim's body.

"We were told to go back to the village and find you. Mister Kuznetsov discovered you were alive. He said to capture you and bring you back to Moscow...or kill you."

"Why is he so interested in me?"

"You killed his son."

"Explain yourself."

"His son was killed during the shootout in Milan. It started with someone shooting the boyevik who tried to grab the briefcase and the mouse." Nikolai looked up at Dan. "That was you?"

Dan didn't answer, just stared back at the man, waiting for him to continue.

"When the shooting started, Kuznetsov's son ran after the mouse to try to catch him. He was shot. One of our boyevik's shot you while you were chasing him. The boss figured you had shot his son. He figured you knew where the mouse was headed. He wanted the information before we killed you."

Dan waited for the story to continue.

"So we took you to Marseille to interrogate you and find out what you knew. After that, we were to kill you." He looked again at Dan. "But you don't know where the mouse is, do you?"

Dan didn't answer.

"When we couldn't get the information from you, the boss told us to bring you back to Moscow. He'd take care of killing you himself." Nikolai shuddered. "It wouldn't have been pretty. He wants his revenge on you. He won't rest until he gets it. If there is anyone close, he will use them to get to you...or kill them to hurt you."

"Has the *malen'kaya mysh'* been located?"

Nikolai shook his head. "Not located, but he has made contact." Nikolai turned to Dan with fear in his eyes. "I don't know where he is or what the plans are. I'm not important enough. I am not lying to you now. If I knew I would tell you." He looked over at Maxim's body lying in the ditch. "I don't want to end up like him."

"Contact has been made. A second attempt to make the exchange will happen. Do you know where?"

Nikolai shook his head vigorously. "No. But we heard Kuznetsov said he would not do it outside of Russia. He wants nothing more to do with foreign countries and their police."

"Where is Kuznetsov now? I didn't believe for a second Maxim's tale about him moving around so much. He's a rich man. He can travel to Paris for a concert. He doesn't run around hiding like a refugee."

"*Da*. He is in Moscow."

"Then it is to Moscow we go."

Chapter 29

Dan had Nikolai drag Maxim's body into the woods. It might never be found, but if it were, there was no identification on it to help the authorities. The more likely scenario would be that the body would become food for animals.

Back in the car Nikolai drove them to Paris. They arrived late the next day, having driven through the night. He directed Nikolai to Luc Tsiganes's shop, L'Art de L'Automobile. Dan had called him earlier and timed his arrival for after the mechanics and the office girl had left.

"Who is your friend?" Luc asked after he let them in.

"Not a friend, but someone who is going to help me."

"And what brings you to my shop? What do you want from me?"

"I need a car. I have to drive to Moscow and I need one of your special cars."

Luc looked dismayed. "I don't make cars for that route. The inspections can be too invasive. It is very hard to do. What are you transporting that you need a special compartment?"

"Some weapons," Dan pointed to Nikolai, "and him."

"*Non*, my friend. That is impossible. Can't he just ride through a checkpoint with you?"

Dan shook his head. "He could give away the game. Better he is not seen. Besides, he's not fond of *gendarmes*, are you?" He turned to Nikolai who looked at him without understanding. Nikolai did not speak French. "I really need your help. And I can pay you well."

Luc showed some interest in that last comment. He thought for a moment. "Could you drive a small delivery van? I could work with something like that."

"*Oui*, I can make up a story for it at the border if necessary."

Luc's face lit up with interest. The challenge seemed to intrigue him. "I can make a false floor, front to back, so there's no change in height to suggest it exists. I can arrange a compartment underneath the front seats. With the seats mounted, no one will be able to see any access point. You'll have to load the compartment before the seats go in and, on the other end, take them out to unload it."

"What about breathing?"

"A vent tube. I can run it up through the wall, behind the front door. It will travel to the rear along the joint between the wall and roof. I'll build a molding that will conceal it. It will come out behind the taillights I'll mount up high. A small electric fan will draw in the air. You'll have to remember to turn it off while going through customs so it can't be heard."

"*Bien*. You are the master."

"This will not be cheap," Luc said, ignoring the compliment for a moment.

Dan waited for him to continue.

"Ten thousand euros."

Dan nodded.

"How will you get your companion to agree?"

"I won't. I'll drug him and he'll sleep all the way there."

"It's a long drive. Over thirty hours."

"We'll go by way of Poland to Lithuania, Latvia and then then to Moscow. That way he'll only have to be in the compartment when crossing into Russia."

The drive was longer but it went through countries that were all part of the Shengen Agreement that allowed open border crossings. The route would avoid Belarus which would add an additional crossing checkpoint to the trip, increasing the danger of exposure.

Luc shrugged. "I don't want to know what you are involved in. It sounds like it could be much worse than what I do."

"It is. But don't worry. I just need your skills at fabrication. The rest is up to me. Do you have a place I can keep my friend? I don't want him to run off."

"You ask too much."

"I can pay you extra for your trouble."

"I do have an attic in the building. You could tie him up there while I find a van and get it ready."

"That's what we'll do."

Dan explained to Nikolai that they were going to get a small van prepared to travel to Moscow. It would be modified so Dan could bring weapons with him. Dan neglected to mention that Nikolai would also be traveling in the hidden compartment.

With Nikolai secured in the attic, Luc went to work. He had managed to purchase a used Citroën Berlingo cargo van. It came with a 1.9 liter diesel engine that put out 71 horsepower when new through a 5-speed gearbox. If driven flat out, it would reach 70 to 75 miles per hour. Its virtues were that it was cheap, reliable, and could be modified by Luc.

Dan helped when and where he could. He knew his way around hand tools and served as a good assistant for Luc, who made it clear that Dan's help would not reduce the price he was charging for the modifications.

"You know, if this works, you could expand your business."

"If this works, I'll be happy to not do it again. I do well with the customers I have and my work never gets connected to their work. We have a trust between us. If any one of them thought to connect me, it would probably do them no good with the authorities and it would trigger a harsh response from my other clients. They don't want to lose their source for such discreet work." He made a sour face. "I don't trust the Russians. They will turn on you in a moment. Their loyalty is only to their gang."

"Maybe you are being a bit harsh," Dan said.

Luc shook his head and continued to work.

Late the next day, Dan went up to the attic after spending hours helping Luc. Nikolai was gone. The bed frame that he had been handcuffed to was broken. The attic window was open. Dan looked out. No one was in sight. He ran down the stairs and out of the shop. A quick search of the block revealed nothing. He swore.

"What happened?" Luc asked as Dan reentered the garage.

"My helper escaped."

"How?"

"Looks like he broke the bed frame and went out of the window, with the handcuffs still on one wrist."

"*Pas possible*, not true. There's no way down from the roof."

"I think he used a downspout and hoped it wouldn't come free from the building."

"*Un homme désespéré.*"

"Indeed. He didn't think it would end well, either with me nor with his boss if he helped me."

Luc's interest in the missing man involved only its effect on the work he had undertaken. What else Dan had to consider was none of Luc's business and he wanted it to remain that way.

"I still complete the project?"

It was a mix of question and statement of fact. Luc's concern now was that Dan would abandon the job and he'd not get paid. He liked Dan and appreciated his business, but Luc was not about to challenge or pressure him. He correctly surmised that Dan was capable of great violence when crossed. A good man to have on your side, but not as an enemy.

"Looks like there's no need for that now."

"But my investment, my time." Luc said in a complaining voice. "What am I to do with this *tas de boue*, piece of crap?"

Dan gave him a sharp look. Luc held his ground. His windfall payout for a week's work was disappearing and he wanted to save it.

"I'll pay you what I agreed. But I'm not driving that to Moscow since I don't have to. You do what you want with it. Sell it or keep it, I don't care. But buy me a car, a sedan and put in a weapon compartment. Just like you do for your Marseille customers."

His eyes were intense. Luc sensed no give in him. He sighed and nodded his head.

When the work was nearly completed, Dan decided to make a call to Jane Tanner. With his memory returned, he knew that the two of them had a special relationship. But that was before Christina. Now he felt a deep conflict between his current feelings for Christina and the memory of his relationship with Jane. They had not been lovers—she was his boss, after all—but they had almost crossed that line. And, as Dan remembered, it seemed as though the line would eventually be crossed. What had the Watcher in Venice said to her? Their lives were entwined.

He shook his head as if to clear it. That seemed so distant now. He knew the feelings had been real, but in the face of his current emotions, now seemed out of place. It would be a dangerous call. Not only for the awkwardness of it but for the concern he had about a breach of security. He still did not know how the exchange had been compromised. As far as he knew, he was the only one to find out about the meeting between Pavlovich and Kuznetsov. Yet, there it was. Nikolai, who had been there, said a Chechen gang had ambushed the meeting. It was that complication that had led to Dan getting shot, captured, and tortured. And the Chechens were still out there.

He dialed the number from a public phone booth far from Luc's shop. On the third ring it was answered.

"Tanner here." Jane's voice came through with a metallic sound from her secure phone.

"It's Dan."

There was a pause. "Dan, you're alive. Thank God! Where are you? Are you all right?"

"I am alive, not speaking from beyond the grave." It struck him how easily he slid into a banter with her. An old habit come back to life.

"Where are you?"

"I can't say right now."

There was another pause on the line. "Well, what happened to you? You've been out of communication for almost a year now. Some here thought you were dead, but I knew you must still be alive. I sensed it. It didn't feel to me like you were dead."

"I was...out of commission...for quite a while. I'm better now."

"Why didn't you contact us? We could have come to you. I was worried sick. Henry said to move on, find another agent, that you were dead. I couldn't...wouldn't do it. He's been angry with me for months. Just a word from you would have helped—"

"I'm sorry," Dan said, interrupting her. "I was not in a position to contact anyone."

"Were you being held captive? I don't understand."

"I'll explain later. It's not important now. Just tell Henry that I'm alive and you don't know where I am."

"Why the secrecy?"

"You may have a mole. A Chechen gang got wind of the exchange in Milan. They blew it up."

"I know about the gunfight. You were there?"

"I was there."

"Did you get hurt?"

"I got hurt."

"And you think the leak came from our group? We went over that problem after you got back from Mexico. It was taken care of."

"Maybe, maybe not. All I know is that Milan was a disaster."

Dan went on before Jane could jump in. He didn't want to discuss possible leakers and intrigue in Henry's office. The line was only secure on Jane's end and at this moment he didn't care about that. He just needed some information. Information that could help him and also let him discover how much a possible mole might know.

"Is Pavlovich still at large?" Dan asked.

"We don't know. We assume so. He went to ground after Milan."

"So, you don't know where he is or where the briefcase is."

"That's right. I'm hoping you do. Let's work together. I can send Roland and Marcus over to help you."

Roland James and Marcus Thomas were ex-Delta Force men who had worked with Dan previously in Europe. Jane had recruited them to the small unit where she worked under Henry Mason's guidance. It was a small, covert part of the CIA, a covert organization in its own right containing secrets within secrets and silos of information. The secrecy helped against broad security breaches but resulted in a Byzantine structure almost too complicated to map out and understand, let alone control.

"I have to work this alone. You just said you had no info, so you can't help."

"I want to help."

"Find the mole."

"I'll talk with Henry. We'll do a thorough review, but I doubt we'll find anything. Henry's going to want you to come in and debrief."

"Tell him I can't right now."

"Why? Is something going to happen? With Pavlovich?"

Dan didn't answer.

"Dan, what's going on?" Jane sounded even more stressed than when she first answered the phone.

"I'll tell you later. If you have no further information, then I have to go. You can trace the call, but I won't be here when you locate it. I'll contact you later. See about the mole."

He hung up the phone. It didn't matter if they traced the call. He would be gone shortly. They could find out he had been in Paris. But even if they arrived before he left, they still had to find him and no one knew about Luc.

The value of keeping some things to oneself.

Chapter 30

Nikolai knew that the handcuffs dangling from his left wrist marked him. Any *gendarme* seeing them would stop and detain him. He would be under suspicion as an escapee. Even when no record of his arrest was found the questions would be hard to answer.

He ran for many blocks before slowing down. He had a coat and kept his left hand stuffed inside, hiding the shackle. He had some money in his wallet. His first stop would be a store where he could purchase a prepaid cell phone. He needed to contact Kuznetsov to warn him and to protect himself from retribution. It would all be Maxim's fault. He was dead so it wouldn't matter to him.

Nikolai's story was that they had captured Dan again, but Maxim slipped up when guarding him allowing Dan to get the upper hand on them. Maxim was killed by Dan on the way to Paris and Dan kept Nikolai prisoner while trying to extract information from him. Nikolai escaped and was now warning his boss. The virtue of the story was that much of it was true, allowing him to more easily maintain it and keep everything straight.

He was only part of the way through his story when his brigadier told him to wait. He would contact Kuznetsov and have him call back.

Five minutes later Nikolai's phone rang.

"He is coming to Moscow?" Kuznetsov asked. "That is good. I will enjoy killing him. I'll do it slowly and painfully." His anger still burned. His only son was dead and the man responsible was coming to him. It was fortunate. His men had failed, but in a way, maybe they had not. The man he wanted was on his way to Moscow. Not yet his prisoner, but Yevgeni knew he would be. Moscow was his territory. He would find the assassin before he could do whatever he came to do. Then he would have his revenge.

Luc found a 1995 Peugeot 405. It was Peugeot's first front wheel drive car. It came with a 1.9 liter engine that made around 90 horsepower. The five-speed manual gearbox helped keep the motor revving and the car moving at a brisk pace, although Luc warned against aggressive driving with the older machine. Blue smoke would chuff out on start-up indicating worn valve stem seals. Dan didn't worry about it. He didn't plan on having the car make the return trip from Moscow.

When Luc had finished his modifications, Dan set out on the long drive to the Russian capitol. Nikolai getting away was a loss. Kuznetsov would be warned of his coming and Dan would have to find the man on his own. The latter wouldn't be hard, but the former presented problems. Kuznetsov would be anticipating him. He'd have his defenses ready. This would make it harder for Dan to capture him. Dan didn't want to kill the man. He needed to interrogate him, to find out where the briefcase was so he could figure out how to get it.

Luc waved goodbye to him, happy to see him go and happy to deposit the two thousand euros. The sale of the Berlingo van would add to that total.

Dan took the A2 from Paris into Belgium and then on to Cologne and Hanover. He bypassed Berlin to the south and headed to Poland on what became the E30 once he'd left Germany. By Poznań, he'd been on the road for fifteen hours and was falling asleep.

He pulled into a travel stop outside of the city. A light snow was falling. He found a parking spot away from lights and leaned his seat back, trying to stretch his tight muscles. The night's cold crept into the car as Dan tried to find some sleep. After three hours, he started the car to warm up the cabin. After getting the inside overly hot, he turned the engine off and tried again to fall asleep.

Sleep wouldn't come. His mind kept going back to Provence and Christina. A few short days ago he was enjoying the peace of her cottage and the joy and passion of her company. Now he was trying to stretch out in a cramped car, on a cold, gray night in Poland. He smiled as he thought about how his quality of life had degraded since the two Russian gangsters intruded upon his hideaway.

Finally he dozed off only to wake hours later shivering. He heated the car once again and, after another three hours of fitful sleeping, he got up and drove around to the restaurant. After a bathroom stop and getting some coffee and a pastry, Dan was back on the road.

The E30 was a four-lane, divided highway. It stretched out before him as he droned on and on through the Polish plains. The day was gray with a north wind blowing off the Baltic Sea. In Provence, the day would probably be sunny with the temperature in the fifties. Here the weather seemed more oppressive, without the hopeful possibilities that one often felt in the south of France.

The Carpathian Mountains were far to the south. To the north, where he drove, the land was flat and wide open. *No wonder Poland could be so easily overrun*. The flat fields, now lying fallow and turning white with snow, would not slow down an advancing army. This was the geography for tank battles with armies advancing behind them.

It seemed dreary to Dan in the monochromatic winter light, and he had to force himself to stay alert. He pushed the Peugeot as hard as he thought prudent. He didn't want to experience a breakdown. Not wanting to risk the attention of the Polish police, he refrained from leading a clump of traffic. Instead he would wait for a bolder driver to cruise past him and then try to follow a quarter mile behind. If the driver braked, Dan would slow to be at a more conservative speed when he reached the same point.

Without his captive, Dan headed for Belarus, it being the faster route to Moscow. He got to the border around noon, just before the Bug River. It was a sternly officious place with long lines of cars and trucks waiting. A serious looking border guard examined his papers with a sour countenance. His passport identified him as Victor James, as did the two credit cards he carried. He explained that he was on his way to Moscow to attend a conference on corporate security in hopes of landing a sale for his company. No, the company did not have the funds to pay for air travel, so, unless he sold a lot of contracts, he was relegated to driving.

Dan smiled at the guard saying he had hopes he would be successful and be able to put the road miles behind him soon. The guard was not impressed, either by Dan's lame attempt at humor, or by his Russian.

"If you speak no better than that, you will not sell much."

"I'm working on it," Dan replied as his passport was stamped and he was waved through.

Belarus was also flat. In fact, the plains ran all the way to Moscow, filled with cultivated fields. Three hours later, Dan arrived in the outskirts of the capital.

Chapter 31

Roman Pavlovich sat in a dreary hotel room in Poldosk, an industrial town thirty-seven miles outside of Moscow. The town housed a sewing machine factory, occupying a full city block. It had been a Singer factory decades ago and still made sewing machines to this day. Huge blocks of apartment buildings erected in the Stalin era gave the town an oppressive look which was only relieved by the closer examination of small churches, an old, pre-revolutionary department store, and the majestic Troitsk cathedral.

Roman had only ventured out to grab some hasty meals and then scurry back to his room where he felt slightly safer. The Russian mafia's tentacles reached deep into society. There could be spies and informants anywhere.

He looked at the metal briefcase sitting in the corner of the room. It had begun to seem like a curse, like the albatross hanging around his neck in the Coleridge rhyme; a piece of writing with which he was vaguely familiar. Worse, that morning a pigeon landed on the window sill outside his room and rammed into the glass, trying to go through the window. Roman was horrified. While not overtly superstitious, he had absorbed certain traditions from his mother and grandmother. A bird tapping on, or flying into one's window was a very bad omen. It often meant death or at least the loss of a limb. Roman had no desire for either.

His situation was dire. He had narrowly escaped death in Milan. He had been on the run since, hiding out, dragging what he now was beginning to think of as the cursed briefcase around with him. It was not the life he had imagined. Yet the metal container still held out hope for riches. But how to cross the divide was the problem. How to convert the briefcase into money?

He cursed his situation and the greed of the mafia boss. If he had only made the exchange, both would have gotten what they wanted. The thought of abandoning the terrible object came to him, but he repeatedly rejected it. He had no work now, no way to earn a living. He was a bureaucrat without any specific skills. At fifty-five, he was past his prime working age. His prospects were dim. Not even a janitor job would be available, most employers wanting a younger, stronger person for that work. No, he'd have to find a way to complete this exchange.

Roman sighed and got up. He slid the briefcase under his bed and headed out of his room. He had found a number for a club in Moscow, one that everyone said was owned by the mafia. He would try to get in touch with Kuznetsov, the man he had previously identified as a mafia boss and the one he had made arrangements with for the rendezvous in Milan. It was the only path open to him.

"I am willing to pay your price for the briefcase," Kuznetsov said after getting on the line with Pavlovich.

Roman had made five different phone calls before getting Kuznetsov's number. He had refused to give out his number because he didn't have one. He was using public phones around Poldosk.

"The problem is how can I trust you to not to just get rid of me and save the money? That is what almost happened in Milan."

"What happened before was that a Chechen gang ambushed both of us. My soldier grabbed you to try to save you."

This story had the virtue of being partly true. All except the part of trying to save Pavlovich.

"It didn't seem like that to me," Roman said.

"That's what happened. You didn't get killed because we fought back. My men were killed including my son. So I have paid a high price for this briefcase. Now we should conclude our dealings."

Roman was quiet.

Kuznetsov continued, "We will make the exchange in Moscow, at one of my clubs. It will be safer for you."

"Safer for you. But there is nothing to keep you from killing me and taking the case."

"You would rather have the Chechens find you? They are probably looking for you as we speak. The longer you wait, the greater the chance of them finding you. Believe me, they will not just take the briefcase. They will take you and kill you slowly. They will blame you for their own comrades' deaths. And they are not very forgiving."

A chill not caused by the grey February day went through Roman. Chechens might be worse than the mafia. Was there no way out? He remembered the pigeon. The omen seemed to be coming true.

"I will call you back. I have to think."

"Do not think too long, *malen'kaya mysh'*. The cat is coming for you."

Back at his hotel room, Roman sat with his head in his hands. He had a strong headache and longed for a large drink. He had to devise a plan to protect himself from both the Chechens and Kuznetsov. *But I'm clever*, he told himself. *I stole the briefcase. I kept it hidden. I can do this.*

Yevgeni Kuznetsov sat back after the phone went dead. Things were complicated. The Chechens were no bluff. They were a presence in Moscow. His organization had fought vicious wars with them over territory. Now they shared Moscow with them. A new Chechen boss had recently arrived. He was a clan warlord. He was nosing around, Kuznetsov assumed, looking for the mouse. He needed to keep him and his men away from the exchange. Once he had the briefcase, he could try to eliminate them.

Then there was the assassin. He was coming. He would try to get intercept the exchange again. The man would locate his headquarters. Would he try to attack there?

Kuznetsov ground his teeth. That's what happened in Milan when he'd killed his son. *He can't get away this time. I'll have my revenge.* He also knew that the assassin, the man who was called Rossignol, was romantically connected to Christina Aubergh. While he had no desire to hurt her (she was such a talent), he knew he could and would use her as leverage against the assassin. *I do what it takes to survive and succeed.* He had operated by that maxim his whole life. If Christina became collateral damage, so be it. He would mourn the loss of her talent, but it would not stop him from exacting his revenge. *Her life for his?* A grim smile played about his face.

When Dan arrived in Moscow, he went to the Arbat House Hotel. It had an attractive exterior and rooms with a hint of pre-revolutionary grandeur. It was located in downtown Moscow which made it convenient for Dan's search. With an adequate bar and a reasonably friendly staff, something not always found in modestly priced hotels in Russia, it fit Dan's needs just fine.

After checking in, his next step was to find Kuznetsov. Dan assumed the pattern would be similar to the mafia he had encountered in Brooklyn. Kuznetsov would have an office at one of the clubs he owned, surrounded by loyal employees, with the *politsiya* paid to leave the place unbothered. He would be in a world peopled with his own, providing more safety than any security agency could offer.

Dan knew of some of the mafia haunts and the restaurants they owned or controlled. No one knew who he was, so he could snoop around. His challenge was to find both Kuznetsov and the mouse. It seemed daunting, but if he found the mobster, that could eventually lead him to Pavlovich and the briefcase. The mouse had no other outlet. Kuznetsov was his only chance to cash in on his stolen property.

Dan spent a week cruising the clubs, working his way from the higher end establishments to the seedier strip and sex clubs. It was in one of the latter, The Pussycat Club, that he learned of Kuznetsov's connection. Now he would hang around for a few days and see who showed up. He knew what Kuznetsov looked like.

During his stakeout, a taxi drove up and stopped on the street across from him. The driver leaned out of his window and fixed Dan with an intense stare.

"You want a ride?" He shouted out.

Dan shook his head. The man was only going to draw attention to him, something he didn't need.

"Are you sure? You want a ride in my taxi." This now sounded less like a question and more like a declaration.

The man waved at him. "Come over. I give you a ride." This last was said in English.

In order to not make more of a scene, Dan walked over to the taxi. The man gestured for Dan to get in. When Dan was in the car, the man turned to him.

He had the eyes. Dan could see it now. The intense look that fixed you. That indicated the person could not only see you, but could see *into* you.

"Are you—?"

The man nodded. "We drive first. It's better to not be seen here."

He pulled out into the traffic and made his way onto *Il'inka* Street. After going a half mile, he turned into a side street and stopped along the curb.

"You are now in one of the dark places in the world."

"Yes, the *Monseigneur* told me. A 'heart of darkness' he called it."

The man nodded. "It is very dangerous for you, but this is where you must be."

“Do you know where the man with the briefcase is? I have to find him.”

“I can’t see him clearly. He is close, but he is not your only task.”

“What else is there to do but secure the briefcase? You must know what it contains.”

“We do. But we are also worried about you. We have pledged to help you. Ever since the Shaman gave you his gift. We are part of your mission, your fight.”

“I’ll be fine when I get control of the briefcase.”

The man shook his head. “There is more here for you to do. The *Monseigneur* told you.”

“I didn’t understand what he told me. ‘Give life to my enemy’ he said. What does that mean?”

“You will know when the time comes. Before it will not make sense to you. This is what we know—understand. It is how you save what is dear to you.”

“What is dear to me? Christina. You know about her?”

The man nodded.

“Is she safe?”

“It is up to you. Right now, she is, but the future…?”

“Right. You don’t see the future in detail.”

Dan choked down his frustration. The Watchers were helpful. They had helped him survive on his missions even when they, like the Shaman, had demanded more of him than he imagined he could deliver.

“Okay. I’ll keep watch for what you say even if I don’t understand. Now, tell me. Where is the mouse?”

“He is being hidden from us. There are powerful forces at work to prevent your success. A man, Lecha Maskhadov, is here. He’s a Chechen warlord and mafia boss. It is very dark around him. He will play a part. You will have to overcome him in the end.”

The taxi driver looked down the street.

“Here, we don’t see so clearly as other places. This is a dark city. The exchange will take place at the Wild Nights Club, not the one where you were waiting. It will be in two days. The hidden man, the one with the briefcase, wants to play a trick. He is afraid for his life. If he does, it will keep the weapon out of the wrong hands and you will have a chance to secure it. But, remember, your work will not be over."

From his attitude, Dan figured the discussion was over. He had the place and the time. That would have to do for now. He would be ready.

Chapter 32

Roman Pavlovich called Kuznetsov the next day. "I will meet with you. This time don't try to do anything but make the exchange. If we both do what we promise, we both get what we want."

"I told you before, we did not try to cross you. The Chechens ambushed our meeting. This time it will be at my club where you'll be safe."

Roman didn't answer. He could only hope Kuznetsov meant what he said. Still he needed a fall back option, something he could use should his life be threatened. He spent the afternoon wracking his brain and by evening, he went out to eat and drink some vodka. A solution had come to his mind. It was imperfect, but it could save his life. Suddenly he felt better than he had for months.

On the day of the exchange, Roman took a taxi to the *Leningradskiy vokzal* or railway station. It was located just outside the Garden Ring, which formed the outer ring road around central Moscow. It had a modestly ornate façade but had the look of so many government buildings, solid and not frivolous. There was a clock tower near the center of the building probably included to help relieve the staid look of the structure. Inside, the architecture was seventies modern with shops located on each side of the main hall. It had the look of an unheated, rundown shopping mall, well past its prime.

The station was located next to *Yaroslavskiy* and across the square from *Kazanskiy* railway stations. The area was called *Komsomolskaya Ploshchad'* or Railway Station

Square. Each of these stations served lines going out into greater Russia in different directions. They reinforced the notion that Moscow was the center of all things Russian.

Earlier in the day, Roman had purchased another metal briefcase and two canisters. Back at his hotel room, he had carefully taken out two of the lethal canisters and put them into the newly purchased case. Then he had put two empty canisters in the original case and locked it closed.

He then went to the train station and rented a locker. In it, he put the case with the two canisters full of their deadly contents. Kuznetsov would be furious at his deception when he discovered it, but Roman would arrange to hand over the last two canisters for a final payment, at the station.

After Kuznetsov left, he would board a train to St. Petersburg and start his journey out of Russia. Along the way, he planned to exit and purchase a car. From there he would drive himself, first to Latvia and then on to Frankfort, Germany where he would catch a flight to London. From London, he could go anywhere and start his new life.

With the two canisters safely in the locker, Roman started out for the designated club. He had decided to not use the front door. Fear of the Chechens made him cautious. Kuznetsov would not do anything outside, but the Chechens might, trying to nab him before he got inside. He guessed they were bold enough to attempt such an act in broad daylight, and in front of Kuznetsov's club. With enough gunmen, they could keep the mobster's security force at bay. The Chechens wouldn't worry about the civilians or the *politsiya*, and he figured, the *politsiya* would not be around, since they seemed to let the Russian mafia pretty much police themselves.

The government, being riddled with corruption, allowed both Russian and Chechen mafias, to operate as long as they understood who had the ultimate power and authority. The Chechen mafia was less tolerated because it had supported the breakaway attempt by Chechnya. However, both mafias were careful not to challenge the areas where the high government officials and their oligarch friends operated. Thus, a semblance of peace and order was established allowing the corruption to continue to line everyone's pockets.

The meeting time had been set for late afternoon, before the club got busy in the evening. Roman hid out behind the club, in an alley. When the meeting time approached, he bribed a worker from the kitchen to let him in when the man came outside to dump some garbage. If he was late, Kuznetsov would wait. What else was he going to do? Roman smiled. He could see the light at the end of his long, dark tunnel. The pigeon would not be prophetic. It was an old-wives tale anyway, wasn't it?

The Wild Nights Club was located in an upscale area with expensive restaurants and stores, but also known as a neighborhood populated by the *bratva*, or brotherhood. The club fit well in its surroundings, being upscale as well as large. Inside it had three separate bars. They ranged from the expensive and classy to the noisy and touristy. There was a quiet bar with posh décor where important people could meet and talk business. They were safe from the possibility of being interrupted by inquisitive reporters or lesser people who were politely but firmly turned away. There was a noisy disco-themed bar that also sported a dance floor complete with flashing lights. Further back in the large building was a strip bar where girls, all young and all with exquisite bodies, pole danced and gyrated. They spent the night getting their thongs stuffed with money—Euros and dollars being most appreciated. For extra money, they would also perform the standard lap dance. Some, for even more money, some would take a patron upstairs to one of the private rooms for an intimate session of sexual activity. The police didn't interfere since the mafia kept things well under control.

Young people who wanted a night out at a disco would spend the evening there, enjoying a sense of living on the wild side, if only more in their imagination than reality. In the end, the drinks were overpriced as were the services of the beautiful girls, but neither the wealthy patrons nor the tourists seemed to mind.

There were also separate rooms on the upper level for private meetings—gatherings that might require more privacy than the business bar. Food and drinks could be brought up in response to orders called in on the house phone. Girls could be ordered in as well to provide atmosphere or enhance the celebration of a completed deal.

In short, the club was the perfect place to make the exchange. It was Kuznetsov's world. *And a perfect place to get rid of this bothersome mouse after the deal is done*, he thought. Unfortunately, the mole in his organization had learned of the meeting place and had informed Lecha of it for a payment of one hundred thousand euros.

Dan watched from his Peugeot. He was parked a half-block away. A newspaper served as a suitable prop for his loitering. He patiently waited. The Watcher had given him the expectation that the meeting was planned for the afternoon. As it grew later, he became more concerned. Had someone changed the plans at the last minute? Moved the exchange? If so, all would be lost. It would be nearly impossible to get the weapon away from Kuznetsov if he managed to get hold of it.

His eye was caught by two Mercedes G Class SUVs that pulled up just ahead of him. The windows were blacked out. It had a gangster look to it. *Chechens?* The hair on the back of Dan's neck stood up. This was a complication he had hoped wouldn't happen. His goal was to nab Pavlovich before he went into the club. If these were Chechens, and they had the same idea he was in trouble. He had only his 9mm pistol. His .M4, with its suppressor, was in the trunk.

He had expected the encounter to be discreet. He would walk up to Pavlovich and quietly let the mouse know that his well-being, his continued existence, depended on him going with Dan. Kuznetsov would assuredly kill him, and Dan was sure he could make that clear, along with the promise that he would do the same if the man didn't go with him. They would get in his car and drive off. Dan would relieve the mouse of his burden and let him go. Now that scenario seemed questionable.

After an hour of waiting, the doors of the first SUV opened. A man motioned to the rear vehicle and five men got out. Nine men, all in long overcoats, not out of place on the cold day, headed for the club entrance. Dan guessed there were automatic weapons under the coats.

Chapter 33

Christina immersed herself in her music after Dan left. She had a concert coming up shortly in Berlin. She was a part of a Beethoven evening. The evening's pieces would include his 3rd Symphony (the Eroica), Egmont Overture, and finish with Christina playing his Emperor Concerto, Beethoven's last and, some say, the greatest of his five.

It was a piece she wouldn't have taken on before Rossignol She was now she liberated from her own prison of technical brilliance. Her grief at Dan's departure, her Rossignol, as she still thought of him, only served to instill more emotion and depth to her music.

Beethoven's Emperor Concerto was revolutionary in some respects. The first movement, the *Allegro*, was longer than the other two combined, the *Adagio* and the *Rondo*. Unlike most of the composers of his time (the early 1800s) Beethoven wrote out all his credenzas, the parts where the orchestra stops and the soloist continues with elaborate flourishes showing off both the instrument and the artist's skill. Beethoven wanted his credenzas to fit with his composition and not have any new "ideas" inserted by the soloist. They were challenging and fiery enough for any artist, maybe made more so, by the need to follow his score correctly.

When Christina arrived in Berlin, three days before the concert, she went to the warehouse holding the collection of Steinways for use by the Berlin Philharmonic Orchestra. She spent an hour playing the pianos before selecting the one she liked. Each had a slightly different tonality. None would be considered wrong or bad, they were, after all, Steinways used by the Philharmonic. But within that group of special instruments were subtle differences and each artist might prefer one over another.

Chloé was with her; ever present, ever patient. She saw Christina's sorrow at Dan's leaving and vowed to assuage it as best she could. She sighed as she watched her artist methodically try out each instrument. Chloé could hear much in music, having grown more sensitive to the level of perfection at which artists like Christina played, but much still escaped her.

If she were honest, she was a bit jealous of Dan's ability to quickly tune into the music at the same level as Christina, even though he played no instrument. He had a sensitivity that was beyond normal. He had sensed that her affection for Christina was multi-layered, with mixed elements influencing one another. For Chloé, it seemed like an unmasking of her hidden love for her artist; something beyond friendship and loyalty.

Chloé felt she belonged to Christina. She had fallen under her spell without Christina even knowing she was casting one. She had decided to link her future with the young, beautiful artist, even if she never was able to fully express the entire range of her feelings. And with that decision, she felt that Christina, in a way, belonged to her.

Dan had been an intruder. He had broken into their pairing. Chloé wasn't thrust out; it was more that Dan had inserted himself, providing another dynamic and giving Christina a new perspective. And with that came their love affair and Christina's freedom of expression.

An ironic smile appeared on Chloé's face as she watched the woman to whom she had dedicated herself. Christina's career was taking off with her new style. Offers, requests, and pleadings were coming in almost daily. She was quickly going to become the hottest ticket on the concert circuit and one of the most sought-after soloists by all the best orchestras.

Now Dan was gone. Chloé didn't wish him harm. He had always been kind and gentle to her, even as he recognized her secret. But he lived in a dangerous world and Chloé knew that there was a very real chance of him never coming back. She straightened her stance. It was her job to help Christina if that came about. She would shore her up, while helping her keep her newly found voice on the piano. That was her mission now.

The night of the concert, Christina sat with Chloé in her dressing room.

"I wonder where Rossignol is now? We could be in the same city and I would not know it."

"He's doing what he left to do. It's best we don't know anything about it. But you shouldn't be thinking about him. Tonight is your moment, your chance to cement your new style. Let them see the full range of your emotion. Certainly, the Emperor is a worthy vehicle for showing off your artistry."

"It is. I can put my sadness into it. My anger and frustration as well." Christina got up. She patted Chloé's cheek as she walked to the door. "Don't worry Chloé. It will go well tonight. Now I have to go walk around. I'll be on soon." She left the dressing room to pace the backstage area, massaging her hands.

The applause was strong but polite when Christina and the conductor walked onto the stage. She shook hands with the first violinist and then bowed to the audience with the conductor. She sat down as the conductor took to his podium. The piece started with three grand chords. The bottom note of the chord was the same as the key. They were open, uncomplicated, inviting and easy to hear. The ear always responded to such "human" chords. In between were rolling flourishes, amplifying the structure of each chord. Her trills were bell-like moments of precision, sparkling gems in a changing light.

After the opening, Christina rested for one hundred measures while the orchestra took up the motifs in the music; ones that would be revisited throughout the piece. She sank into the music. The themes that she was going to play flowed around her as she sat at the piano. The second theme emerged and, after the orchestra played it through, the French horns repeated it in a warmer tone.

Finally, the orchestra subsided and Christina began to play what the orchestra had introduced, elaborating on the themes with flowing credenzas while the orchestra waited for her. They were now backing her up as she played.

The first theme ended in an intense run up the keyboard. At the top it seamlessly transitioned into the second theme. It was like a pianissimo march; a delicate melody that almost sounded Slavic. The music went back to the first theme now, more aggressive than the second one with Christina forcefully attacking the keyboard. She worked the melody with her right hand while her left punctuated it with strong bass chords underneath.

And so it went. Christina put her passion for Rossignol, her anger at his leaving, her heartbreak over the loss of their innocence, into the music. She tapped into Beethoven's joy in the music as well as his anger. She matched the orchestra chord for chord, making the piano stand up to the power of the assembled instruments.

In the quieter moments of the *Allegro*, Christina let all her love flow out in the notes, caressing them, then cutting them off when the composer seemed to call for it. She relished in the rich tonic chords that reappeared, showing off the grand piano's ability to enhance the orchestra. The second theme, whenever it emerged, gave her the opportunity to express her now-frustrated love.

Nearing the end of the *Allegro*, Christina ran through a credenza that spread over the whole keyboard in an energetic flurry of notes which ended in a wonderfully, crystal clear set of trills that slowed down without a hint of losing their rhythmic perfection into the second theme. This time played with a light, staccato touch making it sound like a fairy tale. Again, the French horns warmed the sound.

From there, the orchestra and Christina played duet-like through the rest of the *Allegro*, sometimes backing one another, but more often alternating the motifs. The piano part was dense with notes. Beethoven seemed to have had so much in his head that he almost overwhelmed the instrument with all the notes he wrote down. The movement came to an end with two victorious, grand chords.

As the last two chords struck, Christina looked up triumphantly at the conductor. He let the sound die away to silence as the audience waited for the *Adagio*.

It began with the orchestra playing softly and smoothly, like a wide, gently flowing river that hinted of hidden power while presenting a calm face. Now there were fewer notes, Beethoven letting spaces and simplicity express instead of a flurry of notes. Christina caressed the keys, letting out her longing for everyone to see. She made it her personal love song, which is how she thought the master had composed it.

Her hands were the hands of love as she played. The crescendos were delicate, subdued, with a return to the love song. Tears began to well up in her eyes, but she paid no attention. There was no music to read. It was memorized and coming from her heart. As in Paris, the conductor caught the emotion as did the orchestra. Each instrument section contributed to her ode to love. Gently, tenderly Christina and the orchestra ended the movement.

Without stopping, as Beethoven wrote the piece, the *Rondo* started with a quiet transition to the main theme. Then it took off with a romp into a fiery dance, full of joy and excitement. The music evoked images of a dancing troupe in a town square.

The flurry of notes returned. Christina reveled in them. Her hands flew across the keyboard, the tears now abated. She smiled as her hands danced to the composer's score. Her joy was as infectious as her expression of love. The conductor and orchestra were almost bouncing as they made their way through the movement.

The runs and trills continued through the piece with sudden flourishing stops to let the orchestra pick up the theme. Up and down the keyboard, it seemed as if Beethoven did not want to ignore a single note. The audience could see the smiles on the faces of the musicians as well as Christina.

The piece ended with a short, delicate duet between Christina and the tympani followed by a furious run through the keyboard and two final, grand chords. Christina sat back with a smile on her face. She looked triumphant as the conductor directed the last notes of the orchestra.

The audience erupted. After the hand shaking and bows, they wouldn't stop until there had been four curtain calls. Finally, they closed the curtain with the clapping still going on. Christina's hair was matted with sweat at the edges. Chloé rushed up to hug her and give her a full kiss on the cheek; much more than a polite peck.

"You were wonderful," she whispered.

Christina smiled. "Thank you."

The conductor came up, took her hand and kissed it.

"That was memorable. I don't know when I've been so moved, or had more fun."

Some members of the orchestra milled around, congratulating her. Chloé started moving the throng back to the dressing room. The bouquets would be coming. She knew the routine.

She smiled. Dan was gone, but his contributions to Christina's new expression remained. It had grown since Paris. Chloé could only wonder at where they could go from here. But she was going to help make it happen. She would help Christina hold on to her new emotive style whether or not Dan came back.

Chapter 34

Once inside the club, Roman Pavlovich made his way through the kitchen. He went up to a man who looked like a guard or a bouncer. The man was large and had an imposing air about him. It was accentuated by the bulge of a handgun under his jacket.

"I have an appointment to see Yevgeni Kuznetsov. I'm Roman Pavlovich." Roman clutched his briefcase tightly to his body.

The man looked at him. He took out a phone and made a call. Then he motioned for Roman to follow him. They went up a staircase and down a hall. One side overlooked the disco dance floor, the other was lined with private rooms or offices. Halfway down the hall, he knocked on a door.

"*Da*," someone said. The guard opened the door and motioned for Roman to go inside. He closed it after him.

Roman was now sweating profusely. He stepped into the room. There was a long table with six men around it. Kuznetsov sat at the head. He motioned for Pavlovich to sit down.

"You're late," Kuznetsov said after Pavlovich took a seat, still clutching the briefcase.

"I took pains to make sure I wasn't followed."

"You're safe here. No one can get to you inside my club."

"So you say. I was worried about that other group getting to me outside your club."

Kuznetsov shrugged. *Eto ne vazhno*, it doesn't matter. You're here now." He leaned forward. "You have the material we seek. Let's make the exchange."

"I would like to see the money, please." Pavlovich was nervous. He was in a dangerous situation but needed to show some strength.

Kuznetsov nodded to one of the men at the table who produced a briefcase filled with euros. Pavlovich gestured to see the contents up close and the briefcase was slid over the table to him. His inspection confirmed the presence of the five million. He nodded and closed the case.

"Now your briefcase," Kuznetsov said.

Pavlovich swallowed. This was the critical moment. The meeting could blow up in his face if Kuznetsov reacted badly to his deception. Roman knew the man could not lose face in front of his lieutenants and captains. He had to make Kuznetsov see what Roman was going to propose was a sensible way of increasing his security while keeping to his side of the bargain.

He unlocked the suitcase.

"Mr. Kuznetsov, I have made an adjustment to the exchange. I hope you will understand."

Yevgeni stared hard at his little mouse.

"I am at your mercy, here, in your club." Roman swept his arm around. "There is nothing to stop you from killing me and keeping the money *and* the briefcase."

"What is this change you are talking about?" Kuznetsov's voice held a strong hint of danger and, with it, injury.

"I, I only want one million right now. And for that, I will turn over one of the canisters."

"I see three. What are you saying?"

"One is filled, the other two are empty."

"What are you trying to pull? Where are the other two?" Kuznetsov said in a loud voice. Pavlovich could see his anger rising.

"Sir, I have them safe. I want to meet you in a public space to transfer the other two along with the final payment."

"*Podonok*, scumbag!" Kuznetsov said in a loud voice. "You're just a worm to me. You think you can dictate terms? My son was killed trying to save you from the Chechens!" He was shouting now as he stood up. "Now you want to go out in public? To get murdered by those bastards?"

Pavlovich shrank from his anger.

"Please. I will complete the deal. I made the change to protect myself, not to cross you."

One of the men seated next to Pavlovich reached over and grabbed the briefcase of money and slid it back across the table. He then slapped Pavlovich in the head with enough force to drive the man back in his seat.

The sound of automatic gunfire from downstairs was heard in the room. Two men immediately got up from the table, drawing their pistols, and started for the door. Another closed the briefcase with the canisters.

Lecha entered the club. A bouncer stepped up and confronted the group.

"What do you want?" he asked.

"We're here to see Kuznetsov. Where is he?"

"He's busy. He can't see anyone."

"He can see me. I'm Lecha Maskhadov. Just tell me where he's hiding."

"I don't know you and I don't care who you are. You don't see him. Now you have to go."

Two other bouncers approached.

Lecha smiled. It was a cruel, wolf-like smile from a man who relished an impending battle.

"You will tell me where he is now, or suffer the consequences."

He opened his coat to reveal the Kalashnikov hidden beneath. The bouncer drew a pistol out of his jacket as did the other two. Before they could put their weapons in play, two of Lecha's men opened up with short bursts of their automatic carbines and the three guards fell to the floor.

Patrons screamed and scrambled to get under tables. Two more guards came out from another bar and were immediately shot down. Lecha's men sprayed bullets around the room, shattering bottles and glasses behind the bar. The bartender had dropped to the floor to get out of the line of fire. Two bouncers opened fire from the top of the stairs, hitting one of Lecha's men. The shooters fell in a hail of bullets from the Chechens. Lecha shouted for the men to follow him up the stairs.

At the top, he turned down the hallway. A door opened halfway down and shots were fired. Lecha's men sprayed the hall with machine gun fire and ran towards the door. They burst into the room where Pavlovich and Kuznetsov were sitting. His men opened fire but were outgunned. Bullets from the Chechen's AK47s slammed into them, ripping their bodies open and throwing them to the floor or against the wall. Six of them went down from the automatic rifle fire. Pavlovich dove for cover but not before a bullet tore into his side.

Kuznetsov dropped down under the table and pulled out his .45 caliber Makarov.

"We take Kuznetsov alive!" Lecha shouted as they gunned down the Russians.

Before Kuznetsov could fire, two of Lecha's men dove on him and took away his gun. They tied his hands behind him with his belt. The Chechens started for the door. The first man who stepped into the hallway was killed in a hail of bullets by Kuznetsov's remaining men.

"We need another way out," shouted Lecha. He went back into the room and grabbed one of Kuznetsov's men who was not yet dead.

"Is there a back way out?" he shouted at the man. The wounded man just glared at him and tried to spit in his face. Lecha pulled his pistol out and shot him in the head.

"Break through the wall," he told the men standing with him. "The rest of you keep them from getting to the door. Don't let them come down the hall."

The men in the room started smashing chairs into the wall, breaking through the drywall and plaster. Soon there was a hole large enough to climb through.

Downstairs the nightclub had erupted in panic. The disco floor had cleared in a stampede that left numerous patrons lying on the dance floor, injured with broken limbs. People were pouring out of the entrance and running down the street.

Once the Chechens had gone upstairs people started to run for the doors to escape getting caught in the hail of bullets. Kuznetsov's men gathered at the top of the stairs, exchanging fire with the Chechens down the hallway.

"Go into the next room and do it again," shouted Lecha. We'll hold them off from this room."

When they were two rooms down the hall, Lecha had his men wait at the door. Soon they heard Kuznetsov's men come down the hallway.

"Let them get into the room, then we can control the hallway and retreat to the stairs in the rear. We'll go out the rear."

When the shooting from the room stopped, Kuznetsov's men came down the hallway moving cautiously with guns ready. When they got to the room, they went in. At that moment, Lecha and his men stepped into the hall and ran to the back stairwell.

"You two bring the cars around to the back door," Lecha told the drivers. "We'll hold them off up here. Be ready to pick us up when we come out."

The men ran down the stairs just as Kuznetsov's men came out of the room. The Chechens opened fire and three of them fell, two in the hall and one back into the room. For the next two minutes heavy gunfire was exchanged between the two groups

Suddenly, Lecha heard a call, "Commander!", from the bottom of the stairs. He ordered a retreat, sending the man with the two briefcases and the two men holding Kuznetsov down the stairs. He gave them a minute's head start and then ordered his men to open fire into the hall and room entrance with one last blistering volley. After the volley, they bolted down the stairs, tumbled into the SUVs, and roared down the alley, back onto the Moscow streets just as Kuznetsov's men came out of the exit door.

Dan was unsure of what to do when he saw the Chechens go into the building. Pavlovich had not arrived at the door. He was inclined to let the two groups kill each other. He could nab Pavlovich when he arrived, although the fact that he hadn't shown up yet nagged at him. Something was wrong.

He heard the sound of gunfire coming from inside the club. Moments later people started running out of the building. He started to get out of his car when two of the Chechens ran around the corner of the building and jumped into their SUVs. They made a sharp U-turn and roared back around and into the alley from where they had emerged.

Got to see what's going on. Dan ran to the entrance and jammed his way through the panic crowd trying to get out.

Inside, he saw the bodies lying on the ground. A man came out from a doorway pointing an AK at him. Dan raised his hands.

"*Ne strelyay*, don't shoot."

The man hesitated.

"Where is your boss? We have to help him," Dan shouted.

The man glanced upstairs and Dan ran for the stairs before he could ask any questions. He took the steps two at a time banking on the man's confusion to give him a chance to get out of his line of fire.

Instead of shooting, the man followed Dan. They both got to the room nearly at the same time. It was a scene of carnage. Six men lay shot, two slumped across the table and the rest on the floor or against the wall. Dan looked around. Kuznetsov was not in the room. *They took him.*

He spied Pavlovich under the table. The man was moving. He was alive. Dan knelt down close to him.

"Can you hear me? Did the Chechens take the briefcase?"

Pavlovich nodded.

"Key," he whispered and then groaned in pain.

"What?"

"Key," he said, louder this time. And then, "dacha."

"What key? What dacha?" Dan asked. Roman let out a sigh. "Dacha," he said again, and then his eyes went sightless. Pavlovich's dreams of a luxury retirement ended under a table in a strip club in Moscow.

Dan felt around in the man's pockets and found a locker key. It had the name of the train station on it. Could Pavlovich have kept the canisters there instead of bringing them to the club? That seem crazy, but he'd check it out. He pocketed the key.

He got up as others came into the room.

"I need to get in touch with Kuznetsov's wife. The Chechens may come for her," Dan said to someone who looked to be in charge.

"Who are you and how did you get in?" the men asked. He was angry and suspicious.

"I've been tracking the Chechen gang. They led me here. I think they may go after Kuznetsov's wife. Help me warn her."

"Get out. You're a stranger. We don't deal with strangers. Maybe you led the Chechens here yourself."

"Don't be stupid. If I did, I wouldn't stick around. I followed them here and came in after hearing the shooting."

Sirens could now be heard in the distance.

"You better clean this up. The *politsiya* are coming."

"Get him out of here," the man said, "before I add him to the body count."

One of the men grabbed Dan by the arm and shoved him into the hall. He started walking him down the hall.

“Give me Duscha’s phone number at least. Let me call her and warn her.”

“You know her?” the man asked.

Dan nodded. “Just her number. If I call her, she’ll know who I am,” he lied. “I want to let her know I’ll get her husband back.”

The gangster looked doubtful. Dan hoped he had convinced him that giving out the phone number would be okay. When they got downstairs, the man wrote it on a piece of paper at the front desk. After grabbing it, Dan ran outside. The sirens were closer.

He got into his car and drove off down the street as the police pulled up to the club entrance.

Chapter 35

Dan headed for the *Leningradskiy* railway station. He hoped he would find all three canisters there. That would bring this mission to an end. Or would it? The words of the Watcher came to mind. He guessed his plans had to involve Kuznetsov. Nikolai said the mafia boss believed Dan had killed his son. Such an act would create a vendetta that could only be resolved in blood. As he drove along his mind went over possible strategies.

Secure the canisters first. Then try to figure out where the Chechens have taken Kuznetsov and get to him before they kill him. If they killed him, would that solve his problem? There were others in his family. They would take up the vendetta. While not as bad as the Chechens, the Russian mafia was certainly capable of holding a grudge for many decades. But how to prove a negative?

He shook his head as if to clear it. *First the canisters.* But what did Pavlovich mean by dacha? It had to be important to be his last word on Earth.

He drove down the large boulevard to *Komsomolskaya* Square and turned into a street-level parking area between the station and some shops. He pulled the Peugeot into a space and stopped. There would be some sort of a checkpoint. Security would be checking passengers, more carefully when they entered than when they left.

If the canisters were here, Pavlovich got them in somehow, it should be easier to leave. Would the guards even be looking at luggage on exit? His backpack would pass examination when he entered; there was only a change of clothing in it. He had his documents. But getting out? *Go in and watch how the checkpoint is being operated*. If it looked too dangerous, he'd have to work out another plan.

He slipped off his 9mm along with its holster, stuffed them under the seat, and got out of the car. Inside the station, the security was cursory, and once inside the checkpoint, Dan took time to watch the exiting passengers. They passed out of the station with even less scrutiny. He would be able to leave without complication.

After five minutes of wandering around, he found the lockers. He made a pass of the room and could detect no one monitoring the locker he was targeting. He walked up and unlocked it. Inside was a metal briefcase. Dan slid it out and closed the locker, leaving the key in it. He walked off with a casual pace and headed for the restrooms.

Inside, he locked himself in a stall and opened the case, revealing two full canisters. Dan stared at them for a long moment. *Damn!* That meant the Chechens probably had the third one. His quest was not over by a long shot. With something so deadly, Dan knew that two out of three was still a failure and thousands could die as a result. He had to secure the third canister. He carefully placed the canisters in his backpack and, after putting the briefcase on the back of the toilet, he exited the restroom.

Back in the Peugeot Dan drove down the *Academician Sakharov* Avenue until he reached the Garden Ring, the inner ring road that circled the center of Moscow. He was headed for the U.S. embassy located almost directly on the other side of the city. It was near the New *Arbat* Avenue, a pedestrian street, full of tourists, with sidewalk cafés and people spending time sitting outside when the sun was shining and air warm. Today few would be out in the gray of early February.

The traffic, as usual for Moscow, was terrible. The city, even with its wide boulevards and ever-present Metro, still had huge traffic problems. Dan kept thinking about how to handle the two canisters as he worked his way counter-clockwise around the center of the city.

Drop them off at the embassy? But how?

He could not just drive up and park, then walk up and tell the guard that he had a weapon of mass destruction in his backpack which he wanted to drop off. He would be subdued on the spot and held captive. His cover would be blown, as his actions would reverberate all the way up to the CIA in Langley. It would blow up the whole operation.

When he got close, he dropped off the ring road and looked for a place to park. After circling around for five minutes, he was able to grab a spot. *Got to call Jane.* He didn't want to, but he needed her help to make this handoff happen. With two of them safe, he could then chase down the third canister, which he assumed was in the possession of the Chechens.

"Jane here," the familiar voice said when Dan made the call.

"Jane, I need some help."

"Dan, where are you? What's going on?"

"Just let me talk. I've retrieved two of the three items we're looking for. I need you to arrange for someone to meet me so I can turn them over. I need to go find the third."

"Okay. Tell me where you are."

"Moscow. Get someone here into action and call me. I'll need some way to identify them and I'll direct them as to where we meet."

"Do you know where the third item is?"

"No. The sooner you can take charge of these two, the sooner I can get on it."

"Do you need any help?"

"I feel the same as before. There's no time and I'd rather do this alone. Something's still not right in your area and I don't want to be compromised again."

"We haven't found anything yet, although we're early in our investigation."

"Keep going. And Jane...don't have anyone try to follow me after the transfer. I won't take kindly to that and they might get hurt."

Dan was not in the mood for dealing with anyone interfering at this critical time. "Call me back in an hour," he said.

After Dan hung up, Jane called Henry.

"Dan's in Moscow. He has two canisters. He says a third on is still on the loose."

"I'm on my way," Henry said. He hung up the phone and headed to Jane's small set of offices.

"Does he know where it is?" he asked when he entered.

"No. Right now he needs to get these two handed off. Then he'll go after the third."

"Go after? Does he know who has it? Is it still in Pavlovich's hands?"

Jane shook her head. "He didn't say. I don't think he wanted to stay on the line very long. He's still paranoid about Milan."

"Damn it." Henry paced Jane's small space. "We don't have time for that. Thousands could be killed by just one canister."

"Henry, let's help him hand over the two he has. Then we can work with him to get the other one. First things first."

"Have him take them to the embassy."

Jane just looked at Henry.

"You're right," Henry said. "That's a bad idea." He paused for a moment. "I've got someone in the embassy." His name is Boris. I'll give him a call."

Henry picked up Jane's secure phone and put in a call to the embassy. It was 1pm in D.C., 9pm in Moscow. When he got the duty officer on the line, he had them track down Boris and contact him. Henry had to use his rank to get things into action.

An hour later, Jane called Dan back.

"I've got an asset. His name is Boris. He's in the city and waiting for your call."

She gave him the number and Dan hung up before Jane could ask him any more questions. He called the number she gave him.

"Who am I talking to?" Dan asked when the man answered.

"Boris. Is this Dan?"

"Yes. Where are you?"

"I'm in Shokoladnica, a coffee shop on *Arbat* Street."

"Good. What are you driving?"

"A BMW 328. Black.

"Head to *Ninsky* Boulevard and turn north. I'll call you later."

He hung up and pulled out into the traffic. He had to hurry across the city. He would meet Boris in a public place and needed to get there ahead of the man. An hour later he was parked behind the Metropol Hotel, one of the grand old dames of world-class hotels.

It had survived the revolution and the counterrevolution, while keeping its impeccable service intact. The Soviet apparatchiks who preached the classless society had let the hotel fall into neglect. But when they began to open up to the West, they realized that the Metropol made a great statement of richness, refinement and success. The grand structure was reconditioned back to its former glory and visiting businessmen and officials were directed there.

The Soviet officials also enjoyed the fruits of this renovation as well, consoling their consciences with the fact that the people actually owned the elaborate furnishings and fixtures—the communists had placed a label somewhere on each piece of furniture indicting it was owned by the soviet citizens—even though the people (as in the proletariat) would never enjoy them.

By the time he got in place, Boris, who had kept driving, was now on *Christoprudny* Boulevard, having followed the same road which changed names from Ninsky, through *Christoprudny*, to, finally, *Yauzsky* Boulevard, before crossing the Moscow River.

"Where are you now?" Dan asked after Boris answered his phone.

"On *Christoprudny* Boulevard heading to the river."

"Good. Keep going and turn right on the Embankment road, just before the bridge. Call me when you make that turn." This was the road that ran along the Moscow River as it curved its way through the city.

After making the turn, Boris called and was told to go to St. Basil's Cathedral next to Red Square, which was not open to vehicles. Then he was told to work his way around the square, going north. When he was north of Red Square, Dan directed Boris to head east on *Ulitsa Okhotnyy* and to keep his phone connected. He then had him pull into the street parking between the Metropol and the Karl Marx Memorial.

Dan watched the BMW pull in and waited. *Patience*, he reminded himself. If Boris was followed, he'd see some evidence of the fact. The phone line, remaining open, didn't allow Boris to make a call. Still Dan knew the man would be tracked by his phone. He studied the traffic intently for five minutes.

Then he began to walk towards the BMW. He kept scanning his surroundings, looking for any evidence of surveillance. Nothing. When he got to the car, he rapped on the driver's window and a startled Boris lowered it.

Dan motioned for him to hang up his phone.

"You have a pack for the canisters?"

Boris nodded and pointed to the passenger seat.

"Put it in your lap and open it slowly."

Boris did as he directed. Dan slid off his own backpack and opened it. He took one of the canisters out and handed it to Boris.

"You know what this contains?"

"No."

"That's fine. But understand that it's lethal and can kill you and hundreds around you if you damage the canister. Handle with care. Got it?"

The man nodded. Dan gave him the second one. When the two were safely in the pack, Dan directed Boris to leave on the road he arrived.

"If you or anyone else try to follow me, they'll be in danger of being shot. I'm very good at spotting surveillance and I have no patience for it."

The man nodded.

"Tell Jane you have the two items. Don't describe them over the phone. She'll give you instructions on what to do, if she hasn't already."

"Is there anything you want me to tell her?"

"If I want to tell her anything, I'll call her myself. Now go."

Dan watched him pull out and then walked quickly back to his Peugeot. He'd lose himself in the Moscow traffic while he considered his next move.

Chapter 36

After turning over the two canisters, Dan began to think about the word “dacha”. What significance did it have for Pavlovich to make it his last, dying word? Dan knew Russians who lived in the cities often had dachas. It had something to do with their national character—wanting to return to their peasant roots, maybe. Certainly, trying to stay close to the soil and source of food.

Did the Chechens have a dacha? Somewhere to take Kuznetsov? Doubtful. Or did Kuznetsov have a dacha?

There were two SUVs full of Chechens plus their captive. Cameras in the street would have captured their license plates and pictures of the vehicles. They couldn’t drive around Moscow for long without being stopped. Kuznetsov, even being a member of the mafia, was important enough to have the police mount a search for the vehicles. Especially when the incident would be reported as the kidnapping of a nightclub owner with his criminal connections downplayed.

Duscha might be of some help. It was a risk, but he had no other leads to pursue and didn’t think he had a lot of time. The Chechens would be looking for the other two canisters and would aggressively interrogate Kuznetsov to find them. He was tough, but he’d talk eventually. If he knew, then sooner or later the Chechens would know. The interrogations also could go wrong and he could die. Time was short. Once the Chechens determined they could not retrieve the two missing canisters, they would kill Kuznetsov and disappear with the one they had. Thousands of lives depended on that not happening.

The gangster lived near the *Estate Arkhangelskoye*, now a museum. It consisted of a grand palace with formal grounds surrounding it, all set out in a large forest. It was northwest of the city just over the Moscow River. Thankfully, the residence was not in a gated community, but each mansion was surrounded by serious walls designed, not for looks, but to keep people out and keep them from seeing inside.

Dan cruised past the mansion. It had a gate, strongly made, with surveillance cameras and an intercom to call the main house. He parked up the street on the edge of the road. The Peugeot would begin to attract attention after an hour, so he had to work fast. He checked his .22 caliber CZ with its suppressor. *Hope I don't have to use it*. Killing one or more bodyguards was not a good way to gain Duscha's trust.

He walked back along the road and when he came near the mansion, he ducked into the trees. Thankfully the residents of the community liked the sense of privacy the woods provided and kept large swaths in place offering good cover for Dan as he approached the grounds.

He studied the wall and cameras for some time from the safety of the woods. After a careful search along the wall, Dan found a dark spot where the cameras did not overlap. He jumped up and pulled himself over.

Once over the wall he slipped into a close-by bush and watched the yard. There were cameras on the mansion. He took out the .22 pistol. The sound wouldn't carry to the front gate and certainly not into the house. There were no open windows on the cold, grey February day. He selected one of the cameras and shot it out. The gun gave a short, fuzzy crack similar to a stick snapping.

Inside the mansion, one of the camera feeds went blank. He was relying on inattentive security to give him a few minutes to get into the house before any alarm was raised. He sprinted to the wall of the building.

The cameras on the house were aimed into the yard. If he kept close to the walls, they would not pick him up. He made his way to a set of French doors opening to a sun room. There was no one inside. Dan chanced that the doors were not alarmed since it was daytime. The door handle and latch were lightweight. He took hold of it and, putting all of his weight on it, yanked the handle. The lock snapped and he entered.

Taking a lot of chances. He knew he was operating without proper advance surveillance and information, but he didn't have time to do things more precisely. His plan was to neutralize any inside security and not kill them if he could avoid it. Then he would talk with Duscha. If she cooperated, he could be gone and the men at the gate would never know he had been there.

First, find the security room with the monitors. There would be someone there. He'd overpower them and tie them up. There would be some number of employees in the house—maids, a cook, and perhaps even a butler. *If I can get ahold of one of them, they can lead me to the security room.* Dan didn't relish sneaking around the house trying to find that room. People would be about. It was getting towards dinner time; there would be normal household activities going on.

He moved through the sun room into the main house and a long hallway. The kitchen would be on the main floor. It was probably the best place to start. The evening meal preparation had begun. Dan followed the aroma of the cooking down the hallway, noting doors along the way that he could duck into if someone came along.

He heard footsteps approaching from a side hallway leading towards the front of the house. He ducked into a room. It was a library lined with floor-to-ceiling bookshelves on the two sidewalls. There were two ladders mounted on rails that could slide along the shelving making the upper shelves accessible. Opposite the door were eight-foot tall windows looking out over a formal garden.

With his ear pressed to the door, Dan waited for the footsteps to disappear. They hadn't come past the room he was in, so he was unsure of where the person had gone. He slowly turned the doorknob and pulled the door open a crack. The limited view of the hall showed nothing. He listened for a minute. No sound. He pulled the door further back and looked down the hall in both directions. There was no one in sight.

Dan stepped out and started towards the source of the cooking odors. The kitchen was at the end of the hall, with swinging doors such as you might find in a restaurant. He worked his way to them, pressed against the hallway wall. The doors had round portal-like windows. Once there he chanced a look inside. A man with an apron and chef's hat was chopping vegetables at a table, his back to the door. To one side, a woman, probably the maid, was sitting on a stool drinking a cup of what Dan assumed was tea.

Dan pushed open the door and stepped in with his pistol held in front of him.

Chapter 37

"Don't move," Dan said in Russian, his voice sharp. The maid dropped her cup on the floor as the chef turned with his knife in the air.

"This gun is quiet and will kill you," Dan said to the cook as he pointed his .22 at the man. "Put the knife down and sit. I'm not here to hurt either of you."

The chef's face, which first reflected his surprise, turned to anger. "Who are you?" he demanded.

"Someone who wants to help Yevgeni. He's in trouble."

"He's not here. Why come like a thief?"

Dan ignored the question. "I know he's not here. I have to talk with Duscha so I can go help him. He's been kidnapped."

"*O nyet!*" The maid exclaimed putting her hand to her mouth.

"I'm going to tie you up for a little while," he said to the chef. "It's for your safety and mine. You," he said looking at the maid, "you'll take me to the security room."

He directed the maid to take off the chef's apron and belt. She secured his hand behind his back while Dan covered them with his gun. When she was done, Dan had her sit on the floor while he improved on the chef's restraints. Then he put the chef in the pantry and turned down the flame under the pot on the stove.

"Now we go," he said to the maid.

They left the kitchen and the maid led them to a staircase. Before stepping out of the hallway to the larger space surrounding the stairs, Dan whispered to the frightened woman.

“Where is Duscha?”

“She is in her sitting room on the second floor.”

“Are there any other guards inside?”

“Just the man who monitors the security cameras.”

“Children?”

The woman shook her head. “The daughter is at school. She will be home in half an hour.”

“Okay. Let’s go. They went up the stairs. At the top, the maid turned left and went down the hall. She nodded towards the door at the end of the long corridor.

“You go first,” Dan said in a whisper.

She took a deep breath and turned the knob.

A man was sitting back in a chair asleep. His hands were folded across his large belly. He sat up when he heard the door open.

“Irina, what are you—”

He stopped short upon seeing Dan behind the maid with his pistol pointed at him.

“*Tsi shih nah*, quiet,” Dan commanded.

The man started to pull his pistol out of his holster. Dan shot him in the arm. The maid let out a stifled scream.

“*Sshh*,” Dan said to her.

He stepped to the security guard and took away his gun before he could try to use it again.

“Come over here,” Dan said to the maid. Take his belt and tie him up like you did the chef.”

The woman fumbled around and finally complied.

“Who are you?” the guard asked.

Dan shook his head. There was no time to talk.

“Give me your apron,” he said to her.

After she took off the apron, Dan tore it into strips and used it to, first tie a wrap around the man’s bullet wound. Next, he tied his feet together and left him hog-tied on the floor.

He leaned down to the man. “If you raise an alarm, people will get killed, you among them. I’m not here to hurt anyone, just to get some information and then I'll be gone. Keep quiet, and no one gets hurt."

With the guard secured, Dan motioned the maid to leave with him.

"Now we see Duscha."

She led Dan down the hall in the direction they had come. They passed the grand staircase and continued to the other side of the house. The maid stopped at a door part of the way down the hall and nodded.

Dan motioned for her to open the door and go in. When she did, he followed close behind her.

"Irina, what is it?" Duscha looked up from a newspaper she was reading. "Who are you?" she said in alarm after seeing Dan behind the maid. He had pocketed his weapon but he knew his strange presence was still startlingly out of place.

Dan motioned for the maid to go to a second chair near where Duscha was sitting.

"Who are you and how did you get in? I'm not expecting anyone. I've ordered the guards to not let anyone in."

"You were called then? You know what happened at the club?"

She nodded all the while eyeing him cautiously.

"Are you one of them?" she asked.

"*Nyet*. It was Chechens. A gang captured your husband. They want something from him. Something he won't be able to give them." Dan paused. "The result is that he could be killed."

"How do you know this? What do you have to do with me or my husband? How did you get in?" Her questions came in rapid fire. She seemed, to Dan, to be headed towards panicking.

"Stay calm," he said. "I'll explain as best I can. I don't have much time so you need to answer my questions."

"First, tell me how you know about me, about Yevgeni?"

"We're both looking for the same thing."

She studied Dan, her face shifting from impending panic to confusion, then calculation.

"The same thing. You are also after *malen'kaya mysh'*?"

Dan nodded. He held her gaze waiting for her to process the information.

"You..." she stood up. "You...are you the assassin?" Now more forcefully, "Are you the one who killed my Vasilij?"

Dan shook his head, "Nyet. I was there, but I didn't kill him. The Chechens ambushed the exchange and one of them killed your son. I was shot by one of your husband's men."

"You lie!" she shouted at him. She collapsed back in her chair. "Why help him...if he had you shot?"

"Because helping him may help me find what the mouse had."

"It is not with *malen'kaya mysh'*?"

"No. He's dead."

Now Duscha seemed to have gathered back her composure.

"Why should I help you? You say that you didn't kill Vasilij, but I don't believe you. And you and my husband want the same thing. I can't help you find it or take it from him."

Her face was now set hard as she glared at him. Dan had to admit that she had backbone. She was no shrinking violet.

"First," he replied, "I may be the only one who can save his life. Second, you are not safe. If the Chechens are thwarted, they may exact revenge, not only on Yevgeni, but on you and your daughter. Do you think you are safe here? I got in. They also could."

He stopped and waited. The woman obviously needed to process what he was telling her, but he was getting nervous about spending more time in the mansion. If the guards came back, there would be bloodshed. He wanted to avoid that, if possible. He had no quarrel with Kuznetsov's wife or her guards. He just needed information from her.

"What is it you want to know?"

"The mouse, as you call him, said the word *dacha*, just before he died. It was his last word. It had to be important. Maybe it is where they took Yevgeni. Do you have a dacha near here? Somewhere isolated where they might want to go to hide out and interrogate you husband?"

"We do." She started to get up, but Dan put out his hand to stop her. She sat back down.

"Tell me where it is and I'll go there."

"I can send Yevgeni's men, at least fifty of them. They'll go and free Zhenya. We don't need your help."

Dan shook his head. "If you send men, the Chechens will hear them coming. They'll kill Yevgeni before anyone can get to him. Even if your men drive off his captors, they won't leave your husband alive."

Duscha's face now showed alarm and panic again.

"What can I do?"

"I can go. It is what I do. You were right about one thing. I am an assassin. This is what I do. I got in here and could have killed everyone in the mansion without the guards at the gate knowing. I can kill the Chechens and get to Yevgeni."

"You won't kill him?"

"No, I told you. I am only interested in what the mouse had."

"He will not let you have it."

"He's not in control right now. And I will save his life." He waited for a moment. "I need to hurry. Tell me where the dacha is now."

After a moment's hesitation, Duscha gave him the directions. It was ninety kilometers northwest of Moscow near a lake and nestled up against a large forest preserve. Dan listened as she rattled off the directions.

"Please don't kill my Zhenya," she said. Her eyes met his in a pleading look.

"I will do my best. I'm going now. If you don't want anyone killed, wait ten minutes before freeing everyone. Irina will show you where they are."

He turned and ran down the hall, down the stairs and out through the sunroom.

Chapter 38

The Chechens drove out of Moscow and headed to the dacha. Lecha knew they needed to get off the road quickly. The cameras would have shown the two Mercedes leaving the club after the shooting. The *politsiya* would be looking for them. Once at the dacha he would have time to get the information he needed to find the two missing canisters.

The entrance gate was unlocked since the dacha was empty. They drove up to the house and stopped. An older man came out to greet them. It was Yevgeni's caretaker. Lecha stepped out and showed the man his Kalashnikov. The man immediately turned and started to run back to the house. Lecha fired a short burst and the caretaker fell on the front steps.

They dragged Kuznetsov into the house and tied him to a straight backed, wooden chair. Lecha sat down in another chair in front of him. His ten men spread out to relax, some of them looking for food.

"Two of you go back out to the main gate and keep watch," Lecha said.

"What do we do if someone comes?"

"Stop them, stupid. You can tell them that Kuznetsov sent you to secure the dacha and make sure no one broke in."

"They'll believe that?"

"Tell them to go find Kuznetsov to confirm the order. They won't find him. If it's any of his gang, just shoot them."

He turned back to his prisoner.

"Now, you are not so tough, eh? Not the big Russian mafia boss, *pakhan*. You belong to me now. You will give me what I want and maybe I let you live. If you don't, you will die painfully."

Lecha leaned close and Kuznetsov spit in his face. The man sat back. His eyes grew even darker. He balled his right hand into a fist and swung it into the side of Kuznetsov's head. The blow knocked the man and the chair over. Lecha motioned for one of his men to pull the chair upright.

"Tell me where the other two canisters are hiding. I don't have much time. You will tell me in the end. But you can shorten your pain if you want."

"I don't know."

His words came out muffled. His face was already beginning to swell from the blow.

"That is not an acceptable answer."

"I was trying to find out where the mouse was holding them when you came in and killed him. Now it is lost forever."

Lecha got up and started to pace around the room. One of his men offered him a glass of vodka. They had discovered Yevgeni's liquor cabinet.

"Soften him up," he said to one of the men. He poured himself a glass of vodka.

As he walked out through the front door, Lecha heard the dull thumps of fists hitting Kuznetsov along with the man's grunts of pain.

He looked around. Regular citizens who had more modest incomes, but still enough to afford a dacha, settled for smaller cottages in dense village-like settings. They always included a garden, however tiny. If you were wealthier you would have a larger lot with an outbuilding, such as a small barn. You might even have some chickens, but always the garden to grow your vegetables and potatoes.

This dacha was much grander. It had a full-sized barn. There was a pasture with some goats grazing, along with a cow. Next to the barn was a large chicken coop penned in with wire mesh to keep out foxes and raccoons. It was in a solitary location. There were no other compounds within hearing or sight. *Just the getaway for a rich gang leader. And useful for me.*

He lit a cigarette and stood smoking on the porch while the beating went on inside. The air promised bad weather. Lecha could feel the dampness in the wind.

Finally, he flipped the cigarette into the yard, drained his glass, and turned to go inside. Kuznetsov's bloody head hung down, his chin resting on his chest. There was blood on his wrists where he had strained against the ropes.

"He is still alive?"

The man grinned at Lecha. "Of course. He didn't say much, though."

"I didn't want him to say much. He's a tough guy. It may take time to break him, but he will tell me where those canisters are before the night's over."

The afternoon was beginning to fade to evening. A light snow began to fall. Lecha could tell it would be strong tonight. A proper Moscow winter snowstorm.

"Have one of the men bring in more wood and start a fire. It's getting colder outside."

The man looked at him questioningly.

"There are no other dachas near to see or smell the fire. Besides, the caretaker would use a fire when the nights got cold."

The man nodded and disappeared. Lecha filled his glass with more vodka and sat down to look at Kuznetsov.

Yevgeni slowly stirred. He looked up at Lecha with eyes barely opened. The swelling had almost shut them.

"*Yebat' tebya*, go fuck yourself," he said. His words were slurred.

Lecha smiled.

"Still the tough guy. I can start cutting off parts of you—your fingers, your toes. Eventually you will tell me, but what will you look like when you do? Of course, you could bleed to death and we don't want that." He stood up. "I think we'll just continue for a while. There will be a storm tonight. No one will be coming out in it, so we have all night to ourselves. I expect you'll tell me before morning."

"I told you, I don't know where they are."

Lecha looked at him with his wolf-like smile. "Yes, you did. But I don't believe you."

He turned to walk away.

"Bring two buckets of ice water. Throw one on him to get him fully awake. Put his feet in the other. We'll see how much he likes the cold."

Lecha walked into the kitchen to look for food. His men had been drinking and they would soon need something more than vodka.

Later that night Lecha sat back in front of Kuznetsov.

"Do you remember now?"

The man shook his head hardly able to talk. He shivered almost uncontrollably.

"I have a new idea." He cupped his hand under Yevgeni's chin and forced his head up. The man's face was bruised and bloodied. His shirt had been torn off of him and his ribs were purple from the beatings. Lecha looked close into Yevgeni's eyes, which were almost closed from the swelling in his face.

"Listen carefully. I know where you live, where your wife and daughter live. If you haven't told me where to find the canisters by morning, we'll go there. I'll take them and make slaves out of them. I'll send them to Chechnya and further south. They might bring a good price."

Kuznetsov could only growl. His body twitched and the growls turned to grunts of pain. Lecha stood up and smiled.

"Stop," Kuznetsov said in a weak voice.

"You want to tell me something?"

The man nodded. Lecha walked over to him.

"A key," Kuznetsov whispered through his puffed lips. "He had a key...train station locker...don't know which one."

"You are sure you don't know?"

Kuznetsov tried to nod his head.

"You killed him before we could find out or get the key. It may still be on him."

"And the police have it now."

Kuznetsov tried to nod again.

"Don't kill my wife, my daughter. That is all I know."

"We will see."

Chapter 39

Rashid sat in his office in Riyadh. The mission to acquire the canisters of anthrax had stalled. The exchange in Milan had blown up and, Lecha, the man Bulat had sent had retreated back to Chechnya. The Italian police suspected it was something more than a drug deal gone bad but had no leads to follow.

And here he sat in Riyadh, unable to do anything, while Bulat's warlord now was headed to Moscow to try to match wits with Kuznetsov. Both of the Chechens felt the only path to find the man with the canisters was through the Russian gangster. Rashid was beginning to regret his decision to work with Bulat. He hadn't known at the time that the man who held the canisters would seek out the mafia. Now it was too late to switch horses. He'd have to ride this one out as best he could.

He picked up his cell phone and placed a call to Bulat in Grozny. The phone had encryption software installed. The arms dealer had a similar phone on his end.

"Update me," Rashid said when Bulat answered.

"The man we seek is going to try to make an exchange again with the mafia. Lecha's men will be there. This time we'll succeed."

"What about this third party, the assassin?"

An unknown person had triggered the blow up in Milan. In the back of Rashid's mind, he wondered if this was the same person that blew up his plans in Mexico. That was an expensive failure, in money, manpower, and time.

"We don't know," Bulat said. "From what I've learned he may be dead. Kuznetsov's men captured him and I don't know his fate. But Lecha will be on the lookout in any case."

"Maybe you should be there at the exchange yourself. I don't have any patience for more mistakes."

Bulat ended the call without responding. He wanted to stay at arm's length from Lecha who was not subtle and left a big trail behind him, usually in dead bodies. But Rashid was the most important customer he had. And he was Rashid's best source for what the billionaire needed.

Rashid had made it clear that he would put up with no more procrastination. He didn't want to hear how Bulat had to rely on Lecha. He didn't want to hear more about Lecha or anyone else's attempts to find the canisters. He wanted results. He was unhappy that more and more people seemed to be getting involved in what was supposed to be a very clandestine operation.

Bulat couldn't disagree. The operation had become messy and might easily lead back to him. Lecha's source in the mafia had confirmed the existence of the assassin. He apparently wasn't dead. Bulat hadn't let Rashid know that fact in their phone call. He didn't want to deal with the man's reaction. Rashid might get cold feet and abandon the effort. The potential loss of payout was significant.

Navigating around government agencies was dangerous enough in his work as an illicit arms dealer. An assassin, working under contract for who knows what group or government agency, presented another level of threat. There would be no way to guess to what lengths someone like that would go.

Rashid was right about one thing. He needed to know more. He placed a call.

"*Da*," Lecha said when he answered his phone.

"Tell me what's going on," Bulat said without identifying himself.

"We have one canister. Two are missing."

"What happened?"

Lecha recounted his ambush at Kuznetsov's night club.

"Do you know where the canisters are? Do you know where the mouse is?"

"The mouse is no more. Our host, the Russian, says the mouse had a key to a train station locker. We need to get the key, if it's still on him."

"Talk some sense into our host. He must have connections and can get us into the morgue. We have to recover the mouse's clothes. We'll find the key. But don't do anything right away. I'm coming."

"How quickly? We don't have time to wait."

"I'll fly up tonight. Meet me at the airport. In the meantime, get a contact name. We'll set it all up tonight so we can act first thing in the morning."

He hung up the phone. This might be the break he needed. He grabbed his kit bag and headed out of the door.

Lecha went back into the room where Kuznetsov was being held.

"I'm going to need something from you," he said to the mafia boss. "Give me the name of someone who can get me into the morgue to see the mouse's body, and his clothes."

Kuznetsov looked at him with a question in his eyes.

"The key you talk about may be in his clothes. If we can get it, your family may yet live."

Lecha grabbed a piece of paper and pencil. Kuznetsov mumbled out a name through his swollen lips.

"A phone number? I need a way to reach this person."

"My phone," he said.

Lecha grabbed the phone and went through the contacts until he came to the man. He wrote down the number. After thinking for a moment, he pocketed Kuznetsov's phone.

"I'll call him from your phone. That way I'm sure he'll answer." Lecha pulled Kuznetsov's feet out of the bucket and turned to his men. "Keep him alive. I'm going to try to get the key we need. I'll call you about what we do with him."

He waved his hand towards the captive. The dismissive gesture spoke volumes about Yevgeni Kuznetsov's fate.

Chapter 40

Dan raced out of Moscow, pushing his Peugeot to its limits. Snow was beginning to fall. He drove on the M11 past the Pushkin International Airport towards Lake *Senezhskoye*. His mind was the mind of a warrior, a killer, anticipating a deadly mission ahead; resolved but with no firm plan and no clear idea of how to succeed. In spite of his focus, images of Christina flickered into his consciousness, her face filled with light and joy. *Don't go there. This is no time for reverie*. He forced his thoughts back to the dark path before him.

Before reaching the lake, he headed north on a rough, local road, then turned off on an even rougher road which turned to dirt. From there he made another turn, deep in the forest onto a dirt two-track, which, according to Duscha accessed only two dachas. Theirs was the last one.

It was now dark. He turned off the headlights as he got closer. He didn't know when he would reach the dacha and didn't want to alert anyone as he approached. Even with the storm, Dan could still discern the road as it cut a path through the dense stand of trees. When he saw a short side trail, bridging the ditch and going into the woods, he stopped and backed the car down it until it was hidden from the dirt road. Facing out, it would be a quicker exit, if he was fortunate enough to need one.

He opened his trunk. Inside was a duffel bag containing a sniper rifle, a suppressed German H&K PSG-1 which fired a NATO 7.62 round. He also had his M4 and 9mm pistol, both with suppressors. After some thought, Dan selected the M4 and the 9mm pistol.

Snow was now falling harder. The night was getting colder. The storm seemed to be increasing in strength. The wind had increased in strength; the snow was coming down faster. *It'll help conceal my attack*. The sound of the wind rushing through the pines was growing louder. This was not going to be a quiet snowy evening.

He zipped up his jacket against the storm and grabbed his final item, a pair of night vision goggles. Then he closed the trunk and started up the road. If a car approached, he'd have time to head into the woods before being seen. With the wind, no one could hear his footsteps on the dirt road.

While he walked down the rough road, Dan tried to formulate a plan. As usual, there were too many unknowns. He would have to operate extemporaneously. How many times had he done that? He'd lost count. *One day that's going to catch up with me*. Yet there was nothing else to do. Overall, the goal was to rescue Yevgeni and capture the one remaining canister. How to do it was the problem.

He guessed there was no more than ten Chechens, having seen them depart in two SUVs. He needed to take down as many as possible before a firefight erupted. Even outnumbered, Dan didn't fear a gun battle but he didn't want collateral damage (Kuznetsov or the canister). Breaching the canister would be a disaster, even out here in the forest.

The sound of the wind kept increasing as it blew through the forest. Dan almost didn't hear the engine. He saw the flash of the headlights up ahead, around a bend, just as the engine sound reached him. He dove off the road and threw himself into the brush at the edge of the trees. The SUV flew past him. He couldn't make out if anyone but the driver was in it.

Are they moving him? Dan dismissed the thought. Both SUVs would have left if they were taking him somewhere, or if they had finished their job and Kuznetsov was dead. He stood and started up the road again. Hopefully, both of his objectiives were still at the dacha.

Ahead, he could barely see the cement columns framing the entrance drive with the metal gate attached to them. He veered off into the woods. The wind and snow kept increasing in strength. He jammed his hands into his pockets to keep them from freezing. If he had to spend the night outside, he would be in danger of serious hypothermia. The recollection of that terrible night fleeing from his captors, almost freezing to death, rushed back into his mind. He shivered long and hard. *Put that out of your mind. That's the past. This is the present. You have to execute a plan, any plan, flawlessly if you want to survive.* He forced himself to calm down. He was cold, but he could operate in the cold. He'd do what he came to do.

Take out as many as I can before I'm discovered. That was the basis of his plan. They'd all be well-armed and capable fighters. *Start with any guards at the gate. That'll be the easy part.* He approached the gate from the cover of the woods. The storm, while making him cold and uncomfortable, masked his approach.

There were two men hunched against the wind at the gate. They were smoking and stamping their feet. They had carbines slung over their shoulders. *Not on alert. Probably pissed at being left out here.* They were easy prey, but they'd be calling to get relieved before too long. Dan couldn't imagine them spending a two or three-hour shift outside in this weather. *More like an hour at best.* He didn't know how much of that assumed hour he had left. *Act now and then get to the house.* He didn't relish waiting outside in the storm for a change of shift.

Dan shouldered his M4. With the suppressor, the shots would not be heard above the storm. He settled his tactical scope on the first man. His finger caressed the trigger. The gun made a wet sounding pop. The man's head exploded and he fell sideways. The second man jerked his head around in surprise. At that moment, Dan's second shot hit him in the chest and he went down. Neither man had time to level their rifles. *Two down. How many more?*

He headed towards the house. Without knowing when a shift change would occur, he needed to strike quickly. Using his night vision goggles to illuminate the dark, Dan headed to the back of the building, looking for the power connection.

Before cutting the power, he located a rear door. Once he had cut the power, the men inside would go on alert. He had to strike fast and hard before they had time to figure out what was going on. Being outnumbered, speed was his ally. He would use confusion to move the odds in his favor. *Cut the power, go in with the goggles, kill anything that moves.* He needed to reduce the number of defenders before any effective response was mounted. It sounded simple but Dan knew it involved a lot of shooting which meant a lot of bullets flying around. He had to make sure he didn't intercept any of them.

He tested the door and found it unlocked. Dan crept back to the electrical box. The storm continued unabated and the snow was growing deeper on the ground. *Time to move.* He pulled the lever to its off position and ran to the door.

Chapter 41

There was a flurry of shouts from inside when the lights went out. The fireplace gave off flickering light which hardly illuminated the large room. Dan entered through the back door. There was a hallway leading to the kitchen off to the right and the main room straight ahead. He could clearly see five men milling around. *Got to get out of the hallway.*

As he went forward a man came walking down the hall with a flashlight. Dan immediately shot him. The light clattered to the floor. Dan ran forward and fired at two figures as they started for the hall. They both fell, their weapons clattering on the wooden floor. In the main room the firelight was too blinding with the goggles on. Dan hit the floor as shots rang out. He pushed up the goggles. He'd be on even ground now, visually.

He could see a muzzle flash coming from his left side. He was lying behind a large, stuffed chair. It didn't give any ballistic protection but kept him out of sight. He twisted around, staying behind the chair and got off a shot. He heard a weapon hit the floor. It sounded like a pistol. Now shots rang out from behind a large couch placed in front of the large fireplace. The bullets ripped through the chair Dan was lying behind. He slithered away from the chair towards the opening to the kitchen.

Once around the corner of the entrance, he braced himself against the door frame. It was thick and made of solid wood. It would stop a bullet. Multiple shots would chip away at its narrow sliver of protection but it was better than nothing. *One behind the couch, where are the others?*

With the first shot, Yevgeni swung his head around towards the hall to the back door. *Someone was here, to rescue him?* His numbed mind tried to figure out what was going on. He was being rescued, but he could be killed in a firefight. He lurched to the side, rocking the sturdy wooden chair to which he was bound. He lurched again, grunting in pain. The third try saw the chair tip over, throwing him to the floor with a violent thud.

Dan had heard the chair fall. The sound came from one side of the couch, near the fireplace. *Yevgeni?*

One of the shooters started spraying the main room with automatic fire. He was in a side doorway, probably a bedroom. The man had no target. He was just hoping to hit something. Dan waited putting his sights on the doorway. When the man popped his head out to see what damage he had done, Dan fired. The man's head flew back and his body crashed to the floor. His Kalashnikov fell from his hand with the barrel laying in the doorway.

One of the Chechens shouted out. Another responded. They discovered, as did Dan, that there were only two of them left. And Dan now knew where they were. One was in another doorway to the left of the main room. The other voice came from above. *There's a loft*. That made his situation more dangerous. The shooter in the loft would have full visual over the main floor.

Dan crept back through the kitchen. The man in the side room had seen Dan at the entrance to the kitchen. He'd be focused there. If Dan could get back to the hall and go forward without him hearing, he could attack from a new position. The hallway ended at the main room. The upper floor covered the rear part of the dacha with the main room being double height. There was most likely a balcony overlooking the living room. Dan couldn't step out into the main room without being killed.

Eliminate the ground floor shooter first? The man upstairs couldn't effectively shoot through solid wooden floors and hit anything, especially if Dan didn't stay in one spot after taking a shot. Dan entered the hall and crept forward. No one was moving or making a sound. The shooter in the side room was being cautious. The man upstairs probably understood his advantage and was going to wait for the attacker to make the next move.

Dan waited, hunched against the wall. There was no movement. After a long minute, he changed his plan and crept back down the hall. There might be a rear staircase. If so, he could get to the upper floor and surprise the shooter.

Behind the kitchen, there was a side door leading off the hall. Dan gently opened it to reveal a narrow staircase that went up and turned upon itself. He started up the stairs. He stepped on each tread near the casing, not in the middle. He couldn't risk any creaking boards. He would be at a serious disadvantage if the shooter met him on the stairs. It took two long minutes to climb the steps.

The two Chechens called out to each other. Dan assumed they were discussing what to do, how to flush him out. They spoke in Chechen but there were a few words similar to Russian to confirm that was their purpose. Neither was willing to move from their positions so everyone was holding tight for the moment.

He forced himself to not hurry. It seemed as though every nerve ending in his body was firing. Any moment the upstairs shooter would get the same idea Dan had gotten. He would look to see if there was a back set of stairs. Dan had to get to the top before the man came looking. But he couldn't make a sound; that only would bring him faster. His breathing was coming in harsher gasps. *Too noisy. Calm down.* He forced himself to settle his breathing, to find a calm place just as he had to do when sniping in a stressful situation.

In a slightly calmer state, he arrived at the top of the stairs. There was another door. The landing was tight. Dan carefully worked his M4 to the ready position. He'd have no time once he opened the door. It would be who shot first and best. He hoped the element of surprise was still on his side.

After taking a breath and exhaling slowly Dan opened the door and swung the M4 towards the balcony rail as he dropped to one knee. The Chechen spun around firing on full auto. The shots went high and Dan put five rounds into his torso. The man flipped over the balcony rail and dropped to the main floor with a thud.

Dan ran forward. The last shooter needed to be taken out. Dan had the dominant position, but only if the man revealed himself. When he reached the balcony, he heard glass breaking. He was trying to escape! Dan ran down the stairs and out the front door which exited to the side of the main room.

Once outside, he flipped down his goggles and started around the house. The snow was flying sideways in the fierce wind. When he came around the corner, he saw the man jumping into the second Mercedes. Dan unloaded his magazine at the vehicle, spraying the driver' side. There was no movement at the vehicle. Dan ejected the spent mag and loaded another. Then he walked forward, approaching the vehicle from the rear quarter. With the M4 held in his right arm, he opened the driver's door. The dead man flopped out to the ground.

Chapter 42

Dan walked slowly back into the dacha. He felt drained. Nine men, killed by his hand, lay strewn about. He didn't regret the killing, but had to admit it took something out of him. He felt hollowed out.

This life he now found himself living felt a bit alien. Yes, he had all the right instincts, honed over years, necessary for survival in this violent world. But the contrast between this violence and the peaceful, more contemplative world he had recently inhabited with Christina now presented itself to him in a clear and stark manner. He couldn't escape seeing the differences nor the ramifications that lurked behind this recognition.

All the men he had killed just now...and what was Christina doing? She had finished practicing, had made some dinner, and was probably relaxing by the fire with a glass of wine. Sitting alone or maybe with Chloé. Was she thinking of him? Did she miss him and wonder what he was doing? He shook his head. She could never imagine what had just taken place.

He stepped back into the main room of the dacha and walked over to the chair where Yevgeni was tied, still laying on its side. He pulled the chair upright. Yevgeni looked up at him with his dark eyes, through his puffy face. He was alert now. It was as if the shootout had energized him.

"You save me so you can kill me?" he asked.

Dan didn't answer. Instead, he went around to the men lying on the floor. Two were still alive. He asked them where the canister was. The first man couldn't speak. His lungs were filling up with blood. Dan took out his pistol and put a bullet in his head. It was more an act of mercy than an execution. The second man had been shot in his gut. He was going to die without serious medical help, which Dan was not able to supply. The rules were starkly clear—kill or be killed. He asked him about the canister.

"*Yebat' tebya,*" the man replied and tried to spit at him. Instead of spitting, he only dribbled a mixture of blood and saliva down his chin.

Dan stood up and, without comment, put a bullet in his head as well.

He walked over to Yevgeni and sat down on another chair in front of him.

"Water?" Dan asked.

Yevgeni nodded his head and Dan went to the kitchen to retrieve a bottle of water from the refrigerator. He brought that back along with a bottle of vodka. After giving Yevgeni a drink of water he held the vodka bottle to his lips. The Russian took a healthy swig and began to cough.

"Too much?"

Yevgeni shook his head. The fire gave a low, flickering light to the room. Dan got up and put more wood on it.

"So, what now?" Yevgeni asked.

"I need to retrieve the third canister," Dan said

"You have the other two? The ones in the station?"

Dan didn't answer his question.

"Where is the third one?" he asked.

"Gone. It's with that Chechen dog, Lecha."

"Where did he go?" Dan tried to remain calm, but he was now anxious. Had that been Lecha in the car that drove past him? If so, he had a good head start. Dan needed to know where he was headed.

"To find the other canisters. Someone is paying him for all three and he doesn't want to come up short."

"I asked where is he going?" Dan voice now held a measure of menace in it. Whether or not Yevgeni could recognize it Dan couldn't tell.

"Don't you know? To find the little mouse's key." Yevgeni tried to smile through his swollen lips. "They know about the key and a train station. But they don't know which one. The *malen'kaya mysh'* told me about the locker. We hadn't gotten to the point where he was going to tell me which station it was in when the Chechens attacked."

Yevgeni coughed and spit up some blood.

"You want another drink of water?"

He nodded.

"But you know, don't you?" He tried to smile again. "You have them, so they won't find them. You've won."

"I have to get the other canister. It can still do a lot of damage."

"They will come back here, whether or not they find the canisters. They'll kill me. Then they'll kill my family."

"They won't kill you."

Yevgeni looked at Dan. "Because you will do it for them?"

"I'm not going to kill you," Dan said. The words surprised him as they came out of his mouth. But it was what both watchers had said must happen. Dan couldn't see how that was going to work, even as he said the words.

"You play with me? I would kill you, if I could...right now."

"I didn't kill your son."

"So, you say. But you were there."

Dan nodded. "I was there. I was after Pavlovich, the mouse. I was concentrating on him as he ran away when someone shot me. The shot that killed your son came from the other building, from the Chechens."

"Who shot the giant? That started the gunfight."

"That was me. I couldn't let him take the canisters, with or without Pavlovich." Dan leaned close to Yevgeni. "I'd do it again. But I had no reason to shoot your son. I was only after the canisters."

"We were both after the same thing, only I lost a son. It looks like you won."

"I haven't won until I get that third canister. It can still kill thousands of people. And you know the terrorists will use it."

"I don't care what they do with it. It was going to make me a lot of money."

"And how much money will it take to compensate for losing your wife and daughter, on top of your son?"

"Fuck you!" Yevgeni scowled at Dan. "If you're going to kill me do it. If not, untie me. I'll freeze to death if you leave and the fire goes out."

Dan paced around the room, his mind racing. This was what the Watchers had told him about. Somewhere in this moment was the opportunity to make peace with his enemy. But where? How? There was something to be done here before he could chase the canister. He turned back to Yevgeni.

"How will they try to find the key?"

"I gave Lecha the name of a contact to get access to the morgue, to go through Pavlovich's clothes. They'll have to wait until morning." He paused for a moment, studying Dan. "But they won't find the key, will they?"

Dan looked at the gangster. He was recovering his strength, even without medical help. Dan could tell he was evaluating his situation. If he believed what Dan said, he'd be figuring out how to turn the fact he wasn't going to be shot to his advantage.

Dan stood up and went around the room, gathering the weapons from the dead gangsters. He piled them in a corner, taking one Makarov 9mm pistol back to his seat in front of Yevgeni. He slid out the magazine and checked it. There were five rounds left. He cleared the chamber and then shoved the magazine back inside the grip. Then he put the pistol on the side table.

"You going to shoot me with that? Make it look like the Chechen's executed me?"

Dan didn't answer. He sat looking at Yevgeni, using his increased sensitivity to plumb the man's thoughts while he pondered what to do next. The body gave away what the mind was thinking. He studied Kuznetsov's body. The face would give clues, even when bruised and swollen. Dan was sensing his way forward with no clear path to guide him.

"I can't spend the rest of my life looking over my shoulder to see if you're coming," Dan finally said.

Kuznetsov smiled. "I know about Christina," he said.

"That's part of my problem with you."

"I can't watch for you every day as well. One of us has to kill the other."

"Maybe so."

Dan stood up and took out his knife. Kuznetsov gave him a wary look. He stepped forward and cut the man's bindings. Kuznetsov rubbed his wrists, getting his circulation going.

"Neither of us has to die. At least, by each other's hand," Dan said.

Kuznetsov looked up at him but didn't answer. He slowly stretched out his body while remaining in the chair. He'd been tied to it for hours, while being beaten. Now released from that prison, he enjoyed being able to move his limbs.

This is the moment. Dan knew it and the shock of knowing it so clearly stunned him. He sensed the possibility of settlement between them, but also the dire risk he had to take. But he had to act. Any future with Christina depended on it. He turned to go. He took five steps and heard the unmistakable sound of the pistol's slide being racked, chambering a round in the Makarov. Dan stopped but didn't turn.

"Do you wish to die? Commit suicide? You want me to help you?"

Dan slowly turned. Kuznetsov was standing with the pistol aimed at his chest. He studied the gangster even more closely, looking for clues as to how this would play out. His eyes slid over Kuznetsov's figure; how tight he gripped the pistol, how his finger was positioned on the trigger, noticing the tension points in his torso, the shape of his mouth, the set of his jaw and then, his eyes. Dan looked deep in the gangster's eyes. He locked onto them with his own, making the man return his intense gaze.

"I told you, neither of us has to die."

"I don't see it that way. But I don't understand why you didn't kill me."

"I gave you life. I didn't shoot you when you were in my power. I cut you loose so you wouldn't freeze to death. From this moment on, you don't have to look over your shoulder for me. If I felt I had to kill you, I would have done it then, just like I killed these others, including the last two that were wounded."

Dan paused for a moment. "Yevgeni," he said, using the man's first name, "I gave you life. Now you can give me life. It's the only way. If I didn't kill you, when I had full power to do so, you can trust that I won't in the future. If you don't kill me now, when you have the power to do so, then I can trust you won't in the future."

"You are a crazy man."

"Maybe, but this seems to be the only way out without one of us killing the other. Giving each other life. I can see that there is honor in you. That honor drove you to seek your son's killer, but it also can correct your path if it's wrong. You also understand beauty. I can sense that in you. You can understand my relationship with Christina."

Would Kuznetsov agree? Dan was strangely calm as he stood before the man who had vowed to kill him and now had all the opportunity he needed.

"Is it because of the woman, Christina?"

"Maybe partly. It is also that neither of us should die for a misunderstanding. We live with enough death."

"You use this to make peace with me? You think this will allow you to go back to your life with her? You think you can leave all this behind? I don't know your name or who you are, but from what I've seen, you are well-practiced. An experienced assassin. Someone like you doesn't get to retire."

"Perhaps. The issue of the moment is whether or not you'll return the gift of life that I gave you."

"I put the gun down and you won't kill me? Kuznetsov asked.

Dan smiled. "Why would I? I already passed on the chance to do so, easily, at my leisure, in any way I saw fit. No, you are safe from me. You should understand that."

Kuznetsov studied him. Dan could see his mind, which was clear now, in spite of the beatings he had suffered, turning over the point Dan made and comparing it with what Dan had actually done.

"You take a big risk. I'm surprised you haven't been killed before this. But I will take you up on your offer. You might be helpful to me in the future."

He flicked the safety on with his thumb and stuffed the pistol in his belt, letting out a grunt as his ribs protested.

Dan felt the tension drain from him. He had held it in, not wanting to display any doubt or fear. He stepped forward and reached out his hand. Kuznetsov took it.

"This doesn't mean we are on the same side," Yevgeni said.

"No, we're not," Dan replied.

"How did you know about the dacha?"

"Your wife told me."

"Duscha? You talked to her?" His voice held both a question and a menace.

"I got into the house and talked with her. No one was killed. I convinced her that sending your men to assault the dacha would result in you being killed. I convinced her that I could rescue you."

"You set this up—the rescue—to make peace with me?"

Dan shook his head. "To find the third canister. Saving you was secondary."

Dan looked around the room.

“I need you to tell me which morgue Lecha will go to. I’ll intercept him.”

“You alone?”

“I took out nine men here. I think I can do it alone. You should get the rest of your gang out here to clean up the mess. It may be hard even for you to explain this to the authorities. Make sure your wife and daughter are protected as well. Your mansion is not as secure as you think.”

After getting the names of the hospital and the contact, Dan left to retrieve his car and head to Moscow.

Chapter 43

It had been over a week since Dan had left. Christina had not received a word from him. She remembered that he said he wouldn't call, but she still felt disappointed. Chloé had taken to visiting more frequently. She was solicitous, seeming to be worried about depression engulfing her star. Christina felt it as well. It was like a dark cloud advancing on her, turning her world of colors and light to one of differing hues of grey.

To find solace, she turned to her beloved piano. Practice consumed her most days, even when she felt she was only going through the motions. She worked at her scales, the études, the musical exercises that kept her sharp and her hands and fingers well-conditioned.

She had begun to expand her repertoire to include pieces that offered more opportunity to express the emotions she now wanted to show to her audiences. There were the Brahms piano sonatas. Christina always enjoyed the faster, more challenging movements where she could let her prodigious skills show. Now she reveled in the slower movements as well—the *andante* and *adagio* sections. Here she could express her emotions, give voice to her feelings over what had taken place and how her heart had been opened, enlarged, and also wounded.

One of her new favorites was the short Impromptu in G flat by Franz Schubert. It was a love song, tender yet full of strength. It featured a simple, gentle melody along with three-finger *arpeggios* all played by the right hand without stopping through the whole piece. The left hand provided wonderfully clear bass notes to underpin the rolling sound of the right hand. Schubert's handling of the melody allowed it to stand out clearly from the cascade of notes that swirled around it.

She also began to work on Schumann's *Gesänge der Frühe*, Songs of Dawn much to Chloé's objections. It was one of Schumann's latter coherent works as his mind became increasingly disturbed. A few years after composing the piece he would attempt to drown himself. Many critics held the view that the composer's growing insanity affected his work, but Christina, along with a small group of critics valued the work and saw it as a culmination of much of where Schumann had been headed throughout his composing life. She felt the pain and isolation he expressed in the piece and wanted to convey that to her audience.

Chloé would listen to her play when she was at the cottage, but both knew that she could not replace Christina's Rossignol. His listening skills far surpassed what Chloé could bring. She quickly learned to not comment, but just to listen and provide companionship.

"I'm finding new music," Christina said after one practice session in which she began two new pieces.

"I know. The range of your expression has grown, so your selection of music must follow. This will be a triumphant year for you."

"Maybe. It will be most triumphant when Rossignol comes back." She sighed and got up from the piano. "I don't know if I can go on without him."

The two walked into the living room. A cold dread now spread through Chloe. She had to keep her friend from thinking such thoughts.

"You can go on. Whether or not Rossignol returns. He would want that. He always encouraged you to express what you had inside to the world. He helped bring that out in you and now you must not let it go."

Christina took her friend's hand.

"I know you're right. But it is hard. I want to believe he's coming back, but I know nothing of the world he went back to, the world he lived in before he came to me. It could take him away from me...and that strikes fear in my heart."

"He'll return," Chloe said. She didn't fully believe that, but sensed Christina needed to hear it.

Lecha arrived at the *Vnukovo* airport southwest of Moscow. This was where the flights from Chechnya arrived. He parked and called Bulat. There was no answer. He looked up flights from Grozny and found one getting in at 1am. He leaned back in the Mercedes SUV and tried to relax. The odds of finding the key were slim. If anyone had gone through Pavlovich's pockets, they would have found it and would be going to the station to see what was inside the locker.

The thought of bribing one of the police crossed his mind, but he dismissed it. The canisters would probably look sinister enough to require a call to the FSB which would put them out of reach. Whoever had employed Bulat, was going to have to be satisfied with one canister.

Lecha anticipated a fierce argument with Bulat regarding payment. He'd wait to discuss the issue. First, they had to see if they were going to be lucky. Lecha was not in the mood for compromise. He had taken losses while Bulat had sat back playing the middle man, the broker. Lecha had the wives and families of his dead men to pay compensation to. He could feel his anger growing. He had power. Bulat had to recognize that. Bulat may have wealth, but he was a businessman, Lecha was the fighter, the man on the ground, on the front lines. He should get the lion's share. If the deal turned out thin for Bulat, so be it. Lecha was not going to be denied full payment.

At 1:30 in the morning, Lecha's phone rang.

"Da," he said after answering.

"Are you at the airport?"

"In the parking lot."

"I'm out front, pick me up."

He drove around to the terminal and Bulat got in the SUV, throwing his bag in the back seat.

"I'm lucky to get here. The flights are starting to be canceled with the storm. You have a contact?"

"Yes. We must wait until morning when he comes on duty. He'll get us into the morgue. It's located in the basement. They have a locker for the dead man's clothes. He warned me that the police have already gone through it."

"You're saying there's no key?"

Lecha shrugged. "The man didn't say the police found anything. He may not know."

"Where is Kuznetsov?"

"I have him at his dacha. It's isolated, so no one will disturb me there."

"You're sure he doesn't have the key or the other canisters?"

Lecha nodded. "We interrupted his interrogation of the mouse. I'm convinced he doesn't know where the other two are. We were very persuasive."

Lecha went on to explain the interrogation and his threats to Kuznetsov's family.

"The threat to his family loosened his tongue. He gave us the name of our contact. That is the best we can do for now."

"Let's go to the dacha. I will want to talk with Kuznetsov myself. I've done business with him before. I can act as an intermediary, trying to save him from you. We'll see if there's any more information to be gained."

Lecha shrugged. He didn't expect anything to come of it, but they had time to kill before they could get into the morguc. Then there would be the discussion of payment with one canister being all Bulat would get out of the deal.

On their way, Lecha placed a call to one of his men at the dacha. There was no answer. He tried another, no answer.

Bulat looked over at him. "No answer? Something wrong?"

Lecha didn't say anything. Something *was* wrong. He accelerated the big Merc. He'd find out soon enough. The snow was still falling and beginning to drift with the wind.

"Be careful, you don't want to wreck in the storm."

When they got to the local road, Lecha told Bulat to get two AKs out of the rear compartment and bring them up front along with extra magazines.

"You think Kuznetsov's men are at the dacha?"

Lecha kept his eyes forward, pushing the large vehicle down the narrow, bumpy road.

"Maybe. It's not right that two men didn't answer their phones."

A mile from the dacha, Lecha turned off his headlights and drove slowly forward.

"We get to the gate, have your rifle ready," he said.

"What do we do if Kuznetsov's gang is there?"

"We kill them."

Bulat charged the AK and shifted it in the seat so he could fire.

"If his gang is there, we get out and split up. You go to the right, to the woods, I'll go to the left. From there we start the killing. Put extra magazines in your pockets."

They turned into the gate, which stood open. Lecha's guards were not to be seen. The other SUV was in the front with its door open. Lecha pulled up and both men got out with the Mercedes between themselves and the building. Once out of the SUV, they saw the dead man hanging halfway out of the shot-up SUV.

No sound and no lights came from inside. The dacha looked empty. The wind and snow blew around them in a confused swirl. After studying the building for any signs of an ambush, Lecha motioned for Bulat to follow him. He dashed around the building to the back door. After Bulat caught up with him, Lecha carefully opened it and went down the hallway. There was a smell of death inside, blood, urine, and feces. He'd smelled it many times before in the war with the Soviets.

A dwindling fire remained, still radiating heat, trying to fend off the growing chill in the room.

After a careful search revealed no one, Lecha turned on the lights. He could see bullet holes in the walls, the furniture. There was blood on the floor and signs of bodies being dragged. The two men went to the front door. Outside on the porch they could see a blood trail going off to the right, away from the car parking area in the front. Bodies had been dragged outside, probably into the woods.

"You want to follow?" Bulat asked.

Lecha shook his head. "I know what I'll find. My men have been killed and hidden in the woods for the scavengers."

He turned back inside. Bulat followed and closed the door to the howling wind and snow.

Lecha looked around. How did this happen? Kuznetsov's men? How could they surprise his men? Kill them all? He shook his head. Maybe his men had killed Kuznetsov when they had come under attack. His hands gripped the AK tightly.

He'd get his revenge on the family. He would deliver on his promise. He would capture them and take them south, into Chechnya and Dagestan. He'd sell them, the wife and the daughter to someone who'd sell them further south. They would disappear into a life of sexual slavery and torment. He ground his teeth. It was the best he could do if Kuznetsov was already dead. He only wished he could watch their degradation.

It was now 3:30 am. Lecha went back to the SUV with Bulat following. Lecha knew Bulat was concerned that things had gone awry.

"We still meet the man at the hospital," Bulat said, partly a question, partly a statement.

"*Da*. Then I will take my revenge."

"What will you do? Your men are gone."

"I will take Kuznetsov's wife and daughter. He is probably dead, but it doesn't matter. I promised this if he didn't cooperate, and now I'll deliver."

"But his men will be there. They'll be expecting you. We need to take the canisters south, get them out of Russia so I can deliver them to the customer."

"You may have only one to deliver."

"Let's hope not. That would be hard to explain."

"That is your problem, not mine."

"At least agree we get out of the country with what we can get, one or more of the canisters. Then you can work out your revenge. You will need more men. You will need to come back later. Now is not the time to be hurrying. Better to plan your actions."

Lecha didn't answer. He knew Bulat's advice was correct, but his blood called for swift, brutal action.

Chapter 44

After Dan left, Kuznetsov called one of his *Brodyaga* and told him to assemble as many men as he could and get them to the dacha as fast as possible. When they arrived, they dragged the bodies out into the woods. Then they drove back to Moscow to Kuznetsov's house. He had them set up guard around the property. Then he made a call to the contact he had given to Lecha.

"*Da*," said a sleepy voice."

"This is Kuznetsov. When do you meet the man who called you?"

"He said he would meet me at 8am."

"You didn't tell him there was no key?"

"*Nyet*. He wants to look for it, I don't want to get in his way. I said only that the police had gone through the clothes. I didn't know the results."

Kuznetsov hung up. Would Lecha come for him by himself? He doubted it but he had to make sure his family stayed safe. He would go to his home, leave some of his men there to guard Duscha, then go to the hospital. Maybe he could get back the two canisters that the assassin had recovered. The third one was with Lecha. There was a possibility he could retrieve all three.

But he didn't want to have an encounter in the hospital. He would wait outside. Lecha would not find the key and would return to his vehicle. Kuznetsov could ambush him there and get the canister. The assassin was the wildcard. He didn't know how he would handle the situation.

Dan stopped in the parking lot at the hospital. It was large, but there were few cars in it at this time of the morning. He had a view of the main entrance. He put the seat back and tried to relax. *Rest while you can*. It was a mantra he had said to himself more than a few times.

Kuznetsov would be busy waiting for his lieutenants and then cleaning up. Dan wasn't sure whether or not he would come to the hospital to attempt to retrieve all three canisters. He might think Dan still had two and he could get the third from Lecha. While he seemed to have made peace with Kuznetsov, he had no illusions that the man wouldn't try to take the canisters from him by force.

Lecha would know by now that something had gone wrong at the dacha. Would he just head back to Chechnya when he couldn't find the key? That made sense. He wouldn't know who had gotten the key and therefore the canisters. He didn't know Dan was part of the picture. Lecha might think Kuznetsov's gang had attacked his men at the dacha. With no answers, there was a good chance he would head south to complete his delivery with the arms dealer, Bulat.

A dark Mercedes GL Wagon drove up to the hospital. Dan recognized it. Two men got out. They left the vehicle in the drop-off zone, telling the door guard they would only be a few minutes. Bulat handed the guard two 500-ruble bills to insure his agreement. The hospital employee arrived a few minutes later. When he walked in, Lecha went up to him.

"Fyodor?"

The man looked startled, but nodded. "I thought we were to meet at 8am."

"We came early. Show us the clothes."

Lecha took hold of his arm with a tight grip.

"Come with me," the man said nervously.

He led them to the front desk and asked for passes for the two men.

"They have to identify a body," he said to the woman at the counter.

After signing in, they walked to an elevator and headed for the basement.

Once in the basement, Fyodor took them to a locker room. It was next to the room where the bodies were kept. He opened the locker that held the last belongings of Roman Pavlovich. Inside were his coat, shirt, pants, underwear, shoes, and socks. The men spent ten minutes rummaging through the clothes, finding nothing.

"You didn't know there was no key?" Lecha's voice was threatening.

Fyodor cowered and shook his head.

"I had no reason to look. I didn't know anything about a key. The police told me nothing. I am nobody. I just take care of the dead, send them to be buried or burned as directed. The relatives claim the belongings. I have nothing to do with them."

Lecha gave him a long, hard look but didn't answer. His explanation seemed credible to the warlord. He turned to Bulat.

"What we seek isn't here. We can't get to it. You may as well fly home."

Bulat looked angry. "My buyer will not be pleased. He wanted all three canisters."

"The other two are gone. If they were in the locker, the FSB has them by now. It's best you go back to Grozny."

"No planes will be flying today. I ride with you."

Lecha could see that Bulat was not going to let the canister out of his sight. He'd ride with him to Grozny where they would conclude their deal. There, Lecha would get the money due him.

They walked out of the hospital into the still-strong snowstorm. Dan had recognized both men as they went into the hospital. He waited, knowing they would not be successful in their search. As they climbed into the

Mercedes, he started his Peugeot. This was his chance to get back the third canister. He would head them off near the exit where he could ambush them without immediately setting off alarms. As he was about to drive off, he noticed a sleek, bright red Mercedes GLS drive up. He had seen such a vehicle at Kuznetsov's mansion.

"Damn!" Dan said. Kuznetsov was going to try to take back the canister. It looked like Milan all over again: three parties each vying for the canister. Only now in Moscow with the police not far away.

He grabbed his rifle and stepped out of the Peugeot, gasping at the cold wind that swept across the empty lot. He rested his weapon on the hood of the car and aimed for Kuznetsov's tires. He'd take the Russian out of the picture and then go after Lecha. No one would hear the suppressed rifle shot over the storm. His first shot hit the pavement somewhere near the front tire. Dan didn't wait, but sent another round which burst the tire. As the SUV started to slide, he hit the left rear with another shot. The Mercedes skidded to a stop with both left tires punctured.

Dan jumped back into his Peugeot and pulled out of his space. He reached the exit as the other Merc, driven by Lecha, headed down the highway. He guessed they were headed for Grozny which was over twenty hours away by car. It would be longer in the snow storm. He would have to follow and try to intercept them later, on an empty part of the road.

The snow slowed him down. The Peugeot didn't have the four-wheel drive and ground clearance of the G Wagon. Soon Dan was falling farther and farther behind, his car no match for the more powerful, better equipped Mercedes. Finally, he lost sight of them and was beginning to flounder in the deepening snow.

They could turn off anywhere and I'd never know. He pounded the steering wheel in frustration. After two more treacherous miles, he admitted defeat and pulled off the highway. He didn't want to get stuck and risk an encounter with authorities.

He found a hotel and checked in. After locking his door, he undressed and took a hot shower. He let the water run over his aching body, trying to wash away the killing and his frustration, until the tap began to run cold, which wasn't nearly as long as he would have liked. Getting out, he dried and dressed again.

He went to the window and stared at the snow through the street lights, still coming down. It made the lights glow with halos of light reflected off the snowflakes. A nice scene to watch while one was warm. The moment was dampened by the intruding thought that a weapon of mass murder was on its way to Chechnya. He would follow. Lecha would go to Grozny. Dan knew that was where he had his headquarters. Bulat also centered his business in the city. *Guess that's where I'm going next.*

What he hoped would be a quick acquisition of the cannisters and making peace with Kuznetsov, the two acts which Dan had hoped would free him to return to Christina, now had turned more complicated. He had made peace, but he still had to get his hands on the third cannister. The professional in him felt it was an untidy end to his mission to leave it in the wrong hands. He also felt, even more deeply, a revulsion at letting the criminals and terrorists win. It was going to take more time. He had a nagging fear that events were going to drag him further away from what he desired, a life back in Provence with Christina and the ties to this violent world severed.

He sighed and picked up his phone to call Jane. Maybe she could locate where Lecha did business and save Dan the time and danger of asking questions one probably shouldn't ask in Grozny.

Chapter 45

The next morning Dan set out on the now-plowed roads. In five hours, he was out of the snow as he headed south. He drove the M4, a modern, four lane highway, out of Moscow. The sky remained gray and dismal as he drove, but the roads were clear. He slept in the car that night, starting the engine every three or four hours to warm up. By four in the morning he was back on the road.

The road went south, but veered west to pass through Rostov-on-Don, the city at the head of the Sea of Azov which emptied into the Black Sea. South of Rostov-on-Don, he turned onto the E50 which headed eastward to Grozny. The E50 was two lanes, but well-paved and very straight. He made good time now, south of the winter storm and arrived in Grozny around 5pm. It was already dark.

Jane had located Lecha's center of operations. It was in a warehouse south of the center of town, just north of the *Sunzha* River. The warehouse was one of a dozen near the rail yard. It was a good place for a part-time smuggler and warlord to locate with run down, partly empty buildings and few surveillance cameras about. That made it perfect for Dan as well.

He found a room in the Caucasus Hotel. It was a plain, two story building patronized by Chechens more than tourists. Although Dan couldn't pass as a local, his rough clothes would not stand out in the hotel. It was just north of the central part of the city where the Islamist Cultural Center was located.

Grozny had many bright, newly constructed buildings built since the civil wars with the Soviets in the 1990s and early 2000s. However, one could still see the bombed-out shells of buildings and the cleared lots that testified to those conflicts.

After getting something to eat, Dan retreated to his room to review his options. Bulat and Lecha were not from the same clan. Clans were everything in Chechnya. They came before national interests. The two would have an uneasy time working together.

The Chechen leader, Kasanov, had come to power after the wars and had ruled with an iron hand, capturing and murdering his opponents and dissidents. He was probably involved in many illicit activities but remained popular. His support of the Russian president earned him some respite from Russian repression. That fact alone gave him status among Chechens.

Ironically for a people with such a reputation for violence, Grozny had become reasonably safe. Most men were armed and considered it their duty to protect women. Lawlessness on the streets was not abided.

Dan knew he had to insert himself when the canister was exchanged between the two men. The trust between them would be tenuous, tempered by the fact that they were from differing clans. *Probably no outstanding feuds.* Dan remembered one analyst telling him the Chechens were masters at holding grudges. Honor was of paramount importance to them and disputes between clans, especially where some code of honor had been breached, could go on for hundreds of years, not just a few generations. The two men's business arrangements would always have a level of uncertainty for that reason. Could he exploit that issue?

He sighed. This was the third opportunity which came at an exchange. It seemed that Dan could only find an opening during these attempted transfers. *How many times will this situation occur?* He was running out of opportunities to exploit. *I'll go to the warehouse early tomorrow and see what develops.*

Lecha and Bulat arrived in Grozny early that morning. They went to Lecha's headquarters. Bulat was slightly nervous. Lecha had said that the details of their deal needed to be discussed. A quick exchange and completion of their business without any conflict seemed to be in doubt.

After settling into a room above the warehouse, one of the men laid the metal briefcase on the table and left. Another brought in a large metal tray with a coffee pot and two cups. He set these on the table and left. Lecha opened the briefcase and turned it around for Bulat to see.

"So many lives, for one of these," he said.

"Yes. But this one canister can claim thousands of lives." He stared at the sealed metal tube. It looked sinister to him. Probably because he knew its contents. "Yet it is only one third of what you were to deliver."

"It cost me nearly twenty good men. I have to answer to their families, and I have to provide for their families. That will not be cheap."

Bulat sensed what was coming next. "I contracted with you to get three canisters for a half million euros," he said. "You got me one. You were paid a quarter million up front." He paused for a moment as if to think through an offer. "I'm prepared to pay you the remaining quarter million, even for only one third of the goods. That's in recognition of your losses."

He saw a thin smile appear on Lecha's face. Both men were still in their coats. The day was cold and a space heater had only recently been turned on and was now trying hard to raise the temperature in the room. Bulat took a sip of the hot coffee.

"You think you are being generous? I wonder how much you are being paid by whoever is going to receive the canister. And what risk did you take?" He put his cup on the table and leaned forward, his black eyes now alight with energy. "I took all the risk. I suffered the losses, while you sat back, here in Grozny, making calls."

Bulat stared back. He knew not to let the warlord intimidate him. That was Lecha's standard practice. He used his reputation as a fighter and ruthless killer to cower others into acquiescence. Bulat was not to be shaken so easily.

"I offered you the job. You took it willingly. You knew Kuznetsov was involved. That is why I hired you. If Pavlovich had contacted me, I could have bought the canister directly from him. I wouldn't have needed you. You wouldn't now be standing to make a half million plus the extra one hundred grand I already paid for your losses in Milan."

Lecha reached out and closed the briefcase. He pulled it back away from Bulat. Bulat didn't move or change his expression. He needed to work things out with Lecha peacefully. He was in the man's headquarters, and exiting without an agreement would not be easy. From past experience, he knew that Lecha's technique was to first try to intimidate the other party. The man was not subtle.

"I could, perhaps, offer you more. It would depend on what my buyer agrees to. He will not want to make full payment to me for just one canister. I'm losing out on this as well."

Lecha snorted. "You have not lost men. Don't speak to me of your losses. You are getting much more for doing nothing."

"Lecha, if I didn't have the contact. If my buyer hadn't come to me, you would have not had this work." Now Bulat leaned forward. "You only have the work because of me."

"And I lost men because of it."

"We are in a dangerous business. Death is always a possibility. You led your men. Getting the briefcase from Pavlovich, not letting Kuznetsov get it—that was your job. You knew what was going on before you took the work. You even had an informer to help you."

"There was something else. Someone else."

"What do you mean?" Bulat asked.

"In Milan. The first shot did not come from my men."

"Kuznetsov? He knew you were there?"

Lecha shook his head. "From a third party. There was someone else there. I'm sure of it." He gave Bulat a hard look. "Did you send someone to watch me?"

"No. I hired you and expected you to complete the job. Sending a third party would only complicate things."

"Yet there was someone else. Maybe they got the canisters, not the FSB."

Bulat put up his hands. "What does it matter now? Those two canisters are gone. We will not find them.

"Yes, you are right." Lecha leaned forward again. "But it doesn't change things. My men are still dead."

Bulat sighed. "What do you want?"

"An extra million Euros."

Bulat's eyes widened. "On top of the two hundred and fifty thousand I already gave you?"

"On top of that and the two hundred fifty thousand you still owe me."

"You want one and a half million for one third of the goods? Three times what you contracted for?"

Lecha nodded. "It is fair. I lost three times the number of men I expected to lose."

"I can't do that. It's too much."

"I'm sure you can do it. I'm sure you've been paid more than that amount. You make less, but not all deals can be so profitable for you. Especially when they don't work out well."

"It didn't work out well because of your mistakes."

Lecha closed his hands into large fists and set them on the table. "Be careful, my friend. You should not insult me, especially when I still hold the goods. If you don't agree, I can always sell the canister back to Kuznetsov. I'm sure he would pay a million and a half for it."

Bulat's position was not good. He recognized it. "If you highjack me at the end of our deal, we may never do business again. You understand what you are risking? The work I provide for you makes you rich. Makes you influential. You want to go back to smuggling caviar?"

Lecha smiled. "Caviar is not so bad. The money may be less, but there are fewer guns and gunfights."

"And you remain a man of smaller influence. It is my money, from the work I give you, that makes you so powerful. Remember that."

"So, we need one another. I don't disagree. But the blood of my men calls out for more money."

"Here is what I'll do," Bulat said. "I will give you the two hundred and fifty thousand now. I have it here." He reached into his coat and pulled out a large, thick envelope. "Tomorrow we can go to the bank and I will draw out five hundred thousand more. I will pay you a total of one million euros, even though I take a loss on this deal. Accept that and we can continue to do business."

"Put another two hundred fifty in it and we have a deal."

"One fifty."

Lecha stared at Bulat. Bulat knew he was evaluating how firm he was.

"Okay. Two hundred fifty thousand now and six hundred and fifty thousand later, from your bank."

Bulat smiled and slid the envelop across the desk.

"We will meet tomorrow," Lecha said.

Bulat nodded. "You have the two fifty as my token of good faith."

"I will hold the briefcase until tomorrow," Lecha said.

"You can trust me. We'll do business again."

Chapter 46

That night Bulat met with his men. He briefed them carefully. If the opportunity presented itself to not pay the full 1.15 million euros, he'd take it. Lecha was not the only warlord he could work with. Short of killing him which would ignite a blood feud between their clans, he would watch for an opportunity. With the canister in his hands, and not controlled by Lecha's guns, the warlord would be more pliant in his demands. Bulat would make it up to him with the next deal.

The next morning, Dan drove across the river to the warehouse district. He found an abandoned building near Bulat's headquarters. After going inside, he made his way to the roof with his H&K sniper rifle.

He watched as men arrived and went inside. Finally, Lecha showed up. Dan was now on high alert. Another SUV drove up; Bulat got out and went into the building. After fifteen minutes, the two men exited and walked to their separate vehicles. At that moment, three black SUV's drove into the compound and spread out in a line. Lecha's men looked over at the vehicles, their weapons now drawn.

A dozen men jumped out on the protected side of the arriving SUVs and opened fire on Lecha's men. Most of them went down in the initial burst of automatic fire. Lecha was caught out of his SUV, but crouched down behind it.

Bulat's vehicle was in no-man's land, in between the newly arrived SUVs and Lecha's vehicle. His men got out between the two, shielding themselves from the three intruding SUVs. They hunkered down, not wanting to draw fire to themselves. The attackers were focused on Lecha's men.

Dan watched the attack from the rooftop. *Kuznetsov? Did he drive here to get revenge?* He held his fire. As he was watching someone crawled over to Lecha's SUV and opened the rear door. They reached inside as the bullets flew overhead in a furious back and forth.

Dan could see the man crawl back and slither over to Bulat's vehicle. It looked like he had the briefcase with him. New shooting came from the upper floors of the warehouse. Kuznetsov's men were now pinned down from this new round of fire. Increased shooting came from Lecha's men, both on the ground and from the second floor.

In the confusion, Bulat's men got back into their SUV and they accelerated away from the shootout. Dan watched them go around the corner of the warehouse. He got up to go, just as an RPG was fired out of one of the upper windows and destroyed the rear-most SUV. Kuznetsov and his gang scrambled into the two remaining vehicles and roared off, while still exchanging shots with Lecha's men.

The canister! Bulat snatched it, right out from under Lecha's nose. Dan ran to the stairs and took them two and three at a time down the four flights to his Peugeot. He had to catch up with Bulat if he was going to get the canister.

He floored the sedan and raced out of the warehouse area onto the local street. He could see the SUV disappearing down the road, moving fast. Where are they going? Bulat couldn't stay in Grozny. Lecha would come for him, if he hadn't been killed. And if he were, Bulat still had Kuznetsov to worry about. The man seemed to be on a search and destroy mission after suffering at the hand of Lecha.

The SUV raced through Grozny and onto the E50, the main road going east. *He's heading into Dagestan. Where could he be going?* Dagestan was more dangerous than Chechnya. It was one of the centers for smuggling along the Caspian Sea. Caviar was one of the favorite items. It could be purchased for five hundred euros per kilo and when it got to one of the capitols in Europe, it could fetch up to three thousand euros.

There was, however, a darker side to the smuggling business which included men, woman, and children, often from Uzbekistan, to be used as slave labor and sex slaves in Russia and eastern Europe. Some of the women and children wound up in the Middle-Eastern states along the Persian Gulf.

Dan raced after the SUV, the Peugeot slowly losing ground to the more powerful machine. When Bulat had to slow down, Dan was able to close on him and so kept the fleeing arms dealer in sight. In a little over two hours, they turned into the port town of Kaspiysk, located on the Caspian Sea. *He's going on a boat? Clever. Lecha won't be able to follow. South to Azerbaijan?*

Dan drove carefully, not wanting to give himself away. He was pretty sure that Bulat didn't know he was on his tail. The man would be worried about SUVs, containing either Lecha and his men, or Kuznetsov and his gang.

At the harbor, the SUV drove out along a dirt road to a quay across from the commercial docks. Moored out there was a forty-foot cabin cruiser. It looked out of place in the harbor filled with old freighters and a few rundown fishing boats.

Dan parked at the shore and watched. The men exited and boarded the cruiser. Dan got out with his duffel bag and walked down to the dock. There were two fishing boats tied up. One was locked up with no one about. There was an older fisherman on the second boat.

Dan stepped aboard with his bag. The startled captain turned from his net mending to see a 9mm pistol pointed at his chest.

"Not a sound," Dan said in Russian.

"What do you want?" the man asked.

"You are going to take me out to sea. We will follow that cruiser across the harbor." Dan gestured to the luxury yacht out on the quay.

The man gave him a questioning look.

"Nothing will happen to you if you follow my directions," Dan said.

"My boat is too slow to follow that yacht."

"You will try. And you will do as I say along the way. *Vyponimayete*? Do you understand?"

The man nodded.

"Start the engine and head out."

The captain did as Dan told him. With the engine running, he cast off the lines and the old fishing boat headed out from the harbor. They passed the cruiser with Dan watching from inside the half cabin. The crew were untying the yacht from the dock as they motored past.

"Go straight out and when the cruiser comes out, turn in the direction they go, but do it slowly."

"They will get away from us quickly. This old boat only goes seven knots. They can go twenty or more, I'm sure of it."

"We just keep them in sight."

A plan had formed in Dan's mind. The old fisherman was right. They would never know where the yacht went after it got over the horizon. They would be out of sight after they put about three miles between them. He'd have to do something before that. He was encouraged that the sea was quite calm. The Caspian experienced long periods of little wind, mostly in the summer. Calm days appeared however, through the whole year, even in the winter.

Rather than turning north or south, the yacht motored past the chugging fishing boat and kept on a course straight out to sea. The crew and passengers paid little attention to the old boat as they churned past.

Getting out of sight of land before they turn. The fishing boat kept a similar course. After rocking side-to-side from the wake of the passing yacht, the old boat settled down to follow the steadily disappearing yacht as it motored away.

"Lock the wheel down," Dan directed.

The captain tied a length of rope to the wheel, holding it straight. Dan took out his H&K. The yacht was now a half mile ahead and getting smaller. Dan motioned for the captain to slow the boat to an idle and come forward with him. At the front of the boat, he had the man lie down. Dan lay down behind him and rested his rifle across the man's back, aiming it through a forward scupper hole.

"Lie still or I'll knock you unconscious," he told the now confused and frightened fisherman.

Dan sighted the yacht through his scope. He could see the man at the elevated helm. There were other men about lower down on the rear deck. They were holding bottles, passing them around in a celebration.

Don't celebrate too soon, Dan thought.

He turned his aim back to the man at the helm and slowed his breathing. The familiar tunnel between himself and the target emerged, shutting out everything around him. His heart rate slowed and, letting out half a breath, his finger closed on the trigger.

The bullet slammed into the back of the helmsman, throwing him against the wheel. His body bounced back off of it and fell to the deck with one arm hanging over the edge. The men on the lower deck looked up in shock. One of them ran up the ladder to grab the helm. Dan's second shot dropped him and he fell back down to the lower deck. Men now dove for cover, some going inside the main deck cabin.

Dan now sent round after round into the fiberglass hull of the yacht, above and below the waterline. Another man, one of the crew, ran up the ladder. He reached the helm just as Dan shot him. He then put a series of rounds into the control panel and throttle lever. The yacht slowed and stopped. It turned sideways. Dan ejected his spent magazine and shoved a new one into the weapon. He now took advantage of the exposed target and began sending rounds into the hull at the waterline and below. The fiberglass construction would not present any obstacle to the 7.62mm rounds. They shattered the glass hull ripping open numerous holes to the sea and continued inside, causing more damage.

Return fire started coming from the yacht. The shooters had only the fishing boat to target. When Dan saw a muzzle flash, he fired through the fiberglass sides of the yacht which offered only the illusion of protection for the shooter. The few shots that hit the fishing boat either rang off the steel sections or lodged with a dull *thunk* in the solid wood frame. Dan and the old captain could not be seen by any of the shooters.

Soon there was no more gunfire coming from the yacht. Dan allowed the fisherman to get onto his hands and knees. He watched with Dan as the yacht slowly began to list to one side. Dan kept a watch through his scope. If anyone came on deck, he was going to make that their last act.

Only one person attempted to. He must have been one of the crew. He ran to the stern and tried to let down the dinghy. As he was working the winch, Dan's shot took him out. The dinghy hung lopsided, partly lowered to the water.

Another crew member ran up the ladder to the bridge. He worked at the controls and Dan shot him. *Trying to get the pumps working. Can't have that.*

The list increased and the stern began to sink lower into the water.

"Are you going to save them?" the fisherman asked. He was a man of the sea and must have felt the strong commitment to rescue other seamen from drowning.

Dan gave him a long, hard look. "*Nyet*. They are bad men. They would cause much death and destruction if they got away. I am at war with them." He locked eyes with the old man. "You understand war?"

The man nodded. "They are in Allah's hands then. What do we do?"

"We watch until it is over."

He thought he could detect a shiver from the old man.

"And after? You kill me as well?"

Dan shook his head. "You have done what I told you. You will live."

A half hour later, the few remaining men started jumping overboard into the cold waters as the yacht tipped further on its side. Dan was satisfied to see that no one carried a briefcase or cylinder with them when they left the yacht. The stern, now awash, sank even lower and finally the luxury yacht rolled to one side, tipped up its bow, and, with a jet of air forced out of the cabin, sank under water.

"We go now," Dan said.

He and the captain walked back to the helm. The man turned the old boat around and started motoring away. His face dark with confused emotions. Dan could sense them. There was relief that he would live, anger at leaving others to drown, and questions about who Dan was and what the whole event had been about.

"You have many questions. I sense them. I will not give you answers except to say that those were men who would kill thousands with what they carried on the boat. It's gone now, to the bottom of the sea, ruined by the water and never to be used. Don't morn them. They are not worth it. Better to celebrate that you have been spared today."

He looked towards the shore. "You must go south now and drop me off somewhere else besides the harbor. There may be people waiting for us there. People we don't want to meet."

Fifteen miles down the coast, there was a stretch of beach with some empty beach houses behind it. The fisherman idled the old boat near the shore.

"I can't go any further. I'll run aground."

“This will work. You have any plastic on the boat?”

The man nodded and produced a large scrap of plastic sheeting.

“Give me your phone,” Dan said.

The man handed him his cell phone. Dan wrapped his clothes and his coat along with two phones in the plastic and stuck them back in his duffel bag with his weapons. Then he took the power cord from the boat’s radio.

“This and your phone will be at the front door of one of those houses,” he said pointing to the beach homes.

Next, he took a thousand euros out of his bag and handed them to the man. The captain shook his head.

“I cannot be paid for what I did today.”

“I’m paying you for your fuel, for the plastic, and for taking your phone. That is all.” He stuffed the bills into the man’s coat pocket. “Do what you want with it.”

With an average monthly income of around two hundred euros, it represented a sizable increase in the old man’s finances.

Dan dropped over the side. The water was chest deep. He pushed off from the boat and waded to the shore. He looked back to see the boat reversing and turning to the north.

I’ve got an hour head start in the worst case. Better get moving. He lurched through the water and sprinted across the rough sand beach. When out of site, he stopped and put on his still-dry clothes. After leaving the old captain’s phone and radio power cord at one of the houses, he started jogging to the west. In an hour he was away from the fields and houses following a road leading into the dry foothills.

Chapter 47

Got to find some cell reception and arrange for an extraction. Dan continued to jog along the road. A farm tractor approached from behind, barely faster than he was running. Dan waved the farmer down.

"Can I ride on the wagon?" He spoke in Russian.

The farmer looked at him suspiciously for a moment and then nodded. Dan climbed onto the wagon with the farmer watching him. After he sat down, the man started up again. Dan tried to relax as he bounced around amid the pile of hay. Along with the hay, there was a butchered hog, which Dan guessed the farmer was going to sell in the next village.

"*Izvinitye*, excuse me."

The farmer turned to look at Dan.

"Is there cell phone service in the next village?" Dan took out his phone and pointed to it.

The farmer nodded without speaking and turned back to the road.

Better drop off before the village. Dan didn't know what the farmer was thinking. He was sure the man didn't think he was Russian. Whether that helped or not, Dan couldn't guess. The farmer would tell the local official, and whether that person was a clan leader or part of the official police wouldn't matter. Even with Dan's ID, his duffel bag would be enough to lock him up and call in other authorities.

The wagon lumbered on for a half hour. When they came to a rise, Dan saw houses a mile ahead in the valley. He slipped off the back of the wagon and dropped into the ditch along the side of the road. Hopefully the farmer would not look back until he got to town.

From his position on the rise, Dan could get a signal. He dialed Jane's cell.

"Who is this?" she asked after answering the call.

"It's me. I need a pickup."

"Where are you?"

"Dagestan. An hour west of Kaspiysk."

"You sure know how to get around. Did you accomplish your task?"

"Sort of."

There was a pause.

"What does that mean?"

"Better to tell you in person, later. Can you send someone for me or do I have to walk to Tblisi?"

"You're on foot? That would be a tough walk. There's no road link and you'd have to cross some high mountains, in the winter."

"Forget the geography lesson. I'm familiar with the terrain. Just tell me what you can do. I don't think it's a good idea to just hang my thumb out. Things were pretty hot when I left Grozny. Same as when I just left Kaspiysk."

"All right. Hunker down. Stay in cell range. I'll call you back in an hour."

"Don't be too long, There may be people trying to find me." He paused, then added. "And Jane, don't send someone I don't know."

He clicked off the phone and started into the hills. He'd get hidden higher up, but still in cell range, and wait. There was always the waiting, ever since sniper school.

Half an hour later a police car heading to the village drove past the spot where Dan had exited the wagon. *Someone got called. They'll be looking around town for me*. Unless the fisherman raised an alarm, which was possible, Dan's presence on the farm wagon wouldn't merit a major search of the surrounding territory. Still he knew he had better keep a watch through the rest of the day.

After another twenty minutes Dan's phone rang.

"Marcus and Roland are on their way tonight. I've arranged a private charter. They'll stop in Frankfurt and then Tbilisi. From there, they'll rent a car. If you're heading west, there's no road going over the mountains into Georgia. If they use the roads, they have to go north to Chechnya, almost to Grozny, before heading east."

"That might present problems. Those two don't look like civilians."

"I got them to let their hair grow a little longer. They don't look quite so soldier-like now."

"I'm not sure you can cover that up. But I like your choice. I can trust those two."

"Can you shelter in place for a few days?"

"Not much shelter, but I can make do. Hopefully a storm won't come through."

"Sit tight. I'm having Fred research if there are any off-road routes over the mountains. It might not be quicker, but they won't run into any police. It's pretty desolate on that border."

Dan ended the call. Much as he enjoyed hearing Jane's voice, it wasn't a good idea to stay on the line too long. *Never know who's listening*. He leaned back against a rock and let his body relax for the first time in twenty-four hours. Between Yevgeni Kuznetsov, Bulat Zakayev, and Lecha Maskhadov, events had gotten very complicated. He was lucky he had been able to navigate through them without getting caught in the middle.

He had no idea whether or not Lecha was still alive. Bulat had been until the yacht sank. Dan guessed the fisherman probably went back to pick up the survivors. He would not ignore the waterman's code. It didn't matter that Dan had said they were bad. Dan was an outsider, so why would he listen to him?

He felt reasonably sure the canister had gone down with the yacht. The depth where the yacht sank was around eight hundred feet from what Dan could remember. The Caspian was up to two thousand feet deep in some areas, but that was further out from shore. Still the yacht was well below the depth that could be reached by a normal scuba diver. It would take a deep diving professional and a lot of support equipment to locate and get to the yacht.

Would the fisherman find the survivors alive? The water temperatures this time of year were fifty to fifty-five degrees; cold enough to kill you in a few hours. Some might be saved. That fact sat uncomfortably with Dan. The job hadn't been fully finished. *Maybe they'll kill each other*. Lecha could find Bulat and, if he survived the sinking, kill him for trying to skip out on him. He was not a man to entertain the explanation that Bulat just wanted to save himself from Kuznetsov's attack. Bulat took the canister. That might be enough for Lecha to exact his revenge even if Bulat protested he planned to make the payment in full. Maybe Kuznetsov could then finish his mission, killing Lecha?

Dan shook his head. It was all conjecture. The fact remained there were too many loose ends and the canister at the bottom of the Caspian was one of them.

He hiked further into the hills until he found a shallow cave cut into the hillside from centuries of erosion. He was in a shallow depression. No one could see him. He began to scrounge around for scraps of wood. The surrounding hills provided enough shielding that he felt he could risk a fire to stave off the night's chill. It would get down to freezing and he didn't want to have to spend the whole night tramping around to keep warm. The fire at the entrance could give him a few hours of sleep and the rocks, when heated, would keep his cubby above freezing. Things were looking up. If one had low expectations, little comforts could bring much satisfaction.

There'd be no planes. Even if Bulat had been saved, he would not want authorities to get too involved in his situation. Uncomfortable questions would come up. While both he and Lecha wielded some influence, at least in Grozny, in Dagestan, Bulat was not on such sure footing. Lecha had connections with the smuggling business, but Bulat had done little arms business in Dagestan.

Chapter 48

As soon as Dan ended the call, Jane went over to Henry's office. Both rooms had been swept again for bugs, with negative results.

"Just got a call from Dan," she said as she barged into the room.

Henry looked up at her and motioned for her to take a seat. He was on the phone but quickly finished his conversation. After he had hung up, he looked at his assistant. Jane knew she was barely hiding her enthusiasm.

"Did he recover the third canister?"

"He didn't say. The line was not secure. He's in Dagestan, an hour west of the Caspian. I need to get him out."

"We can send a pickup team to Georgia."

"That's a problem. He's on foot and there aren't any roads linking Georgia and Dagestan directly. He'd have to go through Chechnya.'

Henry stared up at Jane.

"He's on foot and from what he said, things got hot in Grozny and in the port town in Dagestan. It didn't sound like hitching a ride would be a good idea."

"Take a step back. What was he doing in Chechnya and Dagestan?"

"Chasing the third canister."

"And he didn't indicate he recovered it?"

"Not directly." She sat down and leaned on Henry's desk. "Look, he's on foot. The territory is hot right now. He has a thin cover story at best, especially why he's in Dagestan." She paused for a moment to collect her thoughts. "A security systems sales consultant would not be hitchhiking in Dagestan. I want to send a team to Georgia and have them drive to meet him."

"Through Chechnya."

"They'll be fine. They won't be stopping."

"Who will you send?"

"I want to send Marcus and Roland. Dan trusts them."

"He's still worried about a mole, someone trying to subvert the mission?"

"Milan was FUBAR, you know that. People here knew something about it was suspicious. Why would they suspect it was something other than an Italian problem, a drug deal gone bad? He has reason to be suspicious."

"And we've taken steps to make sure we don't have any leaks."

"He doesn't know that. Henry, we're wasting time. Let me get started on sending Roland and Marcus. I need to hurry."

"What's their cover? We don't have time to build anything elaborate."

"They'll be reporters doing a story on how Chechnya has come back from the war and is a wonderful place to visit. Anyone asking will like the idea of a puff piece on the country."

She was almost squirming in her seat. There was much to do and she needed to get it done that day so the two men could fly that evening.

"Okay. Get your team on it."

"Thanks. Can you get me a Gulfstream for tonight? Something like a G550?"

"I'll see what I can come up with."

Jane almost flew out of Henry's office.

She called Roland and Marcus and told them to meet her at the private air terminal at Dulles that evening. Next, she set her team on producing some ID documents showing both men to be employed by a media outlet. The cover wouldn't hold up to any serious checking, but would satisfy any authorities at a checkpoint or traffic stop.

Later Jane drove to Dulles airport. When she arrived, Roland and Marcus were waiting in the general aviation lounge. They got up when they saw her enter. She motioned them down one hallway to a small, private room. Inside were a table and chairs with coffee service set up along the wall. The curtains were closed. Jane put her briefcase on the table and opened it up.

"I've got a Gulfstream 550. It will take you to Tbilisi, Georgia. You leave in one hour, 10pm."

"We're going to get Dan?" Roland asked.

She handed the two men their individual packets.

"Your IDs. You'll rent a car and drive to Dagestan. I've got maps showing you the route. Your cover is that, you, Marcus, are a journalist writing a puff piece, all sweetness and light, about Chechnya. And you," she turned to Roland, "are the photographer. I've got some equipment for you." She handed him a professional hand-held camera.

"I don't know how to use this," Roland said as he turned the device over in his hands.

"You've got thirteen hours to study the manual and learn. Your packets contain passports and employee IDs. And we have cover in place for a first level of check on you. Your documents won't survive any deeper checks so stay out of trouble."

"Easier said than done," Roland replied.

"How do we find him?" Marcus asked.

"Get to Kaspiysk and call him. He'll direct you from there. He's holed up west of the town. We're not sure where but he says he can stay there undetected. He doesn't have any supplies, so you want to get to him as quickly as you can."

"Who's searching for him and do we take any weapons with us?" Roland asked.

"We don't know exactly who's looking for him. It could be the Russian mafia, a Chechen gang, or the arms dealer. She paused, then added, "Or the police, both Chechen and Russian."

“What the hell kind of mess did he get into?” Roland asked.

“I’ll let him tell you. Just get to him and get him out. The plane will wait at Tbilisi. If you run into trouble, call. Your phones are encrypted so we’re reasonably sure of a private conversation. You know though, there are no guarantees, so watch what you say.

“Any questions?”

“Weapons?” Roland repeated his question.

“I can give you sidearms with magnetic holsters. You can attach them on top of the frame, out of sight if someone sticks a mirror under the car.”

Roland furrowed his brows. “We’ll need more than that. How about two Uzi’s? They don’t take up much room when folded and we can hide them along with the pistols.”

“They both use 9mm ammo so that helps consolidate the load,” Marcus said.

“You can hide them?”

“Enough so Russian checks won’t find them,” Roland said.

“Okay.” Jane opened her cell phone and made a quick call. We’ll have two out here in half an hour. Any more questions?”

Marcus raised his hand, seeming to parody a schoolboy asking his teacher a question. Jane nodded at him with an exasperated expression on her face.

“I was on a hot date when you called. Can you call her and tell her I’m so important that my country had to send me on an emergency overseas mission to save lives, but I’ll be back to take up where we left off?”

Jane smiled at him. He was a warrior through and through. Over six feet tall, but slightly smaller than his counterpart, Roland. Both extremely lethal, yet they had never grown out of their schoolboy humor.

“No, I don’t think I can tell her all of that. But I can send her some flowers and tell her you miss her.”

"That'll do. Thank you, ma'am." He wrote the woman's name and address down on a piece of paper.

"Roland, do you need any help in your love life?"

"No, Miss Jane," Roland replied, picking up on Marcus's play. "I'm good. The women wait patiently for me."

"Good." Jane got up. "The plane's outside, you may as well board. You're going to be wheels-up as soon as the weapons get here." She looked at her watch. "Probably a half hour." She shook the men's hands. They were large, but gentle, gripping their boss's hand. "Be careful and bring yourselves back safely. No international episodes, please." She didn't smile at this last comment.

The men nodded.

"See you in a couple of days," Roland said.

Chapter 49

Christina sat at her piano, playing scales in a desultory manner. Her heart was not in it. Chloé watched from outside the practice room. A jumble of emotions stirred inside her. She felt badly for Christina's sadness. She felt a guilty relief that the man was gone. And her hopes for a closer relation with her employer and friend kept rising to tease her.

She took a breath and stepped into the room. She put her hand on Christina's shoulder. The woman stopped playing and leaned her head to one side, against Chloé's hand.

"You miss him."

"Do you think he'll come back? It's been two weeks now."

Chloé didn't answer. She felt afraid of giving away too much.

"He said he had to close things up, to end any threats to him...and possibly me. He could be in danger and I'd never know it." She turned to Chloé, "I have a bad feeling. He's in danger and I can't help him."

"There's nothing you can do at this point. You just have to go on. Maybe he'll come back, maybe not."

Christina looked up at Chloé. "That's no help. Of course, those two options exist. But I can't help thinking the worst is going to happen."

"And what is that?"

"That he won't come back, not because he doesn't want to, but because he's been killed or captured like before."

She paused. "And I won't know where he is or how to help him."

"Christina, he lived in a violent world, from what we can tell—"

"He's not a bad man. I know that deep down."

"But he's involved with bad men and no good can come of that."

"Oh, you're no help," she said as she got up and left the room.

Chloé followed her out.

"I didn't mean to upset you. I know you miss him."

Christina looked at her assistant.

"We were in love. What we had was not a fling."

"You saved his life from what you told me."

"Yes, and he opened up my heart...and career." She looked at Chloé, her big eyes pleading for understanding. "He has an amazing gift. All the more unusual since he's not a musician. He can listen to me and know when I've gotten to the heart of the music, gotten to the composer's soul, if that's possible. He spoke of what he heard in layman's terms, but his words struck to the core of whatever I was playing."

She took Chloé's hands.

"He helped me discover a new level of expression and interpretation in my music."

"And that seems to be paying off. We need to go over your schedule. More and more demands are coming in. Right now, you are a hot property. I'm fielding calls from five continents and hundreds of people wanting to propose marriage."

Christina gave her assistant a sad smile.

"Save me from those, please."

"You know I will. I'm here for you. I'll always be here for you."

Chloé wanted to say more, but caution held her back. Dan had told her he understood the full range of her feelings for Christina and warned Chloé that Christina did not think of her in a romantic way. The words rang in her ears and she didn't say more. Maybe being this important to Christina was enough. Maybe it would have to be enough, at least for now.

Later that week, Christina went into the village. Chloé had gone back to Paris for the week and would return on the weekend. She was sitting at a table in the restaurant on the main square when the Monseigneur came in.

His eyes were sharp and penetrating; something she had noticed in their previous meeting. She had also seen that same intensity in her Rossignol. It confused her because this man was part of the church, a man of peace. He walked up to her but didn't sit down.

"You again," Christina said in a cold voice.

"I know you think badly of me. I tried to tell you some truths about the man you harbored. I was indelicate, impolite. For that, I apologize. May I sit down for a moment?"

Christina nodded to a chair across from her.

The priest sat down and took off his hat.

"I know some things about the man who left you. Some of them, I can tell you, but some of them I can't."

"You know about him? Have you heard from him? Is he alive?

"He is alive. I am not in communication with him, but I know he's alive."

"How do you know this?"

The priest pointed to his head; a gesture he had used in their earlier meeting.

"As I told you, I know things. There are others like me who know things. That is as much as I can say. This man has completed his mission as best he could. He has given life to his enemy and with that made you safer."

Christina looked at the man, who was not only a priest, but a Monseigneur, a man who commanded great respect. She felt a pang of embarrassment that she hadn't given him much of that in their previous meeting. Since that time, she had not communicated with anyone about the Monseigneur, preferring to put aside what he had said.

"Is he coming back? You said he had completed his mission, as you call it." She knew her voice expressed her hope in his return.

"That I can't see. I see that he has had a deep effect on you, but you still need to guard your heart."

"Will he call me? I haven't heard from him in over two weeks now."

Monseigneur Louis-Marie Chicon shook his head. He looked sad. Christina wondered if it was because he was hiding bad news or because he could not participate in the affairs of the heart as normal people do—people who fall in love with one another.

"I expect that you will hear from him. What will be the outcome? I don't know. I just know that you are vulnerable to being hurt and I don't want to see that happen. I also want to allay your fears about his welfare."

He stood up and put on his hat.

"*Prends soin de toi*, take care. I am here once a month. Father Lucien knows my schedule. If you ever want to talk, I will make time for you. You are very special to this man. And he is very special to so many people in this world."

Without waiting for more questions, he turned to go.

Chapter 50

Rashid flew to Baku, Azerbaijan. He had insisted on meeting Bulat face-to-face. Bulat had relayed what had taken place since Moscow and how the third canister had been lost. Rashid took two bodyguards with him and a small, wiry man known as Scorpion. He was not large, but he was deadly. His body was sinewy and taut, full of surprising strength.

The two bodyguards, although much larger in size, showed him much deference, preferring to stand apart from the man. Scorpion had a thin face with a long nose. His hair and eyes were black as coal. His face showed no emotion. While his small size might allow him to move unnoticed in a crowd, a good look at his face, into his eyes, left one with no doubt that this was a man to be avoided.

He was an assassin. He had many ways to kill someone. It was said that he had poison daggers inserted under his finger nails, and one rake of his hand across your exposed skin sentenced you to a painful death. The Scorpion did nothing to dispel the rumor.

To Rashid the man showed deference. Not only because Rashid paid him well, but because he respected Rashid's single-minded purpose of bringing jihad to the infidel. The Scorpion was not overly religious, but he felt the centuries-old insult of the west's dominance over Islamic countries.

He had no respect for fellow Muslims, and Arabs in particular, even though he counted himself a true-blooded Arab with descendants living in the Arabian Peninsula that he could trace back a thousand years. These Arabs had sold out their heritage and their mission to get along with the west for monetary gain. In Rashid, he had found a rich Arab who manipulated the west in order to gain from them the funds with which to wage war against them. All the while the fools never recognized him as their enemy. Such deadly deception was something the Scorpion could admire.

They met in a rented house. Bulat was nervous. Rashid's men had disarmed his bodyguards. They sat in a plain room around a dining table, western style. In one corner, not at the table, sat a small, evil-looking man who kept staring at Bulat.

"You have cost me much loss of money. Money I paid for goods not delivered."

"I can pay you back," Bulat said. His voice betrayed his nerves.

"And that makes everything all right? The canisters are lost. One to the bottom of the sea and the other two may be in the hands of the Americans or the Russians."

"At least I kept it out of Kuznetsov's hands."

Rashid held back his sudden surge of anger. He should kill Bulat's guards and let the Scorpion terminate the man slowly and painfully.

"If he had the canister, I could have purchased it from him. Your actions closed off that possibility." His voice was low and flat, without any emotion.

He paused to pour himself some tea. None was offered to Bulat who he saw was beginning to sweat in spite of the cold winter day.

"Here is what you are going to do. You are going to recover that canister. I won't pay for the work. You will have to do that. And you will have to figure out how to do it on your own. There are technical divers in the world that can work at those depths. Get the permits. Hire the divers. You are recovering remains from the sunken yacht. When you have the canister, contact me and I will meet you here again."

"That will be an expensive operation. And one that could expose me to publicity. In my work, one doesn't need publicity."

"In your work, one can't have failure. It can be fatal." Rashid pointed to the small man in the corner. "Do you know who this is?"

Bulat shook his head, but his face betrayed his suspicions.

"Yes. It is the Scorpion. He exists. He is real, he is deadly, and he can inflict a lot of pain. One doesn't always get to die quickly. One can, under the Scorpion's ministrations, die slowly and...very painfully."

Rashid now slammed his hands flat on the table with a loud bang. Bulat jumped in his chair.

"You do not get any more money. What you get in exchange for the canister, is your life. I get the canister or you get the Scorpion."

He held Bulat's eyes in his dark gaze. "Am I clear on this?"

Bulat nodded.

Rashid dismissed him with a wave of his hand.

Before his meeting with Bulat, Rashid had talked at length with Lecha Maskhadov. He made sure Lecha would not ignite a feud with Bulat. Maskhadov was an unpleasant person, brutish and disrespectful but he would acquiesce to Rashid's orders. The last thing Rashid needed was a feud to derail Bulat's recovery efforts.

Lecha had held Kuznetsov captive with the possibility of getting information about the other two canisters. And then it had all gone wrong. Rashid needed the details so he could better understand what had happened.

"Maskhadov thinks there was only one or two who killed his men and rescued Kuznetsov," Rashid said to the Scorpion. "He thinks Kuznetsov was freed during the night and, afterwards, called in his men to clean up the dead bodies."

"It's an interesting idea," said the Scorpion. "It would take a very lethal man to accomplish that."

"The snowstorm would have helped hide his actions."

"While making them harder, as well."

Rashid's mind went back to Mexico. That plan had gone wrong. Someone had gotten wind of it and it had cost him his investment in the fighters smuggled into the country as well as Tariq Basara, a true believer and faithful warrior. He had hated to eliminate him but had felt it necessary to obliterate his tracks in the aftermath of that debacle.

Then there was Frankfort. Someone had known of his plans. From what he could learn it had been only one or two men who had killed and disrupted the dozen or more men that had attacked the airport.

And only one man had later killed Jabbar Khalid in Marseille. And then had escaped with a whole block of enraged Muslims looking for him.

Were all these events connected?

Rashid relayed his thoughts to the Scorpion. The man listened silently, without expression.

"You think there is one man, an assassin of great skill, behind all these plans gone wrong?"

Rashid nodded. "It's a possibility. Kuznetsov and Bulat supplied material for the Frankfort attacks, but they would not sell out. It would mean the end of their business."

He paused to think.

"The Swiss banker, Aebischer, who we used in our projects, would also not have said anything. He had always been a reliable conduit for money."

"You both speak the same language, even if he is an infidel."

"He is not political, and, yes, we do. But since Frankfurt, he has disappeared from the face of the earth. I cannot locate him through any of my contacts. His daughter now resides in his Swiss mansion. She runs a recovery home for abused girls and runaways."

Rashid thought for moment.

"What is interesting is that she has such sophisticated security on the grounds. It seems well above her expertise or need."

The Scorpion shrugged. "Perhaps. She is now wealthy, is she not?"

Rashid nodded.

"You want me to find this assassin? Before we know whether or not he exists?"

"I'll put my resources into learning more. You put your resources to work as well. And if he exists, as I suspect, you need to eliminate him."

"An assassin to kill an assassin." The thin man smiled. It was a cruel smile without warmth. "It will be a worthy challenge."

Chapter 51

Marcus and Roland drove north from Tbilisi and took a road that followed the Terek River into the hills through what is called the Dariali Gorge. They were heading towards one of the few border crossings going over the mountains dividing Georgia from Ingushetia.

As they approached the border with Russia, they drove past the Dariali Monastery. It was built near the border checkpoint in hopes that it would create a peaceful atmosphere in this area that had been filled with so much violence in the past. The checkpoint was busy with many lorries going in both directions. The explanation of writing a travel article was not questioned and they passed through with a cursory inspection.

Beyond the checkpoint they turned east on a paved, but secondary road that snaked through the mountains. They wanted to avoid going through Vladikavkaz and getting stopped at more checkpoints. The road wound, serpent-like, up and down the hillsides and through tiny villages. If anyone was out, they eyed the two men with open suspicion. Finally, the road turned north and the mountains receded.

They crossed into Chechnya without stopping, both Ingushetia and Chechnya being Russian provinces. Their route avoided more built-up areas, passing through a series of small towns on the main road heading to Grozny.

They passed Grozny to the south and made their way to the port of Kaspiysk. When they got there, they called Dan and, following his description of the road, they closed in on his location two hours later. They were driving slowly west when Dan called again.

"I can see a car leaving a trail of dust. Stop so I can tell if it's you."

Marcus stopped the car.

"I got you. Wait there for a half hour, I'll make my way to the road. I should be a mile ahead of you."

After waiting, they drove slowly up the road. They were near a rise, when Dan popped out of the ditch. He got into the back seat and Marcus turned the car around.

He looked over his shoulder at Dan. "You're a mess," he said.

"Don't smell so good either," Roland added.

"Try being on the move for four days and then camping in a cave—not a good one either—for another three, waiting for you two. What took you so long?"

"Funny man. Jane had to convince Henry to send us in to rescue your ass," Marcus said over his shoulder.

"You complete your mission?" Roland asked.

"Pretty much. But there's loose ends."

"We going to tie them up?" Roland asked.

Dan shook his head. "Not this time. I've done all that can be done. Now we need to get the hell out and let things settle down. You got some water?"

Roland handed him a plastic bottle. Dan took a couple of long drinks and sighed.

"Needed that."

It was late afternoon. Marcus drove off the road onto a faint two-track that took them around a hill and out of sight of the road.

"We should spend the night here and drive back in daylight. Less danger of ambushes," he said.

Roland took out some power bars to go with the water and the men settled down to get as comfortable as they could in the sedan.

"So, what needs settling down?" Marcus asked.

"There are dead bodies in Moscow, outside of Moscow, in Grozny, and in the Caspian Sea."

"You've been a busy boy," Marcus said.

"What's in the duffel bag?" Roland asked.

"Clothes and weapons. Got an M4, an H&K PSG-1, and a .22 CZ."

"Can't carry that around in the back seat. We'll never get through any checkpoints," Roland said. "Got to hide that 9mm you're carrying as well." He pointed to Dan's coat pocket which showed the outline of a semi-automatic pistol.

"You get much hassle on the road?"

"No. But I'm worried about going back through the same crossing only a day later with another person. We may be remembered. They'll want to know why we're leaving so soon and who you are and why you're with us."

"That's a problem for sure. Not sure I want to go further into Russia though. And I know I don't want to go west through Ingushetia. That only gets us to Azov and the Crimea."

"You still got some ID with you?" Marcus asked.

"Yeah. But I still don't like spending so much time in Russia."

"Maybe we hoof it over the mountains?" Roland asked.

"Maybe," Marcus replied. "Let's get past Grozny first, then we can decide what to do."

At the first crack of dawn, they went back to the road and continued their journey.

"We took a longer route to get here but avoided Nazran and Vladikavkaz. Go back the same way?" Marcus asked.

"Damned if I know. You didn't run into trouble, go take it."

"No trouble. Got lots of suspicious looks, especially when we passed through the villages," Marcus said.

"Sounds like as good a plan as any," Dan said.

He leaned back and closed his eyes. He had had little sleep for four days and decided to take advantage of the few more hours he'd have in the car to relax.

When they started down the road into the mountains, Dan woke up. He couldn't sleep with the car navigating the twisting road. There were switchbacks climbing up the slopes, only to snake down the other side, all of which kept him awake. Marcus was driving at an aggressive pace, but not one that abused the rental car too much.

As they neared a small village, they came around a corner and saw some vehicles parked along the side of the road about three hundred yards ahead. Men in a mix of military and civilian uniforms stood around. Marcus stopped the car.

"Looks like a checkpoint ahead," he said. "I see weapons on some of the men."

Roland and Dan leaned forward to look. The men at the checkpoint were now all looking at the car.

"They'll probably shake us down for money," Roland said.

"More than that and they'll most likely find the weapons."

"No way we can let that happen."

"We turn around, they'll pursue. We'll be target practice for them," Dan said.

"They could call ahead and get the road blocked if we turn and run," Roland answered.

"Not any good options," Marcus said.

"Let's go forward and try to bribe our way through. I can speak enough Russian to get by. How about you two?"

"I can speak a bit," Marcus said.

He put the car in gear and they slowly drove forward.

"What about your weapons?" Roland asked.

"We'll keep them on the floor. They're more likely to want to look in the trunk."

"We got our clothes bags there. The weapons are under the car," Roland said.

"Not much help there. You got a sidearm on you?"

Both men nodded. There was no panicking. The checkpoint was a problem; one to be solved.

They pulled up and stopped as one of the men signaled. There were six men. The leader stepped forward to the driver's window, while the others watched. They were standing around one of their vehicles, a four-door pickup truck. They were all watching the car.

"Where are you going?" The militia leader asked when Marcus lowered the window.

"Tbilisi," Marcus replied.

"You have identification?"

Marcus nodded. "In my pocket." He put his hand into his jacket and took out a leather folder. Opening it, he took out his passport and media company ID. He handed the documents to the leader of the group.

"You just entered Russia earlier yesterday. Why do you leave so soon?"

"We came to pick up our fellow worker." He gestured to Dan. "He needed a ride back and we were near, so our company asked us to pick him up."

Marcus was at the limit of his Russian. The militia leader gave him a long, questioning look.

"You drive from Tbilisi to where, Grozny? To pick up someone? Why don't they just fly from Grozny to Tbilisi?"

"I can't fly on airplanes. They make me sick. I go everywhere by car or train. No flying," Dan said from the back seat.

"You have ID?" the man asked. He turned to Roland as well. "And you?" He held out his hand.

Both men reached into their pockets, took out their passports, and handed them to Marcus who passed them to the man at the window. The man looked at them for a long time. Then he stepped back from the door.

"Out of the car," he commanded.

Chapter 52

"Time to go into action," Dan said under his breath. "On my mark."

The three men stepped out of the car. Interest among the men watching had intensified, although no one had unshouldered their rifles.

The three stood outside of the car. The militia leader motioned them to put their hands on the car, turning their backs to him. He was pulling out his sidearm when Dan grabbed him and put his gun to the man's neck. Marcus and Roland drew their pistols. The militia now leveled their weapons.

"Put your guns down or I shoot him!" Dan shouted out in Russian. He put the pistol to the side of the man's head as he held him around the neck with his left arm. The man tried to wriggle loose.

"Stand still or you're dead," Dan said in his ear.

There was confusion on the part of the militia. Dan repeated his order. Roland and Marcus were now crouched down behind the engine of the car with their 9mms aimed at the group. Some of the men started to lay down their rifles when one of them raised his weapon and fired a shot at Dan. The shot went wide.

Marcus and Roland didn't hesitate but started firing at the men. Two of them dropped. The others scattered, running for cover. Two more were hit and fell to the ground, wounded. Dan fired and the militia leader collapsed, his head blown open by the pointblank shot. Dan let him drop.

"They'll be calling for help. We can't stay," Dan shouted. "Marcus drive, Roland and I will try to keep them pinned down. Let's get the hell out of here."

The men threw themselves into the car and Marcus roared ahead. Both Dan and Roland kept up a withering level of fire, emptying their magazines as they accelerated past the checkpoint. Everyone crouched low, Marcus barely looking over the windshield as return fire followed them down the road, blowing out the rear window and shattering the windshield.

"Everyone okay?" Dan called out.

Both men responded in the affirmative.

"Can't see shit out of the windshield," Marcus shouted.

A bullet had caused a spiderweb of cracks distorting his view. Marcus was leaning his head out of the side window, trying to see. They careened around a corner and into the village. There were a few people out who stopped to stare at the car as it sped along the main street.

"We got to get off the road quickly. They'll be coming after us. They'll set up a roadblock ahead," Roland said.

"How close to the border are we?" Dan asked.

"Hell if I know. It's south, over that range to our left," Marcus shouted. "If I remember right, we can hike south until we come to the highway Roland and I drove north on. That takes us back to Tbilisi."

"Take the next road or trail going south. Let's drive as far up into the hills as we can, then go on foot," Dan said.

He glanced back and could see the pickup with some other vehicles coming after them.

Marcus turned onto a dirt two-track. It went through the farm fields and into the forested hills beyond. He drove with punishing speed over the uneven terrain. Looking back, Dan could see their pursuers make the same turn.

"We didn't fool them. Flog it for all it's worth."

"Drive it like you stole it," Roland said.

"Kind of what we're doing. This one ain't coming home," Marcus replied.

He was panting with the effort of keeping his head outside while controlling the steering wheel to not have the car turn over or lurch into the ditch. In the backseat Roland and Dan held on trying not to get thrown into each other or out of a door.

The forest now closed in on the sides. The two-track began to snake its way upslope and got rougher as it climbed the hill.

"Not much more to go," Marcus said.

Dan could hear the motor laboring, the wheels spinning as the trail degraded.

"When we stop, get what you need from the trunk and let's get into the woods. We can set up and go after them long range."

Finally, the car started to spin its wheels and slewed sideways, sticking its rear up against a boulder.

"End of the line. Let's move!" shouted Marcus.

Everyone jumped out. Marcus ran to the trunk and opened it. He and Roland grabbed their bags. Dan took his duffel bag as he exited the car and the three sprinted into the woods.

Once in the cover of the trees, Dan pointed south, up the slope, and they started jogging through the forest. It was older growth with enough clear ground on the floor for them to jog forward. They heard the pursuers pull up and stop. A few shots rang out and a voice shouted out in Chechen. Dan guessed someone was telling them to stop firing blindly into the woods.

They couldn't see what was going on so Dan had them stop to listen. Dan whispered to the two men.

"Probably dropped off some men to follow in the woods. We left clear marks in the mud along the side of the road, so they'll know where we entered. The rest will come forward in the vehicles. Let's keep going. We need to find a defensible position. Then we can take out the ones following in the woods as they advance."

They continued forward more slowly and more quietly. After crossing a semi-open area, they stopped behind a rock outcropping. It was shallow but offered bullet-proof cover, if one kept one's head down. They had only a small visual between the trees to the two-track, but could easily see anyone approaching from the woods.

Dan took the H&K out of his duffel bag and assembled it while Roland commandeered the M4.

"Damn, we brought two UZI's and now they're stuck under the frame of the car," Marcus said.

"Not as good a weapon as the M4 for reaching out any distance," Dan said.

"We're going to get bracketed by the men in the trucks if they slip past us," Roland said.

"Can't be helped. They'll still have to get out and come to us. We don't need the trail anymore."

"Be on our turf then," Roland said. "I like that better." He hefted the familiar M4. "We got enough rounds?"

"Not for a lengthy stand-off. Enough to take care of this threat, hopefully," Dan said.

Roland reached past Dan and took the remaining magazines and stuffed them into his pockets. Dan did the same with the magazines for the H&K rifle.

"You boys are well armed and I'm stuck with a pistol?" Marcus said.

"Roland, give your buddy your 9mm," Dan said.

"Fuck that. Give him yours."

Dan sighed. He took out his 9mm and handed it to Marcus. Then he took his .22 caliber CZ and put it in his coat pocket.

"What is that a pea shooter?" Roland asked.

"It'll work if they get close. Last resort weapon."

"Let's hope we don't need that," Marcus said. "Thanks for the extra gun.

"Two pistol Pete," Roland said.

At that moment, the pickup came into view.

"Don't shoot," Dan said. He didn't need to tell them as the vehicles went past too quickly to get off any shots.

"Wait for the ones in the woods," he said.

The banter stopped. The men each found a spot from which to watch and shoot. No one moved as they waited for the engagement with the enemy.

"On my shot," Dan said. He scanned the edge of the denser part of the woods through the scope of his carbine.

Two men emerged. Dan held still, waiting. There would be more. In a moment three more came out. They were disciplined enough to fan out.

"You start on the left, I'll take the right," Dan whispered to Roland. He knew Marcus wouldn't fire, the pistols not being as accurate as the rifles.

Dan moved his sights from the right most man to the next in line, getting a sense of the swing. He wanted to take at least two down before they could react and find cover. Then he swung his rifle back at the man on the right.

That familiar sense of a tunnel arose and flooded out everything else. He squeezed his hand gently in almost a handshake with the rifle's pistol grip. The HK gave a muffled bark and the head of the man on the right exploded. Before he hit the ground, two more shots rang out and Dan's next target dropped with a shot to the chest. Roland's shot dropped the man on the far left. Two men dropped to the ground, but not before Roland hit one of them. He yelled out as he twisted in the scrub. The last man had scrambled behind one of the few trees.

The forest was still. The two rifles had their suppressors attached. Dan was fairly certain the men in the trucks, now ahead of them, had not heard the shots.

"What now?" Marcus asked.

Dan called out in Russian for the man to surrender. If he came out with his hands up, they wouldn't shoot him. Otherwise he would die.

He repeated his offer, letting the man know it was his last chance. Otherwise they were going to separate and come at him from many directions.

An AK 47 came flying out from behind the tree.

"I'm coming out. *Ne strelyayte*, don't shoot."

"*Publishno zayavit*, come out!" Dan shouted.

The man emerged with his hands in the air. He walked forward to the rock outcropping.

"What the hell do we do with him now?" Roland asked.

"We tie him up. He'll be able to make his way to the trail but it will take him an hour or more. We'll be long gone by then."

"Not kill him? That's what he wanted to do with us," Roland replied.

"It's easier this way. We didn't have to take the time to flush him out in a gunfight. I might have saved your ass from getting shot."

"Not by this bozo."

"Let's get on with it," Marcus said. We still have the pickups to deal with."

"One of you get the belts from the others. We'll use them to tie this one up."

The man stood still, his eyes wide with fear. Dan guessed the English was causing him some confusion. He probably expected rival clan members, not Americans.

After tying the man's arms and hands behind his back, they bound his legs so he could barely walk. It would lengthen the time it took for him to get to the road. They grabbed his cell phone and left him standing in the field.

They moved south, up the slope, into the denser forest. The enemy was somewhere ahead. They had to locate him before he located them. That was the primary rule of engagement: not get surprised by your enemy.

Chapter 53

The three men advanced in silence. They moved methodically, searching ahead for signs of the other group. They stopped to listen every fifty yards and communicated with hand signals and a few whispers. They were in their zone. Marcus had relieved one of the pursuers of his AK and spare magazines.

They heard it at the same time—muffled voices ahead. Then a car door slammed shut off to their left. They crouched low in the brush, listening and trying to guess the number that faced them. They put their heads close together.

"We go around them?" Marcus asked.

"We could," Dan said.

"They might come at us from behind," Roland said. "I don't like having to keep looking over my shoulder while we hike out."

"Only if they know we've gone past them," Dan said.

As they were whispering, they heard the sound of twigs snapping. The men were advancing.

"They're going to try to pinch us. They think the group following is still behind us," Marcus said.

"Fools," muttered Roland.

"We don't have the high ground, but we'll have the advantage of surprise," Dan said. "We spread out but stay in sight of each other."

"If they'd stayed where they were, they wouldn't get killed," Marcus said in a whisper.

"Their choice," said Roland as he moved to one side.

"Wait for my shot," Dan said as the men separated.

The militia would be coming at them from up the slope. Dan knew his team's advantage would be short lived and they had to make the most of it.

He watched through the trees. The sounds of movement got closer until finally a figure emerged, then another. The militia were pushing underbrush aside as they made their way down the slope towards the waiting men. They were not focusing ahead to see the men they were approaching. They were letting the immediate effort of working their way through the trees and brush cause them to focus only a few feet ahead as they walked.

In a moment, more men appeared. They were in a partial line, not far apart, with a few behind. When there were five in sight, Dan squeezed off a round at one of the men in the center of the group. The man's head exploded and he fell limp to the ground. Marcus and Roland fired almost immediately and two more men went down. The three continued to fire, dropping all five of the men before they could retreat or find cover. There were shouts from the rear, men they couldn't yet see, and more shouts from the pickups to their left.

Dan motioned to Roland, who was on his left, to come towards him. Then he waved Marcus to move away from him. The three men quietly edged to the right, keeping spaced apart but within sight of each other. They set up a flanking position now to the side from where they first fired. The militia would focus on the down slope area from where their men had been shot. The problem for them was that Dan and his two companions wouldn't be there.

The three waited in their new position. It sounded like the men from the pickups had joined the remainder of the group. They now were advancing to the point of the initial ambush. This time the men were on full alert. They had stopped talking and were moving more slowly and carefully, trying to not get surprised again.

Dan could see the figures through the woods. Not fully exposed, but fleeting as they passed through the underbrush.

Got to take a quick shot when I get a look. He couldn't wait until all the men were exposed. He only hoped Roland and Marcus would get visuals on the targets as well.

A silhouette showed through the branches. The small twigs and leaves wouldn't throw off his shot. Dan fired. The figure cried out and dropped. *Probably wounded.* The others fired as well. There were more cries as men were hit.

The remaining men must have dropped to the ground. Dan couldn't see anyone and heard no sounds. He waited. *Patience. Let the enemy show first.* After two long minutes he heard one of the militia call out to the others. *Checking to see who's hit, who's not.* Between the accents and his limited Russian, Dan couldn't follow the communication. But it seemed to him to be an assessment of their situation and what they should do.

The three men waited, silently watching. They were the predators now. The militia members were the hunted, and they knew it.

Dan turned as Marcus made his way over to him. He moved through the brush without making a sound, not compromising their position.

"Think their enthusiasm is gone?" Marcus whispered.

Dan nodded. "Probably discussing whether or not to get back to the pickups and leave."

"They'd leave the others behind?"

"Come back for them when they think we've gone. They seem pretty sure we won't stay around."

"Let's let 'em go and then we can get on our way as well."

"Copy that," Dan said.

They waited for another five minutes. There was more rustling ahead, but it receded, indicating to Dan that the militia were moving to their vehicles. Finally, they heard the trucks start and move down the road, back in the direction they came. Roland came over from his position. For a large man, he moved silently and effortlessly through the brush.

"They've gone. We go now?"

Dan nodded. "Onward through the mountains. Just like in The Sound of Music."

They started back up the slope. Roland and Marcus looked at Dan.

"You guys are cultural illiterates," Dan said.

"If it ain't by Iron Maiden or Judas Priest," Marcus said, "we probably don't know it."

The men hiked on, working their way up the crease in the mountains, using the natural fold that provided a route up to the ridge. When the terrain began to steepen, they moved to their right and continued on their way towards the ridge, which now had begun to level out before them. Near the top, the woods thinned again, presenting high pasture. They followed trails left by sheep or goats.

Just before the ridge, they saw a herder's cabin nestled up against the woods. It was late afternoon. They approached cautiously and found it empty. The animals now were all back in the valleys.

"Let's stop here for the night. We can keep watch in shifts, but we'll get some sleep. Better inside than out."

"You got that right. Gonna be cold up here tonight. We need to get across the border and down into the valley before any serious snow comes. Otherwise we could get stuck," Marcus said.

"Not a good place to get to be," Roland replied.

The men filled their water bottles from the springhouse they found at the rear of the cabin. Inside, they ate some rations and drank the water. Then they tried to settle down and make themselves comfortable.

"How the hell are we going to get out of Tbilisi?" Marcus asked. "We lost our passports at that ambush."

"I've got the solution," Dan said.

"You got a solution for everything, don't you?" Roland challenged him with a smile on his face.

"Sometimes I do," Dan replied. He reached into his coat pocket and produced three passports. "Voila!" he announced.

"How the fuck did you get those?" Marcus asked.

"After I shot the guy, I reached into his pocket and grabbed 'em. Figured we could use them."

"Aren't you the boy scout. You think of everything," Roland said.

"Snipers. Always thinking ahead, always prepared. You should try it sometime," Dan said.

"Go fuck yourself," Roland said. "I'll take the first watch." He got up, put his coat back on, and grabbed the M4. "Better watching outside."

"I'll relieve you in three hours," Marcus said. "We'll let Dan take the third watch since he saved our passports."

"Thanks for nothing. That'll be the late night one."

"Think of it as the early morning one," Roland said as he stepped out of the cabin.

The next day dawned clear and cold. The three men hiked arduously and in two hours were rewarded with a stunning view from the ridge which represented the border between Ingushetia and Georgia. The valley stretched out below them. They could see the road which followed the Terek River. High fives were slapped all around. They packed their weapons in their bags and started downhill. In four more hours, they would be crossing the river and catching a ride back to Tbilisi and the waiting jet.

Marcus took out his cell phone and made a call to Jane, confirming that the jet would be there to take them back to the States.

"Tell her I need to be dropped off in Paris," Dan said.

Marcus looked at him in surprise.

"Some unfinished business. I'll call her when I'm done and we can meet."

"Tell her yourself," Marcus said.

Dan shook his head. "Don't want to start an argument.

Marcus relayed the message and hung up the phone.

"I think she's pissed at you. You've been pretty mysterious since you emerged from your cocoon. Where the hell were you anyway?"

"You don't want to know. It's above your pay grade."

"Screw you. We rescued your ass and now you don't show any respect. Typical Army fuck. Not recognizing their betters."

"I'm sorry. I truly appreciate you two saving me from certain death. I'm going to put both of you in my will. But I'm not saying when. You might have me whacked."

"No, our job is to babysit you and—look out for your ass. Jane seems to be under the illusion that you're special and need protecting. I understand a sniper needs our protection, but I'm not so sure about the special part."

Dan laughed. "It's good to have you guys around." His face turned serious. "And I can't think of two better men to have in a firefight."

"Don't go getting all maudlin on us," Roland said.

"I won't but, man, I didn't know Delta Force guys could use such big words."

Roland punched his shoulder as they marched down the hill.

Chapter 54

The Gulfstream landed at Orly airport in Paris. A car from the U.S. embassy met the plane. Dan's duffel bag was put into a larger diplomatic case and loaded into the car. Dan got into the back seat and they left the airport.

After clearing the airport, the car took Dan to a Metro stop and from there he rode the subway to the *Gare du Nord* train station. He bought a ticket to Marseille but exited at Lyon. From Lyon he rented a car under his passport alias, Victor James.

After driving around Lyon to check for tails, he headed south on A7 towards Orange. From there he took a labyrinth of winding roads to the little village of Vachères, near *Parc Naturel Régional du Luberon*, and Christina's cottage. It was dark when he arrived in Vachères. The *Monseigneur* waved him down as he drove through the village.

"Come with me before you go to Christina's cottage," he said.

Dan parked and the *Monseigneur* led them to the small restaurant. They took a table at the back and sat down. The waiter followed and the clergyman ordered a glass of the local *Côtes de Provence*. Dan waited until the waiter had left.

"You knew I was coming." By now Dan was not surprised at the intuitive skills of the Watchers, nor their unfathomable ability to communicate over distances.

The *Monseigneur* nodded.

"I see that you completed your mission to the best of your ability. And, just as important, you gave life to your enemy, made peace with him."

"That was a perilous moment, *très effrayant*."

"That act will prove useful in the future."

"You can see the future now?"

The *Monseigneur* smiled and shook his head. He waited to answer as the waiter brought his glass of red wine.

"*Non*. But that does not mean we don't have clues. With your actions you gained an ally. That is always useful in a war."

Dan rubbed his eyes and sighed. He was tired. He longed to embrace Christina, to hold her again, to show her he had kept his promise and returned.

"Do you have something to tell me or are you here to just welcome me back?"

The *Monseigneur* kept smiling. He showed no irritation at Dan's somewhat rude remark.

"Of course, I welcome you back. But there is something more serious to my visit."

He took a sip and savored the flavor of the wine. Provence wines tended to be less alcoholic than U.S. or Australian wines, which were generally more robust. They had more subtle flavors that encouraged leisurely tasting.

"There is a very wealthy Arab—"

"Rashid. We think he's involved in financing terror operations. We cannot find where he is, but my guess is that he's somewhere in Saudi Arabia."

"You are correct. He's well hidden from us as well," the *Monseigneur* said.

"What about him?"

"We sense he suspects a single operator, or a small group of men are responsible for disrupting his plans."

"But he doesn't know who? He doesn't know about me?"

The *Monseigneur* shook his head. "But there is danger. He will be looking for you. He will be looking for anyone who is connected to you. If he discovers your identity, anyone close to you is in danger."

"That's why I stay out of sight, with aliases. Only a small group of people know who I am."

"He has hired someone to find you."

Dan looked at the *Monseigneur*. The man was correct. Someone actively out looking for him, marked an escalation of danger.

"And you know who this is?"

"He is called Scorpion. He's very deadly. He is a dark, evil soul. We can't see into Saudi Arabia well, and so only know when he ventures out. Recently he and Rashid met with Maskhadov in Baku. That meeting had to be about the results of your actions. That is when Rashid activated the Scorpion."

"Do my people have a file on this Scorpion?"

"A small one. But you should get them to work on it. We can't see what will happen, but I warn you that you will probably confront this Scorpion somewhere in the field. I also must warn you that Christina could be in great danger if he discovers your connection to her. His soul is dark. He not only kills but seems to delight in torturing his victims, leaving them in a condition that terrorizes those connected to the unfortunate person."

The worry nagging Dan in the back of his mind, the danger he brought to those around him, now rushed forward.

"You sense the truth of what I am saying."

"I do," Dan responded.

"We will do what we can to protect her. We can try to shield her from any intrusion, but a fortress built around this area would register with the Scorpion. He's in touch with dark forces, even if he doesn't fully know how they work. He would get suspicious and investigate further."

The *Monseigneur* paused for a moment.

"I see that I have made you uncomfortable with this information. It is not what you hoped. My...our...aim is to not give you comfort, but help, where and when we can. Remember what the shaman, Tlayolotl, told you. 'You are the tip of the spear'. We can only provide help and support."

He finished his glass of wine with a last swallow and stood up.

"Do not tarry here too long. It only brings more danger. Rest and prepare for what must come next. You are the warrior. Many rely on you."

He gave Dan a nod of his head and turned and walked out. Dan sat for another hour deep in thought.

Finally, he stood up, paid the bill, and left. When he got to Christina's cottage, he drove up slowly and got out. At the door, he could hear the sound of her playing. He stopped to listen. He didn't recognize the piece but it was filled with more emotion than the ones she had been playing when he first came to her cottage.

Drawing a deep breath, he opened the door.

Chapter 55

Christina did not hear the door when it opened. When she finished the piece, someone spoke from the living room.

"That was beautiful."

Her heart raced. She stood up and stepped into the front room. There he was, just standing there. She hesitated for only a second to absorb the reality of his presence and then ran to his arms.

They embraced long and tight without words, each wanting to meld into the other, to join themselves. She turned her head to him and they kissed long and deep.

"Rossignol, I knew you would come back. Chloé said you might not, but I knew you would."

They kissed again. She pushed back to look at him.

"You were successful? The threat is over? I was so afraid that you might get hurt. You are all right?"

"So many questions. But I'm here, so they don't matter now."

She pulled him close again.

"Yes. They don't matter now."

She began to pull at his coat.

"Take that off. It's warm here. More so now that you're back. Did you eat? Can I make you something?"

Dan smiled. He handed her his coat, sat down on the couch, and looked around. As Christina hung his coat on a hook, she caught him looking at the room.

"This is home...for the two of us," she said.

Dan smiled. His eyes scanned the familiar details of the space. Christina went into the kitchen and got a bottle of red wine. She came back with the bottle and two glasses.

"What did you have to do? I didn't hear from you and was so worried. But I never lost faith."

"I don't want to talk about what I did. But you were busy? Tell me about your concerts and what you're working on."

"I played Beethoven's Emperor in Berlin. I received rave reviews."

She talked at length about other concerts, the new music she was working on, her face beaming. She was happy to be back with her Rossignol and sharing her world with him.

"The public seems to like my new, more emotive style. I'm no longer called the 'Ice Queen'." She gave him a coy smile.

"You were never the Ice Queen. You had emotions. You just kept them bottled up."

"And you helped me release them. I tried to explain it all to Chloé. She understands a little, but not fully. I think she's a bit jealous of our relationship."

She snuggled closer to him on the couch and took a sip of wine.

"She's a loyal and loving friend. You could have no better for a personal assistant."

"I know. But she will have to get used to sharing me with you."

She leaned over and kissed him long and hard. The wine glasses, on the table, were ignored. Finally, Christina pulled back, stood up, and took Dan's hand.

"Come. You're tired, you're tense. I can feel it in you. Come to bed and I'll make all the tension go away."

In the bedroom, she unbuttoned Dan's shirt and helped him take it off. She pulled up her shirt and threw it in the corner. Her breasts pushed against her bra as her breathing became heavy. Dan reached around her and unhooked the strap. It fell away. She pushed up his undershirt and slid it over his head. They came together now flesh to flesh. Her breasts pressed against his chest. Without letting each other go, they shuffled to the edge of the bed and half fell onto it.

A flurry of hands went to work, removing each other's clothes. It was unspoken and automatic that each undressed the other. The time for speaking was past. Their bodies expressed their feelings without words; their desires, long pent up, were now to be released.

Sounds came from each of them as they stroked one another—soft, but, animal-like. Not words, they were the overflow of ecstatic feeling issuing forth in utterances more profound than mere words.

When she was ready, Christina lay back. Her body opened to him, wanting to receive, to encompass him and his energy; to capture it and hold it inside her. He slid over her and they began to move together in a thrusting rhythm. It was steady and slow, building in tempo as the pressure built inside each of them. Christina wrapped her arms and legs around Dan. Their climax came together, with both crying out.

Neither spoke as they lay back partly entwined. She could feel him now beginning to relax, his muscles not strained or tight. His body carried scars. Before those blemishes frightened her. Now she saw them simply as part of the man she loved. They spoke of the dangerous world he had inhabited. Now it would be different.

They would be at peace in their hideaway. He could now travel with her, help her in her work. Help her to reach new heights of expression. Whether he drew it out of her, or just inspired her to find it within, she knew her skills could express what she felt with her man. She could bring this new openness and energy to the pieces she played. The great composers all had much passion for their work. She was more attuned to it now. She could see it in the subtle parts of their music. Her Rossignol would help increase her connection to the masters whose music she played.

She reached over to Dan and started to caress him. She was hungry for more of him. He had almost dropped off to sleep, but responded. They touched one another, stroking the parts they knew stimulated their pleasure. Soon their passion rose again and they locked together in a strong thrusting rhythm until that passion overflowed into climatic release.

When they were done, Christina snuggled close against Dan's neck and they talked about little things—flowers in spring, the wood pile, going wading in the stream near the cottage with its clear, cold water, lying in a sun-drenched field, smelling the lavender that grew so abundantly in this part of France. There were whole fields of purple that bloomed from June through August. During those times the air was filled with the gentle fragrance. Their talking slowed down until they fell asleep in one another's arms, fully satiated, fully satisfied.

The next morning, Dan woke before Christina. He quietly dressed and went to the kitchen to put on some coffee. Then he went into the bathroom to take a shower. Half way through it, Christina stepped in with him and proceeded to soap him down. She rubbed her body over his, their skin sliding over each other. He couldn't resist and massaged her firm breasts with his hands tracing their outline and shape. All this touching energized them and they quickly rinsed, dried, and jumped back into bed to continue their tryst.

When they were done, Dan put his clothes back on.

"We can't run around naked all day, jumping in and out of bed."

Christina gave him a look at once coy and lustful. Their eyes met and she knew that her's projected a sexual energy. She made no attempt to hide it. She could feel its animal-like intensity burning inside of her.

"I think that would be perfect. I'm willing to take the day off from practice so we can celebrate your homecoming. Tomorrow Chloé will be here, so we'll have to act much more decorously."

Dan looked at her. Christina couldn't hide her awakened sexuality. Certainly not with Dan. She kept that part of her hidden from others, except for the new expression she put into her music. But with Dan back, it came to the forefront and she had no desire to restrain it, reveling in the lustiness she felt with him. He threw some clothes at her.

"I'll make us some breakfast. I'm starving, how about you?"

She nodded and began to get dressed.

After some coffee and small talk, Dan made an omelet for two. When they had eaten, they sat quietly. Christina began to feel a sense of nervousness. He was quiet. And seemed to be retreating into himself.

When he didn't know who he was, he was a simpler man to deal with. Now there were so many conflicting issues. A sense of dread began to grow in her. Could he be satisfied being her partner, her lover, while she pursued her music career? She pushed those thoughts back, not willing to let them spoil the happiness she felt at his return.

"Let's go for a walk," he said after a long period of silence.

She nodded and they put on their coats and started across the fields. It was a bright day, cold, but not too cold. It was still winter with the air crisp, but the dreaded mistral was not blowing.

"Does your mind go back to the things you had to do while you were away?"

Dan thought for a moment. "It's not easy to turn those things off. They sit hard in my memory, solidly imprinted."

"But you can't live with those piling up? How do you let them go?"

"They fade a bit over time. And I find other things to do so I don't have to reflect on them too much."

They continued in silence. Her dread continued to grow. He was not a man to sit around while she developed her career. He was someone who took action. He'd taken it after recovering his memory. His actions had taken him away, but he had come back like he had promised. She couldn't imagine what he had encountered, what he had done. And she sensed he would never tell her. The world he lived in was so different, so alien from hers. What would come next for them?

They continued, hand in hand, making small talk. Christina sensed there was something else. Something not yet said, but waiting to be spoken. They returned to the cottage and stepped back inside. It was warm and cozy. The fire was still going. Christina went over to it and added some logs.

"This is a comfortable place is it not?" she said.

"Yes, it is."

She screwed up her courage. She was afraid. She feared his silences, but needed to address her fears. She needed to know if her man was back.

"Can you be happy here, with me? I know you love me and want me. I know we are good for one another. Will you stay now? Is your other life behind you?"

Dan took her hand and led her to the kitchen table. They sat down.

"I do love you. I hope you believe that."

He paused. Dread filled her. It was now front and center. She knew it showed on her face.

"You...you...aren't staying?" There, it was said.

He shook his head. "I can't."

The tears started. She didn't cry but her eyes welled up and spilled over, sending rivulets down her cheeks. She wanted to cry out against what she had just heard, to try to push the words back, out of existence. But they had been said. He had said them and they couldn't be put back.

"My world brings danger to you. I want to stay with you, be your muse, be a boring gentleman farmer, go to your concerts, make wine with Émile, go boar hunting with him..."

"But you would get bored?"

"It's more than that. There are people out there, dangerous people, who want to attack me. If they found a connection between us, they would attack you to get to me. I can't let that happen."

"You said you could put that world behind you. It doesn't have to be your world anymore. You said you love me and I love you, so I'm willing to be at risk."

Dan shook his head. "I don't think it will let me go. You don't know what these people are capable of." His eyes were full of sadness. "I can't put you in that position. You have to live in a different world from me. I can't let that world intrude on you. With me gone, you are safe. The longer I stay, the less safe you become."

He took her hands in his. "If anything were to happen to you, I couldn't live with that."

She had no words. She just looked at him, her tears flowing. She wouldn't cry out. She was not going to break down like a child, but she couldn't mask her pain.

"How...how...soon are you going to leave?"

"It's better I go now. To prolong this departure will only make it harder."

She forced herself to speak. "Will I ever see you again? Can you come to see me once in a while?"

Dan looked at her. There was no good way to do this. No way to separate themselves without pain. But it had to be done right away. He had known it this morning when he had awakened. It was not so much that he might get bored by being here while Christina pursued an increasingly busy and successful performing career. It was the danger he posed to her.

He was trapped by the life he had chosen. There was no turning back at this point. Somewhere along the way, a line had been crossed and he hadn't recognized it. Or had he just not cared to notice? Maybe it had been in Brooklyn, when he had found the vengeance he had sought for his wife's murder, but no way out of the trap that he had put himself into.

This woman, with whom he had fallen in love, who had saved him, he now had to protect, even if it broke both of their hearts. What had happened to Rita in Brooklyn, he could not let happen again.

"No. To come back would only keep us connected but also would not allow you to move forward. As much as it breaks both our hearts, there is no future for us together."

Her sobs started now. Dan sensed she had been holding them back, but could do so no longer. He got up from the table, kissed her on the head, and walked out of the door.

Chapter 56

Christina sat at the table and cried as Dan closed the door. She let go of her restraint and the tears flowed. She cried for the injustice of it all; for how he had hurt her. She cried for how he was right. Deep inside she knew he would never be satisfied with the life she had imagined in her *naiveté*. She didn't fully understand the danger he spoke of, but she knew his was a violent world. An assassin, even of bad men, could not lead a normal life.

After crying herself dry of tears, she walked into her music room and sat at her beloved piano without moving. Then she started with some scales, playing them in ascending and descending runs. Her fingers moved fluidly over the keyboard. Her mind began to quiet and relax. The runs increased in speed until they were a rippling cascade of notes going up and down. She modulated the key and continued, going through all twelve keys. Next, she played the scales, this time hitting four notes simultaneously with each hand, moving up and down the keyboard in ever more aggressive strikes and going through all the keys again.

Dan drove to the village, his heart dark, his mind almost blank. Once there, he took a piece of paper from the glove box and wrote a note addressed to *Monseigneur* Louis-Marie Chicon. He stopped at the church and gave the note to the priest with instructions to give it to the *Monseigneur* when he returned.

Then he drove back to Lyon.

"The Scorpion." Dan said.

"Who's that?" Jane asked.

Dan had called her while on the train from Lyon to Marseille.

"An assassin who's on the hunt for me. Have Fred and Warren get on it."

"How do you know this?"

"Watchers."

Jane didn't need him to ask more. She had experienced their insights in Venice.

"You know who hired him? They don't work for themselves."

"Rashid. I may need to find him as well. It seems he is the one behind much of what we've disrupted."

"Cut off the head...?"

"You got it."

"Where are you now? I was more than a little upset when you made the plane land in Paris. I wanted you back here in the States, to meet with you face to face. Henry is pissed, to say the least."

"Tell Henry I'm fine. If you want to visit, come to Milan and I'll meet you there."

Dan changed trains in Marseille for one that went to Milan. From there he boarded a train to Venice which arrived at the *Stazione di Venezia Santa Lucia* out on the causeway at the entrance to the city. The whole trip took eleven hours. From there he took a bus to the *Marghera* district outside of Venice. After getting off in a commercial part of the city, Dan placed a call to Marco. He was a local hustler who Dan had hired to keep an eye on his residence.

When he had first arrived in Italy, Dan had purchased an isolated mansion: one left behind as the neighborhood around it had become more industrial. Dan paid a premium price to purchase it and keep it from destruction. It stood out in the commercial area, but at the same time was unexpected. One would not be looking for a residence in the area. The property allowed for excellent security to be set up. In addition, he had Marco who logged any suspicious activity. While Dan was away, he wanted to know if anyone showed undue interest in the property, or worse tried to set up surveillance on it.

They met in a small park.

"You have been gone a long time. I didn't know if you were coming back."

"You received the money on time, each month?"

Marco nodded. "I did. And I kept watch."

"You and your gang?"

"I delegate the work sometimes. I told you that."

"As long as your men are circumspect about it. I want no talk about the stranger who wants his house to be watched over. Such talk raises suspicion in other people. Makes them wonder who lives there and why they contract for such services."

"My boys are good. I impressed upon them that you are a dangerous man. One to not be crossed. Some of them have met you and they concur. It helps the newer members to understand the situation."

"Good. Now what do you have to report?"

"Things have remained quiet. There have been no repeat visitors or passersby. I have a list of license plates that might be suspicious. It's a bit long—almost two years long."

He reached into his coat and pulled out a folded sheet of paper. Dan took it and put it in his pocket.

"But none of these came back?"

"A few. But there was no serious repetition. The passing-by may have been random. I had the plates copied because they weren't local cars."

Marco seemed to hesitate for a moment.

"Things get more expensive. There are other opportunities for my small enterprise. This activity takes time from pursuing them." He paused.

"You want a raise?"

Marco nodded.

"Remember," Dan said, "this work is clean. You have no worries about breaking the law. No chance to get into trouble with the *piedipiatti*." He used the slang word for cops.

Marco smiled. "We are good at what we do. We stay off the cop's radar. I don't worry about them."

The conversation continued for a few minutes longer, an almost friendly give and take as Marco negotiated a raise with Dan. Dan knew he would agree to it, but he had to make Marco work for the raise, so that he would appreciate his victory.

With the meeting over, Dan walked to the mansion.

Lecha placed a call to Bulat. The warlord was in a deadly mood. Bulat had used the ambush by the Russians to take the canister and hadn't paid him. He was going to collect.

"*Da*," said Bulat when he picked up the phone.

"You have the canister, and you have my money."

Bulat didn't say a word.

"Did you hear me?"

"I heard you. I got out of there when Kuznetsov attacked. I took the cannister to keep it from him. He was after you. I wasn't going to stick around and get killed, or let him know I was involved. I don't need him as an enemy."

"Yes. You took off like a frightened woman...with my canister. The one my men paid for in blood. Now I want my payment." This last he said with in a low threatening voice. "Or, I want my canister back. I can sell it myself."

"I can't do that."

"What can't you do—pay me, or give me back the canister?"

"Both. I already paid you too much and you botched the job a second time. I flew to Moscow to deal with this personally, only to find your men gone and the canister missing—again."

"So you took it. Now I want it back."

"You can come and get it. I know where it is."

"Don't play with me. I have no patience for it. Where is the canister, if you don't have it?"

"It's at the bottom of the Caspian."

There was silence on the line.

"Do you take me for a fool? You dumped it in the sea?"

"Someone attacked my boat, sank it and the canister went to the bottom. I barely escaped with my life."

"Get a diver. Bring it up."

Bulat's voice was almost condescending in tone. "It would take a major expedition. It is very deep, beyond normal dive depths. Without such effort, it is lost. Perhaps forever."

Lecha was quiet for a long moment. Finally, he said, "Blood must be paid for blood. Without the canister or money, I will require your blood. You do not want to get into a war with me."

"There is something else."

"What could that be?"

"Think about the events. There was someone in Milan. Someone took the first shot and you said it wasn't one of your men. Then you capture Kuznetsov. You take him to the villa. When you come back your men are gone and with all the blood around, I am sure they are dead. How did Kuznetsov do that? His men? Maybe. But maybe it was someone else.

"Then we meet in Grozny," Bulat continued. "Kuznetsov ambushes us, but someone else followed me to Kaspiysk. My yacht was shot up and sunk by a single shooter, from a fishing boat. Someone who could shoot well. He wasn't a local. The fisherman who runs the boat rescued me. He said it was one man, a foreigner."

Bulat paused to let that fact sink in.

"One man sank a boat with a rifle. That is not a normal man."

"So, there was a third person involved. Perhaps he has the other two canisters. Why is that important to our situation? It is still blood for blood with me."

"In the dacha, I saw a newspaper clipping. It showed a man with a woman, a concert pianist. The man's face was circled. He was someone important to Kuznetsov."

"I didn't see it."

"You wouldn't notice something like that."

"My informant, the one in Kuznetsov's gang that we were paying, spoke about someone Kuznetsov captured. The man said Yevgeni thought his captive knew where the mouse was, where the canisters were. He apparently killed one of his captors and got away. My informant said he spoke with the other man who had captured him."

"There you go," Bulat said. "That is your man. That is the one you should exact your blood price from."

"But I can't find him. I can find you."

Bulat felt himself go cold. He was not without defenses. In his work, arms dealing, one had to be ready to defend oneself with violence. But getting into a blood feud with Lecha would be disastrous. It would mean many casualties and losses for his business. No one would want to deal with him anymore. It was going to be bad enough after word of this debacle got out.

"The man is connected to the pianist," Bulat said, keeping his voice calm. "You find her, you can find him. She gives you leverage and, if you can't get to him, she gives you the blood you seek. He's the one to pay, not me."

"Maybe, for now. What is her name?"

"Christina Aubergh."

Chapter 57

The next day, Dan took a bus to the *Stazione di Venezia*. He wanted to walk this city he had fallen in love with, to soothe his heartache and find some peace. Maybe it wouldn't come, but he could not stay in his house, sanctuary though it was. From the train station he boarded a *vaporetto* or water bus and rode it to St. Mark's Square.

He would have a coffee at one of the restaurants lining the square, then walk the back streets, almost alleys, until lunch. He would find a small *ristorante* that only the locals would patronize and then walk the afternoon away. There were favorite spots off the tourist paths that he enjoyed. He had come to feel they were his private spaces with only a few, if any, people about, all of them locals.

After ordering his *café Americano*, he sat back to watch the tourists. There were fewer, it being winter. Then from across the square, their eyes met. It was the old gypsy woman selling scarves. Her face was stern and her gaze intense. Dan could sense an urgency in her gaze. Something was amiss. Something that needed his attention right away.

Without waiting, he put some money on the table and left with his coffee unfinished. When he got to the woman, after a quick glance around, she put her face close to his and spoke into his ear.

"You have to return to the pianist. She is in grave danger."

He turned his head to give her a sharp look.

"The Chechen warlord. He is coming for her. With men in two vehicles. He is looking for revenge. Hurry, there is no time to waste."

She pushed him away, not giving him time to ask any questions. Dan started to speak. She shook her head.

"No speak. Go. Strike. You have to save her."

She motioned for him to go.

Dan turned and walked quickly away, barely keeping himself from running. He didn't want to draw attention to the old woman by bolting from her as if she had done something wrong. When he got to the waterside, he hired one of the speedboat taxis. He couldn't wait for the *vaporetto*. At the station, Dan gabbed a taxi. He got dropped off two blocks from where he lived and ran the rest of the way to his home.

Upstairs he grabbed a change of clothes and opened his weapons vault. He chose his M110 with a suppressor to go along with his suppressed M4 and his CZ 9mm. Stuffing the gear into a bag, he went to the garage. He unlocked the Peugeot 607 and put his bag in the hidden compartment between the trunk and back seat.

The Peugeot had been modified by Luc Tsiganes in Paris. It had a rebuilt V6 now equipped with a supercharger, special intake, and exhaust systems. Along with the engine modifications, Dan had the suspension, tires, and brakes modified. The work resulted in an inconspicuous car that was a match for any sedan on the highway. The only clue was a slightly more aggressive stance and exhaust note, which didn't register with most people.

He drove out of the city and headed at high speed across Italy to the coast where he drove the winding, treacherous road that followed the cliffs. It was night and the later it got, the faster Dan drove. Being midweek and deep into the night, he gambled that the *polizia* would not be very present. Along the way he hooked up with a Maserati Quattroporte. He kept up a rolling race with the driver who was probably surprised that some bland looking French sedan could keep pace with his expensive machine.

Dan assumed the Maserati driver was using his radar to watch for the police, the same as Dan. With no alarms sounding, they ate up the miles as best they could on such a tight road. They slowed only when they passed near or through the coastal towns of Savona, Albenga, Andora, and Ventimiglia, skirting north of Monaco and through Nice. Next came the cities of Cagnes su Mer and Cannes. At Cannes, the Maserati turned off. Dan kept going and turned north near Aix-en-Provence, bypassing Marseille. From there he drove over increasingly narrower, less traveled roads, forcing the Peugeot to its limits around the turns and down the few short straights until he entered Vachères.

As he passed through the square, a man stepped out in front of him with his hand raised. It was the Monseigneur. Dan screeched to a halt and he walked up to the car.

"I know about Lecha," Dan said. He didn't have time to talk with the priest, even if he was a Watcher.

"Come with me for a moment." He pointed to the side for Dan to park. "It is important."

Dan ground his teeth and started to protest but the *Monseigneur* cut him off.

"Do as I say, then you go do what you have to do."

Dan pulled over and got out of the car. The priest led him into the church and into his office.

"I don't have time. I have to get to her before she's hurt or taken."

The priest didn't respond but reached into a drawer and pulled out a sheath knife and held it out to Dan.

He looked at it. It was in an odd sheath—one that couldn't fit on a belt. The loops were all wrong.

"What's this? I don't need this." Dan's voice was now angry.

“It was my grandfather’s. He was a young man, a teenager, during the Nazi resistance. You attach it to your wrist. Take off your jacket and pull up your sleeve.”

“I don’t—”

“Pull up your sleeve,” the *Monseigneur* now repeated in a commanding voice.

He strapped the knife to Dan’s arm.

“You trigger it by flexing your wrist and forearm. Be careful, it is sensitive.”

He showed Dan how to make the motion. When Dan tried it, the knife shot out into his palm. Dan looked at it closely. It was razor sharp.

“My father said his father, my grandfather, killed many Germans with this knife. He said it must remain very sharp. To let it get dull would be to dishonor the knife and the work my grandfather did with it. I kept it for years, but being a priest, I have no use for it. I fight evil on a different front. It is time for it to go to someone else. You are that one.

“But—”

“Take it. It may be useful to you before this day is done.”

Dan threw his coat back on and started for the door. After opening it, he turned.

“Thank you. I hope I’m in time.”

“She can be saved, but it will challenge you.”

He ran out to the Peugeot and headed for the cottage.

Chapter 58

During the frenzied drive, Dan went over all the destruction he would unleash on Lecha. He alternated between those dark thoughts and the fear that Christina had already been hurt or taken away. Along the way, he tried to calm down. *Do what you're trained to do. Methodically, professionally, without mercy.* The best way to rescue Christina was to be the professional assassin. Calm and cool. *Now's not the time for emotion.* He kept up that mantra as he drove more quietly to the cottage.

He parked a half mile away on a small pull-off. He put on his camo coat and opened his gear bag.

Lecha had driven to Vachères with six men in two SUVs. The informant said that was where the captive had escaped. He wasted no time in forcing an unfortunate resident of the town to tell him where Christina lived. As he left the village the *Monseigneur* watched from the door of the church.

Lecha drove up the entrance lane and stopped at the cottage.

"Two of you go to the end of the drive and stand guard. Anyone comes, you kill them." He pointed to two more men. "You wait outside here and keep watch. Same orders. Kill anyone who comes.'

He motioned for the other two to go inside with him.

They burst through the door with their weapons out even though they didn't expect any defense. Their actions were meant to terrorize and subdue anyone inside.

Chloé was sitting at the kitchen table. She looked up and screamed in shock at the intruding men. Christina was in the music room playing. She heard Chloé scream and got up from the piano. Seeing the strange men, she stopped at the doorway of her room.

"You're the pianist," Lecha said with a cold, evil smile.

Christina stood with her large eyes opened wide and said nothing.

"Come here and sit down," Lecha said pointing to the couch. "You too." He pointed at Chloé.

"What do you want?" Chloé asked. "We have no money on us. You can take what little we have."

"I don't want your money."

"What then?" Chloé asked.

Lecha could see her fear deepen as she imagined what other horror might befall them if he was not there for robbery. His smile broadened. Striking fear and panic in others pleased him. If he could capture the assassin it would make the day perfect. As it stood, taking the pianist would be a satisfying second. He would make sure the word got out to this mystery killer. He would make sure that he understood he had caused the death of this girl. He would make sure the assassin knew she would have a painful and defiling experience before death released her. Blood for blood.

"What is your name?" He directed his question to Christina.

She swallowed and spoke in a barely audible voice.

"Christina."

"What? Speak up, girl"

"Her name is Christina," Chloé said. "She's famous. If you harm her, you will be in big trouble."

"You are a mouthy one, aren't you?"

Chloé didn't respond but Lecha could see her fear struggling with her attempt to be strong.

"I am not talking to you."

He stepped over and slapped her on the side of her face. Chloé flopped to one side from the blow.

Christina screamed. “Don’t hurt her!”

“I will do whatever I like. To her and to you.”

“But what do you want? We haven’t done anything to you. We don’t even know who you are. I play music. That’s all I do.”

“Blood for blood,” Lecha said almost under his breath.

“What? What have we done?” Christina asked again.

“You must pay the price for what someone else has done.”

The two women looked at him uncomprehendingly. It didn’t matter. He had decided to take them away, so he could exact his revenge slowly. They would come to understand, and with that understanding, would know they were without hope, completely at his mercy. And mercy was not something Lecha felt inclined to offer.

Christina began to quietly sob. Chloé looked fearful, but still defiant.

Dan decided against the M110. He would take the M4 and his CZ. He headed into the field to cut through to the driveway. Lecha would have lookouts or guards at the end of the drive. He’d take them out first. He had no idea of how many fighters the warlord had brought. The Watcher spoke of two SUVs, so he estimated six to eight men. *Eliminate as many as possible while I’m not discovered.* It would make the latter stages of his attack easier.

The point was to not harm Christina during the rescue. If Lecha felt he had no other options, he was capable of killing Christina just to hurt him. That was why he came to Vachères. The first challenge was if they were still at the cottage. If they were, he would do what he had always trained to do—kill the enemy.

He slowed as he approached the line of trees marking the driveway. For the last fifty yards he crawled on the cold, frozen ground. He couldn’t see through the screening, but that meant he couldn't be seen. When he reached the trees, he carefully worked his way partly through them and saw the two men standing in the drive. *They're still here*. He felt a surge of elation that he was not too late.

The men were facing the road. Their rifles were on their shoulders, their hands in their pockets. They talked and occasionally stamped their feet. Standing in the cold was not pleasant and they clearly were not enjoying the assignment.

I'll solve that, Dan thought.

He took aim at the man farthest from him. He would have the best chance to dive for cover once Dan fired, so he had to be taken first.

The M4 made a muffled *spat* and the man's headed exploded. Before the second man could fire, Dan's shot hit him in the side. He was turning to the direction of the shot. He spun around, still on his feet, and Dan's second shot hit him square in the chest, throwing him to the ground.

Dan lay still listening. No sound came from the cottage. The lane made a turn on its way to the house, so no one up there could see what had happened. If they hadn't heard, Dan still had the element of surprise on his side. He got up and went back into the field. He started for the cottage, moving as quietly as he could through the stubble left from the fall's harvest.

The trees at the field's edge shielded him from the drive, but they ended at the cottage. The field ended at a fence. Beyond the fence was a grassy yard and the gravel drive, opening into a wide turn-around at the front door.

He slipped into the trees and brush before getting to the fence line. Now he approached from the cover of the trees. He saw two men standing around, similar to the ones he had just killed. They also were cold and not very alert. One was looking away from Dan towards the barn and fields that went up behind the house. The other was looking down the driveway. Between them and Dan were two large G Wagon SUVs.

When Dan was forty yards away, he stopped. He couldn't risk getting closer. The shots weren't hard, but the vehicles offered potential cover. If there was return fire, those inside would hear it. He could not be sure what Lecha's response would be.

The two men were talking. As Dan was going over his options, one of the men started walking towards the side of the house.

They're splitting up. Maybe going to patrol the perimeter.

Dan couldn't let that happen. If he got inside with anyone outside still alive, he risked a counter attack and gunfight. The damage to the cottage would be huge and Christina could be shot.

Dan raised his M4 and centered his sights on the man starting his round. His pace was steady which made it easy for Dan to maintain a target on his head. He stroked the trigger. The M4 spat out its deadly sound and the guard's head erupted with blood and brains. He collapsed to the ground.

The second guard dropped behind the SUV just as Dan's second shot flew over his head. He reached over the hood and loosed a short blast of automatic fire from his Kalashnikov. Dan didn't flinch. The guard's shots were not well aimed. Dan fired two rounds which skimmed over the hood of the SUV and hit the man in the temple as he started to duck down behind the G Wagon.

They know I'm coming. Dan jumped out from the trees and started running for the door. Speed was now needed. *Got to avoid a stand-off. He'll use Christina as a bargaining chip.*

As he approached the cottage, the door opened and a man jumped out. Dan sent a short round of automatic fire into his torso throwing him back against the door and to the ground. He didn't break stride as he ran forward.

He burst into the room, ready to shoot any male present, and stopped. Chloé was in the room, alone, sitting on the couch.

Chapter 59

Surprised?" The voice came from the music room. Suddenly, Christina's face appeared. A man's arm was around her neck, a 9mm pressed up against her temple.

"I think you should lay down your weapon," the voice said, "if you want her to live."

"Who are you?" Dan asked. He looked around. Were there any other men inside?

"A better question is who are you? You have done great harm to my clan. Killed many men, interrupted my getting the canisters."

"I work for people who don't want those canisters used. They kill indiscriminately, hurting innocent people."

"So you kill to keep that from happening."

"Not innocent people."

"And yet, you involve innocent people. I'm guessing this woman, your pianist, has no idea of who you are and what you do. I'm surprised you thought you could have a relationship with someone like this and not bring trouble down on her."

"What do you want? The canisters are out of reach. I can't even get to them."

"Yes, I'm sure. One I know is at the bottom of the Caspian. The other two—who knows? But that is not what I want." Lecha paused for a moment. He tightened his hold on Christina's neck.

"Don't hurt her," Dan said.

"Blood for blood," Lecha said.

"What?"

“You heard me. Blood for blood. You killed many of my men. I can’t return that in the same way. But I can extract some payback. She pays for your killings. That is what I want.”

“No! She’s innocent. She had nothing to do with those things. That’s between you and me.”

“You say so, yet here I am. You took from me. I take from you. Innocence doesn’t matter. Only whether or not the payback is sufficient.”

“What if I offered to trade for her?”

Dan looked around. Was there anyone else in the cottage? If it was just him and Lecha, there was a chance he could prevail.

“What can you offer? You said the canisters were out of reach.”

“Myself.”

Dan let that statement sit out there for a moment. “It’s me you want. I trade Christina for me. You let her go and I’ll give myself up to you.”

“You are not in a position to bargain. You think I’m a fool? I let her go, you start shooting. You might have killed my guards outside, but I am not as easy to overcome as them. He tapped Christina’s temple with the gun’s barrel. A whimper escaped from her lips.

“No, you lay down your weapon and give yourself up, then I turn the woman loose.”

“Both of them?”

“Both of them. Of course, they can’t leave until we’ve gone. I want to take you somewhere so we can spend time together.”

“How do I know you’ll keep you end of the bargain?”

“You don’t. But what choice do you have? If shooting starts, I start with Christina. So, even if you kill me, you will have killed her by your choice. Probably the other woman as well.”

As Lecha finished speaking another man stepped out from the short dividing wall separating the kitchen from the living room.

"All right. I give you myself, for the lives of the two women. Do we have a deal?"

"A deal."

Dan kept his eyes on the guard and slowly set his M4 on the floor. The guard said something in Chechen that Dan couldn't catch and Lecha stepped out from behind the wall. He was only an inch or two shorter than Dan, but with a thick, solid body. He gave the impression one could hit him hard in his torso and he would just shrug it off before delivering a bone-crushing blow with one of his meaty fists.

Lecha walked forward with Christina still held in front of him.

"Turn around," he said. "Put your hands behind your back."

"Let the women go."

"First I secure you. I take no chances. You have killed too many of my men."

Dan turned around. He heard the man from the kitchen step forward.

"Put your arms behind your back," Lecha said again.

The guard slid a pair of plastic cuffs over Dan's wrists and pulled them tight. Next, he reached into Dan's coat and pulled out his 9mm. After patting his torso and legs, and checking his pockets, he pronounced him safe.

Lecha pushed Christina onto the couch. He pulled a chair over from the kitchen and pushed Dan into it.

"You have me. Now let the women go."

Lecha smiled that smile without any warmth and stared back at Dan.

"Did you really think I would let them go? Now I have the best prize. I take all of you with me. We go somewhere quiet. I let you watch while I take these two." He gestured to Christina and Chloé. "Then I make you watch while I kill these two. I start with this one." He pointed to Chloé. "Then, before I kill you, you will see this one," he touched Christina's hair. She shrank from his hand. "You will see me disfigure her, cause her pain she's never felt before, and then I kill her."

His face turned hard as he looked at Dan. "Then I kill you and my vengeance is complete. Blood for blood."

"Bastard, son of a whore. Your word is no good."

Lecha stepped forward and swung his fist at Dan's face. Dan tipped his head to one side and avoided a direct blow which would have smashed his nose and probably knocked him out cold. A long, red scrape opened up on the left side of his head where Lecha's fist glanced off of him.

"My word is not for you, infidel, killer of my men. My word is for my people. Now I have you and, even better, I have something you love. Maybe love more than your own life, since you were willing to give it up. This makes my victory more complete."

He turned to his guard. "Tie these women up as well. We go soon."

"What about our comrades?"

"We have to leave them. We'll take both vehicles. One of the women in each and this man in mine."

After the guard had secured the two women, Lecha went into the kitchen and opened a bottle of wine. He took a large swig.

"I drink to my success." He took another swig. "I drink to your misery." And another. "I drink to your pain." And another. "And, finally, I drink to your death."

He put down the bottle and came back into the living room.

Chapter 60

While Lecha had been gloating over Dan, describing his revenge in graphic terms, terrorizing both Chloé and Christina with what he would do, Dan arched his wrist and flexed his forearm as the Monseigneur had instructed. The knife slipped into his hand. He worked it against the plastic which gave way to the sharp blade.

Dan kept his hands behind his back. When Lecha was finished with the bottle of wine, he put it down.

"Stand him up," he told the guard.

Dan glanced at Chloé and caught her eye as the guard came over to where Dan sat.

He reached down to yank Dan up by his arms. Dan sprang forward, bringing the blade up and into the man's chest. He struck in the middle, under the ribs and thrust upward, into his heart. There was a cry and the man crumpled as his heart was cut open.

Lecha reached for his pistol just as Chloé lashed out with both feet into the side of his knee. Lecha lurched sideways with a startled shout and his shot went wide. He swung towards the couch and shot at Chloé. At that moment, Dan was rushing forward to close on his enemy before he could aim and fire again.

Lecha was swinging the gun back to shoot as Dan reached him. His left arm blocked the gun which fired, the bullet going past Dan's left side and tearing his coat. Lecha's left hand swung down to deflect the thrust of Dan's knife but he missed his arm. The blade struck low in his abdomen. Dan's thrust continued going up through his intestines and belly to finally stop at his sternum.

The gun dropped from Lecha's hand. He fell back against the wall, clutching his middle as his viscera spilled out around his hand. He looked down almost in wonder and then looked at Dan, who stood before him, bloody knife in hand. He locked eyes with Dan and slid to the floor. Groans escaped his mouth, his hands futilely tried to keep his insides in place, while his legs twitched spasmodically.

It was over in seconds. Christina was yelling. Chloé had sunk back in the couch. A stain of blood seeped out of her left side.

"Chloé's been shot!" Christina screamed. "Help her!"

Dan went over to Chloé and leaned close to her.

"Look at me," he commanded her. Chloé looked up at Dan. Her breathing was coming in rapid gasps.

"Breath steadily. You won't die." He grabbed a pillow on the couch and pressed it on her side. Chloé yelled in pain.

"Push here. This will slow down the bleeding."

He put one of Chloé's hands on the pillow.

He turned to Christina, "Talk to her. Keep her calm."

He jumped up and ran to the bathroom. There he grabbed two towels and brought them back. He pulled Chloé's shirt up and examined the wound.

"The bullet pierced you, but just barely. It passed through your body. I don't think it hit any organs or ribs. You're fortunate."

"It hurts," Chloé said in a raspy voice.

"I imagine it hurts like hell. And you'll have a scar to talk about when it's healed."

Both women stared at him.

"But you did good. You saved my life and Christina's. I might not have gotten to him before he shot me if you hadn't kicked him in the knee."

"Shouldn't we take her to a hospital?" Christina asked.

Dan shook his head. "There'll be too many questions. Questions that won't be good for you. She'll heal. And I'll make the rest of this go away."

He stood up and looked around the room. There was blood on the floor from both men, blood on the wall where Lecha had fallen, and blood on the couch. Outside there were five dead men and blood on Christina's front door.

Lecha was still moving and groaning. Dan went over to him and, taking out his 9mm, put a bullet in his head. Christina cried out in shock at the sound of the gun.

Dan went to the bathroom and found a roll of tape. He wrapped it around Chloé, holding the towel in place. Both women sat still now in shock. Dan brought them water in two glasses. He made Chloé take a drink. Christina just held her glass in her hand staring off at nothing.

"Here is what you will do," Dan said to both women. "You will take your car and drive to Vachères. Go see the *Monseigneur*. He knows what has taken place. He will guide you so Chloé gets some care and the police are not brought into this."

Chloé barely nodded. Christina now turned her gaze to Dan. Her large, brown eyes were wide with a fearful look. She stared at him. Dan could see her incomprehension. He sensed she could not process what had just taken place—the malevolent words from Lecha about what he wanted to do, his enjoyment at the horrors he would bring to people who had done him no wrong, and the brutality he would inflict on her and Chloé.

Dan looked into her wide eyes and saw no understanding. He saw no recognition of him. She looked at him now like he was a being from another world. Someone alien to her. He turned away.

"Where are the car keys?" He said in almost a gruff voice.

"On the kitchen counter," Chloé responded, her voice hoarse from the pain. Christina said nothing.

Dan grabbed the keys and brought them over to the couch.

"Go now. Get Chloé some help. I'll take care of this before you get back."

Christina put on her coat like she was sleepwalking. She draped Chloé's coat over her and they both walked out the front door. Christina let out a muffled cry as she saw the dead men at the front of her house: one riddled with bullets at the door, the other two with their heads blown open.

Dan walked with them and helped Chloé into the passenger seat.

"Remember, go to the *Monseigneur*, not the police."

Christina looked at him over the top of the car. Their eyes met. She was looking at a stranger. This man, she didn't know. He seemed alien to her now, strange and terrible. He did violent things. She had never thought such a world existed except in movies, yet here it was in her house. She shuddered. This was someone else. Her Rossignol was gone. Had he ever existed outside of her imagination? She dropped her gaze and, without a word, got into the car.

Dan understood her look. His world and hers would never meet. He was thankful for that. But he could not be a part of her world. He was trapped in his own. Words wouldn't come. There was nothing to say—nothing he *could* say. He watched as Christina lowered her eyes and got into the car. She headed down the drive where one last horror awaited them. The two dead men at the end of the lane.

When the car was out of sight, Dan started across the fields to find Émile. He would get him to help remove the bodies. He'd try to clean everything up as well as he could and then he had to go. He didn't belong in this world anymore.

After hauling the bodies into the woods with Émile, Dan headed for Marseille. He needed to find someone. Someone he hoped could give him some information.

Chapter 61

Christina drove herself and Chloé to the village. They stopped at the church. When they pulled up, the Monseigneur was standing outside, as if expecting them. He immediately went forward to help Chloé out of the car. He brought the two women into his office and had Chloé lie on a couch. Then he called the local doctor and instructed him to come to the church with supplies to tend to her wound.

Christina sat in the corner, her eyes vacantly staring at the wall. There was too much to process. The extreme violence seemed to have frozen her mind. Then this cleric, who seemed to know things, who seemed to be a part of a war, was now involved in her life. How much had her world changed? Could she ever recovery some of her previous life here in Vachères or was all of that now lost?

She got up and knelt over Chloé who was struggling to remain calm.

"You were so brave," she said to her. "I don't think I could have done that."

Chloé gave her a weak smile. "I'm feisty, you know that. Your gift is music, mine is being feisty and not letting people bully us...me or you."

Christina smile at her friend and gave her a kiss on the forehead. She got up and turned to the *Monseigneur*.

"You have some water for her to drink? And I need a wash cloth and water as well."

"Of course." He brought water and a cloth and Christina tended to her friend.

The doctor arrived and went to work on Chloé's injury. After disinfecting the wound and bandaging it tight, he pronounced her safe. The bullet had passed through and she had suffered no internal damage. He left her with some pain medication and spare bandages, and departed with instructions to see him in a week. It was clear that he had a special relationship with the *Monseigneur* and there would be no police report.

"You will spend the night here. I have a room with two beds. Tomorrow you can go back to the cottage, if you want to do so. If not, you are welcome to stay as long as you like."

The women nodded.

"I'll have some food brought to your room so you don't have to go out."

He led them down the hall to another room that served as a bedroom for visitors. After Chloé was in bed, the *Monseigneur* motioned for Christina to come with him. They went back to his office.

"Dan, your Rossignol, gave me this note. I thought you might want to know what it says. He left it with the priest when he departed from you."

Christina stared at him for some time. The parting had been so painful but the subsequent events had proven her Rossignol, Dan, right. His world would not release him and it should never collide with hers. There was no coexistence. Finally, she reached out her hand.

"*Monseigneur*," the note began. "I must leave the woman I love. The woman who gave me my life back. It was painful for both of us. She may never understand why I did what I did, run from her. You, however, do understand. You are part of the battle I and others wage against the darkness of evil. Our paths may never cross again, but I ask, no, charge you, to watch over Christina. Protect her from the dark forces. Deflect them away from her so she can flourish and grow in her artistry. She has so much to offer the world. Watch over her."

Christina looked up.

"It is yours to keep if you like," the Monseigneur said.

"*Merci,*" she said. She folded the note back up and held it tightly in her hand. After a moment, she reached out and handed it back to the priest. "It is for you, not me."

A few hours after leaving the cottage, Dan parked his car in the *quartiers nords* neighborhood of Marseille. He walked to a seedy bar he remembered and sat down. He told the bartender he needed to talk with Gaspard. The man said he didn't know anyone by that name. Dan gave him a long, serious look.

"I don't have a lot of time. Gaspard knows me. Tell one of his men to relay the message that Abdullah wants to talk with him. It's the Abdullah who did him a favor a few years ago."

The bartender shrugged his shoulders and said he could ask around. Maybe someone knew this person.

"I'm sure you can. Tell them I'll be here tomorrow night. Same time."

He gave the man a large tip and left.

The next night, as he expected, two men came up to him, one on either side, as he sat at the bar nursing a beer.

"Are you the one looking to talk with Gaspard?"

"That's correct."

"Come with us."

They led him outside where one of the men frisked Dan. After removing his 9mm, they had him walk between them. They covered five blocks and came to one of the many high-rise apartment buildings that disfigured the neighborhood. They were built without any attempt at grace or art; tall rectangular structures designed to maximize their holding capacity, not enhance the cityscape.

Twenty flights up in the slow elevator, they emerged and the men led Dan down the hallway to a corner apartment. After knocking, they opened the door and ushered him inside.

The fat man was sitting at his dining table, this time with only a bottle of red wine, having apparently finished his meal. He looked up with his black eyes shining out from his puffy cheeks.

"It is the same man, but not Abdullah. Who are you this time?"

"Victor."

The man motioned for Dan to sit.

"Have a glass of wine with me."

Dan started to refuse, but then thought the better of it. Hospitality was a big thing with Gaspard.

He took the glass in hand. Gaspard raised his glass.

"*À ta santé*, to your health."

Dan took a sip, while Gaspard took a large swallow.

"You did good work for me before. Do you want more work?"

Dan shook his head. "No. I need some information."

"Just like before. We can make a trade."

"No. I helped you a great deal last time. I only need a little information and should not have to work for it."

Gaspard put down his glass. "Tell me what you need. I'll decide whether or not you have to work for it."

Dan looked into his eyes. He trusted that his heightened sense would let him know if he was going to get an honest response from Gaspard.

"I want to know more about a man called the Scorpion."

He studied Gaspard as he waited for an answer. The man took another drink from his glass and set it down.

"I have heard of him. He's not in Marseille if that is what you want to know."

"I'd like to know where he is, but I don't expect you know that. What do you know about him?"

Gaspard thought for a moment, then spoke. "Since I can't direct you to him, I won't ask for a favor…now. Maybe later, since I expect our paths may cross again."

"So, what can you tell me?"

"He's illusive, subtle and very deadly. His victims often don't appear to be victims. That is one of his specialties. The others are terrors to behold after he is done with them.

"Some assassins are blunt instruments. Deadly, but unsophisticated. They leave a large trail of debris behind them, *très mauvais*. He can be precise and leave little to no trace of his work when he chooses to."

"What's he look like? Can you describe him?"

"He's Arab. Slightly built with a cunning visage. Dark eyes and countenance, a large nose placed on a narrow face. Someone you would instinctively not want around your loved ones."

"Who does he work for?"

"Anyone who can pay him. Although I think a wealthy Arab is the one who uses him the most."

"Rashid al-Din Said?"

Gaspard raised his eyebrows slightly and gave Dan an appraising look.

"Interesting that you know of him. It makes me wonder who *you* work for. You and the Scorpion are in the same business I suspect. Maybe I should be cautious of you?"

Dan gave him a faint smile. Gaspard was dangerous in his own territory but was, in the end, a local hood interested in his turf, protecting it and profiting from it. Any larger activities Dan sensed were of little interest to him.

"No. You are safe from me, as I expect, I am from you. We work in different arenas." He dropped his smile. "But you do have information that sometimes can be useful and I am grateful that you share it with me."

"Victor—that's you name now, correct?"

Dan nodded.

"I am not a charity. I don't work for free. We can help one another out. If you can't help me by what you do, then I expect you can find a way to pay me. We can have a good business relationship going forward."

"I agree. For now, let's see how useful your information can be."

"That is fair. The Scorpion leaves almost no trail. But one can find it if one looks carefully."

"And you have seen it?"

Gaspard shook his head. "No, but now that we have talked, I will look for it. We have a large Muslim community here, so he may have support. He may communicate or visit. Either way, I will be sure to hear of it." He took another sip of wine.

"Good. Do you have some something to write with?"

Gaspard motioned to one of his men to bring him paper and pen.

"Here's how you can reach me."

Dan wrote down a phone number. It went to an answering machine that gave no hint of its location. Dan regularly checked it and returned the calls necessary.

"This number is secure. You can leave a message or a phone number and I will get back to you. No one has access to this machine but me." He paused, then added. "And no one can hack into it. I've had the best in the business set it up."

Gaspard rose. "I think I am correct. You work for important people."

Dan got up as well. They shook hands and Dan turned to go.

"One thing," Gaspard said as Dan reached the door. He stopped and turned. "The rumors of razor blades under his finger nails are true. And the Scorpion has another specialty. As well as leaving no trace of a murder, he is adept and willing to kill someone slowly and painfully if the fee is high enough. Rumor has it that he can take a month or longer if paid well. Be careful. I would not want to be one of his victims. He is a thoroughly evil man, *un homme mauvais*."

Chapter 62

The next day, Jane called and said she was on her way to Milan. Dan met her and they drove to his residence outside of Venice. The trip passed in silence. Jane attempted some casual conversation but Dan didn't respond beyond a few monosyllabic words.

That night they went out to eat, again mostly in quiet. Jane didn't try to fill the silence with empty words. She seemed content to be a silent companion, letting him work through his thoughts. After, they went back to Dan's house where Jane opened a bottle of wine.

"Can you talk about things now? Tell me now where you were for so long?"

Dan began in a low voice to relate the story of his capture, escape, loss of memory and Christina. He stared into the room as if talking to himself as he recounted the events. He left out the details of where she lived, saying it was only somewhere in France.

He touched lightly on the details of his relationship with Christina, but he sensed Jane could understand the depth of their involvement. It was not something Dan could hide as he spoke about her. He needed to explain what drew them close and what drove the separation and its accompanying pain.

"That was another world—the one without my memory. I seem to be trapped in this world now. A prisoner with no normal life available to me."

Jane looked at him. Dan could see her concern and affection. She had not shown offense by Dan's depiction of his affair. She seemed to accept the depths of their passion.

"I'm not sure what a 'normal' life is," she said when he had finished. "Maybe it's because I haven't led one."

"Normal...that would be a partner, a family, holiday visits to other family? I guess that would be normal," Dan said.

"You only have your sister," Jane said. "Do you need to go see her, spend some time in Montana?"

Dan shook his head. "It would be nice to do that once in a while. But I don't need that now."

Dan went on, explaining how a Watcher, the gypsy woman in St. Mark's Square, had told him of Lecha and the danger to Christina. He related his attack and rescue of the two women.

"You offered yourself up?"

Dan nodded. "For the two women, yes."

"That sounds like an incredibly foolish thing to do. To put your trust in such a man."

"I didn't see any other way forward. I had the knife, which I knew gave me a chance."

Jane shook her head but kept silent, waiting for Dan to continue.

"It was violent. It was bloody. Much of the evil the world can hold crashed into Christina's life that day. She looked at me like I was a stranger, someone she didn't know." He paused to catch himself. "It struck me to the core. What I had to do to save her opened up a fissure between us. There was a separation, a gulf, deeper than I could ever have imagined. She saw it."

Dan's distress was clear to Jane. He rescued the woman who had saved him, the woman he had fallen in love with while he didn't know who he was. He had offered himself up to certain death, a sacrifice for her. Now she looked at him like a monster from another world. Yes, he had saved her, but the violence involved in that act seemed to have been too much for her. Jane guessed she saw him to be part of a terrible world, one that she wanted no part of.

"You both had a basis for a relationship when you didn't know your identity. I'm thinking you seemed like an innocent to her then." She paused, then risked another comment.

"But you weren't. I told you once that I gave up a normal life to do this work, to fight the evils we find in the world. I warned you it would be the same for you. You had already worked your way into a trap pursuing your revenge for Rita's death."

He turned to her. "It was either let her death go unpunished or exact my own payback. I don't regret what I did."

"I don't regret the decision I made as well. But with those decisions, we lost the ability to lead normal lives, whatever that means."

She risked reaching for Dan to touch his cheek. Her heart went out to him. But her practical sense told her to be cautious. He had been in love. The woman he spoke of had saved his life. He had tasted normalcy and the pleasures it brought, at least until his memory had returned.

Jane sensed he could never be satisfied with such a life and maybe he recognized that as well. It was partly why he had left the woman—not only to protect her, but because he would eventually feel confined, stifled by so quiet a life.

"You are a warrior. You respond to the call to battle. The sidelines are not where you want to be. Roland and Marcus are the same. Even myself and Henry, in our own way, respond to that call. We don't live normal lives and would probably not be happy trying to do so."

Dan looked at her. "I know you're right. It's just I have this feeling that something's lost. I saw it in Christina's eyes. Maybe it was lost with Rita. I don't hear her speak to me so much now. She's faded and that makes me sad." He stared out into the room.

"She may fade, but she'll never be lost to you. Your present life now speaks more loudly to you. The path you've chosen, the choices you've made...they *should* speak loudly as they are who you are now. But you are also who you *have* been, what you have experienced, so that will remain." She paused, then added, "And we will remain."

Dan smiled and glanced at her. "What the old woman, the Watcher, in St. Mark's Square said to you."

Jane nodded. "You took me to meet her. She said our lives were entwined."

He nodded.

Jane held back from embracing him. He had been lost, to her, to himself, to the mission. Now he was back—wounded, but back. She would be patient. There was time for their relationship to grow again, after more healing. For now, she would hold on to those words.

She realized that she was clinging to that promise. What the old gypsy woman, with some strange power that Jane didn't fully understand, had said to her, had become a beacon of hope for her. In a life that held little promise of what Dan lamented...normalcy.

"So now what do we do?" Dan asked.

They had finished the bottle of wine. Dan was beginning to get a headache and was already uneasy with all the self-reflection he had done. He would find a way to put aside his grief. Christina had to fade into his past now. It never would have worked, he told himself, even without recovering his memory. He wasn't wired to be a simple farmer.

"We fight bad guys. You are the tip of the spear, like your Shaman said. Henry and I, Fred and Warren and the others, we're the shaft. We drive back the darkness so others can live normal lives."

She raised her glass to Dan and drained it.

"We go back to the fight."

The End